THE INDUSTRIALIZATION OF THE
CONTINENTAL POWERS
1780–1914

The Industrialization of the Continental Powers 1780–1914

CLIVE TREBILCOCK

LONGMAN
London and New York

Longman Group Limited
Longman House
Burnt Mill, Harlow, Essex, UK

Published in the United States of America
by Longman Inc., New York

© Clive Trebilcock 1981

First published 1981

British Library Cataloguing in Publication Data

Trebilcock, Clive
The industrialization of the continental powers.
1. Europe – Industries – History
I. Title
338'.094   HC240   79-41543

ISBN 0-582-49119-3
ISBN 0-582-49120-7 Pbk

Set in 11/12pt Linotron 202 Garamond No. 3
Printed in Singapore by Huntsmen Offset Printing Pte Ltd

To my parents.

Contents

List of Tables

LIST OF TABLES

CHAPTER FOUR
Russia

CHAPTER FIVE
Austria-Hungary, Italy, Spain

CHAPTER SIX
Anti-Models

LIST OF TABLES

CHAPTER SEVEN
Statistics and structures

List of Maps

Acknowledgements

We are grateful to the following for permission to reproduce copyright material:

Cambridge University Press for an extract and five figures from 'Agrarian Policies and Industrialization' by A. Gerschenkron from *Cambridge Economic History of Europe*, Vol. 6 edited by M.M. Postan and H.J. Habakkuk; The Economic History Association and the author, Dr. R. Fremdling, for eight figures from 'Railroads and German Economic Growth' from the *Journal of Economic History* Vol. 37 No. 3 (September 1977); Harvard University Press for fourteen figures from *French International Accounts* by H.D. White published by Harvard University Press. Reprinted by permission of Harvard University Press; Oxford University Press (New York) for five extracts and eight figures from *Banking and Economic Development* edited by R.E. Cameron; Princeton University Press for a table of figures from *An Economic History of Spain* by Jaime Vincens Vives with the collaboration of George Nadal Oller translated by Frances M. López-Morillas, copyright © 1969 by Princeton University Press. Reprinted by permission of Princeton University Press.

The author also wishes to express his gratitude to the following authors for their generous permission to quote from these unpublished Ph.D. dissertations:

M.K. Anafu, 'The Co-operative Movement in Reggio-Emilia, 1889–1914' (Cambridge, 1980).

P.W. Gattrell, 'Russian Heavy Industry and State Defence, 1908–18' (Cambridge, 1979).

C. Kent, 'Camille Cavallier and Pont à Mousson: An Industrialist of the Third Republic' (Oxford, 1972).

M.J.F.X. Soltys, 'Austrian Agriculture: Lower Austrian Estates and the Peasants, 1751–87' (Cambridge, 1978).

I am particularly indebted to Pam Mills, Helen Hatfield and Shirley Gilbey for converting my tiresome longhand into efficient typescript. And my special thanks is due to Pam Judd against whose caring hand and endless patience the process of checking and cross-referencing eventually capitulated. To my family goes the award for forbearance: they endured the pangs of composition with a stoicism that was mostly benevolent and always resourceful.

Preface

There are many economic histories of Europe. There are narrative surveys of individual countries, collections of essays about many countries, summaries of fact with a continental span. Generally, the available works have surveyed and recorded, but rarely have they proved rich in explanation. And rarely have they approached the field of European industrial history with an explicit or consistently maintained intention to offer a comparative style of analysis. The central tenet of this volume is to concentrate upon analysis and explanation within a broadly comparative and *inter*-national framework of argument. It provides fact and hard record where these are needed, and sufficient to permit the student a sense of what simply happened – or, given the historian's usual limitations, what *probably* simply happened – but its main purpose is to argue, to propose a case.

For this reason, since the construction of a case relies upon the best available data, the unearthing of additional evidence, the most ingenious interpretation of given points, considerable reliance is placed in the ensuing chapters upon the incorporation of research material from the specialist journals, and, occasionally, from unpublished monographs. This reliance is probably more marked than is conventional in most textbook treatments but it is consistent with the major strategic objective of this particular textbook. And it is consistent, too, with the belief that research findings should be made available to the student in a form which is both generally accessible and clearly related to the pre-existing body of knowledge within the field. So there follows from the ambition to provide explanation, a need also to provide synthesis.

There is of course the danger that a design which purports to offer explanation across a continental sequence rife with inconsistencies and deviations from the norm will, in fact, lay clear only the inner, indeed the very close, boundaries of our ignorance. That is a risk which will probably not be avoided – and certainly not so in its entirety. Comparative economic history, at least in its present rudimentary state of development, has an inherent tendency to find things which do not fit, to produce national results which do not conform to global models. But, of course, in comparative studies, it is not only the comparisons that matter; the contrasts and the contradictions are quite as significant, and perhaps, since they are usually more numerous, they are also *more* significant. The models, after all, do not exist simply to fit. They exist to be tested. And to be refined until they do fit; or until they must be rejected and the process of design recommenced. So merely to press the comparisons along clearly defined thematic lines is in itself a useful exercise – to hold a number of questions in consideration while they are pursued and matched against a very wide set of national instances, and to make frequent inter-reference, might well possess the double investigative virtues of consistency and penetration. And if the result is merely a clearer map of where the frontiers of ignorance actually are, there should be some value in that. On the way to this destination, moreover – if it *is* the destination for this analytical venture – there are likely to be some roads, highways as well as pathways, which might both benefit from the traffic and entertain the traveller.

The general area requiring exploration is well known and requires little justification. The period from the late eighteenth century to the First World War has become generally accepted as the foundation phase of European industrialism. Within that period the European nations, among them the greatest, were the 'less developed countries' of their time – measured then, not, as is the 'Third World' now, against the communal sophistication of the industrial West, but against the prosperity of the off-shore factory economy of the industrial pioneer, Great Britain. The problems around which analysis revolves, therefore, are the problems of development – as to why industrial capitalism rooted more tenaciously in some quarters of Europe than in others, or as to why some nations produced communities of dynamic capitalists and some did not. Since the First World War the problems for the larger European economies have lain in the sustaining of industrial growth, not in initiating it. So the period at least has a coherence and a distinctive unity about it.

If these desirable characteristics are to be duplicated in the following analysis, a definite marching order is clearly required. There is a need for orderliness. Since the purpose of the undertaking is primarily analytical, separate sections are provided in Chapters One and Six which, respectively, lay out the models and methods employed in the body of the argument and then, in the second case, summarize the findings as they compare with these conceptual starting points. These sections are deliberately different in quality – dealing, as it were, with matters of design rather than with matters of performance – from the 'country' chapters which follow. In these latter sections a combination of geographic, thematic, and comparative approaches is employed. The nation-state remains the most convenient and also the most defensible unit of analysis, so, with the necessary qualifications generated by recent research, this familiar form has been retained for the basic chapter structure. However, the student, with his attention focused upon the practical issues imposed by essays and examinations, and also the teacher, with his interest concentrated upon lectures and current research questions, tends in practice towards a preoccupation with *themes* which have international scope. Hence, each chapter is broken into a series of readily identifiable segments, separately titled, and easily matched as between countries. These cover the 'large issues' such as state intervention, resource constraints, entrepreneurial behaviour, financial provision, and the rest, and locate them at appropriate points *both* within the analysis of national cases *and* within the construction of an overall analysis. Within this system, a line of running comparative comment is maintained. This is strengthened by grouping the coverage of the three lesser powers – where the nature of the literature and of their shared problems favours a more direct comparison – within a single chapter structure. This unit plays national cases against one another more explicitly than is administratively possible with the bigger – and more written-over – economies. It is probably the only generally available exercise of its kind. Rather similarly, the final analytical chapter, takes the results from the foregoing units and forces them into a more demanding confrontation with the guiding concepts than is perhaps usual. The order of march is then completed by a statistical section which again has an analytical organizing principle; it arranges the statistical data clearly around the same models of backwardness and development which have been employed in the text. Here, too, commentary sections are provided which describe the degree of fit – or looseness – between the qualitative and the quantitative measures.

If some things are intended to be unusual, the whole thing is designed to be easily usable. Analytical sections are clearly labelled. Country units are arranged in a simple and familiar way. They are then ranked according to a distinctive principle: a hierarchy of backwardness which commences with Germany and ends with Austria-Hungary, Italy, and Spain. Themes may readily be followed through and between the country units. Research findings are distilled to an assimilable form. The aim is to provide signposts and charts to several different types of pattern. Even the mapping of the ignorance frontiers has a direct utility – if, at least, there is any guide to be found in the widespread, if hardly confident, undergraduate preoccupation with what exactly might *be* the legitimate areas of debate. Certainly there is a point in knowing which questions may be usefully discussed and which it may be wiser not to confront.

Primarily, the readership is imagined as an undergraduate one, though, with many degree courses widening to include options in European economic history, not necessarily a specialist undergraduate one. Moreover, the treatment has been cast to make the work suitable for some sixth-form use and for many of the further education categories which fall between these two. Many institutions in further and higher education now offer courses in international economic history, historical development studies, or comparative industrialization; and, in particular, the trend towards comparative economic history is strengthening and will continue to do so.

For this audience, this book attempts to offer, neither a selection of 'useful facts' nor a structure of fixed opinions but rather an intelligible analytical system – even if it may be as a system of doubts – with which the phenomenon of industrialization may be explored.

Note In order to maximize access to further reading material for students, the references provided cite works written in, or translated into, English, wherever possible. However, given the intention to follow the current research as far as is feasible, this curb on language cannot always be sustained. In such cases reference is made to the work in the original language on the assumption that it is useful to know where and when, and by whom, the findings were made, even if they cannot be examined at first hand.

CHAPTER ONE

Historical Models of Growth

Symbolically, the European civilization of 1914 could be represented as precisely by the steam-hammer or the steam warship as it had once been by the cathedral spire or the knightly banner. Modern technology had established itself across wide areas of a continent dominated, only decades previously, by the feudal lord and the urban guild. There were engineering works in Spezia and Tsaritsyn, automobile factories in Vienna and Milan, dreadnought yards in Fiume and Ferrol. In the great coal and metallurgical complex of Rhine-Ruhr, Europe could boast the world's most concentrated and integrated industrial area. And at St Etienne, Hayange, or Décazeville, the French industrialists had created a handful of manufacturing installations which could rival any in existence. To the casual glance, it might appear that industrialization had overtaken Europe from the Mediterranean to the Baltic, from the Channel to the Danube. But, clearly enough, industrialization did not possess the same value wherever it touched. A machine-shop in Budapest did not possess the same significance as a machine-shop in Birmingham or Berlin. Despite the outward similarities, industrialization in Europe was a phenomenon of very variable pace and intensity, offering radically different prospects of wealth and power as it crossed frontiers and resource areas. To begin with, it may be useful to provide a rough outline of the divergent pattern of achievement among the main industrial contenders.

Within this period some areas of the continent did manage to graduate from industrial infancy to flourishing, if early, adulthood. For them, the process of advance was relatively gradual; they were not so far behind Britain — the international exemplar in the manufacturing arts — that the business of economic modernization had become an institutionalized technique. Parts of France and segments of the German states, for instance, displayed, as early as the middle eighteenth century, an apparent potential for industrial growth that resembled the British capabilities of the same era more than fleetingly. Yet it was another century and a half before the French and German economies were safely entrenched within the high-technology stage of development, equipped with the chemical, machine-tool and engineering factories which picked out the leading economies of the pre-1914 world. Generally speaking, their rate of industrial advance had quickened – after an extended period of economic preparation – around the fourth or fifth decades of the nineteenth century. In the process, they had drawn as selective, if not systematic, imitators upon the technology and experience supplied by the industrial prototype across the Channel. By 1914, however, they had no further need to imitate. Within limits, by European standards, and with Germany decisively leading France, these countries – the long-run developers – could be described, by the time of the First World War, as the successful economic powers of continental Europe.

For another group of countries, including tsarist Russia, the Austrian section of the Habsburg Empire, and freshly united Italy, industrialization followed a different pattern. In these cases the early industrial stirrings were much weaker; the industrial surge at mid-century was much less pronounced; and the major part of growth inside the period was concentrated within the thirty years before the First World War. Among this group, the level of backwardness – set largely by the ballast of semi-feudal agricultures and the economic deadweight of large peasant populations – was more pronounced and the base from which industrialization commenced much lower than was the case for the early developers. Partly because of this low starting point, partly because of their ability to extract aid of a technological, financial, or entrepreneurial type from their continental predecessors, as well as from Britain, the initial development of this group exhibited a tendency to be more rapid and compressed than anything which had gone before. It is from growth patterns like these that notions of the 'big spurt' or the 'big push' in industrial expansion derive. But if the growth rates veered upwards for these countries, their problems of backwardness remained acute, and in few cases had the former suppressed the latter by 1914. At the end of the period, this group could claim a partial success in industrialization. Its members had achieved a form of economic adolescence, sometimes tempestuous as with Russia, sometimes demure and withdrawn as with Austria.

Behind the adolescents came the problem children, the sick offspring of the old regimes, struggling for survival by dint of modern economic achievement. Among this group, Spain and the Habsburg satellites, especially Hungary, provide typical cases. Here the proto-industrial activity came late in the period and the degree of under-development was so severe that the possibility of leaping out of backwardness astride high industrial growth rates was remote indeed. At the outbreak of the First World War, the degree of industrial achievement in these areas was small, and much time would elapse before it could be otherwise.

Even from such a cursory inspection of the continent's manufacturing attributes, it is obvious that nothing so monolithic as 'an industrial revolution in Europe' occurred in the nineteenth century. The experience of industrialization was most certainly not uniform between countries; instead, there was an immense variety of growth rate, technological advance, and managerial expertise. Nor is it obvious that single countries had their industrial 'revolutions'. For the most successful of the early developers – particularly the off-shore manufactory of Britain — modern research insists that industrial growth was gradualistic, evolutionary, achieved not in the violent spontaneous outburst of revolution, but in the plodding long run. Illumination for the industrial path-way was provided not by the 'thunderbolt from a clear blue sky' but by decades of candle-ends. Naturally, this does not mean that all economic modernization must be gradualistic; for the later developer, able to 'borrow' and to implement complete industrial systems in short order, the prospects of a 'big push' certainly become more feasible. Correspondingly, the middle group of countries did experience a pace of development which could be energetic. But it could also be — and frequently was — restricted by sector, or by region, in a style which could leave huge backward agricultures more or less intact, or relegate whole tracts of the nation to the status of undeveloped areas within the host economy. The scale or extent of such growth may fall short of the 'revolutionary'. And, for the *very* late developer, the shortfall will be even more acute, since the advantages of 'borrowing' will be extensively qualified by the rudimentary economic equipment of the borrower. For this third category of country, persistent economic deprivation, rather than any species of sudden industrial onrush, remained the problem.

In order to assess such widely differing cases, and give due allowance to the various degrees of industrialization achieved in Europe, a number of measuring tools are required. For the individual economy, a method of analysis is needed which will detect the presence or absence — and if presence, also the quality — of the materials for growth, and will distinguish between the various stages of development within the economic system. Further, we need to allow for the varying levels of backwardness *between* countries and for the effects that the given distribution of European backwardness had on the industrial growth of the various national economies. Stock must be taken not only of the physical resources, or the lack of them, but also of the social endowment which will supply, or fail to supply, an entrepreneurial shockforce which may be able to innovate a way past the obstacles imposed by the allocation of resources. In addition, there must be a place within our assessment for an element of politics; for it is an often-neglected feature of economic development viewed historically that a political preference — frequently for the maintenance of social stability or for an improved military capacity — may close or open an economic option. Similarly, in the reverse procedure, economic events — as the determinist thinkers have more widely publicized — may create political problems. Yet, if the policy of nation-states both influences, and may be influenced by, industrial growth, it is not always the case that industrial growth is a national phenomenon. Some allowance must be made for the fact that economic advance may be highly regionalized, and that an industrial region in one country may compare, and may co-operate, more closely with an industrial area in a foreign country than it does with its own agricultural hinterland. Thus, industrialization, in this sense, may be more a European experience than a national one, though still by no means a uniform experience.

Various models or analytical constructs are available to the economic historian which attempt these tasks of measurement, naturally enough with fairly diverse amounts of success. In this study it will be convenient to employ, in particular, three formal models and to link to them a pair of hypotheses of somewhat more humble theoretical pretension. It does not necessarily follow that all will function satisfactorily within their own terms of reference, but, for the purposes of this analysis, the points at which they fail may be no less significant than those at which they successfully reflect reality. In each case, the analytical tool will be used recurrently so as to provide a number of refrains running in parallel through the argument.

THE ROSTOW MODEL: THE AIRBORNE ECONOMY

This is a reasonably simple – some would say crude – 'stage theory', dividing the process of industrialization into a number of distinct – most would say over-distinct – phases.[1] The initial phase from which the expanding economy must emerge is that of the 'traditional society', a benighted world 'based upon pre-Newtonian science and technology'. If all goes well, this dim scenario is exchanged, in the fullness of real time, but fairly briskly in Professor Rostow's analysis, for the 'preconditions' stage, a form of industrial apprenticeship in which the qualifications for industrial growth are painstakingly gathered together. After this grooming process, comes, somewhat less spontaneously than the traditional industrial revolution but hardly less explosively, the stage of 'take-off'. At this point the manufacturing sector lifts away from its econom-ic base in the same style as an aircraft from its runway or a missile from its launching pad. Perhaps the choice of analogy is revealing: in place of God's thunderbolt descending we have Man's vehicle ascending, and although the operation of each is fairly abrupt, one clearly requires more preparation than the other. The most significant characteristics of 'take-off' are: its short chrono-logical span, requiring 'lift-off' to be effected within two or three decades; a doubling in the proportion of national income productively invested; and the growth of certain major industries to form 'leading sectors' within the econ-omy. As the analogies proliferate, the economy then moves forward into the next stage: after 'taking off' like a missile it is required to embark upon the 'drive to maturity', a process of ageing and increasing sophistication under-gone by fine wines, favourite pipes, and, it would appear, economies. In this state, at any rate, the process of industrial growth becomes 'sustained', or irreversible. When it has been sustained for a sufficiently long period, a final stage, the *terminus ad quem* of the model, will be reached: this is the age of 'high mass consumption'.

Whatever its drawbacks – and they are considerable – the Rostow model possesses one obvious, if humble, advantage: it offers a highly *generalized* vision of industrialization which touches upon the actual industrial fortunes of a number of European countries at a variety of points. As long as it is construed in these very general terms, some few statements of moderate utility may be derived from it. Allowing overlapping periods, it would seem safe to say that a sizeable group of countries experienced something like a 'preparation' phase, or a 'proto-industrial' phase, or, to employ Rostow's term, a 'preconditions' phase, at some time within the period 1800–70, a burst of more rapid growth, reminiscent of a 'take-off' phase, at some time within the period 1840–95, and, for a few, the initial suspicions of the 'drive to maturity' at some time within the period 1870–1914. But as an approach, this is painfully non-specific, and the over-lapping time periods adopted here allow an extremely generous degree of latitude which, though necessary if the Rostowian system is to be made to produce a description of 'European' range, jeopardizes accurate analysis.

Perhaps the drawbacks are more obvious than the utility. Briefly, the model is too explosive, too neat, and too monolithic; it postulates growth which is rapid, but, at the same time, orderly in progression, and derived from a limited number of sources. Although a preparation phase is built into its structure, the major requirement is that the critical work of industrialization should be executed to the short order, within two or three decades. This runs clean counter to the growing preference among economic historians for the application of an evolutionary mode of interpretation to a growing number of historical cases. And, in terms of record, the requirements for the successful short-haul 'take-off' seem to have been fulfilled in few detectable instances. Certainly the belief that economies may within thirty years double their rate of 'productive' investment – from below 5 per cent to above 10 per cent of national income in the basic interpretation[2] – has met with remarkably little authentication of a convincing historical type.[3] In the observed cases the time required for this process – in so far as the data reveals it – appears to considerably exceed thirty years, thus arguing for an important 'stretching' of the 'take-off' process.[4] Furthermore, the identification of the 'take-off' stage by associating with it the emergence of 'leading sectors' has proved to be a good deal less than foolproof, since, as is fairly obvious, major industries have a perennial tendency to move forward into dominating positions, before, during, and after 'take-off'.

Excessive neatness as a complaint attaches most damagingly to the proto-industrial phase of the model. It is possible, by abstracting from Professor Rostow's various descriptions of the preconditioning equipment, to establish a schedule itemizing at least its more important components.[5] These prerequisites would appear to be:

(a) a transformation in agriculture (or 'agricultural revolution'), yielding higher productivity on the land and thus freeing surplus labour, food, and raw materials for use in industry;

(b) an accumulation of social overhead capital, mostly in the form of transport-related facilities (such as ports, docks, canals, or railways) which would act to extend markets, allow supply and demand to interact quickly and efficiently, and move in raw materials at tolerable prices and move out bulky industrial products at tolerable costs;

(c) a development of the ancillary services for industry, most especially banking;

(d) the presence of entrepreneurs willing to take risks in non-conventional fields;

(e) the presence of initial minima of skilled labour and power resources;

(f) an increased exploitation of domestic raw materials or an increase in the importation of foreign ones.

Most of these are formally described as 'preconditions' by Rostow; others are suggested less explicitly; and the schedule is not exhaustive.[6] However, the factors listed above are representative of the Rostowian interpretation and provide a fair mark upon which to direct counter-arguments.

Logically, if the conceptual neatness of a separate, self-contained preconditions stage is to lend a *justified* shapeliness to the analysis of industrial growth, we might require that two simple criteria should be fulfilled. Firstly, that the various prerequisites should be unique to the proto-industrial stage; secondly, that they should be unique as a collectivity: they should occur at no other stage of the growth process and they should certainly exhibit no mobility in any numbers.[7] Additionally, we might expect that if the preconditions are genuinely necessary for industrialization, they should be noticeably present in all countries which do industrialize. But, in fact, Rostow's brainchildren measure up to these requirements in disappointing style. Even the most casual review of nineteenth-century economic development will reveal that many of the factors described by Rostow as *pre*conditions may occur at almost any stage of the growth process, often well after the economy has embarked upon 'take-off'. Thus in Russia, the lending of capital, 'on long term, at high risk, to back the innovating entrepreneur'[8] through an effective native banking system did not develop in advance of the industrial spurt of the 1890s, but in the 1900s, when the spurt had already begun to slow. Similarly, Russia's agricultural transformation is difficult to detect: it certainly did not precede 1890; it may have arrived with Stalin's collectivization programme of the 1930s; or, as some would argue, it may be yet to come. In Italy also, agriculture has presented a problem: here industrialization occurred against the backcloth of savage rural poverty, in the south most especially, and both the industrial achievement and the agricultural problem have persisted into the present time. If the preconditions can appear in so capricious a manner, and sometimes scarcely appear at all, then clearly the descriptive accuracy of the model is placed in doubt. By the same token the neatness of the distinct stages is revealed as no more than an intellectual elegance bearing small resemblance to the indistinct, overlapping, and wayward reality. It was perhaps this overdeveloped elegance which drew from Alexander Gerschenkron the pertinent gibe that those things which were not prerequisites must presumably be post-requisites.[9]

The joke is a good one but the point is real. It is a feature of the Rostow hypothesis that it succeeds in conveying the impression that the preconditions are indispensable to industrialization, that in their absence it is impossible, and in their presence, it becomes, if not inevitable, at least probable. The qualifications within the model are profuse, but if it does not carry this meaning, it is exceedingly difficult to imagine what it does mean. It is possible, as H. J. Habakkuk has argued, that the only true meaning is negative, namely that 'the conditions favourable to growth are so varied. . . . that it is not possible to give a list of essential requisites that is more than a string of platitudes'.[10] But it is probably necessary to test the hypothesis at its own valuation if its implications are to become clear. Taking the impression that is conveyed, therefore, we could agree that it would be highly convenient if there could be a schedule of prerequisites, a list of essentials to be checked off, before industrialization could occur. The analyst would be provided with a measure of success that could be applied to the performance of any industrializing economy in its pre-'take-off' stage. The imminence of 'take-off' and the rate of progress towards it, could thus be assessed for any historical case. But if the prerequisites are, in reality, highly mobile between the various stages, the predictive potential of the model, together with its utility as a test for the efficiency of the proto-industrial economy at once disintegrates. If prerequisites can so easily become post-requisites, they can tell us little that is essential about the immediately pre-industrial phase of European economic advance. In fact, it would seem more likely that the preconditions are less the basic qualifications for industrial growth than integral components of the growth process itself, appearing more distinctly as an economy proceeds from backwardness towards full industrial modernization but wholly capable of appearing at different stages in different countries. What Rostow has identified as preconditions are in reality the stripes upon the industrial tiger; they are essential identifying features of the animal, but they have no independent life as prerequisites for its existence.

Finally, there is the problem of the model as monolith. According to the Rostow interpretation, the model indicates a *single* highway which leads from the traditional society to the era of high mass consumption, and every aspirant economy, after having been issued with the standard development equipment, must tread this road. But any inspection of the various preconditions — the thriving agricultural transformations, the swelling social overheads — will reveal that they do not bear a great deal of resemblance to the actual physical endowment possessed by most of pre-industrial Europe. Countries with acute capital scarcities, like the German states in the 1840s, countries with deeply stagnant agricultures like Russia or Italy, could not pay the toll on Rostow's highway and did not pay it. Yet they achieved, in varying degrees, a measure of industrialization. Clearly there must be *alternative* routes, devious by-roads — the forced taxes levied on a subsistence agriculture to produce artificial 'surpluses', the specialized development banks designed to alleviate capital shortages, the economic management provided by the state as a replacement for defective private enterprise — which lead to the same destination. The uniformity imposed by the Rostow model is, therefore, a false uniformity; in the actual, highly varied world, as Gerschenkron has pointed out, there tend to be 'substitutes'[11] for Rostow's preconditions, methods, more or less contrived, for

7

circumventing bottlenecks in the supply of prerequisites. And it is likely that in each country, special deficiencies in resources, particular social or cultural characteristics, or specialized political objectives, will necessitate a highly individualistic mixture of 'substitutes'.

Given the deficiencies of the Rostow model as a description of the speed, stages, or uniformity of industrial growth, its overall utility is brought into question. But it does fulfil certain functions. The first is negative: it provides a cautionary reminder that it is dangerous to over-dramatize the rate of industrial advance. The rest are more positive. A set of *ideal* preconditions is, at least, placed among the analyst's instruments of measurement. Reality may well be different, but many of the 'substitutes' found in the actual world will possess a clear relationship to the original precondition, and will constitute a makeshift approach to the same problem. The amount of deviation between the precondition and the 'substitute', the degree of contrivance which must go into the making of the 'substitute', will thus reveal important facts about the economic and institutional sophistication of the country under review. Moreover, the absence of a precondition may be more significant than its presence. When an economy is growing imperfectly, any laxity in the development of a particular precondition, or approximation for it, may provide the historian with some indication, if not a complete diagnosis, of the weaknesses responsible for the unsatisfactory development pattern. Finally, the concept of the leading sector has some virtues, if employed with care. As long as the fortunes of lesser industries are given due weight in any macro-economic assessment, it may be analytically useful to associate a particular era of economic advance with a concentration upon a specific set of manufacturing sectors. No doubt this is a good deal less impressive than the full apparatus of the airborne economy, but it is distinctly more functional.

THE GERSCHENKRON MODEL: THE DEPRIVED ECONOMY

Where the Rostow model looks forward in its economics to the avidly consuming society, and in its terminology to the space age – is, in a sense, pulled out of shape by its objectives – the Gerschenkron model looks firmly backwards. Indeed, it deals with backwardness, and its emphasis rests more heavily upon the beginnings of growth than upon its long-term objectives. For this reason, perhaps, it may commend itself to the historical analyst. It will be commended also by its well-developed flexibility and its modest expectations. Nothing as sophisticated as the preconditions – with their proliferating transport systems, their reforming agriculturalists, and their enterprising businessmen – is postulated as the starting point for industrialization. It is recognized that, in most of nineteenth-century Europe, industrial growth issued from a context of economic deprivation. Therefore, it is expected that backward countries will produce approximations or 'substitutes' for the more rarefied preconditions if they are to conquer their disabilities. But the necessity to contrive substitutes is not made a uniform requirement. It is conceded that there are many *degrees* of backwardness and that the economic characteristics and policies attached to backward states will vary accordingly.

Any model which assumes under-endowment as its starting point in assessing the economic life of nineteenth-century Europe possesses clear advantages over systems which seek from the outset to identify the materials of progress. For the historical detail provides more evidence of backwardness than of glowing industrial prospects. Observe the countries which feature in this survey. France, in breaking down the restraints of the *ancien régime*, forged new social and ideological fetters which hobbled her manufacturing potential. 'Germany' before 1870 was divided into miniature principalities and splintered markets. Russia before 1861 was a feudal society deeply resistant to innovation, economic or otherwise, and it improved only very slowly after 1861. The Austro-Hungarian Empire remained down to 1914 almost as chronically divided in economics as it was in politics. Northern Italy in 1914 was separated virtually by an economic universe from the underdeveloped desert on its southern doorstep. Much of Spain on the eve of the First World War was still more or less as the decline of the seventeenth century had left it. It is the special achievement of the Gerschenkron model that it has traced operational connexions between such measures of deprivation and modern industrial growth.

In doing so, however, it features a style of economic advance no less discontinuous and no less rapid than that envisaged by Rostow. The deprived economy is made to leap out of backwardness. It does so, its protagonist argues, because of the major paradox implicit in backwardness itself: that, as other countries advance and backwardness – an affliction largely defined by the progress of others – deepens, the underprivileged society becomes increasingly sensitive to the contrast between its own feebleness and the prosperity or power being generated elsewhere. As the gains to be had from industrial growth spiral upwards, and are increasingly publicized, the tension within the backward economy mounts progressively until, finally, it is expressed in some extraordinary effort to bridge the gap, a sudden lunge for the benefits of industrialization.[12] The agency for this swift remedial thrust is most usually the state, and naturally so, since governments are both especially attuned to disparities in international achievement and can command the resources needed for the extraordinary efforts to obliterate them. Moreover, the level of output from which the lunge develops will be so low that quite modest absolute increases in industrial production will create very high percentage rates of growth. This conclusion to the hypothesis, placing so much emphasis on the lunge or 'big spurt' as the natural concomitant of backwardness is – as will later emerge – the weakest part of the model. Nevertheless, in the process of linking economic backwardness to rapid industrial advance, Gerschenkron does produce an explanatory system of considerable ingenuity and usefulness.

The general assumption is that the greater a country's backwardness, the more rapid will be its initial industrial development. However, a number of operational rules are suggested which deal with more specific aspects of the growth problem. A free adaptation might run as follows:

(a) The more backward the country, the more sophisticated will be the industrial equipment which it selects for its manufacturing début. This will be so, because the backwardness of follower countries is itself partly defined by the advanced nature of the technology at work inside the leader economies. By purchasing or copying modern machines the backward country can obtain segments of this technology. And within the deprived economy the high-quality equipment will naturally produce a disproportionate effect and will assist in pulling the borrowing country abruptly forward into the industrial race.

(b) For similar reasons, there will be a relationship between the degree of backwardness and the scale of industrial enterprise chosen by the developing country. Again, the follower will imitate the most modern and efficient organization of work that the advanced nations have to offer, and will implement it unencumbered by the clutter of obsolete plant which often constrains the older economies. At least, the backward economy has the advantage of a clean start and can select the most efficient large-scale industrial systems from the international stock.

(c) The backward economy will tend to use not only modern equipment arranged in large units but also generous *amounts* of the new technology. Its need to compensate for the shortcomings of its labour supply in numbers and in skills will require every effort to replace men with machines.

(d) The backward economy will tend to emphasize the heavy or capital goods industries and to choose these for its technological vanguard. Considerations of prestige will reinforce this taste for the most formidable industries of the era, but it is not irrelevant that such industries offer the follower country the most swift means of narrowing the gap between itself and the advanced nations.

(e) The backward economy will tend to require a great deal of assistance of an institutional kind. In a context of medium backwardness, where shortage of capital is often the major bottleneck, this assistance will often take the form of innovation within the banking institutions, producing a specialized industrial investment bank which may prove successful in cracking the bottleneck. In a context of chronic backwardness, where additional deficiencies – most likely in market demand and managerial skills – will be added to those in capital supply, there will be little alternative to the use of the state as the co-ordinating and managerial agency.

(f) It is implicit in much of this that agricultural change will play little part in the surge out of backwardness. For it is largely an unresponsive and inflexible agriculture which is the conditioning factor in rendering, and keeping, a country backward. [13]

A vital point emerges instantly from this model. Elements deemed essential in the Rostow interpretation are here barely mentioned. Where Rostow places the 'agricultural transformation' high on his list of preconditions, Gerschenkron despairs of aid from this quarter. Some other contribution must take its place. Where Rostow demands a supply of creative capitalists, Gerschenkron's context of backwardness makes their presence improbable. Some other agency must take their place. Clearly, the central issue again concerns the practice of 'substitution'. It is present either explicitly or by assumption in most areas of the Gerschenkron model. And it is carried a long way. A backward country can substitute for an indigenous stream of innovation by importing advanced technology, for the accumulation of capital by attracting foreign funds, for a sufficiency of skilled labour by extensive mechanization, for the services of an entrepreneurial ginger group by state action. Given the meagre initial endowments, such devices might well shunt the deprived economy into a burst of intense activity. And if Gershenkron is correct, we would expect that the element of contrivance would be more pronounced and the industrial burst more rapid in a country of severe backwardness, such as Russia, than in a country of moderate backwardness, such as Germany. But we shall have to suspend judgement as to whether these effects were most evident of all in countries of most chronic backwardness, such as Spain. For the time being, it is sufficient that Gershenkron provides us with a model which does not require the developing economy to emulate the acrobatics of Rostow's prototype but views 'the industrial history of Europe . . . not as a series of mere repetitions of the "first" industrialization but as an orderly system of graduated deviations from that industrialization'.[14] This is a superior idea, even though the concept of 'orderly deviation' may perhaps show signs of strain when applied to the least privileged European economies of all.

MANAGEMENT MODELS OR MODEL MANAGEMENTS?

Discussion of objective physical endowments or constraints – raw materials, labour supplies, investment capital, or the lack of them – plays a justifiably large part in the historical assessment of economic growth, but it does not tell the whole story. In particular, it would fail to explain the behaviour of economies such as the Japanese or Swiss, which, in spite of indifferent natural resources, have created very specialized and very successful versions of industrial and commercial prosperity. We require, therefore, some instrument of measurement capable of assessing the *non-economic* variables, of analysing the elements which react to, and react upon, the objective physical factors; we need, in other words, a means of describing the behaviour of entrepreneurial groups. For it is most certainly true that a gleeful exploitation of promising economic opportunities is by no means the only possible relationship between the industrialist and the resources; rather this relationship may range anywhere between entrenched conservatism in the face of apparently enticing prospects and sustained ingenuity in the teeth of almost unrelieved adversity.

Social characteristics may exert an influence upon the course of industrialization at least as powerful as any derived from the more basic economic equipment. Mobile or fluid societies, in which the talented individual may rise by achievement irrespective of background, will provide a wider field for

11

entrepreneurial recruitment than hierarchic or 'fixed' societies. Open societies will respond to the success of industrialists, as indeed to the success of other groups, by absorbing the newly wealthy easily into their upper ranks. Closed societies, by contrast, will recognize only a narrow range of functions, frequently agricultural or military functions, and will actively deplore the pursuit of wealth or influence by unconventional means. Both the form of social organization, therefore, and the climate of opinion, within which entrepreneurial behaviour occurs will function – by extending or withdrawing the social returns to enterprise, that is, status, office, or noble title – as an important determinant of industrial activity.

Preoccupations of this type were systematized most usefully by the American sociologist, Talcott Parsons. Every society, said Parsons, possesses a set of 'role expectations', defining the roles which the individuals within the society expect one another to perform. The society protects this series of role expectations by its system of rewards and retributions. Together, the role expectations and their protective mechanism constitute a 'social value system' which has a substantial ability to condition the activities of society's individual members.[15] Consequently, for the entrepreneurial objectives to be effectively pursued, it is necessary that the fundamental behaviour patterns of capitalism – risk-taking, profit-motivation, the impersonal non-familial organization, and the rest – should interlock smoothly with the society's prevailing value system, and should receive the 'social approval' of the community. Deficiencies in the social approval for capitalist endeavour may leave the businessman stranded as an ambivalent, or even, at worst, destructive element in the growth process. This will be particularly so since the capitalist will not only suffer the constraints imposed by anti-capitalist values but, as a member of society, sharing some of its assumptions, will, at least partially, *concede* the force of these values. Necessarily, such contradictions in attitude must reduce entrepreneurial efficiency. In these terms, it is entirely possible for an economy well endowed with natural resources and scientific skills to be situated within a community possessed of a pre-industrial value system. Such a community would be likely to cherish a set of *non-capitalistic* motives, ideals, and goals, achieving satisfaction, for instance, in the solidarity of the community, the security of the family, or the observance of religious dictates rather than by the exercise of competition or the acquisition of profit. Attaining satisfaction of the first type, however, would make economic modernization a painful and frustrating process at best. In reality, nineteenth-century France exhibited a range of characteristics not dissimilar from those of the pre-capitalistic society. Conversely, it is also possible for an economy with very meagre natural advantages to be situated within a community which expresses an unusually high social approval for industrialization. In reality, the Japan of the 1870s and 1880s, menaced by the encirclement of the colonial powers, did not diverge greatly from this description.

To the Parsonian structure has been added in recent years an attempt by the French scholar Raymond Aron to create 'a sociological theory of growth . . . which would combine economic analysis and historical narrative'.[16] Aron, like

12

Parsons, concentrates upon 'the attitudes of economic subjects', most relevantly here upon the opinions and preconceptions of the entrepreneurial force. He selects particularly those attitudes governing: the appetite for progress and change; the interest in science and technique; and the habit of economic calculation. Clearly the forces which impel entrepreneurs towards an interest in these areas are important, and bear examination:

(a) The desire for change and innovation is largely a function of the social value system and here Aron makes little improvement on Parsons' more precise formulation. However, he does add the suggestion that the rate of population growth might strongly influence a society's tolerance for change and innovation.

(b) The interest in science and technique is obviously dependent upon culture and education. Here there are significant differences between nineteenth-century economies. The range might run from the society of the northern states of the USA with its assiduous cultivation of science and its eye for the practical applications of education, to the French society of the Second Empire and Third Republic with its traditions of liberal education and its continued preference for 'humane studies' or *culture générale*. These attitudes are essentially neither capitalistic nor anti-capitalistic, but one is manifestly more conducive to industrial development than the other. However, it is also clear that the educational preferences of a community are again much influenced by its social value system.

(c) The habit of economic calculation will run most fluently within the framework of a relatively rational and predictable system of administration and justice. Capricious or unstable government does not make for the balanced formulation of industrial plans by businessmen, and militates against their assumption of long-run commitments. Calculation is also concerned with incentives and rewards; it will function smoothly only under a system which provides more reward for more effort. A landholding system which permits landlords to profit disproportionately from the labours of tenants, or a fiscal system which minimizes returns to further effort will deter the habit of calculation for gain and growth. Legislation can, all too easily, produce such unwelcome effects. [17]

Generally speaking, the Aron model provides slight refinements for some segments of the Parsonian system as it relates to the businessman, but does not alter the overall direction for the analysis of entrepreneurial behaviour.

Much more determined attempts radically to amend the entrepreneurial explanation issue from quite other quarters. It seems that any analysis which features the quality of entrepreneurship, and the social forces controlling it, is apt to arouse violent passions. A number of basic positions are possible. The entrepreneurial or managerial hypothesis can be repudiated as a Trojan horse infiltrating the defences of 'objective' economico-historical method. When a phenomenon cannot be explained in terms of physical resources or the available economic theory it is convenient – over-convenient, say the critics – to fix the explanation upon the human variable in management. This is obligingly unquantifiable, and hostility towards explanations which employ it is bound up with the frequently encountered suspicion of all factors which resist statistical evaluation. Among the modern school of 'new economic historians' a not dissimilar outlook prevails: here the immeasurable entrepreneur is either discounted entirely or deemed to possess a uniformly and persistently rational economic intelligence – which is the next best thing to discounting him entirely.[18] In whatever fashion it is occupied, this position allows attacks to be mounted upon the entrepreneurial explanation as an untrustworthy outsider.

The second position is employed to launch a frontal onslaught. Under fire from this quarter, any theoretical system seeking to describe the forces controlling entrepreneurial behaviour may be cut down as irrelevant since it is held that the entrepreneur *should not* conform to any social orthodoxy or any other conventional restraint. This heroic view of entrepreneurship, often associated with the writings of J. A. Schumpeter, interprets innovation as a 'distinct *economic* function'[19] and holds that it is precisely the entrepreneur's task to fulfil this function regardless of prevailing orthodoxies. Unsurprisingly, Schumpeter compares his entrepreneurs to warriors, a 'stratum of capitalist society which exists by entrepreneurial achievement as the knights of the Middle Ages existed by virtue of a certain technique of warfare.'[20] The justification for these pioneering spirits lies, in fact, in their combative unorthodoxy, in 'creative destruction', the forceful substitution of innovational for traditional patterns; and, as the economic and social climate swings round to favour the new ways, their importance *diminishes*. Within these terms any society whose value system did control the activities of its entrepreneurs to the detriment of the 'distinct economic function' would be judged simply to possess no entrepreneurs worthy of the title.

The third position is equipped with more sophisticated weaponry, and is occupied by those intent upon sapping the value-system defences with technical subtlety. Led by Gerschenkron, they argue – correctly – that the concept of social approval has exaggerated the cohesion or uniformity displayed by societies in their attitudes to economic change, as to most major issues.[21] It is more likely that such attitudes will exhibit a pronounced diversity: social approval may be extended by some groups, withheld by others. 'A single system of dominant social values', concludes Gerschenkron, 'is little more than a fiction'.[22] Allied to this argument are two further hypotheses. There is the suggestion that social disapproval has no power to prevent innovation since, within an entire constellation of *various* social groups, the pattern-breaking entrepreneurial minorities will be governed by their *own* sets of values, and will earn approval for their actions from *some* other groups, if not from all. And, secondly, there is the principle of substitution, invoked once more to support the proposition that, since industrialization has manifestly occurred within societies featuring a high level of disapproval for modern capitalistic organization, there must be methods for overcoming whatever disability this lack of sympathy represents. In consequence, it is not possible to regard social approval for entrepreneurial endeavour as a prerequisite for modern industrial growth.

The final position forms the marshalling area for an entrepreneurial counter-attack. Whatever the qualifications advanced by the various schools of critics, one simple point might bear renewed emphasis: the objective economic endowments, the quantifiable resources or 'inputs' which figure so largely within the 'new economic history' possess no life of their own; they exist only to have decisions taken about them by the entrepreneurial task force. If there are dangers in loading all blame or all credit upon the entrepreneur, it is still true that, in the final analysis, all economic processes must focus upon those who supply the *decisions* governing productive activity. And historical observation would suggest that, whether they deserve the name of entrepreneur or not, the decision-takers are by no means always efficient innovators or relentless maximizers of profit. For instance, a considerable act of faith – and it is nothing else – would be required for the analyst to believe that the progress of innovation in the nineteenth century was a smoothly internationalist exchange with entrepreneurs of one nationality responding rationally and rapidly to demonstrations provided by entrepreneurs of other nationalities. Professor McCloskey finds it 'hardly credible that such a large reward for imitation would go unclaimed'.[23] But if imitation was a fact of nineteeth-century technology, this by no means rules out considerable variations in the perception and competence of the imitators.

It remains possible, therefore, that analysis of the differing skills in decision-making available to the various economies – and often concerned with similar resources or techniques may help to explain their differing economic fortunes. That given, it is the disparity between countries in the decision-taking powers which becomes the puzzle. And here considerations of social approval, educational preference, and governmental rationality may well assist in explaining the behaviour of businessmen who in one country may act with faultless enterprise and in another with little of the opportunist, and less of the heroic, in their style. Even if Gerschenkron is right to argue that the uniformity of attitude inherent within a society's value system – and thus its power to control growth – has been much overrated by some historians, his comments constitute, nevertheless, a modification rather than a demolition of the Parsonian approach. For if a single, comprehensive adverse social value system emerges as an unlikely barrier to successful industrialization, the *balance* between the various value systems maintained by society's constituent minorities may certainly influence the efficiency of the manufacturing community. Each society necessarily will contain a multiplicity of contending interest groups with competing value systems; and its industrial performance may well be determined by the relative strengths of the systems favouring capitalistic growth and those opposing it.

When entrepreneurial values represent a minority element within a social structure which generates disapproval from a wide *range* of groups, it would seem reasonable that industrial growth should be of modest dimensions. Limitations upon entrepreneurial recruitment, credit supply, and market demand, among other features, would prevail as long as disapproval covered such a range, and the entrepreneurial values commanded only minority sup-

15

port. Value dispositions of this type would surely possess the power to dampen, if not to suppress, growth. Similarly, the capacity of any system of 'substitutes' to overcome this form of disapproval must be doubted. Gerschenkron points to the investment banks in Germany and the imperial bureaucracy in Russia as examples of entrepreneurial substitutes.[24] But it could as easily be proposed that the German Great Banks represented simply one *expression* of a value system endowed with a preference for organizations of large scale and 'Reich-building' potential, rather than any substitute for existing values (see below, p. 00). In Russia, on the other hand, it is surely a feature of pre-revolutionary economic history that the use of state entrepreneurship *failed* to commend the idea of industrialization to large portions of Russian society. Indeed, non-industrial and explicitly agrarian values remained sufficiently strong to *moderate* state policy, ensuring that Count Witte's programme of modernization did not extend so far as to tamper with existing relationships within the agricultural sector. Nor, indeed, is the state apparatus itself wholly independent of the values prevalent within the society it administers: there is no surety that those who control the apparatus will partake only of 'progressive' entrepreneurial values. Even at the level of state enterprise, therefore, the possibilities for change are not entirely insulated from the orbital pull of social values.

In the final analysis, therefore, it is true that some of the most important issues in economic development must be resolved outside the realm of purely economic calculation. Allowance must somehow be made for human factors in management which may be family-centred, deployed for state aggrandizement, simply irrational, or wayward in some other style, rather than obediently trained to the mechanical retrieval of capitalistic profit. The models of entrepreneurial behaviour remain useful in permitting a schematic approach to these intricate issues.

A POLITICAL REFLECTION

The role of the government, no less than that of the individual is subject to expectation in the models we have described. Gerschenkron expects that the state will take up a position of major organizational importance within the economic structure of very backward countries. Aron has argued that the state should provide rational administrative, judicial, and fiscal systems as part of the framework for efficient private enterprise. In both cases, the political arm of society is drawn into the economic analysis to perform a specific task which lies outside the competence of any other agency. Too often, that is the only form of recognition extended to the political element by the economic historian. The area of interaction between the political operations of the state and the economic operations of the industrial sector has been strangely neglected in the subject's research activities.[25] Yet it is not necessary to take on board any kind of determinism to recognize that economic processes in the nineteenth century often carried weighty political implications. Nor is it necessary to desert the proper realms of the economic historian to recognize that political decisions greatly affected the capacity for economic growth.

Illustration of the first type of connexion, running from economic towards political affairs, is not difficult to find. Thus the French Revolution was about rural poverty and dear bread as much as it was about privilege, the Rights of Man, or Robespierre. In Italy the goal of unification achieved political pre-eminence, not least because of the need to reduce the disastrous gap in economic achievement between the country's northern and southern parts. And in Germany the formation of the Empire was not unrelated to the needs of the Rhineland industrialists for a nation-sized market, as the belligerent diplomacy of the Reich in the years before the First World War was not unrelated to the appetite of German heavy industry for foreign markets and domestic battleship contracts.

Equally clear on the historical record are the political events which controlled the processes of economic change. The French Revolution of 1789 with its emphasis on liberty and equality, and its stress upon the small man in' politics and economics, introduced into the social value system of nineteenth-century France a peculiarly atomistic individualism (see below pp. 135–9) which had definite consequences for the country's industrial prospects. Once again, it was the political objectives of the tsarist autocracy after its humiliation by Japanese forces in the war of 1904–05 which diverted many millions of roubles from the economic tasks which had claimed them in the 1890s to the apparently unproductive business of swingeing rearmament in the decade before 1914. Alongside these dramatic cases, it is as well to place the salutary reminder that all the actions of government, however humdrum, have an economic outcome, however minor.

Any survey of nineteenth-century industrialization should, therefore, reserve a capacity for the occasional political reflection. It will not always prove possible to trace an operational connexion between economic and political events, and it would be unnecessary, as well as impossible, to maintain a political narrative alongside the economic analysis. But the points of contact are worthy of more note than they commonly receive.

AN ANTI-NATIONAL SUGGESTION

Most surveys of European industrial development assume that the national boundaries define entities which undergo a more or less uniform experience. To a certain extent this study will make no exception to the general rule. The reasons are obvious: the nation represents the most convenient unit of organization for economic data, as for most other kinds of data; the accumulation of economic-historical records has been divided up, traditionally, on a national basis and the collection of such records has often been carried out by the national administrations; and in so far as political or social forces affect econ-

17

omic growth, these tend to be strongly flavoured with nationalistic peculiarities. However, there are some grounds for a certain measure of rethinking.[26] It is clear that, in the early nineteenth century, the defining feature of industrialism was not its national organization but its occurrence within a series of 'enclaves' scattered across Europe. Initially, the major pockets were formed by the textile towns of Lancashire, the Rhineland, and Alsace, even of the Salerno region to the south of the continent and the Moscow—Ivanovo region to the north. These areas shared a common technology based mainly on cotton spinning, a common large scale of factory organization, and a common range of product. And they provided certain complementarities for one another. Lancashire supplied much of the technology for the continental centres, and the British cotton areas also contributed direct consultancy services in the shape of itinerant industrial experts like Milne and Holker in France or Ludwig Knoop in Russia. In return, the towns and cities of the Rhineland based their spinning economies on cheap British yarn and thus provided a useful outlet for Lancashire. There were natural economic connexions between these areas, and, in a real sense, they possessed more affinities with one another than, let us say, Manchester did with southern Cornwall or the Duchy of Berg with the East Elbian grainlands. Nor was this effect restricted to cotton and the early nineteenth century. The diffusion of technology from Britain and the transcontinental wanderings of British industrialists continued down to the First World War and touched a range of industries stretching from machine-tools through railway engineering to the manufacture of heavy artillery and super-dreadnoughts.[27] Up to a point at least — though blockages in the flows of innovation could occur, and entrepreneurial shortcomings remained a problem in some areas — the technological development of this period contained pronounced *international* implications. This does not mean that the technology was wholly transferable between economies, nor that imitation was in any way automatic. Value systems and factor endowments[28] played their part in channelling and metering the flows, but there can be no doubt that they existed, nor that they provided a neglected set of connexions between widely separated industrial concentrations. Furthermore, these economic complementarities probably tended to strengthen as the century progressed: witness the growth of Rhine-Ruhr as the industrial heartland of Europe with its arteries and supporting organs running into Holland, France, and Austria;[29] witness, too, the important part played by French capital, capitalists, and contractors in the development — especially transport development — of Spain, Italy, Hungary, and Russia.[30]

Perhaps even more emphasis should be laid upon these international connexions, given the strong opposing tendency at work within many European economies: the tendency for divisions between advanced and backward sectors to become increasingly acute *inside* the political boundaries. Thus Russia, Italy, Spain, and the Austro-Hungarian Empire each possessed deeply divided economies by 1914. Economic 'dualism' became the common problem, splitting the manufacturing and traditional sectors apart, as the scarce resources inseparable from the state of backwardness became the object of competition between the two. As the more profitable industrial areas gathered in all available slack in capital and manpower, the poverty of the traditional sectors grew progressively more intense.[31] This competition for resources between the sectors outweighed the prospects for any productive interaction between what should have been complementary components of the same economic system and left the older component to assume the status of a 'stranded' region. Industrial growth in a context of backwardness carried the unfortunate implication that some sectors were likely to *stay* backward, their economic deprivation only deepening as innovation proceeded in neighbouring departments or provinces. And, necessarily, as the advanced sectors in various countries expanded in similar style, so they became *collectively* unlike the economies of the grain plains or the olive slopes.

It would be wise, therefore, to qualify the national orientation of this study by resolving to maintain an alertness to the international transmission of resources and to the development of complementary economic structures which happened to straddle political frontiers.

Equipped with concepts governing the stages of growth, the graduated effects of backwardness, and the capabilities of the entrepreneur, we are provided with a set of instruments, more or less primitive no doubt, with which to study the morphology, the quality, and the personnel of European industrialization. Forewarned as to the political conditioning of some industrial advance, and its invariable political content, we may, when necessary, place it within a wider historical context. Reminded as to the particular frontiers of growth, we may, again as necessary, distinguish them from the frontiers of peoples.

An order of treatment is also suggested by those first thoughts. Should not a study of continental industrialization begin with the least backward power in Europe and work towards the most backward, from the most fully industrialized economic system to the least, along a route which by 1914 runs tortuously and roughly from Berlin to Madrid or Budapest, or, more properly, from Gelsenkirchen, Essen, or Dusseldorf to Bilbao or Fiume – and mercifully stops a good way west of the Golden Horn? It is because the following interpretation is built around a system of graduated backwardness that it begins, not, as might be more conventional, with the French economy, an indifferent imitator of the British industrial prototype even in 1800, but with the German, clearly the most formidable on the continental mainland by 1914.

However, for reasons of administration and coherence, the scope of this survey cannot be genuinely pan-European. Some restriction upon the sample is inevitable; here it is thrown around those continental nations which were also great powers. Given the nature of the approach described above, the most suitable subjects will clearly be states of large extent and ambition in which the internal variety of economic achievement is greatest and the association between political and economic stature most keenly measured. Thus Europe's small countries, however prosperous, are omitted. So too, is the British originator of industrial capitalism: the focus of the survey is upon backwardness and thus upon the shared problems of follower economies rather than upon the

19

unique ones of the manufacturing pioneer. Into this rubric, Germany, France, Russia, and Austria-Hungary may be fitted fairly smoothly. The Italian case is a useful one – featuring a nation aspiring simultaneously to the status both of industrial economy and of international power, and achieving both by the skin of its teeth – and may be added without undue strain. The reciprocal – a nation once pre-eminent in Europe and now at best a marginal power seeking in its halting industrialization some, largely ineffectual, compensation for political failure – is provided by Spain. This example of extreme backwardness, coupled with political debilitation, is so valuable for comparative purposes that it is expedient – and narrowly defensible – to include Spain within the community of powers. America is another matter: though undoubtedly an industrial great power and a follower economy, she must be excluded on the grounds of location and of culture. We are concerned with Europe and with the economic fortunes of those special parts of Europe which sought for themselves a world role.

NOTES AND REFERENCES

Full publication details are provided in the bibliography.

1. See Rostow (1960).
2. *Ibid.*, p. 20.
3. See the various national studies in Rostow (ed.) (1963), and especially Cairncross, pp. 240–60.
4. In the case of the UK, the period needed seems to have been between six and ten decades (cf. Habakkuk and Deane in Rostow (ed.), 1963, pp. 74–7); in France close to a half-century (see Marczewski in Rostow (ed.), 1963, p. 123); and in Japan the proportion of net national capital formation to net national product did not exceed 10 per cent until 1931–40, again roughly a half-century after the initial acceleration of industrial growth (see Rosovsky, 1961, p. 15).
5. Rostow (1960), Ch. 3, and Rostow (ed.) (1963), pp. xxiv–xxvi.
6. Compare with these prerequisites the Marxist requirement for an 'original accumulation of capital' in the pre-industrial economy, K. Marx, *Das Kapital*, Ch. 24.
7. Cf. Kuznets in Rostow (ed.) (1963), p. 24.
8. Rostow (1960), p. 20.
9. Gerschenkron (1968), p. 247.
10. Habakkuk (1963), p. 112.
11. Gerschenkron (1962), pp. 46–51.
12. *Ibid.*, p. 8.
13. The above points are largely derived from Gerschenkron (1962), p. 44, and Gerschenkron in Rostow (ed.) (1963), pp. 152–3.
14. Gerschenkron (1962), p. 44.
15. Parsons and Shils (eds) (1951), Pt II, pp. 190ff. Also see Gerschenkron (1962), pp. 52–8.
16. Aron (1967), p. 138.
17. *Ibid.*, pp. 139–41.

18. See, for example, McCloskey (1971), pp. 285–304.
19. Schumpeter (1942), p. 132.
20. Schumpeter (1969), p. 83.
21. See Gerschenkron (1962), pp. 52–71, and (1968), pp. 128–39.
22. *Ibid.*, p. 135.
23. McCloskey (ed.) (1971), p. 287. He is speaking particularly of exchanges between the USA and the UK, but the assumption of an 'international technology' is present within the essay; cf. p. 299.
24. Gerschenkron (1968), pp. 137–8.
25. Coleman (1972), p. 29.
26. See, for instance, Pollard (1973), pp. 636–48.
27. See Trebilcock (1973), pp. 254–72.
28. That is, the supply and relative price of capital, labour, and raw materials.
29. Hauser (1917), p. 22.
30. Cameron (1961).
31. Kelley, Williamson, and Cheetham (1972).

CHAPTER TWO

Germany

By 1914 the legend 'Made in Germany' carried almost as much ominous weight for the island British as did the great warships of the High Seas Fleet.[1] Poised to rival the Anglo-Saxon powers in commercial, imperial, and naval might, the Kaiser's Reich had clearly done a great deal to drive backwardness out of German territory, and, judged by its international strength in 1914, had succeeded more comprehensively in this objective than any other power on the European mainland. If, as Gerschenkron insists, we can in practice rank countries according to their level of backwardness, Germany would be placed in 1914 as the least backward nation on the continent, and might thus represent the most logical departure point for a survey of European industrialization.

The economic power of the Reich, however, was by no means obviously foreshadowed in the fortunes of the multitudinous principalities which, in the eighteenth century, occupied German ground space. In many ways, indeed, the proliferation of states which after 1871 would compose the German Empire, appeared in 1750 to be rather poorly placed in respect of economic potential. The political pulverization of the time prevented free mobility between states, both of persons and products, subjecting the one to restrictions upon migration and the other to the endless hurdles erected by myriad customs authorities. It permitted also the reproduction within each petty domain of an over-decorated administrative pyramid staffed largely by an agrarian social élite undisposed to favour the growth of a nationally coherent or identifiable commercial class. Social relations inside these miniature autocracies were often feudal or semi-feudal, extending in the east to a fully compulsory labour system under which a serf population worked the great estates of the Junker ascendancy. And in the western areas, although the influence of serfdom had been subject to a long process of erosion, the position of the lord remained one of power in matters social, fiscal, or legal. Even the German cities, especially in the Rhineland, tended to be court, cathedral, or university centres rather than the focal points for expanding local trade. Nor within this strait-laced system was any marked disposition towards relaxation evident much before 1800. If anything, the political and economic separatism of the states was reaffirmed with increased emphasis over the eighteenth century. And the so-

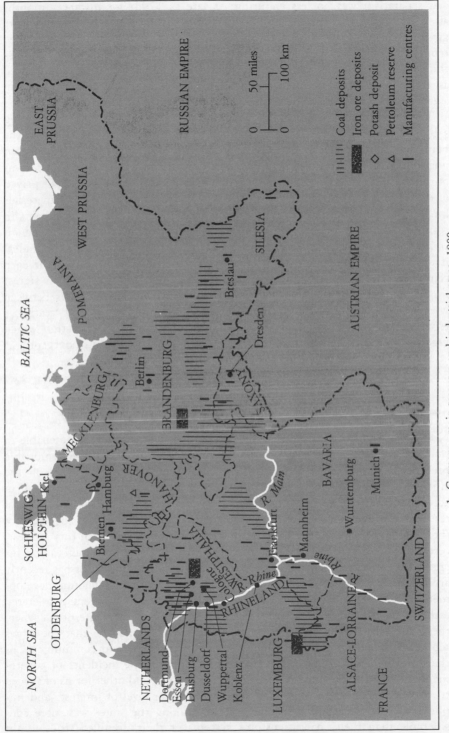

1. Germany: main resource and industrial areas, 1900

NORTH SEA

BALTIC SEA

SCHLESWIG-
HOLSTEIN

OLDENBURG

EAST
PRUSSIA

POMERANIA

WEST PRUSSIA

MECKLENBURG

Kiel

Hamburg

Bremen

HANOVER

NETHERLANDS

Dortmund
Essen
Duisburg
Dusseldorf
Wuppertal
Koblenz

Cologne

WESTPHALIA

R. Rhine

RHINELAND

LUXEMBURG

ALSACE-LORRAINE

FRANCE

Frankfurt

R. Main

Mannheim

R. Rhine

Berlin

BRANDENBURG

SAXONY

Dresden

Breslau

SILESIA

RUSSIAN EMPIRE

AUSTRIAN EMPIRE

BAVARIA

Wurttemburg

Munich

SWITZERLAND

0   50 miles
0   100 km

⫴⫴⫴ Coal deposits
▬   Iron ore deposits
◇   Potash deposit
△   Petroleum reserve
▬   Manufacturing centres

23

cial separatism was no less enduring: as late as 1794, for instance, months after the French had forcibly torn down their social barriers, the Prussian state gave frank legal sanction to the division of society into strict classes, the trinity of noble, burgher, and peasant.[2] If a rational system of fiscal administration or a fluid society willing to reward the commercial talents are counted as useful attributes for industrial success, the eighteenth-century German states could scarcely have been less adequately equipped for growth.

The location of this ramshackle amalgam of states did not help. Occupying a central position between the prosperous trading powers to the west and the benighted absolutisms to the east, the majority of German states had proved unable to tap the stream of seaborne wealth which had created concentrations of capital and expertise in the ports of Britain, France, and Holland. Deprived of the 'commercial revolution' which had provided some of the basic materials for British industrialization, the German states forfeited the improvements in commercial skills, transportation, and the free movement of goods which it could have been expected to encourage. Yet if location discouraged the trader, it attracted the soldier all too effectively. In the seventeenth and eighteenth centuries war appeared as an endemic phenomenon for the German states, imposing high defence costs on strained budgets, souring relations between governments, and thus the prospects for economic integration, and creating – especially in the Thirty Years War – a measure of urban devastation which greatly limited the possibilities for the growth of an indigenous bourgeoisie.[3]

THE OLD REGIME AND THE NEW INDUSTRIES

Not all the characteristics of these pocket duchies were entirely unamenable to economic advance, however. As the German states absorbed the fashionable precepts of Enlightened Despotism, and most notably its emphasis on the efficient organization of available resources, their governments imbibed an accompanying interest in things industrial. Nor were the military interests of the *ancien régime* administrations – which typically disbursed 70 per cent of their budgets on war-related pursuits – at all incompatible with this interest: certain industries could both make rational use of available resources and increase the offensive potential of the state. It may be, as Borchardt has recently argued, that the role of the public authorities in German economic development before 1850 has been overplayed and that the governments, 'tolerated rather than encouraged' industry, even suppressing private enterprises where these cut across their own official ventures.[4] And it may be that the states tended to spend more on the improvement of transport and communications than on the direct promotion of manufacturing. But the incidence of government subsidies, monopoly grants, tariff concessions, and other forms of special treatment for key industries, does suggest a higher level of interest, and implies that the capacity for economic action among the states was more considerable than their chaotic customs systems or their dignified cities might suggest. Nor is this greatly surprising. However necessary it may be that successful economic development should be supported over the long run by a positive social value system, this requirement includes no stipulation that industrial advance must be *initiated* by a 'new' society with freshly woven bourgeois priorities – although some recent writing has virtually asserted as much.[5] Governments, even governments of a fairly hidebound old-regime type, might follow their interest in military capabilities as far as the competent execution of specific industrial tasks. This order of state might dislike free enterprise as much as it disliked civil liberties, but it could see the point of directed enterprise in manufactures such as metals and armaments. Pugnaciously separatist governments and rigidly ordered societies can be seen instead, with only a slight twist of the model, as bureaucratic systems interested in secure administration and in the industrial means for remaining *effectively* pugnacious. In this early type of activity the state does not have to perform as a consciously modernizing agency – indeed the state apparatus continues to employ some very unmodern personnel – but directly and simply in its own military interest. Economic advance thus comes about more as a by-product of *realpolitik* than as the outcome of a deliberate choice within an economic programme.

Nowhere is this more evident than in Prussia. Within its borders the requirements of an expansionist territorial policy brought into existence the most impressive array of development incentives yet seen among the German states, and in one area at least – Silesia – they were notably successful. Behind these devices lay, in the first instance, the absolutism of Frederick the Great with its strongly militaristic orientation. This absolutism not only pieced together a nation from segments of various German duchies but also created, out of necessity, a uniform trading policy to hold it together. Led into economic action by the demands of a political grand design, Frederick was probably the first German ruler to employ economic bricks for shoring up the none-too-secure edifice of state. Unsurprisingly, the economic component of this policy – and even this terminology exaggerates the degree to which a discrete economic element may be separated from the overall policy objectives – was much concerned with war capacity, a form of blood-and-iron mercantilism which was to appear, from time to time, throughout the German industrial process.

By the end of Frederick's reign in 1786, the Prussian economy was already well drilled in self-sufficiency and the military arts. A system of agricultural credit had been extended to the landowners with the intention of improving crop yields and maintaining a ready supply of home-grown foodstuffs. The agricultural labour group, still enserfed but benevolently supervised by the Crown, was already the docile factor of production which the German workforce remained for the great majority of the nineteenth century. And in the more modern forms of economic activity the state found itself increasingly involved: it maintained its own royal shipyard at Stettin and its own agencies for the marketing of Silesian iron ore, together with important monopolies in timber and salt. At the same time, private industrial enterprise was encouraged with the conventional incentives of the old regime – tariff protection, monopoly grants, and cheap supplies from the royal factories. Even in financial affairs there was official activity. In a curious anticipation of the role later to be played in German development by the banking sector, Frederick, as early as 1765, laid the foundations of a state bank, the Reichsbank. At the time, he expressed also an oddly advanced interpretation of the state's role in development: 'If economic enterprise is beyond the power of my subjects', he observed, 'it is my affair to defray the costs.' What remained unspoken, however, was that the Crown was less interested in economic enterprise as a general good or as a modernizing force – witness its unkindness to industrial projects which cut across its own priorities – than as a specific asset for its own policy.

Most interesting of all, however, was the involvement of the Prussian authorities in the promotion of new industries and in the managerial responsibility for such ventures. There would appear to be three major phases in the early development of German entrepreneurship. The first, running from about 1720 to about 1790, involved the recruitment by the state of a small group of competent businessmen as managers for industries in which the government had a special interest. The second, from about 1790 to about 1840, saw the state – primarily the Prussian state – providing its own industrial experts for a select range of strategic industries. And the third, from 1840 to 1914, saw the rise of the private industrialist and financier more or less independent of government interest or intervention. Significantly, it was only this final entrepreneurial phase, accompanied by pronounced social and political readjustments, which produced an extensive form of industrial activity in German territory.

But, for Frederick the Great, faced with a narrow range of manufacturing possibilities and an equally specialized set of industrial objectives, the employment of the nation's small band of efficient firms as management consultants offered the best prospects. Despite his frequently expressed contempt for the merchant class – indicating once more the *limited* desirability attached to commercial activity by the official value system – the King retained a number of houses to pioneer the development of such new industries as cutlery, sugar refining, metals, and munitions between the 1750s, and the 1780s. The most important of these concerns, Splitgerber and Daum of Berlin, controlled eight 'national factories' around mid-century – most of them, predictably, war-related industries – and retained the supervision of the vital armament factories at Spandau and Potsdam until the middle of the next century. In such projects the connexion between Frederick's mercantilist economic interests and his chauvinistic political aims was perhaps most tightly made.[6]

It is, of course, possible to criticize these 'proto-factories' on the grounds that they were over-dependent on courtly or official demand and possessed little custom outside the old regime itself. By the same token, the licensed manufacturers may be compared to monopolists unable to offer much useful example to the private business community. Such industries were thus related neither to the open-market potential nor to the existing reserve of entrepreneurial power, such as it was. They were hothouse plants easily upset by any

26

change in the micro-climate artificially maintained for them by the state.[7] But, on the other hand, the interest of the state, however single-minded it may have been, did introduce new technologies into the available stock, and some demonstration effect could be expected to follow in the medium, if not in the immediate, term. Moreover, the war-related industries preferred by the Prussian Crown appear to have possessed more stamina than the other types of 'proto-factory' and to have convincingly outlived the induced demand of the old regime, carrying their technological advances with them. Finally, this form of development, provided a useful apprenticeship in industrial affairs for the Prussian state, and this was to be exploited after the 1780s.

Upper Silesia, a bare, sparsely cultivated, and thinly populated region, lacking any ready supply of capital or labour, was the recipient of the bureaucracy's increased attention. It became the forum for an ambitious exercise in state-led growth. From the mid-eighteenth century, Frederick the Great had been interested in this uninviting province, and, in consequence, its few industries – particularly iron and linen – had attracted state assistance. The first blast-furnace on German soil was installed in a Silesian ironworks, the Malapane Hütte, in 1753,[8] and labour for the linen manufactories was attracted by a characteristic royal promise of a free loom for each immigrant weaver. But the fullest development of the area came after Frederick's death. Silesia's one priceless resource – its proximity to the Austrian battlefields – was more than sufficient to hold, and to enhance, the government's interest. The element of war preparedness within the earlier industrial promotions emerged with renewed strength in the development of Silesia: the province was to be a Prussian arsenal. Partly for this reason, partly because of the naturally expanding scale of the Silesian industries, the state assumed a much tighter control over the entrepreneurial function. By a device known as the *Direktionprinzip*, the authorities claimed the right to appoint their own directors to the boards of private companies. But, given the shortage of private capitalistic experience in the largest type of industrial operation, the bureaucracy was frequently involved more deeply, drawn into outright control of the more important Silesian installations. Despite the reverence of those at the helm of Prussian affairs[9] for the economic propositions of Adam Smith ('der gottliche Smith'), it was not the non-interventionist philosophy of the continent's foremost advocate of free trade which proved influential in Silesia: here the reforming civil servants of the Prussian Crown put on an industrial cap and became official businessmen.

At this point the government did take the entrepreneurial function upon itself, providing management, capital, and, critically important, technical skill to mould Silesia's scattered mineral deposits into viable industrial concentrations. The most vitally placed of the state industrialists were von Heinitz, head of the Prussian industrial and mining agency, and Graf von Reden, special industrial commissar for Silesia, both appointed in the 1770s. For the technical skills these officials very often looked abroad, taking suggestions, techniques, and sometimes technologists, from France, Belgium, Switzerland, and, above all, Britain. In the 1780s, Berlin despatched Reden himself to join the crowd of Europeans conducting discreet if watchful pilgrimages to the shrines of British industrialization. Judged by the results, Reden must have learned his devotions well for he was able to introduce the iron-puddling process to Silesia only shortly after Britain had pioneered its application, to equip the government ironworks of the Königshütte and the sister foundry at Gleiwitz with the most modern coke furnaces by 1802, and, fittingly, to provide for the great lead plant at Friedrichsgrube, the first British steam-engine in Germany.[10] More than this, he brought over the brother of the British ironmaster, John Wilkinson, to manage the Malapane Hütte and the Scot, John Baildon, to look after the new coke furnaces. Under Reden's management, Silesia was given some of the most active mining concerns and some of the largest and most efficient iron-processing plants in Europe. By 1800 her industrial labour force, together with her mining output, had increased fivefold over the level of 1780[11] and by 1842 one observer could claim that Silesia was 'the equal of England and the foremost on the continent of Europe'.[12] If so, if the first industrial nation was finding a proficient Germanic imitator, it was largely a function of induced growth, of state interest in the task of development.

Certain lessons follow from the Prussian experience. It provides perhaps the first European instance of effective substitution for the lack of an extensive commercial class. Similar contemporaneous experiments in Saxony and Thuringia proving unsuccessful, it was left to the Silesian factories to demonstrate that a form of industrial activity could be achieved even without the development of an independent entrepreneurial group or the possession of lavish natural endowments. In doing so, they supplied, admittedly at a low level of sophistication, an example of entrepreneurial substitution of the type suggested by Gerschenkron for countries of pronounced backwardness. Further, they indicated a second important truth: that politico-military ambitions could play a large part in focusing the attention of the state upon the need for industrial advance. And in the Silesian case it so happens that this was not the only manner in which political considerations made economic growth possible. It is probable that the proliferation of state boundaries and tariff barriers, in other ways major impediments to German growth, here acted to protect the Silesian resource situation, since they permitted concentration upon a region of largely strategic value, sealing it off, insulating it from inter-regional competition and forestalling the drift of industry to the more favoured resource sites of the Ruhr and Rhineland. Within such a context, an especial premium was placed upon organizational skill – which the Prussian civil service could provide – and upon technological skill – which could be imported. And through that technological importation, Silesia became a member of an international manufacturing fraternity, picking up devices and personnel from a common pool, able to produce with her acquisitions factories and mines which convincingly resembled the British prototypes. Substitution, military orientation, and imitation thus suggest themselves as contituents of the classical development mix for the backward country.

However, a cautionary word is in order. If much of the Silesian growth followed from an exercise in entrepreneurial substitution, it is worth noting that this device was applied only to a very limited range of military-related industries. The substitution did not in any way attempt, and would not have welcomed, a thorough-going programme of economic modernization, not even indeed a measure of modernization as wide as that sought by Count Witte's bureaucracy in the Russia of the 1890s. Within German territory, growth of wider scope was to depend upon quite other entrepreneurial resources. It is not true, therefore, that Prussian economic activity witnessed the triumph of state entrepreneurship over backwardness and an adverse value system; it rather saw state entrepreneurship confining itself to economic areas of especial interest to the Crown's policies for internal security and external advantage.

Nor did one Silesia make a 'German' industrial surge. In the first phase of European industrial growth, the initial Kondratiev 'long cycle' of the period 1780–1850, which featured especially the industrialization of Britain and Belgium, *parts* of what was to become Germany were economically active, probably at least as active as the equivalent industrial areas of France. Around 1800, however, it was still a regionally limited activity. Over most of the German states, manufacturing ventures remained small, booms and slumps commercial rather than industrial, innovation scarce, and the market tightly circumscribed. Where there were not enterprising state authorities willing to take a hand with industrial administration, the underdevelopment of the bourgeoisie remained a serious constraint. External trade and export demand grew only sluggishly, producing a limited effect in such manufactures as linen and in the grain sector of agriculture. Where the primary sector had responded to the existence of commercial opportunities, as on the north-eastern plains, it had done so by exploiting the existing feudal relationships rather than by any internal modernization. And over the territory of all German states, some 80 per cent of the population continued to work on the land. As yet, if there were 'intimations of industrialization' (Borchardt) in some areas, the backwardness of most had still to be seriously dented.

WAR AND PEACE 1790–1830: SOME ECONOMIC CONSEQUENCES OF NAPOLEON BONAPARTE

In the decades either side of 1800, war provided a charge sufficiently powerful to disturb this equilibrium. From both the American War of Independence and the Napoleonic Wars, the industries of Lower Rhine, the kingdom of Saxony and Westphalia, won important market advantages. Saxony, indeed, was developing contemporaneously with Silesia, if in a very different style. By 1800 only 20 per cent of Saxons were *full-time* agriculturalists, close to a reciprocal of the figure for all German states.[13] And in the early years of the new century, despite her inadequate capital supplies and her primitive technology, Saxony was contending vigorously with Britain in some lines of textile manufacture and even establishing a quiet supremacy in the European hosiery trade. If, in 1812, one-quarter of Saxon spindles were driven by cattle-power, rather than by steam-power, a superb system of state education offered considerable compensation in the shape of a highly literate labouring and managerial force.[14] Additionally, Napoleon's Continental System, in protecting Saxony from the power of the British mills after 1806, allowed a rapid expansion of modern methods: between 1806 and 1810 the production of machine-spun yarn quadrupled. Silesia, therefore, was not entirely alone; additional manufacturing areas were slowly joining her in the early 1800s.

One of these attracted benefits similar to those enjoyed by Saxony but derived far more substantial advantages from the deeds of the Napoleonic armies. Naturally enough, the impact of the invaders upon the economies of the German states was mixed. For some it was definitely painful. The international diffusion of technology – most important to Silesia for instance – was disrupted; the traditional export textiles, linen, silk, and wool were checked by the British blockade of 1806–13; the occupied areas suffered considerable financial and political impositions; and those areas where economic prosperity was closely bound up with state activity found their growth jeopardized by war needs and war burdens. For others the results were quite different. Thus the Rhineland, which next to France itself experienced most directly the economic influence of the revolutionary and imperial regimes, appears to have undergone a marked improvement in industrial performance. In these border areas the intrusion of the Napoleonic system modified some of the worst features in German economic organization. The restrictive guild structure of the urban trades, the feudal relics in the countryside, the ubiquitous internal customs barriers were broken down by the occupying authorities and, in place of the corrupt native government, an efficient administration and a rational legal code were substituted. A better approximation to the institutional systems within which economic 'subjects' were likely to act in an enterprising way was provided by the invading French. Or, as one recent commentator has observed, the *Code Napoléon* brought with it 'a system of government that was in close harmony with the needs of a buoyantly industrialising economy'.[15]

Certainly, the beneficiaries, the towns of Julich, Krefeld, or Aachen, the mills of the Wupper Valley and the Duchy of Berg, were able before long to present their own challenges to the British superiority in cotton textiles. But war also brought benefits more tangible than those of rational government. With French industries damaged by conscription and British imports curtailed by hostilities, and, after 1806, by the Continental System, the Rhineland became a natural focus for textile manufacture.[16] With Napoleon's armies as customers and French demand eager for their products, these captive cities and factories were provided with a captive market, amounting within the Continental System to some 30 m. consumers. Inevitably, there were disadvantages also: even for the Rhineland the exactions of the French armies could become overbearing or the inflation which France exported excessively burdensome. Admittedly, too, the invaders' administration of a divided Rhineland could set off abrupt locational shifts in the region's industrial prosperity. The areas on the west bank, firmly attached to the French market from the 1790s, enjoyed a relatively stable advance, but the areas on the eastern side – including 'Little England', the remarkably successful cotton manufactory of Berg – sometimes experienced the workings of French economic discrimination from the wrong side of the fence. Such acts of exclusion were perpetrated with little military advantage in mind, but rather because the textile manufacturers of the east bank had succeeded too well, and, in the process, had given their French competitors an unpleasant fright.

On the whole, however, the economic benefits of the French occupation outweighed the disadvantages. On the west bank, the Department of Roer was transformed from an almost wholly agricultural district in 1799 to an industrial concentration employing some 65,000 workers by 1815. Urban centres went through a similar period of spectacular expansion. And none more so than the city of Aachen. Not least because of its Carolingian associations, it attracted especial attention from the new Charlemagne – and found army contracts, subsidies, and prizes showered upon it. The industrialists of the city responded obediently, introducing the first British machinery in 1807 and the first power loom in 1812. Between 1800 and 1807 the number of Aachen's woollen factories rose fivefold and exports to Spain and Russia were well in train by the later date. Significant also was the city's connexion with British technology, no less significant than the relationship achieved by the Silesian industries, and, like it, extending beyond the provision of machines alone. For the growth prospects of Aachen during the early 1800s were sufficient to bring John Cockerill and a team of English technicians to the city with the intention of creating an engineering business which turned out to be one of the most advanced machine-building works on the continent. Cockerill in Aachen, like Wilkinson and Baildon in Silesia was a citizen of an industrial world, moving easily between the manufacturing centres scattered across Europe.

Outside Aachen there was also plentiful activity. Within 80 kilometres, there were the textile centres of Julich and Krefeld, doubling their population during the occupation, as labour moved into their expanding factories. And even the Prussian authorities conceded after 1815 that the expansion of markets under French auspices, though 'procured by force and power politics',[17] had brought considerable benefits to many of the Rhenish textile areas. Kisch has gone so far as to claim, risking an element of hyperbole, that, 'never before, nor for that matter ever again, were the Rhineland capitalists to enjoy a regime so favourably disposed towards entrepreneurial initiative'.[18] This is to underrate, perhaps, the instability of the economic structure created by the Continental System, its erratic price movements, and its alternating bouts of feverish activity and deep slump. But it is certainly true that the structure of embargoes, by removing British cottons from the immediate market, allowed these German areas to acquire vital manufacturing experience in the production of textiles and thus in the technology which offered the most obvious route towards full industrial status. An economic style characterized by large-scale organization, trained labour, and specialized machine construction was amply demonstrated, together with the rewards that accrued to enterprise under

31

rational systems of administration. Of these gains the Rhineland acquired more over the Napoleonic period than any other German region. Moreover, the Rhineland could absorb the institutional benefits of the Revolution and Empire – almost any governmental, legal, or fiscal innovation would have marked an improvement upon the established procedures of 1790–without the political and psycho-social upheavals suffered by the French. It could sequester the Gallic markets without having to absorb the Gallic value system. It could gather the best economic bequests passed on by the French legislators and administrators without inheriting also the economic restraints which the French imposed upon themselves as a result of the revolutionary experience.

The three major growth areas, Silesia, Saxony, and the Rhineland thus provide, by the time of Waterloo, a distinct suggestion that the 'intimations' of economic modernization were strengthening. But they can by no means support any hypothesis of 'dynamic' industrial advance. For, outside these areas, economic life was very different. After the war, the Rhinelanders could only resent the prospect of reunion with the other war-torn and battered provinces. By their standards even Prussia remained backward in 1815. And, if one looks away from the growth points towards the other duchies and principalities between 1815 and 1830, one encounters the materials of economic distress more frequently than those of industrial advance. Many governments had been forced into deflationary policies in an attempt to rectify their war-ravaged currencies. Harvests were disastrously short in 1816–18 and embarrassingly abundant in 1818–25, leaving the rural community with a highly unstable price and food problem. Poverty and emigration were common in many areas. In northern Westphalia and Hesse-Darmstadt in 1818 officials reported 'a wandering spirit . . . the craze to emigrate to America',[19] which stemmed, they argued, from the recent invasion and the consequent decay of trade. It was this period which in Hamburg produced the barely subsistence labour groups who lost a relatively secure economic base, never to regain it. Soaring food prices, rents, and unemployment brought no less than 60 per cent of the city's population to the edge of poverty between 1800 and 1850.[20]

Elsewhere, outside the expanding agriculture of the north-east and the modern industry of the Frenchified border areas, overpopulation was common. Between 1815 and 1850 the pressure of numbers drove some 800,000 persons into emigration, particularly from the Brunswick, Hanover, Baden, Württemberg and Bavaria regions. By the time revolution came in 1848, it had behind it a long pedigree of poverty and immizeration as well as the more commonly emphasized political grievances. Nor were the growth areas themselves entirely untainted by this pedigree. For them, the return to peace meant readjustment to a competitive market and a simultaneous sharp decline in French and German government purchasing. The change could be highly painful: some of the bright new spinning mills could not stand the strain and collapsed; others, cut off from the modernizing flow of British technology for the duration of the war, could now no longer maintain their earlier level of mechanical excellence. Even for Aachen, it proved impossible to renew the challenge to British industry much before the 1830s. And, for the one-time industrial élite of Silesia, the proto-industrial era received an unhappy culmination in the shape of the poverty riots of 1844.

Clearly, then, the German development areas need to be placed in a correct context and a correct perspective. In the first place, if certain regions gained from the Franco-British hostilities while they lasted, these regions also shared in the less pleasant consequences of war. In the second place, the development areas lay among a number of other regions which did not gain greatly from the military conflict, and suffered severely in its aftermath. Indeed it is arguable that, around 1830–40, the western German states were confronting a demographic crisis which was avoided only by a subsequent industrialization and its attendant expansion in jobs and incomes. It is certain that the regionalized industrial development before 1830 was wholly insufficient to solve this problem. The gradualistic expansion of German industry, therefore, while accelerating in the later eighteenth and early nineteenth centuries, had by 1815–30 achieved only a partial geographical coverage and a by no means definite security of tenure.

Yet the legacies of war, like its immediate effects, are endlessly complex. Within any analysis of the German economy before 1830, a place must be found for the major institutional reforms perpetrated by German civil servants between 1800 and 1815. Quite certainly, they were introduced under the stresses of war, but their administrative and economic utility far outlived it. Traditional boundaries, traditional practices of government, traditional privileges and monopolies were subjected to critical scrutiny and were swiftly adjusted. During the 1800s, what was once the Holy Roman Empire came under the dissecting knives of the various princes collaborating with Bonaparte and was carved up into a score of modern states. Other territorial rulers fighting Bonaparte were obliged by his acts of reform to offer competition in kind: the proximity of the citizen army rendered innovation unusually acceptable to the controllers of the more archaic state structures. Consequently, the reforming civil servants of many an absolute ruler were set to work upon the creation of a territorial and legal transformation, whittling away numerous peculiarities of the old regime almost entirely. Prince-bishops, imperial knights, and other assorted dignitaries found their privileges cut sternly down to size.[21] In Prussia another monopoly, the restrictive framework of the urban guilds, was attacked between 1807 and 1811 and most of it destroyed – although even here certain limitations endured until mid-century, and in Saxony into the 1860s. Rural reform, beginning in Baden in 1783 and sweeping over most of the German states between 1810 and 1850,[22] accompanied the increasing liberalization of commerce and industry. Again, the most important measures came in Prussia. Here, even in the 1770s, noble and bourgeois estate owners, tempted by the lucrative grain trade to England, had pressed for the modernization of rotation and cultivation systems. They had been impeded, however, by Frederick the Great's policies of peasant protection. With an increasing appreciation of the superior productivity of free labour in the 1790s, such restraints in turn began to yield; the royal domains were, in fact, the first to discharge their peasantry from feudal services and to liberate peasant land for consolidation into individual holdings. At this point, however, fears of peasant impatience, and perhaps insurrection, prevented the diffusion of the reforms beyond the palisades of the royal estates. It was quite clearly Bonaparte who removed these final barriers. The military collapse of Prussia at Jena and Auerstädt made internal reconstruction imperative and its agricultural component, a design for extensive emancipation, was rapidly formulated in the decrees of 1807, 1811, 1816, and 1821. The reformist schedule was completed in Prussia by the educational provisions of von Humboldt (1810), adding an element of change which possessed obvious relevance for future generations of Prussian businessmen and officials.

The largest effect of the wartime reforms was to create a measure of economic mobility in the rural sector. But it was a partial mobility only. The major beneficiaries of the Prussian provisions, for instance, were the more substantial peasantry. Just as the first shoots of reform were evoked by French expansionism, so its fruits fell in much the same direction as those released by the revolutionary land settlement in France, towards the 'bourgeoisie rurale'. By 1816 about 70 per cent of the larger peasantry, controlling the great majority of all peasant land, had already freed themselves of feudal obligation, 'by a combination of commutation payments and land transfers'.[23] In contrast, the smaller peasantry, immensely more numerous but holding only a fraction of total peasant land, 'the rural masses between the Elbe and the Vistula',[24] had to await the 1850s and 1860s before the miraculous cloak of emancipation swept over them. Agricultural reform here entailed strong polarizing movements among the peasantry. As the wealthy grew more prosperous, the small unfree cultivators of the east, still tenants-at-will, were progressively transformed into a captive wage labour force between 1816 and 1860, perhaps forfeiting considerable portions of their land in the process. Mobility, therefore, had some limited and specialized meanings in the Prussian countryside in the half-century after 1807. But, however constrained, it almost certainly opened new prospects for agricultural *output*. If the smaller peasant elements suffered a loss in acreage as a result of the reforms, the general efficiency of agriculture was raised as the bigger peasantry gained independence, control over their own plots, and the ability to produce for the market. Simultaneously, the great estates of the east absorbed the extra land gradually surrendered by the lesser peasantry in exchange for their freedom, and then smoothly took aboard their redirected labour power. New prospects for economic activity also opened in other directions. The provisions in respect of urban manufacturing released the constraints imposed by craft antiquarianism and illiteracy and sketched some fresh outlines, at least tentatively, upon the industrial slate.

These measures constitute in many ways 'Germany's' best answer to the French Revolution. It was not a bourgeois revolution, and even R.R. Palmer finds his ingenuity stretched to the utmost in the attempt to fit it, rather unsuccessfully, within his considerable collection of 'democratic revolutions'.[25] It was a revolution from above, carried out by governing élites and professional administrators. And it followed, probably, less from their liberalism than from their recognition that the redefined or besieged states produced in the

34

course of the Napoleonic campaigns could not be governed by the conventional processes. War, in this sense, compelled a rationalization of institutional
and legal structures. And, as in Silesia, a political predicament led to developments of economic utility.

But how much utility? The guild regulations had always been difficult to
enforce and it is unlikely that they could have proved major obstacles in the
way of healthy industrial advance. Similarly, the effectiveness of peasant
emancipation was at best ambiguous in economic terms. In order to secure his
freedom the peasant was required, as was usual and reasonable, to pay compensation to his former overlord. But in Prussia, for instance, this compensation could take the form, in the case of manorial land, of redemption dues
payable over onerously long periods, or, in the case of non-hereditary peasant
holdings, typically on the great estates of East Elbia, could involve the forfei-
ture of up to two-thirds of the existing plot in order to obtain title to the
remaining one-third. The thousands of serfs with no claim to any form of land
– again heavily concentrated in the eastern provinces – lost their feudal common rights and became merely landless labourers. On the face of it, the price
paid for emancipation was high: the redemption payments could drag on for
twenty-five years or more; the total surrender of peasant land may be estimated as high as one million hectares; the eastern serfs lost traditional certainties and gained very little.[26] But in practice, a number of considerations acted
to modify the weight of the exaction: it does not seem to be true that emancipation within German territory was simply an amendment in legal nomen-
clature involving heavy real burdens for the peasantry, as it undoubtedly was in
Russia after 1861. To begin with, the creation of the *Rentenbanken*, financial
intermediaries which provided redemption payments for the landlord in the
short term but allowed the peasant to spread repayment over a considerable
time span, *eased* the problem of those facing cash outlays. Secondly, the huge
transfer of surrendered land which could have occurred in the east seems not to
have done so in practice, and it is unlikely that more than 3 per cent of
peasant land was lost in redemption surrenders.[27] Even for the least prosperous
rural groups there was a hint of a silver lining. Although the small peasants
and cottars indisputably sank after 1816 into the great morass of the eastern
agricultural proletariat, they were able, by accepting the status of employees
'bonded' to the estate owners and bigger peasants, to obtain a tolerable
measure of security, reasonably living standards, and a small allotment for
livestock and arable cultivation. Garden plots supplied by the new landlord-
employers, together with the potato crop which made maximum use of these
small holdings, constituted something like salvation for the eastern peasantry.
Provided with these new opportunities, freed of the responsibility and cares of
inheritance, they appeared to proclaim at least a measure of satisfaction by
establishing one of the highest rates of population growth to be found among
the rural communities of nineteenth-century Europe.[28]

Yet it is by no means possible to construct statements of a generally optimistic nature for the whole of 'Germany'. Although it may be permissible to
modify the most severe assessments of emancipation in some particulars, it

remains true that the level of agricultural efficiency achieved by the various states in the post-reform decades varied very widely indeed.

If there is a discernible trend within the experience of the territories, it would appear to be a split one, favouring, on the one hand, the more substantial peasantry, better able to handle redemption payments, and, on the other, the great eastern estates, now provided with a guaranteed and numerous labour force. In the south-west, a region of dwarf holdings and heavy over-population, the fragmentation of plots and the accompanying attachment to common rights had progressed too far for reform to offer any useful prospects of economic advance. In the centre and south-east, the opportunities for con-solidation of holdings opened up by the tenurial adjustments were not acted upon until the late nineteenth century. Only in Hanover and the north-west did a wave of enclosure follow closely upon the liberation movements, and here the peasants farming substantial plots were much in evidence. Only in the east did large-scale capitalistic producers working for an expanding market and employing wage labour strengthen their place within the primary sector, and here Junker pre-eminence was forcefully restated.

In agriculture, as in industry, it would seem that the legacy of war was an untidy one. Just as some manufacturing areas were pushed into activity by war conditions and others damaged by them, so the major tenurial reforms – by far the most important of the legal and administrative adjustments precipi-tated by war pressures – fell with unequal weight upon the rural sectors of the various states. As industrialization affected some districts and left others im-mune, so agricultural advance 'took' only in a limited number of regions once emancipation was accomplished. Therefore, the agrarian reforms of the early nineteenth century did little to reduce the intense regionalism of German economic development.

It would scarcely be realistic, therefore, to speak of a uniform 'agricultural transformation' as a characteristic of German farming in the period down to 1850. Nor was extreme variation in performance between regions its only peculiarity. Even within those areas which did expand output considerably, there was little noticeable improvement in agricultural technique. An in-creased enthusiasm for the cultivation of more arable furrows had been evident in the late eighteenth century, and, even in their reformed state, the most progressive areas continued to increase output simply by expanding the culti-vated acreage. Few increases in yields were recorded until late in the century. Even in the north-west, enclosure proceeded by the division of common land and the ploughing up of marginal land to produce, still within a three-field structure, a greatly increased crop-bearing area. This commenced a process of new settlement in the region which continued down to the Second World War.[29] As arable yields were slow to rise, so meat production found it dif-ficult to keep pace with population: the supply of meat per head, thanks partly to the stock losses of the war years, was no more generous in 1850 than in 1800. Finally, in the 1840s, in the last vicious swing of the famine cycle, German agriculture demonstrated that it was still capable of collapse: the potato blight of 1845–46 and the scanty grain harvests of 1846 and 1847 combined to create starvation conditions. Nevertheless, the record was by no means wholly bleak; there were real achievements in German agriculture before mid-century. As the three-field system gradually gave way to new crop rotations in the third and fourth decades of the century, root crops did greatly expand their share of the total harvest – from 3 per cent to 24 per cent in Prussia between 1800 and 1840 – thus permitting vegetable output to keep pace with population advance and at least lessening the reliance upon the performance of grains. Moreover, the expansion of the cultivated acreage, even without increased yields, did succeed in maintaining 'Germany' in a position of almost complete self-sufficiency in foodstuffs down to 1850, very much as the British primary sector had done upon the threshold of another industrialization a century earlier. Thus, during the period 1816–65 total German population expanded by 59 per cent but was sustained by an increase in agricultural output of 135 per cent.[30] In addition, German agrarian producers managed to supply an export balance of grain, wool, and timber which provided a highly useful counterbalance to the imports of raw materials and semi-finished products required in the early stages of industrialization.

THE SEARCH FOR THE GERMAN 'TAKE-OFF'

Even given the highly chequered form of agricultural and manufacturing expansion, it is precisely 'the early stages of industrialization' which form the central preoccupation of German economic history in the period 1830–50. With at least a certain measure of proficiency establishing itself in the primary sector, with the growth areas in manufacturing now increasingly soundly based, with the recessional characteristics of the post-war years fading, the more adventurous among the economic historians have tended to look for evidence of dynamic growth, perhaps of 'take-off', commencing in the 1830s. They have discovered a variety of promising indications: a fairly wide assortment of textile factories, a renewed spate of canal building, a measure of railroad construction, the first clear upswing of the industrial cycle in 1834–37, and the rearrangement of Germany's chaotic markets into the tidier inter-state organization of the *Zollverein* or Customs Union from 1834. Undoubtedly there was an upward movement in economic activity in the 1830s. It included probably the first wave of innovation that was felt, in one form or another, across most of the German states. The first railroad was constructed between Nuremberg and Furth in Bavaria in 1835; some 240 kilometres of new canal and 700 kilometres of improved waterway were created, mostly on the North German lowlands; and new financial institutions were introduced into such commercial centres as Berlin and Leipzig in the decade or so before 1840. Such activity – particularly the activity in the railway and textile sectors – has convinced Professor W.G. Hoffmann for one that the commencement of German 'take-off' might be located within the years 1830/35 and the completion of the process within the period 1830/35 – 1855/60.[31]

Among most economic historians, however, a preference has grown up over the years − expressed by Clapham, Schumpeter, Gerschenkron, and, most recently, Borchardt among others − for locating the acceleration somewhat later, in the 1850s. It is not difficult to see why. If the new textile factories of the 1830s were the familiar capitalistic evolutions in the Manchester style, the network of domestic and craft production which expanded *alongside* the modern concerns belonged to a much earlier mode of production. And before 1850 the modern scale-intensive organizations worked much less to replace the proliferating craft system than to replace British imports. Therefore, the major part of German textile output to mid-century, was associated with a form of production which, across most of Europe, was distinctively *proto-industrial*, composed of small units of low capital intensity and basic technology, easily reproduced. Within this domestic system, there was a long-standing attachment to traditional products − such as linen − and to traditional methods − such as hand-spinning. According to Schmoller machine-spinning did not definitely replace the hand methods until 1870, and the mechanization of weaving followed more slowly still.[32] Nor was the emergence of the railroad with its valuable and stimulating demand for fuels, metals, and machines very much more sudden than that of the heavily mechanized cotton mill. By 1840, after all, the total track laid throughout the German states was a meagre 549 kilometres, and the highest peaks of construction and investment in transportation were not reached until the 1870s. Mechanization in the general context was everywhere impeded − as it was in France − by the pattern of resource endowment. Plentiful supplies of wood fuel and water power encouraged prolonged commitment to the old technologies, while the power source of the new industrial practices lay on the geographical margins − for Germany in the coal deposits of the Saar, Silesia, and the Ruhr. It is not greatly surprising, therefore, that in 1840 the industrial horsepower of the German states should have amounted to a mere 6 per cent of the British power facilities.[33] From such evidence the impression which is conveyed is less one of discontinuous advance as one of gradualistic change, a further lengthy phase in the gathering of economic strength, not much more than an exploratory flexing of the industrial muscles while the encumbering fat of the traditional practices slips very slowly away.

Even the modification of the German market structure seems not to have delivered the shock to the economic system which might have been anticipated. The economic fragmentation which accompanied the political particularism of the states persisted in its debilitating existence until 1 January 1834. On that date *Zersplitterung* formally yielded to *Zollverein*,[34] and at least the prospect of a unified 'German' market, based upon the Customs Union and surrounded by the moderate Prussian tariff of 1817. In theory, the German entrepreneur was provided with an expanded market,[35] with horizons extended in time and space, and with increased competition to invigorate the strong and drive out the weak. And, in fact, the potential for integration did gain in credibility when the foundation of the Union attracted as contenders for membership enterprises of Belgian, Swiss, and Austrian origin, anxious to

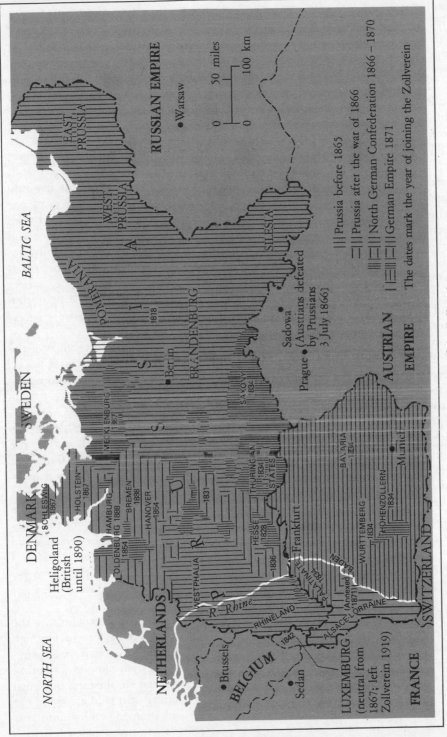

NORTH SEA

BALTIC SEA

DENMARK

SWEDEN

RUSSIAN EMPIRE

• Warsaw

EAST PRUSSIA

WEST PRUSSIA

POMERANIA

SILESIA

BRANDENBURG

• Berlin

SAXONY 1834

Sadowa (Austrians defeated by Prussians 3 July 1866)

Prague •

AUSTRIAN EMPIRE

MECKLENBURG 1867 1868

Heligoland (British until 1890)

SCHLESWIG 1867

HOLSTEIN 1867

HAMBURG 1888

BREMEN 1888

OLDENBURG 1854

HANOVER 1854

THURINGIAN STATES 1834

1831

NETHERLANDS

WESTPHALIA

HESSE 1828

R. Rhine

RHINELAND

Frankfurt

PALATINATE 1834

1836

• Brussels

BELGIUM

1842

• Sedan

LUXEMBURG (neutral from 1867; left Zollverein 1919)

ALSACE-LORRAINE (Annexed 1871)

BADEN 1836

WÜRTTEMBERG 1834

HOHENZOLLERN 1834

BAVARIA 1834

Munich •

SWITZERLAND

FRANCE

||| Prussia before 1865

≡||| Prussia after the war of 1866

≡||| North German Confederation 1866 – 1870

≡|||≡ German Empire 1871

The dates mark the year of joining the Zollverein

0   50 miles
0   100 km

2 The formation of the Zollverein

39

exploit the new source of demand. Not only was it demonstrated once more that a major change within one European economy represented a significant event for the international association of manufacturers; it also seemed probable that, if the foreign interests derived benefits from the reform, the *Zollverein* would offer even more attractive prospects for its German participants.

It is indeed true that the years after 1834 saw the spread of modern large-scale enterprises to new areas. But the part played by the *Zollverein* in this diffusion may easily be exaggerated. Two influences have worked in this direction. Firstly, the contemporaneous upswing in railway construction in the 1840s would itself have accounted for a proportion of the industrial advance, and it is likely that its largest effect would have fallen in the area of demand, exactly that most influenced by the customs reforms. Parallel causation would thus have been present, making it all too easy to ascribe the effects of one stimulus to the operation of the other. The contemporary economist, and chief architect of the *Zollverein*, Frederick List, perceived the interdependence and argued that the Union was important only in conjunction with the railways; he saw the two as indispensable counterparts or 'Siamese twins'.[36] More modern research is able only to perpetuate the ambiguity: 'It may even be,' writes F. B. Tipton, 'that the railway increased internal trade *despite* the hesitation and delay of the *Zollverein* in achieving its objectives. . . . If both were necessary, the *Zollverein* alone may have been less than sufficient.'[37]

It is exceedingly difficult, therefore, to allocate the industrial changes of the 1830s, or 1840s mainly or exactly to the rising level of economic integration. Secondly, there is the complicating effect created by the political propagandists and fusionists who saw the Union, then and later, as a first step on the path to a German Reich. Thus Professor W. F. Bruck wrote that List's conception of the *Zollverein*, 'made him the great fore-runner of Bismarck as founder of the German Empire'.[38] There is, of course, some truth in this: the common tariff system did tie independent states together after a fashion and created an embryonic sense of unity. And there were certainly political overtones of the type associated with an awakening German national consciousness embedded within the design of the Customs Union. List himself saw the *Zollverein* as a weapon for use against the international supremacy of the British, a weapon for Germans 'debased to be carriers of water and hewers of wood for the Britons . . . treated even worse than the downtrodden Hindu'.[39] However understandable all this may be, it acted to confer upon the *Zollverein*, for political reasons, a unity and integrity which the economic reality did not possess.

In fact, it is extremely doubtful whether the contemporaries who saw the *Zollverein* as the vehicle either of perfect internal free trade for the German states or of nascent political strength for some German collectivity were anywhere near the truth. The Union was, after all, somewhat slow in gathering its members together: the first four years saw substantial enrolments, but until 1851 the important regions of Hanover and Oldenburg still held aloof and the powerful north coast centres such as Hamburg and Bremen – remaining true to their international connexions and preferring their industrialized British colleagues as trading partners – were not fully recruited until the 1880s.[40] Not much before 1860 was the degree of cohesion sufficient to give physical reality to the concept of a distinctively 'German' market area.[41] And by this time many of the important innovations which *might* have been diffused by a major alteration in the market structure had already occurred. Slow progress was also evident in the *Zollverein*'s mode of operation, which was seriously affected by interstate disagreements. One important commercial code, for example, first proposed in 1836, was eventually ratified in 1861.[42] For similar reasons, most attempts to co-ordinate economic policy and legislation between states met with little success. The separate states tended to regard the Union as a means of informing one another of their intentions in this department, little more: certainly the right to *act* unilaterally was jealously guarded.[43] And the form of action was conceived by most governments as an experiment in fiscal rather than commercial policy, intended primarily to raise revenue. Certainly, *Zollverein* tariffs were insufficient to provide effective 'infant industry' protection; even the iron manufacturers went without tariff duties until 1844, and lacked successful protection well beyond this.[44] Given the persistent frictions between states and the limited nature of their objectives, the potential offered by the Union for political agreement and economic integration may be treated with some suspicion.

In fact, the context for enterprise formed by the *Zollverein* was a market which gradually became coterminous with an entity ripe for nationhood, scarcely a glittering novelty in nineteenth-century Europe. It broke down old barriers and created an important new market shape, but its contents will not support the implications pasted upon it by many commentators. It could not stimulate growth, only release what potential for growth already existed. Schumpeter judged this correctly, if clumsily: 'No great effect is attributed to these institutional changes. . . . What they immediately accomplished was to only remove the fetters from the things initiated in and crippled by these fetters.'[45]

Germany's equipment in machines, transportation, and markets, therefore, left a good deal to be desired in the 1830s and 1840s. Even towards the end of the 'take-off' period chosen by Hoffmann, grave weaknesses remained. Modern industries such as metal-processing were still restricted to the traditional locations and did not begin the vital migration to the rich resource areas of Rhine-Ruhr until the 1850s. For the great majority of Germans everyday life continued to be dominated by the traditional occupations: the rural motif was imprinted on most forms of activity, and almost concealed others. Even Prussia in the early 1870s was scarcely less rural than at the end of the Napoleonic Wars, her agricultural population having declined merely from 73.5 per cent to 71.5 per cent of the total in the years between 1816 and 1872. Nor was agriculture much more willing to give up capital than it was to surrender people. With the influence of the landed aristocracy continuing paramount, the most common form of investment activity remained attached to mortgage business and to official securities. In Prussia in 1835, for example, the total value of mortgage bonds amounted to two-thirds of the entire state debt,[46] and the transfer of funds from agriculture to manufacture was strongly resisted by the agrarian interests. To be sure, a number of private bankers across the German states – the Rothschilds and the Bethmanns in Frankfurt-Main, the Schicklers in Berlin, Parish and Heine in Hamburg – were moving towards industrial interests from the 1830s. The Rhine-Ruhr machine industry and the Rhenish railways certainly benefited from the financial assistance of such concerns – in this instance the local family bank of Abraham Schaaffhausen – well before 1850; and by 1852 three of the greatest industrial concerns in Rhineland-Westphalia, the Kölner Bergwerksverein, the Phönix Ironworks, and the Stolberg Zinc Company very largely owed their existence to the aid of the private bankers.[47] But the single source for this thin flow of industrial capital lay within an assortment of local capital markets based on personal contacts and interfamilial links. The system was wholly informal and even the soundest industrial concerns – if they lacked the appropriate connexions – could encounter difficulty in extracting bank credit from it. What is more, it was neither sufficiently extensive nor sufficiently robust to guarantee any continuity in the supply of funds for industrial use: in the late 1830s, most especially, the capital situation for new flotations was very tight. It was not that capital was not ready; it was simply that it was not ready for industrial purposes. The cumulative effect of these various weaknesses is to suggest that the period down to mid-century, although it may have seen significant innovations and reforms, remained at best one of preparation.

It was perhaps, appropriate in a grim style, that the expansion of this type of industrializing economy should have been temporarily halted in 1848–49 by an *agricultural* depression of the most traditional variety. And it is also significant that this occasion was to prove the last upon which such an effect could operate. The crisis signposts clearly enough a point of important transition. But under its pressure, the most modern textile and machinery factories, together with those banks like Schaaffhausen which had contracted industrial affiliations, experienced, for the time being, very grave problems of liquidity from which they were rescued, in many cases, only by assistance from the state governments. At mid-century, therefore, an economy which some believe to be virtually airborne, proceeds rather with the clumsy gyrations of a novice birdman than with the powerful elegance of a sky-bound missile. And the birdman still had good soil on his boots.

An early 'take-off' hypothesis contrasting Germany's rapid development in the second half of the nineteenth century with her backwardness around 1800 – thus highlighting all possible elements of discontinuity – would appear to feature a badly misplaced emphasis. Similarly, statements like the recent one from Tom Kemp that, 'Within the space of a generation Germany was transformed from a collection of economically backward states . . . into a unified empire driven forward by a rapidly expanding industry on an advanced technological base'[48] contrive to isolate the events of the decades after 1850 from the long-drawn-out preparation phase of the previous century. It should be clear both that there was much preparation and that it was not complete by 1830, or even by 1850.

From mid-century, however, the final adjustments were made. Admittedly, many of them were based upon the intensification of earlier trends, but the intensification was in itself vital. Mechanization and factory organization spread across more trades. The *Zollverein* recruited a more formidable list of members. Railway construction had created a more impressive network containing over 6000 kilometres of track by 1850, and the service it provided had registered a definite impact upon the cost of bulk transport. Continued extensions to the system were made throughout the 1850s and accelerated strongly in the 1860s adding a further 21,000 kilometres of line between 1850 and 1875. As the rails went down, so the vital demand initiatives, compelling the main heavy industries to respond with increased output, emanated from the transport sector. And, after a slow start, the coal and iron industries did indeed begin an expansion in answer to the signals from the railroads, and the machine-building industries also commenced upon a healthy upswing. It is probable that around 1850/60, if no earlier, the railway industry in Germany achieved the combination of high growth rate and physical size which might qualify it as an appropriate 'leading sector', and as a powerful source of spreader effects. Certainly the 'fit' between the graph of producer goods output and the graph of railway construction for the period 1850–70 is very close, far better than for the period 1835–50.[49] It would seem, therefore, that Schumpeter's choice of this upswing period as the beginning of the 'railway Kondratiev' – implying a general industrial 'long cycle'[50] driven by the railroad – has a good deal to commend it in the German case.

But it was not simply that around 1850 the railway industry in Germany reached a critical point in its ability to influence the economy. There also occurred a remarkable expansion within the banking system, creating between 1848 and 1856 a very comprehensive structure of industrial credit and lifting the traditional restraints upon the flow of capital to manufacturers. A number of the banking innovations were centred around Cologne where the attractions of the Rhenish-Westphalian coal and iron resources were beginning to tempt financial palates. The first industrial investment bank, the Schaaffhausen'scher Bankverein, was formed in the city in 1848 from the crisis-torn remnants of the private bank of similar title, and, six years later, the Bank für Handel und Industrie zu Darmstadt was created, with the participation of Cologne interests, to deal in rail and industrial stock.[51] In 1856 an institution with a similar brief, the Diskonto-Gesellschaft, was formed in Berlin by a reorganization of David Hansemann's existing *Kommandit* concern.[52] As these banks were designed to deal primarily in industrial investment, so, in the same period, a number of going financial concerns – including the Mitteldeutsch Kreditbank, the Leipziger Anstalt, and the Berliner Handelsgesellschaft – moved decisively into industrial business for the first time. It is probable that this new departure in finance was based upon Belgian example – the Société Générale de Belgique had taken up industrial finance from 1820 – and upon accurate observation of German needs in both banking practice and credit supply, rather than upon imitation of French developments. The Crédit Mobilier, often held up as an European exemplar in industrial finance, was created only in 1852, rather too close in time to the German innovations and somewhat after the first of them.[53] What is certain, however, is that the political fragmentation which had plagued German economic development in some respects, turned out to be a positive advantage in the money market. Where, in other countries, conservative central banks could restrict the incidence of banking innovations – as did the Bank of France – the financial entrepreneur in Germany had only to cross a state boundary to escape such controls and find conditions fit for his talents – as several Prussian financiers manifestly deduced. Under these favourable conditions, the bank with industrial interests developed more rapidly and more comprehensively in Germany than in France. By the end of the 1850s the progress of the financial sector within the German states had moved so far that only a few gaps remained for subsequent treatment – mainly by the creation of the Deutsche Bank and the Dresdner Bank in the early 1870s and the Nationalbank in 1881.

The German pattern of development was here very different from that of the British prototype. Britain had faced an industrialization of low cost, a technology of low capital intensity, and had acquired both by recourse mainly to the savings – personal, familial, or local – amassed by entrepreneurs and by their thrifty reinvestment of profits. Bank participation was usually employed, at most, in the provision of short-term working capital and rarely in connexion with long-term fixed capital formation or share ownership. For Germany the informal sources of credit were less generous, the resevoirs of savings which could easily be tapped for industrial purposes far fewer, and, crucially, the level of capital intensiveness implied by the current technology far higher. Specialized financial institutions willing to make funds available for long-run capital formation, although only beginning their career in the 1850s, thus offered better growth prospects than the German economy had yet experienced. The best of the German businessmen, particularly the Rhenish group, had realized as much and had emphasized the need for financial institutions fit to counteract the problems in the supply of industrial credit. Here contemporary observers were anticipating Gerschenkron and urging the development of 'substitutes' in a condition of backwardness. Many present-day analysts would agree that they pointed a discerning finger at a central weak point of the pre-1850 economy; it is, for instance, clear that the acceleration of the 1850s was directly related to changes in the structure of credit. Certainly, also, the subsequent development of German industry down to 1914 with its high degree of 'bank domination' would suggest that a crucial corner was turned around 1850 – and on the corner was an industrial investment bank.

Whether the period 1850–70 could in consequence be deemed one of 'take-off' remains, nevertheless, a moot point. There was, indeed, the emergence of a plausible 'leading sector' in the railroad industry. There was the development of the modern financial auxiliaries for industry. There was the presence of a group of dynamic private entrepreneurs involved in the heavy industrial promotions of Rhine-Ruhr, replacing the state initiatives which had previously bulked so large in this area of technology. But it is noteworthy that, within the strict Rostowian interpretation, most of these effects – the accumulation of social overhead capital, the provision of auxiliary services, the emergence of entrepreneurs in non-conventional fields – are attached to the 'preconditions' rather than to the 'take-off' stage of activity. Once more the stages overlap in a highly confusing manner. Looking in the other direction, it is obvious that, even in 1870, the completeness of Germany's industrial advance is subject to a number of qualifications. The older industries such as textiles were only just about to achieve a comprehensive measure of mechanization: as late as 1882 one-third of all textile workers were still employed within the domestic system of employment, testifying once more to the enduring qualities of the traditional technology. Similarly, the definitive replacement of wood by coal as a fuel for power-using industries remained a matter of contention into the 1860s. And, in the primary sector, the agriculturalists, after having brought about some measure of 'transformation', were poised not for a graceful withdrawal but rather to make very considerable demands on both German economy and German society, threatening on occasion to overbalance the entire industrial structure. Both the proportion of the population remaining in the rural areas – still 42.5 per cent as late as 1882[54] – and the weighting of the agrarian elements within economic policy-making constitute suspiciously heavy ballast for the airborne economy. Once more, the interpenetration of stages and the admixture of traditional elements with modernizing influences might suggest a gradualistic approach as the most prudent.

That is not to say, of course, that the 'German' economy of the 1850s does not accelerate. The motive power that had been accumulating since the late eighteenth century was translated into a definite forward surge between 1850 and 1914. But the surge was based upon the amplification of existing capabilities; it did not follow from any major discontinuity in economic action. Thus the growth rate of the net national product would probably have averaged about 0.5 per cent between 1830 and 1850, risen to 2.4 per cent per annum for the period 1850–70, and then risen again to 3.12 per cent per annum for the years 1896–1913 – a reasonably orderly progression. This gradualistic interpretation of German industrial growth is echoed by F. B. Tipton's useful attempt to construct an integrated 'consensus' description of the economy's long-run performance: his reading of 'yearly estimates beginning in 1850', suggests 'a nearly constant growth rate for the entire nineteenth century', and he emphasizes that this 'nearly constant long-term rate' is applied to the decades on *both* sides of 1870.[55] Nevertheless, it is clear that, for the historical investigator, one major change did occur around 1850: the central problem in the analysis alters; it is no longer to discern the quality of Germany's industrial apprenticeship but to determine what factors underlay the notably confident maturing process of the next sixty years. The question is not whether industrialization is established upon German territory but why by 1914 it is more securely established there than in any other continental country.

GROWTH PATTERNS OF THE STEADILY ACHIEVING SOCIETY

In general outline, the profile of the post-1850 economic expansion is particularly sharply etched. The 'railway Kondratiev' pursued its upswing until roughly 1870, maintaining, together with its influential dependants – mining, metallurgy, and machine-making – a solid base for vigorous expansion. Throughout this period changes in technology and modifications in industrial organization provided a fairly steady supply of growth materials. In the early 1870s, however, a number of non-economic events, mostly associated with the successes of the Franco-Prussian War – the rout of Napoleon III at Sedan, the surrender by the French of a lavish war indemnity, the joyful foundation of the *Kaiserreich* – superimposed themselves upon the cyclical boom of the late 1860s and created a bout of unusual economic euphoria. Before long, this found outlet in a speculative bonanza (*Gründerzeit*) which doubled the capital of German joint-stock companies between 1870 and 1873 and then, inevitably, moved on into an equally spectacular collapse, featuring a torrent of bankruptcies and a rush of deflation, both economic and psychological (*Gründerkrise*). It may have been appropriate that the powerful German expansion of 1850–70 should have culminated in an outburst of lusty over-enthusiasm – rather than in the entrepreneurial malaises or the agricultural diseases which plagued the British and French economies at this time – but it was no less final. Or so it seemed in the early 1870s. In fact, however, the 'Great Depression' which afflicted the world economy in the period 1873–96 rarely lived up to its reputation and within German territory signally failed to do so, touching there only lightly. True, unemployment was widespread during the 1870s and the effects of the *Gründerkrise* persisted throughout the decade. Prices and confidence remained low. Growth possibilities within the railroad–iron–coal complex were temporarily exhausted. And even the efficient German entrepreneurs resorted increasingly to cartel alliances, defensive amalgamations aiming to compensate for unattractive prices by collective action. Recovery was much longer delayed than it had been in the lesser troughs of 1857/58 and 1864/66. But these symptoms scarcely outlived the 1870s and recovery did come for Germany more quickly and more powerfully than for many other countries. The metal industries received the considerable impulsion of the new Gilchrist–Thomas process from 1879 and the 1880s saw extensive if jerky activity in textiles, coal, gas, and railroads.[56] New technologies such as chemicals, dyestuffs, and electrical engineering moved forward to replenish the stream of innovation, exerting great influence in the two decades before 1914. As growth picked up, the cartels adjusted their previously defensive posture to a more aggressive, market-seeking attitude. From 1882 to 1896 industrial output grew at an annual average of about 4.5 per cent, very close to the performance of 1849–73, and somewhat better even than the average of 3.1 per cent per annum achieved in the good years 1896–1913. Neither the Great Depression nor the need to amend the economy's technological base did a great deal to interrupt the progress of the German economy.

46

A special place in the generation of this momentum needs to be awarded to the metals—mining sector of the economy. Growing rapidly both before and after 1880, this group achieved its maximum leverage after 1895. In this period, metals assumed pride of place as the largest branch of manufacturing, increasing its share of output from 19.8 per cent in 1895 to 25.1 per cent in 1907 as textiles fell back from 19.8 per cent to 16.0 per cent. Soaring demand for the products of the mining—metals group, as these materials became essential components for consumer durables as well as for capital goods, touched off 'the largest and most sudden change in the structure of the labour force and . . . the first (such) truly "national" change of the century'.[57] In every industrial region of Germany metal products composed the most rapidly expanding segment of manufacturing. The suitability of Germany's powerful equipment in the mining—metals group for the requirements of the technological phases on *either* side of 1880 contributed a notable stabilizing influence to the growth patterns of the Reich down to the century's turn. After this point overcapacity in the heavy industries became a characteristic German problem, but, before the 1900s, more equilibrium was gained from the mining—metals sector than was lost by it.

But the sustained development after 1896 – if it proceeded a trifle more slowly than in the 1880s – contained features that were more novel than the great residual force of the mining—metals sector. This upswing carried the new high-technology manufacturers upwards, not merely towards a position of prosperity, but, on the eve of war, to one of world pre-eminence. Thus the German electrical engineering industry, the biggest and costliest of the newcomers, began its expansion only in the 1880s, but by 1913 easily led the world schedule of exporters, controlling over half the international trade in electrical products.[58] In 1895 this sector employed some 15,000 workers (0.33% of employed male workers in manufacturing), yet by 1907 the number had risen to 50,000 (0.84% of employed male workers in manufacturing). Meanwhile, in the early years of the new century, the German chemical industry constructed a virtually complete monopoly of the European commerce in fine chemicals. By 1907 this sector was the world's largest producer of chemicals with an annual product worth some $300 m., more even in value than the output of the formidable German machine industries.[59] In sulphuric acid alone Germany produced 30 per cent less than Britain in 1900, 60 per cent *more* in 1913.[60] And, in the very demanding sector of dyestuffs, German pre-eminence was again global, and especially unchallengeable; by the early 1900s the Reich economy housed no less than 80 per cent of all world production in these commodities.[61] Whether monstrous aggregations of capital like electrical engineering or chemicals or more modestly scaled industries like dyestuffs – or equally optics and precision engineering – these new manufacturing systems acted as the technological 'carriers' for a fresh Kondratiev upswing[62] commencing around the mid-1890s, a powerful descendant of the railway-induced upsurge of the 1850s and 1860s. If the mining—metals group provided a steady underlying impulsion for German output growth down to 1900–10, the new advanced industries supplied the multipliers to demand, the sources of technological renewal and structural adjustment which were required in an economy so forcefully committed to constant industrial refurbishment.

Nearing 1900, some ripples of uncertainty did begin to infiltrate the current of technology-based expansion – there were disasters in the financial arena, reaching out in 1901 to engulf even a member of the great investment banking fraternity, the Leipziger Bank – but, even these disturbances failed to erode the underlying durability of the new German industrial structure; paradoxically enough, indeed, they worked to reinforce it. The already highly integrated German business system reacted to the warnings of instability by commencing a movement towards yet more extensive mergers. The period around 1900 is characterized by the evolution of gigantic forms of business organization. In the electro-technical industry, the firm of AEG amalgamated with that of Union Electric, the business of Siemens and Halske with that of Schuckert, forming two massive combines controlling between them, among other things, some 40 per cent of German power supply. From about 1909 organizations such as these carried the provision of electrical power into German industry with an impetus that was difficult to resist. In coal, the gigantic Rhenish-Westphalian Coal Syndicate had existed since 1893 but was modified and greatly extended in 1903. Within twelve months, moreover, this strengthened dinosaur of the pits had acquired an equally vast colleague in the metal industry, the Stahlwerksverband or Steel Works Association, a cartel organization which controlled 84 per cent of total German steel output. In explosives and chemicals, the German province of the industrial empire represented by the Anglo-German Nobel Dynamite Trust controlled a veritable army of factories.[63] And in this area even the state took a hand, driving the whole of the potash industry into a single cartel (the *Zwangsyndikat*) in 1910 by a deft manipulation of the legislative controls. Between 1900 and 1914 amalgamations of this calibre produced a manufacturing structure of remarkable stability and durability. The community of interest established between giant industrial groups helped maintain an equilibrium of prices and a constraint upon the depressive tendencies induced by over-competition. With this equipment, the German economy was able to sustain conditions of industrial prosperity – if with an underlying threat of overcapacity in the manufacturing sector – until war intervened. Nothing resembling the speculative excesses and consequent instability of 1900/01 – which had particularly rocked the machine and iron industries – recurred in the years down to the war. Improved organization coincided with buoyant demand and falling unit costs to produce a context in which economic activity remained high and the downswing – even in the trough year 1907 – comparatively suppressed.[64] Even the Stock Exchange panic of September 1911 owed more to international politics than to the state of domestic industry.

The pattern of German economic growth between 1850 and 1914 consists, therefore, of two, technologically distinct, surges of expansion, separated by a phase of short-lived recession. The lack of any extended chronological lapse between the first and second technological phases – the first and second 'industrial revolutions' – is notable. Quite unlike Great Britain, which endured a considerable interval between the two instalments of technology, Germany was well qualified to manage the transition smoothly, employing the momentum built up with railways, iron, and coal to sustain the leap into chemicals, electrics, and engineering, and enjoying the compression or 'telescoping' of growth phases which is often the advantage of the later developer.

Moreover, this pattern of advance, taken together with the proto-industrial activity before 1850, fits fairly closely with the outline for European expansion sketched out by Kondratiev's scheme of international 'long cycles'. The first of these, moving into upswing in the late 1780s and tailing off in the early 1840s would include, neatly enough, the industrial stirrings in Silesia, Saxony, and the Rhineland. The second, moving strongly up from the 1840s to 1873 and then swinging down to 1897 would correspond with the accelerated surge of the mid-century and the 'little depression' of the 1870s – though not so neatly with the 'early' recovery of the 1880s. The third cycle swinging up from 1897 to 1914 and plummeting down after 1919, would find strong echoes in Germany's achievements with the new technologies, and also in her post-war disruption. In each of these cyclical upswings, Germany's level of success is strikingly high. The immediately pre-industrial activity is probably very nearly as marked as that of France before 1830, although France is usually counted as a more advanced economy in the early nineteenth century. The performance of the railroad – iron – coal group at mid-century surpassed that of any continental rival by a handsome margin. And the German contribution to the 'high-technology Kondratiev' at the century's end could be approached only by that of the USA. By a similar token, the downswing of the crucial second Kondratiev affected Germany much less severely than it did other advanced nations, although in the downswings on either side of this one, the country bore at least its share of the burden. Not entirely coincidentally, it may be noted, the formation of the Reich, by which Germany became a nation and the German market an entity, corresponded almost precisely with the onset of the 'little depression'. However, if the circumstances surrounding the victory at Sedan helped to unleash overspeculation and recession, if the foundation of the Reich involved an economically damaging war (in a rather unusual sense), it is probable that the benefits of unification were felt in the economic resilience of the 1880s and 1890s. Arrival at nationhood may thus have acted to emphasize both the downswing of the second 'long cycle' and the upswing of the third.

The various phases of this powerful industrial expansion were associated with marked regional shifts in the location of the major centres of industrial production; the expansion was not a nationally uniform experience even if it profited by the processes of national unification. The industrial accent moved from region to region; de-industrialization proved entirely possible; and so too did the emergence of deprived economic regions characteristic of the dual economy. Tipton argues that in Germany the evolution of industrial growth was 'competitive rather than complementary' and embodied a type of specialization which caused regions to become progressively more unlike and progressively further removed from the national average.[65] Unlike Russia, Italy, or Spain with their massive and enduring territorial imbalances, Germany appears to have passed through at least *two* distinct forms of regional dualism over the course of the nineteenth century – the first, involving the growth within a generally rural economy of compact manufacturing centres like those of Silesia, Saxony, or the Rhineland, the second setting large, highly specialized regions of heavy industry against large and equally specialized regions of innovation-*resistant* agriculture. At first, increasing regional specialization was associated with economic progress, particularly between 1770 and 1860, and especially with the emergence of the Kingdom of Saxony as the primary manufacturing centre among the German states.[66] But from the 1880s and 1890s regional imbalance took on a sharper edge. Only with the Kondratiev upswing of the late century did industrialization become distributed in a wide *national* dispersion, and, from that point specialization for some regions – notably the eastern regions struggling to avoid the 'contagion' of economic modernization – became merely a synonym for economic backwardness. Within this overall structure, there are some important emphases. Censal material may be recalculated to yield employment shares in relation to economic sector and geographical region; and from these a scale of regional economic specialization can be derived. Some of the results are surprising. Economic specialization, as measured by the share of industrial employment in the total employed labour force, is shown to have been restricted in the Rhineland before 1840, in Westphalia before 1861. By contrast, the Kingdom of Saxony retained its edge in industrial employment over both regions, the great showplaces of German manufacturing, as late as the 1860s and 1870s[67] (see Table 2.1). Once more the inherent gradualism of the industrial transition receives due emphasis. Not until the period 1882–1907 did the Ruhr definitely replace Saxony as Germany's largest industrial district, a function of the great turn-of-century boom in the metals–mining and new technology groups. On the other hand, the latter parts of the specialization process provoked a re-emergence of German dualism in pronounced form: the eastern plains may even be placed among the classically 'stranded' regions of the economic world, emptied of resources by the appetites of more advanced neighbours. According to Tipton, 'Berlin's self-feeding growth hindered developments in the East in much the same way as the expansion of Paris has been held to have injured the provincial areas of France, and the extension of the railway system to have hampered industry in southern Italy.'[68] Like the American or Italian south, the German east was economically penalized by the survival into industrial times of an antiquated social ascendancy. The outcome was that, alongside the enormous development of the western manufacturing centres, 'low income and depression in the East probably resulted in less than optimal growth in Germany'[69] as a whole. Even the rise of the continent's most formidable manufacturing economy produced nothing as simple as an 'industrial nation'.

The remaining problem of explanation, then, is to demonstrate why the German style of industrial growth from 1850 was such a strong one in many sectors – but why also it remained so strongly influenced by pre-industrial

Table 2.1   Industrial employment, Kingdom of Saxony and districts of Düsseldorf – Arnsberg
(Ruhr), 1861–1907

	Kingdom of Saxony		Düsseldorf – Arnsberg	
	Nos.	% Total employ.	Nos.	% Total employ.
1861	546,000	51.2	362,000	46.9
1882	747,000	56.4	629,000	57.3
1895	998,000	60.2	896,000	62.2
1907	1,295,000	63.9	1,427,000	67.9

Source: Tipton, (1976), App. Tables P and V, pp. 185, 191.

motifs in many others. Discussion of such issues has often brought into play
hypotheses which combine elements of technology and autocracy and emphasize some aspect of Germany's economic 'discipline', her economic 'efficiency',
or even her 'commercial grip on the world'.[70] In order to establish some prospects for analytical precision the method adopted here is to arrange the major
hypotheses in a roughly ascending order of plausibility and to review each
one critically. The resulting deductions may support the ranking order selected *a priori*, or they may point towards an alternative schedule of growth
ingredients.

FACTOR ENDOWMENT: MINERAL ILLUSIONS VERSUS DEMOGRAPHIC REALITIES

Perhaps the simplest interpretation of Germany's industrial prowess places
much emphasis on the excellence of the country's natural resources. Despite
the fact that this argument has encountered in its career a good deal of opposition from historians concerned to exalt the role of the state in German development – and thus to minimize natural endowments in favour of artificial
devices[71] – it has survived more or less intact and is still commonly encountered. Unfortunately, it is constituted of a generalization which treats the
country's natural endowments as a homogeneous block; and it involves a considerable disregard for chronology. It is true, of course, that Germany did
possess, concentrated in the great fields of the Ruhr, about one-half of all
continental coal supplies, but, that happy accident aside, her resources were
not distinctly superior to those of neighbouring France, usually counted a
country poor in resources. 'As is well known', Thorstein Veblen superciliously
wrote – for it was not well known – 'the Fatherland is not at all specially
fortunate in natural resources of the class that count towards modern industry.' Even as regards coal – scored by Veblen as 'by no means . . . better than
second best'[72] – it is noteworthy that by 1914, German seams were becoming
increasingly difficult to mine and were requiring considerable inputs of capital, a feature commonly used in *excuse* for the poor efficiency of French coal
extraction.

Nor were other resources scattered abroad in a display of natural liberality. In 1850, it has been argued by Professor W. N. Parker, Germany lacked most natural endowments *except* coal.[73] And there is truth in this: Germany possessed at that time – mainly in the Siegerland – very inferior iron-ore deposits by the standards of the current technology and was driven to import large quantities of material from France, Luxemburg, and Sweden in subsequent years. It was not until 1870, and only by the employment of armed force, that this problem was partially resolved with the annexation of the Lorraine ore reserves. And it was only by a technological advance, the Gilchrist–Thomas process of 1879, that ores of high phosphoric content, previously considered markedly inferior, were converted into an industrial asset. Similarly, the German stocks of potassium and pyrites, which have traditionally attracted much admiration, were of little use in the early stages of industrialization. They emerged as important only at the end of the nineteenth century when the chemical industry became a leading sector. Earlier on, this industry had established itself not upon German but upon *imported* raw materials, often British coal-tar products. Even in agriculture, the German endowment, naturally predestined to poor soils and low yields, was inferior to that of France. Yet a predominance in agricultural efficiency was established over France from early in the nineteenth century. And, by 1914, Germany was the only major European nation to have improved her cultivation by the intensive use of artificial fertilizers.

Those who argue that Germany was not disproportionately blessed by nature, and that consequently her unusual industrial success did not stem simply from initial endowments would appear to have a case. After all, the country was well on the road to industrialization before her material resources were properly utilized, and, even if these had been smaller, it is improbable that her industrial objectives would have altered. Dynamic industrial advance may as readily lead on to the discovery and exploitation of raw materials as vice versa – and this sequence is perhaps the more likely of the two.[74] Certainly, the examples of phosphoric iron ore and potassium suggest that resources became usable because growth occurred, not that growth occurred because raw materials were plentiful. Even in cases where there prove to be few raw materials to discover and exploit – such as Japan or Switzerland – economic advance of an energetic type may refuse to be obstructed. And in countries where uneven industrial development *does* appear to coincide with poor resource endowment – as in France – the true problem may be not so much physical shortages as that the resources which are available are simply being utilized inappropriately or insufficiently.[75] Moreover, the shortage of a resource, or its poor quality, or its high price, may provide an inducement for the replacement of the 'inadequate' endowment by technical ingenuity quite as easily as a plentiful supply of cheap raw materials may provide an inducement for the energetic industrial application of such assets. The blend of resource endowment with industrial performance may thus be varied in a very large number of ways. Lavish endowment does not guarantee high performance. Meagre endowment does not necessarily constitute a sentence to low growth rates. And what may appear lavish endowment may have to be revised downwards when the chronology of growth and innovation is properly allowed for.

In respect of one resource, however, Germany was fortunate: she was heavily supplied with people. The population within the territory which became the 1871 Reich grew at 0.8 per cent per annum average in the 1850s and at 1.4 per cent per annum average in the years immediately before the First World War, giving a total population stock of 35 m. in 1850 and 47 m. by 1904. In some respects this was also an ambiguous endowment. Both large and small populations may confer benefits (and disadvantages) upon industrializing economies. Communities of large size or rapid expansion, on the one hand, may provide extended markets, augmented labour supplies, and increased scope for the division of labour; on the other hand, they divert funds from investment to consumption, exert downward pressure on the growth of *per caput* income and impose upon the economy a high 'dependency cost' by adding non-productive individuals at either end of the age range. Contrariwise, communities of small size or low growth rate, in the first place, offer few obstacles to the growth of *per capita* income, thus permitting high rates of savings, and, potentially, of investment. Yet, in the second place, such communities may provide little actual *stimulus* to investment in the form of swelling demand or expanding labour supply. Additionally, they may cause income to be distributed more equally, thus perhaps further curbing the propensity to *mobilize* investable savings. In practice, it is likely that the advantages of a strongly expanding population are, within limits,[76] more positive and direct in operation than the benefits of a slowly growing population. For one thing, the population which expands gradually may accumulate plentiful savings but exerts little pressure to ensure that these are productively *employed*. On the other hand, the population which grows rapidly defines certain requirements – for foodstuffs, living space, or employment – which an economy may ignore at its peril. Thus, in the German states, demographic expansion produced impoverishment in some regions before 1850, but also created opportunities and needs which acted as stimuli to economic advance. For German agriculture in particular, the growth in numbers provided a taxing but galvanizing experience. With a 59 per cent increase in population between 1816 and 1865 superimposing an augmented internal demand upon the existing requirement to export primary products – the chief means of payment for essential imports of foreign machinery – agriculture could scarcely afford to remain quiescent. Significantly, too, the areas of most rapid demographic change – Silesia in the 1820s, Westphalia and the Rhineland after 1840 – were also the areas of most rapid industrial advance. Here the arrival of factories and ironworks broke down existing modes of employment, and with them existing social constraints, eliciting a demographic expansion which, in turn, provided the industrial installations with workers and the local economy with consumers.

Nor were the size and rate of advance of the German population its only positive attributes. It was also highly mobile. Unlike the French cultivators, the German agricultural population was not inextricably attached to the '*vie paysanne*. In France, the system of equal inheritance, guaranteeing a plot, however miniature, to each heir formed the major constraint binding the peasant to the land, but in Germany this system – though present in some south-western areas – was much less common. In many regions, single-heir inheritance encouraged younger sons to leave the land. And in the hard areas of the eastern provinces, affection for the life of the landless bondsman wore progressively more thin from mid-century. In consequence, very considerable internal migrations of labour took place across German territory between 1870 and 1914. Where before 1850, the 'wandering spirit' had pointed migrants towards America, the new employment opportunities with which the economy had answered the expansion of numbers, now drew them into Rhine-Ruhr. Almost the whole of the natural increase in the eastern provinces, for instance, was surrendered to the industrial west in the forty years before the war. By 1900 no less than half the workers in the manufacturing towns of the Rhine-land were eastern migrants, and, by 1907, the census revealed, only 52 per cent of Germans lived in their place of birth.[77] Among the pits and foundries of Rhine-Ruhr this mingling of eastern and western industrial components produced an identifiable industrial tribe, the 'Ruhrvolk'. And these long chains of population movement, thrown across the states, acted to bind more tightly together the areas unified by tariff in 1834 and imperial decree in 1871. Germany's rise from a fragmented collection of principalities and markets to an empire and economic colossus owed not a little to this mobility of population. As Wolfgang Köllman wrote, 'these movements may well be regarded as one of the most potent forces in the development of the specific German national consciousness prior to World War I'.[78] Not only is German industry provided with a valuable labour input but industrialism, via migration, is associated with the very specialized development of German nationalism; an economic and social force assists in the shaping of a political one.

However, the purely economic consequences of the migrations were sufficiently considerable. Moderately priced labour was available to German employers throughout the years from 1850 to 1914. And the migrant groups tended to be of the optimal working age and of more than usually enterprising spirit. The census of 1907 revealed that the proportion of self-employed individuals, white-collar workers, administrators and professional men was higher among the immigrant populations of the larger cities than among the native-born.[79] Moreover, the influx of easterners, whether its members enjoyed upward social mobility or not, needed to be housed. As the recruitment to the urban industrial areas swelled – by 1910 over 20 per cent of the German population lived in cities of 100,000 persons or more, and only 40 per cent in communities of under 2000 individuals – the demand for non-agricultural accommodation expanded alongside it. In most years after 1870 this demand was insistent enough to claim between one-quarter and one-third of total net investment for embodiment in housing. Quite possibly, as Borchardt argues, the result was to designate the building industry as a leading sector, its spreader effects reaching out to the brick, glass, cement, gas, and water industries, and, after 1880, establishing contact with the important high-technology disciplines of electrical generation and electrical engineering.[80] Such effects may begin to suggest that mobility of population could be economically more significant than population size: certainly 'movable' populations like the British, American, German, or Japanese have been more consistently associated with industrial success than the 'immovable' populations of countries like France or Russia.

In general, however, the distribution of physical resources – whatever the resource – seems to provide no direct clue to the style of German development. The country possessed some vital growth elements (such as coal), lacked others (such as high-grade, non-phosphoric iron ore), acquired a few (such as the Lorraine deposits), and appreciated the utility of a few more only with the passing of time and technology (such as the potassium reserves). In most cases the possession or non-possession of the endowment was less important than the decisions taken about the problems – the early development of the chemical industry or the indifferent quality of agricultural land, for instance – by entrepreneurs, officials, or legislators. Initiatives were required that could produce industrial development and so the exploitation of existing and recognized natural resources. Technological advances were necessary before previously sterile or unrecognized deposits could be converted into usable industrial inputs. More technological ingenuity was required to 'substitute' for resources that were almost entirely lacking: thus where Britain could acquire essential nitrates by sophisticated trade relations, Germany in the early 1900s contrived the Haber–Bosch process to extract nitrogen from the air. Even as regards the population resource, its most attractive characteristic – mobility – followed less from the intrinsic nature of the endowment than from the legal and entrepreneurial context in which it was placed. As countries like France and Russia so painfully demonstrated, the mobility of populations – whether moderately small or overwhelmingly massive – revolved, in the first instance, around the existence of suitable tenurial arrangements and the provision of comprehensive transportation systems. Naturally, neither private nor official decision-making need have been consciously formulated for these purposes; it is rather that efficient performance in a number of activities – entrepreneurial, scientific, legal – led on to the release of resources for further efficiency in industrial application.

TRANSPORTATION: RAILWAYS VERSUS WATERWAYS

Where natural bounty is not advanced as an explanation of Germany's early growth, a man-made contrivance is often proposed in its place. The states are said to have profited to an unusual extent from the railway construction of the period 1850–70 and Germany's initial development is associated more closely with the 'railway Kondratiev' than that of any other country with the possible exception of the USA. There is a great deal to be said for this view. Where the French railroad system in its early stages was deployed as a structure of spokes radiating from the administrative centre and neglecting the manufacturing regions, there was, from the beginning, a close association between German transportation and German manufacturing. Here the newly laid tracks turned Lower Rhineland and Westphalia into Europe's most compact economic unit, with feeder lines running towards the ore deposits of Luxembourg and Alsace and connecting with the water communications of the Rhine. Stitching up a second industrial belt, further railways linked together the manufacturing areas between Saxony and Silesia.[81] Together, these two industrial blocs accounted for half the iron and steel manufactured on the continent by the late nineteenth century. In Germany, the transport and locational possibilities opened to industry by the railroad were clearly very developed indeed; haulage costs per kilometre were alone reduced by some 80–85 per cent upon the advent of the steam locomotive. Moreover, the relevance of the railway sector as a source of spreader effects for industries such as metal-processing and machine-building is clearly established: by mid-century, for example, engineering works involved in locomotive construction existed in most German states. The case of the 'railway school' of historians, led by Schumpeter, is without doubt a strong one.

But strong qualifications are also required. For one thing, the orderliness of German railroad development – real enough when opposed to the French – is easily exaggerated in the absolute scale. Thus Thorstein Veblen could write: 'The railway system was laid out under State surveillance on strategic lines',[82] and promulgate an assessment that was faulty on almost every count. In fact, construction was rarely governed by a systematic single design and rarely centrally supervised by state governments. Only a few individual administrations were involved in railway design more or less from the beginning: Hanover and Baden – with a miniature railway enthusiast as Margrave – were conspicuous examples, constructing their own public lines, and both Bavaria, which took over privately-built lines in 1844, and Prussia, which guaranteed interest on all railway investment from 1842, were committed to intervention, if less deeply. Altogether, the various governments had provided about one-half of all railway investment by 1850. But the fact remains that the great majority of pioneering construction in the great majority of states was initiated by uncontrolled private interests.[83] Certainly by the time that the German railroad system was provided with a central controlling agency – in the shape of the Imperial Railroad Office of 1873, though the reality of control was to elude the agency for years – much of the basic railroad network had already been completed, and completed under independent auspices. Even when the imperial state did commence upon its own large-scale construction from the 1880s, the initiative for the work frequently emenated from private interests pressing upon the government agencies. Furthermore, the design for a nation-wide public enterprise, which Bismarck greatly favoured and Veblen enthusiastically described, proved simpler in the planning than in the execution. The Imperial Railroad Office encountered much opposition from the various state administrations and was forced to spend many years in purchasing determinedly independent railroad systems. Eventually, it acquired some 12,000 kilometres of private track between 1879 and 1884 and the final 3400 kilometres in the ensuing twenty years. Outright nationalization and the creation of a world exemplar for successful public enterprise – as the German railways famously were by 1914 – was a long and slow process which neared completion only around the turn of the century.[84] The description of a unified and rationalized railway system, with strong suggestions of state supervision, is not therefore especially accurate for most of the period between 1850 and 1914. And with no question, the provision, if not the ultimate control, of the German railroads fell mainly in the private sector, with some of the frictions, inefficiency, and corruption which this usually implies in construction projects of such scale.

Nor is the economic record attained by the railways in their own operations of invariable excellence. In the flat terrain of Prussia, where railways were built comparatively early and cheaply, and the main export routes via Hamburg and Bremen ran conveniently close, the railroad network did turn out a financial success. Consequently, the Prussian railways could afford to provide concessionary freight rates for industrial products and especially for export consignments. Other states, however, built their tracks later and more expensively, encountered natural obstacles, and suffered from Prussia's grasp upon the export/import routes.[85] As a result these states could scarcely afford to favour industrial freight in the Prussian style. Sound profitability for them was a difficult and distant goal: in the early 1900s the joint revenue yield of the Bavarian, Baden, Saxon, and Württemberg railway systems reached only one-half of the Prussian receipts and Württemberg actually recorded deficits.[86] In this respect nationalization had brought little improvement. Indeed Schumaker in 1912 concluded that, 'in the lesser German States the nationalization of the railways has proved a bad bargain.'[87] It would appear, therefore, that, during the early years of the Second Reich, the efficiency of the railroad network, like many things in Germany, could still vary greatly between the individual states. The politics of particular states could also prevent the railways striking with unerring accuracy to the heart of market or resource areas. This was especially so in the east where the Junker nexus set up in opposition to the modernizing impulses released by the railways.[88] And, naturally enough, where the lesser state systems were under pressure to raise revenue, but could not raise sufficient, their service to industry suffered in consequence. What was true for Prussia, therefore – and then outside the Junker east – was not necessarily true for all Germany.

Finally, it is a marked feature of the German transportation industry before 1914 that the railway sector was by no means unchallenged in its pre-eminence. Just as traditional manufacturing methods remained to obstruct the path of the modern factory until late in the day, so a less advanced form of transport facility – the canal – persisted in competition with the German railways. Where Britain permitted the railway to steam headlong over the canal interests and to push the waterway network into premature obsolescence, Germany – like America – retained an extensive and sophisticated canal network alongside – sometimes literally alongside – its railway tracks.[89] In the

United States this partnership of canal and railroad has prompted much recent speculation among economic historians that the railway's contribution to economic development may have been overstressed and that of the canal underplayed. Professor Fogel has even argued that, in the absence of railways and employing the existing canal system for transportation, 76 per cent of America's cultivated land would still have provided its support for the industrializing economy, and, given another 8000 kilometres of canal in place of the railroad system, 93 per cent of cultivated land would have remained in production.[90] If the 'railway school' of historians can be so attacked in their American citadel, it is perhaps possible that a second country, with a developed condominium within its transport industry might offer grounds for similar hypotheses. Certainly, Alfred Marshall noted in the early twentieth century that German railroads ranked second only to the American, and then, significantly, went on to record the strengths of the German canal system.[91] At the least, the thesis that Germany might also have profitably constructed additional canals instead of succumbing so energetically to the fashionable lure of steam is an attractive heterodoxy.

With its vast internal river system based on the Rhine, Elbe, and Oder, each with its network of canal 'spurs' Germany is perhaps a better choice for such a proposition than even America.

But so much is conjecture. What is not is that the canals of Germany continued to offer a range of essential transport services down to 1914 and beyond. Throughout the period the waterways were able to maintain artificially low freight rates which provided a hidden subsidy to industry. Compared with railway charges, these rates were highly competitive: by 1914 the Rhine, providing 480 kilometres of clear water from Rotterdam to Mannheim, and flowing straight past the factory wharves of the Rhine-Ruhr complex, formed the cheapest major transport system in Germany, its rates lower than those of any other waterway and *half* those of the railway route.[92] Cargo could travel down from the great Ruhr port at Duisburg to the sea at Rotterdam far more cheaply by water than by rail. Not only the economy but also the geographical spread of the German water transport system commended it to industrialists. By 1914 the Rhine terminus was gradually inching down the map, the way being opened for the 1000-ton barges past Mannheim and on towards Strasbourg. At a time when German manufacture was carried on at an average of 320 kilometres from the sea, the waterways straightened, deepened, and cleared, allowed maritime influences to penetrate to the heart of the industrial districts. On the Rhine system, the *Rheinseedampfer*, vessels of river *and* sea, could bring wheat, ore, or petroleum directly into Westphalia and the Ruhr, while sea lighters and their special *Rheinseeschlepper* tugs could carry the products of Rhine-Ruhr downstream, out through Rotterdam, and directly, without transhipment, to the ports of northern Europe. As the traffic swelled, inland ports handling more tonnage than many ocean harbours grew up along the German waterways and canals; sleepy riverside towns acquired grain elevators and electrically powered dock machinery and transformed themselves into the world's best equipped inland anchorages. The greatest of them, Ruhrort—

Duisburg, the dockland of the Ruhr, could already handle 2000-ton barges by 1914. Dusseldorf and Mannheim came close behind, and Cologne, 240 kilometres downstream, was just graduating into a fully fledged seaport, despatching its steamers to England and Scandinavia. At the mouth of the Rhine, Rotterdam had already become an extra-territorial German port, exchanging freight between ocean-going vessels and the barge trains from Mannheim and Duisburg. Canal extensions gave German cargoes passage into Switzerland and France, while, in the north, other man-made links carried traffic from Hamburg and Stettin into the German hinterland. As a final bonus, the waterway system contrived to visit most of Germany's resource areas: the Rhine flowed past the coalfields of Rhineland–Westphalia, the lignite deposits south of Cologne, and the iron-ore deposits of the Siegerland above Koblenz, while its tributary the Mosel darted south to skirt the coal of the Saar and the iron ore of Lorraine. Given these various attractions, it is perhaps not surprising that the German canal and waterway system on the eve of war was transporting more tonnage per kilometre than the railroads and was maintaining its growth rate in freight carried at a far higher level.[93]

There is no doubt that the capabilities of the water system constituted for Germany a source of economic strength. The barges divided the work rationally with the railway trucks, taking for themselves the bulk cargoes on long-term demand and leaving to the railroads the traffic with a higher return and lower demand horizon. If the British had employed their canals and railways in an equally sensible fashion, the economy would have been richer by some £7 m. per year according to one contemporary computation.[94] But such a marked dualism within the transport sector does modify the supreme importance attached to the railroad system by some analysts. And it did retain within the transport resources a method of haulage which might be cheap and accommodating but which offered to the manufacturing industries a much smaller measure of technological stimulation than did the railway method. Although the freight service provided by the canals was efficient, their backward, sideways, and forward linkages with the rest of the economy were weaker than those of the railroad. In this sense, a large element of traditional methodology was kept up within the German transport sector down to 1914.

Generally, there can be little dispute that the railroads made the more considerable contribution to the growth of the period 1850–70. Quite apart from their impact upon freight costs and technology growth, they clearly acted as the critical determinants in the regional location of industry. When administrative friction halted rail construction, industrialization could be blocked, as in the east, or even reversed, as in the Eifel region. Areas of difficult terrain could prosper and find entrepreneurs if the railways came, as in the Saxon Erzebirge, or decline and shed enterprise if they did not, as in the Eifel.[95]

Recent research has gone yet further, turning the econometric weapons against their American pioneers and beginning to query the *general* truth of Fogel's notion of railway 'dispensability'. Specifically, his central proposition that 'no single innovation was vital for economic growth'[96] has drawn heavy fire. In Germany, in particular, it has proved impossible to diminish the scale of the railway innovation. Fremdling has clearly shown that German rail construction claimed enormous shares of total net investment between 1851 and 1879, averaging 17.6 per cent over this period and attaining peaks of 19.7 per cent in 1855–59 and 25.8 per cent in 1875–79;[97] he concludes that 'between 1840 and 1880 no other modern sector in Germany accumulated capital on this scale'.[98] Not only was this leading sector very large, but its linkages with other industries were also strong, notably stronger than in the American case. In Germany at least, railway demand *did* prove a vital educational experience for both the engineering and metallurgical industries, virtually creating the modern sectors of each.[99] German rail demand for pig iron as a percentage of total domestic consumption of the commodity was between two and four *times* greater than the equivalent US percentage between 1840 and 1855 and over one-fifth greater in 1855–60 (see Table 2.2). This was probably due to the favourable German tariff system – which allowed free importation of pig iron – and thus enabled domestic manufacturers of railway ironware to capture a large share of the home market in transport equipment than their American counterparts had seized in the USA. But, whatever the reason, the outcome is clear: the railway 'multiplier' in Germany was large and the 'extraordinary importance' of railways to German economic growth receives new and authoritative confirmation. Despite the promising indications, the room for railway revisionism in Germany turns out to be limited.

Table 2.2 Railroad derived demand for pig iron as % total domestic consumption of pig iron

USA		Germany	
1840–45	3.5	1840–44	15.4
1846–50	6.4	1845–49	22.9
1851–55	10.7	1850–54	24.6
1856–60	17.4	1855–59	21.5

Source: Fremdling (1977), p. 593.

Even then, however, the portrayal of the iron roads as sovereign 'carriers' of German development – the tendency rightly dubbed by Fogel, 'the hero theory of history applied to things rather than persons'[100] – is certainly an inflation. They were not entirely well organized; they were not entirely profitable; they were not by any means without competitors. Nor *could* they have acted as carriers of economic development *tout court*. It is, after all, highly tautologous to derive the development of several manufacturing industries from the development of a single transport industry; and it says nothing about first causes. Just as the transport industry provided markets, services, and an example of enterprise for the manufacturers, so it, too, required inputs of capital, labour, and enterprise from some quarter. To credit railroads with an almost independent propulsive force gives no clue as to the origin of these vital factors. Put another way, the 'railway Kondratiev' is not explained solely by the railway. As with the problem of natural resources, there is a deeper level to which analysis must penetrate.

MANAGEMENT: ENTREPRENEURIAL INDIVIDUALISM VERSUS CARTELIZED COLLECTIVISM

At first sight, it might appear as if that level were inhabited by the German entrepreneur. After all, he was the economic decision-taker who contrived to convert – often by science applied industrially – Germany's moderate resources into outstanding manufacturing success. Highly adventurous private business-men and bankers were required to engineer Germany's 'transport revolution' And, in the annals of rumbustious free enterprise, it is perhaps the German businessman who is popularly supposed to rival the American prototype most closely.

However, he did not begin to do so, in any numbers, until the 1840s. Before then, the German technical journals suggest only a disturbing state of entrepreneurial ignorance.[101] Businessmen were clearly investing in manufac-turing ventures at this time, but the majority of them, operating commonly within family businesses, concerned themselves with the modest issues of commercial or organizational change rather than with the central problems of technological progress. The great innovators – Harkort, Borsig, or Egells in the machine industry, Krupp or Mayer in metallurgy – were few and far between. Wide-ranging change did not come until the 1860s. Then, with the advent of the new steel technology, a wave of industrial mergers swept across the economy. Procedural and organizational innovation combined as heavy industry was rapidly shuffled under the hand of entrepreneurs like Thyssen, Stinnes, Haniel, Funke, Pastor, Böcker, or Mannesmann.[102] Huge vertical in-tegrations were formed as the managerial motif, the direction of the individual promotor, came to count more in industrial affairs than any other. Many of the great named empires of German industry originated in these years. At the same time, an element that was to mark the whole of German economic growth became increasingly evident through the 1850s and 1860s – the ele-ment of rapid technical progress. From 1850 through to 1914, the level of capital intensity in German industry was maintained at an unusually high point, and although it climbed most sharply in the years nearest 1914 – the rate of growth in the stock of capital rising from 2.3 per cent per annum in 1850–75 to 2.7 per cent in 1876–1895 and to 3.4 per cent per annum in 1896–1913 – it was already well established by 1860. With the labour force merely doubling in size in 1850–1913, the proportion of capital stock to labour force increased at the high annual average rate of 1.6 per cent per year from the mid-century to the First World War. This would imply that German entre-preneurs first became highly responsive to the opportunities revealed by scien-tific investigation in the 1850s and 1860s. And it would imply also that they *remained* consistently sensitive to technological prospects from that point on-wards, in clear contrast to their cautious British rivals of the period 1870–1914.[103]

The outcome of the German responsiveness to the opportunities for indus-trial innovation was a startingly high level of capital formation. Rising from 14.4 per cent GNP in 1851–70 to 24.1 per cent GNP in 1891–1913,[104] German gross capital formation represented the largest investment effort in relation to national product of the era, easily outpacing that of Britain, France, and even the USA. The pattern is similar for net capital formation with the German levels outstripping the British in every decade between 1861 and 1910 (See Table 2.3). What is more, this effort was heavily concentrated upon fixed capital in industry and transport – investment of this type accounted for 62 per cent of total net domestic capital formation by 1901–13. The implications are that capital could hardly have been scarce in the German economy after 1850,[105] that means now existed to direct it accurately towards industry, and that entrepreneurs were notably swift to claim it for absorption in new technology.

Table 2.3 Net national capital formation as % Net National Product: Germany and UK, 1851–1910. Annual averages

	Germany		UK
1851–60	9.4		
1861–70	11.9	1860–69	10.0
1871–80	12.1	1870–79	11.8
1881–90	11.1	1880–89	10.9
1891–1900	13.6	1890–99	10.1
1901–10	14.4	1900–09	11.7

Sources: for Germany, calculated from Mitchell (1975), pp. 781–5; for UK, Kuznets (1961), Table UK-1, p. 58.

The explanation most usually advanced to account for the alertness of Ger-man businessmen features the excellence of their educational background. German schools, polytechnics, and universities, it is suggested, contrived not only to train scientists capable of conducting industry-related research but also industrial managers capable of appreciating their discoveries. Certainly, the apparatus of educational provision within the German states was very lavish, many of the individual governments acting upon Bismarck's dictum that 'the nation that has the schools, has the future', decades before he formulated it. Thus Saxony started upon the creation of trade schools in the eighteenth cen-tury, and by 1872 possessed a remarkably comprehensive system of education with compulsory attendance and a scholarship path leading from elementary through technical to polytechnic schools – and all at a time when Britain possessed neither compulsory attendance nor a national system.[106] By 1905 the Reich could offer a system of vocational education, matching a technical school against virtually every rung of the conventional education 'ladder' Commercial and industrial 'continuation' schools were provided alongside the general primary schools, higher commercial and industrial schools alongside the general secondary schools and the great technical high schools, the *technische hochschulen*, on a par with the universities.[107] In order to provide sufficient recruits for these industrial academies, the imperial state offered inducements both practical and social: six years of technical study brought exemption from two years of military service and a much-coveted commission in the army reserve (together with uniform).[108] Although the state did not originate many of the technical institutions – most were private creations – they did have its close attention. Indeed, interest was such that from 1872 to 1914, the official outlay on the educational count added almost as much to the imperial budget as did the Reich's military spending.[109]

From a precocious stage in Germany's growth, the relationship between the educational structure and the business world was a tight one. As early as 1828 an overtly technological manifestation of this fact occurred with the foundation of Liebig's chemical laboratories at the University of Giessen, an institution which was to provide a flow of discoveries vital for the initial development of the German chemical industry.[110] By mid-century the work of the universities was affecting a wider technological range, taking in textiles, dyestuffs, agricultural chemicals, glass, and steel. By 1872 a single German university, that of Munich, contained more graduate research chemists than all English universities put together. Within this explosion of industry-related education and research, the academic instructor was clearly an essential component. Significantly, he was seen, according to Hauser, not as in France, as a simple functionary rarely consulted by businessmen, but as 'an obligatory auxiliary of the public services and great industries.'[111]

Flows of scientific knowledge and of trained personnel on this scale should have produced definitely positive effects upon the industrial sector: for Germany, distinct advantages over the main manufacturing powers of Europe should have followed. Measured against the British educational provision, with its more or less comprehensive divorce between technology and science, industry and universities, the German system did indeed score heavily. It excelled, also, precisely where the French system failed: in the application of science to practical problems. Although the French might take initiatives in theoretical science they lacked the skills of the applied variety: they defined many of the ground rules for chemical manufacturing yet continued to make the poorest explosives in Europe. Appropriately, where the French were the first industrialists to introduce theoretically trained chemists into factories, the Germans were the first to employ specialized research teams. However, the record is not without its flaws. There have always been some, usually Anglo-Saxon, doubts as to the degree of regimentation and standardization implied by the German educational preferences. Early in this century Alfred Marshall recorded these qualifications, although he also observed, without apparent irony, that organized efforts were being made to inject a measure of spontaneity into German curricula.[112] And, much more recently, W. N. Parker concluded in his study of the Lorraine ore fields – where, after 1871, French and German technologists faced one another across the new frontier – that the French engineering education, with its wide-ranging and theoretical sweep, was no less effective in its practical consequences, and possibly even more effective, than its tightly focused and highly vocational German counterpart.[113] But, even conceding these doubts, it is impossible to dispute the judgement that the German educational system was tailored, with unusual precision, to industrial needs. The narrow division of labour employed in German factories did in fact *require* highly specialized (or tightly focused) technicians. Similarly, a technology that was naturally imitative needed industrial researchers and managers who could produce adaptative innovations rather than make penetrating insights into new principles.

Many of Germany's industrial achievements followed not so much from discovery as from the swift application of methods and mechanisms developed elsewhere. Aniline dyes, the generation and conveyance of electric power, the Gilchrist–Thomas process for iron manufacture – each basic to Germany's late-nineteenth-century pre-eminence – were French and British, not German, discoveries. The essential connexion between foreign invention and domestic innovation was the German research team. For the chemical industry this was particularly the case. Aniline-violet dye processes from Britain, fuschine processes from France, were worked over indefatigably in the laboratories of Frankfurt or Mannheim, and perfected for profitable exploitation. By 1900 German chemical firms were deploying research groups up to fifty or seventy strong, allowing them to carry out what research they wished, and *expecting* to discard 90 per cent of the results.[114] Using these methods the Badische firm at Ludwigshafen produced artificial indigo after seventeen years of research. Unsurprisingly, such scientific application prompted Professor F. Fischer to write in 1897: 'It is generally recognised that the German chemical industry owes its preponderating position to the high scientific preparation of its collaborators.'[115] In metals it was the same. The Westphalian steelmasters made none of the new discoveries, but were quicker than any foreign rivals in applying them. The sleight of hand was again managed through the research laboratory. At Essen, Krupp maintained, to the usual high standards of the armament manufacturer, research capacity worth £100,000; it was described by a British competitor as 'an immense physical and chemical laboratory . . . such as is possessed by no university in the world'.[116] Scientific investigation was thus at the epicentre of German industrial growth. And it was placed there by education, and, even more significantly, by educated management. As Hauser shrewdly noted, the society in which education is so emphasized becomes not so much a superior intellectual community as a medium for the deep penetration of scientific ideas and their application to a very wide variety of tasks. One of the most curious applications demonstrates the thoroughness of the penetration. In the 1900s the German chemical industry obtained a French discovery – grapes from the Côte d'Or – and began to produce with its wines superior to those turned out by the famous ignorance and uncleanliness of the French peasantry. Hauser's reaction, appropriately for a native of Alsace, was the appalled witticism, 'vive donc le bourgogne allemand'.[117]

The deduction would appear to be that, in the German entrepreneur, we have a decision-taker of rare qualities: superbly, if narrowly, educated, technically qualified, respectful of – and eager for – scientific assistance, gifted at the translation of scientific discovery into industrial practice. Within an economy propelled by technical change to an unusual degree, does one need to look further for the chief agency of progress? Unfortunately, the answer is in the affirmative. For a country so well equipped with managerial material, Germany was extraordinarily sparsely endowed with outstanding entrepreneurial figures; the heroic capitalists of the USA – Carnegie, Vanderbilt, Morgan – or the scarcer British industrial captains – Armstrong, Lever – find very few German equivalents.[118] It is possible to identify the buccaneering activities of a Thyssen, raiding the pits of Rhine-Ruhr from his base at the Mulheim Steelworks; or of a Stinnes building up a coal empire which amounted to a personal dominion over the southern Ruhr; or of a Rathenau, creating in AEG with a rare eye for the mass market, one of the largest electro-technical concerns in the world. But individualistic operators of this type do not represent a norm even for the highest levels of German business activity. They were never common in Germany, but, after the speculative mania and collapse of the early 1870s, they gave ground increasingly to managers who preferred collective action to the jungle law of the independent capitalist.[119] The team element, already so pronounced within German research activity, spread to dominate also German management. Even where the opportunities for individual entrepreneurship were greatest – among the many concerns and varied technological possibilities of the light manufacturing sector – earnings from innovation remained remarkably low.[120]

It becomes clear, therefore, that some force must have interposed itself between the supply of highly trained managers and the exploitation of the market by individualistic capitalists. That force was the cartel. As a form of collaborative industrial action, the cartel allowed firms – while nominally maintaining their independent existence – to come together in agreements designed to control prices and markets. Beginning in the depressed conditions of the 1870s, and with the heavy industries, the cartel increasingly captured the initiative from the independent businessman. The cartel was the exact antithesis of the entrepreneur – who combines in one person the functions of financier, shop manager, merchant, and salesman. Fragmentation of the decision-making process was the mark of the cartel: commercial decisions were appropriated by its professional administrators at cartel headquarters; production decisions were governed by its technical staff; financial policy was largely controlled by its bankers. Further, these decisions were not taken within an institution that was by spirit enterprising; on the contrary, the cartel was a deeply conservative organization aiming at the orderly exploitation of consumers and markets, the elimination of competition, and the pooling of profits. Most entrepreneurs who were sucked into the mill of the cartel were ground down into safety-conscious industrial functionaries. And the technically adept managers and researchers, instead of being allowed free rein as individual profit-seekers within a competitive market, were inserted into their specialized slots within a massive and hierarchic industrial mechanism. Naturally, a handful of manufacturing virtuosi, the Krupps, Thyssens, Haniels, and their colleagues, guarded their independence, but even they, while expressing dislike for the cartel, were forced to accept its facilities for certain of their products. It would seem, therefore, that despite the considerable promise offered by the German education system, and despite the thrusting reputation of German business, the individual capitalist in Germany enjoyed a somewhat limited heyday: it lay between his apprenticeship in the 1840s and his eclipse by the cartel in the 1870s or 1880s. As Schmoller put it in the early 1900s: 'A large portion of the freedom of trade and free economy on which thirty years ago we prided ourselves has been buried through the cartel, not legally but in fact.'[121]

If the Parsonian method of analysis is to be operationally useful, it should be able to absorb these peculiarities of the German entrepreneurial endowment, matching them to the characteristics of the German social value system. This does indeed seem to be the case.

In Germany any large-scale organization – the army, the bureaucracy, academe – which contributed to national prestige stood high in social approval. The creation of the Reich in 1871 naturally placed a premium upon any agency which could work to reinforce the viability of the new Empire. Consequently, business achievement could most easily command social respect if it were conducted on a massive scale, if it achieved national significance, and if it strengthened the sinews of the Reich.[122] Such a calculus explains why Schmoller could claim, on behalf of the great German entrepreneurs that he was 'not a *mere* money-maker but on a level with the best generals and statesmen in talent, in character and in achievement'.[123] An industrialist of suitable qualities could be accredited status on a par with the feudal aristocracy, and the role of entrepreneurship thus sanctified by association with the traditional state-building forces. The nobility, as David Landes observes, sneered discreetly if at all, and the middle class took the manipulation seriously.[124] Unlike France, therefore, Germany possessed a set of past attitudes and role expectations centred on respect for the state and for military achievement which could be translated productively into industrial terms. Particular traditions could be utilized to connect large-scale industry with national objectives, thus providing an *alternative* to the equally traditional, but far more constraining, familial goals of the small producers. If pre-industrial values, together with a multitude of miniature concerns, persisted within German industry, the objectives and expectations of familial business were not permitted to dominate the industrial community as they did in France. For, given the presence in the market of very few ventures of middling size, the numerous small concerns of conservative outlook could be matched by equally numerous monster concerns linked to national aspirations and politico-military objectives.

The difficulty was that the innovational value systems attached *solely* to big business: the criterion of national significance could be fulfilled, the interaction of industrial and political élites facilitated, the relationship between Ruhr

66

and Reich sustained, only within the ambit of the most massive industrial organizations. Yet, clearly, a mere handful of individual entrepreneurs actually possessed the capacity to construct *personal* empires of appropriate scale. For most, once they had progressed beyond a certain point, further advance towards the desirable level of bigness posed formidable problems. Usually these were solved by a single and direct tactic: an act of surrender to the cartel. Membership of the cartel could provide the final, otherwise unattainable, element of size and prestige – participation in the control of the entire national market for a given commodity. Or, alternatively, it could offer a haven for manufacturing concerns already grown unwieldy in the pursuit of bigness. By definition – through its supervision of the Reich's market or very large provincial markets – the cartel achieved national significance. And within its own schedule of priorities, the element of market domination carried more weight than the margin of profit earned. Where such considerations could predominate, the independent capitalist was left with little elbow-room.

A possible conclusion might be that the style and pace of German growth was derived not so much from a particular type of entrepreneurial behaviour as from a particular institutional device. Certainly, both the behaviour of German businessmen and the cast of German social values suggest that the contribution made by the classic entrepreneurial type was of limited duration and subject to marked decline after 1870. However, it would obviously be mistaken to regard the entrepreneur and the cartel as mutually exclusive economic forces; clearly the cartel was not an anonymous and autonomous monster but was directed from within by its own team of business administrators. If, as the cartel strengthened its hold from the 1870s, the majority of industrial managers became prudent specialists, a band of entrepreneurs of an entirely new type was thrown up inside the cartel. They were not numerous. And, although they matched the equally thinly populated society of industrial barons in dynamism, responsibility, and risk-taking, they lacked large resources or ownership interests of their own. Probably, they would have considered themselves as career bureaucrats within industry. Individuals like these were the architects of the great cartels – Hammacher, designer of many of the original coal syndicates, Emil Krabler, promoter of equally many, Anton Unckell, leader of the Rhenish-Westphalian Coal Syndicate for over a decade, and, most successful of all, the Kirdorf brothers, the great diplomats of cartelization in the Ruhr mining region.[125] These men were entrepreneurs in the *promotion* of cartelization, continuing in their own actions the traditions of the pre-1870 period, even as they helped to suppress this tradition for the rest of the business community.

BUSINESS ORGANIZATION: BENEFITS AND COSTS OF INDUSTRIAL GIANTISM

If there were opportunities for enterprise within the German cartels, it remains true that the process of cartelization worked to reduce the *total* scope for entrepreneurial action. To what extent did it offer compensation? If the entrepreneurial capabilities of the German economy were negatively affected by the cartel movement, were there also positive attributes which followed from a collectivist and co-operative form of industrial activity? Marshall considered that the major characteristic of German growth, its high rate of technological change, was precisely such an attribute. For the cartel, by imposing a common set of manufacturing conditions upon its members, proved highly effective in eliminating obsolescence in its satellite factories. The responsiveness of cartel managers to technological opportunities was also maintained at a high level by unremitting pressure from headquarters. Similarly, the rapid rate of growth in industrial capacity – admittedly hovering close to *over*capacity in the years before 1914 – owed a great deal to the accumulative and self-reproducing nature of cartelization and to the safe environment for investment which it offered its expanding list of members. By extension, the exuberant German export drive of the 1900s – an antidote for overcapacity – was closely related to the 'dumping' of products at artificially low prices which the cartels practised in their overseas markets. Some of the identifying features of the expansionary German economy were, clearly enough, cartel-inspired.

If the individual entrepreneur was not the major influence acting upon the design of the German economy, the collective form of enterprise might establish certain claims to this title. Certainly, in Hauser's assessment of the 'colossal' scale of German economic activity, the cartel was an integral part.[126] In its fullest incarnation it was a totally binding collective agreement into which member firms entered, retaining their individual status but bowing absolutely to cartel headquarters over the subject-matter of the agreement. This would include: the fixing of prices; the setting of a production quota for each member, to be exceeded only under penalty of a stiff fine; and the complete surrender of all sales decisions to the central sales bureau of the cartel. For these various processes to function effectively the product under scrutiny clearly had to be, as far as possible, homogeneous. Consequently, since the market agreement attached to the product and not to the industry, a single firm might belong to several cartels, a different one for each of its main manufactures. Whatever the article, however, the objective of the cartel was, invariably, the stabilization of the market. In pursuit of this goal, every item of cartel operation was subjected to a tight discipline: as Hauser wrote, the cartel 'leads the partners with a lash'.[127]

Perhaps unsurprisingly, these features accumulated into a still more powerful characteristic, a tendency to encourage industrial integration, and, eventually, giantism. The structure of the cartel frequently induced the larger members to buy out the smaller ones in order to acquire their production quotas, and to achieve an advantage in independence and market power over other cartel members. In this way, some two-thirds of the lesser coal mines within the Rhenish-Westphalian Coal Syndicate in 1893 were cannibalized by 1914. Rather more sophisticated was the form of integration operated particularly by the iron and coal cartels across the industrial frontiers. Here a 'pure' concern – that is one devoted *only* to iron or coal – would be impelled to go 'mixed' – that is, to acquire its own coal-mines for fuel or its own blast-furnaces as outlets for its pit output – by the high prices charged for coal by the mining cartels or the attractive quotas offered to 'mixed' plants by the metal cartels. Similar pressure upon the price of vital inputs by cartels could often force non-members to join, or stimulate them into becoming massive and independent conglomerates, usually the only viable alternative to surrender. The cartel thus introduced into the German economy a powerful dynamic of integration both for members *and* for outsiders. This has a clear bearing upon the extraordinary German business structure with its heavy layers of very small and very large concerns and its very thin layer in the middle. By 1914, 95 per cent of enterprises in industry and mining employed less than 10 people, but 50 per cent of the entire workforce was employed in installations housing more than 500 persons. Integration had accounted for the businesses of middling size. Once again, the basic industrial equipment of Germany was profoundly affected by the cartel.

To begin with, in the 1870s and 1880s, cartelization had been concerned only with the fixing of prices on a minimum and mandatory basis. Before long, however, cartel managers realized that price levers were insufficient to control sales and markets, and that additional powers over output were essential. This perception introduced the quota-setting cartel which proliferated throughout the 1870s and 1880s. Adequate controls over production were provided by this innovation since it allocated strict market shares to all member firms, but it left a great deal to be desired in the supervision of sales. Solution to this problem waited upon the invention of the syndicate form, delegating to a central marketing agency the entire output of the cartel members. This proposal originated with the coal industry in 1887 and was applied widely during the 1890s, especially in regard to the Westphalian Coal Syndicate of 1890, the huge Rhenish-Westphalian Coal Syndicate of 1893 – controlling 87 per cent of the coal cut in the Dortmund region – and the Pig Iron Syndicate of 1896. Between 1897 and 1914 syndicatization swept over virtually the entire range of German raw material output, penetrated the finishing stages of heavy industry, and even began to affect some consumer goods sectors. Its wide popularity is revealed by the count of cartel formations in the 1890s and early 1900s. By 1896 there were 250 cartels, one-quarter in the iron and chemical industries; by 1895 there were 385 cartels, covering some 12,000 separate factories, and with the iron and chemical industries still claiming the leading shares. Finishing touches to the imposing structure were given in the remaining years before the First World War.[128] By 1904 the German economy possessed in the Stahlwerksverband, one of the most important pre-war creations, a fighting organization of world stature, fully capable of confronting the might of United States Steel (1901) to which indeed it was in part a reaction. In coal, similarly, cartelization had rooted so deeply that, by 1908, the entire industry was disposed in an echelon of powerful regional syndicates.[129] To such, by now almost conventional, forms of integration a logical elaboration was added at the end of the period – an *inter*-syndical conciliation board designed to concert the export activities of the various associations. It gave rise, not unreasonably, to the assertion that German industry was becoming a 'cartel of cartels'.

But this was not all. Alongside the cartels, and stimulated by them, were other forms of amalgamation. The German economy, it seemed, was becoming populated by a limited number of industrial species, most of them monstrous. The electrical engineering industry, perhaps the major growth industry of the 1890s, organized itself with desperate energy into seven groups, covering twenty-eight large companies by 1900, and, by 1910, had further convulsed into the gigantic duopoly of Siemens-Schuckert and AEG. A similar process of outright consolidation, reaching beyond cartelization, went on in chemicals, banking, and shipping. In chemicals the two great firms of Hoescht and Casella came together in combination in October 1904, and, almost simultaneously, a triple alliance was struck between BASF, Bayer, and the Aniline Dyes Manufacturing Co. These were true fusions, the culmination of a process of amalgamation which might also be seen as a process of drastic 'industrial simplification'.[130] So simplified was German industry as a result that one contemporary observer argued that, 'the individual enterprise has ceased to be the unit of German industry to a large extent'.[131]

From this it should be clear that the German economy of 1914 partook more of the nature of a collectivist—collaborationist system than it did of the competitive and individualistic style of capitalistic growth found predominantly in Britain, France, or America. But to conclude from this that the cartel was responsible for most of the more positive aspects of German industrial advance before 1914 would be a rash deduction. The cartel, after all, meant radically different things at different times, and brought other qualities than rationality of large-scale enterprise to the German economy. At some points, indeed, it probably brought more damage than benefit.

In terms of motivation and conditioning stimuli, it is possible to detect three major phases of cartel growth. The initial upsurge of the 1870s came about as a response to the low prices, overproduction, and furious competition of the time. As great firms like the Phönix Ironworks or the Rheinische Stahlwerke were forced to reduce their capital, and others like the Dortmunder Union recorded heavy losses, cartels sprang up in serried, defensive ranks. No doubt many analysts have exaggerated the depth of the German depression partly in order to present the cartels as 'children of bad times', but it is beyond argument that, during the 1870s at least, they did emerge from a context of business disruption. The first phase of cartelization was not a healthy rationalizing exercise carried out with confidence and an eye to market advantage; instead it was a conservative avoiding action designed to ward off crisis by force of numbers. As a form of association it could contribute little to the dynamic growth which characterized the German economy for the major part of the pre-war period.

Both in this early stage and later, the resort to cartelization, as a defensive parry in the repertoire of business tactics, possessed a particular appeal for the banking community. Once a financial entrepreneur had risked his capital in some manufacturing venture, his prime concern was for its safety; and the security of the industrial asset was best guaranteed by steering it towards the safe haven offered by cartel membership. Banks also preferred, again largely for reasons of risk-aversion, to invest in 'mixed' concerns, those with capacity in more than one branch of manufacturing. Since cartels habitually allocated larger shares of the market to mixed concerns, the financiers could secure additional risk-barriers for their industrial protégés by surrendering them to the care of the industrial associations. It follows as a natural consequence that the German investment banks constantly encouraged their industrial clients towards cartel membership and openly supported firms active in cartel leadership. At all points they would have viewed this policy as a means of minimizing risk rather than of maximizing growth. At points of market recession, however, they proved especially sensitive to the cartel's talents for limiting their liabilities.

In the second phase of cartelization, from the late 1880s to 1900, the more elaborate schemes of risk reduction were less necessary. Among cartel members, certainly, the patterns of behaviour moved from the defensive to the determinedly aggressive. Policy now aimed deliberately at the objective of monopoly power and pursued it with some violence. Cut-throat pricing was employed to ruin outsider firms – as the Pig Iron Syndicate attempted to do for years by persistent under-cutting of the independent Kraft Ironworks. Alternatively, vital raw materials could be denied to non-members – as the Phönix Ironworks discovered to its cost. Not unnaturally, terms such as 'power-hunger' or 'terrorism' were frequently used in criticism of cartels like the Pig Iron Syndicate or the Coke Syndicate. Even a concern as prestigious as the Gelsenkirchen Coal Co. admitted in 1902 that its 'chief and fundamental object was the attainment of a position of conspicuous power'.[132]

But what was attractive to cartels was too frequently damaging to the economy; perhaps the most obvious drawbacks of cartelization are associated with the era of power-seeking. If the cartels managed to acquire, in some measure, stability of prices and of markets, the results, for customers as well as for competitors, could be highly unpleasant. Since cartels concentrated upon the extractive and semi-finished product industries – that is, near the beginning of the product line – they were well placed to hold their customers – usually manufacturers further down the line – to a form of price-ransom. Integral to this tactic were the opportunities created for the cartels by the *Kaiserreich*'s policies of tariff protection. The levy imposed upon imported materials gave the cartels every incentive to inflate their co-ordinated price for a given commodity to a point only marginally below that charged for the foreign article *after* it had attracted tariff duty. The exclusion of interlopers at which protection aimed also greatly assisted the cartels in their tight supervision of domestic prices. Effectively, the additional price margin created by protective duties provided a comfortable field of manoeuvre for organized business developing a taste for exploitative policies. And, naturally, domestic customers who might seek escape from cartel price policies by resorting to overseas sources of supply

— especially tempting for raw materials — would find themselves prevented by the springing of the tariff trap.

Clearly the abolition of competition in the name of stable markets did not protect the *client* from anarchy in prices. In 1899, for instance, the Dusseldorf pig-iron firms simply decided to reduce output by 45 per cent and to increase prices to match. After the boom of 1899–1900 most heavy industrial cartels were accused of raising prices too rapidly in the upswing and reducing them too slowly as the cycle turned and dipped. And these were only the more spectacular incidents in a long-drawn-out tale of complaint from cartel customers. Nor were high prices the only subject of such complaints. Cartel insistence on the *differential* between prices — a special 'dumping' level for overseas sales but a much higher one for domestic purchasers — was also greatly resented. When, for example, the foreign customer for sheet-iron could purchase for 100 marks the ton, materials which cost his German rival 140 marks, it is not difficult to perceive the basis of the unease. With some articles, indeed, the differential was so great that it paid German users to *re-import* 'dumped' cartel products. But even this stratagem could not prevent German cartel policy from raising up low-cost foreign competition against Germany's own finishing industries. 'Dumping' of German wire created effective nail industries in Holland and Belgium, while the cheap exports of German steel conjured up barge-building yards in Holland and presented British shipbuilders with a welcome, if unexpected, subsidy. Very often the foreign competitor could then proceed to under-cut the German final producer. Over-priced supplies for domestic industry, over-generous assistance to overseas rivals could only harm Germany's economic prospects. In its power-seeking phase, therefore, the German cartel movement probably provided less of value for the economy than in its defensive and reactive phase.

Only in their third incarnation did the cartels discover a definitely creative form. The change followed not least from the official response to the cartel problem, aired in Reichstag debates at the turn of the century and formalized in the Government Inquiry into Cartels in 1903. While accepting the necessity of 'dumping' and exonerating some cartels from charges of profiteering, the Inquiry deplored the absence of co-ordination between cartels and customers, and the lack of a systematic relationship between raw material, semi-finished, and final product prices. It noted with dissatisfaction the damage to the producer at the end of the chain. And it singled out coal, coke, and pig-iron syndicates for special censure.

The cartels' response to this embarrassing scrutiny was to discover a new sense of responsibility. The reformed cartel was to aim at moderate and stable prices under all conditions. If the movement began as an antidote to ruinous competition and became a market power system, it embarked from 1900 on a programme 'to assume marketing functions whose object was above all the stability of the economy'.[133] A major influence upon these new tendencies was the Rhenish-Westphalian Coal Syndicate which presented itself to the Inquiry as a model cartel, devoid of the appetite for monopoly prices and mindful of other industrial interests. Its chief executive, Emil Kirdorf, was either a man ahead of his time or an inspired propagandist. Whichever he was, both the commissioners and other cartel managers believed him, each, in their different ways, eager to find an exemplar for acceptable cartel behaviour. Consequently, the first major cartel formed after the Inquiry, the Stahlwerksverband of 1904 came under some pressure to embody the new principles. In the event, it promised to pursue 'a stable price policy in co-operation with other great combines', to 'hold a middle course', and 'to take great care not to put the economic power inherent in the Steel Works Association against the political authority and power of the State'.[134] It embodied, however, a device designed to rectify perhaps the gravest flaw revealed by the self-examination of the early 1900s – the problem of the 'dumping' price. Under the new code of conduct, the cartels, Steel Works Association included, were to reduce their prices to home consumers if their products were to be incorporated in a commodity destined for export; in other words, the cartels were to provide rebates for exporting industries. This system became a formidable weapon of exportation. It allowed German locomotive producers to drive French engines out of Spain, and almost out of France; it made a British dyestuffs industry scarcely worth while; it overcame every Italian tariff and converted this market into a testing ground for German manufactures. As before, cheap raw materials could be poured out of Germany, killing the preparatory industries in other countries. But now the rebate system extended the slaughter to the transforming industries. Instead of penalizing the German exporter, the reformed cartels placed an instrument of economic warfare in his hands. Where 'dumping' had been formerly a symptom of Germany's economic overweight, dangerous to some of her most vital industrial organs, it was now adjusted to become a means of poisoning the opposition. Clashing interests in the overseas markets were refashioned to form a concerted policy of German exportation. In one instance – that of the Stahlwerksverband – the cartel not only provided a rebate scheme for customers, and negotiated its own rebates with raw material cartels like the coal syndicates; it also provided a central export agency to handle the overseas business of all members and levied a tax upon them in order to provide funds for the conduct of the export battle.

From 1900, therefore, the cartels were steered away from the particularist interests of belligerent economic satrapies towards the social duties of responsible industrial communities, content to create their mayhem abroad. This growing dutifulness was probably a function of the increasing spread of cartelization and the natural balance forming between the conglomerates. It was seemingly for this reason that German heavy industry gradually adopted and administered – though admittedly under some pressure – a code of business behaviour that, in most countries, had to emanate from the state authorities. But, so much conceded, it is still true that these desirable conditions were achieved only in the last years before 1914. The earlier phases of cartel activity have a good deal less to offer the industrializing economy. It would not seem, therefore, that a convincing explanation of Germany's economic prowess could be associated with the behaviour of her cartels much before 1900.

THE STATE: MYTHS OF THE DIRECTED ECONOMY

If neither resources nor railways, neither entrepreneurial decision-takers nor associative policy-makers, hold the key to the German growth-style, it might be logical to look towards an institutional force of still larger scope than the cartel – the state itself. Certainly, some earlier economic historians have deduced from the orderliness of the cartelized economy that the influence of the bureaucracy had been at work, and, although there is little in this, the role played by the state in whistling the cartels to heel in the 1900s – tactfully but no less effectively – is, to an extent, suggestive. In a similar vein, Professor W. F. Bruck, in writing on the theoretical background to German cartelization, observed: 'Private interest as the fundamental principle was always a stranger to the German mercantilist, state-socialist mind. The idea of state interference was always congenial.'[135] Such views have, of course, made frequent appearances in German economic history, and they have covered much more ground than merely the relationship between the state and the cartels. At the outset, however, it is important to record that a body of opinion exists which would allocate more influence in the design of German economic growth to the government than to the cartel. That it would also allocate more influence to the state than to *any* other factor, is worthy of investigation.

A respect for state economic power is traditional within German historical studies.[136] Thus Bruck, writing as an émigré in 1938, observed that 'mercantilism is the key-note of Prussian Germany'.[137] At very much the same time, Thorstein Veblen contended that: 'The economic history of the new era might well be written as the history of the economic policy of the Prussian State and the Prussianised Empire.'[138] And writing with a propagandist's hostility just before the First World War, Henri Hauser had categorically stated that: 'No kind of national activity is even conceivable there outside the framework of the state.'[139] The sources for such views are fairly clear. To begin with, there was precedent: Brandenburg-Prussia, Silesia, and Frederick the Great's mercantilism; obviously enough, the state *had* been important in German economic affairs. Then, more recently, there was the merely ephemeral importance of political and economic liberalism in the second third of the nineteenth century; surely, this indicated the implausibility, within German territory, of any form of economic growth other than one influenced by the state? And, finally, there was the political and international context for the Second Reich. In this area there was a great deal of evidence – drawn from outside the economy – to support the belief in a dominant state. Any observer of the political situation who noted the virtually unlimited powers of the Imperial Chancellor disposed opposite an almost fictitious constitutional assembly, might be forgiven for arguing that there could be no sphere of policy in which the Prussian executive would not claim a dominant role. Even the fact that Germany developed so robustly – and simultaneously – both as an international power and as an industrial economy might suggest that *Machtpolitik* spilled out of one area into the other. In short, the belief in an economically 'dominant' state is derived partly by analogy from Germany's political development. Nor does it eschew borrowings from political theory. Studies of the German economy are frequently, if obscurely, prefaced by statements from Hegel, Fichte, Kant or Nietzsche designed to demonstrate the central importance of the *Machtstaat* within their thinking, and, by extension, within German thinking generally, including, naturally, economic thinking.

The fallacies of the approach lie chiefly in the implied conviction that what is true of politics is necessarily true of economics, and that the values specified by a nation's political theory will necessarily translate more or less directly into its economic action. In each case the method of translation is left in studied vagueness. The method of Bruck or Veblen is often to *infer* action in the economic sphere from data of a wholly non-economic type, to establish implied qualitative similarities between wholly distinct areas of thought or action. The facts may well be very different.

Initially, it should be recognized that 'state intervention' is not a constant economic input either over time or between countries. State economic policy is no independent or mobile variable but rather a function of the constitutional type – from imperial autocracy to constitutional democracy – bureaucratic composition, and social structure of *particular* states. And all of these determinants are subject to modification over the decades. The pronounced variability in the content of state intervention is well displayed in the divergent economic attitudes struck by the early-nineteenth-century German states, ranging from the military *dirigisme* of Prussia through the near-Smithian doctrines of Saxony to the wavering and inconsistent programmes maintained by the socially split governments of the southern states. Similarly, the thrust of official policy may often be conditioned less by antiquated decision-making than by internal frictions within the administration, frequently by conflicts between central and regional levels. Again, the German states of the proto-industrial era provide good examples. In Rhineland–Westphalia, industrial and financial innovation numbered among the casualties trapped in the cross-fire between the strong and modernized local governments of the post-Napoleonic period and a Prussian central government bent upon making its writ effective in reconquered territory. Later, in the east, the local Junker administration resisted Berlin's plans for industrial development not only because such schemes represented the familiar catechism of terrors – cities, socialism, Jewish speculators, Polish workers – but because they opposed central government power to local semi-feudal autonomy.[140] These, however, are all 'supply' characteristics, affecting the quality of state economic policy at source. But state intervention is affected also by 'demand' considerations. Some kinds of economy (mostly backward) or some stages of growth (mostly early) may *require* state assistance; others may render it almost entirely marginal. Whether 'supply' or 'demand' in type, however, these consideration are far more likely to affect official economic policy than the reflections of political thinkers or the implications of foreign policy.

Within these terms, state economic action in the German lands would appear to break down into three sub-periods: a period of high need and qualified response, 1790–1840; a period of declining need and potentially increased response, 1840—70; a period of low need and declining response, 1870—1914.

Before 1840, as we have seen, the importance of state action in growth areas like Silesia — and, less successfully in Thuringia and Saxony — was of considerable significance. Within the context of backwardness prevailing at that time, it is exceedingly unlikely that an alternative source of enterprise of equal strength could have arisen. But it is worth considering for a moment the nature of the Prussian state. As a military absolutism served by a ministeriat and bureaucracy largely composed of Junker *agricultural* interests, it was attracted only to a particular type of industrial development, that with military utility. Outside this area, the authorities contributed little in the way of investment or encouragement to private entrepreneurs. In some cases they even expressed hostility to major innovations in industry or transport, and they were notably suspicious of the railways at the outset.[141] Within their own sphere of control, they approached increases in the currency supply — important for the level of economic activity — very cautiously, and the authorization of joint-stock companies with the utmost reluctance.[142] Even the liberalization of trade carried out by Prussia, as by most German regimes in the period 1810—45 — and deriving from the lessons of the Napoleonic period — was conducted with a strict attention to 'beneficial' restrictions and with an eye to commercial advantage rather than to the prospects of industrialization and growth of the national economy.[143] Furthermore, as the mid-century approached, the political preferences of the Junker groups definitely restricted the scope for economic advance. As servants and representatives of absolutism the Junkers opposed co-operation with the Prussian representative assembly, the United Diet, but as administrators they needed the tax increases which lay in the gift of the politicians. In the event they allowed their distaste to outweigh their responsibilities, and, in consequence, the Junkers were obliged to reduce official spending on a number of fronts. Fiscal policies favourable to industrialization were thus a casualty of the confrontation between Junker authoritarianism and embryonic democracy. The point is made that, within an autocratic state, the existing balance of political and social vested interests may *limit* industrial advance in some sectors while promoting it in others, almost always areas where authoritarian and industrial goals are rendered compatible by military or diplomatic reasoning.[144]

This should emphasize that the state is not a wholly autonomous force in economic affairs but rather a reflector of other forces, of group interests within society. For Germany, important changes occurred in the balance of these forces in the 1840s, and these, appropriately enough, altered the cast of official economic policy. As the threat of political upheaval increased throughout the decade, the landed classes and the middle classes began to discern in one another undreamed-of virtues. A new alliance was formed, combining authoritarian with bourgeois elements, against the menace of peasant and proletariat. By modifying the vested interests of the previous four or five decades, it created a climate more favourable to industrial advance. Even the Prussian Junkers were affected by the new sentiments,[145] and as their new friendships helped to refill their revenue coffers, official spending for economic purposes increased dramatically between 1849 and 1856. Significantly, the revolution-ary context in and around 1848 acted to remove some political impediments to growth immediately prior to the industrial acceleration of the 1850s.

The German governments were thus developing a potentially expanded capacity for economic action in the crucial period 1840–70. Yet, paradoxical-ly, most modern authorities discern a diminution in state activity after the heyday of Silesia and military-related industrialization.[146] These two proposi-tions are not incompatible: although the readiness of the public authorities to supply economic intervention may have been growing, the demand for them to do so was shrinking. After 1840 the alternative source of enterprise, which had previously been lacking, began to develop in the private sector. In close synchronization the state-supervised economy of Silesia began to wilt as the new capitalistic ventures of the Ruhr and Rhineland expanded, taking up the available supplies of capital and skill.[147] Silesia was soon outpaced. The moral might be that state-led growth is better than none, even if pursued for non-economic reasons in rigidly defined territories, but also that when private enterprise develops strongly the same state effort may become redundant. Worse, it may even become restrictive. The Silesian case suggests as much. Here, the wave of capitalistic promotions which immediately swept the pro-vince once the principal state controls were abolished in 1864 provides strong indications that the apparatus of official supervision had latterly *reduced* the growth prospects open to the region. Consequently, there are some grounds for asserting that the hand of the state had become a dead one by mid-century.[148]

The conclusion is not entirely a fair one. If credit is given to the work of the 'official industrialists' in Silesia, at a time when the climate was unsym-pathetic to economic advance, credit must also go to the very different state agencies which operated within a steadily improving climate after 1840. Appropriately enough, as private entrepreneurs emerged to take up the reins of industry, these bodies tended to act as instruments of advice and guidance rather than of mandatory control. The most important of them were the Zen-tralstelle für Handel und Gewerbe created in Württemberg under Ferdinand Steinbeiss in 1848 and the Gewerbeinstitut of Prussia, directed by Peter Beuth. In the two or three decades after 1850, these organizations did much good work. Scholarships were dispensed to promising innovators like the gunsmith, Gottlieb Daimler;[149] subsidies were provided for competent en-trepreneurs like the engineer, Borsig; exhibitions of new machinery and indus-trial processes were arranged to catch the eye of the German businessman.[150] It was all most useful, but it was, very definitely, a much less direct form of involvement in German industry than that practised by a Reden or a Heinitz; Professor Fischer has aptly christened it a species of 'benevolent bureaucracy'. However, qualified though it may be, it is not consonant with descriptions of an official 'dead hand'. There was a decline only in the most regimented, the most 'Prussian' form of industrial involvement. Other new forms continued into the second half of the century and were productive. The problem, in so far as a problem remains, is that these methods are not easily reconciled with traditional expectations as to the behaviour of 'authoritarian' German states.

Still less so are the actions of the imperial régime after 1870. It contented itself, in this third phase of German state activity, very largely with the administration of the economic 'framework' – the tariffs, currency measures, company legislation, or social security provisions – that virtually every late-nineteenth-century state, whether *laissez-faire* or *dirigiste*, counted as part of its bailiwick.

The general intent is permissive rather than propulsive, aiming primarily to establish the conditions within which capitalist enterprise might thrive, rather than directly to promote this enterprise, or to extend state commitment. In this at least the authorities enjoyed some modest success. By 1907, although the imperial government through its railroad and coal-owning interests, remained the largest industrial employer in Germany, the private sector accounted for some 90 per cent of total industrial output. The Hohenzollern Reich would thus approximate more closely to a private capitalistic model of economy than to any other.[151] The freedom of the Wilhelmian industrialist from state oversight – if not from cartel oversight – was scarcely less than that enjoyed by his American, British, or French competitor. Perhaps the most dramatic proof of this is supplied by a notable confrontation of 1904 between the King of Prussia, coal merchant, and the coal kings of the mineral syndicates. The incident arose out of an attempt by the state to gain control of the Hibernia coal-mine – a vast enterprise accounting for 7 per cent of the entire Westphalian cut – in order to defend the coal-consuming public and railroads from the enthusiastic pricing policies of the syndicated pits. The great banking houses lined up on either flank, the Dresdner backing the Crown, the Diskonto–Gesellschaft siding with the syndicate, and imperial, industrial, and financial forces joined in battle. When the mêlée cleared, it was obvious that the state had acquired no more than a minority of Hibernia shares: big business had dared to defy big government and, for all practical purposes, the authorities came off worst. Nor was it for the last time. In a return match over similar ground in 1912, the Crown, still dissatisfied with the level of coal prices, took its Ruhr mines out of their agreement with the Rhenish–Westphalian Coal Syndicate in an attempt to exert pressure upon the private coal interests. Despite the threat of an independent 'official' coal price, no perceptible change in syndicate policy was achieved; the cartel merely declined to experience the pressure. It would appear, therefore, that, not only were the economic objectives of the Reich very moderate ones but also that, as private enterprise expanded within the carapace of cartelization – outgrowing any appetite for official guidance or advice as it did so – it was able to set its own capitalistic limitations upon the range of official industrial policy. As the need for state intervention declined, so did the state's response. But this was not all: the state's *capability* to act also declined.

At the same time, the official interest in industrial affairs itself underwent modification. Around mid-century, the Junker groups had found some tactical convenience in a closer alliance with the commercial classes. But in the de-

cades after 1870, the swelling pressures of agricultural recession, combined
with the awesome advance of German industrialism, pointed up the need for a
restatement of Junker autonomy. One sequel during the 1890s was the
'purification' of the Prussian civil service – epitomized by Puttkamer's purge –
which gave to the administrative structure a reinforcement of authoritarian
elements. The agrarian groups, least committed to industrial objectives, were
thus strengthened in the central control-room of the Reich. Consequently, the
restored Junker pre-eminence acted – as did the influential gentry nexus within the tsarist bureaucracy – to restrict the state's will to promote industrial
advance. It is even possible that this 'Junker limitation' – qualified as it was in
the second phase of German state intervention – was more pronounced in the
imperial era than in the years after 1780. In the early stages, as the Junkers
perceived, the military dividends to be derived from industrial promotion
were high, but after 1870, they could contend that the momentum of the
German economy was sufficient to provide for adequate military capacity even
in the absence of official encouragement. From this point, the Junkers might
continue to make concessions to the business lobbies, on the usual military
terms, but they would now provide their largesse only in exchange for direct
economic pay-offs to the rural sector. Furthermore, their own need for special
treatment was rising steeply: the fortunes of the Junkers estates – affected by
the swingeing price declines for grains 1870–95 – were under more immediate threat in the late nineteenth century than in the late eighteenth. Official
interest was therefore increasingly preoccupied with subjects other than expanded interventionism in industry.

Given the resilience of the German economy, the strength of its 'collective
enterprise', and the changing preferences of the high bureaucracy, it was
perhaps true, as Riesser shrewdly noted, that, 'unless demanded by imperative
reasons . . . in the interests of national self-preservation . . . nationalization represents but a backward step from the economic point of view'.[152] He spoke of
nationalization, but the restraints might also apply to many lesser forms of
official activity.

Contemporary attempts to argue the opposite case have not lasted well.
Even Hauser's points, though strident, were ineffectual. The state, he pointed
out, was at the head of the German banking system – but so it was in most
countries.[153] The state held the balance between industries and between cartels – but this function of arbitration, of 'holding the ring' was a commonplace even in *laissez-faire* economies. The state, through the railways and the
armed services, was a major customer for the metal and chemical industries –
but official contracts of this type also played a significant part in such anti-
dirigiste economies as the British or the French.[154] The state was the largest
single employer in Germany – but, as the Hibernia incident revealed, the
employment of coal-miners did not carry with it the power to persuade coal
syndicates. Very little of substance emerged from analysis of this type.

Actual proof of official economic interventionism of a mandatory kind is a
rare commodity for the years 1870–1914, although there is an abundance of
legend. Most of the available comment relates to a limited number of themes:

cartel policy; the supervision of foreign investment; social security provision; defence policy; tariff policy.

The outcome of the government's attempts to curb the coal syndicates do not suggest that the Reich succeeded in producing a comprehensive or effective cartel policy before 1914. Even Professor Bruck, who advanced the expectation that official influence might be revealed behind the cartels' schemes for the 'organization of demand', proved unable to detect it, and instead admitted that the bureaucracy's attitude towards cartelization remained highly ambivalent down to the war.[155] A tendency to accept, and in practice to support, the existing cartel interests, while at the same time proclaiming the principles of free trade, typified the state's uncertain and contradictory methods of dealing with the combines. Similarly, any attempt to meddle directly with the business structure was put aside in favour of indirect methods exerting influence over the cartels through the imprecise mechanisms of general commercial and transport policy. Some expert opinion of the early 1900s believed that the measure of effective supervision which resulted was entirely inadequate, and advocated the assumption of far stronger powers. The best evidence that even Hauser can lead on this count is the *proposal* in 1912 that an imperial cartel department *ought* to be created.[156] Among the published surveys, the most striking features remain the frustrated expectations of those who seek evidence of governmental dabbling in cartel affairs and the frequent demands of the realists that a larger official stick should be wielded against the conglomerates.

Allowing Germany's reputation for diplomatic expansionism in the period before 1914, we might expect that, if state activity in economic affairs were to exist anywhere, it would surely exist where the possibilities of economic gain and diplomatic gain combined – as they clearly did in the area of foreign investment. Yet the ratio of German home investment to foreign investment was 2 : 1 against overseas lending in 1886–90, and *advanced* to 9 : 1 against in 1906–10.[157] In general, investment was permitted to serve diplomatic purposes only once domestic capital needs had been met, and only then after careful selection of the securities involved. For these critical decisions, the government preferred to rely upon the judgement of private bankers and investors, rather than to rest the whole matter upon its own policy initiatives. Further, the close relationship between the German investment bankers and their industrial colleagues ensured that the majority of German overseas lending was angled towards the acquisition of markets rather than of political advantage. The diversion of funds for diplomatic purposes was, consequently, almost as much the exception in Germany as it was the rule in France. However, it did, on occasion, happen. A number of instances can be cited, most of them well known. For example, from the 1880s an official ban on lending to Russia was imposed with the intent – counter-productive as it turned out – of compelling a closer political dependence. Similarly, loans to Serbia were blocked in 1893 and 1906 in an attempt to modulate the Balkan operetta to a financial tempo. Conversely, loans were promoted for political purposes: secret funds were made available to Italy immediately upon her recruitment to the Triple Alliance in 1882, and, much against their inclinations, the Berlin financiers were induced to provide substantial loans for Turkey from 1888.[158] More notoriously, where imperial or colonial opportunities offered, Germany, always abashed by her lack of international endowments, did not hesitate to employ investment power as a means of self-advancement. Hence the active official approval given to the operations of the Deutsche Asiatische Bank in China during the 1900s. Hence, too, the use of the financial weapon by the imperial government to further German claims upon Morocco after the Anglo-French Declaration of 1904.[159] Taken together, however, these adventures would represent only a tiny percentage of total German investment. They consumed less in volume, were more cautious in commitment, and were subject to much less overt state direction than the massive overseas lending operations of the French. In reality, the foreign investment of supposedly statist Germany was more open to the influence and judgement of private enterprise than the foreign investment of supposedly free-enterprise France.

With social policy, it might be assumed, the ground should be firmer. Were not Bismarck's designs for social insurance, embodied in the legislation of 1883 and 1887, prototypes for European practice, and firmly in line with the concept of a strong caretaker state? But here, of course, politics does enter with a vengeance. For the social insurance scheme, in fact, formed part of the 'double-edged sword against socialism', and was designed more as a tactical manoeuvre than as an economic innovation. Intended at one stroke to make atonement for the Chancellor's earlier onslaughts upon the Social Democrats and to undercut their reformist plans, it implied very little about the state's true view of its responsibilities towards industrial labour. This, for the most part, continued to regard the manufacturer as the proper master within his own house. When, during the tenure of the brilliant von Berlepsch at the Ministry of Commerce, or within the phrasing of the imperial law of 1891, official policy did appear to swing towards a full-blown theory of social trusteeship, it is significant that the industrial interests became noticeably uneasy, and, before long, that the state's new activities diminished sharply. Although further attempts to extend social insurance were made after 1900 by Posadovsky, Bethmann–Hollweg, and Delbruck, the state could scarcely be said to have followed a consistent policy fired by a sense of economic or social purpose. Rather it based its social policies upon the balance of forces within the Reichstag, applying the tools of interventionism only when political advantage dictated.

Within the defence sector, one of large financial commitment for most nineteenth-century governments and one strongly connected to important manufacturing sectors, political advantage is popularly supposed to have evoked especially considerable action from the *Kaiserreich*. Sophisticated political research has recently done much to perpetuate this emphasis either by arguing that an expansive military–imperial policy was employed by the regime as a means of uniting the privileged conservative and bourgeois echelons against the Social Democrats, and thus defending their privileged position,[160] or by proposing that lavish naval expenditure was designed to create a 'bourgeois' battlefleet as a means of rallying the middle parties to 'a plebiscitarian Kaistertum', and thus bolstering the failing popularity of the regime.[161] It is something of a surprise, therefore, to find that economic research has chosen a precisely opposite emphasis, and that quantification of Germany's military effort serves only to stress its modest dimensions. True the Reich increased its defence spending between 1875 and 1908 far faster than did comparably advanced nations such as France or Britain: by 150 per cent against 70 per cent and 65 per cent. But the German national income shares allotted to defence activity were low: 3.3–3.8 per cent between 1891 and 1913; and they were easily surpassed by social, economic, and environmental expenditures, with 5.4 per cent of national income claimed by social services alone in 1913. Of the increase in imperial expenditure 1871–1913 over one-third went to social services, one-sixth to urbanization, and merely one-fifth to defence. Whatever the political deployments woven around the *Tirpitzplan*, the correct economic valuation is in fact that 'the military effort of Imperial

Table 2.4 German government expenditure on total defence and total social insurance as proportions of total government expenditure and GNP

	Defence		Social insurance	
	% TGE	%GNP	%TGE	% GNP
1872	–	8.3	–	–
1881	25.1	2.5	–	–
1885	–	–	–	0.3
1891	25.4	3.3	5.1	0.7
1901	22.5	3.4	8.7	1.3
1907	21.2	3.5	9.6	1.6
1913	21.6	3.8	10.3	1.8

Source: Andic and Veverka (1964), Tables A–9, p. 247; A–30, p. 269. *Note*: social insurance is but one element in total social service expenditure (see Table 2.5 below)

Table 2.5 German total government expenditure by function at current prices, 1913; and as proportions of total government expenditure and GNP.

	Total govt	Admin. etc.	Law and order	Defence	Economic services
DM (m.)	7478	695	560	1819	904
% TGE		9.3	7.5	24.3	12.1
% GNP	14.8	1.4	1.1	3.6	1.8

Source: Andic and Veverka (1964), Tables A-18, p. 258; A-21, p. 261, with additional calculations for social service components.

Germany was based on a slender material foundation'.[162] (see Tables 2.4 and 2.5).

At first sight tariff policy offers much less scope for revisionism. Here the German state exhibited no lack of initiative in the years after 1870. As world prices slid away, Germany joined the widespread return to protectionism. Tariffs were introduced by Bismarck in 1877 and 1879, revised in 1885 and 1887, refined by Caprivi in 1893, reformulated by Bülow in 1902 – a record fit to establish Germany among Europe's most heavily defended economies. And with some duties – mainly those on grain imports – rising by a factor of five between 1879 and 1887, there can hardly be reason to question the state's degree of commitment. What remains at issue is rather the mood and purpose of imperial tariff policy: whom did it protect, why, and with what benefit to the German economy?

Much has been written to suggest that German tariffs were merely an extension of the Reich's bellicose diplomacy, a family of trade relations derived from a species of political objectives. This is the flavour to Bruck's assertion that Bismarck, 'subordinated . . . free competition and protection . . . to the idea of the authoritarian and monarchist state of Prussian temper'.[163] But was this so? Did German tariffs make specifically 'authoritarian' or 'offensive' statements in the international trading forum? Were they, among all European tariffs, related in some unique way, to the broader aims of *Machtpolitik*? It would not seem so. Many states, not usually associated with the appetites implicit in *Machtpolitik* – France, Italy, USA – employed tariffs in this period. All states, Germany included, were reacting to a common international problem – the sustained decline in primary product prices as new transport systems opened up the world's cheapest sources of supply from the 1870s. Thus the French government inaugurated a punishing level of protection from 1881 and built it up by stages until it issued in the formidable Méline tariff of 1892. A year earlier the Russians had introduced the phenomenal Mendele'ev tariff. And in the same decade, even free-trade America introduced its trump cards in the shape of the McKinley and Dingley tariffs. States of many political colours turned to fairly radical systems of protectionism within this period. In part, at least, Germany reacted to this general trend and did not generate any

Environmental services	Debt services	Total social services	Social Assist. and Insurance	Health	Housing	Education
328	422	2749	1181	272	31	1265
4.4	5.6	36.7	15.8	3.6	0.4	16.9
0.7	0.8	5.4	2.3	0.5	0.06	2.5

particularly independent style of fiscal aggression. It is not clear that any special elements of *Machtpolitik* need to be attributed to the German version of this widely dispersed economic terminology. When the economic problems against which the tariffs were designed to guard were so considerable, it is unlikely that any diplomatic explanation of fiscal policy will prove sufficient.

But in one way at least the German tariffs possessed authoritarian implications. These had much less to do with industry than with the interests of the Junker élite. Where industrial advantage would have required free agricultural importation, with the consequent transfer of resources from primary to secondary employment, the actual objective of early German tariffs lay in much *expanded* agricultural protection. Marshall believed that these tactics restricted the expansion of the German market more severely than the abolition of the Reich's tariffs could have achieved. Moreover, the primarily agrarian bias of the duties encouraged producer nations to place retaliatory penalties upon the industrial exports so vital to German prosperity. Not until 1893 did the industrial products receive any useful protection of their own. And just how useful it was may be debated. For, alongside an over-protected high-cost agriculture, Germany was now given a heavy manufacturing sector cumbrously maintained in overproduction and secured in excessive prices. If the Reich kept up an interventionist record in tariff policy, this had little to do with the promotion of economic growth. Rather it aimed at the conservation of outmoded economic interests and its results rarely proved of benefit to an expanding industrial economy.

Indeed the force of the state's economic role in the period 1870–1914 is qualified by nothing so strongly as by the insistent penetration of official policy by the agrarian elements. Schumpeter even contended that the Reich government did everything in its power to *stifle* industrialization in the interests of the Junker nexus.[164] No doubt this is an overstatement, but the implied pre-eminence of the agrarian squadrons was real enough. It is quite certain that the Junkers contrived – largely via the imperial tariffs – a quite remarkable restatement of agrarian values and ambitions and successfully imposed them upon Europe's most robust industrial economy.[165] Their price for allowing it to remain robust was uncomfortably high. Before 1870 they had not favoured the protective measures for which the industrialists clamoured, but with the advent of the agricultural price crisis, they underwent a rapid and comprehensive conversion. An identity of interest between agricultural and industrial producers was forthwith discovered, and then formalized as the 'solidarity bloc' or the 'agrarian–industrial complex', the negotiating basis for the tariffs of 1879, 1885, and 1887. Its keystone was a compact between iron and rye: a monopoly of the domestic market was reserved for the Westphalian iron interests and in return enhanced grain prices, essential subsidies for the appointed Junker life style, were passed on to the great estates. However, for most other industrial producers the compact entailed higher metal prices, and for most other agricultural producers, higher feedstuff prices. For the economy at large there were the additional impositions of higher wages, pushed up by agricultural prices; a restriction in the labour outflow from agriculture; and higher agricultural production costs, pushed up by the tariff's leverage upon manufactured inputs for the farming sector. As an exchange for dearer rye it was not a pretty bargain.

When the 'solidarity bloc' trembled – as it did when the interests of the resurgent industrialists and the still depressed agriculturalists parted company in the 1890s – the full might of the Junker camarilla was revealed. Caprivi's 'new course' in tariffs, offering reductions in German agricultural protection against freer overseas passage for the Reich's manufactures, incensed the Junkers. Rather than sacrifice before industrial altars, they countered the 'new course' with their own 'Kanitz motion'. It was a stroke of unbridled economic egocentrism, a proposal to levy protective duties of 100–115 per cent on grains, and, effectively, to attach an immediate 7 per cent surcharge to the nation's food bill. Although this extraordinary exploitive coup collapsed in due time, the Junkers did make it impossible for Caprivi to control a cabinet and court well packed with agrarian sympathizers, and forced him into resignation in 1894. His successor, Hohenlohe, fared little better. And, finally, when Bülow became Chancellor in 1900 he recognized that no room for manœuvre remained. Committed to a programme of naval construction and colonial expansion he had no choice but to solicit the traditional militarism of the Junkers. They, however, suspected that a connexion necessarily existed between naval expansionism, colonialism, and the terrors of free trade, and, quickly scenting a divergence between imperial interest and their own, they occupied their defences and set their terms – enormous agricultural indemnities in exchange for compliance in the nation's maritime ambitions.[166] When Bülow bowed to pressure and rendered the required policy in 1902, it necessarily included one's of the world's most formidable fiscal prophylactics for the grain sector. German arable farming thus became, as the century turned, the biggest agricultural hothouse maintained by any of the advanced nations. Once more the violent particularists of the Junker *apparat* secured their private protectionism and turned their uniformed backs upon economic efficiency.

Given the nature of the imperial state, little could have been done to prevent this outcome. Junker methodology was one of political terrorism: to achieve their economic ends these pillars of conservatism composed the most bloodthirsty threats; to withhold taxes from the Treasury or recruits from the army; to obstruct the much-prized naval programmes of their bourgeois adversaries; even, unthinkably, to join the Social Democractic Party.[167] And these constitution-shaking devices were launched not from some remote corner of the body politic but from deep within the framework of government itself, from the Court, from the bureaucracy, from the white-liveried aristocracy of the Gardes du Corps and the élite Kürassier regiments.[168] Civilian governments could scarcely contend with this form of pressure. And the industrialists did not care to. Still quaking at the thought of organized labour, their wish was to retain a relationship, at almost any cost, with the massive stabilizing force of the Junker echelons. For very similar reasons, the peasantry, fearful of a labour movement which proclaimed them an outmoded and dispensable class, acquiesced in an agricultural movement which claimed to preserve the homogeneity of the rural community while most obviously profiting a mere fraction (see Table 2.6) of its landholders.[169] The balance of these fears and aggressions acted to destroy an industrial tariff policy within one of the world's most advanced industrial powers.

Table 2.6 Distribution of landed property, 1895: Germany and England (as percentage of total number of properties, and area occupied)

	Germany properties		UK properties	
Size of property (hectares)	Number of properties (%)	Area occupied (%)	Number of properties (%)	Area occupied (%)
0–5	76.5	15.1	51.5	6.2
5–20	18.0	29.0	16.5	8.8
20–50	4.3	21.9	12.8	15.0
50–100	0.7	8.5	15.6	42.6
100–500	0.4	15.2	3.5	24.9
500+	0.1	10.3	0.1	2.5

Source: Eddie, (1967), p. 302.

This was not all: the victory of the agrarians also perpetrated a major disruption within German agriculture. It was by no means an agriculture without potential. By 1911 it led the world in potato production, achieved higher grain returns *per caput* than any other agricultural producer, and maintained one of Europe's best records in the application of mechanical and fertilizer inputs. But at its centre there was a prodigious instability; the Junker preference for rye. The Bülow tariff happened to coincide with an upswing in rye prices (from a nadir in 1894–96) and contributed extra upward pressure until 1914. With the American consumers taking more of prairie output, and poor Russian crops between 1904 and 1908, the way was cleared for Junker rye. Exports increased by a factor of twelve in 1900–13, and, at home, wheat furrows were cleared to accommodate more rye. The wholly irrational feature was that the Junker preference, institutionalized by tariff, bore no resemblance to the pattern of world demand. Rye was an outmoded low-income crop, fast becoming a liability in the market. In the 1900s world consumption of rye contracted faster than that of any other grain, and the huge German exports were achieved only with prices falling relative to other grain prices. The nostalgia of German society for things agrarian, the fears of socialism harboured by industrialists and peasants, the extraordinary truculence of autocratic agriculturalists had succeeded in preserving, alongside Europe's most powerful industrial system, a near-feudal estate economy pledged to a non-viable crop. This was the major achievement of German protectionism.

It would seem, therefore, that it is possible almost to reverse the traditional emphasis: state intervention in German economic affairs proved to be least effective under the Reich and most creative in its earliest 'Silesian' interpretation. The interim period was one of emergence for the private capitalist and of indirect guidance from the state authorities, reflecting fairly accurately the characteristic mid-century alliance between bourgeois and traditional groups. When Junker interests prevailed unchallenged, in a backward economy, useful industrial policies could emerge only as long as the objective of modernization implied some military gain. When Junker interests were allowed to prevail against all challenge, in an advanced industrial economy, the result could only be a series of damaging economic throwbacks. It appears, then, that the nature and utility of state intervention depended, before anything else, upon the balance of forces within the body politic. And, over the years 1870–1914, this was such that the opinions expressed in the castle halls and upon the rye acres of the East Elbean prairies controlled all too frequently the policies meted out to the factories and mines of Rhine-Ruhr, Alsace, and the Saar.

Table 2.7   Total government expenditure as % GNP: Germany and UK

Germany	1872	1881	1891	1901	1907	1913
	7.5	8.8	11.1	16.2	14.4	15.3

U.K.	1870	1880	1890	1900	1910	
	9.0	10.0	9.0	15.0	12.8	

Sources: Andic and Veverka (1964), p. 183; Peacock and Wiseman (1967), pp. 37, 42.

Consistent with this valuation is the rather surprising result, obtained from investigation of German national accounts, that the total weight of imperial expenditure within the Reich economy was, at best, moderate. As Table 2.7 reveals, the shares of total German state expenditure in GNP, 1870–1914, closely shadow those of Britain, classically the premier exponent of *laissez-faire* economics, and draw away somewhat only in the final years before the First World War. This remains so despite a reasonably rapid annual increase (5.1 per cent average) in total official spending during the span of the *Kaiserreich*. Compared over the long run, additions to output in 'statist' Germany and 'free-enterprise' Britain turn out to have been divided 'in almost identical proportions between private and public use.'[170] Ironically then, the combination of advancing private enterprise and conservative social ascendancy – the twin components of the 'industrial – agrarian complex' – succeeded in effectively limiting both the demand for, and the supply of, creative state intervention in economic affairs during Germany's brief explosion of imperial *Machtpolitik*.

THE ECONOMY–STATE NEXUS: A REVERSED EMPHASIS

Much modern writing, especially modern German writing, has sought not so much to redirect the traditional emphases concerning state–economy linkages

87

as to turn them entirely upside down: in place of government policy which dictates economic advance, we are offered economic conditions which control the formation of state policy and even of states. Such considerations form a useful appendix to any study of the Reich's economic role, not least because they suggest a substantial modification of German historical preferences.

Perhaps the most ambitious example of the genus has been the attempt by Hans Rosenberg to prove that long waves in economic growth, such as the Kondratiev cycles, may directly generate accompanying long waves in political and social affairs.[171] One such long wave, the German Great Depression of 1873–96, Rosenberg claims, provides a satisfactory explanation for the rise of protectionism, for the advent of the Social Democratic Party, for the development of social insurance and the other Bismarckian antidotes to socialism, as well as for the Junker *revanche*. Bismarck's cautious foreign policy is seen as a product of economic embarrassment at home, and Wilhelmian aggression as the result of increasing domestic prosperity after 1896. Ingenious as this may be, the factual basis for it appears very weak, not least because the existence of a 'Great Depression' in Germany is a highly dubious proposition in itself. Only the rise of protectionist politics can be traced directly from economic disaster; for something of the kind befell the Elbian grainlands. In other sectors, however, there was little sign of sustained economic disruption. Seven years of stagnation may have followed the *Gründerkrise* of 1873, but industrial growth resumed strongly after 1882. Unemployment and social distress were no more obviously characteristic of the period 1873–96, than of the years 1849–73. And it was much more probably the franchise extensions of 1866 and 1871 than the rigours of depression which galvanized popular politics and parties.[172] As revisionism goes, this is not particularly successful.

A more controlled attack has been mounted against a similar target by Böhme.[173] The hypothesis is not deficient in novelty; it ascribes the *formation* of the Prussian-centred Reich almost entirely to the operation of economic forces. Before 1871, Böhme argues, Prussia was not well regarded by the other German states and the political influence which they acknowledged was Austrian rather than Prussian. Economically, however, Prussia far outstripped Austria. Accordingly, the Dual Monarchy attempted to counter this threat to its leadership by the formation in the 1850s of a greater customs union which would overshadow the Prussian-based *Zollverein*. Its failure – which was total – followed largely from the operation of an arbitrary economic force, the great slump of 1857. With this crisis the possibility of an Austrian solution to the German problem was definitively smashed. In this analysis, the German states chose to group themselves around Prussia, not because of her military prowess nor out of imperial idealism, but simply because she represented the most attractive available trading partner. This would seem to underrate the potency, during the 1860s, of that remarkable military cocktail, composed in equal parts of von Moltke, needle-guns, Krupp artillery, and railway timetables, but it has undeniable precision and symmetry. So too does Böhme's second major proposition: that the nature of the Empire once formed, was transfigured by another bout of economic crisis. Here he picks up and amplifies a contention of Rosenberg's. In both theses the collapse of 1873 occupies a central position. According to Böhme, it was the *Gründerkrise* which permitted Bismarck to execute, in very short order, the switch from free trade, with its liberal–bourgeois affiliations, to protectionism, with its conservative–agrarian affiliations. In this interpretation, the vital directions chosen by the Prussian-centred Reich were sign-posted by economic crisis. The state reacted to economic forces rather than imposed its will upon them.

There is no denying that Böhme's hypothesis is more rigorously and clearly constructed than Rosenberg's, and its detail certainly suggests that specific economic incidents produced political changes of large magnitude. The virtue consists chiefly in the close logical connexion which is constructed between the economic stimulus and the political response. But in a more general sense, Rosenberg's 'long wave' hypothesis also possesses merit. For instance, it might plausibly be argued that the two major upswings in German economic advance between 1850 and 1914 caused adjustments within the international power balance to which governments had no choice but to respond. By 1885 the industrial hegemony maintained by Britain in Europe was under challenge; for the first time in continental history a major industrial power was confronted by one of roughly equal potential. Necessarily, the transition from hegemony to divided rule entailed strain. Although political and military circumstances might offer a large number of detailed options, the disposition of economic forces could point towards rivalry, and even conflict. This economic pressure might be an underlying one, able to guarantee no specific outcome, diverted no doubt by the day-to-day decisions of politicians and generals. But none of these necessary qualifications rules out the existence of such a force. After all, there is significance in the fact that the two major contenders for economic supremacy in the late nineteenth century, the Yankee states and Bismarckian Germany, were the first nations to win wars with 'industrialized' armies, with forges and firepower.[174] As the power of German forges grew, it was not unnatural that the European alliance system should be redrawn to accommodate the displacement. And, during the second upswing from the 1880s to 1914, German forges vied with British forges in an arms race which was as much a confrontation of industrial capacities, as much a competition of manufacturing economies disputing world markets, as a competition of nation-states disputing international precedence. The components of the arms race, the dreadnoughts and battlecruisers, were not only units in the power calculus; they were also the appropriate symbols of commercial rivalry. As guardians of the sea-lanes and shepherds of the merchant fleets, they possessed a more directly economic relevance than any of the twentieth-century weaponry which has succeeded them. Some connexion between the upsurge of German economic power and the formulation of offensive German strategies – a connexion which nevertheless stops well short of the determinist assertion that economic forces 'cause' wars – would be difficult to deny.

An intelligent and much-neglected thesis of Robert Brady's[175] would support an analysis of this kind. Brady also argued that Germany's style of industrialization possessed a peculiarly developed relevance for general Reich policy:

in short it posited expansionism. German industrialization, it seemed, shared a characteristic of economic modernization which we have encountered before: it ignored national boundaries, and proceeded upon a continental rather than a national supposition. This was particularly true of transportation. Even if the German railroads acted initially as a unifying force, it was not long after 1850 before they assumed an entirely different significance. Lacking any concrete national boundaries, Germany formed the true railway cross-roads of Europe and the natural scale of her networks – unfortunately constricted by frontiers which flew in the face of engineering – was continental. Such political constraints directly conditioned the aggressive railway policies pursued by Germany against her neighbours, most notably the preferential freight rates virtually dictated to the Italians and the Swiss. Similar difficulties surrounded the German waterway system which reached westwards into Holland, eastwards into Austria, and southwards into Switzerland and France. Even the main port for the Ruhr was in Holland – at Rotterdam. The arrangement was as irrational and inconvenient as if the industrial heartland of the United States had been separated from its vital auxiliary organs by a system of arbitrary barriers. Denied a genuine empire or an expanding frontier, devoid of an integral economic hinterland, the potential scale of Germany's industrial capabilities was several times too large for her territorial extent.

Industrial enterprises naturally attempted to approximate to the optimal conditions. From 1850 and past 1870, Germany's new industries drifted towards the favourable sites of Upper Silesia and the Rhineland, and in the habitual integrated style of German concerns began to form alliances and associations in these areas. They were, of course, border areas and the industrial alliances that were formed stretched into France, Belgium, Holland, and Austria-Hungary. Among the industries most affected by these geopolitical complications was the vital metallurgical complex. By 1914 imports, not least from French Lorraine and Sweden, composed roughly one-half of total German ore supplies, forming a dependence for which ironmasters naturally sought to compensate with their own international arrangements. Their trans-national tendencies are revealed in the interests of the Thyssen organization in Normandy and French Lorraine, and, most spectacularly, by Fritz Fischer's contention that the acquisition of the rich French seams at Longwy-Briey formed a 'war aim' which was widely entertained well before 1914.[176] Even further afield, economic schemes were spun which ran in parallel with German political expansionism: Krupp looked for ore supplies to the mines of Biscay, while other industrialists, in the early 1900s, found a topical solution in the much-overrated minerals of Morocco. The general tendency of the Reich economy to escape its borders was well captured in Fischer's demonstration that plans to establish a German-led European Economic Association, designed to formalize German economic domination of the continent, were circulating in industrial circles during the last pre-war years.[177] Much the same thread was picked out by Hauser in his claim that, 'Italian, Swiss, and Spanish industries have become branches of German industry . . . Zurich and Milan have become German towns'.[178] It is scarcely unlikely that, at this point, the economic dispositions might help condition the military and political outlook: the significance to the German economy of neighbouring resource and industrial areas could not be discounted; the integrity of the German economic structure required a supra-national assumption, and, potentially, a forceful means of sustaining it. Similarly, it was necessary to provide this structure with markets, some near by, in the countries bordering Germany, others further afield, within the territory of rival economic powers. It was not only the strength and momentum of Germany's economic advance which created problems for the Reich and for envious competitors. The shape and the location of these expanding industrial muscles also raised peculiar difficulties.

The relationship between *Machtpolitik* and economic advance did not follow from the deliberate promotion of industrial strength by a war-hungry state. Rather it appears that German economic growth itself contained implications that made *Machtpolitik* a likely outcome. Naturally enough, there could have been other outcomes. The economic elements do not pre-empt the importance of political chauvinism, military technology, 'war-by-timetable', or the simple concatenation of circumstances. But it might be reasonable to propose that economic conditions helped at least to narrow the options for German statesmen, admirals, and generals.[179]

AN ANALYTICAL FULCRUM

The various correlations between economic and political forms of activity are undeniably important in influencing the style and direction of German economic expansion, the framework through which capacity is expressed, but they do not clearly illuminate the forces promoting the rapid *accumulation* of capacity. The state's economic activities were most useful when few other growth-inducing forces were available and least useful, in the context of the maturing economy, when a multitude of alternative forces were at work. By the century's end the Reich economy was well provided for. Adequate, if not super-abundant, supplies of raw materials lay easily to hand and more had been acquired in strategically placed border areas. But these were only as good as the technologies contrived to exploit them. There were, in some German states, efficient and modern transportation systems. But these were only as good as the industrial structures of which they formed part. There was a very high quality of industrial science. But this was only as good as the capitalists who applied it. The industrial managers were educated to a high level of specialization. But they were only as good as the team within which they perferred to work. The cartel supplied the organizational requirements for disciplined and orderly teamwork. But it was only as good as the tactics conferred upon it; and these could be defensive, offensive, or merely responsible. The state overlooked the cartels, but intervened less and less as time went on. And, its actions were only as good as the traditional ruling élites permitted.

Among these influences, none stands out. Of course, it may be that it was the manner of blending these elements which provided the vital essence of German economic growth. But, on the other hand, it would seem that there is a measure of order, coherence, and direction which is implicit in German development, yet which is not supplied by this mixture. Possibly Gerschenkron's observations on backwardness may provide the missing ingredient. If these are correct, the state may be assumed to play the directing role in an economy of pronounced backwardness. The behaviour of the German economy, featuring active bureaucratic interventionism in the early industrial era, and then a continuous decline in official involvement as backwardness receded, would be precisely consistent with this interpretation. In a situation of moderate backwardness, Gerschenkron expects that the industrial investment bank will take over the directing role. So, in Germany, as backwardness moderates, the investment bank should become more active.

THE EVOLUTION OF THE HYPERBANK

The rise of the *Kreditbanken* after 1848 looks sufficiently promising. And, significantly, it owed little to state assistance: during its initial period of development the Prussian authorities, in particular, were anxious to protect the status of their central bank and, like their French counterparts, were loath to permit any rival financial innovations. However, if banker-entrepreneurs were not entirely free of close central supervision – an essential prerequisite for creative finance – they could at least circumvent it. Thus, Prussian financiers like Mevissen and the Oppenheims were able to function effectively *outside* Prussian territory, under the noses of more accommodating state administrations. Even inside Prussia, the competition of the 'foreign' banks across the state-lines forced the bureaucrats to sanction a handful of joint-stock institutions with rights of note issue.[180] Similarly, the *commandité* bank, a limited form of partnership free from the more onerous style of supervision, made considerable headway in Prussia. Eight of these finance houses were created in 1856, and a near predecessor, the Diskonto-Gesellschaft created in 1851 and reorganized in 1856, was to develop into one of the greatest German investment banks. Just as the German bankers proved more resourceful than the French in evading bureaucratic apron-strings, so they contrived even to extract success from the insecure *commandité* house, a financial subspecies which in France did not survive the deluge of 1848. Furthermore, where the cautious orthodoxy of the French Central Bank succeeded in whipping the finance houses – with a few honourable exceptions – into line, the hidebound attitude of the Bank of Prussia seemed only to provoke German financiers to go far beyond the orthodox in their credit policies. The stimuli – or seen another way, the 'objective constraints' – were not dissimilar, but the entrepreneurial responses diverged widely.

It is important neither to exaggerate nor to underestimate the development of industry-related banking on the eve of unification. Some German houses, especially the Rhenish ones, had maintained interests in industrial and transportation projects for some three or four decades. And the new industrial investment foundations of the late 1840s and 1850s possessed high potential, even if this was not matched in their early decades by high profitability. Throughout the German states there was scattered a force of banker-entrepreneurs, willing to face up to the prevailing obstacles, and able, very frequently, to surmount them. This much rested on the credit side of the bank account. On the other hand, there were governments, like the Prussian, ready to provide a supply of obstacles: central control of an absolutist and restrictive type; rigid curbs on note issue; tight-fisted chartering of new institutions. Consequently, the largest group within the German credit market down to 1870 remained the private bankers. As with other traditional techniques within the economies of the German states, that of private banking possessed a pronounced longevity. That much was recorded on the other side of the account. However, by 1870 replacement technologies were coming to supersede traditional practice over much of the German economy, and banking was no exception; by this time its new order was already past the design stage and well advanced upon the process of development. The true production stage came after 1870, coinciding with the rise of the new Reich. What was produced was a formidable mixture of industrial credit techniques, entrepreneurial daring, and outright bank control of large-scale manufacturing assets.

Conditions were ripe for this development. Railway demand for capital – probably the major initial custom for most investment-style banks – began to fall away after the 1860s and the possibilities for industrial business became increasingly attractive. At the same time, official restrictions upon the joint-stock banks were abolished, and the formation of these institutions freed from impediment. This was fully consistent with the more restrained role adopted by the state during the imperial era. Moreover, it suggested that a particular developmental barrier had been passed; as one stage of backwardness was pushed aside, one institutional force made way for another. However, the reduction of official interventionism did not erode the innovations which had been devised to outwit it. For instance, the tradition of financial competition between the states stood up sufficiently well to ensure a healthy overall sprinkling of investment institutions. After 1870 bank density per unit of German territory or per thousand of German population was maintained at a high level, ensuring ease of access for industrial borrowers.[181] And the industrialists remained the banks' most favoured clients.

From the beginning German investment banks, quite unlike the British deposit banks with their liking for high liquidity and short-term lending, had been attracted by fixed capital investment and its inherently high profitability. Early in the career of the German banks, such profits had been necessary in order to finance the high interest rates which alone could entice German deposits into the bankers' vaults. In this sense, German investment banking developed very specifically from domestic conditions rather than from foreign example. And once begun, it retained this special imprint. Theoretically, the result, the classical mixture of investment and deposit functions, represented a *lower* form of financial development than that achieved by the rigidly demarcated institutions of Britain, the merchant banks, deposit banks, and bill-broking houses. Even in 1914 the great German banks combined all these functions under a single roof. Ironically, the banks which were so attached to German industry, and lent it so much strength, were conditioned in their interests by a certain lack of financial sophistication.

The irony proliferated, however, and in the end, rebounded. For. once the industrial connexion was formed, it led inexorably to an inter-penetration of financial and manufacturing interests that was far from unsophisticated. Broadly, the process of integration contained three stages: first, the banks financed industrial promotions and share issues; next they began to assume a managerial role *over* their industrial clients; finally, they accumulated such large conglomerations of shareholding power that they raised implications for the conduct of the entire economy.

The first transition was in the making for decades. As early as 1837, the Rhineland bankers were involved in the biggest railroad venture of its time, the Rhenish Railway Company, for which they provided services of credit, brokerage, and administration. But that was not all: in return they took stock-jobbing and promotional profits from the enterprise, a high proportion of its share issues – and thus voting rights – and strategic seats upon its directing board. They were interested not only in financial profits but in the benefits of ownership and the power of management. Nor was this appetite peculiar to the Rhinelanders; Leipzig bankers were to be found pursuing attractive portions of the Saxon railway system and their colleagues of Breslau were no less active in Silesia. However, from 1870 the desired menu of profits could no longer be supplied from railways alone, and it was increasingly supplemented by industrial flotations. And, with these, the need for ownership interest was even more pronounced. As industrial lending required the *kreditbanken* to employ their short-term deposits for long-run investments in fixed capital, losses in liquidity and departures from the conventional rules of safe banking were unavoidable. Consequently, some means of providing a hedge against the considerable risks incurred by such tricky manoeuvres had to be devised. Obviously, the best hedge was provided by the creditor securing control over the manufacturing concern in which the investment was placed. Financiers soon found that they could acquire this control by one, or both, of two methods: when organizing a new issue for an industrial client, they could reserve blocks of shares for themselves, or, by insisting upon their dual rights as shareholders and creditors, they could demand representation upon the directing board of client firms. In some cases they went even further: they would offer finance not only for the industrialist bent upon increasing his issued capital but also for the would-be investor anxious to buy shares. In return for this credit – usually up to two-thirds of the share's face value – the bank would require, not the dividend from the share, but the voting rights which it conferred.

Conventional lending to industry through the money market is an impersonal process, but when finance houses were drawn into large-scale invest-ment-credit functions it was natural that they should seek managerial parti-cipation. It became doubly natural when the early industrial ventures failed to make money. In 1872, for instance, the Diskonto-Gesellschaft and the Dresd-ner Bank each suffered heavy losses upon investments in manufacturing and exporting projects. To his basic interest in industrial profits, therefore, the banker added a special concern with the prudence of industrial borrowers. Since this virtue stood at a discount in the 1870s, the bankers sought to encourage its growth by creating their own enclave of good sense within in-dustry. Their consumption of industrial shares and directorships mounted sharply, to such effect that by 1914 a mere 16 of the country's greatest finan-ciers controlled between them 437 industrial directorships. In turn, these ex-tensive connexions provided the banks with a comprehensive over-view of the entire industrial landscape, and thus a wider and safer arena for their own industrial promotions. At this point, the process became self-reinforcing. From their improved vantage point, the bankers adventured more confidently to acquire even larger blocks of industrial securities. And with these they were able to earn higher profits, pay higher dividends, and strengthen their own credit position.

For these reasons, the investment banks took to industrial business after 1870 with scarcely restrained enthusiasm. Between 1885 and 1900 they placed £1200 m. of securities in the market, establishing a peak around 1899–1901. At the century's turn the number of industrial issues handled by the six largest houses rose from 99 in 1895 to 100 in 1897 and 161 in 1899 before falling back to 90 in 1903.[182] The most prolific contributor to this flood of industrial securities was the Dresdner Bank, although the Schaaf-fhausen'scher Bankverein, situated in the thick of the Rhineland industrial complex, probably commanded the greatest number of manufacturing clients. Close behind this pair came the remaining members of the Big Six: the Ber-liner Handelsgesellschaft with its commitment to the heavy industries and especially to coal, the Darmstädter Bank with its particular taste for railways, the Deutsche Bank with its affection for the electro-technical industry, and the Diskonto-Gesellschaft with its very various portfolio, again heavily weighted with coal. Given the increased safeguards of bank participation, the industrial connexion proved highly profitable. Dividends declared by the *Kre-ditbanken* retained an impressive solidity: in only three years between 1885 and 1914 – the downswing years 1892 and 1893 and the crisis year 1901 – did the average return on all credit banks fall below 6 per cent and it was more usually above 7 or 8 per cent. It was this swelling industrial profitability which converted the *Kreditbanken* into the German Great Banks of the pre-war quarter-century.

But profitable investment was not the only concern of such institutions. They had turned to industry for profits. They had invaded industry to protect profits. But once there, they discovered that they possessed power, and power with entrepreneurial implications. Their shareholdings and directorships could be employed not only to protect existing interests but to create new ones, or to generate more stability within the German economy. It is arguable that the banks became the true entrepreneurs of the business community. If the individual industrialist was subordinated to the team, and the cartel squeezed enterprise out of business, the precious drops were collected by the banks. The result was financial entrepreneurship working with industrial materials — *bankinitiative*. It was this quality which persuaded Bruck that: 'These banks *created* the German Industrial State.'[183]

That, of course, was overstatement. There were sectors of industry to which *bankinitiative* did not penetrate. The chemical industry, for instance, possessed its own technological impetus towards consolidation and integration and did not make great use of the banks' entrepreneurial skills. Within the iron industry of the Saar also, the preponderance of great industrial dynasties, the Stumms, de Wendels, or Röchlings, restricted bank infiltration, and the state kept its hand firmly upon the coal-mines of the region. Here there was already a tradition of 'mixed' development, of integration between coal-mines and blast-furnaces, and this pre-empted the speciality at which *bankinitiative* excelled. The financiers were not, therefore, the complete sovereigns of industry; they had to select their territories with care. Some scope was offered to their talents within the industrial complex of the Siegerland. *Bankinitiative* was concerned here, as it was at its best, with the contrivance of alliances or mergers between concerns in different but complementary lines of business. From the 1850s, the mine-owners of the area had enjoyed the assistance, or suffered the manipulation, of the financiers. And by 1900 the Siegerland was festooned with the massive integrated projects which betrayed the hand of the Great Banks.

But these examples, whether open or closed to *bankinitiative*, are almost trivial when compared with the set-piece of the bankers' industrial composition: Rhine—Ruhr. Within the great mineral triangle, the banks provided the vital imperatives to bully and cajole the Rhenish coal interests into a clear mastery of the region's industrial resources, and to combine with them, in the most classic of all the German economy's 'mixed' ventures, a small army of metallurgical concerns. Particularly during the 1890s, as coal prices soared and the furnace masters prospected for likely pits of their own, the banks busied themselves as brilliant intermediaries. A financial hand led the great Phönix Ironworks into a marriage with the Westende coal concern, presented the Dortmunder Union with the Hansemann mine, and introduced countless manufacturers uncompromisingly to the rewards of pit ownership. One house, the Schaaffhausen'scher, pledged to combine firms of maximum possible variety, and having been successful in securing control over the entire unworked coal wealth of Rhine-Ruhr, earned itself the supremely non-financial title of the Mining Bank.

Even in Rhine-Ruhr, however, the possibilities for *bankinitiative* were not limitless. By 1900 the bankers were looking around for new fields. They were discovered in Luxembourg-Lorraine, a region of low costs, rich in ores suitable for the new electric furnaces, and free from the influence of the great industrial dynasties. Here the banks discovered their final pre-war conquests. The

Luxembourg-Lorraine Pig Iron Syndicate was persuaded into existence, at least in part, by powerful arguments from the Darmstädter Bank. And the great migration of the hugely important Gelsenkirchen Mining Company out of the coal industry and out of the Ruhr and into a dominating position among the new metallurgical ventures of the *minette* fields was contrived almost entirely by bank credit. In the most important locational shift of German industry since 1850, as the metal industries swung towards the south-west, the banks again played a central role as participating and directing agencies.[184] Their preference for hybrid industrial conglomerates was written as clearly across the terrain of Luxembourg-Lorraine as it was across Rhine-Ruhr. By 1914 the interweaving of assorted heavy industries into massive organizational patch-works was a pronounced characteristic of German economic life. Clearly, the parallelism between these identifying features of the Reich's economy and the preferences of the bankers suggests a significant and formative relationship.

Another arises in relation to cartelization. The banks were always insistent that their industrial clients should participate in cartel schemes, and for good cause. They reasoned that cartel membership reduced the risks of serious business failure and thus increased the security of their investments. This would become especially true at periods either of market recession *or* of heavy lending. The finance and promotion of cartels, therefore, became matters worthy of bank attention. Especially after 1890, the investment houses worked to place their own directors inside the most powerful cartel leaders – as the Dresdner and Deutsche Banks did with the Gelsenkirchen Mining Company – and upon the boards of outsiders most ripe for cartelization – as the Deutsche Bank did with the Phönix Ironworks. When the Gelsenkirchen firm inaugurated negotiations for the formation of the Rhenish-Westphalian Coal Syndicate in the early 1890s, it received enthusiastic support from the banking community. And when, in the 1900s, a recalcitrant Phönix Ironworks refused to join the Steel Works Association, it found its aloofness frustrated by rapid financial action: the bankers deliberately accumulated Phönix shares and helped drive the firm into the cartel. Often several banks would join forces in order to secure a particularly important industrial conjunction. Perhaps the best example of this device occurred in 1905 in relation, not to a cartel scheme, but to the massive community of interest arranged between the Gelsenkirchen company, the Aachener Hüttenverein and Thyssen's Schalker Grüben.[185] The diplomatists behind this alliance included four banks, the Diskonto, Deutsche, Dresdner, and Schaffhausen'scher, an assortment of size-conscious financial power that could not be matched elsewhere in Europe. That cartels and risk-averting alliances of other kinds were German industrial characteristics by 1914 was due not least to such *bankinitiative*. Not only did the financial houses inject high-quality credit into the industrial structure, they also helped to redesign the structure. If cartels themselves were unfriendly to the entrepreneurial spirit, there is no denying the financial entrepreneurship which went into their creation. And, once established, it was not impossible for the banks to *deploy* their cartel interests in enterprising style.

However, these exercises in sponsored association were not without cost to the banks. As the scale, resources and capital of the industrial clientele expanded, so the lending power of the individual banks were placed under pressure by the borrowers' larger needs. At the best of times, large industrial issues required participating banks to hold heavy capital reserves, and the larger the share issue, the heavier the load. Some banks like the Essener Kreditanstalt increased their own capital many times in order to accommodate their industrial friends – in that case mainly the coal syndicates of Rhine-Ruhr – but such a course could not be pursued indefinitely. From the late 1890s in particular, the demands upon the banks became pressing, not only from their enlarged industrial interests but also from the government and the municipalities, both of which had generated exceptional credit needs over the preceding two decades. The logic of the situation, therefore, pointed towards *financial* integration and the accumulation of larger fund-raising agencies.

Fortunately, for the banks, logic and events were running in parallel. From the *Gründerkrise* of 1873 onwards the downswing of the business cycle had created a supply of weak and failing houses as ripe pickings for the larger and healthier financiers. The crash of 1890–91 had obliged in similar style, providing the Great Banks with an accession of financial assets – and thus with the additional lending power to finance the industrial revival of the following decade. But the largest bonus came with the crash of 1901: it created a shopping list of some 116 failed institutions for the surviving giants to pick over. In consequence, the Great Banks were enabled to absorb the dozen most important joint-stock banks of Rhineland-Westphalia during the early 1900s. By 1911 the total value (capital and reserves) of the captures made by the Big Six came to £137 m., with the Deutsche Bank and the Diskonto achieving the largest individual bags of £49 m. and £33 m. [186]

However, the extension of lending power could not be left to depend only on the happy accidents of economic crisis. Deliberate prospecting was also employed by the banks, imitating the tactics of association already widely used in industry. Communities of interest were established between the Great Banks as between the great industrialists. Directorships were exchanged between banks so as to create interlinked networks of lending power. Cartels of banks were set up for the exploitation of particular industries, as cartels of producers were set up for the exploitation of particular markets. *Ad hoc* bank groups were called together for particularly lavish flotations. And more permanent bank syndicates, akin to the manufacturing syndicates, could be created for specific long-term purposes. Of these various devices, the syndicate became the most powerful and the most popular. Indeed, with the immense demands issuing from capital-hungry industrialists like the electro-technical manufacturers, it became virtually a financial necessity after 1890. By 1910 many individual producers of electro-technical goods were financed by multi-bank syndicates – Siemens and Halske had employed eleven banks in its support group and AEG eight – and the industry's main associations required the collective assistance of fifty-two houses, combined in numerous permutations. The bankers took to the new, and safer, game with a will: in the boom year of 1900 the Deutsche Bank was involved in some 160 separate syndicate projects, and its major colleagues were not far behind. Given the windfalls of crisis, and the collective security of diplomatic contrivance, the Great Banks presented by 1900 no less of a united front than the industrial behemoths which they had helped graft together.

But collective security for the banks extended in its implications beyond risk aversion. By spreading the dangers collectively, the syndicates also permitted individual banks to commit a proportion of their resources to the cultivation of their private gardens. Finance houses were encouraged to group their prize industrial associates into ensembles forming an industrial 'family' specific to each bank. Thus the Deutsche Bank trailed in dependence the electrical interests of Siemens and Halske and Hoch and the steamship interests of Norddeutscher Lloyd, while the Diskonto-Gesellschaft consorted with the Gelsenkirchen Mining Co., the Loewe Engineering Works, the Bochumer Verein, and the Hamburg-Amerika Line. Naturally, some loyalties were split; one bank might be attached to a firm which was also financed by a syndicate containing other banks, but it was quite possible for 'special relationships' to survive under these conditions. As they did so, the banks created not only integration and cartelization among manufacturers but also a type of concentration by agglomeration, with the investment houses acting as nuclei and the industrial ventures as highly varied satellite cells. The orderly *inter-industry* relationships in Germany owed something to this collector's interest on the part of the Great Banks. These 'bank groups' bore some resemblance to the equally orderly Japanese *zaibatsu* or the Russian 'investment groups', but were more numerous and more powerful than either.

By the 1890s syndicated bank power with its numerous attachments running through industry – horizontally to influence complete industries via their cartels, vertically to influence connected industries via 'mixed' integration, and in all directions via the bank groups – represented a unique potential for economic action. Concerns under the influence of a single (hypothetical) bank might dig coal, employ the coal to produce metals, incorporate the metals into ships, manage the shipping lines, promote exports carried in the ships, and, as a bonus, direct colonial investment and condition public opinion. The implicit ability to chart inter-industry connexions, to promote structural change, or to engineer cartelization resided more with the Great Banks than it did with the imperial state. And, once that had occurred, the final transition was completed. As the banks had climbed the ladder of industrial credit into an entrepreneurial occupation, so they ascended a second entrepreneurial ladder, through the twin integrated structures of finance and affiliated industry, accumulating influence as they went, until they reached a position which carried a certain potential for economic management.

These finance houses met, and surpassed, the requirements for a growth-inducing banking structure.[187] They were reasonably free of state control after 1870, and disposed anyway to evade it before this date; their credit policies were generous far beyond the orthodox; their density relative to population was high; the ratio of their resources to national income was high; and the level of monetization they supported was high. But these tests do not fully describe their capabilities. Additional strength was generated by the concentration of financial power and its alliance with concentrated industrial power, a combination of collectivist forces unique in Europe.[188] If this structure surpassed the growth-inducing role it may perhaps have reached the growth-directing role. Standing at the head of a snaking chain of lesser banks and industries, the Great Banks could devise coherent business policies incorporating not only profit objectives but the optimal macro-economic balance and the overall interest of the Reich. This capability underlay Schumaker's famous dictum that the investment banks were equipped to 'carry out their own private economic policy'.

Bankinitiative extended by concentration certainly promised significant macro-economic controls: most importantly it offered the prospect of effective supervision of the investment market, curbing it either in reckless over-lending or in panic selling. And it appeared both symptom of, and sequel to, this developing capability that in Germany the investment banks did indeed contrive to usurp most Stock Exchange functions. Stock management was taken out of the market-place and set – theoretically at least – within a more rational and close-knit system of supervision. With most share purchasing and selling passing under bank scrutiny it would not be difficult to 'steer' the market into equilibrium; by adjusting their own massive portfolios, bankers should have been able to bolster bear markets and dampen bullish ones. In all probability, however, this capability remained potential rather than actual before 1914; the record contains few suggestions that financiers fully comprehended the leverage at their disposal and some indications – notably their over-stoking of the boom of 1900 – that their understanding was definitely limited. However, if German bankers remained fallible in perception, the capabilities of the structure over which they presided can scarcely be questioned. In 1914 no other banking system in the world possessed equivalent weight within the national economy; and since, after 1918, governments and international money flows became the arbiters of a disturbed economic world, the German financial structure of the pre-war years may perhaps be seen as the fullest historical expression of investment banking practice.

The ascent of the bank sector towards – if not quite to – control of the apparatus for fine-tuning the economy imposed relatively few social costs. Despite extremely tight integration among major institutions, outright monopoly was not achieved. Between the Great Banks, competition for business was as fierce as collaboration within joint ventures was close. Areas were reserved, as appropriate, for independent action or for joint operation. And with bank commissions, the banker's price for services rendered, falling to record levels in the 1900s, it is clear that sufficient competition survived to prevent the formation of 'collusive' profit policies. Nor did financial concentration imply a reduction in financial enterprise. It was distinctly adventurous for bankers to encourage cartelization as medicine for an over-producing market structure. Enterprise in the diplomacy of cartelization was a very different commodity from enterprise among cartel members. Probably, the worst that truthfully could be alleged against the Great Banks is the annihilation of the economically useful private bankers. The strong arm of corporate finance did impose that much of a price, but, against the design influence upon the economy which it also imposed, the price was relatively modest.

Naturally enough, the German bankers have been accused of much worse. Even contemporaries were fertile in creating their own unsympathetic revisions for this sector. The nostalgic agrarianism common at the time turned readily upon financial agencies which accelerated an unwelcome industrialization, and could add the damagingly relevant allegation that the great houses had neglected deserving agricultural clients. Probably, the *Raiffeisen* credit co-operatives and the other mortgage institutions served rural interests quite adequately, but this exculpation could not, in fact, rescue the bankers: in the vicious cross-fire between the rival adherents of *Industriestaat* and *Agrarstaat*, theirs remained an uncomfortably central position. Further, critics who emphasized, whether in the agrarian, the socialistic, or the generally conservative cause, the 'dangerous over-concentration' of the banks were greatly assisted by the apparently increasing riskiness of the financial ventures around the century's turn. Embarassingly, between 1893 and 1908, the ratio of immediately available bank assets to all bank liabilities declined from 85 to 62 per cent. Prejudice and pretext thus fused in the demand for bank reform: a powerful opposition vociferously required that investment banks be controlled by law, or forcibly directed towards such proper securities as government bonds, or entirely superseded by a central government body – and achieved, at least, the establishment of the German Bank Inquiry of 1908.

Largely, the opposition was chasing illusions. True, 'riskiness' and 'over-concentration' appeared to combine dramatically just before the 1901 panic when investment banks continued to lend massively even amidst mounting evidence of impending collapse. The failure of the Leipziger Bankverein, the most important before 1914, followed in 1901 from the overextension of credit to a single client in the grain-drying trade. But, as Riesser insisted, the demand for German credit always outran supply, and if a monster system of credit creation had not existed to feed industrial demand, recessions could have been far more severe than, in fact, they were. In this context, customers who demanded capital at times inappropriate for their own business or misrepresented their virtues as clients – as many did in 1900–01 – might escape even the considerable antennae of the Great Banks, through no fault of the financiers.

The 'risk' theory was also prone to exaggeration: if the ratio of ready assets to liabilities was falling, it had scarcely plunged into the dragon's mouth by 1908. Germany's 170 most important banks held resources equivalent to 50 per cent of liabilities at that time, whereas the much admired British banks sported paid-up capitals matching only 10 per cent of liabilities. Moreover, the 'safer' British banks, holding aloof from industrial participation, were often the innocent victims of industrial clients skilled at 'converting' manufacturing credit into speculative funds for Stock Exchange operations. In contrast, the 'dangerous' German banks wielded their industrial connexions deliberately to ensure good husbandry among their manufacturing customers. And if they did not lend extravagantly or dangerously, nor did they pervert the flow of funds to gratify their industrial 'mania'. Most of their deposits came in small instalments from the working reserves of businessmen. In the absence of industrial banks, these sums probably would not have been built into any useful aggregates. And, given their origins, it is exceedingly unlikely that, freed from *Kreditbank* supervision, they would have flowed towards farmers, craftsmen, or government bonds. Investment banks, therefore, did not ruin the market in capital to the prejudice of non-industrial sectors. Nor does it seem that their largely imaginary sins ever earned retribution from vengeful financial gods. Indeed the roster of bank failures – the ultimate test of efficiency – suggests either that the gods were generous to a fault or that the sins were beneath notice. Between 1894 and 1907 when the temptations of large-scale industrial financing and the special appetites of the electro-technical industry were at their most developed, the proportion of German bank deposits lost by financial lapses was a negligible 0.9 per cent of the total.

Economic historians, on the whole, have upheld the outstanding entrepreneurial record of the German bankers and have not followed the lead of the early century revisionists. Admittedly, some have moderated their compliments with the accurate observation that, in the last pre-war years, the bigger industrial concerns were developing their own internal financial resources and *reducing* their reliance upon bank finance.[189] At the same point, undoubtedly, the *sources* of industrial management underwent change and began to slip outside financial control: within large industrial concerns the main concentration of decision-making shifted from the supervisory boards – where the banks were heavily represented – to the administrative boards – where they were not. Furthermore, in the early 1900s the customary balance of power between the largest bankers and the largest manufacturers began to tilt as an increasing number of powerful industrialists achieved access to positions of influence on the directing boards of major banks, and carried out, according to Gille, an *industrial* 'colonization' of the banks.[190] Such a process could well have been assisted by the accumulations of manufacturing power within syndicated industry. Ironically, just as the organizational circuit of the banking institutions reached its widest scope, so the flows of current within it began to adjust, and, in some cases, perhaps to reverse. But in 1914 this was true only for the very largest manufacturing concerns; for the great majority, especially in the new metallurgical regions, the signals from the bankers still represented instructions worthy of respect. Upon the last locational adjustments and technological integrations amidst German heavy industry prior to the First World War, bank finance was still, detectably, a predominating influence. Any reversal of *bankinitiative* is encountered most commonly either in the older industrial regions where the tasks of promotion were long past and the concentrations of industrial wealth longest established, or among modern high technologies of very rapid growth and monstrous capitals. Consistent with this, the great majority of Gille's examples[191] are taken either from the coal-mining industry or from amidst the very few, quite exceptional, behemoths of the electro-technical trade. And even here little can be found before 1905.

Perhaps more generally applicable are the arguments which stress the power of the *alternative* German banking agencies, particularly the much-neglected savings banks and the *Raiffeisen* rural credit co-operatives, which, with the mortgage institutions, handled as much investment as the industrial banks themselves between 1880 and 1913.[192] However, this interpretation seeks, wholly advisedly, to create a correct proportion between financial sectors. No denigration of the Great Banks need be implied.

Although a rarity within the specialist literature, the denigratory approach is not yet entirely extinct. Recently, indeed, it has been revived by the dark rites of the econometricians. Their calculations have suggested that the Great Banks may actually have inhibited German development. By allocating capital excessively to heavy industry and insufficiently to lighter manufacturing sectors, the banks dispensed investment funds 'not strictly in accordance with their marginal product in different sectors'.[193] Quite apart from its failure to distinguish any operational definition for 'heavy' or 'light' industry, this proposition suffers from three crucial deficiencies. Firstly, it entirely evades the issue raised by one important aspect of *bankinitiative* which, scarcely coincidentally, is extremely hard to quantify: the entrepreneurial or 'design' influence wreaked upon the heavy industrial system by the banks. This is simply omitted as less 'relevant to an econometric approach'.[194] Unfortunately, it is obviously one of the strategic objectives of *bankinitiative* and merely to exclude it is to undervalue at the outset what one is purporting to measure. Secondly, the modern revisionists do not test the important possibility that the bankers' low preference for light industry may less have contributed to the frailty of this sector in Germany than have proceeded directly from it. Suggestions do indeed exist that returns to enterprise were particularly poor in this region of manufacturing.[195] Thirdly, and most important, the notion that the biased distribution of capital between the two sectors represented a misallocation of resources depends upon the implicit assumption that risks were distributed between the two sectors in an *unbiased* fashion. This is particularly unlikely. Heavy industry, with its much greater suitability for cartel organization, and for other forms of association and integration, possessed notably superior means of risk *containment*. In creating their 'biased' flow of funds towards this sector, the bankers were merely appraising accurately the real distribution of risk. And it is not accidental that it was precisely within this area that they could most readily employ their managerial or design capability to reduce risks further. Certainly, more substantial charges than the econometric allegation of funds misallocated will be needed if the developmental utility of the *Kreditbanken* is to be convincingly undermined. And it is not without significance that one modern evaluation has taken the opposite road, and, while subjecting the investment houses to thoroughly critical appraisal, has chosen to echo Riesser's classic study of the 1900s, and describe them finally as 'centres of business decision-making', originators of 'a distinctive contribution as *organising agencies*'.[196]

With the investment banks surviving both the onslaughts of contemporaries and the reservations of subsequent commentators it is perhaps safe to point out the considerable affiliations between the preferences of the financiers and the observed characteristics of the Reich economy. The lack of medium-sized firms in Germany reflects, at least in part, the liking of the banks for large manufacturing units. The high incidence of vertical integration follows substantially from the banks' attraction towards 'mixed' industrial properties. The wide spread of cartelization – covering 90 per cent of the market in paper, 74 per cent in mining and 50 per cent in crude steel by 1907 – derives to a large degree from the banks' approval of these stabilizing institutions. Even the rapid pace of German technological change owed something to the banks, since many of them maintained specialist departments for the support and promotion of potentially valuable innovations.

No other agency – whether private-entrepreneurial, state-entrepreneurial, or cartel – could claim a record covering so much economic ground and covering it with so much enterprise.

CONCLUSIONS

Clearly enough, any pattern of industrial growth is composed of highly intricate force conjunctions; rarely, if ever, does a single element so predominate as to become the 'key variable'. But even within intricate force conjunctions, priorities and rank orders exist. Any growing economy must contain opportunities of many kinds – in market demand, in capital availability, in labour supply, in material endowment – and a supply of exploitative agencies, also of several possible species – private capitalistic, corporate institutional, or state institutional. But even so, within the growth system, it is possible to identify emphases which shift between the design influences, the forces which depend upon others but exert more gravitational pull than is exerted upon them. Within German territory these shifts are reasonably clear. Before 1840 the state, whether in the shape of the Prussian Crown operating directly in Silesia, or of the Napoleonic Empire indirectly promoting the textile industries of the Rhineland and Saxony, operated powerfully upon the proto-industrial economy. Between 1840 and 1870, the state gradually reduced its contribution as both private entrepreneurial and corporate financial influences strengthened. During this transition period, the exploitative agency was formed by an amalgam of private capitalists, official advisory agencies, and prototype investment banks. After 1870, this alliance resolved its own priorities: the state element fell away sharply and private entrepreneurs – with a few exceptions – were subordinated on one level to the cartel, and, more comprehensively, to the banker. Apart from a brief mid-century interlude, therefore, the growth of the German economy was strongly influenced by institutional forces. And it is possible to detect changes in the balance of emphasis between these forces.

But how far did these shifts in pattern conform to the various models of economic and socio-economic analysis? With regard to the stage theory of growth with its equipment of 'preconditions' and 'take-off', the resemblance is only passing. Preconditions entered the pattern with extreme timidity and in only a few sectors – notably agriculture – while elsewhere equally essential requisites – such as a fully effective banking system or an extensive national market – were delayed until the 1870s. Overlap between the preconditions and take-off stages was, as usual, uncomfortable, and in Germany proved especially protracted. [197] Take-off itself remains difficult to detect and both the long preparation of technological advance and the long survival of traditional methods (to 1870 at least) suggests gradualism rather than discontinuity as the basic style of growth. Closer affinity with German patterns is achieved by the 'backwardness model'. State operations did prove effective stimuli to economic progress when backwardness was pronounced, and thereafter subsided as it receded. The most modern (that is capital-intensive) technological 'mix', was indeed applied by proficiently imitative manufacturers. Units of the largest scale were indeed extensively employed. And when backwardness receded, leaving a measure of manufacturing development to combine with a scarcity of savings around mid-century, the industrial investment bank did emerge as the most appropriate institutional replacement for the state.

Close parallels were also achieved by the 'social value' explanation of entrepreneurial behaviour. Clearly the attachment of entrepreneurial values to the notion of state-building and thus to the goal of national significance through business success, was a conditioning force acting upon the scale and composition of German industry. And even when the individual manufacturer both fulfilled and submerged these values within the cartel, the financial entrepreneur was able to carry them further. For what could have more accurately summarized the relationship of nationalistic values with business objectives than the interleaved system of Great Banks, controlling private industrial empires fit to serve the Reich, and wielding financial levers capable of influencing its economic course? The investment houses achieved the acme of state-building service: within the business arena they *surpassed* the state in activity and weight. Backwardness models and social value models are thus mutually (and assuringly) reinforcing: components such as state promotion, *bankinitiative*, and largeness of scale are accepted by either model with equal ease. Similarly, the political element, running from the Silesia of Frederick the Great to the *Kaiserreich* of Wilhelm II, relates to the subtly modulating role of the state: in the early decades of the period, political issues *determine* economic prospects, but they are themselves increasingly influenced by economic forces in the last *ante-bellum* years – although the Junkers remain an obstinate and obstructive throwback, placing an outmoded political and social pre-eminence athwart the path of modernization.

Finally, German experience conforms closely to the 'internationalist' model of manufacturing advance. That it did so again possesses relevance for the backwardness model, since international technological diffusion forms the process by which backward countries are *permitted* to pursue imitative modernization. Backwardness sets up a demand for the most modern available technology; international technological flows satisfy the demand. In another sense, however, the determined miniature internationalism of the German states prior to 1870 itself constituted an integral component of the area's backwardness. However, once this was suppressed, and the German nation unified, the internationalism of the Reich economy took on a more sophisticated form, incorporating economic and political ingredients in a particularly toxic cocktail. At the commencement of the growth process the international aspect of technology allowed the German economies to draw *in* vital development resources even though the international aspect of the German states greatly complicated the economic organization within which development occurred. But with vigorous growth established, the Reich economy's orientation turned *outwards* as its economic capacity overflowed the political boundaries. The implications of industrial internationalism were frequently present – but with *zersplitterung*, 'dumping', and economic expansionism, they were not always pleasant.

NOTES AND REFERENCES

Full publication details are provided in the bibliography.

1. The commercial 'scare' both evoked and summarized by Williams' book, *Made in Germany* (1896) may be compared, not entirely fancifully, with the armament 'scare' of 1908–09.
2. Palmer (1964), p. 432.
3. Borchardt (1973), p. 84.
4. *Ibid.*, p. 102.
5. See Palmer (1964), Ch. XI.
6. See Henderson (1960–62)
7. Borchardt (1973), pp. 87–8.
8. Pounds (1959), p. 194. This essay provides a good deal of useful information on the Silesian developments.
9. Most notably the group of reformers around Hardenberg in the 1800s.
10. Pounds (1959), pp. 194–5.
11. Schumpeter (1939), I, p. 284.
12. Quoted by Pounds (1959), p. 195.
13. The proportion of the total labour force employed in agriculture in Silesia in 1787 and in Prussia in 1800 was about two-thirds in each case. Even in 1861 the proportion of the Saxon population employed in full-time manufacturing was twice that for the majority of German states (Tipton, 1976, pp. 18–21).
14. Marshall (1920), App. F, p. 767n.
15. Kisch (1962), p. 326.
16. *Ibid.* Also, Crouzet (1964), pp. 567–88. For a more extensive treatment see Crouzet (1958).
17. Quoted by Kisch (1962), p. 323.
18. *Ibid.*, p. 326.
19. Quoted by Köllmann (1964), pp. 100–1.
20. See Kraus (1965).
21. Palmer (1964), pp. 426–7.
22. Agrarian reform commenced in Prussia in 1807, in Bavaria in 1808, in Hesse

in 1811, in Württemberg in 1819. It had covered most of the western states by 1830, most of the east by the 1850s.

23. Tipton (1976), p. 24.
24. Hamerow (1958), p. 222.
25. Palmer (1964), Ch. XIV. Rather significantly, this chapter is entitled, 'The revolution of the Mind'.
26. For a typically 'pessimistic' interpretation see Kemp (1969), pp. 87–90. Tipton (1976, p. 25) also suggests that the total area lost may have been equivalent to as much as 12 per cent of all peasant land, as of 1859.
27. Borchardt (1973), pp. 97–8.
28. See Conze (1969), pp. 66–8.
29. *Ibid.*, p. 61.
30. Hoffmann (1963), p. 103.
31. *Ibid.*, p. 96.
32. Schmoller (1894), p. 492.
33. Borchardt (1973), pp. 103–4.
34. Earlier pilot agreements had recruited various states to the Prussian-centred customs alliance: the southern states in 1829, Saxony in 1830, Thuringia in May 1833.
35. The number of potential consumers covered by the customs agreements rose from 14 m. in 1831 to 23.6 m. in 1834 (Milward and Saul, 1973, p. 376).
36. Quoted by Brady (1943), p. 109.
37. Tipton (1974a), pp. 201–2.
38. Bruck (1962), p. 38.
39. Quoted by Marshall (1920), p. 768.
40. Schumpeter (1939), p. 280n.; Borchardt (1973), p. 105.
41. Pounds (1959), p. 198.
42. Fischer (1960), pp. 65–89. See also Henderson (1960).
43. Fischer (1963), p. 85.
44. Tipton (1974a), p. 202.
45. Schumpeter (1939), p. 280n.
46. Tilly (1967), p. 154.
47. *Ibid.*, p. 179.
48. Kemp (1969), p. 81.
49. See Hoffmann (1963), p. 105, Graph 3. Hoffmann himself does not' draw this implication from his material.
50. The Kondratiev cycle is of roughly fifty years' duration. Here the period 1843–73 is taken to represent an upswing of the cycle, the years 1873–97 a downswing.
51. See Cameron (1956).
52. The *Kommandit-gesellschaft auf Aktien* or *société en commandité* was a form of association inferior to the joint-stock company. It involved unlimited liability for active partners, limited liability only for sleeping partners.
53. Naturally, this did not prevent *some* German banks from copying French originals: the Darmstädter Bank (1854) was a conscious imitation of the Crédit Mobilier, the first in Europe, and attracted a substantial participation from its Parisian counterpart.
54. Lebovics (1967), p. 34.
55. Tipton (1974a), pp. 197, 215.
56. Schumpeter (1939), pp. 361–6.

57. Tipton (1976), p. 98; see also pp. 97–101.
58. German exports exceeded British by two and a half times, American by three times (Landes, 1969, p. 290).
59. Howard (1907) pp. 58–62.
60. Calculated from Mitchell (1975), p. 460.
61. Howard (1907), pp. 58–62.
62. Schumpeter (1939), pp. 436–48.
63. Reader (1970), pp. 151, 194ff.
64. Schumpeter (1939), p. 446.
65. Tipton (1976), p. 150.
66. *Ibid.*, p. 30ff.
67. *Ibid.*, p. 68.
68. *Ibid.*, p. 112.
69. *Ibid.*, pp. 111–12.
70. See Hauser (1917a).
71. Cf. Veblen (1939). Compare pp. 175 and 180.
72. *Ibid.*, p. 180.
73. Parker (1954), pp. 26–7.
74. Hirschman (1958), Ch. 1.
75. Kindleberger (1964), pp. 17–29.
76. Notably that it should not entirely outstrip *per caput* income growth, nor commence upon strong expansion before income growth has had some chance to benefit from the processes of economic modernization. Many less developed countries of today have proved much less fortunate in these respects than the developing economies of the last century.
77. Köllman (1964), p. 102.
78. *Ibid.*, p. 104.
79. *Ibid.*, p. 103.
80. Borchardt (1973), p. 121.
81. Marshall (1920), pp. 125–6.
82. Veblen (1939), p. 214.
83. See Schumpeter (1939), p. 346.
84. See *ibid.*, pp. 345–6.
85. Marshall (1920), p. 447.
86. Schumaker (1912), p. 46.
87. *Ibid.*, p. 46.
88. Tipton (1976), p. 53.
89. This partnership did not predate 1870. Until then canals offered no genuine alternative to railways. Their development depended upon the growth of a *demand* for the transportation of bulky commodities, and this did not arise until the later nineteenth century. In part also, this demand sprang from the forward linkages of railway growth itself. (Fremdling, 1977, p. 584n).
90. Fogel (1964), pp. 92–110.
91. Marshall (1920), pp. 447 and 499.
92. Hauser (1917a), pp. 122–7. Marshall (1920, p. 125n) gives an alternative estimate that waterway freights were commonly one-*third* of comparable railway rates.
93. Marshall (1920), p. 499.
94. Quoted *ibid.*, p. 499n.
95. Tipton (1976), pp. 131–2.

96.   Fogel (1964), p. 234.
97.   Fremdling (1975), p. 28.
98.   Fremdling (1977), p. 586.
99.   Wagenblass (1973).
100. Fogel (1964), p. 236.
101. Pounds (1959), p. 195.
102. Schumpeter (1939), pp. 355–6.
103. See, among others, Aldcroft (1964).
104. Kuznets (1966), pp. 236–9. And see Table 7.6, pp. 436–7.
105. See Kuznets (1961), p. 65 for the composition of German capital formation. Contrast the (unlikely) view advanced by Kitchen (1978), that capital for industrial investment was in short supply.
106. Sir Swire Smith (1916).
107. US Department of Commerce (1905), Ch. 4.
108. *Ibid.*, p. 8.
109. Andic and Veverka (1964), p. 189.
110. Marshall (1920), p. 97.
111. Hauser (1917a), p. 37.
112. Marshall (1920), p. 129.
113. Parker (1959), pp. 208–10.
114. Hauser (1917a), pp. 40–1.
115. Quoted *ibid.*, p. 40.
116. Sir Robert Hadfield quoted *ibid.*, p. 43.
117. Hauser (1917a), p. 154.
118. Bowen (1950), p. 76.
119. *Ibid.*, p. 77. Cf. Hauser (1917a), p. 26, 'the German has the temperament of the syndicalist'.
120. Parker (1954), p. 28.
121. Quoted by Maschke (1969), p. 257.
122. See Parker (1954), p. 32.
123. Quoted by Marshall (1920), p. 575. My italics.
124. Landes (1965), pp. 175–81.
125. Maschke (1969), p. 244.
126. Hauser (1917a), pp. 27, 45ff., 92ff.
127. *Ibid.*, p. 95.
128. See Liefman (1932).
129. See especially Stockder (1932).
130. Riesser (1911), pp. 721–2.
131. Walker (1906), p. 360.
132. Quoted by Maschke (1969), pp. 251–2.
133. *Ibid.*, p. 257.
134. Quoted *ibid.*, pp. 251, 255.
135. Bruck (1962), 103–4.
136. It is fast disappearing. Note Pollard's emphasis on the internationalism of industrialization; it spread across varieties of states, regardless of political colours or competences. The power of any individual state in the economic arena is thus placed at a discount (Pollard, 1973).
137. Bruck (1962), p. 26.
138. Veblen (1939), p. 175.
139. Hauser (1917b), pp. 258f.

140. Tipton (1976), pp. 112–17, 146–7.
141. Eicholtz (1962), Ch. II. Contrast Henderson (1958).
142. Tilly (1967), p. 157.
143. Fischer (1963), pp. 88–9.
144. Compare Tilly (1967), pp. 154–7; also Tipton (1974a, p. 219): 'In the west expansion of the money supply, the introduction of limited liability . . . the expansion of the railway system . . . were hindered by aristocratic representatives of the central government far more interested in social control than in economic expansion.'
145. Treue (1962), p. 327; Bergengrün (1908), pp. 145–6, 166–7, 218–20.
146. Pounds (1959), pp. 196–200.
147. *Ibid.*, pp. 196, 198.
148. Pounds (1959, p. 198) talks of 'the *stultifying effect* of state control when this had lost its freshness and originality' (my emphasis).
149. Many of the architects of the automobile industry were trained in the weaponry industries. Henry Leland, Ford's first production engineer, was another. See Trebilcock (1969) for further, similar examples.
150. See Fischer (1963), p. 90. Also Henderson (1955–56); and Landes (1965), p. 104.
151. Bowen (1950), p. 71.
152. Riesser (1911), pp. 776–7.
153. Hauser (1917a), pp. 140ff., and generally Ch. IV. The subsection (pp. 142–4) is entitled 'The economic dictatorship of the octopus state'.
154. Trebilcock (1966), pp. 364–79; Crouzet (1974).
155. Bruck (1962), p. 96.
156. Hauser (1917a), p. 144.
157. In the earlier period Germany's total foreign investment consumed only about 5 per cent of the nation's current income, around 1910 only about 2 per cent (Feis, 1961, p. 72).
158. *Ibid.*, pp. 234–5, 319.
159. *Ibid.*, pp. 404–7; Mömmsen (1973), p. 23.
160. Berghahn (1970), pp. 34ff; also *idem* (1971), pp. 592ff.
161. Mömmsen (1973), p. 18.
162. Andic and Veverka (1964), p. 189. National income shares from *ibid.*, Tables A21, A30.
163. Bruck (1962), p. 68.
164. See Gerschenkron in Rostow (ed.) (1963, p. 344). Note also the view of Tipton (1974a, p. 216) that 'the 1879 tariff represents a pernicious influence of the Bismarckian empire, its provision of a field for the more efficient application of pressure by reactionary interest groups'.
165. See Gerschenkron (1943); Tirrell (1951); Pühle (1966); Barkin (1970).
166. Eley (1974), pp. 29–63; Stegmann (1970), p. 179.
167. Tipton (1974b), p. 964. With the eastern provinces controlling 68 per cent of the national conservative vote in 1876, 80 per cent in 1898, and 88 per cent in 1912, the regime had to tread especially warily with this vital reserve of support (*ibid.*, p. 966).
168. In 1913, 56 per cent of officers above colonel belonged to the aristocracy, 50 per cent of General Staff officers (Steinberg, 1964, p. 105). In contrast, only 11 per cent of the senior department heads in the Admiralty Staff, 1899–1918, belonged to the aristocracy (*ibid.*, pp. 105–6).

169. However, recent revisions by J. C. Hunt suggest that *peasant* gains from German protectionism – especially from the meat quotas (1880), aimed on health grounds, against imported foreign cattle but manipulated effectively as exclusive tariffs – have been seriously underrated. Conversely, the extent to which the peasantry served as political 'dupes' of the Junkers has been exaggerated. Easy land purchase, ready credit, and punitive meat quotas may have cajoled the peasantry into a transaction which was for them a rational economic bargain. However, Hunt does not doubt the *generally* destructive effects of German protectionism (Hunt, 1974, pp. 311–31). See also Hunt (1975, pp. 513–30), and Lebovics, *Journal of Modern History*, 41 (1969), pp. 257–60, reviewing Pühle (1966).

170. Andic and Veverka (1964), p. 185.

171. Rosenberg (1967).

172. See Gerschenkron (1963), pp. 405–8.

173. Böhme (1966). See also *idem*. (1979).

174. This is scarcely a description which could be applied to the armies of the Crimean War without extensive qualifications.

175. Brady (1943), pp. 108–23.

176. Fischer (1975), pp. 517–20.

177. *Ibid.*, pp. 517–22.

178. Hauser (1917a), p. 22.

179. Steinberg (1965) provides interesting suggestions that industrial overcapacity encouraged military leaders to provide contracts in excess of strict military needs. Berghahn (1973) develops a similar thesis for the period 1905–14

180. Tilly (1967), p. 158.

181. Cameron (1967), pp. 298–9.

182. Calculated from Riesser (1911), p. 372.

183. Bruck (1962), p. 80.

184. Riesser (1911), pp. 746–9.

185. *Ibid.*, pp. 483–4.

186. *Ibid.*, p. 638; Hauser (1917a), pp. 67–8.

187. Cameron (1967), pp. 290ff.

188. Cf. Calwer (1900), p. 155: 'Berlin high-finance unquestionably dominates the most representative and the largest businesses in every branch of production.'

189. Barrett Whale (1930), pp. 55–8; Marshall (1920), p. 343n.

190. Gille (1973), p. 296.

191. *Ibid.*, pp. 285–7.

192. Borchardt (1973), pp. 150–1; also Barrett Whale (1930), pp. 33–5.

193. Neuberger and Stokes (1974), p. 715. See Fremdling and Tilly (1976) for a spirited and critical reply.

194. Neuberger and Stokes (1974), p. 713.

195. Parker (1954), p. 28.

196. Borchardt (1973), pp. 138, 149 (my emphasis).

197. See Fischer (1963), p. 353.

CHAPTER THREE

France

After Britain, France was the first major nation to seek initiation into the industrial mysteries. Unfortunately, however, Gallic temperaments appear to have proved ill-suited to the experience: in the event, French devotions at the manufacturing shrines secured fewer returns than those won by the British founding fathers and notably fewer than those bestowed upon the more assiduous congregation across the Rhine. Indeed it is arguable that from 1750 France was faced with retreating economic prospects and an economic stature which diminished progressively as first Britain and then Germany passed her by. By 1900 France was clearly the economic laggard among the powers and not even the unusually energetic progress of the *belle époque* could erase the languid and spasmodic growth pattern of the preceding century and a half.

Given French endowments in 1750, this outcome may appear undeserved. At that time the nation could boast a solid proficiency in the agricultural, handicraft, commercial, and maritime disciplines of the era. French science was among the most sophisticated in Europe. French society possessed bourgeois cadres stronger than those of the contemporary German states and well matched with the prosperous middle classes of Britain and the United Provinces. French industrial output as a share of total physical product had begun to increase as early as 1750. And even if this accelerated pace came as a somewhat unexpected sequel to the 'tragic' economic stumbling of the seventeenth century – where Britain could boast some two centuries of relatively unbroken advance – it was nevertheless sufficient to set France upon a path roughly parallel with that of Britain. Indeed between 1716/20 and 1784/88 French overseas trade advanced *more* rapidly than the British (an expansion of 3 : 1 against the British performance of 2.4 : 1) and the rate of growth of French industrial output between 1700 and 1790 probably equalled the British (each averaging about 1% p.a.).[1] Even in cotton, Britain's traditional industrial masterpiece, the French mills more or less matched the advance of their Lancashire competitors over the important period 1700–90 (at an average growth rate of 3.8% p.a.).[2] Of course, French achievements were built upon lower bases than the British and would appear much less impressive if assessed by *per capita*, rather than by total volume, measurement. But it remains

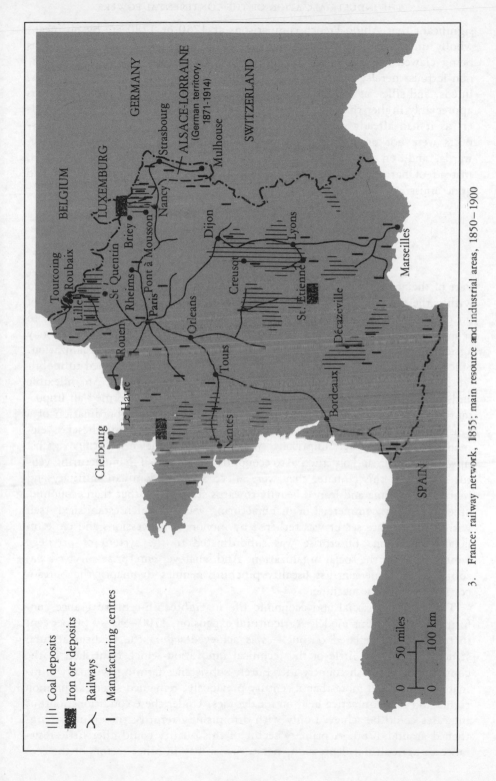

3. France: railway network, 1855; main resource and industrial areas, 1850–1900

Coal deposits

Iron ore deposits

Railways

Manufacturing centres

significant that Anglo-French comparisons at 1750 or 1780 are by no means wholly unfavourable to France, and may even suggest that some ground was being clawed back. Crouzet concludes that: 'France was producing less coal, non-ferrous metals, ships and cotton goods than Britain but more woollens, linens, and silks, as well as more iron. French total industrial production was appreciably higher than the English but production per head remained smaller, as it had already been in the seventeenth century'.[3] On this basis, prospects were not unpromising. Further emulation of Britain offered clear rewards, and, on past record, seemed likely. Yet, a century later, the gap, instead of narrowing, had grown wider and was still widening. What had gone amiss?

THE OLD REGIME ECONOMY

Part of the answer was that in France the growth which did occur was located within the political, legal, and social structure of an *ancien régime* state, or of unstable successor states. Classically, the *ancien régime* is considered hostile to economic modernization and industrial change. Its population was largely agricultural and its agriculture often feudal or quasi-feudal in organization. Since the regime was essentially a military service system, designed to mobilize mass armies upon demand, such dispositions were crucial. An inflexible and hierarchic social structure, dominated by the nobility, formed an important support for a politico-military system based on the subordination of a peasant mass which doubled as a conscript army. Even if middle-class elements existed, they were imprisoned within a social framework fortified against upward mobility and obstructive to economic endeavour. If manufacturing ventures survived this climate, they were affected by its dominant military and hierarchic miasma and leaned heavily towards strategic, rather than economic, objectives. Any commercial or manufacturing venture which established itself within the private sector was tethered by monopoly concessions and close official supervision. Enterprise was subordinated to the system of privilege which made up the social organization. And whatever enterprise survived was subjected to a mercantilist fiscality pinching pennies to finance the bureaucratic and military machine.

The reality of social and economic life in eighteenth-century France conforms broadly to this model. Agricultural expansion, 1700–90 – a 60 per cent increase in the deflated output – was achieved *within* the traditional rural structure and with little of the technical innovation which flourished in the contemporary British countryside. Purely subsistence farming, virtually eliminated in England more than a century previously, remained strong. Common rights and feudal practice held on for decades. Under these conditions, output increases could be achieved only with diminishing returns; these duly strengthened around 1780. A primary sector of this quality could offer little resistance to agricultural depression, nor to instability in other sectors of the eco-

114

nomy. Consequently, in the 1780s French agriculture provided only distressful preliminaries for the collapse of the manufacturing sector later in the decade.

Similarly, the rigidity of French society effectively ruled out the mobility which converted English barbers and blacksmiths into great manufacturers and landowners. When French noblemen like the Comte d'Artois dabbled in industrial venturing, they did so merely as one indulgence of privilege, and they offered no 'demonstration effect' to aspiring capitalists. Open societies are economically useful not because they reduce the social barriers separating the great landed classes from industry and commerce but because they offer lesser individuals both the facility *and* the inducement to rise through their ranks by economic achievement. For the French bourgeoisie, however, the point is almost an academic one since the option came to them only in a tortuously constricted form, snagged with calculations of relative status and burdened with regulamentary purchases of privilege, office, or land. Moreover, for them, freedom in trade was no less scarce than flexibility in society. Choice sectors of the economy were reserved for the socially eminent by the dispensing power of the autocracy. Modern forms of organization and of technology were impeded by the restrictive practices of the guilds. And official disincentives to innovation were imposed by the strict quality requirements of the Colbert code. Increases in industrial output before 1790, like those in agriculture, had to be achieved within a fixed social matrix and a traditional mode of production. Basically, the French manufacturing economy did not evolve or modify; it merely produced more of the same. And, like agriculture, it did this less efficiently towards the end of the century; growth in output slackened from 1750 and dropped to a crawl after 1770.[4] Existing forms of social and economic organization had a *limited* capacity to produce more of the same.

But there was worse. The regime not only had limited powers of production; it also had distinctly unproductive tastes. Enormous Crown expenditures worked to force the national debt up from 1700 m. francs in 1721 to 4500 m. francs in 1789. Faced with such unfortunate accounts, an anti-innovational government had no option but to increase the fiscal burden. And this, since the nobility were widely believed to possess tax exemption, may have exacerbated social tensions.[5] Certainly, the regime then proceeded to make matters worse by using the revenue to fight losing battles. Contrasts with the British performance are here more prolific than parallels. The British had produced an agricultural and commercial, and were well launched upon an industrial, transformation; their wealth was increasing upon the basis of innovation; the wealth purchased unprecedented maritime supremacy; this modern seapower could win wars. Levels of taxation in France and Britain may have been dictated largely by their apparent need to maul one another, but the modernizing economy could better withstand the burden. In contrast, the *ancien régime* economy had to accept military frailty *and* high taxation with reduced living standards – introducing the twin spectres of insolvency and internal political disturbance.

Is it then that the promising French developments of the eighteenth cen-

tury took place as surgical improvements to an arthritic frame, and, as sometimes happens, were rejected and stifled by it? If so, is it possible to talk of
proto-industrial development in late-eighteenth-century France, as one may in
contemporary Prussia? At the outset, however, these questions set up a contra-
diction; for Prussian experience argues precisely that there is no *necessary* correlation between the *ancien régime* and economic lassitude. Calculations of militarism or despotism might induce the old regime state to seek industrial advance for reasons wholly compatible with its fundamental assumptions. Elements of this situation are indeed detectable in France. Fohlen has found in
the last pre-revolutionary years 'a French-style variation of Enlightened Despotism . . . paying special attention to the economy'.[6] The reforming Finance
Minister, Turgot, was an exponent of this policy, aiming in the 1770s at the
suppression of guilds and monopolies and the creation of an open market in
grain, freed from the multitudinous internal customs barriers of tradition.
Calonne, his successor, also took interest in the founding of the great Le
Creusot ironworks and encouraged the pioneering work of foreign industrialists. French governments proved as willing to draw upon the British technological bank as Prussian ones, and industrial advisers like Milne, Holker, and
Wilkinson were brought to France under the auspices of the late vintage *ancien
régime*. Similarly, the Anglo-French Treaty of 1786 was meant to encourage
imitation of British practice. Even in agriculture there was no simple conser-
vationism by the state. Needing to suppress famine (and attendant disturbance) and to increase tax yield, the regime authorized British-style enclosure,
drainage, and land clearance in a number of provinces. Despite peasant opposition, the plan constituted a valid attempt at the creation of a modern market-
economy in agriculture. 'Restrictive' monarchy could thus apparently include,
in its later days, 'a liberal economic regime animated by state impulse'.[7] Old
regime arthritis is then excessively simple as an explanation of the French
problem.

Many of the *ancien régime* institutions were, anyway, more damaging in
theory than in performance. Traditional accounts lashing the 'strait-jacket' of
guild restrictions and Colbertist legislation on to the weakening form of
French manufacturing, have displayed more enthusiasm than accuracy. Guilds
never covered more than a segment of France and left most towns and industries – royal factories, cottage manufacture, new industrial commodities –
entirely untouched. And even the grasp that was real weakened progressively
after 1750. Colbertist restrictions, similarly, were never proof against determined evasion and declined in the second half of the century.[8] Infiltration of
reformist elements into the structure of the *ancien régime* provided a sanction
for this erosion. As the French system incorporated 'enlightened' elements, its
attitude to economic modernization changed, as did that of the Prussian regime upon recognition of the strategic main chance. As industry moved forward, the structure around it changed, and in its last years became increasingly willing to accept a new outline.

Even 'factor endowment' arguments, though they may explain the attachment to economic traditionalism for some decades, lose force around 1780.

True, French timber was plentiful, French coal scarce and dear. Correspondingly, pressure for innovations concerning mineral fuels or mining was much less intense than in a Britain denuded of forest and sprinkled with coal. True, French labour was cheap and plentiful, while British employers suffered frequent and severe bottlenecks around 1750. Correspondingly, French output could be increased without innovation, while in Britain cost-reducing and labour-saving reforms were essential if demand were to be profitably met. For most of the century, the impulsions for 'revolutionary' technological change were weaker in France than in Britain. But around 1770 or 1780 this situation changed. Increased competition from British goods, initially in foreign markets but delivered to the French industrialist's doorstep by the treaty of 1786, began to generate pressures for technological change which domestic endowment had not required. Significantly, French application of British technology accelerated during the 1780s.

On this reading, the constraints – whether economic or institutional – upon French development were crumbling precisely as revolutionary political forces were gathering momentum. The problem as to which impediments *continued* to constrain industrial activity in France down to 1914 gains a new aspect. For it is possible that an economy still contending the industrial race, and perhaps even set to increase its pace, was arrested by a great political revolution, and so slowed over the next quarter-century of war and civil strife, as to emerge in 1815 as the sluggard of the European economy. Here it is not the *ancien régime* but its violent destruction which created the true curbs on performance; and the French revolution, in economic terms at least, becomes a 'national catastrophe'.[9]

Ingenious as this reversal is, it begs important questions. For instance, there is the problem as to whether the revolutionary breakout was itself partly provoked by the economic policies of the declining monarchy. To the extent that it was, the activities of the *ancien régime* state, however revisionist, would once again show themselves to be incompatible with viable and long-term economic advance. Investigation of this problem also sheds light on the wider issues concerned with the economic 'causation' of the revolutionary process.

REVOLUTION AND ECONOMICS I: THE PROBLEM OF CAUSATION

Any survey of this issue revolves uncomfortably about the highly problematic nature of the old regime's failure. Did it suffer economic collapse because of its archaic institutions and policies? Or because it was attempting to *modify* its institutions and policies? Or for entirely separate reasons? Traditionally, much discussion of the problem has focused upon the tax policies of the monarchy. For, clearly, it was the manner in which fiscal issues involved the nobility which, *inter alia*, drove them to demand the convocation of the Estates-General in 1789, and thus set spark to kindling. The implied causation is equally obvious: the nature of the *ancien régime* state as a bureaucratic revenue system provoked inevitable confrontations which in turn worked to frustrate hastily and belatedly conceived reforms. In other words, one cause of revolutionary breakdown was 'inherent in the nature of the old regime'.[10] The central feature in this standard interpretation is formed by the nobility's fiscal privilege, its exemption from taxation, and the twin consequences of this: the acute difficulty of sustaining the revenue state 'when taxation was not levied on the noble classes'[11] and the equally acute social divisiveness created by the privilege. Any attempt to widen this excessively narrow fiscal base would precipitate violent noble reaction – as Calonne's proposed tax revisions of 1786 are widely supposed to have done. On this reading, any growth-inducing characteristics learned by the *ancien régime* were entirely subordinated to its rigid limitations as a fiscal system.

But the reading is an oversimplification. The French nobility was never a uniform and integrated body, a single and identifiable recipient of fiscal privilege. Rather, it was disparate, disorganized, not a little harrassed, certainly not – in Bloch's definition of a social class – a group with comparable incomes and a common way of life. Revolutionary propaganda, particularly that of Abbé Sièyes, portraying the aristocracy as a distinct element, a foreign body within French society, made brilliant polemic but misleading social analysis. In reality, the highly varied constituents of the nobility reunite easily with the bulk of the French populace, making contact at many different levels of wealth. Once this is proposed, it becomes clear that the levels of wealth, and not the titles of nobility, exercised the critical leverage upon fiscal privilege. Exemption from the major taxes of *taille* and *gabelle* were enjoyed as widely by the third estate as by the nobility; the bourgeoisie were at least as likely to hold privileges as their social superiors and perhaps more likely. Similarly, large sections of the French nobility were not exempt from taxation; indeed they were taxed more heavily than their English colleagues. Miss Behrens in her authoritative revision of fiscal exemption concluded that, 'it seem[s] . . . . that the French noble landlords, besides being required on paper to pay a higher proportion of their incomes in tax than their English counterparts, actually often did so'.[12] It follows that the *ancien régime* was not disastrously attached to a fiscal class monopoly, a privileged hierarchy of noble rank. Also, that the tax base was wider (though not necessarily more efficiently exploited) than many have supposed. And, finally, it becomes likely that the discontented nobility of the 1780s were not simply resisting encroachments upon exemptions; they were resisting the genuine fiscal pressure of an increasingly impecunious exchequer.

It was not the 'inherent nature' of the *ancien régime* which attracted their hostility; it was rather the fiscal technology available to any state of the era. Only the very best eighteenth-century administrations could manage a graduated tax system, and then only just; Europe did not witness a general income tax before the days of Pitt and Addington. Certainly, no *pre-revolutionary* government could have contemplated, let alone levied, a graduated surtax.[13] Consequently, for the financial controllers of the late *ancien régime*, virtually the only alternative consisted of low flat-rate exactions – since any impost suitable for the very rich would have ruined the majority. Any improvement in revenue had to follow from limited upward pressure upon this rate or from multiplication of the levies. Unavoidably, either method still left a disproportionate amount of wealth with the very wealthy, but they were very far from equating with the nobility as a group. Any hostility generated by this system should have flowed towards, and if undirected, might have flowed towards, not the entire noble caste, but a very particular aristocratic minority, *les grands*, the high nobility, a caucus of great wealth which *did* stand apart, not only because of birth or power, but because of anomalies in the tax system of the day. The complaint of the noble majority, thus related not so much to the intrinsic antiquarianism of the old regime as to the incidence of the fiscal burden and the inequity of the fiscal system. That is, to the state of the available fiscal art.

In relation to the largest concentrations of wealth, therefore, the *ancien régime* displayed less an overdevelopment than an underfulfilment of its taxation powers. Nor was this the only case. The entire notion of French fiscal absolutism has been drawn into question by recent research; much proves to be amiss with the conventional portrayal of a voracious exchequer screwing up the financial rack with each successive and unsuccessful war until the tolerance of the populace eventually snapped. In fact the burden of taxation in proportion to resources turns out to have been *lighter* in France than in Britain and not to have increased over the century. Mathias and O'Brien calculate (see Table 3.1) that the share of income per head collected as taxes commenced at similar levels in 1730 but then sagged in France while the British share moved smartly in the opposite direction.[14] Further, it is likely that the French taxes, both direct and indirect, were less regressive (that is, secured smaller proportions of their yield from the lower income bands) than their British counterparts. French administrators tried, within the limits of their art, to lighten the tax yoke on the poor, and, in reality, those groups seem to have given up rather small shares of income to the taxman.[15] Quantitative measurement suggests that it was nothing so simple as the runaway career of a bureaucratic revenue state which produced political breakdown. In fact the *ancien régime* may well have taxed too little, rather than too much, for its own good.

There is evidence that the system made efforts to modernize its more inequitable tax practices in its last years.[16] It was the limits of the art which proved the obstacle. Though no government of the 1770s or 1780s could have readily introduced a graduated tax, France had special need of one. But France also faced exceptional obstacles in administration as a result of inherited institutions and practices. Given the low order of the available technology, the officials could do little against the high fences of inheritance. In England, the land tax fell equally on all relevant social groups. In France, traditional practice dubiously exempted some – many more than a noble few – and mysteriously taxed others. And the relevant social groups included not the landed parties of substance but the massed ranks of a land-owning peasantry. Thanks to the hallowed institutions of peasantry and exemption, the major direct taxes, however reasonable their level, were both widely experienced and highly inconsistent. By tradition, too, indirect taxes fluctuated in incidence between town and country, region and region; they were collected not, as in England, by a centrally administered professional bureaucracy but by a network of licensed tax farmers, that is, by applied corruption. Again, inscrutable variety and the ever-present face of malfeasance created legitimate grievances in themselves. Certainly, the mass of the population could find solid cause for fiscal complaint – classically expressed in the *cahiers de doléances* – without exercising their passions over tax levels; they could extract sufficient justified resentment from the privileges of exemption, by whomsoever they were held, or from the infinite vagaries of assessment. Such arguments form the background to the conclusion of Mathias and O'Brien that, 'the political consequences of taxation in France must be judged principally according to the political and administrative hostilities aroused by taxation, not so much by the economic burden they imposed upon the economy'.[17] And of course, there is some defence for the old regime in this. For 'the political and administrative hostilities' compose the subjects of lesser charges than the reactionary and oppressive rapacity traditionally attributed to the system. And it is not easy to see how they could have been evaded. The endlessly ravelled skein of fiscal privileges, collectors' concessions, and provincial eccentricities could not have been unravelled with the means then available. The simplifying strokes of financial innovation had scarcely been conceived in the most advanced administrations of the day, let alone in the labyrinths of an increasingly enmeshed French bureaucracy.

What seems to be emerging is that it was less the size of the aggregate fiscal burden than its *distribution* which most clearly relates to the ensuing political upheavals. The general distaste for the unpredictability and opacity of the prevailing taxation system did not rule out protests against high levels of exaction falling upon *some* groups. And where all these complaints existed in combination, reaction was likely to be most swift and most severe. According to recent revisions, the lower social groups were not especially heavily penalized and the highest in the land largely slipped the net. It was the interim income bands which carried the most fiscal strain, especially the bands of non-exempt noble (and, possibly, non-exempt bourgeois) wealth. Here, grievances were concentrated upon the amounts as well as the style of taxation. Despite their lower assessment of the total fiscal impact on the French community, Mathias and O'Brien conclude significantly that 'direct taxes in France bore more heavily upon wealth and incomes of the more affluent classes than comparable taxes in Britain'.[18] Even within the context of a reasonably moderate aggregate tax burden and a fiscal strategy far from punitively regressive, the noble revolt on taxation remains an intelligible response. And it was provoked not by the taxative gluttony of an insensitive autocracy but by the imprecision of the available fiscal instruments.

If the nobility became politically engaged over taxation, their intention was certainly not to spearhead an insurrection. Nor could they see the rebellious peasantry, the urban *sans-culottes*, or the bourgeois lawyers of the Assembly as

120

Table 3.1   Taxation burden as proportion *per capita* output: France and Britain

	Britain, *share of* per capita output taken in tax	France, *share of* per capita output taken in tax
1730	16	15
1750	18	12
1780	21	12
1790	24	12

Source: Mathias and O'Brien (1976).

in any way acceptable political colleagues. Their role was merely to provide an initial occasion, and, in the summoning of the Estates-General, an opportunity for dispute over constitutional procedures and rights, a platform for the hostile demands of the *tiers état.* Insurrection was to come from elsewhere, from the peasantry and the urban mob. And guidance, officer material for this rank-and-file, was to come from elsewhere again, from the bourgeoisie of the 'democratic revolution'. So, once the occasion was contrived, what were the economic stimuli which galvanized the ranks and summoned the commanders?

For the mass of activists in town and country the economic problem was of the simplest kind: extravagantly rising prices. In the agricultural sector, the inflationary pressures drove landlords to seek increased returns from the leases by which the majority of noble land was exploited. But since the peasant cultivators who held the tenancies and paid the quit-rents had acquired the protection of custom for these transactions, the landlords required additional devices which would permit them to cash in upon the upsurge in agricultural prices. They found the solution in the traditional feudal dues such as *banalités*. Previously declining into atrophy, these were now revived and energetically exploited by a non-cultivating aristocracy which had perceived its seigneurial status to be a negotiable financial asset. Consequently, the eighteenth century witnessed a forceful promotion of outmoded feudal rights, assisted by nice judgments on issues of tenure from the aristocratic cousinhood of the *noblesse de la robe.* As peasant rights were sapped, the agricultural community found its standard of rebellion in the demand for the *abolition* of feudal rights (eventually completed in February 1794). When the harvest failures of the late 1780s placed the peasantry in a scissors composed of declining receipts and escalating feudal revivals, the standard found an army of bearers.

What is important here is that the feudal nature of *ancien régime* agriculture was not in itself the cause of peasant discontent. The feudal aspect of the system was modifying gradually in the early part of the century, and, under equilibrium conditions, would have continued to modify. A 'rigid' old regime characteristic had already proved itself capable of flexibility. The trigger for agricultural unrest was the nobility's *reversal* of this process of autonomous change. And even this did not stem from seigneurial revivalism but from a wholly commercial desire to tap the wealth generated by a developed market economy in grain. It was a choice of financial tactics made for predominantly non-feudal reasons. Other choices were available. The pre-revolutionary peasantry did not object to property rights or to reasonable rents, rather to the 'mysterious' origins of the resurrected dues. Substitution of commutation and commercial rents for these fiscal antiques would have delivered cash to land-lords and worked to avert peasant unrest.[19] Further adjustments to the already diffuse tax exemptions would have appealed to the larger peasants, eroded agricultural solidarity, and perhaps rallied the *bourgeoisie rurale* to the side of the authorities. Without a *uniform* reaction from the peasantry, successful re-volution in eighteenth-century France would have been impractical. And with the landless agricultural population growing faster than the peasant pro-prietors after 1750, the prospects for splitting the rural echelons were real enough. Such manœuvres were not impossible within the final reformist phase of the *ancien régime*. Perhaps the state's fundamental failure lay in omitting to curb the tactical choices of its nobility. Since opposition would flow from this quarter in any event, there could have been considerable gains in currying a measure of peasant favour.

But, ironically, the state's attempts at modernization elsewhere in agricul-ture inflamed rather than mollified rural tempers. For these did not react only to price movements. If the peasantry were outraged by the nobility's man-ipulation of feudal rights, they were deeply attached to another variety of feudal right: their own, the common rights of gleaning, lumbering, and graz-ing. Many peasants depended for survival on these *droits collectifs*, especially peasants with no land of their own – which was the case, on the eve of the revolution, for 75 per cent of family heads on the Flanders coast, 70 per cent in some villages around Versailles, and 30–40 per cent in Lower Normandy.[20] The *ancien régime* bid for agrarian reform – edicts to permit enclosure and encourage the consolidation of holdings, land clearance, and drainage – opposed a defeudalizing intention to the peasantry's breadline antiquarian-ism. Significantly, the peasantry exploited the disturbed conditions of the first revolutionary months to *dismantle* the monarchy's reforms, destroying enclo-sures, restoring common land, and invading forests. Despite this, Lefebvre was of the opinion that 'the policy of the old regime was not badly conceived,'[21] and might have succeeded in its reforms had it emphasized com-mutation and demonstrated that its interest in agricultural change was not to generate more bounty for the aristocracy. Once again, the failure occurs at the level of implementation rather than that of concept.

For the townsmen, the problem, as Labrousse classically argued it, was the dearness of bread.[22] This exactly reflected the agricultural crisis. Indeed, since many peasants were forced to sell their entire crop to meet the claims of landowners and tax-collectors, it was the same crisis. Rural consumers were by no means immunized against high food prices and only large farmers, estate owners, and *seigneurs* rejoiced at the price trend. Yet, naturally enough, it was the towns which bore the brunt of bread famine. It was not that they were unaccustomed to it: over the period 1726–91 the French wage-earner had disbursed an average 50 per cent of his income on bread and in the starvation years 1740, 1749, 1768, and 1775 had, not unnaturally, loaned his share of violence to the accompanying food riots.[23] Acute shortage was no stranger to eighteenth-century France, but that of the late 1780s was unusual for severity and duration. Consequently, the curve of bread prices converts readily into an index of the metropolitan uprising. As the price of a 2-kilogram loaf rose from nine sous in August 1788 to 14½ sous between February and July 1789, the share of the wage-earner's income consigned to bread climbed to 88 per cent, and at its absolute zenith, to a staggering 97 per cent for some urban groups.

Protest accumulated as the price ascent continued, and with almost excessive neatness the Bastille contrived to fall on the day bread prices peaked (14 July 1789). While it lay under siege, the mob was busy prizing hoarded grain out of religious houses and burning the customs posts which had slowed the essential daily flow of wine to a niggardly trickle. To look far beyond the price of food for explanations of the actions of the *menu peuple* is to risk excessive elaboration. For many important outbreaks of violence can be connected with precision to the food issue. In the Réveillon riots of April 1789 the mob broke into food shops but no others. The Women's March from Versailles in October 1789 developed out of a bread riot at the town hall. Even the overthrow of the monarchy and the execution of the King in August 1792 had as prelude food riots of classic type. Clearly, the political sophistication of the *menu peuple* increased with revolutionary experience, but there is little doubt that food prices detonated the early explosions in the towns (as well as many in the countryside) and remained a dangerously delicate trigger mechanism into the 1790s. If feudal rights most incensed the peasantry and drove them into the first successful agrarian revolt of the modern era, the episodes of the urban revolution were closely geared to the cost of living. Pressures behind this inflation were manifold. Partly, they flowed out of the free market in grain, another *modernizing* contribution from the monarchy. Partly, they were generated by the nobility's leverage upon rural costs. But it was not from any special feature of the *ancien régime* system that the disturbance derived.

But if food riots were a commonplace of eighteenth-century crises, they were obviously powerless to evoke revolutionary responses unaided. No isolated movement of peasants or urban artisans, however famished, would suffice. In the earlier outbreaks of the 1740s, 1760s, and 1770s, such movements had been contained because the bourgeoisie had remained committed to the establishment, the army faithful to the monarchy, and the aristocracy indifferent to any interests but their own. But by the late 1780s few of the earlier loyalties endured and the market in protest had widened decisively. Noble interest now pointed to agitation. And, more important, bourgeois commitment had been soured by economic grievances fit to stand with the fiscal, feudal, and farinaceous complaints exercising other sections of the community. It was the flanking bombardment from the more elevated interest groups which gave the food riots of the 1780s their special potency. And most of all, it was the bourgeoisie who provided, in the defection of the intellectuals, the radicalization of the professional groups, and the desertion of the army, the major obstacles to the maintenance of governmental control.

When doctors, teachers, civil servants, and, above all, lawyers – the membership of the Robespierrist *corps d'élite* — discovered axes needful of grinding

123

against the old regime, its capacity for retaliation was extensively damaged and the revolution was equipped with a convincing leadership. 'Revolutionary republicanism', as Professor Palmer correctly observes, 'was above all a movement of the middle ranks of society.'[24] Their propaganda play with aristocratic plots, implicating the many in the privileges of the few, was innovational and their manipulation of the *menu peuple* proved invincible. Clearly, however, they were not such as to agonize over dear bread; their economic interest settled on matters of greater substance. Infringements upon the liberty to trade – state-conferred monopolies, guild restrictions, curbs upon capital investment, and, perhaps especially, upon the supply of credit – form the classical frustrations for an aspiring middle class. And this middle class was aspiring. The economic growth of the pre-revolutionary period had created new elements of commercial wealth, shifts in the distribution of property which would in time require shifts in the distribution of power. It was again the economic downturn of the 1780s – convincing the bourgeoisie that their gains were under threat and their future prospects imperilled by the remaining restrictions of the old regime – which provided a critical moment in the fortunes of a volatile group. If such interests desired constitutional change, it was at least partly in order to set the market to rights. But, once more, the bourgeoisie were pursuing exactly those economic features of the regime which the state had commenced to reform. It was simply that the structure did not modify itself sufficiently rapidly or sufficiently extensively for their tastes. Moreover, violent political protest commonly erupts when the system which is the butt of agitation embarks upon a self-directed relaxation of discipline. Concessions merely encourage further demands, now presented from a position of greater security, for more radical surrender. In so far as the *ancien régime* was responsible for the eruption, it was more in its reformist than in its reactionary aspect.

Economic contributions to the revolutionary causation are thus substantial. Demands for lower taxation, fewer dues, cheaper bread, and freer enterprise provided strands from many social layers which could weave together to entrap the failing authority of the monarchy. And the economic crisis of the 1780s provided a hook upon which these strands might simultaneously catch, strangling the captive. No doubt, economic grievances frequently acted only as catalysts for the expression of deep-running political dissatisfaction. Similarly, it would be idle to pretend that political elements were not autonomously explosive: slogans execrating moderates and royalists, others proclaiming the *sans-culottes* to be 'brothers and liberators' of villager and townsmen alike were increasingly current by 1792, for instance. But the economic materials provide at least *one* explanation of events, its coherence too considerable to be easily discounted, and a segment of any comprehensive explanation which it would be difficult to decry.

However, these materials were not simply supplied by the *ancien régime* administration, by way of a characteristically fossilized *dirigisme*. Its last reformist servants were not entirely unskilled in the design of more efficient taxation, more productive cultivation, or less constricted markets. Unfortunately, however, this official innovation was as apt to provoke antagonism as official reaction. Yet it at least serves to make the point that economic grievances stemmed from no 'intrinsic' peculiarity of the *ancien régime* state. Rather, some complaints were expressed in attempts to *evade* modernizing impulses from the government. Others were triggered by the low speed, not by the absence, of these impulses. Others again followed from processes entirely outside the control of any eighteenth-century regime: thus price inflation was geared to a demographic upsurge which was as old as the century itself.[25] But, clearly, the late French edition of the *ancien régime* was not in itself incompatible with economic progress. The revolution, therefore, so far retains the appearance of a 'catastrophe' falling upon a government which had attempted economic amelioration and which cannot be damned with the simple accusation that it provoked dislocation by an impenitent obscurantism in matters of commerce, industry, and finance.

REVOLUTION AND ECONOMICS II: CATALYST OR CATASTROPHE?

For an event of seemingly calamitous proportions, this economic débâcle evokes strangely little agreement among historians. Some, indeed, contest its existence. Obviously enough, in perpetrating vicious civil strife, the importunate dictatorship of a military upstart, and close to a quarter-century of excessively costly campaigning, the revolutionary processes must have imposed some strains upon the French economy, and are generally conceded to have done so. But to the historical optimist there were equally clear, and more considerable, compensations. Most of these were institutional in form. There was the shining logical clarity of the newly introduced metric system. There was the eradication (though it had been commenced by *ancien régime* progressives like Turgot) of the internal tolls and tariffs which had distorted the domestic market. Similarly, French local government was extensively rationalized. And, above all, so was French law – in the massive systematization of the *Code Napoléon*. If Frenchmen were to fight for the Empire, they were also to be provided with equitable and efficient structures of justice and administration, often seen by economic analysts as providing favourable terrain for the operations of an enterprising business community. In place of overburdensome regulations and unpredictable exactions, Bonaparte and his lawyers resolved to design a society of rational freedoms, of order, and stability, permitting an appropriate return to the actions of every citizen.

Much has been made of such arguments. Professor Palmer has so exploited them as to make the revolution a watershed in the economic, as well as the political, life of France. This emphasis betrays the special interest of the historian of the democratic revolution: if the revolution is to demonstrate its bourgeois character, it should also display economic growth with which this character is well known to be associated. Perhaps it is not surprising, therefore, that few intimations of catastrophe penetrate this hypothesis. Instead, the revolution is made to anticipate Napoleonic rationalization and 'mow down the dense growth of feudal, manorial, patrician and burgher influences,'[26] the sources of local power that were the obstacles to economic change. The guild was one such source of restrictive influence. The revolution – in the great reformist jamboree of 4 August 1789 and over the subsequent months to the decree of Allarde in March 1791 – provided the 'commercial and industrial equivalent of the abolition of feudal rights'[27] and eradicated the guild. In consequence, the field of enterprise was widened (to guildsmen and non-guildsmen equally) and innovation released from the disapproving restraint of traditional craft practice. Similarly, as provincial tariffs and tolls yielded to the centralizing revolutionaries, new national and international markets outside the guild's parochial span became available to French manufacturers. The natural framework for such reforms was one of economic individualism, duly proclaimed by the law of Le Chapelier of 14 June 1791, and reinforced by a complete ban on all forms of economic coalition, whether of labour or capital.

Not only historical optimists but also impressionable contemporaries placed a high value upon this legislation. International industrial exhibitions were convened in Paris in 1798, 1801, 1802, and 1806 in celebration of the economic prospects newly opened to the republic. The gathering of 1798 was told by the Minister of the Interior that French industrialists would demonstrate the superiority of free peoples in free economies; a liberated genius would sweep European markets. And to encourage it further, medals, prizes; and loans were awarded to promising manufacturers as proof that a new order for the public encouragement of the 'practical arts' had arrived. The class of '98, it seems, was headed by a new type of print face and an improved lead pencil. Concluded Palmer, 'A better symbol of a middle class and enlightened world it would be hard to find.'[28]

But, in the ensuing period, Bonaparte attempted to provide better symbols. And these were innovations somewhat larger than lead pencils. With the advent of the Empire, men of essentially practical bent and modernizing ambition came to the fore; spared the frantic pressures of recent years, or, as Palmer puts it, 'freed both from popular demands and from old-noble pretensions, relieved of the fear of both revolution and reaction and protected by armed force',[29] this group settled to the hard graft of codification and the final liquidation, by considered enactment rather than by spontaneous revolutionary zeal, of the last vestiges of the old monarchist order. Bonaparte, Hegel's 'World-Soul on horse back', was pre-eminently a rationalizer, a systematizer, and he had the support of the more solid bourgeois elements most interested in tidying up the revolutionary inheritance. With Napoleon the emphasis of reform moved from rights to efficiency, from principle to practice. Where the revolutionary regimes had slashed at the labyrinthine tangle of old regime laws, feudal custom, and royal decrees, creating light and air but little order, Napoleon sculpted the remains into a disciplined structure. Between 1804 and 1810, in the five great Napoleonic codes,[30] the imperial administrators created the necessary synthesis between the sweeping legal changes of the revolutionary period and the gathering reaction to swingeing reform, plaited together elements from both the old regime and the new society, mixed a blend of authority and equality. Much was borrowed: equal inheritance, already a peasant custom, was converted into an institution; the abolition of slavery introduced in the revolutionary era was given the force of fundamental assumption; the liberalizing thrust of revolutionary legal principle was extended into a comprehensive overhaul of established practice, both civil and criminal. The central principles which emerged were: the equality of citizens before the law, the secularity of the state, the freedom of conscience, the opening of careers to talent and of occupation to free selection. Rights were preserved but given a utilitarian edge. Equal inheritance had the utility that it prevented the recovery of territorial accumulations of power. Freedom of occupation effectively ruled out, on grounds of principle, the restrictions of the traditional guilds. The complete edifice was, at the same time, an extrapolation of the revolutionary measures and a conservative, essentially functional, interpretation of their intent.

Similar characteristics appear in Bonaparte's work as an educational reformer. Here again, he emerges as systems builder and pragmatist. Where the revolutionary legislators had been concerned with mass education, Napoleon gave to the training of Frenchmen a characteristically élitist, utilitarian, and, not least, military, cast; the purpose of his education is to provide a preparation for service to the state and his pupils are intended to be doctors, bureaucrats, and officers. While the Convention had lavished attention on the primary schools, the *écoles communales* , the Empire characteristically abandoned such lowly institutions to the municipalities. The public secondary schools received a little more attention, earning a full reorganization in 1802 and a remit to the Director of Public Instruction. But Bonaparte's most characteristic innovation in this sphere was the *lycée*, a selective secondary school professedly designed to train up a leadership cadre from the sons of officers and civil servants and the cream of the ordinary secondary school pupils. By 1813, the *lycées* were providing probably the most advanced secondary education in Europe and could already boast of some 6000 acceptances by the French universities. In technical education Napoleon was again busy, and in very much the same pattern. His pronouncements of 1803 concerning the *écoles d'arts et métiers* – later to become, in curriculum if not perhaps in output, the most economically relevant of French educational institutions[31] – allocated to them an entirely industrial function but restricted them roundly to training 'les *sous*- officiers de l'industrie'. The grander foundations of the revolutionary period, the Ecole Polytechnique and the Ecole des Mines, the first and foremost of the *grandes écoles*, newly endowed with their strict discipline, their military finery, and their catholic intellectual range, were briefed to pursue the preparation of the élite in appropriately Bonapartist style. Here, apparently, lay the best hope of a task-force sufficiently talented to supervise not only the administration of a rationalized state but also of a rationalized economy.

In the legal and social provisions of both revolutionary innovators and imperial codifiers much of relevance for future industrialization has been detected. The enthusiasts for such causes have most usually been either contemporary propagandists, or, more recently, the designers of wide historical panoramas. In either case there is an evident interest in coupling together political change with economic development, in deducing the incidence of the latter from the extent of the former. But it now seems that even the sober chronicles of the economic historians have fallen prey to very similar temptations. Thus Milward and Saul have contended that the French Revolution, by weakening the ability of traditional agriculture to function efficiently, 'increased receptivity to the economic and social changes associated with industrialization'.[32] Although admitting the small growth in the economy's total output over the revolutionary period, and the relatively modest rate of technological change, they still find sufficient evidence of manufacturing advance – mainly in the mechanization of cotton-spinning in Normandy, Alsace, Picardy, and Paris and in the spread of large-scale factories through the woollen industry of Sedan, Louviers, Elbeuf, and Paris – to place the French industrial revolution 'unhesitatingly' in the period of political transformation between 1770 and 1815. The primary justification for this opinion is that these industrial changes, though 'less dramatic' than their British counterparts, 'constituted a development which had as yet affected no other country on the mainland'.[33]

Undervaluation of the old regime's economic vitality and a corresponding inflation of the innovational activity generated by the revolutionary and imperial administrations are features common to these interpretations. But their peculiarities are more extensive than this. The fault in the Palmer hypothesis, and shared by its Bonapartist cousins, is fairly clear: each one describes a package containing varied administrative and judicial reforms and advances to the proposal that these adjustments held the power to induce economic change.[34] Probably, it is more correct to view institutional equipment of this kind as in itself *neutral*. For although it may create opportunities, it cannot guarantee that they will be exploited. In reality, the economic utility of any given set of institutional provisions will be determined by such variables as a country's factor endowment, a community's system of social values, or the current state of the technological art. The application of a *standard* set to countries differing in these respects – and all countries will differ in some of these respects – would be most unlikely to secure uniform economic consequences. It is particularly striking that the French set gathered a more copious industrial harvest *outside* France, especially in the nearby Rhineland, than in its country of origin. Similarly, it is entirely possible for the output of formidable educational establishments to be reduced, or even nullified, in economic effect by adverse social preferences. These may influence the diversion of highly trained personnel from industrial employment to more prestigious occupations. Precisely such a preference was frequently alleged against the graduates of the *grandes écoles* in the nineteenth century. Again, some forms of high-quality educational preparation may prove more useful to industry at later, rather than earlier, stages of modern economic growth. This, too, was probably true of the rigorous theoretical training provided by the greatest French schools; in all probability it came into its own in the *late* nineteenth and twentieth centuries. Perversely, however, the type of training relevant at lower levels of technological performance may well fail to earn sufficient social approval or official support at the appropriate *time*, and, consequently, will not deliver its full potential in economic impact. This was probably true of the courses offered by the *écoles d'arts arts et métiers* for much of the last century; their graduates, despite the excellent vocational instruction, rarely managed to penetrate beyond the rank of works manager. At best, institutional reforms create economic possibilities; the conjoining of other forces is needed even to convert them into probabilities.

The problem raised by the economic historians, in their conflation of the political and industrial transformations, is even more complex. With Milward and Saul, it centres upon a highly specialized definition of the term 'industrial revolution,' coupled with a tendency — virtually a tradition in French economic history — to emphasize technologically new departures and to pass over the persistent retention of the technologically antique. In fact, the older industrial methodologies *strengthened* their hold upon the French economy until at least 1850. Nor is it immediately obvious why the arrival in France of economic developments so far unknown upon the European mainland should by definition constitute an 'industrial revolution'. A humbler definition – simple technological diffusion, for example – may readily be imagined. And, going further, a definitely pessimistic assessment of economic progress during the revolutionary and imperial eras may provide a more compelling representation of reality than the various attempts to 'industrialize' political change. The elements of such a valuation are easily sketched.

THE TRADE PROBLEM: CONTINENTAL SYSTEM OR DE-INDUSTRIALIZATION?

Perhaps the most significant novelty of these years was an extensive adjustment in the structure of French markets, the effect of which, though much debated, was almost certainly adverse. In the Continental System, Napoleon devised, and in 1806 completed, a structure of protection which was to extend all earlier experimentation with tariffs into an attempt to reserve the entire European market for French manufacturers. Equipped with a dependable reserve of demand, sufficiently large to rival Britain's tentacular commerce, French industry was intended to confront and outface the hostile industrial power. Economic warfare would be directed against Britain in the form most suited to French resources, opposing a continental to a maritime capability, and, at the same time, compensation would be achieved for colonial trade already lost to the British tentacles. As bonus, there was the opportunity to secure French industrial primacy not only against the British but also against promising, if smaller, continental rivals — notably those already active in the Rhineland. Since cotton textiles formed the natural route towards industrialization for European countries, a device which locked out the lethal partnership of John Bull and King Cotton would permit the continent its first experience of modern large-scale production, encourage the accumulation of labour skills, and stimulate the growth of essential machine-building industries. Furthermore, the System would serve as an instrument of exportation for French economic and legal rationalism. The *Code Napoléon* would provide a cohesive socio-legal structure for member states, and rules for the administration and promotion of manufacture would bring the benefits of the free economy to the areas subjected by the imperial armies.

For French industrialists the chief reality certainly turned out to be an innovative and decisive swing away from the long-distance commerce which had been an eighteenth-century staple – the single possession of Santo Domingo had absorbed three-quarters of all colonial trade in 1780 – towards an unfamiliar preoccupation with Europe. As the Royal Navy systematically decimated the French merchant marine from 1793, and neutral traders – primarily Americans – mopped up markets left vacant by French adventurers, overseas commerce progressively diminished, and, in the early 1800s, virtually ceased. Replacements were vitally needed and the innovation of 1806 did not come before time.

But how effective was it? Milward and Saul propose that even by 1801 the loss of extra-European markets had been overcome by the development of the domestic market and of other European markets, a process which the Continental System continued and extended.[35] Probably, this overrates the European prospects open to the French and the security offered by the system. In fact, French external trade did not recover to the levels of 1789 – when it had been close to the British – until 1825; and by this time the British had moved on to achieve exports some 50–60 per cent greater than the French.[36] And the damage was long-term; even in 1880 French exports equalled only 78 per cent of the German by value and 38 per cent of the British.[37] The magnitude of the loss and the forces retarding trade recovery were both very substantial. Maritime commerce in 1789 had constituted the most dynamic sector of the French economy with a volume quadruple that of 1715 and a value exceeding 1000 m. francs; replacement at this level was beyond the capability of the Continental System. Moreover, the excision of colonial trade did irreparable regional damage which no amount of continental expansion could conceal. Great ports like Nantes, Bordeaux, and, especially, Marseilles depended on their connexions with the Middle East, the Barbary Coast, and particularly, through the 'island trade' with the West Indies, Réunion, Mauritius and the settlements in Senegal and India. Manufacturing centres like Grenoble with important drapery and linen trades relied almost entirely upon colonial outlets (in this case Santo Domingo once more).[38] Yet the British response to the Continental System was a naval blockade which successfully interdicted the entire 'Atlantic' sector of French commerce and brought the demotion of centres like Marseilles and Bordeaux from the status of international entrepôts to that of provincial harbours. Population in these 'Atlantic' regions declined; their economic hinterlands contracted as markets disappeared: colonial raw materials for their processing industries, contracts for their shipyards quickly dried up. An enduring *de-industrialization* was the outcome for the southwestern areas and for much of the French seaboard.[39] Promotional industrial effects, the benefits of the new European options, were not spread evenly over the French economy and were, most significantly, entirely denied to what in 1789 had been its healthiest leading sector. That role had to be taken up under conditions of wartime inflation and disruption by the inland centres of the north and east – particularly the Lille–Tourcoing–Roubaix complex and the Alsatian towns – to which the new economic order did offer opportunities. The Continental System thus required a besieged and embattled economy not only to bear the costs of war but to execute simultaneously a painful structural shift, moving the concentration of industrial activity from the coast towards the centre, strongly northwards and eastwards.

While this was progressing, the boycott mechanism did not provide the measure of protection to which it was pledged. Not even the chances of in- dustrial primacy within continental Europe were securely grasped, since by no means all rivals were treated to the discriminatory tactics deployed against the more effective Rhinelanders, particularly against the industrialists of Berg. The inclusion within the tariff structure of Belgium and the Rhine's left bank gave access to a market of 30 m. consumers for manufacturers who could rival those of metropolitan France. Similarly, the textile industries of Saxony and Switzerland were probably conserved by the System, whereas otherwise they might have succumbed to the British onslaught. In this sense France was clutching a nest of industrial vipers to her bosom. More dangerous still was the failure to contain British dynamism: the activity of the British cotton industry was most pronounced *during* the life of the System and its exports after 1806 exceeded the levels even of the recent peacetime year, 1802. Large- scale smuggling and complicated financial transactions brought the fruits of this highly durable prosperity through the tariff wall and deposited them in the centre of the French market-place. And whenever the walls collapsed, as periodically they did, a mountain of British products was ready to slide into Europe. But the final and most vivid demonstration of the System's ineffective protectionism came as, with military defeat, the boycott structure crumbled utterly. At this point a British industrial juggernaut, apparently undented by years of French economic warfare, was able immediately to re-enter the Euro- pean market, crushing many manufacturers into bankruptcy and collapse. Undercutting the Europeans in price, and provided by maritime power with a virtual monopoly of colonial and American trade, the British achieved an ex- port pre-eminence which, for the French, was as good as impregnable. The modern sector of French industry, in the chilly period after the Vienna settle- ment, was revealed as a weakly growth dependent upon the variable and arti- ficial economic climate conjured up by Bonaparte. And, as in military mat- ters, climate control proved in the long run to be beyond the imperial grasp.

As an exercise in the adjustment of markets the Continental System was only partially successful. It could perhaps be argued that the destruction creat- ed by this adjustment fell upon economic sectors that were anyway bound for decline, thus clearing the ground of archaic elements and opening a path for more constructive developments. But, at best, this converts the period 1770–1815 into one of transition for the French economy. There are always costs within major structural transitions, and, in this case, the embarrassment of the Atlantic sector provides them. An 'industrial revolution' which contains such an unusually rapid contraction of a proto-industrial leading sector might be thought unusual. So, too, might one characterized by the economic instability which the Continental System carried as hallmark: the erratic price movements, the bouts of feverish overspeculation, and the periodic fierce slumps – like the savage recession of 1811–12. And, as an exercise in economic warfare, it was pitifully weak. Crouzet concludes that, far from sapping the power of British factories, the System acted to confirm their superiority and to accentuate French deficiencies. While British industrialists shrugged off the continental sling-shots, they were able to enlist a maritime weapon of devastating retaliatory force. This, by 1815, had rampaged so effectively that the de-industrialization which had earlier affected the 'Atlantic' sector now loomed over large tracts of the European economy, and, for France, was only narrowly averted in the years of the restoration.[40] The threat of de-industrialization is clearly some distance removed from the thesis of 'industrial revolution'.

THE TECHNOLOGICAL PROBLEM: THE SEIZED TRANSMISSION EFFECT

War strengthened British industrial supremacy. But it also denied France her share in the fruits of this development. If early European industrialization had depended upon the diffusion of British 'best practice' technology, European warfare easily disrupted this relationship, shattering the fragile international connexions. For these were, in reality, highly personalized: in the 1770s the introduction of the spinning-jenny to France had depended upon the Lancashireman John Holker; in the 1780s the Arkwright water-frame arrived in the baggage of the Mancunian James Milne; while discreet pilgrimages in the opposite direction – to Germany in 1756, to England in 1764, and to Sweden in 1766 – allowed Gabriel Jars to fetch back the coke-smelting process and Jacques Périer to secure the rights to Watt-style steam-engines for his Chaillot works in the 1780s.[41] Such transactions did not survive in beleaguered Europe, and without this replenishment, French technology dropped behind the British, finishing the war some two decades in arrears. Even the 'modern sector' of French textiles employed equipment in 1815 which the British had abandoned in the 1780s and 1790s; and much of this was powered by water or horse, rarely by steam.[42] Over the entire economy, only sixty-five factories employed steam-power by 1820.[43] Not even the wartime pressures for more efficient armament could produce any compensating technological impulsion, as they did in Britain.[44] Where British ironmasters improved the design of artillery and developed advanced methods of cannon-boring – later 'spun-off' to provide accurate cylinders for steam-engines – the technology of the French armouries at Cosne, Tulle, and Maubeuge was scarcely affected by war.[45] Experiments with the British cannon-lathe at the Indret gun foundry failed for lack of high-quality iron supplies. The industrial sophistication of Napoleonic France was thus insufficient to permit the operation of a 'spin-off' effect between military and civilian industries, while Napoleonic campaigns were sufficient to damage the most productive peacetime device for improving technological practice.

THE AGRICULTURAL LEGACY: A FROZEN COUNTRYSIDE

Strangely, as Gerschenkron has pointed out,[46] historians of optimistic persuasion and institutional preoccupation seldom focus upon the revolution's agricultural settlement. Or perhaps it is not strange. For, exactly as reactionary regimes like the Prussian were designing highly efficient agricultural systems, enlightened French administrations were creating a style of cultivation that was to burden the economy throughout its nineteenth-century career. The conventional view is that the revolution, by assuring the existence of the small farm and protecting peasant property rights, worked to perpetuate and solidify a highly traditional agragrian structure.[47] The revolutionary countryside, peopled by free peasant cultivators owning their own plots, and by large groups of landless labourers, was 'fixed' in this shape for a century and more. Against the vast teneurial reforms applied to the serf, or quasi-serf, systems of Europe's more backward economies, clear inferiors to the France of 1789, this was a puny outcome. Why? In the traditional interpretation, the landless peasantry hold the solution; after violent resistance to the old regime's curtailment of feudal rights, they required and received gentle treatment from revolutionary governments, pledged to free trade and the abolition of feudal rights though they might be. It was too late to accept the destitution of the lesser peasantry as an unavoidable implication of agricultural reform, and politically impossible for the new republic to do so. Instead, governments preferred to divide large swathes of land – such as annexed noble or clerical estates – into small peasant plots. Partly, the aim was to swell the ranks of those whose interests were vested in the revolution, partly to orchestrate the peasantry's inevitable decline with an acceptably slow tempo. An uneconomic system of small farms, sprinkled with some retained feudal peculiarities, was the result. Strip farming and open fields persisted and enclosure proceeded with utmost slowness. When it did occur, it was said in Haut-Saône in 1813, to require 'an armed guard on every furrow', and in some regions, common pasture rights survived into the 1930s.[48]

Much of this interpretation is correct. Attempts at defeudalization enjoyed limited success and the peasant micro-plot proceeded in characteristic manner. Innovation, in the shape of reductions in fallow or improved crop rotation, rarely touched it. Consolidation of holdings lay beyond the financial means generated by scattered parcels of land. Average plot size remained sufficiently tiny to guarantee poor productivity performance. And the multiplication of such holdings all over France made millions dependent upon a handkerchief of soil, thus inhibiting the mobility of labour and capital. Yet it was a modernizing revolution – assisted by a system of equal inheritance promoting further fragmentation or *morcellement* – which had secured the micro-plot as an institution of the French countryside.

However, even before such views crystallized as orthodoxy, significant reservations were impressed upon them by the pioneering work of Georges Lefebvre. The revolutionary mythology that the small man came off best, or Mathiez's conviction that the lesser peasantry were converted by the revolution into independent cultivators, had been flavoured with idealism rather than established with evidence. And the peasantry themselves, unable to compel the regime towards large-scale redistribution of land and violently expressing their frustration in 1791 and 1793, provided additional grounds for suspicion. Closer examination of revolutionary land transactions in the Département du Nord revealed that the peasantry had gained twice as much acreage as any other group, but also that the flow was biased towards those who *already* held land: some 13,000 hectares were redistributed to 35,000 individuals, 30,000 of them peasants but only one-third of those *landless* peasants.[49] As appraisal and auction prices were below market values – two-thirds below in Flanders, five-sixths in Cambrésis – and as the paper currency depreciated over the long payment periods favoured by peasant buyers, the moderate cultivators were able to strike a surprisingly attractive bargain with the revolutionary régime. Lefebvre's conclusion was that the main beneficiaries of the agricultural programme were not the micro-cultivators elevated from the landless peasantry, but the *bourgeoisie rurale*, the middling peasantry of some economic weight. If the settlement favoured the small farmer, he emerged from it less small than he began.

No doubt, the truth of the matter is that the agricultural outcome of revolution was not monolithic. A supply of small plots did become available to the landless peasantry on easy terms; but not enough to satisfy large groups who remained landless. The number of small farms did multiply rapidly. And the middling peasantry certainly got the best of the transaction. If this landscape is more complex and its allowance for nuance more generous than the traditional views could manage, the refinement provides scant benefit for French agriculture. Peasant cultivation remained the gainer against all other types, peasant proprietors more numerous after the Revolution than before. If, in the Nord, 'middle-class' land rose from 16 to 28 per cent of the total between 1789 and 1804, the increase in the peasant share more than doubled from 30 to 62 per cent. And, while the substantial peasantry of the *bourgeoisie rurale* had profited most of all, they formed the most tenaciously individualistic, conservative, and security-conscious group among French agriculturalists. For the urban bourgeoisie of the Revolution this result was a political triumph: by nicely calculated economic inducements they had rallied the upper peasantry to their side; by selling confiscated land and abolishing dues and tithes they had contrived a superlative *coup de main*, both ruining aristocracy *and* preserving property; by selecting the more substantial rural groups as beneficiaries they had broken village solidarity and destroyed the communal characteristics of the village economy.

But, in doing so, they imposed high economic costs upon the urban sector and thus upon themselves. For the revolutionary settlement helped fabricate a more individualistic view of agricultural property and attached it to a group of smallholders deeply jealous of their humble economic security. Modestly expanded holdings came to be seen as patrimonies, guaranteeing a degree of independence to the family, not as capital assets to be exploited in the market. Consequently, the 'new agricultural men' of the Revolution – the subsistence farmers of the micro-plots and the avid conservatives of the *bourgeoisie rurale* – emerged as 'small cultivators only marginally involved in the market economy'.[50] Equal inheritance, pressing down on the size of plot, erected further barriers between the cultivator and urban demand, yet in guaranteeing him an allotment of *some* size, perpetuated his attachment to agriculture.

Given this form of agricultural structure, the primary sector could make few direct contributions to the secondary. The diseconomies of scale involved in small plot agriculture produced low levels of profitability, and, in consequence, very little capital surplus was surrendered by the land; in the 1860s, for instance, the Land Tax extracted only 16 per cent of government revenue from this source. Low profits also turned agriculturalists towards self-sufficiency, denying the urban–industrial sector a valuable measure of internal demand. And, in turn, the guarantees of equal inheritance worked against mobility of labour, imposing upon industrialists severe constrictions in the supply of factory workers. Elsewhere, agricultural communities were able to mobilize investment funds, manpower, and markets in the industrial cause, but in France the developmental bounty from the land was much slighter. In effect the 'peasant policy' exercised by the revolutionary and imperial regimes ensured that the Rostowian 'agricultural transformation' – perhaps the most important of the preconditions – could not be successfully implemented in nineteenth-century France. Nor did the raising of a bourgeois cadre within agriculture assist in creating the mobile, aspiring society, escaping the sources of local influence, which features so prominently in Professor Palmer's concept of democratic revolution. Having absorbed an element of change, the French village gained immensely in its power to resist further modification: in 1815, indeed in 1870, its peasant population was as entrenched, as determinedly localized, as it had been in 1789. Unlike the major tenurial reforms carried through by other nations, the agricultural settlement of the revolution did nothing to prevent such an outcome, and much to encourage it.

THE SOCIAL CONSEQUENCES: ATOMISTIC INDIVIDUALISM AND SOCIAL IMPLOSION

It is common ground among historians that generations of Frenchmen since 1815 have looked back to the revolutionary period for precedents and values. There is less agreement on what they found. One possible interpretation is that the revolution 'set' French society in a particular shape and that subsequent observers discovered little encouragement for innovation or change within this static framework. John Christopher has argued that for France the rejection of the *ancien régime* constituted sufficient violent change and inculcated a distaste for further upheavals.[51] This view clearly possesses points of contact with the policies of the restored monarchy, and those of some among its successors. But the revolution also offered other, and more destructive, lessons. Certainly, the requests of the urban middle classes for free trade and the abolition of monopolies had provoked sympathetic action from their republican colleagues. But the businessman also attracted much republican suspicion: in particular, hostility to the large capitalist, whether farmer, merchant or manufacturer, formed a constant refrain throughout the 1790s.[52] One year after the revolutionary outbreak the *National and Anecdotal Dictionary* was defining the large businessman as 'a money monster, a man with a heart of stone',[53] and in summer 1793 this distaste found expression in the closure of the Stock Exchange and the suppression of joint-stock companies.[54] Invariably the butt of criticism was *big* business, *exploitative* enterprise, while antagonism between large producers and small consumers fuelled the discontent. Logically, the sequel was a growth in social approval for the small unit of enterprise, industrial or agricultural. Inside the Constituent Assembly, a society of small producers and independent traders became a widely respected objective, approximating agreeably to the democratic ideal of economic participation for all. Even Napoleon's Code of Commerce of 1808 discriminated against large capital concentrations and effectively limited most businesses to the scope of family firms.[55] Understandably, reformist governments emphasizing the principles of liberty, equality, and fraternity found difficulty in extending unambiguous toleration to economic systems which produced profit out of inequality and subjected the worker to the autocracy of the machine. Whatever the ideological commitment to free trade, displayed by the revolutionary leaders and by their various intellectual heirs, neither group was prepared to translate free trade as 'unbridled capitalism' and each was active in designing limitations upon this form of enterprise – even if the limitations were to remain discreet.

Some kind of solution was found by combining the concept of growth with that of equilibrium: progression towards industrialism was accepted but within set limits and along well-defined channels. Enterprise was permitted only on condition that each exponent avoided damage to the existing framework of society and the *positions acquises* of its members. Economic change was 'unleashed' – in emulation of such characteristic French pursuits as colonial wars, unsuccessful conspiracies, quasi-monarchical republics, and contemplative religion – only on the understanding that it was not to be drastic.[56] Obviously these terms, if closely observed, would limit the quality and utility of enterprise; indeed they virtually constituted a requirement for *timid* enterprise as 'a pre-requisite for the conciliation of groups included in the [social] consensus'.[57] Democratic revolutions may proclaim the rights of man, constitutionalism, and individualism, but these values are by no means necessarily growth-inducing. Constructions may be placed upon them which can impede economic advance as surely as the older restraints of mercantilism.

Of these heroic abstractions, individualism has a special importance for economic affairs. The Anglo-Saxon version of individualism has included the expectation that economic man will act energetically for his own profit but will combine with others for mutual profit. But in France, the revolutionary process shattered the prevailing organic concept of the state and replaced it with an atomistic concept, throwing off as it did so an extremely fragmented or egotistical form of individualism. In expanding the number of political wills to embrace the whole of society, the revolution passed to every individual the right to design his own programme. From this source, concluded observers like Siegfried[58] and J. B. Wolf[59] – who saw the initial decline of French *élan vital* and the first formulations of atomistic individualism as simultaneous and connected events – flowed some of the most destructive effects in nineteenth-century society and economy. Instructive, if unedifying, instances are plentiful. French labour in this period exhibited a marked preference for individual work, as well as a distaste for, and inefficiency in, collaborative large-scale ventures. Peasant determination to stick by the micro-plot – a highly individual possession – survived the attractions of urban employment with almost undented intransigence. And manufacturers went to extreme lengths to protect their firms from the public capital market, from banks, from merger, often from growth, in order to preserve their individualism as producers.

French-style individualism bred a passion for independence, and that, logically, required economic self-sufficiency, which in turn entailed a preoccupation less with risk-taking than with security. And security, under nineteenth-century conditions, correlated readily with thrift. Little farms with gold coin bricked into their mantels or small firms 'drowning in their own liquidity'[60] could be constructed with thrift, but not industrial empires or 'transformed' manufacturing sectors. It is with approval that Professor Palmer asserts that the democratic revolution 'ground up the tissues and sinews of the old order until nothing remained but the individual particles'.[61] But there were real dangers in this: the particles could be negatively charged atoms refusing to cohere in any co-operative endeavour, instead husbanding their energy in polarized seclusion.[62] Individualism, the clarion call of the bourgeois revolution, has more than one value: in economic matters it can create, not *élan vital*, nor risk-taking growth, but the preservation of small property in equilibriated liquidity, above all in equilibriated liquid *security*. With such specialized producers, capitalism's prime sin against the holy growth rate became merely the prime guarantee of individual salvation.

Within this system of values, the smallest unit of effective (and independent) economic activity was the family. Upon it, too, the revolution exerted a critical leverage. French society, under the *ancien régime*, had rested upon the twin certainties of Church and King, but after 1792 it faced, in their absence, a twin negation, with results that profoundly perverted the concept of authority.[63] To begin with, the strongest French political tradition was swiftly forged as a revolt *against* authority. In itself, this greatly complicated relationships between economic interest groups and the state, less productive here than in most other industrial countries. But, more importantly, once all convincing 'extraneous' sources of authority were forfeit, French society sought replacements; and it found them, in an act of introversion, within the family. De Tocqueville, among many observers, noted that France suffered from a deficiency in the intermediary institutions between state and family. In consequence, as the state failed to develop a 'legitimate authority', the family became, 'stronger than the state; it provided a social foundation of extraordinary stability'.[64] This was even worse for business. The fundamental commercial impulsion swung away from an economic towards a social calculus; the entrepreneur emphasized not profit, but the continuity and survival of the family enterprise, the preservation of the industrial or agricultural patrimony against competition or change. Any appetite for security which individualism may have encouraged was much reinforced by these familial preoccupations. For attempts at innovation or expansion might threaten the livelihood of the family: resort to the capital market would ransom its independence; competition would destroy not rival firms, but rival families, and perhaps, even one's own. Within values emphasizing equilibrium, individual security, and familial business there was much that was anti-capitalistic in nature. Here, the daring innovator, the self-made man, the Schumpeterian entrepreneur would be more likely to earn obliquy than renown. By the same token, the requirements sketched out by the sociologists for growth-supporting business systems – that they should distribute rewards and status according to occupational achievement[65] – are here only conspicuous by absence. A society holding these values might well expect to create an economy of slow growth.

But of course, the revolution did not conjure these socio-economic characteristics from some historical void. Elements of the problem existed before 1789. The bourgeoisie, already widely established in commercial if not in industrial activity, had brought, from their peasant origins, concepts governing the role of the family, the nature of work, and the desirability of thrift. Further, they had noticed that if social status could not be earned by business achievement it could be won by social emulation, by the purchase of land and the speedy imitation of the aristocracy's *rentier* relationship with it. Given the post-revolutionary constraints upon manufacturing enterprise, this habit was to persist even in a world much pruned of aristocracy. The eighteenth-century merchants of Bordeaux, Rouen, or Le Havre won status from a society which distrusted their commercial origins only by the purchase of office or the acquisition of the best inland estates; and they set a pattern for many nineteenth-century imitators. But all such precedents were vastly strengthened in appeal by regimes which summarized, approved, and defined the pre-eminence of the bourgeoisie. And, in the revolutionary catechism, they were equipped with new sanctions commanding near-universal respect.

Or were they? In recent years disrepute has fallen upon the complicated apparatus of analysis by social values. The (mainly American) school of historians and sociologists who built the machinery between the mid-1940s and the mid-1960s has received the ritual, deft, scholarly kiss of death: the compliment that their work has been useful in 'provoking discussion'. Admittedly, some of their more rarefied hypotheses possessed the ring, and all the historical force, of readings from everyman's basic primer in social psychology. But many of their descriptions – as the better class of sceptics are coming to admit – capture an entrepreneurial reputation that is 'not entirely undeserved'.[66] The 'fit' between the suggested social values and the actual behaviour of many – if by no.means all – French concerns is too close for out-of-hand rejection of these working postulates (see below, pp. 188ff). Final judgement on the matter will be delivered as the argument develops. But even the superficial record permits some suggestive generalization. For instance, it is clear that by 1900 France had contrived an equilibrium between industry and agriculture by diluting the expansion of industry. French manufacturing, facing a force constellation quite unlike that confronting its German counterpart, could readily tolerate an agriculture whose links with the national market were tenuous. Similarly, agriculture could bear with an industry shot through with non-capitalistic and familial characteristics. It is no accident that Clapham's venerable description of French growth – 'industrialization without Industrial Revolution' – conforms as readily to the social value hypothesis as to the quantitative measurements of the new economic historians.

Disputes in specific interpretation may remain, but the overall burden of evidence concerning developments in trade, technology, agriculture, and society in the thirty years after 1789 does not favour the 'optimistic' or 'dynamic' assessment of the revolution's economic consequences. The slant of the material is towards catastrophe and disruption rather than towards growth inducing reform in society and economy.

IN PURSUIT OF THE FRENCH INDUSTRIAL REVOLUTION

To deny the coincidence of political and industrial revolution in France is to pose the question: when did a distinctive quickening of French economic activity take place, or, if Clapham is to be believed, did it ever take place? The extensive and sometimes violent debate on this topic has been conducted as a three-cornered engagement. A small detachment of 'early starters' has traditionally persisted in locating a decisive industrialization in the years before 1815, having more recently to repulse the 'catastrophic' assumption in order to do so. A somewhat larger, if also somewhat motley, band of 'middle starters' has settled upon the period between 1815 and 1848. And finally the biggest battalion, identifying the critical upturn with the years of the Second Empire, has occupied the period 1850–70. Each group is supported by logistics units deploying the sophisticated modern weaponry of quantitative assessment.

THE FIRST PROTOTYPE: THE 'INDUSTRIAL REVOLUTION' OF
1770–1815

Although the early start hypothesis has been touched upon in its connexion with political change, its economic claims require more specific attention. They are based upon a restricted set of tactics: a distinction between the concept of industrial revolution and the concept of 'take-off'; a concentration upon a small number of 'key' technologies; an emphasis upon long-run statistical series. Milward and Saul have argued that the French economy was unusual in failing to exhibit a parallelism between the introduction of mass production technology and the onset of high growth rates; therefore, they claim a disjunction between the incidence of 'revolution' and that of 'take-off'. This allows them to contend that the introduction of English-style technology at the end of the eighteenth century constituted the revolutionary phase for France and that the more rapid growth of the 1850s did not 'have much in common' with the British 'take-off' of the 1780s and 1790s.[67] Thus encouraged, they turn to their individual industries and are rightly impressed to find developments – mostly in cotton and woollen textiles – as yet unprecedented in Europe. This kind of evidence can be built up quite impressively. Alsatian cotton spindleage certainly doubled, to achieve a total of 1 m., between 1806 and 1808, while the cotton spun by the entire French industry quintupled between 1806 and 1812.[68] Similarly, cast-iron production doubled between 1789 and 1796, quadrupled between 1796 and 1811.

The early emergence of advanced capitalistic plants, Labrousse's 'heavyweight' concerns, is also clearly detectable. The Anzin Mining Company attacked coal extraction in the largest style from 1757, Decretot was said to control the world's finest textile mills at Louviers by 1789; the cotton giant, Richard-Lenoir, constructed the most impressive business success of the revolutionary period on the foundation of 39 establishments and 15,000 employees.[69] Nor can this *pointilliste* approach be dismissed for its lack of macro-economic support; the quantitative surveys of Marczewski and Markovitch have provided the necessary substructure. Very gradual growth and the absence of a definite take-off constitute the main proposals of these econometric surveys. But Marczewski is careful to add that this gradual advance was present as early as 1800, or even 1750; and his first results even suggested an average annual growth rate of total industrial product for the period 1796–1812 (at 3%) higher than that for the years 1855–74 (at 2.72%).[70] Though he preferred to identify no specific take-off period, Marczewski conceded that, were he forced to select a likely date, it would lie around 1750. Reluctantly or not, he eventually speaks out for 'several epochs of brilliant expansion' in the eighteenth century.[71] More ambition is displayed by Markovitch. Though agreeing that the probable French growth rate around 1800 was already about 3 per cent, he claimed that this performance made France the world's *premier* industrial power, surpassed in output by Britain only in the sectors of cotton and coal.[72] The total effect is that of a combined Anglo-Saxon and Slav conspiracy to overthrow the established course of French economic history.

Like many of its kind, however, the *coup* is more percussive than productive. For instance, the Anglo-centric style of assessment employed by Milward and Saul is definitely suspect. Why should economic growth earn the title of 'industrial revolution' simply by its resemblance to the British technological experience of 1780–1815? It is to be expected that the take-off of a follower country should contain ingredients which were *absent* from the experience of pioneer economies. For the nature of technology is to grow more sophisticated with time, and the threshold of industrialization is pushed upward as it does so. What is industrial revolution for a pioneer may be only proto-industrialization for its successors; so that the arrival on the continent of British industrial devices is in itself evidence of no economic process outside that of technological diffusion. The criteria of industrial revolution must be concerned, not with the implementation of a standard technological mix, but with the degree to which an economy employs the 'best practice' of its era.

Still more important, there are doubts as to how precisely French technological experience before 1815 actually did resemble the British. The prototype industrialization had begun with basic industries producing semi-finished materials such as cotton yarn and had then moved on into the mechanization of consumption goods production. But in world markets dominated by the secure British monopoly of basic production, France first chose to exploit her labour advantages in skills and costs to produce high-quality consumption items – as, classically, with the luxury printed cottons from Alsace – and then, subsequently, to move 'backwards' or in Lévy-Leboyer's terminology 'up-stream' into the basic sectors.[73] This was entirely rational: follower countries have to insert themselves into niches in the world economy which earlier developers have not yet entirely occupied. Fulfilment of this requirement will automatically adjust the model of growth pursued by follower countries to a pattern somewhat removed from that of their predecessors; as Crouzet puts it, successful industrialization is unlikely to be 'slavish imitation'.[74] The French adjustment ensured that first-generation industries resembled British manufactures of the second generation, perhaps lending to Gallic technology an aspect of misleading modernism, and concealing its lack of the comprehensive substructure required of a full industrial revolution. In summary, therefore, the arrival of British technology in Europe, however unique, could not (a) guarantee widespread use of current 'best practice', especially since this transmission was much delayed by war, (b) prevent the exploitation of 'downstream' niches even in the absence of the widespread technological base long since secured in Britain.

In fact the exploitation of the French niches left much of the economy in a state of pre-capitalism or commercial capitalism. If specialized consumption items enjoyed success, the entrepreneurs who were active in the promotion of most other commodities were not the manufacturers but the traditional merchant groups, dealing in a wide variety of items and ploughing the returns into land. Even in the textile centres, the mercantile, and not the industrial, forces exercised the major influence upon manufacture; in Lyons, the Guérins and, in Lille, the Crespels dominated the entrepreneurial landscape from a commercial eminence. In the basic sectors, the weaknesses were even more pronounced, if of a different quality. Impressive increases in iron output were recorded, but the few large ironworks like Le Creusot or the de Wendel plant at Hayange experienced difficult years before and after Waterloo. In 1790 these two installations had been the *only* ironworks employing coke-smelting in all France. The great majority of enterprises in iron-making – as in mining, glass production and most other manufactures – remained small, tied to forests for fuel, rivers for power, often to noble estates for both, and for labour, to skilled workers who were part peasant and part artisan. Even in 1814, Jeal Vial considers this crucial basic industry to have been 'essentielle-ment forestière' in organization and style.[75]

Outside these limited growth points, general economic conditions looked distinctly inauspicious. For all producers, markets remained fragmentary and scattered, a series of provincial 'islands' – and so hardly an analogue for any-thing English at this time. The transport system consisted still of a few isolated canals overlaid by a cobweb of indifferent roads; the canal 'fever' of 1760–89 was frustrated by political and financial impediments and produced only one major navigation, that between the Saône and the Loire. Further extension of the waterways was not attempted until after 1820.[76] Capital, with little sur-plus generated either by the mercantile or by the primary sector, remained scarce and expensive. Financial assistance from the banks was unreliable, an occasional rather than routine transaction, secured by the more fortunate in-dustrialists, most usually as a defence against commercial disruption. Mer-chant capital dabbled with manufactures but had not yet made a whole-hearted commitment. Down to 1815, Palmade concluded, 'the progress achieved by industry showed no signs of true, mature, and self-confident in-dustrial capitalism'.[77]

The quantitative results are insufficient to swing this conclusion around. Though interesting, they are by no means beyond contention. Eighteenth-century statistics in particular are suspect, and it is noticeable that Marczews-ki's most ambitious claims – though reluctantly made – are concerned with a 'take-off' located in the most questionable section of his series. Secondly, the figures do not point unambiguously to any single turning point and could be used to support more than one: Marczewski, for instance, concedes a 'first maximum' in French growth rates in the decade *1830–40*. Thirdly, there is disagreement even within the statistical camp: more recent calculations by Lévy-Leboyer and Crouzet have moved the point of initial industrialization decisively into the nineteenth century. Certainly, the case for an early start could not rest upon the statistical data alone. And it is difficult to detect exactly what else there is. An appropriate description for activity in French textiles before 1815 – and perhaps for French economic activity generally for some decades after 1815 – would not be industrial revolution, but rather, as it was for the German states before 1850, proto-industrialization.

THE SECOND PROTOTYPE (a): THE 'INDUSTRIAL REVOLUTION' OF 1830–50

Perhaps the period 1830–50 has more substantial appeal. The pioneering A. L. Dunham cautiously placed 'the infancy and beginning of the adolescence of the Industrial Revolution' within these years; the intrepid Rostow launched his 'take-off' in 1830 and believed the manœuvre completed by 1860; and the eminent Frenchmen Leuillot and Sée detected impressive growth in the major French industries between Waterloo and the revolution of 1848. Repeating the techniques of the 'early start' theorists, the methodology of these authorities usually involves an emphasis upon textiles and sometimes adds an 'argument by example' from the experience of selected factories of high repute. Statistical corroboration is again forthcoming. Markovitch proposes a growth rate close to the British, at 3 per cent per year for the entire period 1800–50 – it slackens only *after* the inauguration of the Second Empire – while Marczewski's results for his critical decade 1830–40 suggest a formidable 5.6 per cent annual average growth rate for the peak industrial sectors and a still impressive 3.5 per cent per annum for all industrial sectors.[78] The consensus here is wider. The early years of the July Monarchy are frequently regarded as a period of strong – if not particularly sustained – economic activity and many observers would accept a genuine acceleration – if not the crucial surge – in the 1830s and 1840s.

However, to rest an industrial revolution primarily upon textile technologies is no more satisfactory for this period than for the years 1789–1815. Indeed, it is *less* satisfactory since the longer an economy lagged behind the British, the less convincingly did textile equipment resemble that of comprehensive industrialization. Such equipment was not 'lumpy', did not require massive investment, and could be disposed in small and inexpensive production units. It could grow by the careful accumulation of units and a gradual reinvestment of profits, that is, by tactics associated with small-scale business, with moderate rather than 'revolutionary' advance, and (by 1830) with a largely pre-industrial level of economic sophistication. This conclusion could not stand if textile expansion had been sustained by capital-intensive expansion in other sectors. But in France the heavy manufactures were notably lethargic after 1815. Of the twenty combined refining- and rolling-mills, the *forges à l'anglais*, established in the iron industry between 1815 and 1823, only five endured the troubles of the 1830s, and the resulting crisis of confidence was not rectified before the railway-led boom of 1845–47.[79] The survivors like Le Creusot persevered, balancing upon fragile profit margins, in an isolation that was anxious rather than splendid. Fortunes improved for Le Creusot only after the works was taken over by the Schneider brothers in the late 1830s;[80] earlier rescue attempts by Chagot and Manby and Wilson achieved little success.

In this context, Rostow regretfully but rightly concluded, 'the development of a modern textile industry . . . did not have a sufficient scale effect to act as a base for sustained growth'.[81] In substitution, he proposed railways. These far exceeded textiles in their 'linkage' and derived demand effects, and they were certainly capital-intensive. Their single deficiency before 1850 was that there were simply too few of them to provide sufficient underpinning for an industrial revolution. Short-haul connexions like the first major rail-link in France, the coal-freighting spur from St Etienne to Andrézieux on the Loire (1828), remained the norm until 1840. At that time only one line, from Strasbourg to Mulhouse, exceeded 100 kilometres in length. Total initial investment in railroads averaged only 34 m. francs per year in 1835–44 (175 m. in 1845–54) but reached 487 m. francs per year in 1855–64, the peak decade before the First World War. Correspondingly, large-scale construction awaited the Le Grand plan of the 1850s: the network expanded slowly from 612 kilometres of track in 1844 – hardly enough for an industrial flutter, let alone a 'take-off' – to 2599 kilometres of track in 1854.[82] In each of the three decades after 1855 building was over three times faster than in the decade 1845–54, and twelve to fourteen times faster than in the decade 1835–44.

Neither does measurement of the 'multiplier' effect generated by the railways yield any substantial results before the mid-century. According to Marczewski's suggestion, some quantities can be placed upon this effect by taking the figures for initial investment in railways and expressing these as a percentage of gross industrial product; the proportions which emerge, 'approximately reflect the development of the railways' direct demand for the goods and services of other industries' and indicate 'the direct and indirect influence of railway construction on economic expansion.'[83] Calculation according to this procedure yields remarkably low estimates for the railway multiplier in the two decades 1825–34 and 1835–44, a notable rise in the decade 1845–54, and a sharp acceleration to the century's peak only in the decade 1855–64. (Table 3.2).

Table 3.2 French railways and industrial production; the railway multiplier

	(a) Initial railway investment (m. current francs)	(b) Gross industrial product (m. current francs)	(c) Multiplier (a) as % (b)
1825–34	4	2,938	0.14
1835–44	34	3,979	0.85
1845–54	175	5,107	3.42
1855–64	437	6,043	7.23
1865–74	236	7,101	3.32
1875–84	398	7,889	5.04
1885–94	280	8,869	3.16
1895–1904	210	10,383	2.02

Source: Initial railway investment from Marczewski (1963), Table 5, col. 1; Gross Industrial Product from Table 1, col. 3

Given these restrictions on railway construction and its multiplier impulses, it is impossible that railways could have exerted a major galvanizing effect upon the French economy before 1855. The quest for a leading sector outside textiles serves only to demonstrate the weak development of capital-intensive undertakings in France before the mid-century.

Concentration upon individual advanced technologies – rightly christened *'industries de pointe'* by Crouzet – establishes very little more. Obviously, France contained large and successful firms by 1820 or 1830, fully comparable with their British or German rivals. Similarly, she possessed industries growing at rates regarded as 'high' or 'modern', say 4 or 5 per cent per year. Silk and cotton were already established among this group, but in the decades 1825–34 and 1835–44, the iron and steel industries added themselves to this advance guard.[84] But alongside the new capitalistic enterprises which drove the growth rate upwards, many archaic ventures and technologies survived, and indeed tightened their grip on the economy. Between 1800 and 1850, water-powered equipment increased in numbers by five times and charcoal-fired forges reached a peak of expansion as late as 1837; at mid-century these tiny metal producers contributed about half of all pig-iron output. Similarly, textiles witnessed 'growth rather than retardation in hand-weaving'[85] and powered looms did not win a clear ascendancy for decades; in Alsace not until 1840–50, in Normandy not until 1860–70, in Lyons not until the 1880s and 1890s. Single centres like the Alsatian cotton metropolis of Mulhouse or the woollen capital of Roubaix, each endowed by 1830 with mechanized, capitalistically organized factory industry, might present a very fair Gallic imitation of Manchester or Bradford. But in the 1840s Mulhouse contained one-half of all power-looms and one-third of all steam-driven spindles in France; outside Mulhouse, even in industrial cities like Rouen or Lille the hand-loom outnumbered the power-loom by 3 : 1. Meanwhile Roubaix, perhaps the most formidable French competitor for British industry in 1830, headed an industry in which power-looms suffered a 1 : 2 inferiority, and the other main manufacturing centre, St Quentin, retained hand-looms down to 1914. As Crouzet rightly concludes, the *industries de pointe* remained 'heavily outnumbered within economies which, in their bulk, were still traditional'.[86]

A marked and enduring dualism therefore existed within the structure of French technology; it was not extensively qualified before 1850, and not eradicated before 1914. In addition, there was a dualism of economic *regions* quite common in the experience of nineteenth-century developers – as the caesura between the Rhineland and East Elbia, metropolitan Austria and the Magyar lands, the Ukraine and Asiatic Russia all demonstrate – and a chronic commonplace for modern underdeveloped economies. It was, however, much less evident in eighteenth-century Britain, another indicator that French industrialization did not *much* resemble the British. For France, the frontiers of industrial prosperity ran between the modern centres of the Nord and Alsace and the backward tracts of the south and west, a disposition permitting the co-existence of model manufacturing towns and regions with areas of the most basic agricultural practice. Consequently, an emphasis upon model factories or industrial concentrations – as with Leuillot's concern with the great manufacturing dynasties of Dufaud and Koechlin, or with the mills of Fourchambault, perhaps the most successful of the metal concerns – produces interesting examples but scant proof of industrial revolution. Indeed, the blend of model plants and dualistic structure is more consistent with growth of gradual rather than discontinuous style. There were, of course, good reasons for the retained traditionalism. If, stimulated by international competition, the more modern technologies were clambering over the obstacles raised by French factor endowment, some of these natural features – dense timber stands, plentiful reserves of water-power, meagre coking coal – proved sufficient to slow their advance and seriously to curb their profitability. But these reasons are arguments *against* an industrial revolution. While they applied, the large modern factory could compose only the tip of the industrial iceberg; below the waterline the tiny organisms of provincial industry persisted, multiplied, and endured the restraints of a frigid economic climate. Occasionally, no doubt, the ice-mountain quaked and heaved, but, before 1850 it did no more than bring forth a shivering industrial mouse.

Nor can the statistics transform it into any more formidable animal. If Lévy-Leboyer and Markovitch produce estimates of 3–3.25 per cent annual average growth in French industrial output 1815–50, Marczewski's computation for the complete period at 2.5 per cent is modest,[87] and Crouzet's at 1.6 per cent positively low.[88] This last is obligingly consistent with the qualitative evidence for the decades to 1850 and the tendency of the Crouzet estimates to rise sharply at mid-century fits well with a later 'turning' or 'take-off' point. Further, Crouzet is able to provide statistical corroboration for the frictional effect generated by traditional industry: if the textile industries are excluded from the measurement of industrial output 1820–60, the advance of the remaining, 'newer' manufactures rises to a much more impressive annual average of 5.5 per cent. The difference between the two rates amounts to a convincing statistical description of technological dualism. Since the Crouzet indices are built up from annual, rather than, as in most cases, decennial, observations, their tendency to dovetail with the qualitative indicators is particularly suggestive.

THE SECOND PROTOTYPE (b): A CONTESTED LANDSCAPE

Outside the 'model plants', 'leading sectors', and quantitative measurements, the wider economic map of the years 1815–48 offers few indicators of a productive industrial landscape. As in Britain, this was an era of deflation. A long glissade in prices caused erosion to profits – particularly to farming profits and landowners' income – and exacerbated the considerable problems already encountered in generating a capital surplus. Exports did swing strongly upwards from their Napoleonic nadir, but, with British competitors sprawled across world markets, proved unable to draw back further ground or additional profits. No more luminous were developments in transport: manufacturers were denied not only a supply of ready capital from the primary and mercantile sectors but also ready access to markets and cheap raw materials. Despite the resumption of canal-building in the 1820s, and the provision through the Bequet Plan of 2500 kilometres of waterway between the central provinces and the northern and eastern industrial regions, it was only under the Second Empire, and after a century of frustrated attempts, that France acquired a basic canal network. With the slow progress of railway construction before 1850, transport costs, in a country where considerable distances separated iron and coal reserves, remained onerous. Heavy freight charges accorded protection to the traditional micro-producers in their provincial redoubts and expensive coking coal continued to discourage innovation. But of all constraints, the most powerful were perhaps the economic policies of the restored monarchy.

It was perhaps natural for caretaker governments, successors to administrations of violent reformism or reckless expansionism, to exhibit a suspicion of innovation. If so, the bourgeois monarchy of the restoration carried what was natural to excess. Restrictions on trade and business as repressive as those of the most obscurantist old régime were imposed in the name of caution and stability. Tariffs were converted virtually into exclusion orders upon foreign manufacturers. *Petite industrie* was wrapped in yet another layer of protection and its antediluvian methods rewarded with undeservedly lavish prices. To these timid governors even the joint-stock company threatened speculative insecurity and the excesses of monster capitalism; accordingly they suppressed it where they could and made company formation subject to the express authorization of the Council of State. Between 1815 and 1848 only 342 ventures survived this test and under 7 per cent of their capital was destined for industrial employment.[89] Growing preferences for small-scale enterprise were thus strongly reinforced by the Restoration's terror of insecurity. Yet the consequences frequently achieved economic havoc. Railway promotion, for instance, was so handled – in fear of potential monopolies – that contractors were permitted only to create limited stretches of track, a stipulation which wrote a rigid parochialism and an insistent factionalism into all exercises in transport planning. State policies of this kind created effective obstacles to the processes of 'industrial revolution'.

But in finance they were more effective still. If the state favoured family concerns which exhibited a high degree of independence from the banks, it also controlled the banks so that they could not properly serve the needs of industry. From Bonaparte's discovery that banks were useful engines of war finance and his consequent foundation of the Bank of France (1800), there developed an excessively tight relationship between finance and government. At the outset, the Central Bank was bound to the official service – Napoleon appointed his own senior officials from 1805 – and made subservient to imperial requirement – in 1814 advances to the state (269 m. francs) were almost three times as large as those to private clients (96 m. francs).[90] Unsurprisingly, the Emperor's final campaigns broke the bank. Historical experience suggests that a measured autonomy for the financial sector is most favourable for the growth and excellence of bank services; French experience suggests that the absence of autonomy is highly damaging to bank development.

Unfortunately, also, the Napoleonic precedent exerted an enduring influence in financial affairs. Hopes of liberalization after 1815 came to nothing, and until 1848 the French government pursued one of the least creative investment policies in Europe. In the official view, the State Bank was as much a servant of the new monarchy as it had been of the old empire. Once this idea was revived, the prospect of a free market in financial institutions – perhaps jeopardizing the primacy of the Central Bank – became repugnant to the regime. Consequently, throughout its tenure, the monarchy sanctioned the formation only of a handful of provincial banks, opened in Rouen, Nantes, and Bordeaux in 1817–18, and a half-dozen city banks, established in the 1830s under officially appointed directors. Transparently, such ventures were intended to harness competition rather than to encourage it. Where genuine rivalry did emerge, as in 1825 with Laffitte's scheme for a special industrial bank, it encountered stubborn official resistance. Funds for French industrialization could not flow freely under such jealous control. Before 1850 they came, in so far as they came at all, from three main sources: industrial concerns in established trades such as textiles; *la haute banque parisienne*, a group of private bankers, often military contractors grown fat on Bonaparte's adventures; and the *sociétés en commandité*, banks employing a form of commercial association which the regime did tolerate, a partnership in which active members had to assume unlimited liability.

The *commandité* bank represented perhaps the only genuine financial innovation of the period 1815–48. Yet, denied the right of note issue, its capital curbed by official regulation, its active protagonists saddled with the enormous risks of unlimited liability, its stability in consequence questionable, it was scarcely an imposing novelty. Until the 1850s it remained the only vehicle available to aspirant financiers, and one or two of these did manage to employ it with some success. The most important *commandité* venture, the Caisse Générale du Commerce et de l'Industrie, was founded in 1837 by Jacques Laffitte to build upon his personal investments in coal, chemicals, glass, textiles, and iron, and to provide a credit service for industrialists. By 1848 this project had twenty-five imitators, and a slowly growing capital market was becoming available to factory-owners.[91] Its support was an important component of the industrial surge of the 1840s. But by the end of that decade, both the efforts of the financial entrepreneurs and the durability of the *commandité* form had proved deficient. The financial crisis which accompanied the political disturbances of 1848–49 afforded the Central Bank an opportunity to restrain rivals now threatening to become over-mighty. Taking vengeance in the name of sound banking practice, the Bank absorbed the entire *commandité* sector in the catastrophic year 1848. As the period began with a strong statement of authoritarianism in finance, so it ended with the most uncompromising tactic open to a central bank: the comprehensive eradication of an independent financial innovation. What small relief had been provided for the credit shortages of French industry – particularly its famine of working capital – was arbitrarily denied. Existing forces encouraging the miniaturization of French enterprise were stiffened as the means for growth were removed from the small industrialist. The 'schizophrenic' development of manufacturing[92] – setting a highly capitalized modern sector, able to signal its needs to the bankers, against an undercapitalized sector of petty capitalism, lacking access to growth capital – is partly explained by the absence of enduring financial innovations.

Given the restrictions upon capital supply, company formation, transportation, and financial development, it is difficult to detect much promise of growth-orientated entrepreneurship in the years before 1848. On the contrary, any tendency towards business conservatism which might have resulted from the revolutionary inheritance would surely have been reinforced by the unattractive nature of this period. Social frictions working against modernization would have exerted most restraint early in the process and there was little enough in the economy of 1815–48 to act as lubricant.

THE RECONSTRUCTION OF THE SECOND PROTOTYPE

Despite the sharp impressions of economic gloom which pervade much of the post-imperial quarter-century, some energetic revisionism has survived. Professor Lévy-Leboyer has added to his statistical good opinions a careful survey which proposes the existence of favourable trends in agriculture and among the *haute banque* during the 1830s and 1840s.[93] Very probably, as Lévy-Leboyer argues, prosperity in the countryside did improve after 1820, for some sections of the community at least, and mainly peasant rather than capitalistic sections. The crucial observation is, however, that any measure of increased rural wealth was generated within an entirely traditional structure of production and consumption (or saving) preferences; it would thus have exerted a limited effect upon consumer demand or capital supply. Too frequently in the nineteenth century, greater prosperity for the French peasant simply entailed greater hoarding, a higher level of immobilized wealth. Rarely did improved prosperity express itself in (or derive from) improved production. If anything, the advance of basic agricultural innovations – cultivation of fodder crops or erosion of fallows – *lost* momentum in the second quarter of the century. Over most of France, for instance, cereal yields scarcely budged from their eighteenth-century levels. In 1840, according to Michel Morineau, French agriculture, 'remained stagnant, retarded, even primitive in the greater part of the territory. . . . There was no agricultural revolution in France but a long period of stagnation of yields'.[94]

More solid grounds for optimism are perhaps provided by the *haute banque*. The traditional antithesis between the old bank and the new, between the conservative merchant financiers of the *haute banque* and the progressive investment bankers of the mid-century *mobiliers* has for some time attracted suspicion. The old bank, David Landes decided in 1956, was in reality 'a malleable and supple institution'.[95] To this view, Lévy-Leboyer has added detailed demonstration that the *haute banque* did indeed support new industries with substantial risk capitals in the period 1815–48. Much of the funding for the canal construction of the 1820s and 1830s came from the revitalized merchant bank sector, and, in the process, valuable experience was gained for the railway flotations of the 1850s and 1860s. Alongside transportation, international trade, insurance, and selected manufactures received attention from these unlikely pioneers of investment banking; the *commandité* banks were joined by a second innovation in a traditional guise. And since the *haute banque* made up the greater part of the private financial sector before 1848, its change in tactics was clearly of the first importance. The submissions upon this point from Landes (1956), Lévy-Leboyer (1964), and Cameron (1967) would appear to constitute an irrefutable case.

However, these financial adjustments, like the agricultural improvements, took place within an institutional structure that was only marginally changed. And whatever the progressiveness of the *haute banque*, its members could operate only within a framework defined by official conservatism. If the Rothschilds proved 'malleable and supple', the landowners sitting on the Conseil d'Etat, and determining the flexibility or rigidity of the complete financial system, were nothing of the kind. Moreover, the 'malleability' of the *haute banque* was subject to definite limitations. The essential working capital requirements of industry, for instance, did not so easily win their support as large and lucrative fixed capital projects. Yet when really generous exercises in the creation of social overheads were proposed – by the mid-century railway promoters – the resources of the private bankers proved unequal to the burden and they made way for the *mobilier* institutions. In the absence of large-scale financial innovation, it would appear that the interests and the reserves of the *haute banque* could support only a *limited* measure of industrialization. The extent to which this kind of evidence can modify the pessimistic assessment of the period 1815–48 must be restricted. Where revisionism applies accurately, it affects tightly defined areas and small numbers of flexible elements within inflexible outer structures.

THE THIRD PROTOTYPE: THE INDUSTRIAL REVOLUTION OF THE 1850s AND 1860s.

The mid-century surge in French manufacturing output represents both the most popular choice for the industrial 'threshold' – it is advocated by Clapham, Morazé, Palmade, Crouzet, and Landes among others – and the best supported. The economic dog days of 1846–48, coming on top of the cyclical crises of 1827, 1831, and 1837, featured profits and output so slashed that even the traditional dynastic fortresses – notably those protecting the textile interests of Rouen, Lille, and Lyons – began to contemplate tactics more venturesome than their habitual manœuvres of defence. And, as the *industries de pointe* regathered their energies, so their isolation within the economy began to break down. The three decades after 1845/54 witnessed the replacement of the original textile vanguard by a new leading sector composed of capital-intensive industries such as iron and steel manufacture, metal fabrication, and coal extraction. Steel changed its status from that of a rare metal in 1850 – when its manufacture was still a monopoly of English masters, the Jacksons based on the Loire – to that of an industrial staple by 1869. At long last, the traditional metal producers – particularly those of Champagne and Franche Comté – began to decline and concentrated capitalism to enter the heavy industries; by 1868 40 per cent of all French iron output could be generated by two vast modern installations.[96] Growth rates in this group were high, ranging between 3 and 6 per cent for most members, but rising to 10 per cent and above for steel and close to 20 per cent for non-ferrous metals.[97]

In addition, jute, sugar, chocolate, and public construction all demonstrated high activity, indicating a convulsion in demand extending well outside the durable goods sector. And innovation extended further still. Crisis in agriculture eventually sufficed to galvanize the rural community into a quest for more dependable sources of income. Around 1850 the responsive regions of the north and east received a bundle of new devices containing fertilizers, drainage techniques, mechanical reapers, and improved ploughs, and, further outdistancing the still backward areas of the centre and south and the archaic areas like Brittany, proceeded to employ the new methods to drive the growth rate of farm income upwards from its 'traditional' level of 1 per cent per annum for the period 1790–1850 to 1.8 per cent per annum for the period 1850–80.[98]

Underlying these powerful trends in both the rural and the manufacturing sectors was a marked upsurge in railway construction from mid-century. Trunk line construction in the three decades from 1855/64 exceeded the provision of the preceding three decades by nearly 700 per cent and of the succeeding three decades by just over 20 per cent.[99] Building of this magnitude produced the nineteenth-century peak for railway investment – at 7.2 per cent of gross industrial product – in the decade after 1855. This boom created many of the strategically most important lines, the connexions from Paris to Marseilles, from the metropolis to the German, Spanish, and Italian frontiers, from Bordeaux on the Atlantic to Sète on the Mediterranean. Investment input and geographical spread were clearly sufficient to exert substantial direct and indirect effects upon the general level of economic activity. Derived demand for railway durables fell heavily upon the capital goods sector, already constituting by the 1840s according to Landes, 'the most important single stimulus to industrial growth'.[100] But penetration of the provinces by the steam locomotive also brought gains to agriculture: increased scope for market-oriented production and a measured improvement in population mobility are both detectable. And related to both was a strong increase in urbanization: population growth in towns with over 50,000 inhabitants was more pronounced in the·period 1851–56 than in any comparable set of years between 1801 and 1936. This accords well with Lévy-Leboyer's argument that the French market – like the 'German' – had to wait until the 1860s before achieving any useful degree of national integration. On this evidence, it seems possible to place France in the company of those countries – Germany and the United States included – which at mid-century experienced a 'railway Kondratiev' with emphatic growth-inducing capabilities.

These promising developments were not unconnected with political changes. The unveiling of the *empire autoritaire* in 1851 revealed not only the glittering accoutrements of Bonapartist militarism but also the tools of economic *dirigisme*. Many capitalists were anxious for a government of strength which would secure order and the resumption of economic life. In return for their support in the difficult months of 1848 and 1849, they received a regime-more disposed to encourage industrialism than any other French administration between 1789 and 1914, and an emperor, who for all his vanities and occasional follies, retained a shrewd eye for the economic main chance. Railway extension and the rationalization of railway operation owed a good deal to the imperial writ. Instead of cautious concessions and parochial administration, the government advocated operation by network or region[101] and threw itself 'full steam into long concessions'.[102] In turn, the stimulation of railroad growth raised financial implications: major projects like the Chemin de Fer du Nord had severely taxed the conventional sources of capital mobilization before 1848 and the vast requirements of the Midi railway venture outran the lending power even of the *haute banque* and the Rothschilds.[103]

It was a problem fit for imperial initiative, and, building upon the liberalization of credit begun by the provisional government of 1848–49, Napoleon once again supplied it. The initial embodiment of Bonapartist finance was the Crédit Foncier, a centralized nation-wide mortgage bank, lured by an official subsidy of 10 m. francs into important work in the rebuilding of French cities, especially Haussmann's reconstruction of Paris, and in other public enterprises. Its twin subsidiaries the Crédit Agricole and the Comptoir d'Agriculture dealt with at least part of the rural problem. But most important, and closer to the stimulus of railway demand, was the Crédit Mobilier, the major financial innovation of the mid-century and the first joint-stock bank in France to practise 'mixed' banking. The essential novelty here lay in combining the conventional management of clients' deposits with the unconventional mobilization of the resultant surpluses as investment capital for businessmen. Intended as a counterweight to the Bank of France – and, capitalized at 60 m. francs, its closest rival in size – the Crédit Mobilier provided a genuine alternative to the restrictive financial strategems of the preceding three decades. Precisely for this reason, of course, the project attracted the long knives of the Council of State and survived to a safe delivery in 1852 only because it carried the personal imprimatur of Louis Napoleon. Commencing business with energy and success in the 1850s and 1860s, it became a European paradigm for the growth-conscious bank, stocking its coffers with scarce investment resources and throwing these open to adventurous capitalists and, pre-eminently, to railway capitalists. Although, in France, no major financial institution specializing in credit for *manufacturing* followed the Mobilier's lead until the foundation of the Banque de Paris et des Pays Bas (1872) and the creation of the Banque de l'Union Parisienne (1904), *mobilier*-style institutions, with the classic bent towards investment in transportation projects, were established in Lyons, Marseilles, and Lille by the mid-1860s.[104] Furthermore, the powerful joint-stock institutions which sailed the calmer waters of the 1860s, now freed from the financial maelstroms of the late 1850s, agencies like the Crédit Industriel et Commercial (1859), the Crédit Lyonnais (1863), or the Société Générale (1864), although later given over almost wholly to deposit and foreign business, did engage in some mixed banking operations early in their careers. If the distinction between the railway-based *mobiliers* and genuine industrial investment banks, or *banques d'affaires*, remained, and in France a considerable lapse of time divided the two, a welcome start had at least been made upon the vital, and long-delayed, work of financial innovation.[105] Also, lasting effects could not fail to follow from the loosening of official controls required by Napoleon's reforms: in 1863 and 1867 specific legislation was framed to facilitate the founding of joint-stock companies, and, in consequence, the next decade witnessed the expansion of the new large-scale finance agencies across the French provinces, while, somewhat reluctantly, offices of the Central Bank trailed in pursuit.

Economically, as in other respects, Louis Napoleon appreciated the utility of bread and circuses. The linked spectacles of the railway bonanza and the financial liberation elicited reponses from many layers of the industrial nation. And these were strengthened and supported both by further doses of imperial largesse and occasional touches of imperial discipline: in the 1860s development subsidies for promising manufactures were balanced by trading agreements with Britain (the Commercial Treaty of 1860) which exposed French industrialists to the bracing effect of vigorous competition. Much-needed adjustments in the direction of capital-intensive growth were thus consequent upon the replacement of an ineffectual monarchy by a confident – elsewhere frequently overbearing – military dictatorship. Advised by practical exponents of Saint-Simonian ideals like the Péreires, Enfantin, Talabot, and Didion, the Second Empire developed a business mind, and put it to constructive use. The revolution of 1848 may have brought agitation and disruption to French economic life in the short term, but it also opened the door to institutional amendments and braver spirits. Before the 1850s were out, the nation's improved economic performance had registered the changes. One could do worse, therefore, than to award new battle honours to the traditional Bonapartist inheritance: as it acquired an additional, if slightly improbable, layer of technological sophistication, the cheque book and the railwayman's cap joined the marshal's baton among the insigniae of imperial office.

Reassuringly, these impressive mid-century developments signal their presence in all the major quantitative surveys. Despite his championship of the pre-1848 economy, Lévy-Leboyer proposes that the turning points of French industrialization were geared to major market changes, the first to 'the traditional rural markets brought together by the railway system.'[106] Before 1850 such a feat of integration was not feasible. More explicitly, Crouzet places the most intense nineteenth-century growth surge between 1845 and 1875, centred on the *empire autoritaire* but spilling over into the July Monarchy and the early Third Republic.[107] And although Marczewski dislikes any nineteenth-century 'take-off' and produces *lower* growth rates (total industrial product) for the three decades after 1845/54 than for the period 1803/12–1835/44, there are some interesting peculiarities to his figures. Firstly, his statistic for the crucial decade 1845/54–1855/64 – a by no means inconsiderable 2.76 per cent per annum (1803/12–1825/34 = 2.86 per cent per annum) – would be unduly deflated by the severe economic dislocation of 1846–48. Rail production, for instance, declined by over 73 per cent in the disturbed period between 1847 and 1850, recovered to the 1847 level by 1853, and improved on this by 67 per cent by the end of the disputed decade. The series at this point may be reflecting not weak industrial energies but the high cost of revolution. Secondly, Marczewski's estimate for net capital formation as a percentage of NNP at no time exceeds the 'bogey' figure of 10 per cent *before* the period 1852–80 (12.1%). Thirdly, he concedes unequivocally that the critical period for railway development and for its impact upon durable production did fall in the three decades *after* 1855/64. Though neither Marczewski nor Lévy-Leboyer is enamoured of a mid-century take-off, there is interest in the modest margin by which their criteria exclude it; indeed the 'fit' between most of the qualitative data and some of the quantitative data for this period could be thought convincing. More importantly, recent statistical measurement, especially that of Crouzet, has broken the monopoly exerted by the 'optimistic' and 'gradualistic' school – proposing *even* growth at *high* rates from the Consulate to the First World War – over the quantitative investigations. Indeed, prospects exist for a new statistical consensus, since, the early decades of the century apart, the results obtained by Lévy-Leboyer are very close to those achieved by Crouzet for the period 1850–1914. Undoubtedly, sufficient quantitative material has now accumulated – which a decade ago it had not – to support a 'pessimistic' and 'discontinuous' interpretation of French development, combining slow growth throughout the century with occasional spurts like those of the 1850s and 1860s.

The admixture of this material to the evidence concerning the improved performance in agriculture, transportation, and finance, blended with generous helpings of perceptive *dirigisme*, produces sufficient beneficial stresses to suggest that 'the great structural mutation'[108] of the French economy might still be placed within the approximate limits of the Second Empire.

If, however, something resembling a 'take-off' was generated in mid-nineteenth-century France, there is very little evidence of appropriately located preconditions. In agriculture, Morineau insists upon a 'recurrence of normal yields . . ., that were identical for three or four centuries' and concludes, unsurprisingly, that, 'the agricultural revolution did not take place in France at the time generally considered as that of take-off'.[109] The agricultural transformation, among the chief of Rostow's credentials for industrialization is thus denied the French economy. Similarly, the flow of innovations within the credit and transportation structures did not precede the 'great upsurge' of the Second Empire but formed an integral part of it. Cameron states explicitly, 'prior to 1848, the financial structure evolved slowly, almost imperceptibly', and that 'major innovations in institutions and techniques were concentrated in the years following the *coup d'état* of 1851'.[110] Similarly, Bouvier is convinced that, 'in the history of French banking, the years 1859 to 1864 are of crucial importance'.[111] No less adamantine are the assessments of railway development: Marczewski rules that 'railway construction could not have had any determinant influence on the economy before 1850'.[112] This leaves little hope for the lesser prerequisites. The scholarly preoccupation with French raw material endowment revolves around not its greatly increased utilization but its poverty in amount and quality. The debate over French entrepreneurship has been concerned not with the emergence of adventurous decision-takers but rather with analysing the relationship between inveterate risk-avoiders and restrictive social conventions. Therefore, it would seem to follow that the mid-century upsurge, *l'essor impérial*, occurred virtually without benefit of preconditions. This, of course, reflects poorly upon the validity of Rostow's conceptual structure – not by any means for the first time – but neither does it leave the solidity of the mid-century boom entirely unquestioned.

THE UNFORTUNATE ECONOMY: THE PROBLEM OF SUSTAINING GROWTH, 1850–1914

In most stage theories of economic development, the transition from the initial industrial leap to the more even jog-trot of sustained advance takes place with notable – if usually mysterious – smoothness. Some break in pace, a momentary hesitation, may be permitted, but there is little room for any more extended pause, and less for any temporary loss of direction. Consequently, French performance between 1850 and 1914 is remarkable for its failure to conform to these athletic norms. True, the new capital goods sectors did generate sufficient impetus for a fairly rapid dash until about 1870, although there are some suspicions of flagging energies in the late 1860s. From this point, however, the economic terrain was so distorted by the eruption of political obstacles – in the shape of the Franco-Prussian War and the humiliation of Sedan – that the prospects of maintaining further advances, even at modest rates, were severely jeopardized. Military ineffectuality carried penalties not only for Napoleon's international fancies but also for his business interests. As war spoils, Alsace-Lorraine was transferred into Prussian occupation, and with it went rich textile industries, important caches of minerals, and no less than four-fifths of the entire French machine-building industry. Iron-ore deposits making up 80 per cent of known French resources – fortunately the vast worth of the nearby Briey basin was not then known – were surrendered, together with their attendant blast-furnaces and steelworks. In comparison with these losses, the war indemnity demanded by Berlin – but easily financed by the European exchanges – fell upon the Parisian diplomatists and bankers rather as an indignity than as a genuine economic hardship.

But to many observers the value of the concessions make of the Prussian War an economic as well as a nationalistic trauma: for them Sedan is the signpost to nine years of negligible growth, falling prices and profits, and rising wages. Here it seems that the political element intervenes once more to encumber the growth path. Yet, more optimistic spirits, including Crouzet and Palmade, have argued that the accumulated industrial momentum was sufficient to carry the economy past the 'accident' of 1870−71, and that serious deceleration occurred only from 1876,[113] or from 1882, when a cyclical crash and a credit squeeze combined with international financial instability to constitute a genuinely impassable hazard.[114] Marczewski's calculations, revealing an easing of railway expansion and a decline in the rate of growth of industrial product from its thirty-year plateau of 2.7 per cent per year to a new level of 2.2 per cent per year, would also suggest that the decade 1875/84−1885/94 represented the critical period of transition. Certainly the short boom near the beginning of this period, 1879−82, implies that a little vitality was left to the economy despite the attentions of von Moltke's armies. But about the 1880s there can be little argument: stagnationist tendencies are much in evidence between 1882 and 1900 and especially within the earlier part of this period. These doldrums derived not only from the business and financial insecurity of the early 1880s, nor only from the European 'Great Depression' of the era, experienced by France most acutely in the early 1890s. They were influenced also by national catastrophe: the French economy it seems, was accident prone, and its slow growth attributable, at least in part, to the malevolence of fortune.

For late-nineteenth-century France was subjected not only to a plague of Prussians but also to the twin scourges of *pébrine* and *Phylloxera*. *Pébrine* spread slaughter throughout the silkworm population and diseased profits throughout the luxury textile trade. More awful still was the corpulent greenfly *Phylloxera vastatrix*, discovered in a Hammersmith greenhouse in 1863, and within months to be found champing its way across the vineyards of the Rhône. From the late 1860s it spread swiftly into the Midi and the Gironde, perhaps aided by the neglect of viticulture brought about by the war; from 1878 it embarked upon the occupation of the Médoc; from the later 1880s it campaigned against the Côte d'Or. As the conquests accumulated, the cost to the French economy rose stupendously. By 1880 between one-half and one-third of the vineyards of St Emilion and Fronsac lay in ruins; by 1882 the Gironde had lost 138,000 of its 141,420 hectares under vine; by 1890 Burgundy had ceded two-thirds of its wine industry to the occupying forces. Recovery, aided by grafts of hardy American vine-stock, came late and sometimes not at all. In the Médoc even the greatest vineyards, like Lafite, exhibited few signs of life before the late 1880s. Some more easterly areas such as the Yonne or the Côte de Dijon never recaptured their former capacity. Lower Burgundy surrendered over 60 per cent of its vine acreage in perpetuity. The sole merit of this relentless aphid was that, in reducing the capability of the vine, it broadcast the attractions of grain-based alcohols, not least those of Scotland. But if the Highland distilleries, secure in the knowledge that *Phylloxera* had little affinity for malt, responded to the new opportunities with enthusiasm, the French had no reason to applaud the gains to mankind in general. *Phylloxera* proved scarcely less costly than the Prussians: it drove a major employer close to destitution, ruined a valuable export trade, withheld an essential ingredient of Gallic spirit and sustenance. When the final bill – for the tangible destruction – was presented it probably exceeded £400 m., approximately 37 per cent of the average annual GDP for 1885–94.[115]

Agricultural cataclysm was not lacking in the most comprehensive politico-economic implications. As the industries previously promoted by imperial *dirigisme* lost way under the timid hands of the Third Republic, as important cereal-growing regions encountered the swingeing deflation of grain prices which accompanied the 'transport revolution' of the late century, the credibility of *laissez-faire* as the governing concept in French trading relations was seriously eroded. Further crises represented by the chronic embarrassment of the silk and wine industries carried this process further, and helped swell the forces pushing the new republican regime towards protectionism. The reconversion to tariffs began in 1881, proceeded through the upward revisions of 1885 and 1887, and culminated in the *pièce de résistance* of the Méline Tariff in 1892.[116]

Such misfortune is indisputable; what is disputed is the point of its termination. Orthodoxy places the watershed in the mid-1890s and the period 1895–1914 as one of rapid growth based upon new technologies such as chemicals, bicycles, and motor-cars. Brisk industrial output certainly appears in Marczewski's series for both of the decades 1885/94–1895/1904 and 1895/1904–1905/13 – at 2.4 and 2.85 per cent per annum respectively – and is concentrated around innovational industries (here engineering, rayon, and electricity are selected as the most promising).[117] Foundations for this development are provided by Lévy-Leboyer: as the growth surge of the Second Empire was based upon the unification of the rural market, so revived activity after 1895 rested upon a second market adjustment – 'urbanization gave the economy its second wind'.[118] The twin upheavals in French supply in the nineteenth century are thus elegantly related to major swings in demand. However, such optimism is not universal: the second upheaval has its detractors. Thus Palmade has detected an *'essouflement'* of French capitalism in the decades before 1914: he sketches a view of failing enterprise that bears an ominous similarity to the 'pessimistic' interpretation of British business practice during the much-disputed 'Great Depression'.[119] Many of the 'failures' perpetrated by the nonchalant British are alleged against the indolent French: the slow substitution of the Solvay for the Leblanc process in alkali production; the poor exploitation of precocious discoveries in dyestuffs technology; the retarded application of 'best practice' in steel-making; the aversion of the banking community to industrial finance.[120] Yet, in some areas, French capitalists clearly outpaced their Anglo-Saxon colleagues. In automobile manufacture for instance, the French dominated the European trade: uncharacteristically large firms (averaging 600 workers each in 1914) succeeded in creating exports which surpassed the American in value in 1911 and 1912; by 1913 their total output was twice that of their British rivals.[121] In the electrical, pipe-making, and specialist metal industries there were also noteworthy exponents of the managerial skills.

Before planting another evergreen debate around the issue of entrepreneurial deficiency, we may note that a measure of reconciliation between these interpretations is not impossible. Crouzet, in his recent quantitative investigations, most interestingly failed to find the conventional economic upturn around 1895. Although he concedes substantial absolute increments to French manufacturing output, and, like Marczewski, draws attention to the singularly rapid advance of engineering sectors between 1896 and 1914, his conclusion from the full range of his extensive series is that, 'the recovery of the *belle époque* . . . appears from these indices as tardier and less brilliant than is generally supposed . . . the indices do not really regain their dynamism until the last pre-war years after *1905* which appears to have been an important turning point'.[122] It is perhaps in this later date that compromise lies. After its accidents of the 1880s, and subsequent subjection to a bout of the *maladie anglaise*, it may well be that the French economy was prone to *essoufflement* in the period down to 1905. It could be – as the econometricians maintain – that there were dynamic sectors before this date; and a more general recovery after it.

The weight of the evidence swings towards the conclusion that industrial growth in nineteenth-century France was indeed hesitant, spasmodic, and slow. It is the 'catastrophic' not the 'dynamic' aspects of the revolutionary period which prevail; whatever growth prospects France had accumulated by 1789 were largely dispersed by 1815. It is arthritis not athleticism which is most evident in French attempts at 'catching up'. And of the various alternatives offered for the eventual transition to industrialization, it is the most delayed which is the most convincing. Even then, once the industrial process is commenced, its equilibrium is by no means secure: the vehicle which carried the economy into 'take-off' in the 1850s, faltered in the 1870s, veered alarmingly in the 1880s, perhaps coasted on reduced power until the early 1900s, and finally discovered a last reserve of thrust merely to overfly a fragment of the *belle époque*. It managed to sustain two growth spurts separated by doldrums and disasters. And in the century-long series even its bursts of energy lose much of their drama; the most obvious feature of Crouzet's charts for major industrial groups (as of Lévy-Leboyer's series from 1850) is their *flatness*. No doubt, even modified spurts and gently ascending output wrought considerable changes upon French society and economy; in terms of past experience, French institutions experienced transformation, even if it came slowly and painfully. Yet any comparative test reveals that French performance, however it may have taxed national energies and tastes, was by the standards of the international industrial community, distinctly modest: Table 3.3 displays a decadal growth rate in French national product lower than that of any other manufacturing nation in the period 1840–1910. And Table 3.4 surveys a large number of economic indicators, invariably placing France low in the industrial league.

FRANCE

Table 3.3 Average decadal growth rate of NNP:
Selected countries (%)

France	1840–1910	18.6
UK	1860/69–1905/14	25.0
Russia	1870–1913	27.7
Sweden	1861/68–1904/13	34.8
Germany	1860/69–1905/14	35.6
USA	1869/78–1904/13	56.0

Source: Kuznets (1956), p. 15.

Perhaps unsurprisingly, the revisionist tactics for the economic history of France appear to be passing out of style: the advocates of 'fast and steady' growth subjected the plentiful jeremiads of the immediately post-war period, and frequently of American authorship, to intense statistical bombardment, only to find, when the smoke cleared, that they had been using blank ammunition. Ironically, the emphasis upon the *even* pace of French industrial development may be construed in support not only of the assessments featuring 'fast and steady' growth but just as readily in corroboration of the pessimistic assertions of 'slow and continuous' advance.[123] More recent statistical measurements have demonstrated that there is no necessary affinity between econometrics and optimism, and that a conjunction between the quantitative

Table 3.4 Selected comparative indicators of economic performance

		France	Germany	UK
Coal output[a]				
(% increase per head,	1850–73	6.12	8.71	–
average per year)	1896–1913	1.74	8.49	
Pig iron Output[b]				
(% increase total,	1851–73	5.2	8.49	–
average per year)				
Industrial h.p.[c]				
(totals, m.)	1913	3.5	8.25	10.75
Steel output[d]				
(m. tons)	1913	5.0	17.0	7.5
Cotton spindles[e]				
(m.)	1912	7.6	10.5	57.0
Central government[f]				
expenditure as % national product	1913	13.3	6.2	7.1
Industrial output[g]				
(% increase average per year)	1860–80	2.4	2.7	2.4
	1880–1900	2.4	5.3	1.7
	1900–1913	3.7	4.4	2.2

Sources [a] Gillet (1969), p. 189.   [b] Fohlen (1970), p. 224.   [c] Clough (1946), p. 99   [d,e] Clapham (1936), pp. 238, 248.   [f] Calculated from Mitchell (1975). Central government expenditure, pp. 701, 702; national product, pp. 785, 790, 797. France = GDP; Germany = NNP; UK = GNP.   [g] Patel (1965), p. 72.

159

and the well-tried qualitative data is by no means impossible. Palace revolutions in historiography may come and go, but the industrial revolution in France remains timid and spasmodic. Perhaps Fohlen's description combines innovation and balance in the appropriate measure: 'Whereas it started in the second half of the eighteenth century, at approximately the same time as in neighbouring England, it proceeded tardily and less completely.'[124]

EXPLANATIONS

The French economic problem between 1850 and 1914 is simply put, if much less simply explained: the industrial system generated a miscellany of growth periods – some offering rapid development, others a small measure of inertial momentum, others again a definite relapse – rather than a smoothly sustained advance. France, it appears, could make industrial beginnings but could not build upon them confidently. If this is revealed by the aggregate measures of industrial output, it is no less obvious on the micro-economic level, with problems of invention and innovation. Here opportunities were missed with almost professional consistency: the French pioneered coke-smelting and investment banking on the continent, but exploited neither fully, nor fast enough; they contrived inventions like Lebon's gaslight and Girard's spinning machine, but surrendered their profitable application to rival economies; they lacked some natural endowments, notably coal, but squandered others, notably the massive water-power of the Rhône and Isère, while nearby Switzerland demonstrated to the industrial world how hydraulic virtuosity might compensate for mineral deficiency. It is a story of unrealized potentials and missed chances, of painful contrasts and lessons apparently unlearned. Many hypotheses have been proposed in explanation of these critical failures in response: shortage of capital, clumsy governments, deficient resources, incompetent entrepreneurs – each has been made to play the pantomime demon in its turn. None has succeeded. And no single-value explanation of this type is likely to succeed. Wherever the answer to the French enigma rests, it will be in a notably complex interplay of forces. However, it is noteworthy that many of the traditional explanations are not as single-valued as they appear; many are double-sided, deeply ambivalent. In fact, they 'explain' very little, but may indicate the areas in which more intricate explanatory systems reside.

POLITICS AND DEVELOPMENT: THE POLITICS OF UNDER-ACHIEVEMENT

The vast pre-eminence of the French revolution, suspended like some threatening crag over most aspects of the Frenchman's life, has clearly helped to suggest that political events might seriously influence the pace of the country's economic pulse. Within the deeds of the revolutionary and imperial administrations before 1815, there was certainly sufficient to stimulate some economic activity and, in the end, catastrophically, to affect most. Probably, the revolution also exerted an enduring leverage upon social values and aspirations – or reinforced selected values and aspirations – which acted to curtail the capability for dynamic entrepreneurship. And in a very general sense the proposition that linkages exist between political and economic processes is obviously uncontentious. But the additional speculation that the detail and chronology of French growth may have been modulated by political affairs – that disagreements in the Chamber obstructed railway growth; that the tensions of 1848–52 delayed the introduction of new metallurgical methods; that the mid-century boom was terminated by the disgrace of Sedan[125] – is less than satisfactory. Certainly, major political embroilments can provoke corresponding economic tremors, but, from 1815 onwards, France is not well supplied with convincing examples. The obstructive and argumentative deputies of the 1830s and 1840s were motivated not merely by political commitment; self-evidently they also possessed and acted upon *economic* interest. Again, the new metallurgical methods had lagged in application long before the disturbances of 1848–52. And the measure in which responsibility for the closure of the growth era associated with the Second Empire may be attributed to the Franco-Prussian War remains entirely obscure. If there is a consensus on this point, it runs against the political interpretation: the conflict between those who argue that the economy was decelerating before Sedan and those who contend that it continued to grow after Sedan is resolved at one significant point – both groups agree that Sedan made little difference.

Furthermore, there is the problem of the 1880s and 1890s. If the economic doldrums persisted until 1900, exactly what political trauma was produced by the Third Republic which could account for it? Surely, the pathetic monarchism of Boulanger did not include a low growth rate among the many discredits in his knapsack. There were other good reasons for the delays in improvement of transportation and metallurgy, and other good non-political reasons for retardation in the last third of the century. An economy with such a consistently low propensity to accept innovation, and to build upon growth, cannot be satisfactorily described simply by a political calculus: extensive economic and socio-economic deficiencies are implied by its performance and are not captured by such a description. Political variables may perhaps act as reinforcing agents, binding more tightly already cramped patterns of development, but they can scarcely take the primary strain when the economic chains themselves weigh so heavily.

TRADE AND DEVELOPMENT: EXPORTS AS A DRAGGING SECTOR?

The reversal of French commercial fortunes during the revolutionary period, coupled with the slow recovery of exports after 1815, has offered tempting contrasts with the experience of Britain, the continent's prime exporter and first industrial nation. Approximately equal commercial capabilities in 1789 formed the introduction to diametrically opposed growth patterns: Britain exploited her trade advantages and became an international manufacturing emporium; France forfeited her advantages and became an industrial laggard. One possible deduction might be that if economies can be export-propelled, they may also be export-restrained. France might then become the classic example of the economy diverted onto the slow line for lack of export traction. Certainly, there were sufficient problems within the economy's export sector. Its contribution to world markets remained insignificant throughout the first third of the century, and despite considerable improvement in trade volumes during the Second Empire – trebling the size of exports – its repressive influence was not eradicated. The important tariff treaty with Britain in 1860, and its successors, did secure preferential trading terms with a number of countries. Duties on imported raw materials were also reduced for the benefit of export manufacturers. The aim, mainly to convert France into an entrepôt for cotton and wool products, was partially achieved.

But the difficulties surrounding the choice of commodities which France might herself successfully export proved more persistent. The commercial 'niche' left for France by industrialization elsewhere was narrow and uncomfortable. In textiles the low wage costs of German and Swiss mills made anything less than bulk production uneconomical, yet Britain, with her vast mechanical equipment, was already solidly established as the mass supplier of cottons. High-quality manufacture offered some prospects but confronted a market circumscribed by elevated prices and less amenable to expansion than one of the British type. Consequently, France exported a lower proportion of output than Britain – one-fifth of cotton production against the British export share of two-thirds by 1850 – and achieved much lower export values – about one-tenth of the British level for cottons in 1827–29, one-fifteenth by 1844–45. Until the *pébrine* epidemic of the later decades, silk – appropriate for the high-quality niche – was the most successful French export. By the 1820s its export values approached half the combined total of all other textiles and by 1845 exceeded the combined total of cotton and linen by a factor of two.[126] Yet the best prospects were also the most limited and specialized. At the end of the century, increased exportation of iron ore, steel, and automobiles – the latter high-quality but also high-technology products – brought some relief, but the pressure behind this reasonably impressive trade upswing was provided originally by a *domestic* boom centred upon an urban expansion which provided the solid substratum of demand for all these commodities. Exports constituted less of a leading sector than a useful overspill at this point.

These facts cause little dispute in themselves.[127] The problematic issue concerns the relationship between these constrained export reflexes and the well-being of the French body economic. Beyond doubt, a flourishing external trade provides a sound base for industrial specialization, extensive division of labour and the economies of scale attached to large-scale production, as well as extensive linkage effects. But the corollary, that an expansive foreign trade forms an essential keystone without which the industrial edifice cannot achieve stability is not convincing. Even in the British case, the expansion of the domestic market played a larger role in the gathering of industrial strength than did the impressive 'commercial revolution' of the eighteenth century. Similarly, the early stages of Germany's rapid industrialization were achieved with little recourse to foreign trade: here it formed not so much a substructure for 'take-off' as an outlet for the overproduction of a mature economy. And, in France itself, since overseas trade remained at a relatively low level throughout the century, it cannot explain – and apparently did not impede – the isolated periods of energetic growth which did occur. Admittedly, export values did increase in these periods, but their gearing to total industrial output remained so weak as not significantly to affect the pace of advance. Unlike Britain, where export booms frequently led domestic recoveries in the second half of the century, it is probable that France experienced export activity as a by-product of 'autonomous' domestic upswings.

There is no doubt that France needed to export. Domestic endowment was by no means lavish and the requirement to purchase large amounts of raw materials overseas maintained pressure upon the import 'trigger', necessitating a compensating reaction from the export sector. Yet there is little reason to believe that the protracted and hesitant start to French industrialization may be traced to the lethargic nature of the export response. If export capability counts heavily at any point in the model of European development, it seems most frequently to be in *sustaining* the continued advance of already prosperous economies. Until 1900, however, the behaviour of the French economy remained uncertain in *both* the early and the more mature stages of development while variations in its progress cannot be convincingly synchronized with variations in export performance. And, in general, it is in any case more likely that the line of causation will run from the economy to the export sector rather than in the opposite direction. Foreign trade is merely one among a battery of possible stimuli to which a healthy economy may respond positively. But within a debilitated economy a strong export stimulus will run to waste and a weak export performance will constitute a symptom rather than a cause of economic drag.

DEMOGRAPHY AND DEVELOPMENT: THE AMBIGUITIES OF UNDER-POPULATION

Unfortunately, unlike the British or German industrialists, the French could not supplement their overseas markets, nor compensate for the lack of them, by exploiting a rapidly expanding domestic market. From 1800 the number of consumers displayed a marked disinclination to grow and the 'demographic surge' frequently associated with the early career of most industrial nations remained conspicuously absent. Understandably, much argument has been spent in the attempt to connect this demographic inadequacy with economic under-performance. Certainly French population and French production appear to have shared a taste for inaction: after ranking in size second only to the Russian hordes in 1800, the French population stock grew only half as fast as the total European community in the succeeding century. Between 1815 and 1914, the Americans managed to multiply by 1000 per cent, the Germans and British by about 170 per cent, and the French by 35 per cent. As early as 1860, in an overturning of supposed behavioural preferences, the French propensity to reproduce was so curtailed that thirty-seven *départements* were unable even to *maintain* their headcount; by 1890 a dozen more were similarly embarrassed.[128] National gross reproduction rates declined from 2.0 in 1801–05 to 1.70 in 1851–55 and to 1.25 by 1914.[129] Consequently, the rate of demographic advance was even more tardy in the second half of the century than in the first: between 1872 and 1911 population increased by only 10 per cent. The contribution of the French to European population contracted continuously – from 15 per cent of the total in 1800 through 13.5 per cent in 1850 to 9.7 per cent in 1900.[130] Appropriately, the total of Germans first exceeded that of Frenchmen in 1870 – with the Germans mustering 4.5 m. men of military age against the French 4.4 m. – and was far ahead by 1914 – when the disparity in potential military strength had widened to 7.7 m. against 4.5 m.

Deficiencies in the supply of soldiery were not the only problems to follow from this predicament. Demographic paralysis fell upon France precisely when she needed additional consumers to help create a viable domestic market. But demand was not the only factor to suffer. Towards the end of the century, serious deficiencies in labour supply began to appear and new industries had often to be based upon a workforce recruited from the four corners of Europe, especially from Spain, Italy, and Poland. Even the exploitation of the invaluable ores of Briey was impeded in the 1880s and 1890s by lack of labour. Ironmasters, faced by local reserves that were both lean and rural, imported Italian miners in large numbers. In Lorraine the blast-furnaces emptied during the potato-picking and grain-harvesting seasons. Nor were such problems confined to the late nineteenth century: French manufacturers had employed foreign labour well before 1850, even the capitalists of Mulhouse relying on German or Swiss workers at this time. Immigrant labour was the badge of French demographic weakness. Of the 14 m. increase in French population between 1801 and 1936, no less than 5.5 m. were provided by immigrants and their descendants.[131] One major industrialist concluded that the national manufacturing problem stemmed from 'lack of workers in coal mines . . . shortages of workers in the steel works, rolling mills, foundries, and construction workshops'.[132] In some respects, therefore, the snagged development of the French economy may have followed simply from a lack of Frenchmen.

However, the double-edged nature of the population endowment affected France no less than Germany. If Germany had to balance the swelling labour force and expanding consumption of her rapidly growing community against its threats to income growth and capital accumulation, France was faced with a balance which reversed the weights. For her it was a question of juggling the assets in *per capita* incomes and savings accumulation against the under-supply in consumers and workers. By mid-century, at least one of the assets had achieved prominence: French savings were notably abundant. Why then were these savings not employed to finance a more emphatic style of industrial expansion?

Of the available explanations two stand out. Firstly it is possible that the rich supply of savings had been acquired only fairly recently. In the second half of the eighteenth century French population had expanded quite strongly,[133] achieving by 1800 a size so large – some 29 m. – that it threatened to litter the threshold to industrialization with demographic obstacles. As the experience of modern underdeveloped countries indicates, this species of demographic endowment depresses pre-industrial incomes and hampers the accumulation of investment power. In France, population, influenced perhaps by precocious experimentation with birth control,[134] may have slid away from just such a conjunction only after 1800. Sufficient capital for industrialization may then have been amassed only as the population stock adjusted to a growth rate at which savings could be maintained and not dispersed in supporting a demographic excess. A slow and uncertain industrial start would be consistent with this model.

Alternatively, the emphasis may be taken from the supply of funds and placed upon the demand for their employment. In a market of miniature producers the high savings rates permitted by leisurely population growth may encourage, not saving for productive investment, but hoarding for reserves. Entrepreneurial expectations are not galvanized by the slow increase in consuming groups and the business community experiences little incentive to call out the savings. In these circumstances, under-investment and under-employment will appear; actual growth in national income will fall below the potential level; capital per head will be formed less rapidly than if the population were expanding more quickly. The particular hazard in this pattern is that it establishes the capacity, but not the incentive, for efficient use of savings.

Perhaps the disadvantages of slow population growth are somewhat qualified: after all substantial savings *were* accumulated, thanks in part to demographic deceleration. The questions hang not over their existence but over the manner of their employment. Moreover, it is probable that French population reserves possessed characteristics more destructive than merely their small size and slow growth. In all probability, the unusually low physical mobility of the French rural community and its unusually high level of self-sufficiency formed more seriously binding constraints. In France, country-dwellers moved away from their smallholdings and towards urban–industrial employment with the utmost possible reluctance. Reflecting this, the rural proportion in total population declined only slowly from 75 per cent in 1846 to 69 per cent in 1872 and to 59 per cent in 1901. Between 1850 and 1872 internal migration did accelerate – Paris and the Nord/Pas de Calais regions recorded population gains of 40 per cent and 20 per cent respectively – and around 1900 it quickened again. But, even in 1910, France could boast only fifteen cities with more than 100,000 inhabitants while Britain and America could each claim 50 of these concentrations and Germany 42. For the majority of Frenchmen, life revolved around the peasant plot or the country town and economic processes focused upon household autarky or the provincial market-place.

Determined action by governments and capitalists might well have circumvented these obstacles. *Morcellement*, the division of French legacies at inheritance, guaranteeing a parcel of property to each heir, was the prime cause of the fixity in population distribution, and the low propensity to consume. It was also, of course, an incentive to keep families small so as to maximize the inter-generational share-out. Government intervention aimed at reforming the system of land tenure and inheritance, though undoubtedly an intricate and politically vexed affair, could have yielded substantial economic returns. Similarly, the facilities for internal migration stood in need of improvement. Even those French agriculturalists disposed to convert themselves into urban workers found the means of mobility inadequate. Railway interests were slow to provide services and were handed misconceived specifications by the official transport strategists. Thus the Le Grand plan, involving a mere 6000 kilometres of track, was proposed in 1832, adopted by the Chamber in 1842, and completed only in 1857. The first attempt at a national communications network, it was in fact much less than national in scope: its design, entailing a number of railway 'spokes' radiating from the 'hub' of Paris, left many important outlying regions entirely untended. Provincial labour could thus flow readily into Paris — as it did during Haussmann's rebuilding under the Second Empire — but only very haltingly to the scattered centres of manufacturing. Saint-Simonian plans for a genuinely 'industrial' system centred on St Dizier and linking Marseilles to Bordeaux and Calais found little sympathy with the officials of the government's transport department, the Ponts et Chausées; instead large tracts of the south and south-west were set in isolation from the north and east, and eastern heavy industry was denied full access to a nation-wide demand. Even the Freycinet plan of 1879, inaugurated as a public works programme to counter the recessive trends of the late 1870s, was subject to substantial operating constraints:[135] although it increased the provision of track from 23,089 kilometres in 1880 to 38,109 kilometres in 1900, many of its facilities were suspected as *lignes electorales*, aimed at political rather than transportational utility.[136] The implications for population mobility were unsavoury: migration became, and characteristically remained, a short-distance affair — frequently between neighbouring *départements* — and frequently incorporating employment choices far removed from industry.[137] Poor transportation was thus an important influence in withholding population supplies from urban–industrial concentrations; and so too was *morcellement*.

Under the pressures created by an inadequate transport system and an unsatisfactory inheritance system, a reformulation of the French demographic problem logically takes shape: that human capital in France was poorly utilized and inefficiently deployed rather than merely undersized. Release of existing population resources would have done much to raise the level of economic activity and to swell the tide of consumer demand.

In theory, both large and small populations, both low and high demographic rates, can accompany, and may not necessarily obstruct, economic growth. On balance, however, the difficulties presented by small populations and low rates were probably the more taxing under nineteenth- (if not twentieth-) century conditions. Yet in France, certain of these difficulties set up a demand for decision-making responses from the institutions of business and government; proficient decisions would greatly have eased the course of growth. Generally, the retarding effects of resource misutilization are easily confused with the retarding effects of resource deficiency, and this confusion is characteristic and perennial in French economic history. In consequence, nature is often blamed for too much.

NATURAL ENDOWMENT AND UNNATURAL PRACTICE

A writer of fables might imagine that, when the creator of France had almost completed his work, he was beset by an egalitarian conscience, and weighing mines carefully against vines, moved to delete the coal. Discovering this after some lapse of time, the nineteenth-century Frenchman could detect no logical point in industry and turned instead to drink. Fancifully put, this is, in substance, a version of French economic history which has found many protagonists.

Until 1870 France had to rely upon foreign suppliers not only for much of her industrial labour but also for much of her industrial fuel: the share of coal imports in total consumption varied from 25 per cent in 1830 to a peak of 45 per cent in 1857 and settled to a more usual level of 30 per cent for the period 1870–1914.[138] In 1912 France was still buying nearly half of her industrial coke requirements overseas, and, with the great majority (82%) of these vital supplies originating in Germany, lay prey to any discriminatory policy which her major continental rival chose to apply. Admittedly, from mid-century the coalfields of the Nord and Pas de Calais were developed with extreme rapidity – achieving growth rates in output scarcely inferior to those of the Ruhr – but these regions constituted only the leading sector of a fuel industry, by no means an industry in themselves. Total French output remained modest by any international standard: even in 1913 the French coal cut was about one-twelfth of the American, one-seventh of the British, and one-fifth of the German. Of all the major powers, France was the only one to suffer such a chronically severe shortage of the nineteenth century's classical mineral fuel. But scarcity was not the only demerit of French coal stocks; what reserves lay in the basins of St Etienne, Saône-et-Loire, and the Nord were extremely expensive to remove. Pithead prices around mid-century were commonly 50 per cent higher than comparable British prices,[139] and transportation from the fields of Ronchamp to the factories of Alsace could double the pithead cost.

In turn, this devalued the worth of the high-grade metal ores from Lorraine and Briey, assets which would have been much enriched by adequate stocks of good coking coal. With the price of French coke very nearly doubling between 1896 and 1900 – from 13½ francs to 25 francs the ton – it was not surprising that the country remained a net importer of iron ore until as late as 1906. Even the vast potential of Briey could only be exploited with painful slowness between the early 1880s – the time of its effective discovery – and 1914 – when it was, at long last, permitting France to export one-third of the iron ore raised. The reserves of Briey carried France from sixth to third place in the world ranking of iron-ore production between 1870 and 1914, but, on the outbreak of war, output per head remained far below the British or the German levels. Nor, alongside the scarce coal and the iron ore that was phosphoric, looted by the Germans in 1871, and expensive to smelt, were there any useful deposits of copper, lead, zinc, or tin. Consequently, even in 1914 immense amounts of varied raw materials, valued far beyond the worth of French manufactured exports, were being imported: where Britain needed only 75 per cent of her manufactured exports (by value) to meet her import bill in raw materials, and Germany 100 per cent, France required 125–135 per cent.[140] Denied sufficient population above ground, it seemed that France was also to be denied any subterranean compensation.

The niggardliness of nature was certainly a problem for French development. But it provides no satisfactory explanation of French underdevelopment. If the resource-endowment hypothesis is put as a *reductio ad absurdum*, some revealing counterpoints are formed. Is it very relevant, for instance, to propose that eighteenth-century Britain suffered from resource deficiency in her inability to grow raw cotton, or twentieth-century Japan in her inability to mine large quantities of vital metals? Yet it is relevant that a France deprived of cheap coal lagged behind Britain in industries where coal costs were not of primary importance: cotton textiles again provides an important example. Comparative testing readily throws up countries with meagre coal endowments which industrialized successfully – like Holland – or even rapidly – like Japan or Switzerland. In reality, resource endowment is linked to industrial development by highly ambivalent relationships. Increasingly, it is fashionable to argue, for instance, that the rich French timber stocks both explained and justified the iron industry's persistent retention of outmoded smelting technology, yet, on the other hand, it was the *depletion* of the timber stands which eventually promoted 'cokeification' in the 1830s and 1840s.[141] Which was the useful endowment: the surplus or the shortage of charcoal fuel? Similarly, if lavish coal deposits can build the muscles of industrial strength, scarce and expensive reserves can as readily stimulate the reflexes of high-technology response – most especially towards advanced methods of fuel economy. Further, since technical change itself has the power to *alter* the relationship between the industrialist's needs for minerals and the economy's supplies of raw materials, it may not be sensible to ascribe inadequate technical progress to weaknesses in natural endowment. Industrial development may as easily define the need for, and promote the exploitation of, the relevant resources as the other way about.

Once again, the genuine determinants of growth are found less in the supply of factors as in the quality of the decisions governing factor use. Recent comment has in fact found little amiss in the French resource equipment. Thus Fohlen has described a France 'wealthy in hydraulic energy and fairly rich in coal';[142] Kindleberger has emphasized the *rapidity* of mining development after 1850;[143] Gillet has portrayed French coalfields outpacing their Belgian rivals – in 1870 combined output from the Nord and the Pas de Calais' reached only one-third of Belgian production totals, but by 1910 comfortably surpassed them.[144] Naturally, the higher the value placed upon such useful assets and creditable exploitation, the more numerous become the doubts concerning the efficiency with which mineral inputs were converted into manufactured outputs. Here it seems, there was less room for credit.

Transportation again proved a case in point, and an especially constricted bottleneck. As Kindleberger has observed, all countries need to acquire scarce materials by trade, and, with bulky commodities, transportation services form an integral part of the process of acquisition.[145] The French, however, were extremely slow to perceive the need for full integration of fuel and communications strategies. Mine-owners, naturally enough, proved an exception and lobbied for better water connexions between the pits and the urban– industrial concentrations. But official response to their initiatives was almost pathologically cautious: coal interests argued for the Canal du Nord from the 1860s, secured the commencement of its first section in 1908, awaited its completion until the 1960s [146] Scarcely better was the provision of rail freight connexions: Paris was joined to the collieries of the Pas de Calais only in 1860, and down to the 1840s had relied for its main fuel supplies upon tortuously water-borne coal from St Etienne. Similarly, until the mid-century, coal travelled to the vital factory city of Mulhouse by road, attracting needy industrialists to the town boundaries for the ritual competitive bribery of the incoming hauliers. Much of Alsatian industry could have been supplied from the Saar or Burgundy, only 190 kilometres distant, but lacked the railroads with which to fetch the coal. Even when, around 1914, the railway companies were able to provide a dependable freight service, they offered no concessionary rates on industrial coke from the Nord.

However, once the appropriate tracks were constructed, a major part of the fuel bottleneck was shattered: between 1840 and 1870 the transport cost of fuel to the factory-owner fell by a factor of seven. In Rouen, once the railway arrived, coal costs slumped to a mere 0.04 franc per kilogram of spun cotton.[147] Clearly, if plentiful French capital had been converted more rapidly into operating social overheads, with less interference from contentious politicians and quarrelsome bankers, the constraints of scarce fuel would have been much relaxed. Improvements in factor use by both public and private agencies, by the Chamber itself, by finance houses and transport contractors would have considerably amended the utility of French factor endowment. Also, international endowment, in the shape of imported coal, would have become available on better terms. Or at least it would have done, but for another set of questionable decisions.

In a country reputedly deprived of coal, it would appear neither necessary nor wise to place tariff restrictions upon coal imports. Yet that, in the early 1820s, the 1830s, and later in 1892 and 1910, was the preference of the French mining interests, and that, under the pressure of these interests, became official policy. In order to preserve the fuel market for domestic producers, a surcharge was deliberately placed upon the coal account of a nation committed to the large-scale importation of fuel. The egocentricity, commercial timidity, and conservatism of French pit-owners was of an exceptional order. But as Kindleberger observes: 'There was very little reason for France to complain of the price of coal since a tariff was maintained on the commodity.'[148] Neither price nor scarcity of coal can be seriously rated as a binding constraint, if the consumer prefers to increase the cost to himself.

Conceivably, however, the reality was less masochistic or irrational than the appearance. Students of the French businessman, like students of his British counterpart, are becoming increasingly disposed to construe the entrepreneur's actions, however unlikely, as commercially sound responses to difficult times or intractable problems. There is some merit in this. In the case of the French fuel industry, the problem lay in the incomplete integration of the coal-producing and coal-consuming sectors of industry; the coincidence of interest between the pit-owners and the ironmasters was much less complete than in Britain, Belgium, or Germany.[149] Deposits of iron were geographically far removed from deposits of coal and the persistent inadequacy of transport between them not only owed something to the conservatism of some businessmen but, *sine culpa*, strengthened the separatism of others. Exchange of investment between the iron- and steelmasters of Lorraine and the coal-owners of the Nord and Centre was minimal. In particular, the coal barons did not take up holdings in metals, as they did in Germany, and thus had no special interest in restraining the cost of fuel inputs. If a model of separate, and partially contending, lobbies is assumed, the paradox of French 'fuel masochism' is largely resolved.

With generosity, similar indulgence may be extended to the ironmasters, the pretext, in this case, issuing less from the separation of industrial interests than from the convolutions of geology. Thus, the slow development of the Briey ore deposits probably owed more to difficulties of terrain than to failings in decision-making. Despite the massed disapproval of Professors Pitts, Parker, and Pounds, it is difficult to fault the argument which emphasizes Briey's geological unfriendliness:[150] in many cases the ground surrounding the mine shafts had even to be artificially frozen in order to immobilize water in the ore-bearing strata. Conservatism in exploitation, and in circumventing the natural obstacles, was more evident in the discouraging assessments of the government's mining bureaucracy, the Corps des Mines, than among the industrial interests like de Wendel or Pont à Mousson – who ignored the official jeremiads and preservered towards paydirt. Properly speaking, the problem here lies neither in endowment – which was rich – nor in the industrial response – which was determined – but in the process and the technology of extraction. Evocation of the relevant objective constraints facing contemporary businessmen – that it was difficult to appreciate the problems of coal-consuming ironmasters when geographically or economically divorced from them; that it was an intricate and lengthy business to raise ore through sodden subsoil – is a valid and useful means of qualifying the strictures placed upon French decision-making in factor use.

Exoneration cannot be complete, however: there is still room to contend that objective factors rank second in importance to the behaviour of entrepreneurial subjects. Thus, divisions of interest between the coal and iron lobbies could be ascribed to inadequate vertical integration even amidst conditions demanding a greater *conciliation* of interests. The absence of such conciliation might then be explained by failures in commercial perception or by an overdeveloped taste for commercial independence, that is, by precisely that form of atomistic individualism which many critical writers have detected in the behaviour of French entrepreneurs. Among the coal-owners, there is evidence that policy-making resembled this less generous description very closely. French mining long persisted as an industry of small private producers: even in 1924 it required some 715 pits to cut 98 per cent of French coal, while in the Ruhr 90 per cent of the region's much larger output was raised by twelve mines. In fact, French coal-owners exhibit unusually clearly the individualistic deficiencies attributed to French enterprise in general: the preference for suboptimal scale, for under-capitalization, for jealously guarded autonomy and the avoidance of bank finance.[151] Geographical separation apart, this scarcely suggests a constituency sufficiently ambitious or sufficiently gifted to create alliances with coal users, and thus to formulate more balanced fuel policies. Its members are, after all, not without guilt. Indeed, their commercial reserve can be linked most damagingly to policies of exploration which answered high demand for coal with lethargic and unenterprising prospecting. Even during the early part of the century the influential Anzin Mining Co. decided to *reduce* its efforts to develop new coal-bearing seams. And, when the Pas de Calais field was eventually discovered in the 1840s, its natural advantages as a latecomer to the European mining fraternity were much diminished by the coal-owners' insistence on traditional methods of extraction.[152] The persistence shown at Briey in the face of adversity can thus be matched by an opposed persistence maintained in the teeth of advantage.

Even in the case of iron-ore extraction, 'optimistic' results are obtained largely by a sleight of hand: the decision-making buck is passed swiftly away from the mining industrialists and left with the mining bureaucracy. Certainly, at Briey, the Corps des Mines can be cast as convincing villains, first denying the existence of the strike, then doubting whether the ore could be mined when it was discovered, discouraging industrial attempts at extraction, and finally parcelling out the ore-fields in undersized lots, thus preventing a fully efficient commercial exploitation. Significantly also, on Gillet's account, the influence of the Corps des Mines was not restricted to the policy of the ironmasters; the advice of its engineers was said also to dominate in the boardrooms of the coal industry.[153] But the implication of this is surely that poor, but influential, decisions controlling raw material availability could issue

171

from quarters *other* than the strictly entrepreneurial. The proposition that French businessmen did not waste French resources but were rather governed by their scarcity and intractability invites a counter-proposal: that adequate French resources were, in important instances, misutilized by decision-takers outside, but close to, the business community. Here the accent is still written against the processes of factor utilization, rather than against the facts of factor supply; all that requires emendation is the identity of the responsible factor users.

Clearly, however, the conventional over-estimate of endowment constraints would be most convincingly sapped if it could be shown that a *proportion* of French industrialists were positively ingenious in their use of these factors and were not deterred by their peculiarities. Obligingly, it seems that some groups did contrive to *solve* problems of endowment supply and to evade the 'objective constraints' with which they were faced. The resource in particular question was coke. And the business decisions concerning it exhibit an intriguing duality, pulled in different directions by different groups at different times, successively exacerbating and mitigating resource deficiencies. In the first instance, the tactics of the coal lobby faced the metallurgical lobby with the 'objective constraint' of dear coke. In the second, an enterprising minority of metal interests developed a counter-tactic designed to circumvent the shortcomings *both* of French coal desposits *and* of French coal-owners: they acquired holdings in coal-producing concerns *outside* France. By 1907, four large French firms were involved in the Belgian Société des Charbonnages de Beeringen and by 1914 French interests possessed 60–80 m. francs' worth of stock in Belgian, and a roughly similar amount in German, mines.[154] Of course, the return on these ventures provided only a fraction of French fuel needs, and it was achieved late in the day. But the device provided an instance of exactly that creativity in factor management which may escape the limitations imposed by underprivileged endowment. If, in the French case, some businessmen employed enterprise and energy to slip the binding constraints, important questions are begged: how restraining in fact were the bonds and why did not more industrialists display ingenuity in breaking them?

If nature was not specifically generous to the French, the suspicion remains that they were less than energetic in exploiting what benefits they did possess. Earlier and more comprehensive attention to social overheads would have eased the scarcity of fuel, while increased co-operation between industrial interests, especially in the reconciliation of tariff claims, would have reduced fuel costs. Potentially, the resource system possessed a measure of flexibility. And in reality, from time to time, it demonstrated a measure of flexibility. When, for instance, French manufacturing did experience growth-bursts, in the 1830s, 1850s, and 1890s, the coal industry shook itself from somnolence and obediently underwent induced expansion: in the 1830s and 1850s the coal tariffs were actually reduced. If the pits and the pit-owners could react to the gadfly of demand on such special occasions, it is difficult to view their limited output simply as a function of natural geological limitations. The answer lies elsewhere, possibly in the thesis that the misutilization of French resources was ultimately more damaging than their meagre size. Such a case would apply not only to coal, iron ore, and bauxite – the two latter all too often altruistically exported to German processing plants where the major proportion of the added value was taken – but also to non-mineral assets. Hence an agriculture, favoured by nature more lavishly than the British, was allowed to stagnate under the system of French micro-cultivation. Hence, art industries like fine silk, in which France had considerable natural advantages and early export successes, were permitted to decline for lack of adequate entrepreneurial participation. Something other than nature's bounty was at issue here. And in these circumstances the exaltation of factor endowment above factor use can perpetrate only the ultimate scientific absurdity: to prefer the value of materials to the values of those who employ materials.

AN ANALYTICAL TURNING POINT

Arguments featuring political, commercial, demographic, or resource constraints emerge as painfully double-edged, as likely to amputate the hand that wields them as to cut to the centre of the development problem. On balance, scarce labour, lean domestic markets, and expensive fuel probably bit more deeply into growth prospects than lethargic overseas trade or the occasional political upheaval, but all these impediments shared an important characteristic: they were subject to counter-action which, in the French case, was either misapplied or not applied at all. It is towards this sector, where conditioning elements influenced the quality of entrepreneurial counter-measures, that the material so far points.

CAPITAL: BANKER'S GHOST

If labour and land raised problems for French growth, what of the remaining term in the classic triad: capital? Were French industrialists restricted in their capacity to outmanoeuvre resource limitations by shortages in this critical facilitating element? More railways, more vertical integration, more investment in foreign coal-mines and more imported fuels, the better evasive measures, were uniformly expensive. Could France meet the bill? Here, as with much of French economic history, there is confusion. On one, very popular, reading, the small French community is notoriously one of impassioned savers, canny and intransigent hoarders. On another, more objective, assessment, the French saved only 10 per cent of their national income in 1871–1911, being surpassed in the race for personal accumulation by the British on 12–15 per cent and the Germans on 15–20 per cent.[155] The conflict may be resolved by the hypothesis that French savings were plentiful only in relation to the proportion productively invested. With a greater equality of income distribution and a lower consumption preference than the British or Germans, this mass of

173

'withheld investment' may well have created the impression of capital abundance – but also the reality of capital immobility. Why was capital immobile? Here again there is confusion. The institutions of French finance, obvious candidates as capital bottlenecks, recorded an extremely chequered performance down to 1914. On the one hand, the French evolved the innovational *commandité* bank and the *haute banque* assumed a newly creative aspect before 1850. On the other, the *commandités* were suppressed in 1848 and the *haute banque* reached only a restricted clientele. Again, once the 1848 revolution had liberated banking from the strictures of the restoration monarchy, a major institutional novelty arose in the shape of the Crédit Mobilier and its imitators. But, on the debit side, this pioneer lasted only a decade and a half before it too was liquidated. Therefore, the efficiency of French capital provision would appear to be controlled not by the size of the capital reservoir but by peculiarities in the mode of saving and by alarming variations in the availability of institutional servicing.

Unsurprisingly, the quantitatively measurable career of French finance between 1850 and 1870 is indifferent. Despite the addition of the liberated *mobiliers* from mid-century, the total size of the bank sector – and thus the scope of the services offered to the investing public and the industrial client – was small. The ratio of bank resources to national income was unusually modest for a great power, lower in 1870 than the Prussian ratio for 1855, and markedly lower than the Russian, American, Belgian, and even Scottish ratios between 1870 and 1914 (see Table 3.5). Given that high bank ratios correlate with high rates of industrial growth in the case of Prussia, Russia, America, and Japan (if not Scotland), some interesting probabilities emerge concerning the relationship between the quality of French capital provision and the rapidity of French industrial advance. At the local level, the probabilities strengthen: the small size of the bank sector was expressed in a low physical density of financial agencies. Down to 1850, regional centres as important as Le Havre, industrial cities as prolific as Mulhouse or St Etienne, lacked most forms of banking facility and could turn only to Parisian finance for assistance. Even in

Table 3.5 Proportion of bank resources to national income: selected countries

France	1870	15.6
England and Wales	1844	34.4
Scotland	1865	80.0
Belgium	1875	40–42
Russia (commercial banks)	1914	61.0
Prussia	1865	31.1
USA	1871	29.8
	1900	63.3
Japan	1878–82	16.1
	1908–12	60.2

Source: Abstracted from Cameron (1967), Table IX, pp. 301–2.

1870, at the culmination of the 'take-off' phase, France recorded one of the lowest bank : population ratios for any developed country, a figure reached by Scotland more than a century before. Well into the century's second half, therefore, French businessmen must have seen external credit as a rare good, and, when they did borrow, encountered provincial interest rates between two and six times the metropolitan norm.

Nor, given the dearth of banks, was credit the only financial commodity in short supply. Money itself was elusive, the proportion of money transactions within the economy abnormally low by international standards. As late as 1857, the smallest French bank-note was the 500-franc bill, and the value of 1000-franc notes in circulation usually provided half the worth of available paper money. Since the average annual income per head was then 200–300 francs, the bank-note for most Frenchmen must have been as scarce as fine claret or generous reactions. In place of paper, the French adored specie. Around mid-century no less than 93 per cent of all transactions were settled in precious metals (in England 35%; in Scotland 10%). To sustain such monetary luxury, France was obliged to hold one-third of the European bullion stock – five times British reserves – and to absorb a phenomenal 40 per cent share of the increase in world gold stocks provided by the Californian and Australian strikes of the century's third quarter. Paper money, of course, saves scarce monetary resources for more useful tasks than the daily exchanges of petty commerce. French financial habits achieved the reverse effect. If, instead, they had included a more progressive note policy, with an English-style paper : metal ratio, sufficient surplus bullion could have been converted to investment – according to Cameron – to produce an annual growth rate 50–100 per cent better than the historical performance.[156] The agencies of French capital supply emerge as undersized, poorly distributed, and deprived, by currency regulation, of vast amounts of potentially investable funds.

It is scarcely surprising that a banking sector so flawed, so thinly spread, and so conservative, should fail to attract the savings that were available. And if the savings were withheld from the banks, their reserves would not be such as to encourage them towards lavish programmes of credit creation for industrialists. At two points in the chain between savings and investment, serious fissures existed. Nor after 1870 was the chain much repaired. Following a common pattern in the economic policies of the French state, the financial initiatives of the Second Empire petered out with the regime's ignominious finale. The new republic was made of more pliable stuff, turning its ear once more to the gilt-edged whisperings of the financial establishment. The pattern of 1870 became, in consequence, the financial equipment with which France had to deal until 1914. At the centre remained the sole note issuer, tetchy and reactionary as ever: the Bank of France. Close to it stood a handful of national deposit banks; in the next rank a larger number of local and regional banks; and on the fringes of the crowd a few specialized institutions for foreign trade or mortgages and a scattering of one or two isolated, truly 'industrial' *banques d'affaires*. Within such a structure, restrictive orthodoxy would meet few challenges and investors find little. incentive for the pursuit of domestic profits.

Speculators or politicians could rattle the broken chain for their special effects, but it would not pull the economy.

The financial preconditioning of France was a lean feast at which only the wraith of sound industrial banking appeared. Significantly, the energetic economic activity of *l'empire autoritaire* coincided with the tenure of a more generous steward, and, by reason of this, the appearance of more robust financial spirits. Equally significantly, from 1870 onwards financial policy reverted to short commons and unsavoury friends.

At this point it might appear as if the behaviour of the industrial decision-takers is explained. With a capital supply so constricted, it was little wonder that businessmen could not afford expensive counter-measures against resource deficiencies. Similarly, Cameron has argued that it was not entrepreneurial debilitation but the failure of French banks to service industry which compelled businesses to remain small and helped breed the reactionary individualism of petty manufacturing.[157] Since the larger, more opulent concerns could attract bank capital more readily than the small fry, the extreme size contrasts within French industry are also accommodated by this explanation. The economic lethargy of France, it seems, may be traced to unhealthy emenations from the bankers' vaults; it is capital-determined.

However, this beguiling view leaves at least one major anomaly out of account. In reality, French savers and bankers were not entirely unskilled at mobilizing generous capitals. From the 1850s the nation developed a mania for *foreign* investment; by 1870 it had despatched overseas one-third of total savings, by 1911 one-half.[158] Scarcely surprisingly, many analysts have concluded that it was this remarkable bonanza in capital exportation which deprived French industry of growth funds. Famously, even Keynes was moved to the sweeping conclusion that: 'No investment has ever been made so foolish and disastrous.'[159] Perhaps so, but the act itself proves beyond doubt that hoarding conventions and institutional rigidities were not insuperable obstacles to capital flows; the obstacles could be overcome once the investors' interest was captured. But why it should be captured by foreign government bonds and not by domestic equities is another, and complex, matter. Initial pointers suggest only a partial explanation. Extravagant foreign investment met French requirements in three immediate essentials: it tightened the large slack in potentially investable reserves; it did this without involving investment in unpleasantly direct entanglement with manufacturing capitalism; yet it did associate national savings with the nation's more acceptable ambitions as an international power. If foreign investment carried more social approval than domestic investment, one of the central contradictions within French enterprise is partially resolved: the prodigies of industrial skill achieved by *émigré* capitalists in the continent's four corners contrast less curiously with the lack of home-grown prodigies. Similarly, if the French realized that their weaknesses in military manpower could be balanced by the international manipulation of capital, the cascade of francs across the council tables of Europe becomes more intelligible. Be that as it may, what is certain is that the general character of French capital supply is given a decisive twist by the peculiarities of style and quality displayed by the nation's overseas lending. Once again the issue moves away from resource size – for huge sums were exported – and settles upon the management of the resource.

Certainly the capital-managers – the bankers – employed the funds which they did attract in some strange ways. Even more noticeable than the fewness of banks before 1850 was the bias in their investment preferences after 1850. Almost casually, the joint pioneers of 'mixed' or investment banking surrendered comprehensive exploitation of this device to their German rivals and abandoned their original purposes. Thus the Crédit Lyonnais, which could have married itself to commerce in no more self-sacrificing a style – it located its first four branches in the abattoirs of Paris and Lyons – soon forsook beef for bulls of a different nature and drifted into the more glamorous world of foreign loans. Even the officially sponsored Crédit Agricole, inaugurated in 1860, appropriately enough for the support of agriculture, fell prey to the foreign temptation: it advanced only 1 m. francs to French farmers in its first decade but 168 m. francs to the Egyptian government in the four years 1873–76.[160] French finance, it appeared, was constitutionally unable to restrict itself to France, the foreign market proving an irresistible lure.

Most simply, this could be explained by a failure on the supply side, amidst the banking community. The bank acts as the arbiter between savings and credit; irresponsibility or irrationality at this point, emphasizing foreign investment when domestic needs were not fully met, could be highly destructive. It is significant, therefore, that French finance houses, permitted service commissions upon foreign transactions as high as 19 per cent,[161] were given considerable incentives to prefer overseas dealing. But whatever the inducements, it remains anomalous that institutions designed to serve a hearty home demand for credit – if Cameron is to be believed – should abandon it so readily. Perhaps it is more likely that the failure lay on the demand side. Family firms may have escaped contact with the banks less because of the latters' inefficiency than because over-cautious manufacturers suspected the 'predatory' habits of the financiers and preferred to draw their capital from reinvested profits. Even large-scale industrialists harboured convictions akin to these. Cavallier of Pont à Mousson judged pithily that 'a Banker supports his client as a rope a hanged man'[162] and the timid metallurgists surveyed by Jean Vial provided plentiful echoes.[163] Concerns as formidable as Schneider-Creusot would habitually finance new investment from profits rather than hawk reputation and independence around the capital market. Given such client-resistance, it is possible that the domestic requirements left untended by the bankers might have remained unserved under any conditions, since they were never worked up into genuine demand. The reluctance of domestic borrowers could well have driven the bankers into foreign pastures. Similarly, the financial interests could legitimately have been deterred by the economic frailty of obstinately self-financing family ventures, a frailty which ironically they were later accused of abetting. Thus Henri Germain took the Crédit Lyonnais to the international markets only after suffering heavy initial losses in lending to the local chemical industries in the 1860s.[164]

Most plausible of all, however, is the distribution of blame to *both* the supply and the demand side: conservative businessmen pledged to financial self-reliance may be ranged opposite conservative financiers preferring foreign profits to unsafe or unreceptive industrials.[165] The relationship between such frail plants is likely to be cross-sterilizing rather than cross-fertilizing. Such an interpretation is persuasively even-handed, although it perhaps leaves a shade more responsibility with the demand side, since the onus was more definitely upon French businessmen to make themselves attractive to French bankers than upon the bankers to overcome the churlish isolationism of manufacturers. Either way, Cameron's proposition that the demand for capital was high in France is badly compromised by this treatment. Nevertheless, if economics were everything, the double-sided explanation would serve quite nicely as a conciliation of many contending views.

Unfortunately, with French investment, economics were rarely everything. Political and military considerations were highly influential in this area and could easily dislocate the interplay of financial supply and demand. Very damaging economically, these interruptions are historically most useful since they create reconciliation between painfully antithetical investment characteristics, between the extreme caution of French domestic investment and the extraordinary rashness of French foreign lending. For where huge sums were remitted to the world's least dependable debtors, to the over-ambitious and perennially bankrupt, to Russia, Turkey, Egypt, and Italy, the non-economic argument has an obvious appeal. In rendering it operational, bankers and industrialists were much less important than, suitably enough, the French Foreign Office, the financial spies of the world, and the enthusiastically venal Parisian press.

By the 1870s, after nearly two centuries of official supervision over the investment market, the success of a French overseas loan was governed as directly by the tastes of the Quai d'Orsay as by the agreement of the Finance Ministry.[166] .The great success in paying off the Prussian war indemnity of 1871 by shrewd use of foreign securities merely strengthened official interest in the management of overseas finance. Until 1914, therefore, French administrators concerned themselves with extracting concrete political advantage from the processes of investment: capital was to be for France what the battle-squadrons were for Britain or the imperial legions for Germany and Russia. By 1908, witnesses to the German Bank Inquiry were describing the financial *Machtpolitik* of France in the Balkans – a heady mixture of financial bargaining, political leverage, and armament transactions – as more formidable even than Germany's own. Poincaré revealed French objectives when he promised in 1912 'to combine with French military power . . . the financial power which is so great an aid to France'.[167] Even the *Finance* Minister, Caillaux, was proclaiming by 1913 that he permitted 'only those foreign loans which assured France of political as well as economic advantages'.[168] When French capital investment was manipulated to procure or reinforce alliances, to furnish military assets to friends or deny them to enemies, it is little wonder that it does not answer to the usual tests of market efficiency (compare Table 3.6).

Table 3.6 Distribution of French overseas investment, 1815–1902: % shares and rank order

	1815–51		1852–58		1858–70		1902	
Spain	(1)	35.0	(2)	27.0	(5)	11.1	(3)	12.0
Italy	(2)	22.0	(1)	28.3	(1)	29.8	(6)	5.6
Belgium	(3)	18.0		1.1		3.3		—
Austria	(4)	10.0	(3)	16.5	(2)	15.0		—
Portugal	(5)	5.0		1.5		–		3.6
Germany	(6)	2.0	(6)	3.8		–		
Russia			(4)	7.5	(6)	7.6	(2)	28.0
Turkey			(5)	6.2	(4)	11.3	(4)	8.8
Egypt					(3)	12.4	(5)	5.7
Tunisia						–		2.1
Balkans						1.4		3.8
South America						–	(1)	30.4

Note Rank numbers are given in brackets. Percentage shares do not sum to 100%. The residual is made up of small components scattered across many countries.
Source Calculated from Gille (1968), pp. 294–5.

Given that the guiding initiatives for this policy originated in ministerial circles, it was of course necessary that the market – the bankers and the investing public – should be 'steered' to the appropriate conclusion. With the financiers there was little problem; even the most reluctant banker had in the end to yield to explicit instructions from the Quai d'Orsay. Thus in 1881 Rothschilds were ordered to abandon the diplomatically troublesome Italians – among the largest and longest French debtors of the century (see Table 3.6) – and wrote obediently to their clients: 'It is certainly painful for us to see our traditional relations with the Italian Treasury slip away, but this is a fact that we have to accept and which is the result of a situation not of our making.'[169] Conversely, when, after the tsarist defeat of 1905, the Rothschilds reckoned that the Romanovs had at last exhausted their credit, and, discreetly, as between dynasties, said as much, a brisk political discipline brought them back into line and into 'the loan which saved Russia'. Seduction of the investing public was somewhat more complex, but, fortunately, talents equal to the task lay within the hire of the French state. The Parisian press was open to bribery from almost any quarter, its journals ready to print good financial opinions – for the Serbian, Brazilian, and Argentinian governments among others – in exchange for hard cash. French officials were fully aware that the Turks had distributed some 3 m. francs among the editors, and, during the critical negotiations of 1904–06, the Russian autocracy dispensed similar largesse with the full knowledge, and presumably approval, of the French Cabinet. Indeed, when faced with the need to mobilize support for the tricky Panama Canal loan of 1888, the government domesticated the device and paid out 7 m. francs of its own money to the newspapers.[170] With the official orchestration of the capital market, the incessant bombardment of the individual investor, and the fabrication of highly coloured financial information, economic

179

rationality inevitably became a stranger to the processes of French overseas lending. The Rothschilds after all, had been right about the Romanovs.

In reality, the map of French foreign investment, was drawn, and redrawn, on the conference table with a diplomat's pen, new frontiers cancelling previous financial relationships or encircling new friends as political affiliations changed. Thus, whatever their glittering financial prospects, German securities were banned from trading on the Paris Bourse after 1870. Similarly, despite protestations from the bankers and the high standing of the debtors, the traditional financial links with Italy and Austria-Hungary were snapped when these countries began to move into the German diplomatic orbit.[171] On the other side, there was the budding romance with Russia. After 1887, when Bismarck, with a miscalculated touch of the financial switch, withdrew credit from the Tsar, the French devoted themselves to the creation of a suitable, imperial bank-roll. The scale was princely: one-quarter of French savings were diverted to Russia, and, by 1914, one-third of the autocracy's overseas indebtedness was controlled by French creditors. The loans were not without stringent conditions, though – significantly – they were scarcely of an economic type.

The French insisted upon the construction of strategic railways, often against opposition from the Russian Finance Ministry;[172] they demanded restrained diplomacy in the Near East; they required universal opposition to Germany. Monetary returns, in contrast, were modest – Russian government bonds averaged 3.87 per cent on nominal capital – and were dwarfed by the immense defaults of the 1914–17 period.[173] By 1919, 82 per cent of French net foreign holdings had been wiped out, the majority in Russia. An important recent revision by René Girault correctly observes that French investors of the time perceived no indications of impending disaster but rather the readily apparent attractions of a genuinely promising economy, and goes on to contend that capitalists drew more generous, if somewhat uneven, profits from their Russian ventures than is conventionally allowed. Even Girault concedes, however, that the industrial investor, having failed to construct at home a manufacturing base sufficiently strong to support large-scale foreign extensions, took second place to the speculative banker chasing the fast franc, and, more damagingly, admits the use of the Parisian press to bolster failing French confidence in the early 1900s.[174]

Quite certainly, the French government in its Russian designs did not have in mind merely orthodox financial dividends. When the time came, seventy German divisions were tied down in the north for three years. For the ministers of Finance, War, and Foreign Affairs, this was reward enough, though, in the end, it was scarcely the style of profit to make bankers or economists swoon. Significantly, also, not all of the recent important investigations of French overseas lending have exhibited rehabilitatory tendencies. Gille's study of the Italian transactions concludes somewhat acidly: 'Apart from the rate of return *which might have, or which should have* determined selection, it seems that, political sentiments affected the French investor most profoundly.'[175] Calculations of security, control by politicians rather than by capitalists, objectives set not in gold but in the coin of alliance and offensive – these, to an extent unequalled in Europe, were finally the controlling guidelines of French investment. As Feis accurately observed, 'French (financial) policy must be regarded as merely one phase of the armed truce that prevailed'.[176] And that, of course, left little room for an economically determined form of investment;[177] and little room either for the idea that the direction of French capital flows was conditioned mainly by inelasticities in domestic demand. Indeed, political pressures created so much *supply* irrationality that even deficiencies within the credit structure might be graded as secondary defects.

This explains why French investment does not accord with the general characteristics of the French economy. But it leaves an important issue unexplained: the extent of economic damage which followed upon over-investment in political capital. It is true that the peaks of foreign investment – in the 1850s, 1879–81, 1886–89 and 1903–06 – coincided with booms or rallies in the domestic economy. However, the implied connexion between overseas lending and domestic prosperity must be distrusted. Unlike its British counterpart, the sluggish French manufacturing sector was poorly equipped to profit from investment-led export growth.[178] It is more likely that the relationship worked in the reverse direction: domestic manufacturing upswings generated surpluses which fell prey to political pressures and were swiftly despatched overseas. The few who noticed such matters were concerned lest such capital 'leakages' should create domestic credit scarcities, as could easily happen when bankers were forced to accept unwelcome or ill-timed business. However, exact measurement of the 'growth forgone' is not easily unravelled.

Theoretically, foreign investment can offer considerable economic benefits. It can employ funds, which may otherwise have lain idle at home, to generate invisible earnings from capitalistic operations overseas, thus supplying credits for the nation's balance of payments. By expanding purchasing power in the debtor country, it may enlarge foreign markets for the creditor's export industries. By increasing productive activity in the debtor country, it may procure more and cheaper commodities for the creditor's import requirements. Overseas investment from Britain reaped most of these benefits in the nineteenth century. But they were by no means inevitable benefits; and they did not accrue to France. Invisible earnings came at very moderate rates of return (declining from an average of 5.5% p.a. 1880–85 to 4.0% p.a. 1896–1902)[179] and defaults were enormous. Exports gained little; French debtors rarely became customers of French industry.[180] Imports gained less; the main debtors – Russia, Turkey, Spain, and earlier on, Italy and Austria-Hungary – reduced their consignments to France over time.[181] Therefore, the propulsive effects theoretically attached to foreign investment were not often attached to French investment. At least it is clear that France did not draw any major economic profit from her capital exports.

Equally, the classical notion that capital moves to where it may be employed most productively cannot be matched with French experience. Once more, politics distorted the process. Capital might buy shipyards and steamhammers; but it could as easily purchase military railways for the Ukraine, artillery batteries for the Bulgars, or harems and battlecruisers for the Sultan. Given that French capital indulged in all these immediately unproductive pursuits, and many more besides, a substantial opportunity cost was inevitably incurred by its use outside the domestic economy. Worse still, this capital did not fulfil the even more powerful classical expectation that it should flow towards the higher return:[182] yields on French foreign investment at the end of the century were on average *lower* than those offered by domestic opportunities (see Table 3.7).[183] The remarkable long-distance drift of French overseas lending towards unfamiliar South American opportunities at the century's turn – by 1902 this category accounted for 30.4 per cent of foreign investment – was sustained by returns certainly no better than those available at home.[184]

Table 3.7   Rates of return on French domestic and foreign investments, 1899

Foreign	Domestic	Rate on nominal capital	Rate on issue price
Russian government		3.87	4.27
Other governments		3.39	3.65
	Insurance & Banks	5.35	5.34
	Railroads	2.58	4.12
	Other	8.88	8.67
Total foreign		3.46	3.85
	Total domestic	3.54	4.28

Source: White (1933), p. 107.

The hypothesis that the investor selects the foreign option only if the yield is higher depends upon the investor being a sound judge. And, after the French investor had been instructed by the government, wooed by the purchased sirens of the press, and advised by the bankers, he was no longer a sound judge. Nor was the investment commodity which he was required to assess accurately represented to him. In the cautious French market, bankers knew that high interest rates signalled danger to small investors and would not sell stocks. Low rates set upon dubious ventures, concealing the true risk and lulling the investor into the sense of security which he preferred, consequently became a stock-in-trade of the financial community. Such misrepresentation provides perhaps the most persuasive explanation for the divergent style of French home and foreign investment: when the yield on, say, a Serbian arms flotation and that on a French railway bond were both 4 per cent, investors could approach the foreign venture *believing* that they were exercising no less caution than in their mild domestic flutters.

According to H. D. White, this manipulation of interest rates by bankers exerted a more decisive pressure upon French foreign investment than any psychological or political influences.[185] However, it is surely true that the initial distortion was caused by diplomatic leverage and that the banks merely accentuated the bias by their unscrupulous handling of interest rates. Moreover, the French state actively connived both at the misrepresentation of the goods and at the innocent investor's appetite for them. No legal requirement was set governing the publication of information about foreign loans, and earnings on foreign government bonds, unlike the profits from comparable domestic securities, were exempt from tax.[186] Given these conditions, it is untrue that funds flowed rationally to meet higher overseas yields and beyond doubt that the same funds could have been used more productively inside France. The difference between the average domestic and the average foreign return (0.08 % on nominal capital in 1899), applied to one-third to one-half of total French savings, would provide a crude minimum estimate of the income forgone and the damage sustained by the French economy as a result of its distorted investment preferences.[187] While physical shape was given to these sacrifices by the decline of Le Havre or Marseilles as ports, or by the poverty of canal facilities in southern and eastern France, the country's capital was constructing harbours from Chile to China, digging canals from the Baltic to the Black Sea. As one acidulated observer summed up in 1900: 'Be you Greek, Chinese or Brazilian . . . the Crédit Lyonnais will make you huge advances, but, if you are French, you will get nothing.'[188] It seems therefore that the diplomats and the bankers must bear a considerable share of the responsibility for creating in France the rare duality, 'financial prosperity, poverty of credit' – and thus a share of the responsibility for the debilitated state of French manufacturing.

It would be foolish to deny this. But it would be equally foolish to accept the further proposition that 'credit poverty' may wholly account for, and may even have generated, the apathy of the business community. This hypothesis is based upon an unsophisticated process of deduction: given that the official regimentation and cosmopolitan tastes of the banking system were such as to squash the home demand for credit, it is assumed more likely that entrepreneurship was poor because of capital scarcity than that capital was scarce because entrepreneurs were too conservative to demand it. In company with this view tends to travel an impressionable valuation of French enterprise, based frequently on suspect materials. It is noticeable for instance that Cameron, who throughout one major study attached a high value to French industrial achievement in non-Gallic Europe, frequently casts the *bankers* as his villians in his subsequent study of French financial and industrial development.[189] But this sequence does not take sufficient stock of the discrepancy between the quality of French enterprise at home and its quality overseas; in consequence, it lays itself open to some damaging rejoinders. If virtuous French industrialists strongly demanded credit, why was it that their suppliers, pioneers of mixed banking, so enthusiastically deserted this custom? If demand existed, why did the industrially oriented credit institutions grow so slowly once they had been established? Why did bank branches proliferate so languidly after 1860 and bank density remain so low to 1914? These features scarcely suggest a buoyant market for financial services.

Above all, it is dangerous to forget that bankers are themselves entrepreneurs: to explain the conservatism of manufacturers by the conservatism of bankers is to commit analytical tautology. The central issue should be posed differently: why did the financial entrepreneurs resemble other French entrepreneurs so closely? What were the motives behind the cautious tactics of the financial community? Why were there so few effective challengers to banking orthodoxy fit to rank with Laffitte or the Pereires? The concluding refrain is familiar: financial resources were not negligible and could have been used to better effect. Decisions taken by financial entrepreneurs – with the Corps Diplomatique serving as auxiliaries no less destructive in their proper sphere than the Corps des Mines in theirs – produced utilization of capital resources no closer to the optimal than the utilization of physical resources by entrepreneurs in industry and transportation. Therefore, interest in measuring the size of the capital resource is less useful than curiosity as to why the decisions were taken. And that requires closer investigation of the decision-takers.

GOVERNMENT: IMPERIAL VIRTUES; DEMOCRATIC DISECONOMIES

Servants of government have many poor decisions to answer for: they left untouched a cumbersome and damaging inheritance system; created, with much dragging of heels, a poorly deployed transportation system; mishandled the exploitation of natural resources; stifled financial innovation before 1850; and distorted capital flows after 1850. In most areas where the French economy suffered embarrassment, civil servants and politicians were to be found making matters worse. And if government was clumsy, it was also big and expensive: as late as 1899 the bureaucracy employed 5 per cent of the working population; military spending at peak points could require up to half the national budget; the cost of past wars and the preparation for future ones commonly consumed 5 per cent of national income; and the bill for all this was the highest level of taxation per head in Europe, together with the absorption of one-quarter of French savings into government bonds.[190] It is perhaps tempting to argue that an agency of such size, cost, and ineptitude might assume much of the responsibility for the low quality of French economic performance. If nineteenth-century governments are permitted the title of growth inducers, it is surely possible that a 'rogue' state might act as a growth restrainer.

However, such a view fails to capture the variety and variability of the tactics subsumed under the rubric of state intervention. Once more, it is wise to remember that the *content* of state action may vary with place, time, political leadership, constitutional structure and dominant social values. Its effectiveness, furthermore, will be much influenced by the size of the administrative unit (and the attendant 'costs of information'), the quality of the bureaucracy, and the suitability for *dirigiste* activity of the current economic theory. In respect to France, a few, but not many, of these conditions have been recognized. Moraze has noted that growth phases 'match' with fluctuations in the state's role; the moderate growth before 1850 with the protectionism and conservatism of the restored monarchy, the mid-century upsurge with the dynamism of Napoleon III, the 'precarious mediocrity' between Sedan and the *belle époque* with the petty-bourgeois characteristics of the Third Republic.[191] Extreme political instability must clearly have rendered the state's economic function more fickle even than the norm. But the rapid alternation of political forms between constitutional monarchies, military autocracies, and unstable republics provides an unusually lucid proof of the 'non-constant' value of *dirigiste* policies under nineteenth-century conditions. Similarly, the penalties attached to an unsatisfactory bureaucracy are revealed with exceptional clarity – remarked upon from Mourre (1900)[192] to Landes (1949)[193] – by the intransigent *fonctionnarisme* of French society.

In France these 'supply' characteristics of state intervention were probably more influential than any 'demand' characteristics: save for a brief period at mid-century, the French economy probably always required more informed and more active state policies than it received. Certainly, prior to 1848, the economic activities of the post-imperial regimes were highly damaging. The Napoleonic Wars had vastly expanded the apparatus of government and opened the bureaucracy to democratization. Yet, as with many of the institutional reforms of the revolutionary and imperial eras, the outcome was to reinforce old ways rather than favour new ones: after 1815 the response of the newly enlarged officialdom to economic change – the social overhead ventures of the July Monarchy somewhat apart – was scarcely less suspicious than that of their Junker counterparts. Joint-stock companies were treated as subversive elements. Mining, under the law of 1810, was submitted to an almost military discipline by the Corps des Mines.[194] Rigid conservatism was the house style of the Bank of France, passionately and violently defended against all impertinent innovation. The period of the bourgeois monarchies was characterized by a system of government constitutionally vulnerable to pressure groups – particularly pressure groups of the *grande bourgeoisie* – who demonstrated great skill in rigging the economic structure for their own conservationist purposes.

Different values and tactics, a different form of state and of state intervention, was supplied by the revived Bonapartism of the Second Empire. No doubt, Gerschenkron is correct in suggesting that Napoleon III utilized the characteristic apparatus of the dictator – the military adventures, the great constructions, the dramatic plebiscites – for a wholly characteristic dictatorial purpose: to keep the political community off balance, and, upon its instability, to establish his own security.[195] But if the imperial vision of a modernized and regenerated France accorded with the dictatorial *Sturm und Drang* it was nevertheless a builder's vision, to Bonaparte specifically so: 'We have immense uncultivated territories to clear, roads to open up, ports to dredge, rivers to render navigable, canals to complete, a railroad system to finish.'[196] And in the economic precepts of the Saint-Simonians there lay to hand a suitable, if crude, theoretical sanction for such *dirigisme*. Naturally, vested interests and inefficiency persisted, and in some areas – notably education – there were larger omissions under the Second Empire than under the First.

But, in general, the military dictatorship assumed economic burdens of a weight attempted by few other French governments before 1914. The railway companies received the most lavish subsidies in western Europe, their numbers rationalized from thirty to six major operators, their concessions extended to an economic scale, and their profits guaranteed. The resulting network was more unified – in administration at least – than the German, English, or American. At least one qualified observer concluded, 'the high prosperity which marked the first years of the Empire was principally due to the expansion of the great railway companies, engineered by the government, and to its protection of their interests'.[197] Given that railways then composed the leading sector of current technology, such intervention was perceptively focused. So too was intervention in the credit market, dragging forward the innovational Crédit Mobilier and suspending the long tradition of indiscriminate official support for the Bank of France. Here political authoritarianism allied itself with the classical growth-sponsoring agency for countries of medium backwardness – the industrial investment bank – and against its more usual friends amidst the financial establishment. In the same spirit of reconstruction, Paris was rebuilt, public works sponsored to combat unemployment, the textile industries subsidized, and the freer trade of the Anglo-French Commercial Treaty (1860) imposed against the resistance of the bureaucratic mandarins, just as the Crédit Mobilier had been imposed against the resistance of the Bank of France. Autocratic leadership, equipped with suitable economic validation, proved capable of slipping the deadweight imposed by a distended and reactionary civil service. Yet its campaigns were not excessively costly: Bonaparte's active economic government never exceeded the levels of expenditure on 'extra-ordinary works' maintained by the late July Monarchy in the period 1845–48, at least not until it was eventually submerged by the warlike extravagances of 1870.[198]

But it was only infrequently that the nineteenth-century French state possessed such freedom of action and significant that a military dictator should prove the most proficient economic engineer among three generations of state servants. More constitutional governments, after 1870 as before 1850, failed to strike a comparably forthright attitude in economic affairs; rather, they merely reflected into official policy the self-interested preoccupations of various economic interest groups. In company with most of French society, these groups held government – with rare exceptions in favour of the hero-emperors – in low esteem. Theoretically, the nineteenth-century Frenchman respected order, *pays*, and the tricolour; actually, he cultivated disorder, characterized government as a robber gull, and exploited the bureaucracy as an all-providing nursemaid. Economic lobbies, in consequence, were 'delinquent communities',[199] skilled at special pleading – for subsidies, fiscal concessions, tariffs – in defiance of the national economic interest. Conflicting groups would produce conflicting claims and weak governments would cobble them together into inconsistent policy. Hence the damaging tariffs on coal represented successive bureaucratic attempts to square the circle, reconciling the demands of the ultra-cautious pit-owners with the needs of the heavy industrial consumers. Such manoeuvres could become pathetically convoluted: under simultaneous pressure from the most advanced and the most reactionary sectors of the metallurgical industries, the state was for long persuaded, on the one hand, to promote the use of wood for iron-smelting and, on the other, to encourage the most modern methods of metal production. Similarly, thanks to the energy of the cereal lobby, the Méline Tariff of 1892 contained an unfortunate bias towards grains and against the converted agricultural products which the market favoured and the more enterprising farmers found attractive.[200] However, economic politicking was not restricted to individual industries; on the contrary, significant portions of the French economy were apt to enter the contest for concessions. At least one major tariff, that of 1881, attempted to meet the requirements of so many interest groups that it came perilously close to self-negation. Economic groups might act as 'delinquents', but it was the state which was goaded into aberrant behaviour.

Official management of the economy, therefore, carried no constant value in French development. Under strong personalities and autocratic constitutions, the state machinery generated a forceful gravitational pull within the economy. In some respects it could be overforceful: in the development of mineral resources, for instance, the First Empire allocated an excessive share of exploration to state geologists and engineers and subjected the private sector to a highly restrictive licensing system. Here, French interventionism was distinctly more penetrative than the German, and less effective. On the whole, however, where German economic *dirigisme* experienced declining demand over time, French policy achieved its best results whenever the executive could secure sufficient independence of economic action. Even its expenditure on armament – which quadrupled between 1855 and 1875 – may have exerted a beneficial counter-cyclical effect in the gloomy decades of the 1870s and 1880s.[201] In contrast, whenever the executive was subordinated to democratic processes, it tended merely to replicate the irrationalities of the business community, pulled hither and thither like a wayward planet. Naturally enough, there were some sectors of its orbit in which the body recovered autonomy; not all were governed by external influences. Military policy was one area which the state was likely to preserve for itself (hence the countervailing force of defence spending even after 1871), while foreign policy was yet more strongly protected. Here, Feis reports that the private pressure groups – the foreign investors' organizations – played a relatively subservient role well into the 1900s.[202] This is to be expected: not even 'delinquent communities' would be likely to overbear the state's authority in its private dealings with other states. Unfortunately, this did not limit the destructiveness of such transactions, even if the intent – to compensate for demographic and industrial *faiblesse* with capital power – was coherent and intelligible. More commonly, however, economic destruction was caused when the administration could not help itself.

If the state was not its own master in economic affairs, it is inappropriate to lay the low quality of economic decisions wholly at its door. Before 1850 and after 1870 the political structure was such as to allow vested interests – the *grande bourgeoisie* and high financiers before 1850, the industrial bourgeoisie and the low intriguers after 1870 – an undue say in the composition of economic policy. In the earlier period, contemporaries referred, like Lamennais, to 'l'autocratie des grands industriels' or complained, like Lamartine, that 'quatre-vingt fabricants de fer tyrranisent impunément le pays',[203] while, in the later, the activities of lobbyists like Paul Barbe ('Whatever Barbe takes in hand prospers', wrote Alfred Nobel enviously, and, in the end, inaccurately) and the perpetrators of the Panama Canal Scandal[204] earned a less formidable and more distasteful notoriety. Initiatives from these 'delinquent' levels rather than those from ministerial or bureaucratic circles account for a significant share of what is often miscalled 'state intervention'. Emphasis should move, therefore, towards those forces which made the business groups delinquent ones, and, at least partially, away from those which rendered the state expensively ineffectual.

MISERABLE CAPITALISTS: A DEARTH OF HEROES

Possibly, then, the influence at the end of the decision-making chain is represented by a peculiar adaptation of capitalist evolution, a species of entrepreneur, native, if not unique, to France. It tended to be small in size, its habitat the modest manufactory, the local bank, or the isolated forge.[205] Its behaviour was reserved, disliking direct competition, stubbornly preserving its own independence, fiercely defending its family from any form of economic subjugation. Its business activity was aimed not so much at profit as at the well-being, status, and integrity of the dynasty and its assets. According to Jean Vial, it survived splendidly among the scattered furnaces of the iron industry, raising generations overdeveloped in expectation and underdeveloped in industriousness, devoid of technical competence and mesmerized by the attractions of high liquidity.[206] And scarcely less splendid were the specimens to be found within the textile industries.[207] Generally, these exponents of petty capitalism have been identified and labelled by the entrepreneurial historians of the 'Harvard School'.[208] The overall conclusion appears to be, that the French entrepreneurial norm was very considerably removed from the heroic ideal.

But obviously there are difficulties. Any comment upon French entrepreneurs en bloc must clearly be impressionistic, while the citation of individual cases, whether virtuous or vapid, involves treacherous problems of selection. Detailed studies of individual industries such as those by Vial, Fohlen, or Miss Kent probably offer the best results, but so far these have run in both directions. Nevertheless, some useful distinctions can be drawn. To begin with, one might argue that the Harvard School differentiated insufficiently between the common or petty capitalist and the rarer 'heroic' type. For it would be idle to pretend that all French entrepreneurs were small and timid. Some like the Péreires or Laffitte in finance, Frèrejean or Talabot in metals, Schneider in engineering and armament, Cavallier in pipes, Citroën or Renault in automobiles, were successful and thrusting by any standards.[209] Yet, if it is unwise to pass over this group, it is also unwise to exaggerate their leverage upon the economy: Vial, in assessing his 'complete entrepreneur', Frèrejean, sets him against the 'routine déplorable' of the 'majorité . . . plongée à plaisir dans l'état d'ignorance' and, in the process comes close to a correct balance.[210] Kindleberger also seeks a judicious mean:

Enlargement of markets, specialization, mergers and competition went much less distance in France than in England. *Exceptions existed especially in the modern industries.* . . . But the period from perhaps 1870 to 1939, *except for steel, automobiles, electricity, chemicals*, was characterized by local markets, production to order, and emphasis on quality. Haunted by the fear of overproduction and collapse of prices, producers held back output and maintained markups.[211]

The petty capitalist remains much in evidence, certainly not suppressing the more adventurous spirits but equally certainly restraining them. Moreover, it is important that large concerns could share the characteristic behaviour patterns of petty capitalism. When the massive de Wendel enterprise could run shy of the capital market until 1908, or the Motte textile dynasty celebrate its proliferation by presenting each new infant with its own woollen mill, the indications are that the values of survival, self-preservation, and familial autonomy might surpass those of profitability or growth in the grandest industrial company. Even at Pont à Mousson, Miss Kent's impressive laboratory for genetic improvement, expansion proceeded entirely by self-finance down to 1905 and managerial recruitment entirely by selection from the ruling dynasties until 1900.[212] Plentiful examples also suggest that capitalists of all sizes were influenced by debilitating preoccupations other than those of independence and dynastic continuity. They tended, for instance, to expend much substance on the acquisition of a social standing which business achievement (unlike *German* business achievement) did not confer. The purchase of land or the acquisition of office were favoured methods, and could tempt the largest interests. Not until the second generation were the younger de Wendel sons excused the army and permitted instead to enjoy the more relevant facilities of the Ecole des Mines. Marriage was another possibility. All de Wendel daughters, down to the second generation, married army officers; only then did one escape into the questionable arms of an engineer. What is remarkable about an entrepreneurial community of this type is not the absence of the entrepreneurial buccaneers, nor even their fewness; it is their isolation among legions of unheroic businessmen, the lack of imitation which they engendered, and even the residual *similarities* in values between grand and petty capitalism. Perhaps the general terrain in which the entire species lived was most accurately identified by Faucher when he wrote, 'in our industrial towns the factory is based on a social state that belongs to a previous era'.

It is indeed arguable that the much-vaunted operations of French enterprise outside France[213] were by no means immunized against these influences, and fell especially prone to them after 1890. The achievements of bankers, industrialists, and investors in Italy – once the largest of French debtors – provide illuminating, if unhappy, examples. Total credit operations on Italian account declined from a peak of nearly 30 per cent of all French overseas investment

1858–70 to not much more than 5 per cent by 1914[214] – and by no means wholly for political reasons. According to Gille, French capital had looked initially to Italian (as to Spanish) investment as a conservative interest, a useful adjunct to the Vienna settlement; then, after 1830, to Roman investment as an exercise in catholicism and legitimacy; then, after 1860, to a unified Italy, favourite of Napoleon III and potential ally. To these versions of Italy, French capital would bring government loans, railways, and public utilities. But when, later in the century, the Italians had domesticated the debt and repurchased the railways, and were anxious for *industrial* capital, French support was not forthcoming; even after 1898, it made little effort to re-enter the Italian market on these terms.[215] Analysis of 1000 portfolios deposited with the Bank of France in 1897 revealed a similar trend: 31 per cent of holdings were concerned with overseas public debts, only 6 per cent with private securities, including industrial equities, and the remainder with domestic interests. In Italy, of course, German bankers throve on the reticence of their competitors, while the French Ambassador regretted the 'timidité de la finance française'. Certainly French investment houses seem to have been no more industrially minded than their investors. Even Rothschilds, railway sovereigns over most of Europe, and especially in Italy, contrived to accumulate their interests in rail-*making* not in France, nor even in Italy, but in *Belgium*. French manufacturers themselves did little better: only the tyre concern, Michelin and the glass-makers, Saint-Gobain set up factories in Italy during the early 1900s, while the single German enterprise AEG accumulated no less than six Italian subsidiaries over the same period. Together, AEG and Siemens monopolized the provision of electrical utilities in Italy, breaking the hold placed upon this market by the earlier French pre-eminence in gas manufacturing.[216] Clearly, the French were prepared to sponsor the economic development of Europe only in a specialized and restricted coin.

Acknowledging the dangers inherent in ideal entrepreneurial types and in generalizations aimed at entire entrepreneurial communities, and allowing for the band of creative 'deviationists', some intriguing features common to French enterprise of varying types nevertheless require notice. There is an avoidance of industrial risk shared by large investors and small producers, a timidity with financial risk shared by merchant bankers and small savers. There is a widespread, if not universal, preference for smallness of scale and an emphasis on familial goals throughout the business range. Pronounced individualism in economic behaviour is ubiquitous and is not distant in kind from the pronounced politicization of international business relations, whether seen in investors' choices or bankers' policies. The inference is that the French business or financial 'subject' subscribed to a set of values that was by no means purely capitalistic, and in some ways pre-capitalistic.

So too did his country cousin. Recently Paul Hohenberg has shown that by 1892 only just over half the 6.6 m. Frenchmen working in agriculture were proprietors in full or in part. But he admits that, if the countryside was not entirely worked by peasant-owners, the influence of this group upon the quality of cultivation remained decisive.[217] Agricultural enterprise was not supplied by the heedless aristocrats who reoccupied the châteaux after 1815 in numbers unseen since Louis XIV captured them for Versailles. The response of agricultural labour to the manpower needs of early industrialization – however large the labouring element in the villages – had been weak. So the main responsibility in adjusting agriculture to an industrial world passed to the peasant-proprietors. It was not met. Holdings remained small; of the 5.7 m. recorded in 1892 less than 16 per cent exceeded 10 hectares. Such small units required labour-intensive operation if they were to be profitable, but the budgetary caution of the peasantry ruled out the large families or the hiring policies needed to sustain labour-intensiveness. Without generous inputs of manpower and skill, the family farms could not tap the markets opened by urban expansion. And without profits from these markets there was little chance of renewed investment in agriculture: by 1914 the French countryside contained half as much capital as the American, and hardly more than the Spanish. Given these choices, only the path of frugality and individualism remained. Polyculture was used to support household autarky and minimize cash outflows. Inheritance procedures generated vendettas counted in decades, and family work systems guaranteed ceaseless labour strife. The most significant output of the peasant plot may well have been dissension as to how it might be inherited. Certainly, other forms of output were not impressive: the farmers of the Third Republic struck the lowest output per acre in western Europe with wheat yields by 1911–12 averaging half those of Belgium or the Netherlands, two-thirds those of Germany or Britain. Once more, according to recent analysis, the limitations upon this performance proceeded from 'timid impulses' rather than from objective bottlenecks.[218]

Timidity was well displayed in French agriculture's unwillingness to release workers: migrants were fewer, and less completely freed, than in any comparable European system. Kindleberger suggests tentatively that elasticity of output was so low that even small migrations out of the primary sector – by transferring factors from the supply to the demand side – sufficed to expand the requirement for agricultural produce and thus, as the profitability of farming marginally improved, to shut off the migration flow.[219] In 1851, 74.5 per cent of the populace still lived in the countryside, or in the characteristic small towns of under 2000 inhabitants, and, even in the period of rapid industrialization 1850–70, the true urban population never grew by more than 3 per cent in any half-decade.[220] As in many parts of Europe, what dribbling off the land there was – mostly from the East, Centre-west, and South-west Massif, and mostly of the least schooled and skilled – was generally regretted as morally and socially debilitating. Well into the Third Republic's span, one of the least flexible peasant communities in Europe was seen as the guarantor of a desirable politico-social equilibrium.

If the values of French businessmen and French agriculturalists are placed together, they compose a significant economic model: that of a small-town economy. The survival of a large primary sector of low output and low income prevented a mass market from emerging; instead its legacy was a system of partially separated provincial markets based upon the transformation of local materials by small-scale manufacturers – miniature ironworks meeting peasant demand for agricultural implements, small mills or mines employing quasi-peasant labour – and located within a regional town economy served by its own small traders, miniature manufacturers, and professional men. Isolation and high transport costs served to protect these systems from the scattered pockets of competitive modern industry. Genuine innovations aimed at the mass market – like the retailing developments favoured by Gerschenkron – were metropolitan phenomena untypical of most French markets; and even they catered for a more elevated social stratum than that served by the retailing systems of late-nineteenth-century Britain. Over most of France, dispersed and fragmented markets formed a natural subsoil for concepts of possessive individualism and of individual wealth destined to grow steadily and without risk or obligation. The bourgeoisies, both rural and urban, who contributed the major components of this model were of a very particular type, far removed from the hard-nosed, achieving middle classes of Britain and the USA. They provide the proof that 'bourgeois values' fail to compose themselves into a single identifiable set; rather there are complete and separate constellations of *various* bourgeois values which may be related to economic growth, or to stagnation, in a manner equally various.

But was the French value-constellation sufficiently specialized to account for the nation's poor record in economic decision-making? Obviously, as an explanation it is superior to many single-track hypotheses. A managerial ethic highly flavoured by atomistic and parochial ingredients might match French economic experience not at one but at many points: in the attachment to local sources of labour, power, and demand; in the poor market for fabricated metal and other capital goods; in the low count of scale-intensive producers; in the underdeveloped clientele for bank-generated credit; in the slow progress of a national communications system; in the inter-regional alienation of coal and metallurgical interests. Nor is this surprising. The entrepreneurial community acts as the factor of production which combines all other factors; if there is any systematic flaw in its decisions regarding that combination, the results will necessarily affect a very wide selection of economic relationships. Yet explanations in terms of social values, assertions of bourgeois reticence, descriptions of miniature enterprise, are open to a common objection: they depict a fixed or equilibrated social system and, apparently, they cannot usefully relate to an economic performance which contained strong *fluctuations*.[221] Despite the static social constraints, and in the manifest absence of social convulsions powerful enough to shatter them, the manufacturing sector – including many family firms – did, after all, achieve rapid mobility in the spurts of the 1850s, and 1900s. If these upswings could galvanize the business ranks, the probability must be that the resistance of the social equilibrium to economic change could not have been serious. But these assumptions will themselves function only if the social value models are *defined* statically; there is no reason why they should not be designed with a dynamic capability.[222] Thus, adverse social dispositions may be deemed to delay and compress growth but not to extinguish it. Then, the materials for growth might accumulate, stacking up against a resistant social barrier, but overflowing when the stream of opportunities exceeded the desire to discount them. An alternation of spurts and stagnant periods – not unlike the French reality – might be a realistic outcome for this type of model.

However, it does not provide a terminus for argument: French entrepreneurial history remains a shooting war with learned articles serving as projectiles. The campaign has flowed both ways, but some identifiable strongpoints have been established, most notably on the border between French and German experience. At an early stage, the opponents of the 'social-value' interpretation enrolled Germany as an ally: its pre-industrial values had also proved strong and durable, and it too embraced a myriad of small firms within its business structure; only the possession of the Ruhr outweighed this Franco-German similarity and permitted the more rapid advance of the northern partner. In this interpretation natural endowment once more triumphs over entrepreneurial endowment. Yet the counter-views are equally, and perhaps more, formidable. By 1900 Germany certainly possessed many small firms, but these were merely the residuals left over from the process of cartelization; in reality, and partly by dint of cartelization, Germany possessed many more *large* concerns than France. Additionally, if Germany succeeded in resource-intensive ventures, she also outpaced France in sectors – like those of banking and exporting – where enterprise counted more heavily than endowment. Even with regard to chemical manufacture, the Germans had initially depended on imported coal-tar inputs quite as heavily as the French. It was technical change, chief achievement of dynamic enterprise, which most strongly supported Germany's late-century advance; and technical change may modify the requirements for resource inputs. On these tests, Germany differed from France not only in material but *also* in entrepreneurial endowment.

Yet even this acknowledged discrepancy can attract optimistic rationalization. The 'inferiority' of the French response is traced not to the social-value system but to appropriate business tactics: cautious innovation, high liquidity, and jealous independence may have provided *proper* measures for survival within an economy of sluggish and depressive tendency; while, in the contrasting case of Germany, the enlarged markets of the new Empire provided a fit context for dashing enterprise. French business selected conservative methods because these suited the bleak mood of the economy; German business directed opposing methods at expanding economic opportunities. Enterprise, it is assumed, is conditioned by the economic environment: the entrepreneur is puppet rather than puppet-master, function rather than fabricator of economic events. Clearly the rationalization may be contested. There is no evidence to suggest that the French economy was *more* prone to recession than its European colleagues: the slumps of 1848 and 1867 were painful, but it would be difficult to establish that they were more intense – and so attracted more conservative responses – than slumps elsewhere. And it may be over-generous to assume that the businessman who, in adverse economic conditions, subordinates enterprise to caution is necessarily acting rationally; he may simply be failing in his primary function as risk-taker. Worse, by seeking refuge against recession in conservative tactics, the business community may merely assist in evoking recession: too frequently anticipation of economic dislocation acts as self-fulfilling prophecy. Among entrepreneurs, then, a predisposition to employ defensive measures might not follow from, but could well explain, sluggish economic performance. Similarly, if lack of enterprise can accentuate economic recession, it does not follow that lack of enterprise is necessarily explained by economic recession. On the contrary, the use of creative business methods – including product, market, or technology changes – can, at least, mitigate recession; and it is arguable that at no point on the cycle are such methods more needed. Indeed, attempts to derive entrepreneurial activity from the economic context may well be *least* satisfactory for periods of economic embarrassment. And all such attempts are open to the *a priori* objection that it is the entrepreneur's task, at least in part, to mould and remodel the economic context.

In this, however, the businessman's capabilities will be controlled not only by values but also by skills. Is it possible that the training of the French entrepreneur, rather than his social assumptions or his market problems, determined the style of economic behaviour? The revolution had included among its socio-economic bequests the great educational innovations of the École Polytechnique, the Conservatoire des Arts et Métiers, and the Écoles d'Arts et Métiers, leaders in European practice until the ascent of the German technical high schools after 1850. Well before then, however, the reach of the French educational system had become suspect. Elementary education attracted few funds before 1815, and, for long after, this facility – probably more relevant for the mass of small manufacturers than were the élite technical schools – remained poor. The Napoleonic reforms had been directed rather towards the grooming of officers and administrators than towards the promotion of wholesale educational advance. And even the economic sensitivity of the Second Empire did not extend to thoroughgoing educational preparation. Among the populace the results were not impressive. By 1835 Lorraine, Franche-Comté, and Burgundy had achieved respectable educational levels, but the national literacy rate probably did not much exceed 40 per cent, the barest minimum 'threshold' for industrialization, according to Bowman and Anderson,[223] and decidedly low for so late a date (England – 65%).[224] It was a performance probably not much better than that of contemporary Russia, Spain, or Naples and clearly surpassed by England, Switzerland, Holland, and Prussia.[225] If French literacy rates caught up fairly quickly after 1835 – the country achieved 80 per cent literacy, the threshold for the high-technology economy, in the 1870s, at roughly the same time as England – their initial retardation could well have imposed entrepreneurial disadvantages during the early phases of industrialization. Vial provides a suggestive echo for this in his description of the metallurgical entrepreneurs who before 1840 displayed little specialist knowledge and left technical matters to their artisan forgemasters.[226]

Even explicit attempts to supply a practical technological education – featuring subjects such as trigonometry, industrial mechanics, and chemistry

— may be questioned. The *grandes écoles*, the Polytechnique and its colleagues, probably did provide tolerably for the highest echelons: selecting upon the basis of mathematical ability, they produced a very wide-ranging curriculum of a highly theoretical nature, a suitable apprenticeship for the commanding generals of the great factories and government departments. But the middle rankers of industry, the foremen and works managers, were reliant upon the Écoles d'Arts et Métiers. While the disorderly hosts of petty capitalism looked to elementary education for basic literacy, large-scale capitalism leaned upon the lesser *écoles* for its non-commissioned officers. And these institutions did not respond convincingly. Despite their practical ambitions, their training remained excessively theoretical. Despite their concentration upon the intermediate range of managers — necessarily a thick layer — their output of graduates remained embarrassingly thin. Just three such schools with some 900 enrolled pupils by 1871 could provide no answer to the problem even of the *sous-officiers* for industry. But still worse was the basic mis-specification of the design: for all their faults, the lesser *écoles* provided a more closely industrial education than any other agency in France, yet they did not aim to place their graduates *above* the middle managerial echelon. Some alumni, of course, had different ideas, but found progress beyond this point difficult or impossible. At Pont à Mousson the remarkable Cavallier managed the ascent, but his successors as Chairman were polytechnicians to a man. At de Wendel only nine individuals from the lesser *écoles* were remembered as significant contributors to company development 1830–1950, and none of these was rewarded with managerial rank.[227] Throughout the metal industries of Lorraine the influence of the *métiers* was more substantial, but their grasp on the top posts was no more secure. Too frequently, this group of industrialists took an over-theoretical education into a lonely manufacturing career and met with social disapproval within the firm. The cachet of the *grandes écoles* with their military and honorific attachments was sufficient to appropriate most management posts that were not filled by nepotism. The supply of a practical industrial education thus remained meagre and erratic while the supply of strategic industrial posts remained a monopoly of status and kin.

The effect of this is not clear. Comparative study of entrepreneurial competence in the adjacent ore-fields of French and German Lorraine seems to show that the generally educated theoreticians of the *grandes écoles* were a match for the vocationally trained specialists of the *technische hochschulen*.[228] Elsewhere, and more generally, however, the catholic spread of the French intellectual style contrived to produce innovations of wide application, probably contributing less to France than to the rest of the world. Even in purely domestic terms, investment in polytechnicians acted more frequently as a subsidy to *culture générale* than to industrial science. Correspondingly, the social status conferred by a *grande école* education could well be inconsistent with its use in industry: many of its beneficiaries withdrew from industrial into bureaucratic or honorary positions, the 'curse of *fonctionnarisme*' maintaining its leaching of managerial talent. And even those who persisted with industrial interests (if, very usually, from the safety of government service) may not have been particularly suited to them. In this connexion, the competitive performance of the Lorraine polytechnicians is less relevant than the fiasco of mineral exploration at Briey. Here graduates of the École des Mines, facing a task for which they were prepared to the highest theoretical level, baulked at the practical difficulties of exploitation and discounted the commercial promise of Europe's richest ore strike; theoretical emphasis fastened upon obstacles and neglected rewards. It was a sequence which might well have prompted Cavallier's denunciation: '. . . it drives me mad with rage to see that in our country where education is nevertheless pursued to a high level, it is so impractical; . . . the young (are) all studying to become scholars, none to do anything practically useful'.[229]

Skills, then, do not separate from values. The provision of technical education in France was subject to the control of social forces: a 'practical' form of training was denied a position of social or economic eminence while a less vocational form of training was rewarded with high rank and social esteem. As the country's real capital was employed, with approval, outside France, so the country's most expensive human capital was employed, with approval, outside industry. Clearly, social values control more than the approval or condemnation extended to capitalistic endeavour: they determine also the range of careers and the array of rewards open to the capitalist. Entrepreneurs cannot easily surmount these constraints. For social values do not deliver merely external judgements upon economic activity, in the style of neighbourhood gossip. As participants in the social system, entrepreneurs will partly *share* these values and will certainly be guided by their operational effects, expressed in educational, promotional, and socio-cultural prospects. Yet it is conceded that the existence of a uniform social-value system is an unlikely event. Groups like the *fermiers généraux* of the old regime could achieve capitalistic success in the face of emphatic hostility.[230] And, even in industrial France, the 'heroic entrepreneur' of the classic swashbuckling type was not entirely unknown. Other value systems than those of the familial, profit-conserving, non-innovating · autonomists obviously existed, and were in contention with the stereotype devised by the Harvard School.

The important issue is the *balance* between the contending systems. 'Deviant' groups or individuals can arise within any set of value systems, but the balance between these systems may still determine whether the entrepreneurial rank and file is receptive, or unreceptive, to the generalship of the entrepreneurial 'heroes'. For France the evidence hints either that divine negligence was as evident in the design of Frenchmen as in the preparation of French geology, or, more likely, that the balance of value systems was tipped towards the conservative. Schumpeterian buccaneers were not absent; the problem lay rather, in contrast to the English case, in the small following of competent imitators that they attracted. From all the vexed literature surrounding this problem perhaps the most useful concluding note falls to Spengler. After a careful parade of exactly those 'objective factors' much stressed in current research – the demographic and capital resources of France – he sets aside these limitations upon growth in favour of more elusive influences: 'French value patterns, French tastes, the heterogeneous nature of France's cultural heritage.'[231] In its attention to both quantifiable and entrepreneurial diagnoses of the French ailment, and, in the judiciousness of its final deduction, this assessment − now a quarter-century old − achieved an analytical symmetry which might well bear reintroduction into French economic studies.

CONCLUSIONS

The battered and tired French economy of the nineteenth century paradoxically forms a sound, if rigorous, test-bed for many of the historical models of economic growth. Concepts of industrial preconditions or pre-requisites, for instance, scarcely survive the experiment: preparation in agriculture, in social overheads, or in banking is clearly deficient, yet the economy nevertheless achieves industrial status. However, this test is not entirely destructive: the weaknesses in the flexibility of the primary, transportation, and credit sectors did restrict, even if they did not prevent, the long-run impulsion of the manufacturing sectors. Similarly, the overall fit of the backwardness model is erratic: France was not a primitively retarded economy; she drew upon a proto-industrial past, a tradition of science, wealth, and military power; therefore, the classic 'lunge' out of backwardness did not lie among her choice of growth styles. Admittedly, the country displayed the classic institutional tools of the nineteenth-century 'follower economy', the investment bank and the interventionist state; yet over the long run she exploited neither device as fully as did her more backward contemporaries. Only in the short run, and at special moments is the fit between this model and French reality sufficiently exact: when both the institutions of credit and of government underwent a limited phase of effective operation around mid century, the economy did respond with a major industrial upswing. Other models find more consistent parallels in the historical data; thus the mid-century growth experience in itself confirms the proposition that the value of statist economics may vary through time and between regimes. The swing towards active industrial promotion by a reconstituted state was initiated, as earlier it had been in Germany, by authoritarian and militaristic interests, and despite the reservations of agricultural groups within the Conseil d'Etat, as unfriendly to economic innovation as any Junker *apparat*. On the other hand, the longer-run ineffectiveness of the French government rested not upon supply characteristics in an era of strong rule but upon demand characteristics in times of democratic administration: here the 'delinquent communities' were the major variables, colleagues in irrationality, if not in socio-economic objectives, for the Junker rye lobby.

Yet if the national administrations exerted a variable leverage upon French growth, that growth was not a national development. In fact the regional models fit French experience particularly well: industrialization is highly fragmented with Alsace-Lorraine, the north-east, and the Nord comparing, and sometimes fraternizing more closely, with economic regions over the Belgian and German borders than with the almost untouched agricultural tracts of the French south-west and centre. Not only in this respect did French development display centrifugal tendencies; there was also its pronounced parochialism, its liability to splinter into isolated local systems of rural consumers and petty capitalists, unsophisticated and largely self-contained industrial domains, contending with one another to withhold capital and labour from the modern sector. However, at the other extreme, and in other respects, the style of French industrialization is almost uniquely cosmopolitan. Centrifugal components of French industry might press towards the frontiers, but other elements of French enterprise crossed them in remarkable volume. In the early nineteenth century, France had drawn heavily upon the stream of technology and technologists flowing out of Britain, but, before long, had created a tributary of her own, irrigating Europe with streams of engineering and ingenuity which somehow could not be conserved at home. Even French science produced inventions of unusually wide currency. And French capital travelled more easily outside the country than inside it. In this sense the international industrial revolution passed *through* France, leaving strong domestic pockets of manufacturing, but mobilizing men and money for a wider, transcontinental task. Arguably, the French industrial revolution was more forceful in its international than in its homespun aspects; more lively as a contributor to European industrialization than as a contributor to French wealth.

However useful these features may be as tests for the various economic models, the overall verdict upon French growth still has a pessimistic ring to it. Brief inklings of a more sanguine quantitative evaluation – originally received as 'almost overwhelming' in their novelty – have been absorbed and adjusted to produce a pattern with a familiar emphasis on gradual advance. The 'steadiness' of growth advocated by the new economic historians has been retained, but so has the slow pace selected by their predecessors. France brackets with England, and also, but less happily, with Germany as an exponent of evolutionary, rather than revolutionary expansion; in France, however, evolution carries more pejorative implications than in the other two cases. Similarly, the hypothesis of entrepreneurial deficiency has been tested, contorted, reviled, and, on the whole, has survived. Kindleberger, after a rapid and abrasive survey, concedes that 'there is substantial evidence in support of the Landes–Pitts thesis' (although he does not find it 'established');[232] Crouzet has combined his carefully controlled statistical explorations with lingering doubts about the quality of enterprise; and, even in agriculture, where the econometricians have detected critical productivity deficiencies, Hohenberg insists upon his 'timid impulses'. It is time perhaps to resurrect the entrepreneurial hypothesis. As a compliment, it would be a small one to expend on a proposal which has endured several decades of hostile criticism, but has shown every sign of persistence.

NOTES AND REFERENCES

Full publication details are provided in the bibliography.
1   Crouzet (1967), p. 146.
2. Marczewski (1961), Table 7.
3. Crouzet (1967), p. 152.
4. Labrousse (1933), vol. 2, pp. 506–8, 548, 555–7.
5. Behrens (1962–3), pp. 451–75. But compare the reality: 'there can be no doubt . . . that the French government attempted to impose a much heavier tax burden on its landed upper classes than did the British government' (p. 463).
6. Fohlen (1973), vol. I, p. 19.
7. *Ibid.*, p. 19.
8. Crouzet (1967), p. 157.
9. *Ibid.*, pp. 173–4.
10. Milward and Saul (1973), p. 251.
11. *Ibid.*, p. 252.
12. The essential reformulation is supplied by Behrens (1962–63), esp. p. 464
13. Even England introduced a graduated income tax only in 1799.
14. Mathias and O'Brien (1976), esp. Tables 5 and 6.
15. Morineau (1972), p. 458. Compare Mathias and O'Brien (1976): 'In terms of social incidence the burden of taxation in constitutional bourgeois, parliamentary Britain was more regressive than in absolutist France' (p. 634).
16. Mathias and O'Brien (1976), p. 629.
17. *Ibid.*, p. 635.
18. *Ibid.*, p. 629.
19. Palmer (1959), pp. 337–9.
20. Lefebvre (1929), p. 310.
21. *Ibid.*, p. 513.
22. Labrousse (1944).
23. Rudé (1954). Also *idem* (1964), pp. 108–22. Compare Rose (1959).
24. Palmer (1964), vol. I, xvi.
25. French population expanded at an annual average rate of 0.31 per cent in 1700 –89 and 0.45 per cent in 1740–89 (Wrigley, 1969, p. 153).
26. Palmer (1964), vol. II, p. 350.
27. Fohlen (1970), p. 204.
28. Palmer (1964), vol. II, pp. 339–40.
29. *Ibid.*, p. 571.
30. The codes, civil, criminal, commercial, penal, and the *code d'instruction criminelle*, collectively given the title *Code Napoléon*.
31. In 1826 the curriculum was defined by ordinance in a shape that was to endure for over a century – 'arithmetic, geometry, trigonometry (as applied to beams and gears) . . . industrial mechanics, physics and chemistry with their industrial applications and the resistance of materials'. Yet even in 1871 there were only three such establishments with a total enlistment of 900.
32. Milward and Saul (1973), p. 254; see also pp. 272–85.
33. *Ibid.*, p. 280.
34. A not dissimilar view is sketched upon a continental scale in Cameron (1961).
35. Milward and Saul (1973), p. 271.
36. Crouzet (1972), p. 115.
37. Clough (1946).

38. Palmade (1972), p. 43.
39. For the most exhaustive treatment of these effects, see Crouzet (1958). The argument is summarized in Crouzet (1964).
40. Lévy-Leboyer (1964), pp. 27–32, 49.
41. Milward and Saul (1973), pp. 274–5, 281.
42. Crouzet (1972), p. 101.
43. Palmade (1972), p. 42.
44. Trebilcock (1969), p. 478.
45. Compare Milward and Saul (1973), pp. 281–2.
46. Gerschenkron (1968), p. 390.
47. See for example Bloch (1960).
48. *Ibid.*, p. 243.
49. Lefebvre (1924), pp. 498–504.
50. Crouzet (1972), p. 114.
51. Christopher (1951), pp. 50–1.
52. Rudé (1964), pp. 118–19, 129.
53. Palmade (1972), p. 35.
54. *Ibid.*, p. 72.
55. Fohlen (1973), pp. 33–4.
56. Pitts (1963), p. 244.
57. Hoffman *et al.* (1963), p. 7.
58. Siegfried (1951), pp. 5–9.
59. Wolf (1951), pp. 19–31.
60. Landes (1951), p. 339.
61. Palmer (1964), vol. II, p. 351.
62. Compare Blondel: 'The spirit of association has remained very superficial with us . . . what we want to learn is not so much how to produce as to how to combine the elements that constitute an industrial operation.' Quoted by Marshall (1920), p. 115.
63. Siegfried (1951), p. 10.
64. *Ibid.*, p. 11.
65. Cf. Aron (1967), pp. 141ff.
66. Crouzet (1972), p. 120.
67. Milward and Saul (1973), p. 255.
68. Léon (1960), pp. 177–8.
69. Palmade (1972), pp. 61–8.
70. Marczewski (1963), pp. 127–8.
71. Marczewski (1961).
72. Markovitch (1966).
73. Lévy-Leboyer (1964), pp. 49, 65, 95, 169, 171, 410f.
74. Crouzet (1972), p. 125.
75. Vial (1967), p. 14.
76. Fohlen (1973), p. 42.
77. Palmade (1972), p. 68.
78. Marczewski (1961).
79. Fohlen (1970), p. 213.
80. *Ibid.*, p. 213.
81. Rostow (ed.) (1963), p. 359. Crouzet's recent quantitative survey goes further, insisting that, in this early period, 'it is the textile industries which had a very

low growth rate and which *acted as a brake*' upon development in other sectors. Far from sponsoring an industrial revolution, the textile sector generated the "phenomenon of braking"' (Crouzet, 1970, p. 272; my emphasis).

82. Marczewski (1963), pp. 129–30.
83. *Ibid*.
84. *Ibid*., p. 128._
85. Fohlen (1970), p. 219.
86. Crouzet (1972), p. 108.
87. Marczewski (1965), vol. 4, pp. cxxxvi–cxxxviii.
88. Crouzet (1970), p. 272.
89. Fohlen (1973), pp. 34–5.
90. Cameron (ed.) (1967), p. 103.
91. *Ibid*., p. 107.
92. *Ibid*., p. 115.
93. Lévy-Leboyer (1964).
94. Morineau (1968), pp. 299–326, esp. pp. 321–2.
95. Landes (1969a), pp. 112–27, esp. p. 120.
96. Fohlen (1970), p. 215.
97. Marczewski (1963), p. 128.
98. Mechanization, however, proceeded slowly: machines cut 3.4 per cent of the grain areas in 1862, 6.8 per cent in 1882, 11.5 per cent in 1892.
99. Calculated from Marczewski (1963), Table 5, p. 130.
100. Landes (1969b), p. 173.
101. Blanchard (1969), p. 104.
102. Quoted by Caron (1970), p. 320.
103. Cameron (ed.) (1967), p. 115.
104. *Ibid*., p. 109.
105. Gille (1973), pp. 274–6.
106. Lévy-Leboyer (1968), p. 801.
107. Crouzet (1970), p. 275.
108. Crouzet (1972), p. 108.
109. Morineau (1968), p. 326.
110. Cameron (ed.) (1967), p. 107.
111. Bouvier (1970), p. 341; also pp. 347–8.
112. Marczewski (1963), p. 130.
113. Crouzet (1970), p. 275.
114. Palmade (1972), p. 124.
115. GDP from Markovitch (1966). Conversion at rate of 25 francs = £1.
116. See Golob (1944).
117. Marczewski (1961).
118. Lévy-Leboyer (1968).
119. See for example, Aldcroft (1964); and contrast McCloskey and Sandberg (1971).
120. Palmade (1972), pp. 206–10.
121. Kindleberger (1964), pp. 298–302.
122. Crouzet (1970), pp. 275–6 (my emphasis).
123. Fohlen (1970), p. 204.
124. *Ibid*., p. 220.
125. See for example, Henderson (1961), pp. 117ff, 167–8.

126. Milward and Saul (1973), pp. 317–23.

127. But see Kindleberger (1964), p. 268 for a higher valuation of the pre-war export boom.

128. Kirk (1951), pp. 315–16.

129. Bourgeois-Pichat (1951), pp. 635–62.

130. Spengler (1951), pp. 404–5.

131. *Ibid.*

132. Camille Cavallier quoted by Kent (1972), p. 100.

133. Henry (1965), pp. 434–56.

134. *Ibid.*, p. 452.

135. Kindleberger (1964), pp. 172; 186–7.

136. Gignoux (1952), p. 108.

137. Kindleberger (1964), pp. 235–6.

138. Cameron (1963), p. 335.

139. *Ibid.*

140. *Ibid.*, p. 334.

141. Vial (1967), pp. 61–5. The rapidity of Britain's transition to fossil fuel may also be ascribed to the early exhaustion of her timber stocks.

142. Fohlen (1970), p. 210.

143. Kindleberger (1964), p. 234.

144. Gillet (1969), p. 190.

145. Kindleberger (1964), p. 15.

146. Gillet (1969), pp. 196–7.

147. Fohlen (1956).

148. Kindleberger (1964), p. 18.

149. Kent (1972), pp. 244–6.

150. *Ibid.*, Ch. 7 provides a most convincing exposition of this view.

151. Gillet (1969), pp. 197–9.

152. *Ibid.*, pp. 182–4.

153. *Ibid.*, p. 198.

154. Kent (1972), pp. 230–9.

155. Spengler (1951), p. 407.

156. Cameron (ed.) (1967), p. 128; see also pp. 110, 117, 297–8.

157. *Ibid.*, p. 115.

158. British and German proportions for 1911 were one-quarter and one-tenth respectively.

159. Keynes (1924).

160. A similar bias is evident within the operations even of the few genuinely industrial investment banks which were created between 1870 and 1914.

161. Christopher (1951), p. 52.

162. Quoted by Kent (1972), p. 125.

163. Vial (1967).

164. Bouvier (1961), pp. 371–81.

165. Cf. Kindleberger (1964), pp. 57–9.

166. Feis (1961), pp. 119–22; Gille (1968), p. 388.

167. Quoted by Feis (1961), p. 123.

168. *Ibid.*, p. 123.

169. Rothschild Archive, cited by Gille (1968), p. 341.

170. A. Raffalovitch, tsarist financial agent, cited by Feis (1961), p. 158n; cf. White (1933), p. 280.

171. Feis (1961), pp. 199–203; 240–2. Table 3.6 further demonstrates that Italy and Austria-Hungary were among the topmost flight of French debtors before 1870. In the Italian case, disagreements over French involvement in Tunisia and contention over Italy's protectionist ambitions had soured the relationship even before the signing of the Triple Alliance in 1882. But motivations remained basically political. French credit was withheld until the qualified *rapprochement* of 1898, but never recovered its former scale and importance. See Gille (1968), pp. 283ff, 365ff.

172. Collins (1973), pp. 777–88, esp. pp. 781–4.

173. White (1933), p. 107.

174. Girault (1973).

175. Gille (1968), p. 393 (my emphasis).

176. Feis (1961), p. 200.

177. Contrast Kindleberger (1964), p. 59, 'the supply of savings was inelastic, the demand inelastic and the only way that the market could be cleared was by foreign lending'. Remarkably, this view entirely omits the political element.

178. Compare White (1933), p. 221. Contrast Kindleberger (1964), p. 58.

179. White (1933), p. 112.

180. Exceptions were usually 'tied' loans. Balkan countries were frequently induced to purchase munitions from their creditors in the 1900s, and in 1908 and 1910 Scandinavian countries had to pay with tariff concessions for their French gold. See Feis (1961), p. 128; Poidevin (1969); Crouzet (1974), pp. 287–318.

181. White (1933), p. 295n.

182. This expectation forms an important assumption of Cameron (1961).

183. White (1933), p. 107. The result is obtained for the complete investment holdings of 1899 if the total domestic and foreign portfolios are compared in respect of *either* rate of return on nominal capital *or* rate on issue price. The poor showing of the foreign portfolio is partly explained by the cautious French preference for low-yielding government bonds. These composed 75 per cent of the French overseas portfolio against 25 per cent for the German and 35 per cent for the British (pp. 110–12).

184. Gille (1968), p. 396.

185. White (1933), pp. 275–83.

186. White (1933), p. 90, but see Gille (1968), p. 388.

187. Further adjustments would, of course, be necessary in respect, *inter alia* of: (a) the capability of domestic investment to create stronger multiplier effects within the home economy than can be achieved by foreign investment with the same sum; (b) the fact that domestic default leaves some capital assets intact and within reach of investors while overseas default frequently places capital assets beyond recall.

188. M. Cawes quoted by White (1933), p. 299.

189. Cameron (1961); *Idem* (1967), pp. 115, 127–8.

190. Cameron (1963), p. 337.

191. Morazé (1952).

192. Mourre (1900).

193. Landes (1949), pp. 45–61.

194. Parker (1959), pp. 201–12.

195. Gerschenkron (1968), p. 333 ('The stability of dictatorships').

196. Cited by Lamèyne (1958), p. 27.

197. Baron Alphonse de Rothschild, cited by Gille (1968), p. 307.

198. Kindleberger (1964), p. 186.
199. *Ibid.*, p. 193.
200. Golob (1944), p. 174.
201. Crouzet (1974), pp. 309–13.
202. Feis (1961), pp. 154–6.
203. Quoted by Vial (1967), pp. 196–7.
204. Reader (1970), vol. 1, pp. 70–1, 154.
205. See, for example, Landes (1949), pp. 45–61; also *idem* (1951), pp. 334–53.
206. Vial (1967), pp. 165–203.
207. Dansette (1954); Fohlen (1956).
208. Notably Professors Landes, Sawyer, and Pitts.
209. Landes (1954), p. 246 conceded a similar point; see also *idem* (1949), p. 50.
210. Vial (1967), pp. 180, 183.
211. Kindleberger (1964), p. 179.
212. Kent (1972), pp. 37, 107–24, 125–30.
213. See Cameron (1961).
214. Gille (1968), p. 391.
215. *Ibid.*, p. 396.
216. *Ibid.*, pp. 380, 391.
217. Hohenberg (1972), pp. 222, 232–6.
218. *Ibid.*, p. 236.
219. Kindleberger (1964), pp. 225ff. However, his discussion does not confirm this suggestion; nor, for that matter, does it confirm any other.
220. Fohlen (1970), p. 203.
221. Gerschenkron (1953), pp. 1–20; esp. p. 12.
222. Sawyer (1954), pp. 277–9; see also Landes (1954).
223. Bowman and Anderson (1963).
224. Webb (1963) estimates French literacy to be: 1835 – 42 per cent; 1847 – 64 per cent; 1867 – 77 per cent; 1877 – 85 per cent; and English literacy to be: 1835/40 – 65 per cent; 1850 – 70 per cent; 1860 – 74 per cent; 1870 – 80 per cent.
225. Dupin (1827), vol. 1, pp. 51–3.
226. Vial (1967), p. 21.
227. Kent (1972), pp. 33–4.
228. Parker (1959), pp. 208–12.
229. Quoted by Kent (1972), pp. 39–40.
230. Gerschenkron (1962), p. 59.
231. Spengler (1951), p. 411.
232. Kindleberger (1964), p. 117.

CHAPTER FOUR

Russia

Where one may debate the relative backwardness of France and the German states prior to 1850, there is no room for argument about the northernmost great power. Only in the Iberian and Balkan extremities of Europe could comparably primitive economic conditions be found, not only before 1850 but until the century's turn. Opinions as to when Russia began to shrug off this incubus are conventionally pessimistic. R. W. Goldsmith describes Russia in 1861 as 'predominantly agrarian . . . without the characteristics of nineteenth century industrialization' and believes her to be 'still an underdeveloped country' on the eve of the 1917 revolution.[1] For Warren Nutter no effective attempt to break out of backwardness is made until the late date of 1928, with the initiation of the First Five Year Plan.[2]

Certainly, the economic assets of the tsarist autocracy in the three-quarters of a century before the Crimean War were scarcely appetizing. Agriculture was paralysed by a vicious climate and by a social structure which retained most of feudalism's least constructive features. While the serf remained a baptized chattel and the lord an irresponsible debtor, there was little chance of improved cultivation. Even the more promising black soil regions were not colonized until the second half of the century. Paradoxically, also, the raw materials in which modern Russia abounds were not available to the economy of 1850. The major part of the natural endowment then lay outside the reach of the main industrial centres with Asiatic Russia monopolizing four-fifths of the Empire's coal, five-sixths of its water-power, and all its tin, cobalt, and tungsten.[3] By comparison, central and north-western provinces contained only inferior deposits of iron ore. Where in Britain and Germany, and even in less favoured France, coal, iron, and people tended to coagulate in reasonable proximity, in Russia thousands of kilometres could separate the population centres from the resource areas. The huge size of the Tsar's domain was thus an integral component of its backwardness. Until a connexion was forged between the high-quality iron ore of Krivoi Rog and the coal of the Donets Basin, industrialization in Russia was a matter of speculation rather than of performance. With railway construction scarcely commenced before 1870 — one line penetrated to the Urals in 1844, another linked the administrative centres of Moscow and St Petersburg by the 1860s – that connexion did not come easily or rapidly. Consequently, indigenous resources were not turned to industrial account. In 1850 a mere half-million tons of coal were raised from Russia's vast subterranean storehouse, one-thirteenth of the British cut. When railway building began in earnest in the 1870s, nearly 60 per cent of the necessary coal came by foreign purchase. Unsurprisingly, manufacturing industry did not thrive under these conditions. Indeed the Russian iron industry, which had led world production in 1780, ran steadily downhill through-

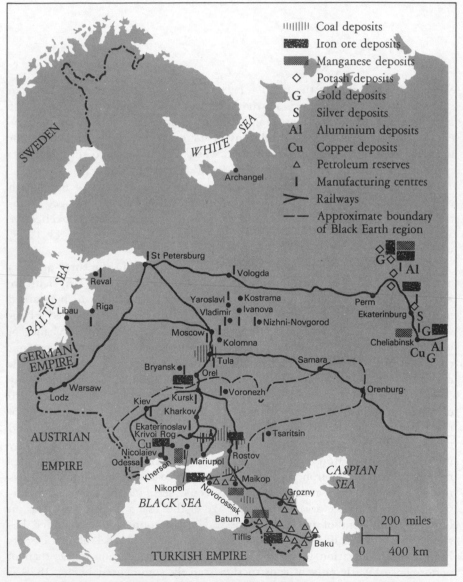

4. European Russia: main railways, resource and industrial areas, 1900

out the nineteenth century's first half: as modern capitalistic ironworks proliferated in the West, the rudimentary equipment of the Urals could account for
only 12 per cent of world production in 1830, 4 per cent by 1858.[4] Hardly any
banks or industrial corporations of note could be set alongside the ironworks,
and factory industry itself was an occasional and sporadic occurrence. Even in
textile manufacture, the usual pre-industrial sprinkling of viable concerns was
cast more thinly than elsewhere in western Europe. By 1850 the entire
Empire could amass only 2000 powered looms against some 18,000 hand-
looms in factory production and 80,000 in cottage production. For the vast
majority of Russians, living on the edge of an industrializing continent, the
limits of experience were still set at mid-century by feudal obligation, com
munal agriculture, and the confines of the village.[5]

EMANCIPATING MOTIVES: FROM TSAR-LIBERATOR TO SERF-REGULATOR

Obviously enough, the problems of Russian backwardness could not be solved
simply by the construction of a railway system, nor by any other single stroke
of 'mechanical' innovation. Among severely backward economies, extensive
social engineering is frequently a prime requisite for industrial advance, and
many observers have placed the nineteenth century tsarist autocracy second to
none in this requirement. It has become widely – if not quite universally[6] –
believed that Russia's retention of a society based on serfdom was incompatible with modern economic growth. If it was important, therefore, to attack
the nation's vast distances with the railway engine, it was also important to
attack its entrenched feudalism with the engine of the law. Superficially, this
was exactly the intent of Alexander II and his advisers in their reformist legislation of 1857–65, the great Emancipation Decree of 1861 standing as
keystone to their efforts. Yet when the more taxing questions are raised – had
the tsarist administrators genuinely perceived that the extirpation of feudalism
was a prerequisite for industrialization? could they claim kinship in reform
with the progressive bourgeoisie of revolutionary France or the clear-sighted
functionaries of beleaguered Prussia? – the answers come as ready negatives.
Although emancipation fell at a critical juncture in Russian economic development, there was nothing of economic motivation in its inception or design.
Although technically reformist, there was little of the progressive in its intent
or provisions. The agricultural economy – virtually the sum of the Russian
economy – supplied few inherent attractions to reform. For all its limitations,
serf labour proved able to generate increases in agricultural output and to
attain productivity levels insufficiently below those of free wage labour automatically to justify adoption of the costlier alternative.[7] Accordingly, non-
economic considerations weighed more heavily within the composition of the
reform measures.

Prime among these was the need to compensate for the declining efficiency

207

of feudalism as a structure of social control and military administration. In the decades before mid-century, commutation had become increasingly common amidst the poor northern provinces as penurious gentry willingly settled for cash in lieu of labour services. By exploiting the loopholes in a crumbling edifice, the peasantry were able to escape the feudal bond – some by a margin permitting town life and non-agricultural employment – in significant numbers. As this increasing social fluidity ate into the internal stability required by the autocracy, an upswing in the cycle of peasant unrest supplied palpable evidence of declining social control, fluttering drawing rooms and ministries alike with whispers of a 'second Pugachev'. To this systematic deterioration, the mid-century decades added coincidental but sharp reinforcement. Harvest failure in 1848 brought cholera and a million deaths in its wake, improving the mood of the countryside not at all. War, completing the apocalyptic company, fell upon the Crimea between 1854 and 1857, unleashing social unrest and breeding significantly fantastic rumours: that military service cancelled feudal obligation; that the French invader, promising emancipation in 1812, had returned to keep his commitment. Judging both the trend and the causes correctly, the Tsar deduced that reform – or something with the appearance of reform – must issue from the government before it was carried to Petersburg on the point of a pitchfork. But the most powerful persuasion flowed directly from the travails of warfare; for unpalatable home truths as well as peasant disturbances had featured among these. The mechanisms of serfdom, designed to field a mass conscript army in support of a military autocracy had turned out the soldiery – and also an ignominious defeat. The system had failed in its fundamental objectives: whatever its surviving economic utility, it could assure neither internal nor external security. Significantly, in the latter areas, the Russian institutions had pitted the slave army of a backward despotism against the military capabilities of two European democracies, second to none in industrial attainment – and the traditional imperial virtues had fared poorly before the representatives of legislative assemblies and high technologies. If the autocracy recognized no economic requirement for modernization, it could scarcely fail to apprehend that the continued viability of the Empire as an international power necessitated emulation of the new processes, for military reasons if no other. Such perceptions were consistent with Russian practice: in the past reform had frequently correlated with defeat, while the military successes of the eighteenth and early nineteenth centuries had acted to muffle the alarum for change.[8]

The motivation behind emancipation thus followed from an appetite for twin securities, the security of peasant equilibrium at home, the security of sustained prestige in the international forum. Unfortunately, these aims were partially incompatible, for international security required at least a measure of economic modernization, while internal security could not readily accommodate the social tensions which modernization entailed. The paradox was not resolved: from 1861 until 1917 Russian industrialization was pursued always in part for military purposes and always within a frame rigidly defined to minimize domestic upheavals. The implications of this are manifold – not least that the contradictory objectives created potentially explosive strains within the social structure – but one important deduction stands clear: that any prospect for economic change generated around mid-century was subject to powerful and longstanding constraints.

Constrained growth from chronic backwardness might serve as a fair description of the Russian economy until as late as 1890. But there remain a few intransigent cross-currents to which it does not do full justice. One is provided by Strumilin's assertion that by the 1840s Russia was sufficiently advanced to share in the movements of the international trade cycle. Between 1800 and 1850 the industrial labour force increased sixfold and between 1820 and 1850, while the total population advanced by only 41 per cent, the community of industrial workers expanded by 180 per cent. On the eve of emancipation, serfs made up only 13 per cent of the factory labour force and the industries with which they were most closely connected were not conspicuously prospering: metallurgy, for instance, performed indifferently between 1800 and 1860, while industries using largely free labour – especially textiles – enjoyed unusual success.[9] Frictions of numerous types emerged from these developments. Free labour groups were established as a contrast, and possibly an attraction, to the largely enserfed workgroups in cottage industry and agriculture. A minority of serfs were set to factory work, but were still required to pay quit-rent to a feudal lord and to resume agricultural labour upon demand, in effect imposing an agricultural 'tax' and an insecure labour supply upon the manufacturing sector. In return, factory industry outpaced serf village production by the 1850s, thus damaging the value of another serf function. Finally, the new industrial developments rendered Russia sensitive to the swings of the international cycle, unfortunately imposing upon the economy during the 1850s a depression that was quite independent of the strains produced by military operations.

These abrasive indicators suggest that an incipient industrial potential played some part in exacerbating the crisis which preceded emancipation: it demonstrated the rewards to freedom, damaged serf manufacture, agitated under the strictures of the feudal code, and loaded its cyclical problems upon an already feeble agricultural economy. The hypothesis possesses force, but topples too readily into overstatement. Phenomenal expansion in the factory workforce can only betray its small initial size, while the enterprises to which the labour flocked were the merest forerunners of industrial capitalism. Optimistic propositions that the Russian economy of the 1840s was sufficiently advanced to share the merry gyrations of the international cycle are subject to the counter-proposals that what the economy was sufficiently advanced to experience was a major international slump, and that it experienced little better for some decades. In reality the issue here is a historiographical one: the determination of some Soviet writers such as Strumilin to extend Russia's industrial revolution backwards, away from the Stalinist 1930s or the imperial 1890s, into the respectable distance of the pre-emancipation past. Necessarily, the effort rests upon an implicitly limited definition of industrialization: not the thorough-going transformation of the manufacturing base but the appearance of new organizational forms and technological processes within the feudal matrix. The specification is again excessively narrow, clearly more redolent of proto-industrialization than of the revolution which its advocates preach. However, Strumilin and his colleagues have succeeded in administering a salutary reminder that even chronic backwardness may not be all-embracing, may include the possibility of *pointilliste* industrial advance. As long as the limitations are well displayed, there is value in the evocation of long-run capitalistic trends within imperial Russia.

THE ENTREPRENEURIAL COMPENSATIONS OF FEUDALISM

Clearly, to focus upon the early industrial achievements of Russia is to imply that, contrary to most expectations, the social structure of the pre-emancipation autocracy may not have entirely excluded the possibility of effective entrepreneurship. Close investigation of this implication has indeed revealed the existence of streams of enterprise flowing from some unusual quarters. Commutation of serf labour duties in the northern regions created security problems for administrators but money economies for budding merchants and mobility for alert peasants. According to Rosovsky, a useful proportion of serfs exploited this relative freedom to pursue fortune in craft manufacturing, factory industry, or even in land-owning.[10] By 1800 cottage industry managed by serfs had already outpaced the state's forced labour factories in supplying the bulk of locally used consumer goods. Similarly, serf-industrialists in textiles proved rapidly sensitive to innovation, employing calico-printing and power-weaving processes well in advance of the official mills. By 1850, Olga Crisp has claimed, important parts of the cotton and sugar industries were of serf origin and an indigenous body of enterprise already established.[11] It was only *after* emancipation that the serf industries declined, and then by no means universally. However, even before 1861 they were not entire monopolists of the commercial arts. Crisp points also to the gentry-entrepreneurs, driven after 1750 by indebtedness and after 1790 by wartime losses, into industrial venturing, usually in distilling or the weaving of uniform cloth. Rural entrepreneurship of either type made excellent sense: with raw materials and subsistence goods close by and good chances of tax evasion, overheads for the serf- or gentry-entrepreneurs were often lower than for their urban counterparts. Protection from sympathetic landlords was not unprecedented, and, for different reasons, neither serf nor gentry encountered the temptation which beset successful urban industrialists – recruitment into the table of ranks and advancement outside the business world. This combination of opportunities, imperatives, and environment, Crisp argues, produced an 'autonomous stream' of modern Russian enterprise stretching back beyond 1861 to the middle of the eighteenth century.

Notable examples of large-scale, even of 'heroic', entrepreneurship were thrown up by this stream. At Ivanovo, as early as 1792, the serf partnership,

Grachev and Granelin, maintained a 600-loom establishment comfortably superior to the best state factories. In 1801, the fisherman's son, Morosov, wishing to escape military service – wisely for it lasted twenty-five years – commenced his own factory with borrowed capital and by 1825 had converted it into the largest mass-producing, steam-driven, cotton textile manufactory within the Empire; by 1852 it employed 2600, by 1897 22,000. Textile undertakings, with their initially modest funding requirements, favoured enterprise from such humble beginnings, yet serf-entrepreneurs also succeeded in notably capital-intensive sectors. The launching of the modern chemical industry in Russia with the foundation of the country's first, and Europe's largest, chromate plant in 1850 was achieved by the serf, Ushkov. Even the early railway projectors numbered among their ranks serfs like Gubonin and Kokorev, or near-serfs like Poliakov and Bloch. If these individuals were the brilliant rarities, the birds of bright plumage and long talons wheeling above the dowdy hedgerow flock, they were emulated by a surprisingly large array of smaller but not insignificant species: serf-entrepreneurs were observed in some numbers by Rosovsky as land-agents, subcontractors, coopers, locksmiths, and jewellers. Whether great or small, these adventurers were necessarily restrained by frictions among which serfdom itself loomed large. Most were concerned with traditional industries of low capital intensity and craft orientation. But the glib assumptions that serfdom composed a desert for commercialism, that pre-emancipation society contained no enterprise-bearing strata, cannot be sustained. These strata may have lain outside the framework of accepted society, but that was not necessarily a disqualification for business success. Some alienation from the dominant social value system, with its agricultural and conservative overtones, was virtually a requirement for active entrepreneurship. Given the prevailing majority values, it was natural, though it was unfortunate, that the nation's nineteenth-century capitalists should have been recruited almost exclusively from minority groups, deviant social categories such as indebted gentry, religious schismatics like the Old Believers in the early decades, and foreign businessmen at the century's close, or from the supremely deviant group of the non-persons, the 'baptized property' of the pre-emancipation era.[12] However, it is an easily and frequently neglected fact that nineteenth-century Russia was not devoid of deviant groups.

CROSS-CURRENTS AND CROSS-ROADS

Persistent eddies of capitalistic development, long-running streams of entrepreneurial replenishment were clearly established within the economy of 1850 or 1860, but, equally clearly, they were insufficient to turn the tide of backwardness. Russia developed sufficiently to experience the rougher aspects of international capitalism and she had recruited a makeshift body of venturesome industrialists, but neither of these achievements could substantially amend her state of underdevelopment. Yet the direction taken by research over the past few decades has raised some interesting implications concerning the cross-currents of the pre-emancipation period. A series of revisionist arguments — the evocation of capitalist development before 1861 by Strumilin; the discovery of matching reserves of native enterprise by Rosovsky and Crisp; the presentation of the Old Believers as entrepreneurial prototypes by Blackwell[13] and Gerschenkron;[14] the suggestions of economic virtues within the serf system from Baykov and Skerpan[15] — have converged in effect to propose for Russian economic development a lesser but intriguing imitation of the 'stretched' form of industrial evolution now commonly associated with the advanced western economies. Even against the substantial odds offered by Russian backwardness, this approach has scored some useful points. Yet it also operates to place the economy of the 1860s even more definitely at a critical point of interchange. For it certainly does not follow that a massive legislative reform, conceived less as an economic than as a military, political, and social safeguard, would automatically foster the development of incipient manufacturing skills. Emancipation, therefore, assumes painfully opposed values within the historical analysis: economically, it is either the liberating force releasing the motors of growth from their enforced inactivity or the barrier to development encircling spontaneous commercial initiatives within the mesh of increasingly taut government; socially, it is either the first hammer blow to crack the prison wall of serf society or a further turn of the bureaucratic screw, locking the rural population into a more comprehensive, if legally redefined, subjection. Either way, its consequences dominate the economic prospects of the three decades between Alexander's decree of liberation and Witte's appointment to the Ministry of Finance.

THE COSTS AND BENEFITS OF EMANCIPATION

Marxist historians, in particular, anxious to establish the orderly progression from feudalism to socialism, have insisted upon allocating a positive economic leverage to the liberation of the serfs. Thus P. I. Lyashchenko, a reasonably typical exponent of this gospel, maintains that emancipation mobilized an army of consumers for industrial goods and a force of landless labourers suitable for conversion into an urban proletariat.[16] Echoes of such views have rebounded for decades, and occasionally a faint resonance may still be heard. Recently, Portal argued that 'the statute facilitated the recruitment of industrial manual labour' and developed a 'more comfortable peasantry . . . a more demanding clientele'.[17] Weaker still, but no less enduring, are the protestations that the abolition of slavery, lacking though it may have been in concrete achievements, nevertheless 'marked the first step', or 'delivered a psychological impetus' towards westernization.

However, comprehensively pessimistic estimates are perfectly possible and probably more compelling. They begin, not with the desirable effects of emancipation, viewed as a system of economic construction, but with the actual mechanisms of liberation, seen as an agricultural settlement. The basic tactic of reform was that the gentry (*pomeshchiki*) should be compensated for the land transferred to the newly emancipated peasantry by issues of government bonds, that is, by a single imperial pay-off; and then that the ex-serfs should repay this sum to the autocracy in fifty annual instalments of 'redemption'. But this procedure was subject to considerable manipulation between the original design of the Imperial Message (1857) and the final enactment of the decree (1861). First thoughts from the autocracy proposed to donate control over land resources to the gentry, bind them to reserve sufficient territory for the peasantry, and permit all migrant serfs to remain in their adopted professions; the final version revealed clearly that the gentry had not admired the autocracy's first thoughts. In the northern provinces, *pomeshchiki*, afflicted by poor cultivatory prospects and a shrinking labour force, demanded heavy cash returns for emancipation and insisted that all serfs, whatever their location and occupation, should collect their allotments and pay their accounts. Where agriculture was more profitable, the gentry echelons required that the new peasant allotments, vital supports for a liberated rural community, should not eat into their valued acres. Such calculations of gentry interest, rather than any concern for a comfortable peasantry or an industrial proletariat, governed the final shape of the emancipation provisions. In order to generate cash for the more impoverished gentry, redemption payments were imposed upon *all* ex-serfs and based upon quit-rents set at rates far above the market value of the land, on poorer soils up to 100 per cent above, in black earth areas usually 20 per cent above.[18] Consequently, the 'liberated' peasantry paid through the nose for inferior land and naturally sank into most illiberal debt: by 1876–80 taxation arrears were equivalent to 22 per cent of budgeted revenue from direct taxes, and in the most afflicted areas to 45 per cent.[19]

As late as the 1890s, famine could double the still massive amount of overdue redemption and force the government to introduce further schemes for extended payment. In order to satisfy the matching requirement of the more substantial gentry for land conservation, the settlement obligingly laid down that each peasant household should receive not a minimum but a *maximum* allocation of plot. Where peasant holdings exceeded this maximum, the lord was entitled to cut them down to size, adding the parings to his own estates. This provision permitted the gentry to *reduce* the land farmed by the peasantry from its 1861 level by 4 per cent in all imperial territory, by 13 per cent in imperial less Polish provinces, and by 23 per cent in the most productive black soil areas.[20] Whereas the subsistence needs of peasant farmers required a land allocation *per capita* of 5 dessiatines of black soil or 8 dessiatines of non-black soil, the actual provision to three-quarters of the liberated serfs was 4 dessiatines per head, or less.[21] Not only were the initial land allocations of the reformed system *below* the survival needs of most recipients; they were also subject to erosion over time. Population pressure within the villages reduced the available supplies of land per head by 25 per cent down to 1881 and by 50 per cent down to 1905.[22] At the century's turn it was unlikely that the peasant, even with the addition of land leased on his own initiative, could amass a cultivable area equal in size to the inadequate subsistence allotments of 1861. For the emancipated household, neither the price of freedom nor the prospect of free cultivation emerged from the settlement in an attractive state; rather, redemption and allotment materialized as burdens scarcely distinguishable from their feudal predecessors in stringency.

Peasant emancipation, therefore, converted all too readily into an exercise in gentry relief. No doubt the reformers had not intended this, but the alternatives facing them were exceptionally unedifying. Influenced at the time by *laissez-faire* ideology, the government could not bring itself to nationalize land supplies. Nor could it simply abolish bondage and leave the gentry in possession of the land; the intent of reform was to avoid a second Pugachev not to provoke one. And, similarly, the possibilities of expropriating the gentry and redistributing the proceeds were minimal: the gentry were the vertebrae of the Empire, the cortex of the bureaucracy, the mailed fist of the officer corps; a second Decembrist revolt was even less attractive than a second Pugachev. So reform had somehow to be translated into an equilibrium between a land-owning gentry and a land-owning peasantry. And of the two groups, it was clear that one enjoyed a disproportion of influence. The gentry possessed the motivation and the opportunity to design an equilibrium for themselves, and when, on top of their earlier triumphs, the administration of the settlement was surrendered to gentry arbitrators, they brought off the coup almost entirely.

For the peasantry, the benefits wished upon them by historical analysts – increasingly 'comfortable' small cultivators, a growing demand for industrial products, a money economy – were not obvious. In fact, the free serfs were transformed into subsistence squatters, eking an existence from inadequate allotments, pouring all available income into the leasing of extra handkerchiefs of land. They were set not so much within a money economy as within a debt economy. And, as a market for manufacturing industry, their shoestring margins were negligible. Yet there was a greater irony still; for if the reform was eventually designed in the interest of the gentry groups, they did not manage to extract much profit from it. Despite the potential gains to estate lands available in some regions, many among the gentry were deeply disillusioned by what they saw as an unjustified sequestration of their wordly wealth, a confiscation of baptized property. As a whole, the gentry class appeared to suffer a loss of morale which some expressed in emigration and many more in economic lassitude and sales of domain lands. By 1877 some 17 per cent of the acres held by the gentry in 1861 had slipped away, by 1916 59 per cent, in the end a larger proportional loss than that experienced by their former serfs. Still more damaging was the failure of the attempt to subsidize gentry deficits by the redemption process: their indebtedness in 1861 was such that not even the massive income transfers of the compensation scheme could extinguish it.[23] The sequel to emancipation was thus the polarization of agricultural interest around the peasant and the state. Gentry lands crumbled into smaller parcels – by 1914 Russia possessed fewer estates over 4000 hectares than Britain – and the class to which Russia might legitimately have looked for agricultural entrepreneurship steadfastly refused to provide anything of the kind. The compromise turned out bitterly for both main protagonists: the peasantry were partially disinherited and wholly subjected to official extortion, while the gentry's liabilities proved too burdensome for the life-saving efforts of the imperial bureaucracy.

In the countryside, however, the state was also an interested protagonist, requiring from emancipation sureties and rewards no less pressing than those sought by the gentry. It desired agricultural tranquillity and effective checks against the transfer of dissension from the countryside to the towns; specifically, it demanded guarantees that its measures of liberalization should not help inculcate the notoriously explosive urban proletariats which had perpetrated such regrettable damage in the West. In other words, tsarist administrators possessed a marked interest in turning emancipation towards the law and order account. Their instruments, easily selected from the existing institutions of peasant agriculture, were the *obshchina* (field commune) and its political counterpart the *mir* (village commune). At the most modest valuation these agencies were intended to replace the *pomeshchik*'s dual functions of policeman and tax-collector. Effectively, they provided the means by which the autocracy obtained its dividend upon emancipation: tighter social control in the countryside.

The field commune was not a universal feature of the Russian landscape — Its share of peasant land varied from 15 per cent in the formerly Polish Ukraine, through 30–40 per cent in Belorussia to over 80–90 per cent in the eastern Ukraine, Novorossiya, and Greater Russia[24] — but where it did hold sway after 1861, it exercised an overlordship distinctly more rigorous than that of the late regime *pomeshchik*. Commune members were subjected to collective liability for tax obligations — so that migration from the village could raise the fiscal burden upon those who remained. Cultivable land was held, not by the individual cultivator but by the commune, and was distributed to each household according to its headcount — so that migration from the household could reduce the land-entitlement of bereft relations. Individual peasants could leave the village only with the consent of the household and of the commune, and, under these specifications, it was not given freely; and even if it were, the state added an internal passport system as a further impediment to mobility. Individual plots could be separated from the communal land store only when the extended and costly process of redemption was complete. While they remained within communal oversight, the allotments were subject to periodic repartition: the problem of balancing swelling village population against fixed land supplies was 'resolved' by calling in the plots and redistributing them in a different order corresponding to the altered composition of households. Further, any change in the status of the *obshchina*, its repartitional practice, or its cultivation was governed by the approval of a two-thirds majority voting in the *mir*. Given the conventional characteristics of peasant communities, this last provision secured a formidable safeguard against all forms of change.

For three decades after 1861 the net effect of the *obshchina* system was to imprison the peasantry in the villages. Delicate but inflexible weights within the commune structure operated to tilt it against all innovation or mobility. As long as the distribution of fiscal burden and territorial gain provided incentives for the conservation of population, land-hungry relatives and tax-conscious elders would block the exits from the village. While allotments were bedecked with redemption obligations and strewn in motley parcels around the villages, a valuable dual purpose was served: the peasant was both anchored by debt and denied the means of effective repayment. Strips could not be consolidated until redemption was complete and could not be improved because repartition – which could transfer land improved by one cultivator arbitrarily to another, without compensation until 1893 and with inadequate compensation thereafter – offered persistent deterrence. Since the land supply to the *obshchina* was constant and population was hoarded to increase the allocation of each household, the system infallibly guaranteed over-crowded villages, low labour productivity, and shrinking holdings; technically, it provided an almost perfect negation of productive agriculture. Justification, both contemporary and later, relied heavily upon social, not economic, calculus: the *obshchina* provided a communal life-raft for those who individually would fall below subsistence; by repartition it provided that each household should be able to bear its fiscal liability. But its main purpose was caught by the (approving) German observer Haxthausen who reflected contentedly that: 'As long as this system exists, no hereditary proletariat can emerge and form itself in Russia.'[25]

But as long as the system existed, it was also a certainty that no surpluses of output, labour, or capital would freely emerge from Russian agriculture; that emancipation would add virtually nothing to the economic integration of the agricultural and industrial sectors. Heavily depressed by the structural primitivism of communal practice, agricultural output for 1860–1913 advanced at an annual average of 2 per cent, barely sufficient to match population, and entirely insufficient when crises of climate or cultivation intervened.[26] Even then, the increase can be traced more to the expansion of tilled acreage – mainly in the south-east and Siberia – than to the indifferent improvement in yield per hectare, a modest average of 1 per cent p.a. 1860–1913.[27] With practised ease the *obshchina* ensured literally that Russia obtained the worst of two worlds: the low land yields of newly settled regions and the poor labour productivity of the heavily populated areas of long settlement. Nor, given the communal way with innovation, was it surprising that the compensating force of mechanization should have touched imperial agriculture only at the end of the period, and only among the industrial crops of the western provinces. Naturally, there were regional variations to the picture. Some flexibility is suggested by the rapid increase in grain exports from the Black Earth belt, but, in reality, this performance did little more than hint at the potential harboured by the Empire's most favoured acres. Even these could do little to lift the national indicators of output and even here changes in institutions and ownership were late and slow. Taken over fifty provinces, the index for output of wheat and rye per head *fell* from 1870 to 1890 (See Table 4.1).

Table 4.1 *Per capita* output of wheat and rye
from fifty provinces; index

1870–74	100.0
1883–85	97.1
1886–90	92.3
1891–95	95.1
1896–1900	97.2

Source: Gerschenkron (1968), p. 223

Denied support from buoyant rural production, the manufacturing sector was denied also the assistance of the surplus rural population. For the landless labourers of Marxist imagination were the very opposite of the *obshchina*'s true members, 'landed' with a vengeance and with shackles. From 1860 to 1913 the share of the Empire's total population claimed by agriculture fell only from 90 to 85 per cent, and around 1900 a census of Petersburg province revealed only 19 per cent of households occupied solely in manufacture against 77 per cent committed to the traditional blend of craft and husbandry.[28] So conspicuously absent indeed was the reserve army of labour that by 1902 industrialists had been driven to locate some 70 per cent of all factories in the countryside, on the peasant's doorstep.[29] Measured as a Rostowian 'precondition', therefore, the emancipation of 1861 resembled the 'agricultural transformation' as shadow resembles solid: a little in outline, not at all in content. Owing to the depredations of the gentry and the requirements of the state, industry could count on no free-market performance from agriculture which would guarantee surpluses of exports, workers, or profits, let alone the creation of internal demand for native manufactures.

However, the market in the presence of the *obshchina* was not free, a feature which both impeded innovation and permitted the commune a single perverse claim to utility. Its forte lay in extortion; if surpluses could not flow, or be permitted to flow, autonomously from the rural sector, the *obshchina* could extract them upon demand. Between 1882 and 1913, for instance, forced levies of grain ensured that cereals composed a steady 46–52 per cent of all exports, holding the share at 42 per cent even in a famine year like 1899. The price, of course, was paid in shortage, and occasional starvation, by the rural poor. Even supplies of capital, in lieu of a rural profit surplus, could be obtained from the same source by deft use of the commune's fiscal pincers. Police powers could be deployed, as they were from 1874, to combine with the *obshchina* organization for more efficient tax collection, and from 1889 the rural chief system explicitly merged the powers of the village arbitrators with those of the police apparatus. At one stroke this provided an extremely successful peace-keeping device and an important instrument of forced draft industrialization. However, if the emancipation settlement supported economic advance only in its most reactionary provisions, the precise nature of this linkage argues that serf reform cannot be construed as a psychological shock leading towards modernization and the western model of growth. The psychic gain to be derived from the exchange of communal for gentry overlordship is both improbable and immeasurable.[30] Moreover, although the *obshchina* supplied the very heart of the liberation settlement, it is not obvious that it relates to *any* of the organs of western economic administration. Like the autocracy's tastes in industrial promotion, it was specifically, not to say extravagantly, Russian in both pedigree and implementation.

If the cause of growth profits in some measure from one coercive aspect of the settlement, the modern sector was as acutely afflicted as the traditional by its other repressive tendencies. To begin with, emancipation imposed direct labour losses on many industries as 'liberated' serf workers were compelled to return to their villages. Abandoned mines and factories – many in the Urals, and the sugar, textile, and machine-building industries elsewhere – were left only with an intermittent productive capability, and the depression which persisted for many industries throughout the decade bit notably more deeply than anything experienced in the West. Within even half a decade of the decree, sugar production had fallen by 23 per cent, machine-building by 30 per cent, from pre-emancipation levels. Forgone output of these proportions was a serious deprivation for industries still struggling to find their feet, while the already questionable labour commitment to sustained industrial work was not assisted by the experience.

However, given that the effects of labour shortage were painful, the problems surrounding the supply of enterprise were more acute and more pervasive. The ramshackle structure of late feudalism had permitted by default a tolerable measure of social mobility. By exploiting the rents in the system, the more alert among the rural community could aspire to the ranks of Rosovsky's serf élite, the best among them commonly moving directly from servile to bourgeois status.[31] But it was precisely the purpose of emancipation, in its oppressive guise of social controller, to stop up such loopholes and apply the uniform restrictiveness of the *obshchina* wherever possible. Its tendency was to create a single-class rural proletariat, approximating varied groups of peasantry to a favoured notional model, that of the state serfs of pre-emancipation vintage. Almost certainly, social mobility out of this increasingly homogeneous agricultural mass became *more* difficult after 1861, and, as it did so, the supply of business talent became correspondingly more constricted. It is likely that the recruitment of entrepreneurs from serf/peasant backgrounds was more extensively damaged by emancipation than by the competition of mechanized industry (which the best of them readily mastered). Portal argues that 'the numerous small businessmen . . . who had raised themselves up to the level of big industrialists' found few successors after 1861; 'an important source of recruitment for the upper bourgeoisie was dried up'.[32] Russia's tiny commercial class expanded between 1850 and 1900 only from one degree of minuteness to another, from perhaps 178,000 members in a population of 68 m. to about 625,000 members among 128 m.[33] The deficiency naturally put checks upon the emergence of indigenous managerial skills and necessitated the much-resented dependence upon foreigners or imperial citizens from the Polish and Jewish minorities. Not only in markets and food surpluses, therefore, but also on the shop floor and in the boardroom, the urban–industrial sector paid heavily for the autocracy's surrender of serfdom. Once again, the new freedoms composed an ill-starred compromise, too much for some – the unfortunate manufacturers who saw their labour force put to rout – too little for others – the potential entrepreneurs denied access to business careers.

The disregard of the emancipation settlement both for productivity growth within agriculture and for resource transfers from agriculture to industry appears paradoxical within a state pledged at least to some measure of economic modernization. The conflict is best resolved by treating tsarist industrialization as a particularly rigid two-sector model. In one sector, agriculture, the imperial administration aimed not at economic growth but at social control. And it was a condition of success in this policy that the rural sector should be protected from contact with its industrial counterpart. Moreover, in order to achieve the political objective in the countryside, it was necessary to eliminate the prospects for agricultural improvement, since these could not deliver economic rewards without heavy social costs. Across the border, in its own heavily policed territory, the industrial sector was accepted not as a profitable asset but as an alien implantation, regrettably necessary for the upkeep of Russia's military and international role. Given these assumptions, the two sectors could not be maintained by the mutual exchange of growth materials; and the only alternative to the free surrender of such materials was the resource raid perpetrated upon one sector for the benefit of the other. Traditionally in Russian history, as Nove has argued, the need for progress has entailed repeated doses of 'developmental serfdom' a tightening of the controls on agriculture in order to collect the forced savings needed for growth.[54] Whenever 'developmental serfdom' was applied, from Peter the Great to Stalin, the resource raid was its inevitable accompaniment. Arguably, the 'serf reform' of 1861 fell within this sequence, its exploitation of the *obshchina* marking a significant advance in oppression upon the best efforts of the late-feudal regime. The reforming autocracy mastered only the vocabulary of liberation, aimed in reality to solve the peasant problem with strong-arm policies disguised perfunctorily in the tissues of illusory freedoms. Outside the extortive capabilities of the new policy – the single point at which 'development' and 'serfdom' fused – it had no positive economic consequences, and was designed to have none. Emancipation should, therefore, be recharacterized as the institutional source of a non-feudal serfdom, harnessing the new peasantry to the requirements of an autocracy prepared only to *coerce* the desired measure of development from its populace.

THE GREATER BENEFITS OF SALUTARY DEFEAT

In most ways the legislative showpiece of the mid-century Era of Reforms was the *least* reformist of contemporary policies; and there is certainly little reason to regard it as a climactic point in Russia's economic development. Better

219

candidates and more creative policies existed in the 1850s and 1860s which had little to do with the problem of the serfs. The conjunction between the Crimean War and the initiation of programmes favourable to industrialization is a case in point. Although war and emancipation were connected by the demonstration of serfdom's military ineffectiveness, a more substantial connexion grew up between the experience of defeat and the delineation of new economic objectives. For it was precisely the superior armament and transportation of the western allies which demonstrated to the Tsar that Russia's deficiencies in railways, steam-engines, iron-foundries, and machine shops could impose costs in a currency which the Empire respected.[35] Thus the only tactic open to the imperial fleet at Sebastopol – since it lacked modern armour, guns, or steam-propulsion – was to convert itself into a submarine reef in a final attempt to constitute a hazard for the allied screw-liners. Military autocracies cannot afford military disasters of such dimensions: failure in the field or the battle-squadron jeopardizes the most cherished assumptions of these regimes and provides the strongest possible incentives for them to rearrange their affairs. In this sense, the imperative behind Russia's nineteenth-century development was a classic shock to the existing socio-political structure, a military intrusion provoking a burst of reactive nationalism in textbook style.[36]

Economically then, the most significant components of the Era of Reforms were those which aimed deliberately at the westernization of finance, technology, and infrastructure. Connexions between these measures and the trigger mechanism of war were particularly clear: the recent hostilities had unleashed such desperate financial stresses – among them chronic budget deficits, a negative balance of payments, and the collapse of the banking system in 1859 – that not only improved methods for the control of public expenditure, but also an expansion of the entire national economy, were required for their resolution.[37] In some sense, the economic modernization of mid-century Russia was instigated by nothing more than the need to repair the monetary damage perpetrated by the Crimean War. Accordingly, from the 1850s, state revenue and accounting procedures were carefully reviewed, and a unified budget of western type established in their place. The European taste for *laissez-faire* was noted and emulated, the autocracy signifying its willingness to participate in the economic life of the continent by severe pruning of its tariff hedge. Industrial experts from advanced economies were recruited to provide technological advice or supervisory skill with substantial concessions and franchises. Most important, the painful lessons in transportation learned in the Crimea were mulled over at the highest level: the Tsar's 'railway ukaz' of 1857 conceded that 'our fatherland, equipped by nature with abundant gifts, but divided by huge spaces, especially needs suitable communications'.[38] For the first time the value of railroad construction as a corrective for extreme backwardness was appreciated and the economic consequences of Russia's vast size subjected to some mitigation. Florinsky argued that railroads were 'the chief single factor in fostering Russia's economic progress',[39] and may perhaps be excused for the thought. Even the problem of funding these schemes attracted modern proposals: in 1859 the Minister of Finánce clearly formulated the need for a banking system fit to support economic development due to 'the revival of industrial entrepreneurship . . . and the anticipated construction of railways'.[40] In 1861 the State Bank was established virtually as a section of the Ministry of Finance. As essays in modernization, these measures betrayed a more determined hand than the provisions of the agricultural code.

Once the economy was provided with at least part of the genuine instrumentation of growth, it responded satisfactorily: between 1861 and 1885 Russia achieved an average annual growth rate in industrial output of about 6 per cent, the country's first respectable performance in manufacturing, and sufficiently powerful to resist the downward leverage exerted upon the economy by the European depression between 1873 and 1882. The increased commercialization brought by railway construction, even to the exchange of agricultural products, generated changes in the flows of capital and demand which particularly favoured the textile industries. Notable expansion in output was achieved in the period 1865–80 – with annual average consumption *per capita* of cotton fabrics doubling between 1856/60 and 1876/80 – and the decade 1880–90 witnessed the consolidation of the large textile manufactories, assisted by tariff protection and the enlargement of the Siberian and Ukrainian markets. Progress in output was matched and supported by rapid modernization of practice: between 1866 and 1879 the number of factory workers serving mechanical cotton looms rose from 94,600 to 162,700, while the rural labour force employing hand-looms declined from 66,200 to 50,200. By the later date, domestic weaving of cotton fabric accounted for no more than one-fortieth of total output and during the 1880s it disappeared almost entirely.[41] This considerable advance in the light industrial sector is consistent with Goldsmith's conclusion, based on adaptation of Kondratiev's statistics for value added, that the food-processing and textile industries formed the main carriers of growth up to the late 1880s.[42]

THE MANAGED ECONOMY: THE FIRST PROTOTYPE

As was implied in the design of the institutions which helped initiate the economic activity of 1861–85, the upswing was by no means autonomous. Supervised development belonged to an extensive Russian tradition which associated the state not only with military functions but with the economic undertakings needed to finance them. From the time of Ivan the Terrible, Russia's geopolitical predicament – vast 'centrifugal' land masses groping for fixed boundaries in a context of open frontiers and perpetual emergency – had required a special response from the state: highly centralized government to compensate for regional fragmentation; a device for attaching scattered populations to a shapeless land mass; a means for providing rapid military response to incursion in the absence of an effective soldier nobility. Serfdom provided the most flexible technology of survival, meeting the specifications of autocracy, land settlement, and military service alike, while endemic crisis conveniently supplied sanctions for dictatorial government and the insistent demands of the bureaucratic revenue state. In consequence, a uniquely strong connexion grew up in Russia between: the military imperative as motive for development; statist direction of the developmental response; forced draft tactics as the form of response; and serfdom as the instrument of the forced draft. It was not unnatural, therefore, that, during the second third of the nineteenth century, an association should persist between military defeat, the *obshchina*'s version of enserfment, and a state-managed style of growth. Moreover, this specifically Russian cocktail – less Molotov than Mordinov[43] – remains compatible with Gerschenkron's staple fare of backwardness. For, in an economy still as primitive as that of post-emancipation Russia, the institutions of moderate backwardness, the great investment banks, would be inappropriate to the task of development and no other agency capable of promoting industrialization could be conceived outside Gerschenkron's alternative source of economic guardianship: the state apparatus. The association of extreme backwardness with pronounced *dirigisme* is thus classically suitable to the Russian case.

However, even in this context, it is not sufficient to consider 'the state' as an economic monolith. Whatever the requirements of defence, and however pressing the issues of backwardness, strict limits to the effectiveness of *dirigiste* policies could be set by the composition of the state apparatus, most notably by the social complexion of the bureaucracy, the staffing of ministries, and the balance between senior ministers. Specifically, the tsarist bureaucracy was drawn overwhelmingly from gentry cadres averse to virtually all social and economic change. Ministers, not uncommonly, would share similar backgrounds and views, and their prejudices could be reinforced by a genuine or contrived reading of their departmental responsibilities. The Ministry of the Interior, for instance, concerned above all with domestic stability, could harbour legitimate doubts as to the social repercussions of industrial (or agricultural) innovation. Much of the Russian state could, therefore, remain *hostile* to economic change well beyond 1861. As industrialization was pursued within a strictly defined area of the economy, so it was promoted only by a narrow segment of government, that concerned with the Ministry of Finance. Controllers of this department became the supreme commanders of the industrial armies, the most powerful among the few protagonists of economic modernization within the Empire. Their position, isolated but influential, conferred upon Russian industrialization an extraordinary unity of direction. Where single value explanations of growth are inappropriate in most development processes, in Russia the views and actions of single individuals exerted far more influence upon development; 'the personal factor in politics or finance had much greater scope . . . than it had in the more democratically organised countries of the west'.[44] But this of course, could impose losses as well as gains. Such officials might be obliged to spend more time fighting their ministerial colleagues than fighting Russian backwardness. They could be – and sometimes were – incompetents or rogues. Or they might themselves remain sufficiently swayed by agrarian values to resist the appeal of thorough-going policies of industrialization. Broadly speaking, this was the case until Sergei Witte took office in the 1890s; prior to his appointment, no finance minister was committed unreservedly to the goal of comprehensive industrialization.

Some indeed were almost comically opposed to it. Kankrin (1823–44), Nicholas I's Minister of Finance, believed that railways fostered rampant social equality, uncontrollable mobility, and the concentration of large numbers of potential insurgents in inconvenient places.[45] While not exactly inaccurate, these should not perhaps be the *only* values ascribed to railroad construction. While remaining hostile to the liberalism of the currently fashionable *laissez-faire* economics, Kankrin could not embrace the *dirigiste* alternative of List because of its whole-hearted commitment to industrial modernization; he resorted, in consequence, to the superannuated forms of mercantilism. More venturesome opinions achieved prominence with the appointment of Alexander II's Minister, Reutern (1862–78). A graduate from the progressive circle of naval bureaucrats, based on the Ministry of Marine, the *Konstantinovtsy*, Reutern was a reconstructed liberal determined to use the constructive freedoms for the purposes of national regeneration. He thus occupies an important transitional rung between Kankrin's antiquated cameralism and Witte's state capitalism.[46] In keeping with this position, and as the first official to attain significance in the handling of industrial policy, Reutern followed a sensible, if unsystematic and expedient, strategy centred upon three imperatives: construct railroads, attract foreign industrialists, employ foreign capital.

Nevertheless, the achievements of the Finance Ministry in the 1860s and 1870s were worthy enough. Major improvements in infrastructure were secured by a determined campaign of railway promotion: between 1862 and 1878 open track increased in length by nearly seven times, from 3,532 to 22,498 kilometres. Regrettably, however, the economy of provision did not match the speed of expansion. The state preferred to avoid direct involvement in the construction and administration of social overheads, and surrendered these functions willingly to private interests. Yet, in its need to assure sufficiently powerful commitment of capital and enterprise, while itself escaping the grimy realities of industrial participation, it surrendered too far: it indemnified contractors against all financial loss and paid the inevitable, costly price. Lines were constructed with expedition but contractors corrupted at the same rate: the lure of easy pickings meant that both the labouring gangs and the government guarantees were worked overtime. The outcome was doubly unsatisfactory: the state paid extravagantly for its transportation, and, at the end of the day, in 1880, the great majority (94%) of all lines remained in private operation.

By contrast, the recruitment of foreign entrepreneurs proved more economical and, probably, also more rewarding. The device, a long-run reflex of Russian development, involved methods – monopoly concessions, taxation exemptions, subsidies – which would have been unfamiliar neither to Peter the Great nor to Stalin (although Reutern never matched Peter's subventions paid in live serfs nor Stalin's spy trials for over-zealous capitalists). But their judicious use in the nineteenth century netted some useful assistance: Ludwig Knoop was drawn from Manchester to preside over the modernization of the Russian textile industry; the Nobels were recruited to tap the oil reserves of Baku, J.J. Hughes to replicate at Ekaterinoslav the metal industries of Ebbw Vale.[47] Of those birds of passage, Hughes was perhaps the most influential. Recruited in 1871, primarily for his skills in the manufacture of armour plate, he transformed his firm – the New Russian Coal, Iron and Railmaking Company – by 1884 into the Empire's largest producer of pig-iron. Two decades later the mills of Hughes and his industrial neighbours in the Ekaterinoslav region accounted for one-half of Russia's steel output. Besides this legacy, Hughes contributed to southern Russia a new town christened eponymously Yuzovo (later Stalino; later still Donetsk), complete with English schools and public houses and a population of Welsh Russians numbering in 1904 some 32,000.[48] However, Hughes' importance was as a missionary, not of Gaelic settlement, but of high technology; he was the first to succeed in Russia with the new methods of metallurgy and thus introduced a demonstration effect of unparalleled value.

As instructors in western 'best practice' methods, foreign entrepreneurs made decisive contributions to Russian technological performance, both before and after 1890. The personification of the diffusion process which British industrialists had brought to France, British and French industrialists to the German states, was in turn conveyed to Russia by migrants from Britain, France, Germany, Belgium, and Sweden. In metallurgy their methods were already far in advance of indigenous practice, in coal-mining only slightly less so, and in chemicals and electrical engineering they were to achieve a further and marked pre-eminence after 1890. However, the chief importance of the foreign technologists was not simply that they were frequently the initiators of new methods, it was rather the collective effect that they could exert as an entrepreneurial community. When foreign industrialists introduced innovations, they did so with a high degree of co-ordination, the community acting with near-simultaneity throughout Russia and ensuring rapid diffusion for devices which in native hands could have remained isolated and unsung. Moreover, the outsiders could offer attributes over and above those of high technology and efficient communication. Groups of wealthy European industrialists were often associated with continental investment banks and could bring a superior capital power to the solution of Russian problems. Both technological and financial gifts were displayed before 1890, most richly in northern Russia and Russian Poland, these regions acting as staging areas for the collection of personnel and experience later employed to carry the revolution into southern Russia – staging area which Reutern did much to build.

Unfortunately, however, the ministerial schemes to meet the Empire's requirements in both railways and modern technology carried daunting price tags, the most basic impediments to the movement for economic reform. Within the autocracy, all large-scale development projects faced a triple financial barrier: a lack of investable surplus for infrastructure creation, an unstable currency, and a balance of payments deficit. In combination, these elements produced the classically vicious circularity of investment needs suffered by underdeveloped countries. In order to finance 'lumpy' social overheads, it was imperative that foreign investment should be attracted; but currency instability acted as a deterrent to external creditors. In order to stabilize the currency, large imports of bullion were needed to bolster the reserves; but bullion inflows could not be obtained while there was a balance of payments deficit. Any determined attempt to reduce the deficit would necessarily involve economies in the imports of capital goods required for industrial development. And development was, of course, the original target of the investment programmes. Attempts to break the circle by raising funds at home proved inadequate: a veritable lake of capital was required for railway construction and even an 80 per cent increase in the soul tax left scarcely a ripple on its surface. Reutern's solution was no innovation: he resorted to borrowing abroad on government account, a course much inferior to attracting foreign capital directly into productive enterprise. As a prop to industrial modernization, the foreign loan was a novelty, but as a general financial standby of the bureaucracy it was an old favourite. Significantly enough, Russia's graduation as an international debtor had accompanied her assumption of great-power status during the reign of Catherine. Over time, the liability deepened and the tortuous commitments of international politics — notably of warfare — had most to do with this. Catherine's adventures in Turkey, Sweden, Poland, and Persia, Alexander I's responses to Napoleon, and the Crimean campaign each marked important stages in Russia's addiction to insolvency. Aggressive foreign policies, however, for a country as backward as the Empire, were more than a strain on the bank balance: by mortgaging credit for more productive purposes, they helped perpetuate an intractable backwardness. Only the occasional and startling defeat provoked reappraisal; the more usual run of skirmishes and excursions merely served to tot up the debts. It followed that, for a finance minister bent on reconstruction, war — in company perhaps with the hostility of his colleagues — ranked as the greatest threat.

Reutern discovered painfully that international crisis could imperil his ability to employ one vital element of policy — foreign borrowing — to finance the others. Admittedly, he was not unequivocally committed to the use of public funds for industrialization, and, at the end of his tenure, Russia still had far to go on the industrial road: in the 1870s, for instance, the Empire produced only 45 per cent of its pig-iron needs, and three-quarters of this amount came from archaic charcoal forges. But, on the other hand, Reutern had by 1879 made considerable inroads upon backwardness: the gold reserves had been augmented, the rouble stabilized, and its international credibility greatly enhanced.[49] Some of the financial underpinnings for industrial advance had been assembled. But these were precisely the features most vulnerable to swings in the international climate, and in international credit. When Russia went to war against Turkey in 1877 the weather duly turned, the foreign credit leaked away, the bullion reserves evaporated, and exports withered. The Reutern system, the first state-managed exercise in industrial advance, could not stand the strain and nor could its architect's claims to office.

THE MANAGED ECONOMY: THE LIBERAL PROTOTYPE

The next manager fit to compare with Reutern exemplified the adage that, in Russia, industrial policy represented no more and no less than the conviction of the Finance Minister. As befitted a professor of economics from Kiev, the new Minister, Bunge (1882–86) was an exponent of liberal philosophies. It is thus somewhat anomalous that his major achievement in office was to drive out the corrupt private railroad interests employed by Reutern and to replace them with state ownership, the beginnings of a process which left 69 per cent of the railroad system in public hands by 1911. In most other respects, however, Bunge resorted to doctrine where Reutern had employed expediency, and in taste he leaned more towards the new economics than the old agrarianism. The key theoretical guidelines employed during this ministry were the assumptions that a sound currency would follow from industrial growth and that a prosperous peasantry would encourage enterprise. In pursuit of these objectives, Bunge dismantled many of the established taxative controls: in 1881 the salt tax was abolished, and in 1886 the poll tax. By 1886 the level of direct taxation was reduced to one-third that of 1862. Nor did the new Tsar offer resistance to these proposals: after the assassination of Alexander II in 1881, he had even thought it prudent to reduce the redemption debt by 9 per cent and to accept the creation of a Peasant Land Bank (1882) as agricultural insurance against a similarly explosive demise. Unfortunately, however, the new economic orthodoxies, as so often, came disturbingly adrift in the unfriendly Russian waters. Bunge's fiscal generosity, almost unique in tsarist (or Soviet) history, had the direct effect simply of sacrificing revenue, while the indirect taxes which were manipulated in an attempt at compensation, could not claw in surpluses sufficiently rapidly to balance the accounts. National expenditure over the period 1866–85 was not in itself disposed to favour experimentation: direct military expenditure had claimed 32 per cent of the budget, while the indirect costs of power politics were represented in a further 28 per cent share devoted to national debt service;[50] in contrast, the allocation to the construction and operation of railways amounted to no more that 10 per cent of the total. Liberal economics and a policy aimed at peasant prosperity could do little in the face of inadequate revenue and rampant military costs. Encountering such insurmountable frustrations, it took less than a war to unseat Bunge. More pressure in the military sector was all that was required and the Afghan and Bulgarian crises of 1886, aided by poor harvests, duly provided it. As the paper rouble sank to an all-time low, Bunge, personifying the fate of liberal policies under Russian conditions, retired from the unequal struggle.

It would not be correct, however, to view the Bunge interlude as one simply of frustrated good intentions, of progressive ideas regrettably nullified by primitive circumstances. For Barkai has pointed out that the orthodox monetary policy of this period contained strong deflationary tendencies;[51] it operated to restrict money supply even during years when potential increases in output needed the support of expanded demand and increased monetary resources. Before 1890, it took disasters or wars to produce currency booms like those of 1853–57 or 1877–78, and Bunge's purpose was, as far as possible, to achieve retrenchment after the printing spree which accompanied the Turkish War. The result was that the money stock actually declined in 1879–91 – by about 1.5 per cent p.a. during the 1880s – before growing at the high annual average of 4 per cent p.a. during Witte's era of liberation, 1891–1903.[52] The monetary squeeze of the 1880s was pressing upon an already stretched currency supply and thus working to *retard* growth and postpone expansion.[53] This was not a case of conditions destroying good policies, rather that liberal economics imposed an inaccurate assessment of monetary needs upon economies in the infant stages of growth. Of course, few alternative policies were available at this time: finance ministers under the sway of balanced-budget philosophies and Gladstonian 'moral husbandry' frequently tended to pursue industrialization with one hand and monetary restriction with the other. Furthermore, there was the additional requirement for Russia to strike a financial style which the capitalistic West – whence came investment and technology – would recognize as sound. If Bunge was prophet of an enlightenment too advanced for Russia's economic capabilities, he was also prisoner of an economic science too undeveloped for contemporary growth requirements.

THE MANAGED ECONOMY: THE BRUTALIST PROTOTYPE

Irony remains in the fact that Bunge's good intentions should have produced so little yield, while the policies of his far from liberal successor should have been rewarded more handsomely. Where Bunge had deserted the mainstream of Russian economic thought – which in both tsarist and Soviet periods flowed sluggishly around the notion of looting agriculture in order to run the rest of the economy on the proceeds – Vyshnegradskii (1887–92) was one of its most enthusiastic passengers. Unlike Bunge, he made no attempt to reform the economic system, merely to subjugate its existing powers to the tasks of amassing gold reserves and stabilizing the rouble. Monetary restrictionism in his hands was tighter even than anything achieved in the preceding era. Yet, on one reading, the ruthless book-keeping of this ministerial accountant yielded dividends. The supreme aim of the calculations lay in the acquisition of gold, and to this all other economic considerations were sacrificed. Grain was siphoned out of the countryside under all conditions: during poor harvests, Vyshnegradskii, with some originality, required the peasantry to export *and* die; during good harvests, as with the bumper crops of 1887 and 1888, or during harvests which paid a belated return on Bunge's policies of peasant aid, the bounty of nature and of irony was sequestered in huge amounts for the national coffers. Massive excises were applied in the Mendele'ev tariff of 1891, less for the purposes of protection than for those of revenue-raising. Together with receipts from taxes, railways, crown lands, even from the ledgers of State

227

Bank and Treasury, the proceeds of these devices were converted into yellow metal. Such energetic scraping of the barrel yielded the desired result: Vyshnegradskii became the first modern Finance Minister both to balance the budget and deliver an annual surplus.

The worth of this achievement is open to doubt. The affinity between Vyshnegradskii's tactics and any structural improvements to the economy was negligible. The incipient boom of the early 1890s owed little to the tariff changes, much more to the railroad construction commenced before Vyshnegradskii's accession. Even the accumulation of revenue was strongly affected by influences outside the control of the Finance Ministry; international politics played a major part, for as the diplomatic alignment shifted, France turned towards a Russian alliance for which she was prepared to extend pension rights. And even if the quest after bullion was successful, the secondary aim of currency stabilization was never achieved, partly because the French diplomatic initiatives stung the Germans into a prolonged speculation against the rouble, partly because Vyshnegradskii preferred to play the exchanges for advantages in gold buying, sacrificing monetary stability to the size of the reserves. In general, it was a policy concerned with budgetary indicators rather than productive power, maximizing the extraction of current resources rather than the creation of new ones. Its budgetary surpluses were paper successes, operating in fact to deflate the economy, and entirely discounting the high human cost upon which they were erected. The more propitious economic changes of the era occurred despite this style of administration and were unusually favoured if they escaped its fiscal interest. Fittingly, Vyshnegradskii's machinery seized when the limits of extortion were reached, and the Finance Minister was ejected not by war or diplomatic fracas but by famine. Breaking in 1891, dearth struck at a peasantry bereft of reserves and drained of every vestige of tax-paying capability. Crucified on a cross of gold, it at least took its tormentor down with it – if only to a directorship of the International Bank.

GROWTH AND THE FINANCE MINISTRY TO WITTE'S ACCESSION

The sum of these three regimes, varying in tactics from the eclectic to the rapacious, was not especially impressive. In 1890 the Russian economy was still overwhelmingly agrarian and severely underdeveloped. Although the finance ministers of the period 1861–91 never viewed the imperial economy as anything other than a primarily agricultural one, they were able to achieve little even in the way of improved rural efficiency. The countryside remained victim to absentee ownership, micro-cultivation, paltry yields, and periodic catastrophe. The peasantry's earth-scratching practice remained unimproved despite demonstrations by authoritarian regimes elsewhere – notably the Japanese in the period 1868–1900 – that intelligent state action could revolutionize agricultural productivity. Campaigns to promote rural literacy, to publicize cultivatory innovations suitable for small plots, or to supply rural credit schemes for peasant farmers yielded handsome returns for other backward economies. In Russia, however, such proposals cut across the imperatives for social control which represented the first charge upon any agricultural policy; within the councils of a nervous autocracy these useful devices were unlikely to find ministerial protagonists. Given this response to agricultural innovation, the policies required for industrial modernization in breadth had little chance of achieving more than a toe-hold within the essentially conservative assumptions of the financial officials.

Nevertheless, the economic events of this period established beyond doubt a single favourable fact: that, in the office of finance minister, the autocracy possessed an enormous potential for developmental action. Fiscally, the powers available to this authority – as Bunge's enormous, if unfortunate, adjustments to the taxation structure fully indicated[54] – were without parallel in Europe. Sacrifices could be extracted from the Russian populace in cash and kind, roubles and grain, in a style which western societies would not readily have tolerated. Agriculture, if not transformed, could be leached for the life-blood of other sectors, and with scant thought for its dependants. A similarly high hand could be taken with vast national resources, distributed at ministerial behest in nationalized or denationalized form, or dangled as incentives before western developers. There were few obstacles to the most flagrant protectionism or the most grasping confiscation. In sum, the imperial order bestowed upon its financial departments a freedom in the disposal of economic resources which carried the implicit promise of induced development. Traditions of fiscal servitude related easily to policies of forced-draft industrialization, while the practice of 'developmental serfdom', at least in its later forms, naturally conferred upon the Finance Minister the responsibilities of developmental tsar. The price, of course, was to court the hazards of war and famine, each able to add the final dimension of unacceptability to the tactics of extortion, to exhaust the gains to be had from compulsion, and, frequently, to unseat the Minister.

The structure which allowed such powers and risks to its director was also necessarily a mechanism for expanding personality into economic policy. Before the 1890s, however, the convictions and abilities of the various incumbents were not such as to expand smoothly into policies of determined industrial promotion. It was not until 1893, upon the appointment to the Finance Ministry of Count Witte, the first dedicated industrializer to hold high office within the Empire, that the system encountered gifts fit to exploit it. But for all that, at Witte's accession to power, the system remained a paradoxical one. No doubt, the economic levers at the Minister's fingertips were immense, his executive discretion rarely circumscribed. But the Minister did not wag the state: both before and during Witte's tenure 'state intervention' remained an insufficiently precise description of the relationship between the autocracy and the industrial economy. For the Finance Ministry which Witte inherited existed *inside* a government and a society deeply suspicious of any deviation from the agrarian norm. Most of the body politic favoured servitude in one form or another, and most of the body social was habituated to accepting it. Development was recognized as a need by some echelons of the administration but resisted in practice by the majority. Implementation of development was relegated to a fragment of the bureaucracy, and its economic plans were necessarily formulated to take account of some very un-modern interests. And these interests remained conspicuously more representative of the imperial state than the Finance Ministry itself.

Effectively, the 'state' consisted of the Tsar, the court, and the ministeriat, few of them unabashed advocates of progress and the life innovational. Nicholas II, Tsar from 1896, drew his inspiration directly from God, or from the charlatans who spoke for God, and the deity, it transpired, was not much interested in industrialization. More earthly, if no more constructive, passions exercised the court: the grand dukes argued that industrialization merely surrendered the nation's wealth to foreigners, and regarded themselves as more proper recipients. For its part, the Council of Ministers carried an unusually substantial complement of intriguers, eccentrics, and criminals. Krivoshein, the Minister of Communications, had extracted more than a purely public profit from the transportation business, while the minor (and fortunately temporary) Finance Minister, Abaza, had proved an inveterate gambler, drawing little distinction between the revolutions of the roulette wheel and those of the Stock Exchange. The avuncular squire, Sipiagin, fond of pranks, conceived the extravagant ruse – for the Minister of the Interior – of despatching the secret police to round up his unwitting friends. Plehve, his successor, was an unpleasant bureaucratic talent who believed that Russia's salvation lay not in industry but in the healthy exercise of a 'victorious little war'.[55] At the War Office, Kuropatkin, rather paradoxically, disagreed: he held that industrialization caused wars, that this was unfortunate, and that it should therefore be avoided. Below these high, if peculiar, levels of government was deployed the hefty phalanx of the gentry-bureaucracy, agrarian in preference and in practice stalwarts of reaction's second defence line. Unsurprisingly, among this intractable and erratic crew, little toleration could be found for modernizing policies such as reformed tariff systems or reconstructed fiscal structures; the only way to secure these innovations was to suborn the captain and work by imperial decree. With officers and artificers of state of such consistent obduracy, any promotional activity that did occur could not be accurately described as state intervention.

Nor, outside the machinery of government, was the social panorama confronting the few agents of economic modernization any more attractive. Here there was little question of a value system unfavourable to industrialization; matters had not progressed as far as this; rather there was scarcely a single aspect of current values which could absorb the concept of industrial work or profit. The capitalistic ethic remained alien to Russian practice: the taking of interest was still widely regarded as usurious; the peasant community suspected the motives behind any large accumulation of wealth; the most widely accepted definition of profit featured the gain which accrued from the simple contract between man, soil, and weather.[56] Standards of commercial honesty were low; the regard for property rights, rocked perhaps by the 1861 expropriation, remained undeveloped; the aptitude for sustained labour, influenced by climatically controlled habits of seasonal employment, was markedly deficient. With the addition of a generous dash of anti-Semitism, together with the contempt for trade which often accompanies it, the obstacles to innovative action become comprehensive. And, in this case, there was little chance of the state moulding or 'crystallizing'[57] the value system into a creative shape. In Germany, the influence of state traditions and ambitions had acted positively upon the value system, but in Russia these features worked to *reinforce* the pre-capitalistic nature of social values.

THE GREAT SPURT AND THE WITTE SYSTEM

Witte concluded from the disposition of the reactionary battalions that 'All thinking Russia was against me'[58], and this – since it omitted unthinking, Russia – greatly underestimated the full weight of the opposing forces. However, in itself this solitary position formed one source of the Finance Minister's remarkable, if complicated, power, established for him an economic significance approached by probably no other single individual in nineteenth-century Europe. Something of this emerges in Witte's own description of his role as that of 'the executive director of the great economic corporation of the Russian people',[59] and in Izvolsky's conclusion that the Minister had been 'for ten years the real master of the 160 million inhabitants of the empire'.[60] At this point, clearly, over-valuation threatens the analyst's fragile craft. The official who acquires supreme executive power, commits himself to outright industrialization, and pursues this objective systematically becomes, with the merest turn of the pen, a hero of planned development. In the hands of his most fervent modern protagonist, T. H. von Laue, Witte has even transcended time; apparently he was, 'a fore-runner of Stalin rather than a contemporary of Nicholas II . . . the *pioneer of all modern experiments in deliberate economic development*'.[61] Accordingly, his policies have become one of the fixed points of Russian economic history in the exceptionally coherent shape of the 'Witte system'. Gerschenkron also has been encouraged by his reflections upon economic backwardness to view the Ministry of Finance under Witte as the supreme exponent of 'substitution', the pilot of Russia's induced development.[62] These views have been persuasively argued, but, in recent years, admixtures of caution, and even of sharp criticism, have modified their status as revealed truth.

It is at least true that the 'system' was based upon a reputable economic philosophy. Before coming to office, Witte had been greatly influenced by the arguments of the German theorist, Friedrich List, and particularly by his concept of the 'national economy'. This entity was designed to serve state purposes, acquiring rapid growth by concentration upon heavy industries, particularly machine and railway construction, and by enforcing present sacrifice for future gain. Light industries, frequently the leaders of growth elsewhere (but generally of more leisurely growth), found little place in this scheme and agriculture almost none; these sectors were merely left to react against the policy leverage applied to the capital goods industries. Similar proposals from the early-century theoretician, Count Mordvinov may also have affected Witte. From such originals he drew an individual and orderly translation, an agenda that was genuinely systematic. Its first priority was that official action should promote *private* enterprise, not an extension of public ownership. Despite the fact that the Russian state sector was proportionately larger than the German by 1890, with the lion's share of the railway, mining, and metallurgical industries, Witte had no ambition to increase its scope. His plan was not to expand manufacture of dubious efficiency and moderate technology but to raise the level of free-enterprise capitalism to the best international standards — and then by taxation to draw back a share of the resulting wealth into the public coffers. Witte's economy was, in consequence, a mixed one, an exercise in 'state capitalism', combining public initiatives with private entrepreneurial responses. Business was to be galvanized by a commitment to railway construction far more lavish than any yet attempted in Russia: the state intended to use the infrastructural impulse to drive the heavy metal and fuel industries upwards along the development slope, while also, more incidentally, creating a favourable context for urban growth. Railway investment formed, for Witte, 'a very powerful weapon for the direction of the economic development of the country'.[63] But it was also an expensive weapon, the cost of which could only be met by the time-honoured expedient of finance ministers: the manipulation of foreign credit as substitute for the scarcity of domestic capital.

Witte, however, intended to improve the design of this traditional dependence: the currency was to be stabilized and the gold standard introduced; and, in consequence of these reforms, international confidence in Russia was to be raised and the flows of *direct* investment greatly increased. In order to ease through the stabilization, special aid was to be given to the main gold-earning industries. As railway investment sparked economic activity, and foreign capital paid for it, the mills of state capitalism would revolve more rapidly, creating employment for a new class of native capitalists. This managerial élite Witte hoped to supply by an expanded provision for technical education. And, finally, in order to safeguard the entire construction, Witte intended to swing the Finance Ministry to the side of peace, curbing the more militaristic spirits of the autocracy and limiting the heavy costs of shooting wars. Undeniably, these propositions achieved a significant degree of interrelationship and logical cohesion.

Furthermore, the Witte design clearly corresponds with Gerschenkron's specifications for a 'substitute' system. One may suspect the exactness of the resemblance since Gerschenkron's original reflections upon backwardness were clearly influenced by the Russian experience; circularity is not entirely absent. Yet Witte's set of substitute policies does appear unusually complete: foreign capital was invoked to substitute for domestic investment; state capitalism for flourishing private enterprise; capital-intensive manufacture for deficient labour supplies; government orders at special prices for the poorly developed market in capital goods. Impressive as they are, however, such statements of economic intention do not guarantee a matching coherence at the level of performance, and it is there that they must be judged.

In aggregate, it is clear that the Russian economy, and particularly its heavy industries, responded positively to these measures: during the Witte era, coal production doubled, while that of iron and steel increased by about fourfold; by 1900 Russia had ousted France from the fourth rank in world iron production and had taken the fifth rank in steel manufacture. The supporting railway provision expanded by 87 per cent between 1892 and 1903, and some advanced technologies crystallized rapidly around the core of the capital goods sector: oil extraction raised its outflow by better than threefold and chemicals by nearly threefold between 1887 and 1898. Foreign capital, the life-blood of this development, pumped in at the phenomenal average annual rate of increase of 120 per cent between 1893 and 1898, and the yearly allocation of funds to new enterprise expanded by sevenfold through the 1890s. The total yield, in terms of income derived from industrial activity, quadrupled between 1888/1893 and 1893/97 (from 42 m. roubles to 161 m. roubles) and, in terms of average annual growth of industrial production, composed a rate of 7.5 per cent, far exceeding Russian achievement for any comparable period before 1914 and establishing one of the most impressive performances in late-nineteenth-century Europe. The record of high-pressure growth is incontestable. What remains at issue is the measure of system in the underlying policies, the degree of 'trim' or balance within the resulting industrial structure, and, above all, the immensity of the final cost to the community.

Critical appraisal of the state's physical commitment to economic affairs does not yield results for Russia comparable with those achieved by recent revisions of German economic history: with the public sector embracing one-third of all land supplies, two-thirds of all forests, two-thirds of the entire railway network, and seven-eights of all telegraphs,[64] as well as the most valuable mines, oil wells, salt and mineral springs, and fisheries, little can be attempted on this front. Instead, concern has focused upon five main areas involving problems of policy design and social gain: the true motives of, and returns upon, the railway plan; the bias towards the capital-goods sector; the high cost of *dirigiste* economics; the 'subversive' effects of foreign investment; the absence of agricultural policy.

RAILWAY PROGRAMMES: PATHWAYS AND PROTO-PLANS

At first sight, Witte's railways appear safe from criticism. By 1892 the main administrative centres had been linked, an initial military capability established, and the grain hinterlands attached to the ports; the remaining needs were primarily to enmesh important outlying regions such as Archangel, Siberia, and the Tashkent cotton fields, and, above all, to provide fully modern double-tracked facilities in European Russia. The programmes of the

1890s met many of these needs by providing genuinely industrial services between the main manufacturing regions and the resource areas of Donets and Krivoi Rog, and by incorporating the new Ukrainian installations within the network. If the first surge of rail construction in the 1860s and 1870s had provided the Empire with its initial long-range communications, the second surge of the 1890s carried construction deeper into the countryside, greatly improving the coverage of services.[65] To be sure, there were costly and flambuoyant failures: the gargantuan Trans-Siberian project, the longest line in the world, proved a 6400-kilometre monster devoid of purpose. The intention, to galvanize an entire economic region with the goad of railway development, although it included co-ordinated plans for population resettlement, mineral extraction, and the expansion of shipping, foundered upon immense expenditures (750 m. roubles, exceeding original estimates by 150%), poor construction (and thus low traffic densities), and, above all, upon the leanness of the eastern markets that it was supposed to unleash.[66] But in European Russia, where Witte concentrated the bulk of rail investment – and three times the track laid on the road to Siberia – a rate of transport growth was attained which no contemporary nation could match (see Table 4.2 and pp. 444–5 below). The proposal to employ railways as the carriers of planned growth applied most readily to these already developing provinces. Generously priced railway contracts supplied valuable demand for their new capital goods industries, while carefully handled freight rates could be manipulated to encourage production either for exports or for stocks. In agriculture also there were major gains: Metzer has calculated that the railways tapping the wheat belt of the south west, the southern regions of New Russia, the Lower Volga and the North Caucasus, as well as the more central rye-raising provinces, played a vital role in improving inter-regional terms of trade and increasing regional specialization of production.[67] At over 52,000 kilometres in length, almost twice the network of 1892, and greatly strengthened in its commercial sections, the path which Witte had intended to cut for private enterprise appeared by 1900 to be well advanced.

Nevertheless, problems of cost, scale, and utility were not entirely suppressed by a rapid rate of expansion and improving market integration. Much of the difficulty lay in railway budgeting, with construction estimates which were both too small and too large: too small for the task they faced, too large for the resources from which they were drawn. Between 1880 and 1900 the imperial purse could spare only 5 per cent of its expenditure for railway development, an amount roughly equal to the returns from the excises on tea, coffee, liquor, salt, and herring.[68] Compared with the vast geographical liabilities of the autocracy, this scale of expenditure, even when enthusiastically deployed by Witte, necessarily implied severe restraints upon railway density: in 1914 the Empire contained eleven times fewer track-kilometres per unit area than Germany and seven times fewer than Austria-Hungary, while, despite the efforts in European Russia, only one-quarter of the existing lines were double-tracked. Nor did the investment which was executed yield by any means rapid returns: completed lines had not only to cover operating costs but also to repay debts contracted to finance the initial construction. This proved difficult: by 1899 the railways sported deficits of some 70m. roubles; no net profit was recorded until 1911; reasonably sound profitability was achieved only just before the First World War.[69] Witte's railroads, then, were not an entirely convincing bargain: they were more expensive than the autocracy could afford and less extensive than it required.

Table 4.2   Russian railways: construction of track and ownership.

Date	Total (versts)	European Russia (versts)	Asiatic Russia (versts)	State lines (%)	Private lines (%)
1886	25,582	24,284	1,298	13.3	86.7
1891	28,809	27,165	1,644	34.7	65.3
1896	37,179	33,676	3,503	61.4	38.6
1901	51,937	43,836	8,101	68.3	31.7
1906	58,285	48,143	10,142	70.4	29.6
1911	61,684	51,428	10,256	69.0	31.0

Note: 1 verst = 1.013 km.
Source: Miller (1926), p. 208

The bargain, moreover, was not entirely an economic one. Recent research has greatly strengthened long-running suspicions that much Russian railway construction derived from military inspiration.[70] Throughout the 1890s the Finance Ministry experienced pressure both from the French government – too frequently its paymaster – and from the Imperial General Staff to embody its borrowed funds in strategic lines. However much the financial bureaucracy might protest that such projects drained the reserves and diverted foreign credit from more productive uses, the autocracy commonly found the appeals of the militarists more compelling. Consequently, lines like that from Orenburg to Tashkent, aimed by the French against British interests in India, or that from Bologoe to Siedlce, intended to accelerate mobilization against Germany and admitted to be 'without economic value for the moment',[71] were constructed *against* the best interests of an industrializing nation. As Witte conceded, 'I tried to develop the railway network as best I could, but military considerations, on whose side his Majesty naturally was for the most part, significantly hindered the building of the railways.'[72] At this juncture, the development programmes of the Finance Ministry clearly collided with the political imperatives of the tsarist regime; more particularly, the designs of Witte collided with those of Kuropatkin, the intentions of the reformist technocrat with those of the conservative general.

Given the thin spread and strained viability of the railway routes, their frequent orientation towards frontiers and garrisons rather than factories and mines, the economy of 1914 can scarcely be described as one fully mobilized by railway development. If further proof is needed, the spectacular wartime disruption of the Russian rail network between 1914 and 1917 surely provides it. With consequences so disorderly and pathways so faint, it is therefore a considerable oversimplification to view Witte's railway programme as a device for proto-planning or as a highway for profitable private enterprise.

THE CAPITAL GOODS SECTOR: BOOM OR BIAS

The enterprise which railway development was primarily intended to activate lay concentrated within the producer goods industries. These, of course, were to provide the power-house of the rapid industrialization which Witte considered necessary. However, if such technologies can deliver rapid growth, excessive emphasis upon them may create grave strains within the industrial structure. By 1901, at least one western source appeared to have detected something of the kind within Russian performance, arguing that 'the Russian industrial revolution has probably been too rapid'.[73] The central problem was that the 'implanted' heavy industries were distinctly more advanced than the general run of domestic manufacturing; the capital goods sector thus lacked the service and support industries which would normally be counted its essential auxiliaries. Despite the advances of the 1890s, the *level* of Russian industrialization remained low, omitting the modern machine-building, electro-technical, and chemical industries which supported comparable heavy industrial conglomerations elsewhere. In Russia, the support was less sophisticated: the most modern steel furnaces might often be charged by massed labour gangs equipped with wheelbarrows. It was consistent with the logic of substitution that, within specialized producer-good technologies, scarce skilled labour should be replaced by capital-intensive and labour-economizing equipment while low-quality labour was applied everywhere else. Probably, Russian industrialization could only have been contrived at an advanced stage of world technological development when equipment suitable for 'substitution' became available. Certainly, the process was closely tailored to Russian requirements.

Though the population of the Empire was vast, the *obshchina*, peasant illiteracy, and social values ensured that labour supplies for industry were scarce, unskilled, and intractable – and, therefore, in real terms *expensive*.[74] Additionally, some important industrial areas combined all these problems with the naturally sparse populations of recently settled territories: Donets, in particular, ranked among the Empire's ten most thinly endowed provinces. Faced with these problems, manufacturers had to spend not only upon wages but upon the recruitment and maintenance of wage labour. The Gorlovka Coal Company, for instance, had built by 1900, alongside its industrial installations, 1300 houses, 6 schools, 2 churches, 1 hospital and a park.[75] Social overhead costs of this kind frequently added a 100 per cent surcharge to money wage bills, making Russian labour in its domestic setting as costly as French or Belgian labour in theirs. But where large labour groups *were* gathered together – most Russian heavy industrial units were very big – it also made sense for the less delicate processes to be executed by mass muscle power. All this made for appropriate substitution but not for industrial equilibrium: a heavy industrial superstructure was balanced upon supports of skills, services, and auxiliary industries which were too slender for safety. The gap between the advanced capital goods sector and all other industrial sectors allowed the one to revolve unusually fast above the others but also maximized its tendency towards instability.

Almost certainly, Witte did too little to fill this gap: his programme concentrated upon the acquisition of the most modern heavy technologies and their combination with Russian labour endowments to the exclusion of important supportive developments in other fields, most notably in extractive and consumer goods industries. His concern centred upon the more prestigious industries of the era, upon the blast-furnaces, steel-mills, railway workshops, and shipyards of the heavy *finished* goods manufactories. Advanced disciplines of this kind often commend themselves to less developed economies since they symbolize an industrial competence which in reality may lie far in the future; they are consequently often pursued with scant regard for genuine economic requirement or endowment. Certainly, the relative neglect of the country's fuel and mineral base, exemplified by Witte's desertion of Urals mining in favour of the high technologies of the Ukraine, suggests that the economic policy of the 1890s was vulnerable to this illusion. The outcome contained many contradictions: hypothetically, the untapped resources of the Urals could have flooded all Europe with cheap iron ore, yet in 1901 Russia was still importing half her ore requirements;[76] at the same time the massive coal reserves of Kuznetsk had been drawn on for only 0.15 per cent of domestic needs while foreign purchases continued at a high level. An emphasis upon the capital goods sector which does not include a sufficient premium upon the vital inputs for heavy manufacture is surely an indicator of misshapen policy.

Internal disproportions thus compromised the balance of the Russian heavy industries. But their major disequilibrating influence within the macroeconomic structure stemmed from the lack of an effective industrial counterweight; without it, the capital goods sector could supply only a lopsided form of growth, confined within a narrow segment of the economy and liable to capsize at moments of crisis. Some form of more laterally extended growth, with several sectors operating to varying and compensating rhythms of activity would have formed a preferable economic system. Here, despite the formidable constraints of the Russian market, the light consumer industries – especially textiles – offered obvious prospects which went largely ignored by the policymakers. Portal points to a period of definite expansion in the cotton sector during the 1880s and to renewed progress after the slump of 1890–92.[77] By the century's end, the textile mills lagged behind the heavy industries only in their capitalization;[78] in equipment they were as progressive as any Russian manufacture, and in scale – the average size of plant employing 600 workers against an all-industry average of 131 – they were, if anything, somewhat ahead. Their survival capability and resistance to cyclical crisis was also notably strong: the severe slump of 1900–02, a disaster for the new heavy industries, affected the lighter industries much less acutely. Nor does the case for these manufactures rest only upon their production performance. Since they were less capital-intensive than the heavy technologies, their expansion would have incurred a lesser dependence on foreign investment and converted the nation's own limited reserves into a more widely spread manufacturing capability. Furthermore, the skill requirements of light industries for both management and labour were more appropriate to Russia's existing supply of human resources. The limitation, of course, lay in the expansion of the market: growth based on consumer industries would have required a matching upsurge in domestic – that is, agricultural – demand. And upon mobility in this sector, as upon railroad development, the autocracy imposed its own specialized array of limitations.

If account is taken of the distortions within and around the capital goods sector, whether the product of political imperative or of economic preference, the operations of the Witte programme across this band of policy appear distinctly less systematic. The growth which it elicited was narrowly and shakily based, neglecting some sectors and forbidding others, progressing not by coherent and orderly steps but by the precarious 'bacchanalian' lunge. It is often said that the Witte system was a 'gamble', staking everything on the industrial *coup de main*, playing for high stakes with small reserves. But, at least in part, the gamble was self-induced: the spreading of resources more widely – if more thinly – across more sectors would have reduced the risk rather than increased it. Perhaps it *is* true that gamblers who play to systems rarely break the bank.

THE COSTS OF DEVELOPMENTAL WAGERS

Modern appraisal of Witte's methods have focused not only upon the gambler's tactics but also upon his stake. It is now common ground that the funds required for development were not amassed by the most upright of financial measures. Witte always claimed that his industrial promotions were achieved without jeopardy to the balance of an órthodox budget. But this was true only in a very limited sense: Witte employed *two* budgets, the ordinary which was maintained in a state of balance and the extraordinary into which were loaded the huge charges of the military, the debt conversion and the railroads. This convenient device allowed such sleights of hand as that of 1900 when a real deficit on the railway account of 31.6 m. roubles was shown as a book revenue of 374 m. roubles.[79] The gamble was thus not supported by a credit that would have been recognized as sound by the international standards of the day.

Moreover, the measure of genuine liquidity attained by Witte was based upon a pair of much-questioned fund-raising ploys: a punitive level of taxation and the use of the gold standard as an international letter of credit, attracting loans from foreign friends. The first has come under attack for its part in reducing even further the possibilities for growth in domestic demand; the second for the vast expense which the conversion of the rouble to gold backing imposed upon the Empire's already strained budgetary capabilities. Kahan has argued that Witte neglected an alternative form of industrialization 'based upon organically developing demand' because he allotted higher priorities to fiscal revenues than to advances in consumption and savings.[80] Certainly, Witte betrayed a strong interest in tax yields, increasing indirect taxes until they accounted for half his revenue and raising the tax burden per head by over 40 per cent above the level of 1885. (6.41 r. *per cap.* 1885; 8.83 r. *per cap.* 1900).[81] But it does not follow that, if he had forgone these tax increases, or even lowered the level of taxation, a spontaneous demand for consumer goods would have arisen in the Russian countryside. Agricultural poverty within the empire had reached such a pitch by the early 1900s that, as Margaret Miller detected, *any* level of taxation would have proved unbearable:[82] trimming the fiscal controls downwards would not have released an 'organically developing demand'; it would merely have reduced the margin by which the peasantry were irretrievably indebted. Furthermore, hypotheses of this counter-factual type emphasize economic alternatives while ignoring political constraints: in reality the fiscal controls were as much instruments of autocratic ascendancy as of budgetary necessity, and of all tsarist policy imperatives, the subjugation of the rural populace is the one least suitable for discounting. The conditions for any useful expansion of domestic demand far exceeded tinkering adjustments to the tax system: wide-ranging agricultural reform, including the abolition of the *obshchina* and the redemption system, was probably the minimum requirement; and any such measure of change prior to 1905 remained politically unacceptable. There were thus few genuine alternatives to fiscal policies which traced a narrow line between economic and governmental requirements, and although, no doubt, socially damaging, could have exerted little further adverse effect upon 'organic demand'. Here Witte deserves defence.

The same may be true of a gold standard policy aimed at acquiring for the rouble a full measure of international respectability; after all, many previous finance ministers had sought this goal only to find it as elusive as Don Quixote's windmills. Once created, however, this respectability was expected to break the vicious circle of backwardness, attracting foreign development capital to a borrower with sound currency and solid reserves. Witte's pursuit of this objective was deft and determined. It began with a counter-speculation on the Berlin Exchange against the German profiteers who had hounded the rouble in the 1880s and secured their complete defeat by October 1894; it continued through three years of export promotion and heavy taxation, and secured a favourable balance of trade and substantial bullion reserves; and it concluded in January 1897 with the successful placement of the rouble upon the gold standard. The sequel was a level of foreign investment between 1897 and 1913 twice that of the years 1881–97.

At the time there were persistent complaints that Russia could not afford the gold standard – the Council of Ministers and bureaucracy, for instance, were dead set against the idea – and it is these which Kahan has chosen to echo. He points out, correctly, that the increased inflow of foreign capital after 1897 was due not only to the gold standard but to fortuitous independent factors: the improving world money-market, the further tightening of the Franco-Russian alliance, favourable interest rates in Russia. His conclusion is that Russia, like France, suffered from a gold obsession: she retained reserves far in excess of the returns brought in by the gold standard, an average above the *statutory* requirement betweeen 1897 and 1913 of 443 m. roubles.[83] Obviously, this was a costly style of administering an already expensive device: lower reserves would have freed much valuable capital for investment purposes. By aspiring to a place among the world's solid currency nations, Russia was seeking a life style beyond her means.[84] But what were the alternatives? *If* the capital-intensiveness of development was fixed by the political constraints on consumer goods expansion, additional capital had to be acquired. It could only be acquired from abroad, and would only come in the required amounts if sureties were offered. *Over*-insurance in this department may not have been imprudent: Witte was, after all, negotiating a remarkably rapid transition for the rouble from one of the world's shakiest to one of the world's biggest borrowing currencies; deliberately lavish guarantees were not necessarily unsuitable here. And to have identified precisely the level of reserves which would have provided the smallest necessary surety to international capitalism and the maximum possible economy to the exchequer was as much beyond the nineteenth-century finance minister as the cure for inflation is beyond the twentieth-century economist.

Too much criticism of Witte's financial policies has revolved around individual measures divorced from their political, social, and diplomatic context. Recent work by Barkai has demonstrated, however, that more comprehensive and certainly more ingenious – though not necessarily more realistic – valuations are possible. While congratulating Witte on becoming the only Finance Minister in the period 1861–1914 to achieve an expansion in the money supply roughly equivalent to the demand – a computed rate of 4 per cent p.a. – he, too, disapproves of the gold standard strategy and the heavy taxation needed to maintain it.[85] Although admitting that the rouble-proofing campaign would have been vindicated had the foreign capital inflows outweighed the production losses incurred by Witte's deflationary taxation, Barkai believes that this desirable result was not achieved. In fact, the Russian national accounts for 1900 show a net deficit on invisible trading larger than the surplus on commodity trading, and between 1898 and 1913 the aggregated current account was consistently in the red – the deficit rising from 1 per cent GNP in 1890 to 2.0–2.5 per cent in 1900, and slipping back to 1 per cent GNP in 1913.[86] According to these estimates, the conversion to gold captured foreign credit to the extent only of 1 per cent GNP per year, encouraging Barkai to the conclusion that, if these amounts were to create a net benefit to the economy, the losses from deflationary taxes would have had to be practically zero.[87] In a country given to the monstrous tsarist imposts, this was clearly implausible.

While conceding that the proper monetary solutions were not available to statesmen reared upon Gladstonian orthodoxy, Barkai does suggest that the alternatives to 'sound' money policies would have better served the Russian needs. If monetary expansion had been generously promoted and a balanced budget exchanged for a modest deficit – he suggests 0.5 – 1.0 per cent GNP – industrialization could have been pursued *without* the immense fiscal burdens placed upon the peasantry. Capital formation and rural peace could have been made compatible. Similarly, the acceptance of flexible exchange rates in place of the gold standard would have stimulated the lighter industries more appropriate to Russia's factor endowments, and, by raising rouble prices, would have boosted farm incomes. Again this is impressive, but does it represent actual possibilities? After all, Barkai excuses Witte on the grounds that he could be nothing other than an economist of his time, a committed budget-balancer. In fact, however, this is over-indulgent. Witte was not the orthodox Gladstonian that Barkai paints: he *did* expand the money supply where his more conservative predecessors faithfully retrenched, and, when the gyrations of the extraordinary budget are remembered, he appears very far from the conventional budget-juggler. The restrictions upon fiscal policy in this area were not those of popular economic theory. What then of sound money and convertibility; did contemporary thinking offer no alternatives in this department? The record again suggests that it did, in the shape this time not of the Finance Minister's eccentricities but of the critical opinions of his adversaries. Devotees of bimetallism like Sharapov – who dismissed gold as 'a slavish and pagan form of money which has outlived itself'[88] or Nechvolodov who complained of its 'heavy yoke'[89] – did not regard a stable currency as essential for economic development. Instead, they proposed a state monopoly of all foreign exchange transactions and aimed both to regulate the rouble's external value and to control the money supply *independently* of all bullion and foreign exchange reserves.[90] Witte's choice of the orthodox solution in this policy area was not solely for lack of alternatives.

Here, Barkai's enthusiasm for one such alternative is marred by two major flaws of procedure. To begin with, his argument, like so many of its kind, fails to develop an adequate sense of the political realities. As these were more powerful than any developmental theory in determining the composition of tsarist industrial growth, so they were more influential than current monetary wisdom in shaping the style of tsarist finance. For the lower level of extortion which monetary expansionism and flexible exchange rates might have permitted would not have accorded with the requirements of social control: rural peace generated by prosperity was less reliable than rural equilibrium pinned down by fiscal extortion. Witte had somehow to contrive a financial formula suited to the requirements of development *and* of authoritarianism; and the resulting compromise was not without its merits. The element of 'sound money' acted to reassure the international financial community; the punitive aspects of taxation retained the confidence of the autocracy; the manipulation of the extraordinary budget achieved *some* of the benefits of deficit spending. Theoretically it was not elegant; economically it was not systematic; practically it bent developmental requirements before political *force majeure*. But as a stroke of expedience it met most of the outstanding claims, no mean feat given the nature of the claimants.

Secondly, the prevailing quantitative attack on Witte's gold standard policies turns out to be less than dependable in its own handling of quantities. Obviously enough, to treat foreign credits worth 1 per cent of GNP as a bagatelle and anything which might be subtracted from it as practically zero is to place a misleading disguise on some very large absolute numbers. In fact, foreign funding which amounts to 1 per cent of GNP, when the GNP is generated by an economy as enormous as the Russian, is very far from being a trifling consideration. Its exact status, however, has attracted diminishing attention as recent research has begun to resolve the issue in a different way: based on more sophisticated measures of capital than those selected by Barkai, this investigation has simply yielded very much larger estimates for the contribution made by overseas credit. Gregory and Sailors suggest that the net foreign investment proportion was in the range of 4 per cent of GNP in 1906 and 2.5 per cent of GNP in 1913; and they conclude, 'these more recent estimates of net foreign investment suggest proportions *double* those used by Barkai'.[91] Expressed more suitably as a proportion of the smaller and more specific aggregate for net domestic capital formation, foreign investment supplied 30–35 per cent of the Russian total around 1906 and about 20 per cent by 1913. But if Barkai under-measures in some cases, he omits entirely in some others. In his account, major additional gains from the Empire's foreign borrowings go devoid of recognition, among them even the important qualitative effect derived from the high-technology content of much of the investment (the shares of foreign participation increase in direct correlation with the technology level of the borrowing industry) and the rich extra reserves won by the reinvestment of profits accruing from previous foreign investment (a practice which McKay has shown to be widespread, see below p. 245). Barkai's claim that foreign investment 'was not a net gain for Russia'[92] can scarcely expect to survive in the company of so many freshly painted indicators to the contrary.

However, if Witte's financial policies prove sufficiently robust to fend off the current forms of criticism, whether of individual fiscal devices or of broad monetary concept, they remain vulnerable to the unexpected attack from first principles. Despite the aggressive taxation, the budgetary virtuosity, the unanimous complaint from conservatives, liberals, and *narodniki* that Russia was being developed too far and too fast, despite the more modern agreement that the state provided the motor power for the expansion of the 1890s, it has duly been alleged that Witte spent too *little* on industrial development. Previously, von Laue had argued that in 1894/95 the economic ministries had appropriated a substantial 52–55 per cent of total budget expenditure (ordinary and extraordinary), while the military departments had taken only 22–29 per cent.[93] (see Table 4.3). However, with the subsequent revisionist swing, Kahan has retorted that the large 'economic' shares were in fact inflated by generous amounts of administrative, and only indirectly economic, expenditure. Employing a more stringent budgetary analysis for 1903, he claims that 36 per cent of expenditure fell to military use, 25.3 per cent to administration, 22.2 per cent to national debt service, and the much more modest allocation of 16.4 per cent to 'economic and cultural' purposes.[94] The implications are, firstly, that the developmental aspects of the 'Witte state' has been greatly exaggerated, and, secondly, that the fiscal extortion which might have found justification in growth-inducing policies was actually denied it by authoritarian and unproductive expenditure preferences.

Much of this is adventurous prospecting and the underlying ice is never firm. Elements neither miraculous nor surprising surround the higher defence charges of the 1900s: the estimates for the relatively peaceful mid-1890s are consistent with the somewhat larger ones (c. 32%) for the turbulent period 1866–85, and indeed with Kahan's figure for 1903, since the statistical up-thrust may be explained by a marked increase in tsarist naval expenditure at the century's turn,[95] a reflection simply of turbulence reviving. Further, the revisionist way with the budgetary categories is at least as curious as von Laue's: if one deals doubtfully with administrative charges, the other treats railway expenditure most curiously, denying it the status of investment 'embodying an economic policy'.[96] Finally, it is probable that Kahan's 'economic and cultural' category requires supplementation from other budgetary heads before a realistic assessment of the state's industrial commitment can be composed. The position of railway investment within these heads is unclear, for instance, and almost certainly requires adjustment. Additionally, both defence spending and railway budgets include large disbursements on capital account – for locomotives, rolling-stock, warships, or artillery – which were intended to assist the heavy industries and should be counted as market-assisting subsidies. The research to establish more exact quantities for the imperial state's involvement in growth-inducing policies remains to be done; it is passably clear, however, that Kahan's 16.4 per cent represents the barest of all minima.

Table 4.3   Government expenditure by category: comparative estimates (%)

	I 1894	II 1903	III 1903	IV 1913
1. General administration	19.0	25.3	17.4	16.4
2. National debt		22.2	15.3	13.1
3. Defence	29.0	36.0	24.8	26.6
4. Productive expenditure	52.0[a]	16.4	11.5[b]	16.9[b]
5. State undertakings			31.2	27.0

[a] Von Laue here aggregates economic expenditure and the service on the government debt since he believes the latter to have been 'contracted largely for railroad construction' (p. 100).
[b] Miller separates 'productive expenditure' and 'state undertakings', thus explaining her small allowances for the first category.

Sources: Col. I: Von Laue (1963), p. 100   Col. II: Kahan (1967), p. 465   Cols. III and IV: Miller (1926), p. 431

Witte's financial management of his limited developer's stake survives the critical assault with some resilience: the internal processes of the 'gamble' should therefore be distinguished in effectiveness from the transportation and capital goods programmes which enjoyed much of the final expenditure. Admittedly, financial policies were as subject to political requirements for fiscal repression as transportation or industrial policies were vulnerable to political emphases upon military railways or non-agricultural markets. But where the railways and the heavy industries were damaged by faults both of concept and implementation, the financial sector was directed skilfully between a series of extremely threatening hazards. The target towards which it was headed, however, was the accumulation inside the Empire of massive foreign holdings. If the handling of this policy was tactically as sound as conditions permitted, other question-marks hang over the value of the strategic objective.

FOREIGN CAPITAL: THE DEPENDENCE IN DEVELOPMENT

Within the development narrative, foreign investment has played the roles both of fairy godmother and first witch, varying from one to the other with taste, politics, and circumstances. In its more sinister personification, its ill-effects are said primarily to be: the creation of a dependence so large that the foreign element cannot be replaced; the subordination of economic sovereignty within the client state; the growth of high-technology 'enclaves' inside the host economy, linked more closely to the needs and facilities of the creditor than of the debtor nation; the repatriation of excessive profits by foreigners. Most of these repercussions have been alleged against Witte's close relationship with foreign capitalists. Some may be dismissed fairly easily. 'Enclaves' did not grow up in the tracks of the western industrialists: the economy was not so deprived that it could not profit by 'spin-off' and demonstration effects from the implantations of advanced capital; and, for better or worse, the regime received from the foreigners the technologies that it desired. Nor were the westerners bent upon establishing enclaves: their investments in social overheads like schools, housing, and transport and in educational programmes for management both served their own manufacturing interests and acted as enclave-averting measures. Similarly, although 'foreign monopolists' excited criticism and apprehension, they did not escape the control of the state: western business ventures were licensed by the Council of State, and schemes which overstepped the bounds of propriety simply did not receive its imprimatur (see below pp. 270–1). The measure of economic sovereignty retained by the autocracy was, in fact, considerable. It pursued a highly independent tariff policy, belabouring the Germans in the 1890s and refusing large concessions to the French even after 1905, while, at the same time, absorbing quantities of 'monopolistic' German and French capital and management. Tied investments – such as those in railways – might go where the creditor decreed, but the autonomy of general commercial and industrial policy was never seriously undermined by the presence of large foreign interests.

Charges of rampant profiteering by the westerners have also proved tenacious, though they are supported by no more convincing evidence. The best stories of capitalistic exploitation, of international banking conspiracy, claim that foreign shareholders extracted massive dividends from their Russian ventures: if the Empire paid through the nose for Reutern's railways, the implication is that it did so again for Witte's industries. Returns could be high, and some may have reached 40 per cent, although they were never consistently as high as the 15–30 per cent mentioned by many sources, and practically never as high as the rates above 80 per cent hysterically imagined by Nesterenko.[97] Even the respected Russian source P.V. Ol' claims as an average no more than a conservative and restrained 5–10 per cent.[98] Similar good sense is evident in J. P. McKay's well-documented demonstration that *entrepreneurial* profits, though distinctly more lavish, were habitually reinvested for growth in Russia, rather than hustled as ill-gotten gains out of the country.[99]

But not all criticisms of 'penetrative' foreign capital are so easily pruned. The size of the foreign-owned sector in Russia by 1900 gave ground for legitimate concern. Soviet sources describe the period before 1914 as one of outright imperialism, and Witte as the chief agent of this invading force, although less doctrinaire observers – notably Gerschenkron[100] – have argued that foreign investment was not an overwhelming element in total industrial investment. Witte's own assessment for 1896 put overseas support at 92 m. roubles and the total of industrial and transportation investment at roughly 290 m. roubles, allocating a share of something under one-third of annual corporate investment to foreign funds.[101] This compares well with modern estimates such as that of H. J. Ellison, conceding a one-third interest to foreign capital by 1914,[102] and with P. V. Ol's longer-established contention that between one-fifth and two-fifths of total corporate common stock fell to foreign investment totalled 2300 m. roubles (the entire *net* foreign debt includ- external sources provided a major but not predominant *tranche* of Russia's growth capital during the period of rapid development. But all-Russian computations of this kind conceal important flaws within the larger picture. In fact, foreign capital was heavily concentrated in certain regions and sectors, invariably those upon which rapid growth was most dependent. Ol' calculated that by 1914 67 per cent of investment in the metal industries came of foreign extraction, but that the comparable figure for the pig-iron and steel producers of the southern industrial belt was nearer 85 per cent.[104] More recent calculations by J. P. Sontag,[105] though based on work by Ol' and Vainshtein, again single out the mining and metallurgical sectors: by 1914 direct and indirect foreign investment totalled 2300 m. roubles (the entire *net* foreign debt including state bonds and allowing for Russian overseas investment was 7500 m. roubles) of which 1200 m. roubles or 52 per cent was claimed by these heavy industrial sectors. Moreover, the foreign interest in *new* industrial capital formation (naturally closely related to the higher technologies) was much larger – 41 per cent of the total 1880–89, 55 per cent 1893–1900 – than the foreign allocation of total stock-holding.[106] Such levels of involvement imply not so much foreign penetration as foreign occupation of selected manufacturing and resource centres.

Conventionally, however, foreign capital offers more than a merely threatening domination to the debtor economy. External credit can mitigate the strains of early industrialization, when the balance of trade is commonly adverse, and may form a superior alternative to swingeing taxation as a means of acquiring development finance. Over the longer run, however, it is important that foreign funds should be replaced by indigenous capital; eventually, at least, growth must be self-sponsored. For Russia, however, the benefits were not easily acquired and the costs bulked unusually large. The country's overseas trade was in deficit in only three years, 1888–1913, and did not require foreign finance to balance the accounts,[107] while overseas borrowing clearly formed an insufficient substitute for the hefty taxes to which the autocracy remained faithful. On the other hand, the foreign participation in the vital high-technology sectors was so immense that the chances of buying out the foreigners over the medium to long term – short of an unimaginable act of political expropriation – were distinctly bleak. Further, the concentration of funds in key areas acted to expose precisely the companies most responsible for Russia's industrial performance to the cruellest swings of international confidence. The great industrial centres of the Ukraine were virtually paying groundrent to the investors of France and Belgium; any palpitation in Paris or Brussels was thus relayed, more or less directly, to the boardrooms of southern Russia. And if foreign investment was subject to the abrasive action of international investment cycles, it was not immune from the corrosive effect produced by international politics. The spearhead of industrialization was easily blunted by this force: the earmarking of finance for military objectives, the tacking of non-economic conditions to industrial credit transactions, the manipulation of loans for diplomatic advantage, all compromised the efficiency of the capital inflow. The foreign capitals attracted by Witte were thus too substantial for comfortable repayment, too concentrated for business equilibrium, too politically sensitive for economic efficiency.

But what was the alternative? It remained preferable to import foreign capital rather than foreign goods: the overseas credits at least created employment, drew technological expertise in their wake, and generated a potential for the export of manufactures, if not to Europe, at least to Asia. Witte's conviction that foreign capital provided the only means to bridge the gap between the advanced and the backward country rested on these considerable assumptions. Yet, if this logic carries power, it remains true that the foreign dependence, imposed upon the tsarist economy an ineradicable measure of vulnerability. Demonstration of this proved sharply destructive to Witte's plan: the international monetary crisis of 1900–01 snapped many of the country's supply lines and plunged the heavy industries into recession. Such breakdowns were in fact built into the 'Witte system': sooner or later, as the investment cycle revolved, it was bound to bring a phase of poor confidence in overseas ventures, and, when that occurred, the Russian capital goods sector was, equally, bound for disaster. It was at this point, in particular, that the lighter industries, with their lower capital needs, might have offered some easing of the Russian problem. However, if the Witte system, with its actual priorities, tended systematically to create violent economic breakdown (thereby throwing further doubt upon its viability as a *growth-inducing* system), it seems that it did so in classically paradoxical style. For, if in absolute terms, and in terms of industrial equilibrium, Russia's foreign borrowing was excessively large, it is possible that in other terms – relative to the national accounts – it was too small to do enough good. Even allowing a net foreign investment proportion of 2–4 per cent of GNP, the impact made by foreign credit on the vastness of the Tsar's economy was necessarily limited; and at least *some* force remains to Barkai's conclusion that, 'Tsarist Russia was, for better or worse, going through its industrialization process by relying almost entirely on its own resources'.[108] It may be that the real dangers of the foreign dependence outweighed the quantitative benefit; or that a less capital-intensive form of growth would have reduced both the dependence and the risks to a less damaging balance. Even if the qualitative technological return on the overseas financial connexion is taken as its major residual virtue, doubts remain as to whether the technology involved was the most economical for the nation's purposes. As the Russian railways were too big for the imperial pocket but too small for the imperial geography, so Witte's employment of foreign capital was too extensive for industrial equipoise, too restricted for a comprehensive exercise in internationally funded capital formation. Allowing that the bargain may have been necessary for Russia, it may, nevertheless, have been struck at a less than ideal rate.

AGRICULTURE: A NEGLECTED CULTIVATION

If Witte's judgement concerning foreign capital was suspect, his judgement concerning agriculture was rarely even exercised. Here there were no bargains. In a system aimed at promoting economic advance, the primary sector was simply omitted. No doubt, the hostility of the Tsar, ministers, and landowners severely impeded the possibility of agrarian change, but Witte himself displayed little interest in the topic. The Listean maxim that the good which accrued to industry accrued automatically to agriculture served *in place of* an agricultural policy. Throughout the 1890s Witte was 'glad to leave the peasantry to the revenue–extracting powers of the Ministry of the Interior';[109] he turned to a close investigation of the subject only in the 1900s, and, for the most part, after leaving the Finance Ministry.[110] Not that change entirely absented itself from the Russian countryside during the Witte period. Yields rose – at their customary slow pace – not only because of extensions in the cultivated acreage at the territorial fringe but because of an alteration in the agricultural centre of gravity. The central provinces, previously the Empire's major granary, proved ill-equipped – due to low rainfall and a predominance of *obschchina* land-holding – to weather the serious crop failures of 1891. Correspondingly, there was a shift in emphasis towards the south – where productivity expanded rapidly in the 1890s – and the main burden of grain exporting passed to the Don and Kuban territories, to Bessarabia, and the regions around Ekaterinoslav and Kherson. As this physical shift occurred, it was paralleled by modifications in entrepreneurship within these provinces: sales of noble land to the bourgeoisie multiplied, and leadership in agriculture passed slowly from the gentry to the new agrarian middle class. Such alterations suggested an incipient modernization within the primary sector, but they were, in fact, the very earliest and faintest heralds of change. In comparative terms, Russian cultivation remained among the world's least satisfactory. Of the twelve main wheat-producing countries, Russia ranked tenth in yield per hectare, surpassing only Spain and British India. And if by 1900 the Empire had become the world's largest producer of sugar beet, her yields per hectare for this crop were less than *half* those of any other cultivator, Italy alone excepted.

It was in peasant agriculture that stagnation was most endemic. Certainly, during the century's final decades the hold of the *obshchina* upon the rural community loosened somewhat, and the trickle of migrants to the towns swelled perceptibly. But the shift was a small one: the urban population was expanded only from 12.7 per cent of the total in 1890 to 14.3 per cent by 1910. True too, that a thriving peasant land market grew up as households turned to additional non-agricultural pursuits – domestic service, rural crafts, and part-time industrial employment – in order to generate extra leasing power. But this was an expedient desperately contrived as counter-measure to insistent land-hunger. Such tiny adjustments were examples of peasant enterprise in evading the restrictions of an official settlement which had yielded only slightly since 1861. Even when Nicholas II assumed the throne in 1896, and cautious man that he was, forgave all land-tax, poll-tax, and quit-rent arrears as the price for a peaceful coronation, he was careful not to touch the redemption system, still chief support of the *obshchina*. Within this enduring carapace, the great majority of peasant agriculture persisted throughout the 1890s in the ancient three-field format, making little use even of rotation or grass-sowing. The individual cultivator, forced to sell his crop immediately after harvest, served still as prey for the local factors, while the marketing of the peasant sector remained very poorly developed. Handling and storage facilities for that portion of the crop which did escape from the villages advanced so little that the autumnal freight both overtaxed the new transportation system cruelly, and ran to waste prodigiously. Russian grain, like peasant cultivation, acquired a deservedly bad name.

This state of affairs followed not from Witte's agricultural policy but from his failure to develop one. The only state-sponsored changes in this sector during the 1890s consisted almost invariably of increased oppression. Alongside the maintained burden of redemption debt, considerable additions to indirect taxes – quintupling their yield between 1881 and 1895 – were made by both Bunge and Witte. These impositions bore heavily upon peasant purchases. Similarly, the huge tariff of 1891, introduced by Vyshnegradskii and retained by Witte, reinforced the upward thrust of peasant living costs, placing imported inputs for agriculture – including fertilizers, implements, and machines − beyond the reach of all peasants and reducing the animal stock − and thus the natural fertilizer supply − which could be sustained by imported feeds. However, worse even than the devices of fiscality were the regime's devices of exportation. Witte, following Vyshnegradskii, applied the forceps to agriculture with a vengeance. The massive shares of crop exported − 20−33 per cent of the wheat produced in 1893−1912, 24−37 per cent of the barley cut − bore witness not so much to increasing productivity as to the increasing efficiency of state procurement. If peasant consumption had been maintained at the standard of the 1870s throughout the Witte period, calculated the German observer Fajans, the 'exportable surplus' actually taken by the state would have been reduced by 71 per cent.[111] Between 1883 and 1896, it is probable that the already chronic levels of peasant consumption were depressed by a further 20 per cent, culminating at a point in *per capita* provision around three-quarters or four-fifths below that of the most ill-fed western European countries.[112] With peasant population swelling by 58 per cent (from 50 m. to 79 m.) between 1860 and 1897, while the cultivated acreage expanded by only 15 per cent, increasingly pressed agriculturalists found it difficult to attain subsistence production from existing plots yet confronted land prices which soared by more than 120 per cent between 1868/77 and 1888/97. The rural community was thus placed by the finance ministers, and especially by Witte, in an early version of the 'scissors'. On one side there were inflated tax and tariff burdens, rising rents and land prices, and the unvarying burden of redemption. On the other side there were falling receipts due to diminishing grain prices, and the great forced surrenders of grain to the state. By 1900 the result was that the most important sector of the economy both as employer, with 80 per cent of the population dependent upon it, and as contributor to national income, with half the total dependent on it, was virtually bankrupt. A system aimed at growth had succeeded, it appeared, only in cutting down the economy's most substantial support.

For agriculture the Witte system was a disaster. Where the French had responded tamely to agricultural interest groups and let sleepy peasants lie; where the German state demonstrated how to preserve a forceful agricultural sector within an advanced industrial economy, if at some cost; where, further afield, the Japanese state had provided classic instruction in the stimulation of peasant economy, Witte showed only what damage could be achieved by the *lack* of specifically tailored agricultural policies. Through the *obshchina* the autocracy employed the communal pressures for purposes which reversed the priorities of more constructive regimes − not to sponsor change but comprehensively to obstruct it. Through the redemption system, grain extraction, and fiscal levers, the state worked systematically to impoverish the majority of the agricultural population − a goal which could have no place amidst the individualist somnolence of the French countryside and one which even the unscrupulous Junkers would not have dared attempt. Through forcing a land-hungry peasantry to participate in a half-century-long real-estate transaction with a land-weary gentry, the autocracy connived at the rupture of the only available chain of command within Russian agriculture: the bond between lord and serf, broken in 1861, was given no successor. The actual tasks assigned to agriculture were the traditional ones: to stagnate, to remain subservient, to render tribute. And there was a wide band of conservationist opinion, parts of its very highly placed, which was determined, like its German counterpart, to maintain agriculture in these tasks, as the true base of Russian society. Even progressive thinkers were unusually affected by such views: the *narodniki*, for instance, believed that the venerable communal devices of the *mir* and *obshchina* would allow Russia to pass directly from agrarianism to socialism, avoiding the aberrational stage of urban capitalism. So widespread was the belief that the 'true base' of agriculture actually formed a substratum to society, to be kept where it belonged, at the bottom, in a position of subjection, that ideas aiming at the *development* of agriculture found themselves in foreign soil. Consequently, the bureaucracy issued, not agrarian policies, but politico-social policies inside agriculture. Nor, unlike their German counterparts, were these policies which envisaged agrarianism threatened by encroaching industrialism; rather, they saw the security of the state threatened by the agricultural mass, all too easily converted into a sickle-waving insurrection or a flag-waving proletariat. Limited by such social and political assumptions, finance ministers faced unenviable choices: effectively they could pursue economic goals without the participation of agriculture or they could pursue larger economic goals at the expense of agriculture.

However, economic, as distinct from politico-social, alternatives probably existed. No doubt the contrary is often argued, relying commonly on three assumptions: that, alongside foreign loans, agricultural 'surplus' constituted the only readily available source of investment credit for the autocracy; that exports from the primary sector provided the only means to finance imports of western capital goods; that forced savings marked for Russia the only path towards eventual industrial gains. But such proposals again assume that the pattern of advance was *economically* fixed, where, in fact, equally plausible models of humbler design would have lowered requirements both for agricultural exaction and for western technological imports. Moreover, the era of forced sacrifices for future gain proved a historical illusion. In 1914 agricultural commodities *still* provided five-sevenths of Russia's total exports, and, between 1900 and 1914, wheat alone constituted an average 48 per cent of exports. Manufactured products, in contrast, composed less than 8 per cent of total exports in 1914[113] (see Table 4.4). This was perhaps an overlong period – since 1888 – in which to be demanding agricultural forfeits in the name of future industrial prosperity. In principle, substitutes for the resource raid upon agriculture could have been found, and, as the post-1905 experience demonstrated, in practice some substitutes could entice cultivators into more positive responses. As so often, Witte's horizons were in fact circumscribed more closely by political than by economic parameters. Until such time as the wide range of conservative opinion was confronted by extreme social unrest and convinced that the existing agricultural system provoked more dissension than it suppressed, no amendment to the 1861 settlement could have commanded adequate political support. It was the capability of pre-1900 agricul-

ture to scrape a living and its failure to collapse entirely into patently dangerous subsistence crisis which held the political checks in place and prevented
the application of development policies to the rural sector. Under these conditions, Witte had little option but to recognize the limitations upon the possible: to maintain and extend the traditional work of extraction.

Table 4.4   Exports by category of commodity, as a percentage of total exports

	1894/98	1899/1903	1904/08	1909/13	1913	1914	1915
Foodstuffs	59.5	58.7	59.9	60.5	,55.2	54.7	50.2
Raw materials and semi-manufactures	34.9	34.4	33.0	33.2	36.9	36.5	36.0
Animal products	2.1	2.2	1.7	1.8	2.3	1.5	0.1
Manufactures	3.5	4.7	5.4	4.5	5.6	7.3	13.7

Source: Miller (1926), p. 46n.

Yet, despite the qualifications, the record insists that Witte's intentions
were eventually frustrated by the coincidence of severe strains in two policy
areas: foreign investment and agriculture. If the end-of-century international
tensions served to cut Russia's vital credit lines, the bad harvest of 1897 and
the famine of 1899 finally drained the agricultural reserves of taxable income.
With its two main sources of funds interrupted, the gambler's wheel slowed.
Witte did not finally relinquish the table until 1903, but from the moment
in 1899 when he felt it necessary to reduce railway expenditure – an orthodox
retrenching error according to Barkai[114] – the 'Witte system' was effectively
shut down. At least six years of recession involving widespread strikes, plentiful bankruptcies, and frequent insurrection provided emphatic confirmation of
its closure.

The schedule of achievements is a mixed one. The railway programmes
forming the system's central supports had been vigorously promoted but had
encountered military limitations. Errors had been made with the management
of the capital goods industries, but, here again, manufacturing requirements
had collided with political imperatives. In contrast, Witte's financial policies
had contained brilliant touches of manipulation and held a fast course through
troubled waters. His reliance upon foreign capital had not achieved such
equilibrium, but was in principle a logical sequel to the choice of industrial
policy. In agriculture, where politico-social impediments were greatest and the
room for promotion least, the new policies merely offered an improved institutionalization of rapacity. None of these devices were especially innovational:
the emphasis on railway development was taken from Reutern, the state's
responsibility for key sectors from Bunge, the tariffs and the tactics of extortion from Vyshnegradskii. Within a broader tradition, the 'Witte system'
could be seen as yet another instalment of 'developmental serfdom', blending
economic advance and social aggression in the approved Russian style. Perhaps
the sole novelty was the manner in which the various elements were combined

and focused sharply upon the objective of industrialization, and in the clear-sighted administrative ruthlessness of the implementation. However, in terms of economic performance, results varied from sector to sector: financial policy, for instance, emerged as more intelligently constructed than industrial policy. Between sectors, the major shared characteristic was the damaging role played by *non-economic* forces. In the end, the contest between the reformist ambitions of the tiny bureaucratic élite and the reactionary inclinations of the majority echelons within the state apparatus was resolved in favour of the latter.

Efforts were made by the modernizers to escape the autocratic bonds and even, by wielding economic power as a curb on ill-considered political reflexes, to reverse the traditional nexus. Witte's schemes for international disarmament and his independent diplomatic initiatives (amounting on occasion to careful 'releases' of Russian war plans) were characteristic of this process. Unfortunately, such tactics were self-limiting, since interference with the fixed preferences of the tsarist system led inevitably to a conservative backlash. Growth-conscious officials were necessarily encouraged to prize away the political barnacles, but the margin of error was very small and the ship of state harshly unforgiving to an excessively reformist helm. Even such political counter-manœuvring as Witte attempted attracted great hostility and to have done more – for instance to press the cause of agrarian reform – would merely have precipitated an earlier crisis. As it was, Witte's downfall was certainly in part due to a 'financial policy [which] encroached too much upon Russian policy in general'.[115]

However, the boundaries of Witte's success were not only defined by external pressures; assumptions internal to the system proved equally confining. It was, for instance, unsatisfactory to require that state power should lay a path for enterprise in a society with a chronically low regard for business achievement. Unsurprisingly, the response was deficient, dragging the state into a more *dirigiste* role and further away from the intended 'mixed' model of state capitalism. Similarly, the belief that industrialization *could* be pursued within the unmodified tsarist superstructure led to a discount being placed upon the necessary underpinnings in social engineering and educational provision. Although Witte expanded technical education (increasing the number of technical schools from 8 to 100, 1894–1904), and increased investment in elementary schools helped to drive the literacy rate upwards (from 22 per cent in 1880 to 68 per cent in 1913 as measured among military recruits),[116] the quality of the provision and the level of official commitment both remained low. Expenditure on elementary schools during the Witte era (150 m. roubles) made up only one-eighth of the amount spent on the railroads. The virtually unqualified insistence upon agricultural underdevelopment and heavy industrial overdevelopment – even allowing for political constraints[117] – suggests an economic scenario lacking in subtlety.

The concept of growth underlying these assumptions is, perhaps necessarily, simplistic: it deals in primary colours (rapid growth; large-scale industries; heavy plant) and extreme options (a looted agriculture; huge tariffs); there is little shading or compromise; useful tinkering is discounted in favour of dramatic gestures. Generally, Witte's system travelled far and fast but not sufficiently deeply into Russian economy and society. Partly the values of the regime prevented it from doing so, partly the selection of methodology was autonomous, following from the poorly developed state of the economic art at the end of the nineteenth century. Experience has proved that selective methods of state intervention based upon capitalistic participation (the sole recipe available to Witte) can offer little answer to problems of severe backwardness; the most comprehensive planning methods of the modern bureaucratic state are scarcely equal to these puzzles. Strong elements of anachronism inevitably pervade the 'Witte system', therefore: many of its stresses arose from attempts to confront issues for which the remedies had not yet emerged. As Prince Mencherskii acutely saw, 'Witte [was] an insufficiently contemporary Minister of Finance, and too much a future one'.[118] In this interpretation, close to von Laue's vision of Witte as a 'precursor of Stalin', the developmental tsar was precocious in the scope of his economic vision but equipped with the all too frail economic instruments of his day.

However, more fundamentalist renderings are possible. The 'Witte system' can be seen merely as a pragmatic approach to certain easily perceived developmental tasks. Heavy finishing industries were selected for growth only because these were the technologies most obviously displayed by the successful economies of the time. Surplus was extracted from agriculture because, as a resource bank for the secondary sector, it was the nearest to hand, the most familiar, and seemingly the most logical contender. The extraction was forcible because, for the autocracy, this was the most traditional, acceptable, and dependable manner of accumulating resources. Coercive methods predominated simply because coercive power was the least complicated form of power available to the nineteenth-century state. The bureaucracy both better understood how, and was better equipped, to coerce than to construct. And the less advanced the bureaucracy, the more attractive became the policies of coercion as against those of economic calculation. Consistent with this interpretation is the revisionist assessment of the Witte system put forward by J. P. McKay. Where both Witte's admirers and detractors formerly accepted that his policies constituted some form of developmental plan – whether they commend or condemn, they assume it to be a systematic design – McKay suggests a less structured approach in which Witte's programme ceases to be a comprehensive economic plan and becomes instead, 'a well organised and resourceful . . . *public relations campaign*'[119] to encourage private enterprise. This valuation removes the state from the position of economic director and places it on the periphery of economic activity: since it does not possess the instruments to elicit growth, and indigenous enterprise does not have the ability, it constitutes itself a lure for an external body of developmental expertise. On this reading, the paraphernalia of *dirigisme* – the government contracts, the tariffs, the gold standard – are not components in an economic grand strategy but diplomatic ruses designed to create an attractive and reassuring environment for the foreign industrialists who are to be the real architects of Russia's industrialization. The contrived budgetary equilibrium, the dashing counter-speculations, the glossy circulars strewn across the European exchanges compose a propaganda displaying Russia's golden opportunities to the world's investors and entrepreneurs. Coercion at home, financial diplomacy abroad represent a tactical combination which might plausibly fall within the competence of a late-nineteenth-century government. Certainly, this assessment ascribes to the 'Witte system' a proper flavour of its time and does not require that the 1890s should have witnessed the untimely manifestation of a Stalinist spirit intent upon a preview of the Five Year Plans.

RECESSION, REVOLUTION AND RECOVERY

The economics of repression and foreign dependence contained sufficient dangers of their own: modesty of design did not protect the 'Witte system' from final and rapid decay. As Margaret Miller detected, Witte's policies were perennially committed to 'speculating in futures'.[120] Ultimately, the railways would pay their way and the foreign technologies strike indigenous roots, but, in the interim, there was the risk that the state's exactions would 'outrun the stage to which the sentiments of the people had attained'[121] – a very delicate description of revolution. By the early 1900s those sentiments were very strained. Harvest crises at length combined with rural pauperization to light the insurrectionary fires which the *obshchina* was supposed to prevent. For the first time since 1861, the agricultural rampage of 1900–2 and 1905 gave shape to the recurrent tsarist nightmare, while the rural poor left the shape of their grievance in no doubt: they seized gentry land for grazing, gentry timber for fuel, gentry houses for bonfires, spectacle, and protests. At the same time, strikes broke out in the Don industrial region and by 1903 the Empire was strikebound from Kiev to Baku. Underlying these outbreaks was an economic situation of considerable gloom. In agriculture, debt, taxation, overpopulation, and famine provided a ready explanation for the disruption. In industry, the starvation of foreign capital bore down upon producers almost as savagely as the dearth of grain upon the rural community. During 1902, the worst year, some 2400 industrial concerns closed down, including one-third of the mining ventures at Krivoi Rog, and one-quarter of the country's largest metal producers.[122] The average annual rate of growth fell to a point 82 per cent below the pre-crisis level,[123] while industrial unemployment rose to the novel heights of 90,000.

Share prices declined spectacularly, those of the Donets coal concerns, for instance, sliding from 680 to 210 on the exchanges. As rural *jacqueries*, industrial strife, and production failure combined, the populace showed their disapproval in traditional style: the Minister of the Interior, Sipiagin, and the Minister of Education, Bogoliepov, were assassinated. Lacking Witte's pacific – if meddlesome – diplomacy, Russia sought Plehve's remedy of the 'victorious little war' against the Japanese in 1904, and met disaster. Admiral Togo's elegant destruction of the imperial fleet at Tsushima was not only a blow to the autocracy's international prestige but also a threat to its domestic security. Incensed by the savagery of military repression in the countryside, and by military ineffectiveness in the Far East, angered by the failure of Russian arms, and the expense of maintaining them, the disaffected populace combined to extend riot, strike, and the odd assassination into fully fledged revolution. By the time its tide had reached flood and begun to ebb, in December 1905, some £200 m. in damage had been suffered. With such events for an epilogue it might indeed seem, as Henry Adams believed, that the Witte era composed merely, 'ten or fifteen years of violent stimulus . . . resulting in nothing'.[124]

The implication of this remark is that the Witte experiment was consistent with earlier attempts at modernization within a determinedly reactionary empire: all tended to fail amidst dramatic upheaval and resurgent backwardness. But such assessments are based upon a misreading of the period 1900–06. For all their dislocations, these years did not witness a reimposition of backwardness, nor could they easily have done so. By 1900 considerable new industrial possessions – the metallurgical works of the Ukraine, the oil wells of Baku, the shipyards and engineering works of the Baltic littoral – had been superimposed upon the more traditional attributes of the central textile-manufacturing provinces and the Urals mining regions. The new furnaces recaptured an extra 5 per cent of world iron output, 1880–1900; the new oil installations surpassed all other producers for a brief moment around 1900; the new engineering shops could meet all the Empire's railway requirements and begin to meet its industrial requirements. If the country remained a predominantly agricultural swamp, industry could provide points of solidity, fit to serve as foundations for later manufacturing constructions, and even under the flux of recession, many of these points remained solid. If the heavy industrial concentrations suffered, they mostly weathered the onslaught, and, in the meanwhile, proved that they did not provide the only supports for the manufacturing economy. Despite the general downswing, profits in the oil industry continued to rise. The few embryonic advanced technologies like chemicals and electric power remained active. Lighter manufactures like textiles experienced only a temporary check to their fortunes and recovered rapidly. Even the coal-mines managed to make ground against imported supplies. All producers faced deflationary pressures, but the Russian price fall was little worse than the British, American, or German, and these countries were not brought to ruin in the early 1900s. Naturally, the infant Russian manufacturing economy had less resilience than its western competitors, and the psychological impact of recession upon its apprentice industrialists was probably larger *pro tanto*. Certainly, the opposition which the 'Witte system' had attracted from both intelligentsia and backwoodsmen discovered additional justification, while the hostility of the peasant community to all forms of official policy was greatly strengthened. But still the economy retained strong reflexes for growth: the industrial performance of the period 1906–14, resuming production at the substantial pace of 6 per cent p.a., gave the measure of these longer-running capabilities, the more so since this output record was achieved against a *declining* trend of direct institutional participation by the post-Witte Finance Ministry.

The period 1900–6 thus forms a hiatus or caesura in the Russian growth process; it does not bring Witte's policies to total destruction, nor prevent their legacy being transmitted to a successor-economy of strength and viability; it does not whistle in backwardness nor deliver the usual, derisory curtain-call to the traditional Russian development-play. As Lenin fully realized, the Witte era had accumulated equipment and expertise which could not be expunged merely by a cyclical downturn. Probably, Russia experienced not a single industrial revolution, but discreet *periods* of industrial transformation, and of these periods, the years of induced development, 1892–1903, and of autonomous development, 1906–14, were important examples. Witte's achievement was to preside throughout the period in which Russia was first turned decisively towards industrialism, and, by that count, a period which can be compared with the years of rapid advance in the 1930s and after 1950 as a critical formative phase in the maturation of the Russian economy.

1905–14: THE LAST PROFITS OF TSARDOM

The economic system which spanned the period between revolution and world war was an unusual one in Russian, and in global, history, and no close cousin to its predecessor of the 1890s. Its prime objective, the maintenance rather than the initiation of technological advance – even if under adverse circumstances – was a comparatively modest one, but the fulfilment of this task was to represent the last chance for the capitalist economy in free-market Russia. Further, this opportunity was seized with an energy uncharacteristic of earlier business activity and the market was suspended between the *dirigisme* of the Witte state and the *dirigisme* of the Soviet state in an interlude of rare liberation. For growth in this period, although borrowing much of its momentum from Witte's achievements, depended to a much lesser degree upon measures of state promotion, the tactic of 'substitution' favoured by Witte declining after 1906 for want of an authoritative sponsor. In consequence, a series of major questions hang over this period: firstly, to what extent were the 'substitutes' of the 1890s now supplanted by the development of the originals for which they had acted as proxies, the autonomously generated 'prerequisites' arriving belatedly upon the Russian scene?; secondly, to what extent did the Russian economy desert its special authoritarian or 'dominant' development pattern and approximate more closely to a 'western', or perhaps, in imitation of the foremost continental producer, to 'German' patterns?;[125] thirdly, to what extent did tsardom neglect each of these alternatives, and discover instead an institutional *replacement* for the state as controller of economic development?

The areas in which pre- (or post-) requisites may have emerged are fairly clear. Changes in agriculture, introduced as sequel to the revolutionary outbreaks of 1904–05, could have provided opportunities for a genuine, if incipient, transformation in the primary sector, involving amendments in tenure, cultivation, and factor mobility. A measure of native entrepreneurial development could have followed upon the educational improvements sponsored by Witte and the demonstration effects provided by foreign industrialists. In turn, this might logically have issued in improved tactics of business organization. Finally, the induced rise of capital-intensive industry during the 1890s might logically have drawn into existence as a post-requisite, the financial auxiliaries of a modern investment banking system. In a subsequent growth phase this apparatus might itself convert to a growth-leading role, and, in so doing, bring an element of 'Germanized' *bankinitiative* to the direction of the tsarist system.

AGRICULTURE 1905–14: THE RISE (AND CYCLICAL FALL) OF AN INNOVATIONAL PEASANTRY

Equal measures of energetic face-saving and silent, if almost total capitulation, comprised the autocracy's early answer to the agrarian revolt. Surrender was not quite entire: the most persistent insurrectionary demand aimed at the comprehensive redistribution of all agricultural land, especially noble land, and although this came close to realization in the winter of 1905–06 – with a distraught regime drafting the requisite legislation[126] – the autocracy in the end contrived an evasion. In the following spring, with the imperial soldiery proving themselves more of a match for ill-disciplined incendiaries than for Japanese infantry, the state was able to shelve its desperate concession and leave the issue of redistribution to await Lenin's attention in 1917. However, before this belated success in peacekeeping, the government had retreated at almost every point. The Imperial Manifesto of February 1903 deplored the disturbances which 'hindered attempts to improve popular welfare', pledged continuing support for the *obshchina* – and then abolished the commune's joint responsibility for taxation, generally regarded as one of its indispensable supports.[127] Similarly, the decree which followed the General Strike of October 1905, thundered out the penalties for violence, and then rewarded violence by initiating the abolition of the redemption system (at an eventual cost to the exchequer of 80 m. roubles in sacrificed repayments).[128] Still more damaging to the regime, was the renunciation of the *obshchina*: a mere two years after the Tsar had named the peasantry a perpetual estate, the single institution of immutable agrarian subjection lay under sentence of dissolution. After 1905 the traditional interpretation of the *obshchina* as a collective security system offering viability to breadline communities was no longer tenable: insurrection finally supplied the necessary proof that communal practice generated land-hunger and disaffection rather than equilibrium and docility. At this point, since even reactionary opinion possessed direct interest in swiftly relinquishing a pacifier now turned powder-keg, the prerequisite for agrarian reform was at length fulfilled: in November 1906 Prime Minister Stolypin was able effectively to dismantle the communal system amidst very nearly general approval.

The results were far more radical than any achieved by the provisions of the emancipation settlement. With the peasant able to choose his place of residence and allotment land subject to sale as private property, the way was opened, for the first time in Russian history, towards independent cultivation for the market by small' but integrated peasant farmsteads. Communal plots could now be transferred to individual ownership and scattered strips grouped into coherent holdings upon formal demand from the household head. If the demand was made at the time of scheduled repartition the commune could only accede; if it were made at another time the commune could retain control of the strips upon payment of compensation to the peasant; if the transaction concerned land which had escaped repartition since 1887, the transfer to individual ownership was automatic. All such emergency provisions were codified into law by 1910, constituting, at least superficially, a charter for successful cultivation by an independent peasantry.[129]

But by the time the charter was compiled the autocracy had emerged from its humiliated posture of 1903–05. It had denied the peasantry their chief objective – land redistribution – and forced them to settle for second best. By 1906 Stolypin could bend concession to the government's advantage and insist upon 'order before reform': martial law and punitive expeditions preceded land reorganization for many a discontented province. Even the substantial peasant, chief beneficiary of the reform, was induced to do the government's work: a cleverly formulated 'wager on the strong' sufficed to create a prosperous rural echelon whose property-owning interest succeeded the *obshchina* as the regime's antidote to unrest in the villages.[130] Certainly, the Stolypin measures did not favour all peasant groups equally. Small cultivators received merely a chance to convert their holdings into cash and thence into a ticket of passage for the city. Their rapid exodus from the villages – with 72 per cent of departures in 1906–14 falling within the short period 1908–10[131] – graphically illustrates the impossibility of viable cultivation for the lesser peasantry. Middling peasants did not fare much better: rather than face the twin uncertainties of single-handed farming or urban employment, they huddled within the scattered debris of the communes[132] – particularly in central, eastern, and south-eastern regions – until Stalin completed the work of destruction in 1928. It was towards the remaining minority – the 2½ m. households who requested consolidation between 1907 and 1914, the 24 per cent of household heads who constituted themselves independent farmers in European Russia by 1915 – that the reforms were angled and the benefits directed (see Table 4.5). It was in its emphasis upon this group that the Stolypin reform proclaimed itself, like its predecessors, a policy of the autocracy rather than a policy of the peasantry. For the measures of the 1900s were as heavily encrusted with *kulak* interests as the measures of the 1860s with gentry interests – and in each case the security of the tsarist superstructure was the prime objective of the governmental reformers.

In economic terms, however, the Stolypin settlement suffered much less damage by its autocratic origins than did the legislation of the 1860s. For the

Table 4.5   The rise of independent peasant farming as proportion of all peasant households

% In private hereditary tenure by 1907	% Leaving the commune in European Russia 1905–16	% In private hereditary tenure by 1 Jan. 1917	% Remaining in communal tenure by 1 Jan. 1917	% Farming new enclosed holdings by 1 Jan. 1917
c.20	24[a]	51[b] 52[c]	49[b]	10.5[d]

Note: The total number of households was 14 m. on 1 Jan. 1917.

Sources: [a] Lyashchenko (1970), p. 748.   [b] Pershin (1925), p. 324.   [c] Robinson (1932), Ch. 11   [d] Pershin (1922), p. 7.

period 1907–14 can present real claims as one of the very few phases of successful agricultural advance recorded in Russia before the 1950s. And, given the continued degeneration of the gentry – if not of some aristocratic – estates, it was a success largely, and, for Russia, uniquely, created by a free peasant agriculture, an economic system unknown before 1905 and impossible after 1917.

The classic formula for a productive peasant agriculture – applied in the nineteenth century most brilliantly by the Japanese and the Danes – contains a number of essential terms: sufficient credit provision to finance peasant requirements in land, fertilizers, animals, or implements; a supply of innovations suitable for small-plot cultivation; a means of publicizing these innovations; a level of rural literacy sufficient to ensure that the innovations may be understood. Before 1905, tsarist agrarian policy supplied little in the way of such assistance; after 1905 its reserve began gradually to thaw.

Official efforts in credit provision were of the longest standing and accumulated to substantial dimensions in the pre-war period. After a rather ineffectual start in the 1880s, the Peasant Land Bank was permitted by a revision of statutes in 1895 to advance funds to communes, peasant groups, or individual peasants for land purchases, or, alternatively, to acquire land for later resale in the peasant market. During the disturbances of the 1900s, its lending power was almost doubled and between 1905 and 1907, in a determined campaign to assuage peasant land-hunger, its plot acquisitions were increased by half and its Peasant Land Fund extended by a factor of eight. In 1906 the autocracy further topped up its acreage reserves by donations of appanage, state and cabinet domains. But the most important development in the bank's short history came in a radical change of lending pattern after 1905: credit supplies were distributed during the 1890s so as to give communes a 56 per cent share, peasant groups 42 per cent and individual peasants only 1.3 per cent; by 1913 these allocations had swung about to give individuals 87 per cent, communes and groups a shared 6.4 per cent.[133] Since the poorer peasantry could not afford even the 10 per cent of the land price left uncovered by the bank advances, transactions concentrated overwhelmingly upon the more substantial cultivators selected as the spearhead of Stolypin's policy. Nor did this group profit simply from the refashioning of Land Bank credit. A parallel expansion among small rural banks offering complementary services, mostly modest finance for the purchase of livestock or equipment, also looked to the higher peasantry for custom. These institutions assisted not only in the production of the crop but also in its sale, frequently pitching the transaction in regions of grain deficit. For the peasantry these intermediaries became agents both of technical improvement – through the financing of methods previously forgone for lack of cash – and of economic improvement – by liberating the peasant crop from the tyrannous monopsony of the local grain factor. The evolution of these petty credit institutions or popular co-operative banks proceeded slowly down to 1905 and with extreme rapidity thereafter; fifty years of development had produced only 1,629 institutions by the year of revolution; a further decade took the total to 14,502 and the clientele to 9 m. households. Proof of the government's newly creative agrarian policies was provided by its relationship with the rural banks: balances from the state coffers were transferred to the co-operatives and their central financial organ, the Moscow Narodny Bank (1912), while in 1910 a special section of the State Bank was created to deal directly with the 'peasant banks'. The forthright extension of the credit arm into the pre-revolutionary countryside was one of its most promising features, a notable innovation releasing peasant cultivation from constraints both of supply and demand.[134]

Care was taken by the state to ensure that the new credit flows found suitably efficient customers. Its Committee of Land Reorganization, created in 1906 to supervise the consolidation of all holdings acquired by the Land Bank and to provide mediation upon all issues of consolidation and between all classes of landlord, worked with some success to encourage the enclosure and integration of plots separated from the communes: by 1916, 60 per cent of all transferred allotments had been consolidated to various degrees and in a process which was steady and even, showing little tendency to fall away.[135] The autonomous small farm (khutor), under Russian conditions a considerable novelty, now became the highest form of consolidation; under Stolypin's terms it ranked as the preferred client of the credit agencies and represented at least one form of agricultural progress to which the autocracy had reconciled itself. Although the regime by no means became avid for agricultural innovation, there were also signs of decreasing hostility elsewhere. If the Japanese-style promotion of 'best practice' cultivation found little replication within the empire, some advance in agronomic sensitivity is suggested by the increase in the numbers of agricultural experts attached to the Ministries of Justice and Agriculture from 210 in 1906 to 12,600 in 1914.[136] Contact between peasants and specialists had become a 'mass phenomenon' by 1914, according to the great agricultural analyst, A. V. Chayanov.[137]

No doubt, the measure of change actually achieved by official sponsorship was modest, but the supply of advice did flow in the same direction as the peasantry's responsiveness to changed opportunities, itself surprisingly positive. When permitted a freer rein, the more substantial cultivators rose well above the witless earth-scratchers of legend: they proved able to extract multiple crop rotations and a grass harvest from their consolidated holdings and to convert their new credit supplies into extra draft power, improved tools, and, most importantly, into fertilizer. As the Japanese had shown, large inputs of fertilizer formed the most effective connexion between small plots and high yields. The rapid increases in Russian manure imports after 1905 – from 0.2 m. poods in 1904 through 7.3 m. in 1907 to 27 m. in 1912[138] – suggests that something of this relationship was grasped in pre-war Russia, if on a much smaller scale. Even among the higher agricultural technologies some progress was recorded. Although the value of agricultural machinery employed by each peasant household still averaged only a single rouble's worth in 1911, the sale of equipment from *zemstvo* stores after 1905 had displayed the upswing characteristic of the period – from 6¾ m. roubles in 1907 to a value of over twelve billion roubles in 1911 (compare Table 4.6). Certainly, the behaviour of agricultural output is consistent with an improvement in the quality of cultivation: the index rises far more steeply in the decade after 1905 than in the decade before, from 88.1 in 1895 to 104.5 in 1905 and thence to 149.5 in 1910 and 166.7 in 1913 (1900 = 100).[139] Bumper harvests were frequent in the years immediately before the First World War, and the marketing of cereals by farmers expanded in matching style. Metzer's calculations reveal a larger advance in the commercialization of major grains, measured by the percentage of the harvest sent as rail freight, between the half-decades 1901–05 and 1906–10 than between any comparable periods since 1878 (see Table 4.7). His revisionist conclusion that, 'the realization of these gains reveal that the rural sector in the late Tsarist Russia was indeed respon-

Table 4.6 Imports of agricultural machinery into Russia (tons)

1886	4,097
1890	7,520
1900	38,035
1907	74,603
1908	67,780
1909	100,000

Source: Kennard (1911), p. 272

Table 4.7 Shipments of major grains as proportion of harvest (%)

	Metzer estimate	Lyashchenko estimate
1878–85	28.6	
1886–90	30.3	17.2
1891–95	30.8	17.6
1896–1900	32.8	20.5
1901–05	37.0	21.4
1906–10	42.3	27.2
1911–13		18.5

Source: Metzer (1974), p. 544; Lyashchenko (1970) p. 517.

sive to economic opportunity and behaved rationally, economically speaking'
will stand as a general summary of the improved possibilities for peasant agriculture, at least of the post-Stolypin period.[140]

If this amelioration of rural production did indeed involve a significant
proportion of the peasant community, some detectable upturn in farm
prosperity might be anticipated. Rough indicators both of peasant savings and
peasant consumption duly confirm this possibility. Assets entrusted by small
cultivators to the petty credit institutions achieved phenomenal growth in the
post-revolutionary period: while total deposits reached only 7 m. roubles in
1905, far inferior to the 77 m. held by the ordinary savings banks, the figure
had soared to 73 m. by 1912, easily surpassing the diminished total of 61 m.
roubles now deposited with the non-agricultural savings institutions.[141] Similarly, the Post Office Savings Banks, designed to dip the rural pool, experienced a 'vast increase' in deposits, even at reduced interest rates. The majority
of all Russian savers were small-scale depositors, but by 1912 the rural saver
was less small than his urban counterpart, salting away an average nest-egg of
190 roubles against the townsman's 173 roubles.[142] Significantly, the rural
savings institutions were most developed in regions with a high count of
independent peasants, particularly in the south which, according to Margaret
Miller, witnessed a 'mass transition to the individual system of land-
holding'.[143] Naturally, peasant consumption is even more difficult to measure
satisfactorily, but evidence exists of increased purchasing both in light
manufactures and in grains. Particularly compelling are the marketing indicators for rye, the preferred peasant cereal: the share of the domestic market in
the total rye trade was by 1910 much greater than its cut of the total wheat
trade (83.9% against 61.3%) and the commercialization of rye advanced faster
than that of wheat between 1901–5 and 1906–10.[144] The commonly encountered argument that Russian agriculture in the decades before 1914 advanced only in quantitative terms, raising more crop but doing so within a
fixed cultivation structure, therefore probably underrates both the enterprise
and the prosperity developing among the larger peasantry.

In the brief interlude before war intervened, these new capabilities began to
generate in agriculture the classical transfer surpluses for the manufacturing
sector. Unprecedented mobility of labour resources was achieved: the flight of
the lesser peasantry supplied a workforce for both urban and craft manufacture. And it was a workforce sufficiently numerous to permit the first substantial exploitation of labour-intensive processes, mitigating the earlier dependence upon capital-intensive heavy manufactures. Rising farm efficiency, coupled with excellent harvests down to 1913, also began to provide 'non-
artificial' food surpluses, most dramatically displayed in the record grain export figures (847 m. poods) for the bonanza year 1909. And, not least, the
strengthening rural prosperity laid the foundations for expansion in the
domestic consumer market. The abolition of redemption liabilities alone do-
nated a 15 per cent increase in purchasing power to some 160 m. consumers
between 1906 and 1910,[145] and increased agricultural receipts further fat-
tened pocket-books. Industrial response to this swelling demand came, logi-

cally enough, from the craft manufactories closest to the rural sector: *kustar* production expanded to account for about 30 per cent of total manufacturing output by 1914.[146] In sum, a much-needed broadening of the Russian economic base may be traced from the agricultural advances of the post-Stolypin period. What is more, growth on a wider front derived not from the forced draft, familiar in the Empire's experience, but from autonomous changes associated with consumer industries, widening markets and employment, and accelerating urbanization. This proliferating economic activity is very clearly revealed in the marked acceleration in railway traffic between 1905 and 1913 (see Table 4.8). Such a mixture might readily imply a 'normalization' or 'Westernization' of Russian growth patterns.

Table 4.8 Increase in railway traffic by category of commodity, 1905–1913

Commodity	% Increase
Coal	118.5
Ores	142.4
Iron manufactures	116.4
Petroleum	17.5
Building material	166.7
Manufactures	40.8
Cotton	57.6
Hemp and flax	23.3
Cereals	34.1
Oil seeds	83.4

Source: Miller (1926), p. 210.

Nor need optimistic or revisionist assessments of the post-1905 era necessarily stop at the socio-political barrier, as many have done. Further progress has, of course, long been impeded by the stern guardianship of Lenin, since, in his concept of the differentiation of the peasantry, the Bolshevik ideologue appropriated Stolypin's 'wager on the strong' as a convenient means both of crystallizing the distinctions and widening the fissures between the various agricultural ranks.[147] It followed from this increasing polarization of interest that any economic utility attained by Stolypin's remedies was cancelled by their cataclysmic political implications: the introduction of class war into the countryside and the kindling of resentments which would eventually blow the autocracy apart. However, alternative explanations have been available for many years and have recently enjoyed forceful and imaginative restatement.[148] In broad terms, these assessments suggest that no peasant category in pre-war Russia – neither the strong nor any other – ever constituted a coherent class or was composed over time of a relatively fixed selection of households or families. Instead, the membership of such categories was subject to 'multidirectional and cyclical processes of socio-economic mobility',[149] that is, it was highly fluid, with families typically passing through several categories at various points in their career. When family size was small and its average age low, the household struggled with plots, capitals and income which were all modest. But as family size and age increased – carrying more children into the productive bracket – more land could be worked and leased, more capital employed, more income generated. Eventually, the household reached its zenith of age, work-capability, and prosperity. But soon after this point, the new adults deserted to commence their own families; the property was divided (frequently before the parents' death); and the life-cycle recommenced. Consequently, a household which at an early stage in its growth might command only the 0–3 dessiatines of cultivated land normally available to the lesser peasantry could, by an upward mobility unimpeded by rank barriers, attain *kulak* status at a later point, farming perhaps 25 dessiatines, leasing land and hiring labour.

Ever since the work of the neo-populist school at the beginning of this century, through that of the Organisation of Production theorists of the 1920s – pre-eminently Chayanov – down to the modern protagonists like Crisp and Shanin, this basic model has found firm advocates. What to their Marxist-Leninist opponents is a property table displaying peasant differentiation, is to these observers a frozen dynamic, a fixed schedule of assorted households which were, in reality, not fixed at all but busily passing different bench-marks in their careers. If their alternative view is correct – and their statistical results demonstrate very high correlations between sown area, family size, family age, and income – important political consequences follow. When *kulak* or 'strong' peasant status is a function of family size and age rather than of transmitted privilege, and the chance of attaining that status is open to younger and poorer households, the prospects for class war and potentially explosive social frictions are much reduced; inter-generational rivalry, though likely, is scarcely of the same order. Any agricultural upheaval which did occur within this system would require a more proximate and shattering detonation directed at the entire rural community, though no doubt impacting with special intensity upon the currently least protected. In the crises of 1905–6 and 1917–20, as Shanin emphasizes, it was the unanimity and not the frictional divergence of peasant responses which was remarkable: between 1905 and 1907 only 1.4 per cent of agrarian disturbances involved outbreaks of inter-peasant warfare and the '*kulak* uprising' of 1917–19 proved equally insubstantial.[150] Within these terms, the Stolypin reforms may be relieved of the conventional political costs; their economic virtues are not jeopardized by the revolutionary's time bomb planted next to their heart.

The cumulative effect of the research conducted by Millar, Crisp, Metzer, and Shanin, when combined with longer-running observations, is to suggest an upward reappraisal of agricultural performance in the final tsarist years. However, like all optimistic valuations of Russian economic achievement it must not go too far. Renovation and innovation affected only a minority of agricultural producers; the larger part of the countryside remained as intransigent as ever; and the great numbers of middling peasantry who clung to the withered stalks of the commune provided a universal summary of peasant conservatism. For their part, the gentry muddled on, sold up, or went broke, while the largest cultivators with estates over 1,000 hectares were reduced in number to less than 10,000 by 1905.[151] In turn, the agricultural bourgeoisie could not expand sufficiently fast, nor lay its hands on sufficient land to make a difference.

Statistical testing may also suggest a certain *lenteur* in the pace of change. However pronounced the rural exodus after 1905, for instance, the surrender of agricultural labour between 1880 and 1913 was still distinctly modest by the standards of economies undergoing 'modern economic growth' (MEG) and the rural labour share in 1913 remained close to the level of the pre-modern economies. Similarly, despite cultivatory improvements, the gap in labour productivity between agriculture and industry *widened* substantially throughout the period 1880–1913 and at its end the indifferent productivity performance of the countryside (an annual growth rate in labour productivity of 0.3 per cent p.a. 1880–1913 compared with 2.7 per cent p.a. in manufacturing) persisted as a deadweight dragging down the economy-wide productivity growth rate.[152] Nevertheless, there is little point in allowing unchanging elements to entirely obscure developments of genuine and unusual promise. With all allowance made, it remains reasonable to argue that *by comparison with Russia's own agricultural past* (perhaps a more worthwhile yardstick than that of MEG), the period 1907–14 brought a rare enlightenment to the rural landscape, removing some of its most restrictive conventions and bestowing upon it at least some of the characteristics of a growth-supporting agriculture. If it was not transformed, it was at least usefully modified.

ENTREPRENEURSHIP: RUSSIFICATION AND TRUSTIFICATION

After 1905, according to one recent interpretation, the large-scale industrialists of Russian origin were 'aroused from their traditional quiescence' and transformed into 'an active public force, vigorously debating economic issues and propounding policies in the common interest'.[153] If so, the period before 1914 must have witnessed not only modifications in the supply of agricultural products but also in the supply of businessmen. For, ever since 1890, and before, the bulk of managerial initiatives within the heavy technologies had emanated not from native groups but from the foreigners recruited by Reutern and Witte. True, home-grown entrepreneurial prospects were arising with increasing frequency in other fields. The emergence of a prosperous and generously proportioned cotton textile industry proved the existence of Russian business talents. And in the craft or *kustar* sector, the slight relaxation of the *obshchina's* hold in the 1890s, its seams creaking under the pressures of overpopulation, provided renewed opportunities for the peasant-industrialists, natural descendants of Rosovsky's serf-entrepreneurs. After several decades of retreatism, the emergence of the *tysyachnik* hinted at a resumed expansion of rural capitalism in Russia. By 1900, for example, one such venturer had secured control of twenty manufacturing villages in Kostroma province and set their production of wooden implements on a business footing. Similar, if less ambitious, activists were to be found supervising the fabrication of nets, wheels, and sleds in Yaroslavl or Nizhni-Novgorod, nails, locks, and knives around Tula or Vladimir.[154] And even beyond the world of cotton mills and cottage crafts, the heavy industries did not form prohibited terrain for all imperial citizens. Thus the Poles, usually as engineers, and the Jews, usually as commercial and financial managers, had infiltrated even the most modern plants by 1900. The southern industrial region was subjected to a veritable invasion of Polish engineers during the 1890s and, by the end of the decade, two of its most important metallurgical concerns, the Dnieper and the Nikupol-Mariupol, sported wholly Polish managements.[155] Frequently, however, as minorities much discriminated against, these 'deviant' capitalists needed to win their initial promotion at the hands of enlightened foreign employers. With that qualification, it appears that the Russian entrepreneurial community of 1900 did indeed contain groups deserving of advancement. Their further progress depended primarily upon expansion in consumer demand – increasing opportunities for the lighter technologies – and improvements in 'technological literacy' – qualifying native managers for the heavier manufactures.

Before 1905 these conditions were not fully satisfied and the foreigners remained in possession, especially of the capital goods industries. Of the fourteen major steel-producing concerns created in southern Russia between 1888 and 1900, for instance, all but one involved heavy foreign participation.[156] And what was true of steel was only slightly less true of coal – where in 1899 three-quarters of Russia's soft coal was raised by fifteen companies, ten of them foreign;[157] of shipbuilding – where foreigners supervised almost every yard from Riga to Odessa; and of engineering. Typically the alien entrepreneurial presence consisted of foreign graduates from leading continental engineering schools who had earned promotion within Russian-based firms. Certain Russian plants like the Huta-Bankova or Donetz Steel in metallurgy or, in coal, the Rutchenko and Gorlovka mines, acted as practical training grounds for these recruits. They tended to be young, aggressive, promoted and demoted quickly, and lavishly paid: even a foreign foreman could expect to earn more than a French cavalry officer. Russia's adopted entrepreneurs were not then akin to the timid micro-capitalists of French domestic industry nor to the industrial bureaucrats of German domestic industry; rather they were the archetypally rugged profit-maximizers of capitalist legend.

Generally, they served Russia well, both up to, and, in fewer cases, after 1905, setting a standard difficult for native talents to match. The technology they brought could not have been developed indigenously at the time, and the production costs achieved with it were significantly lower than the prevailing Russian average. Connexions between Russian subsidiary and western parent firms frequently permitted the implantation of processes scarcely familiar even to the advanced economies: the Alexandrovskii Steel Works, for instance, acquired the Gilchrist–Thomas method of steel manufacture only three years after its discovery.[158] And the price for such services, with dividends held at modest levels, and profits and even salaries often reinvested, was not extravagant. The adopted entrepreneur thus worked creatively within the Russian development pattern, generally with propriety, rarely abusing his undoubted technical superiority to bleed either the customer with prices or the economy of profits.

However, if economic growth were to establish firm roots in Russia, some 'nationalization' of enterprise was essential. Ironically, it was provided, and indigenous capabilities released, by the disturbed political conditions of the early 1900s. Xenophobic and anti-capitalistic aspects of the upheavals despatched a few foreign industrialists by assassination and many more by hurried departure westwards; they thus created an instantaneous supply of job-opportunities for promising Russians.[159] Moreover, western managers were far more expensive than Russians – the Rutchenko mine, for instance, had spent virtually all its profits on western management services in the 1890s – and the pinched financial conditions of the times favoured economy. By 1914 therefore, the pattern of management in the advanced industries had swung towards a widespread use of Russian personnel, guided, often rather remotely, by a task-force of highly experienced westerners, operating usually from some central base such as an investment bank or industrial mother-firm.[160]

But merely to Russify the names on the office doors was obviously insufficient; the new managers needed also to be given appropriate qualifications. However, social and educational currents in the 1900s were relatively favourably disposed for this task. Evidence from savings and bank deposits suggests that the small Russian bourgeoisie – the natural recruiting ground for the managerial echelons – underwent some expansion at this time. Facilities for instructing apprentices for the business profession were also improving. In the pre-war years, basic educational provision expanded particularly rapidly: outlays from the zemstvos on primary education increased by 400 per cent between 1905 and 1914, and, at the national level, the Ministry of Education increased its budget allocation 1906–13 from 2.1 to 4.6 per cent of the total.[161] The resulting literacy rate (measured by the proportion of military recruits who could write) moved up sharply from 30 per cent in 1888 to 60 per cent by 1907[162] and may have reached 68 per cent by 1913,[163] well over Bowman and Anderson's literacy 'threshold' for the primary industrial society[164] (see Tables 4.9 and 4.10). An impressive array of technical schools assisted in grinding this basic literacy to an industrial cutting edge.

Table 4.9   Percentage of literacy for total population of Russia in 1897

	Urban population	Rural population	Total population
Males	54	25	29
Females	36	10	13
Total	45	17	21

Source Kahan (1971b), p. 367.

Table 4.10   Percentage of literacy among military recruits, 1880–1913

1880	22	1900	49
1885	27	1905	56
1890	32	1910	65
1895	39	1913	68

Source: Kahan (1971b), p. 367, citing Rashin (1958), p. 582.

Nor were they alone in this. Many western-owned businesses acted virtually as academies for Russian industrialists, not simply by providing a managerial 'demonstration effect' but by deliberate campaigns of instruction. Even tours of secondment to the continental parent firms were provided for the most alert trainees: budding entrepreneurs might learn hydraulic engineering at Barrow,[165] metallurgy at St Etienne or Essen.[166] International support for Russian managerial standards could also be achieved in other ways. Some family concerns despatched their brighter sons on technological tours of Europe's leading factories and polytechnics in order to keep abreast of best practice. The important textile dynasty of Prokhorov detailed one such disciple for an itinerary which included Moscow University, the Mulhouse School of Chemistry, and the Alsatian cotton mills before reclaiming him as head of the business – and founder of its chemical laboratory.[167] Such long-range educational inputs seem to have been remarkably common by the 1900s: of 519 students attending Leipzig Commercial High School in 1903 no less than 110 were Russians, and there is no reason to think Leipzig untypical of the great German schools. Not unreasonably, an American report concluded in 1904, 'Russia probably profits most in this international educational game'.[168] With the western nations providing valuable supplementation for Russia's deficient training capabilities, the technical transfers inaugurated more than a century before by Wilkinson, Baildon, Jars, and von Reden, proved still to be active on the eve of the First World War. For the Romanov Empire the return on both indigenous and international efforts to improve the quality of its human capital was the training of an independent entrepreneurial force against perhaps the highest odds in Europe.[169]

Of course, the quality of the managerial graduates was highly variable and McKay's bulging dossier of names and careers is properly uncomplimentary about the incidence of 'insouciance and malfeasance'. However, this formidable list also contains instances of highly competent Russian entrepreneurship and is careful to award due distinction to those who had worked or studied in western Europe.[170] Almost certainly, the proportion of the total constituency represented by those dependable individuals increased as 1914 was approached. Fairly convincing evidence that large-scale industrialists adopted independent and strong-minded policies has emerged from Ruth Roosa's investigation of the final pre-war years: these businessmen were sufficiently confident both to demand the abrogation of inefficient state enterprises and bureaucracies and to advise the substitution of coherent planning measures for the sterile retrenchment into which the post-Witte Treasury had again fallen. The late tsarist business community thus discovered a collective identity (institutionalized in the Association of Industry and Trade of 1906) and a noticeable voice, and was not reticent in using either against the residual constraints of the old regime.[171]

While Russian entrepreneurs learned the delights of top-flight boardrooms and public policy statements, important modifications to business organization were occurring which reflected both the process of 'westernization' and the special requirements of the domestic economy. Cartel groupings in Russia, as in Germany, grew up as 'children of bad times' – here the early 1900s – and expanded to unusual dimensions during the period of management transformation after 1905. The appearance of such monstrous organizations might suggest that Russian business had embarked upon the 'Germanized' path of autonomous capitalistic integration. Furthermore, when the state under Finance Minister Kokovtsev exchanged promotional for austerity tactics, the business community had necessarily to develop some form of defensive vehicle. On the other hand, pressures that were neither imitative nor protective evoked quite other affinities between the Russian business predicament and the large-scale business organization. High costs in recruiting and maintaining labour indicated the wisdom of scale-economies. The low quality of manpower necessitated that it be employed in large quantities. Heavy industry, under Russian conditions, was both labour- and capital-intensive, and the combination pointed unequivocally towards large units. The scarcity of management resources necessitated that they be spread over the largest possible accumulations of labour. And, finally, within the restricted Russian market for heavy goods, commercial deployments of a monopolistic or oligopolistic kind probably represented the most economic scale of manufacture; when these markets approached the monopsonistic, such integrated business forms also provided suppliers with valuable bargaining power.

Yet, if these were the peculiar specifications for the rise of indigenous large-scale industry, they emerged remarkably late in the day. Necessarily, any form of industrial combination made slow initial headway against the highly developed frictions of the Russian market-place: the persistence of small-scale manufacture, the absence of a tradition in collective action (most un-German), and the hostility of a state suspicious of concentrations in either labour or capital (again un-German). In fact, it took economic crisis to demonstrate the suitability of large-scale enterprise in Russia. But, even then, big business did not sweep the board: the business structure was not revolutionized; rather it remained dualistic. *Kustar* manufacture persisted as a crude reminder that smallness also paid, right down to 1914. Moreover, by permitting the peasant economy to generate its own clothing, machinery, and implements, the *kustar* sector did nothing to create interdependence between agricultural markets and factory suppliers and much to maintain small-scale and large-scale industry as irreconcilable antagonists, with the former denying the latter an important share of domestic demand. As in Germany, the retention of artisanal industry was reinforced by powerful social sanctions. Populist thinking, in particular, insisted that, in order to escape the slave-wage systems of the

West, the Empire should retain the special relationship between the labour force and the village, and, if industry were essential, between the labour force and village industry.

Such views proved persuasive and did much to prejudice government and people in favour of *kustar* goods, *kustar* fashions, even *kustar* schools and museums – and, in scale terms, in favour of industrial miniatures. It followed not only that many enterprises remained small but that the industrial territory between the artisan workshops and the great trusts remained largely unfilled. Where in Germany the middle ground was cleared by the expansion and carte-lization of medium firms, it was in Russia a form of prohibited terrain. By 1914, therefore, the Empire possessed not one but two uniquely indigenous business forms, one rooted in the Russian past, the other seemingly repre-sentative of the Russian industrial future. As the adjustments in entre-preneurship were qualified, so too were the adjustments in the structure of enterprise.

Nevertheless, if traditional retentions survived in business as well as in agriculture, the reasons for allowing them entirely to obscure new departures are no more compelling. After all, when in 1910 Russia could boast a larger section of its workforce employed in ventures with over 500 workers than could America – 54 per cent against 33 per cent – enterprise on the biggest scale was obviously not languishing.[172] By comparison, Germany employed 50 per cent of its workforce in units with more than 500 workers. The organiza-tion of the Russian syndicate, the most frequent form of integrated structure, with its production quotas distributed among member-firms and its sales con-ducted through a central agency, also strongly resembled its German counter-part. In vehemence, too, there was a similarity, for, from 1902, the Russian syndicates employed market-dominating tactics very like the German cartel methods of the 1890s. Typically, the metal syndicate Prodameta aggressively occupied 74 per cent of the market for its product range in the early 1900s, and then, after a brisk engagement with the rival Krovlya syndicate, moved on to a virtually complete monopoly. Very high market shares were similarly obtained by Prodameta's many colleagues: by 1908 the iron-ore syndicate Pro-darud had 80 per cent, by 1913 the copper producers syndicate, Med had 94 per cent, and, as early as 1907, the rolling-stock syndicate Prodvagon had achieved 97 per cent.[173] Without doubt, these monsters were more monopo-listic than their nearest German equivalents. Yet their militant tactics seem rarely to have tipped over into economically destructive behaviour. Even dur-ing the supposedly highest state of imperialist monopoly capitalism, the 'ex-ploitative' steel companies struck some curiously unrapacious attitudes: be-tween 1900 and 1914 they actually *lowered* their prices by 20 per cent.[174] This unusual modesty of deportment probably relates to the efficacy of state control over the registration and capital of the companies involved. For its part, the government learned in the 1900s to regard cartels as agencies assisting the regulation of the economy and not as engines of intimidation, to approve useful combinations, and to move decisively against immoderate ones. Thus, when southern industrial interests attempted to form an immense American-style steel trust in 1908,[175] or when the two important engineering concerns Kolomna and Sormovo attempted a comprehensive merger in 1913, the state simply withheld its approval and the arrangement was suspended.[176] The degree of extortion practised by Russian cartels before 1914 does not seem to have been excessive and the elements of aggressive expansion and economic responsibility seem to have been maintained in an approximate balance.

By 1914 the Russian business structure had developed into a thin-waisted hourglass shape, a design which appeared to meet many of the Empire's manufacturing needs. At the bottom, peasant requirements were served by small-scale enterprises living close to their markets. At the top, particular problems of scale elicited answering innovations in scale, and, it would seem, at tolerable social cost. Small industry was powered, especially after 1890, by one swelling tributary of the autonomous entrepreneurial stream, and another by 1905 was assuming the load of large-scale industry. *Kustar* remained intransigently Russian in style, but the modifications to the bigger enterprises, though suiting domestic needs, were no less reminiscent of western development models than the parallel adjustments in farming practice. 'Trustification', it seemed, had lifted the Russian economy an evolutionary stage into the world of modern business organization, while 'Russification' had gone some way to providing the native risk-takers needed to guide it through this uncharted terrain.

INVESTMENT BANKS: THE RISE OF FINANCIAL ENTREPRENEURSHIP

As state organizations are to primary backwardness; investment banks are to secondary backwardness. Such is Gerschenkron's formula, and in post-1905 Russia it appears to work through with exemplary neatness: chronic economic deficiency and the *dirigiste* remedies for it both retreat; growth of autonomous type gradually gathers pace but is not yet firmly established; banks are attracted to direct and encourage this growth. Indeed, in Russia the introduction of investment banking proceeded more rapidly and smoothly than in France or Germany; here there was none of the suspicion or obstruction of a puzzling new financial institution experienced by the earlier developers, rather a deliberate and energetic application of a proven development tool. Naturally, then, the 'westernization' of the Russian banking sector involved a larger measure of conscious imitation than was the case with the agricultural and entrepreneurial adjustments. And, by the same token, the element of 'Germanization' was stronger since the copyists of investment banking techniques tended to look for lessons to Europe's foremost exponents of industrial finance.

Given this borrower's relationship, it is not surprising that the Empire's smooth assimilation of modern banking methods came at a late point in tsarist industrial development. During the early part of the nineteenth century, when modern financial institutions were beginning their development in western

271

Europe, the Russian financial structure remained lean, specialized, and almost wholly official, lending mainly to the nobility in the vain hope of preserving the great estates. In this first phase of bank expansion, the cause was hopeless, the debtors undependable, and the banks usually bankrupted. In this period, moreover, the autocracy's financial policy had not yet shrugged off its old-regime restrictiveness: even the first truly mercantile venture, the State Commercial Bank (1817) was permitted to lend only to members of state-controlled guilds; generally, banks were still regarded as weapons against usury rather than as agents of credit creation.[177]

Not until the financial crisis of 1857–59 did a second bout of renovation occur. At this point, various land banks were created to meet the continuing demands from the nobility, and, under the approving eye of Reutern, a selection of large deposit banks grew up during the 1860s, turning increasingly to industrial business after 1875. As they involved themselves with many of the Empire's largest and most modern concerns, these deposit institutions formed the nucleus for the expansion of the 1900s. But initially their role was limited: until the 1890s they assisted industrialists only with working capital and import credit; more lavish aid with fixed investment came only in the Witte era, and, more especially, after 1905. Before the new century, moreover, a substantial place within the financial community was occupied by the Muscovite banks, unincorporated family concerns staffed by local textile magnates and far less enterprising than their counterparts in Petersburg. These institutions distrusted investment in newfangled industries (even railways), made little attempt to offer extended credit, and less to influence the behaviour of their industrial clients.[178] Deficiencies of this considerable scope were made good before 1900 by the activities of an unusually active State Bank. Created in 1861, virtually as a subdepartment of the Ministry of Finance, this central agency enjoyed a successful promotional career well into the 1900s: from the start it traded as a commercial bank, making advances to small and medium industry and to the smaller municipalities; from the 1880s it acquired control over all credit and financial transactions; from 1888 it moved into the direct financing of the grain trade; from the mid-1890s it greatly expanded its already generous credit services to agricultural and industrial enterprise. The new Statutes of 1894 (drafted by a reformer of the Witte coterie, Professor A. I. Antonovich of Kiev) empowered the bank to extend credit into any sector of the economy and inaugurated the most characteristic financial innovation of the decade, the industrial-commercial loan secured by real estate or industrial assets. By 1897 ordinary discount operations occupied only 50 per cent of the bank's business – against 70–90 per cent for the German Reichsbank – with the large remaining share going in credit operations of many types. Interests in coal, iron, sugar, and oil industries were won by this means, and the central bankers were not above protecting them by appointing official directors to the boards of their industrial clients, exactly in the style of an investment bank.[179]

Yet for all its energetic policies, the Russian State Bank, unlike its European colleagues, took care not to impede the development of the private financial sector. Ministers like Reutern and Witte, absolute masters of the bank, actively encouraged the growth of financial competitors and the bank itself did much to protect them in troubled times. In the financial crises of 1899 and 1912, for instance, the provision of unsecured credit for the independent banks and the organization of the prophylactic financial syndicate, aptly known as the 'Red Cross of the Bourse,' marked major rescue operations by the central bankers. Clearly, this dynamic, interventionist, and competitive institution diverged markedly from Cameron's ideal model where independent bankers advance unhindered by official prying and central bankers keep their own counsel. Equally certainly the results of this divergence were *positive*. The explanation is that the laws of backwardness may bend the requirements for a growth-inducing banking structure: where backwardness is so pronounced that the state becomes the only influential exponent of advanced ideas, the autonomy of the private financial sector ceases to be an asset; the criteria of Cameron and Gerschenkron collide. But the corollary to the existence of the growth-inducing *central* bank is, of course, the late development of the independent investment bank. Thus, the Russian financial structure in 1900, dominated by the State Bank and its satellites, the Peasant and Noble Land Banks, formed a sandwich garnished exotically by the overseas banks of the 1890s, the Loan and Discount Bank of Persia (1894), and the Russo-Chinese Bank (1895) and randomly by an assortment of municipal, savings, and mortgage banks, but filled with a meagre portion of private joint-stock banks, still only forty-three in number.

After 1905, however, the proportions changed: in the Empire's most important era of financial development, the 'filling' of independent banks swelled greatly and the State Bank, though not entirely displaced, unprotestingly made room for it (see Table 4.11). The centre of the expansion was St Petersburg where the methods of continental mixed banking were preferred to the cautious liquidity ratios of Moscow, and railway promotion, industrial credit, and fixed investment ranked high in the loan ledgers. Credit policies were highly adventurous – the share of loans granted against non-guaranteed securities by Petersburg bankers rising from 37 per cent in 1893 to 76 per cent in 1914 – and distinctly innovational – the Petersburg financiers intended to control the entire investment cycle, supervising the issuing, buying, and placing of securities in the best German style. And they were highly successful: where all joint-stock banks increased their share of Russian discount and loan operations from 52 to 60 per cent and their share of Russian bank assets from 59 to 68 per cent between 1893 and 1914, the Petersburg banks advanced more spectacularly from 14 to 44 per cent of the all-Russian total for discounts and loans and from 23 to 34 per cent, of the all-Russian total for bank assets, even over the shorter period 1900–14. By comparison, the State Bank managed only to keep its share of discount and loan operations stable at 20 per cent after 1893, and allowed its control of bank assets to fall from 19 to 16 per cent. [180] The upsurge of large-scale joint-stock banking in the western capital thus marked both a major quantitative shift within the financial sector and a vital qualitative improvement in the autocracy's financial maturity.

Table 4.11   Increase of capital in private banks and State
Bank at year end 1900–12 (m. roubles)

End year	Total of deposits, capital, current accounts Private banks	State banks
1900	1165	223
1901	1180	239
1902	1257	292
1903	1395	286
1904	1464	310
1905	1340	319
1906	1468	304
1907	1569	284
1908	1789	265
1909	2175	329
1910	2816	316
1911	3206	313
1912	3952	317

Source: Miller (1926), p. 149

For, as the investment banks assimilated an increasing share of the financial market, they turned increasingly towards managerial participation in industry. Partly, this was in compensation for the large withdrawals of foreign capital during the crisis of 1899–1901, partly it was in response to the widespread accumulation of industrial interests built up by banks during the 1890s. In 1898 the St Petersburg International Bank held one-quarter of its total securities in industrial shares and bonds, the Commercial and Industrial Bank 62 per cent. Portfolio concentrations of this size outgrew their status as investments and became management certificates encouraging bankers towards more direct involvement in industrial affairs, frequently the modernization or improvement of their industrial clients. After 1905 the largest investment houses, the Russo-Asiatic, the St Petersburg International, and the Azov-Don became directly and deeply interested in coal-mining, silk production, and the exportation of grain and sugar. Shipbuilding, engineering, and armament production also came in for much attention and the fastest-growing industries of the era, glass and cement, were closely allied to the financier-entrepreneurs. Perhaps most important of all were the imaginative and risky projects to develop the railways, cotton-growing, and cotton-processing industries of the Urals. An area of the economy neglected by the 'Witte system' was thus picked out for attention by the successor system of bank promotion. That the financiers held the entrepreneurial whip-hand in these transactions was never in doubt: the bankers instructed the manufacturers 'as if they were bank officials'.[181]

If that has a surprisingly Germanic ring to it, other aspects of the Russian bank structure compare surprisingly well with the best European models by 1914. Independence from excessive state oversight was never a genuine problem, although some liberals thought it was. The generosity of credit provision – whether from public or private sector – cannot be faulted. The ratio of bank resources to national income was very high, about 61 per cent by 1914 (commercial bank resources only), comparing well with the likely figures for Germany and Britain and comfortably surpassing those for France.[182] Inevitably, given the Empire's huge extent, bank density results were less impressive, but, even in this department, the autocracy enjoyed a better ratio of bank resources to population in 1914 (0.17) than France had achieved by 1870 (0.12).[183] Only in the case of currency circulation does the comparison run severely to Russia's disfavour: the volume doubled in 1894–1914, but many segments of the economy either remained outside the money-exchange system entirely or persisted in treating paper roubles as gold certificates rather than bank-notes. This deficiency apart, the Tsar's financial institutions in 1914 technically resembled some of the continent's most potent growth-inducing agencies, their entrepreneurial capabilities comparing not too distantly even with the masterly powers of Berlin high finance.

THE AMBIGUITIES OF 'WESTERNIZED' GROWTH

On the best reading, therefore, and it is at present a deliberately optimistic reading, the Russia of 1914 possessed economic characteristics which suggest that industrial take-off of an autonomous and not unconventional type, though clearly not achieved, might at least have been imminent. This view is not inconsistent with the results obtained in Gregory's recent testing of tsarist growth experience against the 'modern economic growth' experience of the advanced nations: broadly, the outcome was that Russia had probably not achieved MEG by 1914, but in some respects was not far removed from it. A tentative conclusion is reached that 'the differences between the structure of Russian industry after 1900 and the structures of the advanced countries were not too significant', and the final suggestion made that remaining constraints might be traced to a dualistic tension between 'a fairly modern industry and a backward agriculture'.[184] Certainly, the key to the growth of the period 1906 –14 lies in its dualistic nature, but the dualism is more widely spread than Gregory implies. It covers, in fact, most economic departments: in agriculture, a modern sector of integrated farmsteads opposed a traditional sector of dirt-scratching cultivation; in entrepreneurship, a modern sector of trained technologists opposed a traditional sector of corruption and incompetence; in business structure, cartel opposed *kustar*; in markets, the spread of urban demand opposed the persistent tastes of the rural 80 per cent; in financial administration, the new industrial banks opposed the orthodox austerity of a revanchist Treasury. The traditionally pessimistic assessment of the pre-war period is achieved by selecting the emphasis in each case from the second of these terms. And it is strengthened by discounting all growth possibilities on the grounds that they were subsequently shattered by seven years of war and revolution. By contrast, the optimistic view puts the stress on the first terms and is able to present them as requisites ('pre' or 'post') of some kind, at least related to the qualifications which compose Rostow's general certificate of industrialization. In this intepretation, a genuine industrial dynamic of developing power and long-run potential is frustrated by the tragic interruption of European war. There is clearly something to be said on both sides of this duality: Russian backwardness in 1914 did indeed remain substantial, but, on the other hand, substantial breaches in it had also been made. Similar ambiguities attach to the concepts of 'westernization' and 'Germanization'. With cartels, investment banks, heavy industries, and consumption simultaneously expanding, and strong appeals for agrarian and artisanal conservation arranged in descant to this theme, it would be difficult to deny some parallels between the new Russian course and the German model of growth. However, for all the much-needed illumination that these comparative assessments throw upon the real economic achievements of the late tsarist period, they remain abstractions of western European growth superimposed upon intractable Russian conditions. It is not so much that Russia thoroughly 'westernizes' or 'Germanizes' in this limited period; it is that these concepts when applied to the autocracy's performance after 1905 find some points of contact where only a decade or so previously there were none. But the contact is only at points, not at surfaces, and the points shift. Between the points there was much that persisted in unwesternized and unmodified form.

Despite the cultivatory merits of the Stolypin reforms, for instance, the match between the agricultural transformation of theory and the Russian reality remains distinctly imperfect. The size of the 'worst practice' sector needs no emphasis, nor that the majority of output was derived from a production structure thoroughly immunized against external instruction. The fault of the new measures was that they provided neither sufficient instruction nor sufficient means to reduce peasant resistance to instruction. Stolypin's general strategy regarding the reform of peasant plots was permissive rather than mandatory, while the commitment of agronomic resources to the vital tasks of agricultural propaganda never outgrew the exploratory stage before 1914[185] (or indeed, 1934). And even if the reform failed to unleash class war in the countryside, there were other kinds of political cost which it did not escape. Thus the release of the lesser peasantry from the countryside provided recruits not only for the manufacturers but also for the socialist agitators. An unstable, extremely dissatisfied, and quickly replenished stream of labour flowed into the cities and congealed into precisely the kind of proletariat which the regime had long feared and against which, employing 'police socialism' on the one hand, and *agents provocateurs* on the other, it now mobilized its most bizarre methods of social control.[186] No less troublesome was the effect on the rural community which stayed behind: for them the dominant fact was that the settlement had transferred to the peasantry *en masse* insufficient land reserves to extinguish traditional preferences for solutions featuring drastic reallocation of agricultural property, most especially aristocratic property. Some households might profit immediately from Stolypin's provisions and many more might hope eventually to profit through family mobility, but, for the majority, the more obvious and immediate expedients retained their attraction. With the estates and imperial lands in 1905 still covering as much ground as 6 m. peasant holdings,[187] enough bait remained to establish redistribution as a concrete and enduring preoccupation of most small cultivators. Even amidst peasant communities that were *not* permanently differentiated the preference for territorial adjustment at a stroke could be powerfully held under such conditions. Furthermore, by permitting these economic grievances to combine with the gravest constitutional issues of the day the regime most ineptly attached high political costs to its rural policies. Given that the Duma was deeply committed to swingeing land reform and had floated redistribution bills in 1906 and 1907, the autocracy blundered critically in its responses: it tacitly approved the assassination of Herzenstein, the peasants' champion in the Constitutional Assembly, and it incorporated the Duma in its 'solution' of the agrarian problem simply by dissolving it. With these strokes the quest for land reform was irretrievably linked with that for constitutional government: the nation was now committed to achieve agrarian *and* political democracy, for one was not possible without the other.[188] The reforms of 1905–14 could, therefore, create much more than zero change in cultivation yet still fall short of agricultural transformation; similarly, agricultural and political change could be explosively related by mechanisms quite other than those of Leninist differentration. The Russian agricultural 'pre-requisite' in 1914 was only partially complete but almost wholly volatile: its economic worth was real but constricted, its political implications such as to damage its technical viability. The combination does not suggest autonomous growth, and is certainly not 'western'.

In fact, the terms 'westernization' and 'Germanization' are not in themselves unequivocal. The interpretation adopted by Gerschenkron – and so far employed here – is that economic growth contains an inherent bias towards normalization or congruence: as growth proceeds, Russian economic man should produce patterns and institutions resembling those created to the west and south. But there are alternatives: western patterns may have flowed less readily from the designs of native Russian capitalists than from the forcible imprint of foreign interests, heedless of growth norms but conversant with the profitable devices of European industrialism. Westernization of this variety was not produced by the tsarist economy's self-directed drift into conformity but by the intrusive activities of immigrant adventurers. Naturally, this suggestion does not apply to agriculture – which had problems of its own – but it requires testing against the other indicators of pre-war resurgence.

At once, the fact that many Soviet economists have referred to the period 1900–14 as one of 'economic imperialism' (and to its immediate predecessor as the phase of 'pre-monopoly capitalism') invites attention.[189] For the implication is that the economy of 1905–14 was at the same time a subject of westernization and an object of western imperialism. The underlying evidence for this supposition is contained in the very high correlation within the empire of cartel organization, modern technology, and foreign ownership. Scale-intensive organization turns out to represent not only an appropriate response to Russian factor endowment but also the size preference of international monopoly capitalism; much of the Russian business structure was not in fact Russian in any real sense. The great trusts like Prodvagon or Produgol were less symptoms of westernization than satrapies of Parisian high finance. Fittingly, the tsarist armament industries were scarcely less internationalist than the conferences upon disarmament summoned by the same Tsar: major contracts were shared out between the affiliates of the great British triumvirate, Vickers, Armstrong-Whitworth, and John Brown on the one hand, and of their foreign rivals Krupp and Schneider-Creusot on the other.[190] Traditionally, oil marches with armaments in the vanguard of multinational enterprise, and the 'Russian' oil interests were no exception: the fields were partitioned between the Swedish Nobels, the Dutch Royal General, the English Shell, and the Russo-American General Petroleum companies. But perhaps most striking of all were the pan-industrial exploits of the French-owned Bonnardel Group. Fastened around the Huta-Bankova Steel Company – 'the nerve centre of a vast informal organization'[191] – this octopus sent tentacles into the metallurgical, iron, copper-mining, and machine-tool industries; by 1914 it stretched across Russia from Poland to the Caucasus and consumed no less than 18 per cent of French investment in Russian industry. With its miscellany of possessions disposed around an entrepreneurial hub, it resembled the German 'bank group' in shape and strategy, but, in ownership, it was foreign to the core. The 'autonomous' recovery of Russian manufacturing after the state's abdication of economic control was, in fact, largely directed by external agencies such as these. Russification of management touched only part of the structure while design and ownership resided elsewhere.

This was the burden of contemporary comment – much from Duma representatives – which viewed the great syndicates not as indicators of an adapting economy, but, quite unequivocally, as the parasites of international capital. A venerable tradition was thus inaugurated which is by no means absent from modern scholarship: one recent observer still found the trusts to be 'deadly organizations . . . creating the machinery for an extraordinary degree of foreign control over Russian economic life'[192] No doubt, this estimate seriously overrates the lethality of the syndicates, but it accurately represents their pedigree: anything that was 'westernized' or 'Germanized' about them related less to the increasing flexibility of Russian growth than to the overseas diffusion of the advanced European economies. And there was nothing novel about this: Russian business practice had been amended by outsiders ever since the time of Peter the Great.

Industrial monopoly was not of course the only game favoured by foreign capital: the financial sector offered attractions at least as powerful, and, after the manufacturing recession of the early 1900s, a definitely more generous measure of security. Industrial crisis by no means terminated the participation of overseas investment; it merely led to a discreet rearrangement of its form. The upshot was naturally that the Russian investment banks were not what they first appeared: by 1916, 45 per cent of the capital of the ten largest banks was foreign-owned; and of these the Private Commercial Bank had 57 per cent of its capital answerable to Paris, the International Bank 33 per cent answerable to Berlin.[193] Moreover, much of the capital that was not placed in bank shares after 1905 was placed *through* bank mediation, seen by interested parties as a useful buffer between the foreign investor and the Russian industrial equity. In turn, this encouraged overseas investment banks administering the capital at source to become interested in the finance houses handling it at destination. After 1907 when banking syndicates were increasingly employed for large industrial projects – apparently as a stroke of 'Germanization' – they were rarely composed simply of native concerns, much more frequently of overseas and Russian houses acting in concert. The foreign collaborators – most usually the Banque de Paris et des Pays-Bas or the Société Générale – underwrote the necessary capital and placed the equities overseas; the Russian collaborators found the investment opportunities, managed local negotiations, and received one-third of the profits. Much of the entrepreneurial impetus behind Russian *bankinitiative* was therefore non-Russian; sometimes, indeed, it was so forceful as to entirely escape even the enveloping decency of the syndicate cloak. In the final pre-war years, the Crédit Lyonnais ran its own Russian brokerage service, matching Russian opportunities directly with French capital and eliminating the native financial intermediary. Even more dramatically, foreign bankers sometimes proved able to precipitate major adjustments in the Russian financial structure. In 1909 the Banque de l'Union Parisienne contrived to force three Poliakov banks into a merger as the Moscow Union Bank.[194] Typically, the Russian 'great bank' not only contained much foreign ownership capital but also transacted much business with foreign funds, and exercised its entrepreneurial functions under the scrutiny, and sometimes the lash, of the foreign banker. If Russian finance houses resembled their French or German counterparts, this was not least because these counterparts were actually present within the Russian financial system – not to speak of the banking offices of Petersburg – in some strength.

The Russian state might well have been concerned about this foreign presence. But, in fact, its means of controlling the Russian financial sector were more considerable than talk of Kokovtsev's orthodoxy might imply. For if Witte's downfall had removed the Finance Ministry from the lighted stage of the Russian economy, it had rapidly discovered a means of re-entry to the theatre, and its path lay squarely through the box-office. The key to the state's retention of economic leverage lay in the State Bank and the 'Treasury balances'. For the central bank achieved more than discreet non-interference in the expansion of the private financial sector: through its guardianship of the state budgetary surpluses – the 'Treasury balances' left on deposit by the exchequer – it controlled a vast proportion of total financial resources, and, by converting part of these into credits for the joint-stock banks, disposed of an effective prerequisite for successful investment banking.[195] By 1914, the Treasury deposits were ten times larger than equivalent holdings at the Bank of England, composed 20 per cent of all Russian bank resources, and allowed the bank to devote 75 per cent of its business to the creation of credits for the investment houses.[196] Alone among European central banks, the Russian contender remained the economy's *main* source of investment support for finance, commerce, and industry. Without its management of the Treasury balances, the more adventurous credit policies pursued by the private finance sector after 1899 probably could not have endured. *Bankinitiative* then depended not only upon foreign entrepreneurial drive but also upon the fund-raising of financial bureaucrats.

Official capabilities of this power have encouraged Garvy favourably to compare the Russian State Bank of the pre-war years to the Soviet 'monobank', the entirely integrated and omnicompetent financial monopolist of the NEP period. As early as 1895 de Cyon had described the central bank as 'the *sole banker* of 129 million Russians',[197] a proposition supported not only by its direct aid to other banks (it supplied initial capitals as well as Treasury credits) but also by its huge assets and liabilities (larger than those of any other Russian institution) and its preponderant share even of total branch offices (one-sixth of the total, again the largest single contribution). Next to the Finance Ministry itself, the State Bank gradually became the autocracy's most powerful instrument for the exercise of *dirigiste* policy. In no other European country did the central bank make such a substantial and wide-ranging commitment to the servicing of the private sector, and in no other case did it become the chief agent of the government's programme of economic promotion. Its relevance for the development of 'Germanized' investment banks is clear: as Aghad concluded, 'the St Petersburg banks are Russian in appearance, foreign as far as their resources go, *and ministerial as far as risk bearing goes*'.[198]

On closer examination, therefore, the application of a 'western' or 'optimistic' model to the Russian economy of 1905–14 throws up some sharp discrepancies. Autonomous preconditions do not fully emerge: they are uncompleted, or they are counterfeited by what is in fact a revised form of institutional 'substitution', or they are mimicked by foreign participation. What appears 'westernized' is too often rawly western, insufficiently absorbed or domesticated; the true texture of the economy adheres more closely to a specifically Russian, and familiar, consistency. 'Worst practice' agriculture persists, as it has for centuries, as a glutinous impediment to progress. Foreign capital provides the hard core of state finance as it had done for Catherine, the hard core of development finance as it had done for Witte; all that is changed is the mode of its employment, whether casually concealed in great cartels or intricately embedded within the investment banks. Imported entrepreneurial skills continue to form a solid managerial layer: as business direction is Russified, the foreign banker smoothly replaces the foreign industrialist as major controller of business resources. To be sure, as McKay insists (and as the Soviets now more than insist) the Russian banking interests retained a sufficiently commanding entrepreneurial voice to prevent the ultimate concentration of monopoly capital power in foreign hands, but little evidence exists to suggest that the native financiers were ever anything more than the subordinate collaborators in the partnership.[199] And, finally, the highly durable connexion which had existed between economic development and state power since the time of Ivan the Terrible continues to resist corrosion: the official pressure for modernization, admittedly less pervasive, less vocal, and more circumspect than in Witte's day, merely chooses a different style of expression; instead of the stentorian vocabulary of the Finance Ministry (now grown petulant), it selects the quieter tones of the State Bank. This adjustment was neither so successful nor so innovational as to require an upward revision of the government's role in late tsarist economic development: after all, the State Bank was still trying to elicit growth from the *private* sector and to do so by a fairly basic expedient – the disbursement of development subsidies. Equally certainly, however, the imperial 'monobank' was no unworthy successor to Witte's Ministry of Finance. In the end, peasant agriculture, foreign techniques, overseas capital, and state promotion compose a growth formula peculiarly Russian in flavour.

A MILITARY EPILOGUE

In order to claim the growth patterns of 1905 – 14 more comprehensively for Russian primitivism than for advancing westernization, the presence of a final element needs perhaps to be established. tsardom's habitually pronounced conflation of economic advance and military gain. True, these years are not conspicuously suitable candidates for yet another of Professor Nove's bouts of 'developmental serfdom'. Most notably, the administrative framework is relaxed rather than tautened and the use of forced savings to finance growth in military capability is set on the retreat, not the advance. But after the ignominious failures in the Far East, the need to reburnish the faded emblems of military prestige was real enough. Even though armament spending was postponed in the penurious months after Tsushima, it did, consequently, recover to extravagant heights in the years prior to the First World War. The intentions for military reconstruction were certainly sufficiently lavish: the proposed budget of 1913 set aside some 4,184 m. roubles for the defence programmes of 1908 – 13[200] – equivalent to 35.4 per cent of national income for 1913 – whereas Witte's efforts in railroad construction were costed only at 1,691 m. roubles[201] – corresponding to 25.7 per cent of the national income for 1900. Similarly, the Small Military Programme of 1910 allocated 1,265 m. roubles to defence needs over the ensuing decade,[202] the Small Shipbuilding Programme of 1912 devoted 421 m. roubles to five years of warship construction, and the projected Great Naval Programme of 1911 – 12 entrusted 2,000 m. roubles to a twenty-year scheme of maritime support. Shortage of funds and the untimely eruption of war ensured that the amounts spent were substantially smaller than these colossal estimates,[203] but they remained sufficient to establish military construction as a major characteristic of the period. Large increases in Russian steel output – achieving a 50 per cent advance in 1910 – 13 – owed much to the demand of dockyards and armouries. And, by 1913, as Falkus has recently emphasized, a powerful defence boom was undoubtedly contributing to the high current levels of national income.[204] During 1914, military consumption rose to absorb 35 per cent of the tsarist regular budget, and, in its disastrous autumn, defence requirements not only filled the armament factories but spilled out to occupy, 'all facilities of the larger metal-processing and metal-construction plants, the Sormovo, the Bryansk, the Kolomna and others'.[205]

This pronounced activity in military production conforms well with a Russo-centric rather than Euro-centric model of development: traditional bellicose tastes do indeed infiltrate the processes of supervised growth in the approved tsarist style. However, as industrial predecessors like eighteenth-century Prussia or even mid-nineteenth-century France had demonstrated, militarily accented policies could contain growth-inducing capabilities of their own. By 1900, this affiliation had, if anything, strengthened: foreign capital and expertise had combined to place upon international offer a 'package' of weaponry technology very much more sophisticated than the conventional manufacturing practice of the developing economies. Exporters were increasingly willing to supply complete production systems as well as hardware items, and importers were increasingly anxious, in the contentious quarter-century before 1914, to secure domestic sources of armament production. Clients for military reasons, the lesser economic powers could acquire 'best practice' technologies (as defence industries must necessarily be) with more than military significance. The 'gap' between the imported weaponry technology and the resident manufacturing technology could be so disposed as to encourage important transfers of practice, machines, and materials from the 'military' to the 'civilian' sectors. Effectively then, pre-war armament development generated an overseas transmission of high-quality engineering practice, a communication of first importance for continental (and Atlantic) technology, and well in line with earlier, if more peaceful, diffusions of itinerant engineering innovations.[206]

Tsarist Russia – alongside colleagues in underdevelopment such as Italy, Spain, and Austria-Hungary – was a natural recipient for this transmission, and attracted armourers from all over Europe to supply it. Most in evidence were the French and the British. A wide selection of heavy industrial plants with defence-related interests, including the Nevsky Steel Casting and Forging Works, the Putilov Armoury and the Franco-Russe and Bryansk establishments worked in collaboration with the major French armouries, Schneider-Creusot and St Chamond. Similarly, Clydeside shipbuilders like John Brown and Co. and William Beardmore and Co. or Sheffield steelworks like Thomas Firth and Co. were involved in dockyard and armoury schemes from Riga to Odessa. But probably the most complex and technologically important of the Russian defence projects involved either the British consortium of John Brown, Armstrong-Whitworth, and Vickers acting together, or Vickers acting alone. Most notable of these involvements were the Nicolaiev dockyard scheme of 1910–14, intended to provide a much-needed overhaul for Russia's backward shipbuilding industry, and the Tsaritsyn arsenal project of 1913 promising, 'a private factory such as no other nation possesses, excepting England . . . the most recent, the most modern, and most effective which could be provided in any country in the world'.[207]

Such defence programmes necessarily created repercussions far overspilling the armaments sector. The most modern shipbuilding knowledge was made available to Russian firms by patent agreements which supplied designs, guarantees of quality, and expert supervision. Cadres of skilled labour and management were despatched to Russia as instructors and selected Russian engineers sent back to the West for remedial training. Equipment from the best British, American, and German manufacturers was imported to make the arsenals model plants, exemplars in technological practice for the bulk of Russian heavy industry. Novel demands entailed in 'creating a new industry', as Vickers found at Tsaritsyn, squeezed innovative responses out of Russian suppliers, particularly in metallurgy and hydraulic engineering. And this effect the Russian state was careful to preserve: it explicitly required that the armourers should, as far as possible, secure supplies of materials and machines from home industries. Cranes for Tsaritsyn were obtained from the Sormovo and Kolomna works while contracts for machine-tool motors, locomotives, turbines, and generators were placed with Russian manufacturers. These orders swelled Russia's meagre market for capital goods and imposed tasks of a rigour which could touch off important learning processes among newly fledged manufacturers. Home suppliers were thus both led by example in high-quality technological practice and subjected to demands so tightly specified that manufacturing capabilities were forced upwards. Improved performance came by way of direct acquisition of innovations, by demonstration effect, and by derived demand. Transfers of this kind formed an extension of the technological importation of the Witte era, now working through to the more sophisticated disciplines with which Russia was still ill-provided and for which, as international conditions deteriorated, she developed increasing need.

Historically, developing countries have experienced difficulties in the creation of the large capital goods industries, and, in Russia's case, the 'Witte system' was designed specifically to counter these problems. The absence of such technologies, Rosenberg has recently argued, may deny to the developer an important source of innovation, but their successful propagation may bring to the formative stages of manufacturing major advances in the practice of machine-producing and machine-using industries, 'an external economy of enormous importance to other sectors of the economy . . . a capital-saving process for the economy as a whole . . . an upward shift to a new production function'. The one central requirement for these connexions to occur is that, 'capital goods producers must be confronted with an extremely large demand for their output'.[208] Clearly, in the years before 1914 the defence industries constituted a particularly advanced capital goods sector and one for which governments were more than usually prepared to provide large guaranteed demand. Given the high research-intensiveness and the technological fertility of this sector, the leverage extended upon the machine industries would be particularly strong. And by the 1900s the general run of Russian producer goods industries were probably subject to fewer constraints than during the Witte era: the more widely based development of 1908–14 had both improved the supply of 'inputs' and established a healthier balance between heavy and light manufactures. Further, the capacity of the defence industries to generate 'spin-off' transfers conferred upon them an especial knack in resolving their own input problems.

Late tsarist policy did therefore contain the traditional connexion between militarism and development. But, in this case, the potential economic utility of modern defence technology to the Russian economy was particularly high. Unfortunately, however, in practice, western 'spin-off' probably arrived too late to produce any *enduring* industrial effects: dependent upon renewed defence activity after 1908, it operated for only a few years before being disrupted by the especially chaotic conditions of the imperial war economy. With its pre-war installations and transfers scarcely complete on the outbreak of war, with the supplies of expertise and equipment interrupted, any further spin-off could only be generated with domestic resources.[209] Russia thus provides a good instance of the dictum that an economy may benefit from the technological benefits of war preparation, only if the physical damage and disruption of overt hostilities are avoided.[210]

CONCLUSIONS: RUSSIA, BACKWARDNESS MODELS AND SOCIAL VALUES

In the Russian example, Rostowian analysis is even less useful than in the fatter pastures of western Europe. Backwardness ensures that 'preconditions' are entirely foreign to the Russian scene before 1890, and that the evolutions of the early 1900s are to a significant extent counterfeits. Gerschenkron's claims for 'substitution', in contrast, find their best material here. And in almost every other particular, it seems, the scheme of backwardness receives resounding Russian authentication: the dominant state, the capital goods industries, the advanced technologies, the swollen business units, and the ill-tended agriculture are probably more vividly displayed here than in any other case. But in several important respects, the model is awry: it overvalues the instruments at the disposal of a late-nineteenth-century bureaucracy and mis-identifies the scope of the economic role that the officials were equipped to play; and it exaggerates the neatness of the transition from a state-dominated phase of chronic backwardness to a bank-dominated phase of moderate backwardness. As with most theoretical structures involving staged divisions, the boundaries prove inconveniently flexible. With the state retaining an initiative through the central bank and the investment financiers maintaining an independent voice, the identifying features of *two* stages of backwardness are merged in the period 1905–14. Here, perhaps, the special circumstances of the late developer, able precociously to adopt the advanced methods pioneered by the industrial forerunners, exerts not an organizing but a dislocating effect on the patterns of the model, hurrying the economy's progress through the backwardness stages and producing 'hybrid' agencies or 'inter-stage' institutions (e.g. bank-and-state) as the supervisors of development. That is, the ability to borrow development techniques allows the latecomer to 'telescope' or merge the institutional devices which are supposed to attach to *separate* stages of backwardness.

Gerschenkron, it appears, does not allow sufficiently – in any but his earliest stage of backwardness — for the highly eclectic style into which the international borrowing of techniques may fall. The international element is particularly strong within Russian development, supplying capital, technology, and management. Clearly, the expansive or diffusive nature of modern economic growth is not confined to the earlier stages of Europe's industrialization, nor to the lighter technologies of that period. However, Russian experience demonstrates very clearly the ambivalent nature of the 'internationalism of the Industrial Revolution'. For it would be idle to pretend that, despite the ministrations of massed foreign funds and manufacturers, the type of economic development achieved by the autocracy in 1914 was anything other than deeply and peculiarly Russian. Here the central paradox would appear to be that the national state was insufficiently powerful to procure, from its own resources and skills, a full measure of industrial growth, but was equipped with sufficient political strength to place a particularly individual imprint on the variously sponsored growth which *was* achieved. The selection of sponsors, spanning government ministries, foreign bankers, immigrant industrialists, and native financiers did not include, until a noticeably late date, a force of Russian industrialists sufficiently large to suggest that entrepreneurship had at length outgrown its attachment to deviant minority groups. In this connexion, Russia provides useful corroboration for the hypothesis that adverse social values may delay and obstruct economic development but will rarely, if ever, suppress it. It is thus incorrect in roughly equal measure *either* to contend that the most grave social deficiencies may well entirely frustrate the ambition to industrialize or to deny that such deficiencies may permit industrialization only of a cramped and distorted kind.

NOTES AND REFERENCES

Full publication details are provided in the bibliography.
1. Goldsmith (1961), pp. 441, 443.
2. Nutter (1962).
3. Baykov (1954), pp. 140–3, 146–7.
4. Ellison (1965), p. 527.
5. Nor were these horizons much broadened by education. The autocracy preferred the concept of social control to that of human capital. Consequently, the total number of pupils receiving education at all levels represented a mere 0.49 per cent of the population in 1834, 0.7 per cent in 1856, and still a far from lavish 6.12 per cent even in 1914 (see Kahan, 1971b, pp. 365–6, 373). Even in

1896 I. I. Yanzhul lamented 'the general illiteracy which distinguishes our country from all other civilized countries', cited in Anderson and Bowman (eds) (1971), p. 5.

6. For a contrary view see Baykov (1954), pp. 138–9; also Skerpan (1964), p. 211.
7. Struve (1913), pp. 103–12.
8. See Nove (1972), pp. 79–97.
9. Strumilin (1969), pp. 158–78.
10. Rosovsky (1954), pp. 207–33.
11. Crisp (1976), pp. 13–15.
12. Although the serfs as members of Russia's most numerous social group can scarcely be deemed to constitute an oppressed or deviant *minority*, they were subjected to pressures similar to those encountered by minority groups: deprived civil status, wide-ranging bans upon alternative careers, low opportunity costs upon careers outside commerce, and, perhaps, in consequence, high 'need achievement'. It was the special achievement of the imperial autocracy to create an oppressed majority.
13. Blackwell (1965), pp. 407–24.
14. Gerschenkron (1970), pp. 18–23 *passim*.
15. Baykov (1954); Skerpan (1964).
16. Lyashchenko (1970), pp. 394, 418.
17. Portal (1974), pp. 159–196.
18. Gerschenkron (1968), pp. 177–9.
19. *Ibid.*, p. 212.
20. *Ibid.*, pp. 167–8.
21. *Ibid.*, p. 182.
22. *Ibid.*, pp. 192ff.
23. Emmons (1968), pp. 398, 421–3, 434–43.
24. Gerschenkron (1968), p. 185. After emancipation perhaps some 70–80 per cent of all peasant land in the area of European Russia lay in communal tenure.
25. Cited *ibid.*, p. 191n.
26. Goldsmith (1961), p. 442.
27. *Ibid.*
28. G. Rimlinger, (1961), p. 213.
29. *Ibid.*, p. 212.
30. Compare the belief of some contemporary reformers who held, like Reutern, that emancipation would provide the 'moral kinetic energy, the psychological foundation' for economic progress. Cited by Kipp (1975), p. 455.
31. Portal (1974), p. 166.
32. *Ibid.*, p. 163.
33. *Ibid.*, pp. 161, 170. The totals are derived by aggregation of the membership from Russia's three industrial and commercial guilds.
34. Nove (1972), pp. 94–5.
35. Miliutin (1959), pp. 206–8.
36. Rostow (1971), pp. 24, 60–2; von Laue (1963), pp. 5–6; Kipp (1972), pp. 210–25.
37. Kipp (1975), pp. 442–53.
38. Quoted by von Laue (1963), pp. 6–7.
39. Florinsky (1953), Vol. II, p. 934.
40. Quoted by Garvy (1972), pp. 878–8.

41. Portal (1974), pp. 164, 170–3.
42. Goldsmith (1961), pp. 442, 460.
43. Count S. N. Mordvinov, statesman and economist, anticipated List as the ideologue of the 'national economy'.
44. Miller (1926), p. 116.
45. Nove (1972), pp. 87–8.
46. Kipp (1975), p. 437.
47. Von Laue (1963), p. 13.
48. Westwood (1965), pp. 564–9; McKay (1970), pp. 297ff.
49. Von Laue (1963), pp. 17–18.
50. *Ibid.*, pp. 22–3.
51. Barkai (1973), pp 339–71.
52. *Ibid.*, p. 364.
53. *Ibid.*, pp. 354–7. Note, however, that Barkai's propositions regarding the money supply have been undermined by recent research in two main respects: (a) the hypothesis of monetary constraint will function only if prices are assumed not to be flexible downwards. If downward price flexibility *is* permitted any shortage of money would be met by a decline in the general price-level and equilibrium between the demand for, and supply of, money would be automatically re-created. This process might contain lags, perhaps featuring temporarily high interest rates, but the evidence suggests that these lags were short. The constraint on growth exerted under such conditions would be minimal. Historically, of course, prices were especially flexible downwards during the world 'transport revolution' of 1870–1900. See Gregory and Sailors (1976), pp. 836–51. (b) It is clear that Barkai made quite inadequate allowance for bank deposits in his definition of money supply. Once these are calculated and introduced into the total monetary aggregate, the supply constraint again disappears. See Drummond (1976), pp. 663–88. If allowance is made for both falling prices *and* enlarged bank deposits, the money supply for the 1880s does not contract by 1.5 per cent p.a. but *expands* by 2 5 per cent p a. (Gregory and Sailors, 1976, p. 845). The matter is still under contention, and, doubtless, there will be yet further elaboration. In the meantime, these important reservations require acknowledgement. And, in any event, even the revised growth rate of 2.5 per cent p.a. for the 1880s is lower than the rate of monetary expansion required for rapid industrial development.
54. And witness Witte's introduction of a liquor monopoly in the 1890s, rapidly to become the Tsar's largest single money-spinner.
55. Cf. von Laue (1963), pp. 199–202.
56. Gerschenkron (1962), pp. 59–61, 126–7; *idem* (1968), pp. 136–8, 251.
57. *Idem* (1962), p. 71.
58. Cited by von Laue (1963), p. 141. The remark was made, originally, of the gold standard policy.
59. Cited *ibid.*, p. 35.
60. Cited *ibid.*, p. 164.
61. von Laue (1964), pp. 52–3 (my italics).
62. Gerschenkron (1963), pp. 158, 167–8.
63. Budget Report of 1894, cited by von Laue (1963), p. 78.
64. US Department of Commerce and Labour (1905a).
65. Metzer (1974), p. 535.
66. Von Laue (1963), pp. 232–5.

67. Metzer (1974), pp. 537–49.
68. Kahan (1967), p. 466.
69. Miller (1926), p. 199.
70. Collins (1973), pp. 777–88.
71. Cited *ibid.*, p. 781.
72. Cited *ibid.*, p. 783.
73. *Economist*, March 1901.
74. McKay (1970), pp. 244–8ff.
75. *Ibid.*, pp. 244–8, 260–7.
76. Von Laue (1963), p. 236.
77. Portal (1974), p. 164.
78. Crisp (1976), pp. 36, 38ff.
79. Von Laue (1963), p. 281. The total revenue for the 1900 budget was probably about 1114.2 m. roubles but was displayed as 1704.1 m. (p. 282).
80. Kahan (1967), p. 462.
81. *Ibid.*, pp. 462–4.
82. Miller (1926), pp. 137, 297.
83. Kahan (1967), p. 475. Gregory and Sailors (1976, p. 850) have contested this point, arguing that Russian reserves were not significantly greater than the international average and that *total* Russian reserves were not overloaded with gold. In contrast, their main constituent was foreign currency while gold remained relatively scarce.
84. Miller (1926), pp. 110–14.
85. Barkai (1973), pp. 344, 358.
86. *Ibid.*, pp. 361–2.
87. *Ibid.*, p. 366.
88. Cited by Garvy (1972), p. 889.
89. Cited *ibid.*, p. 890.
90. *Ibid.*
91. Gregory and Sailors (1976), p. 847; but see more generally, pp. 846–51.
92. Barkai (1973), p. 362.
93. Von Laue (1963), p. 100.
94. Kahan (1967), p. 465.
95. *Brassey's Naval Annual*, 1898, p. 37; 1903, pp. 28–9.
96. Kahan (1967), p. 465.
97. Nesterenko (1954), p. 29.
98. Cited by McKay (1970), p. 74.
99. *Ibid.*, pp. 348–9, 352–3, 366–7, 383.
100. Gerschenkron (1963), p. 388.
101. See von Laue's translation of 'A Secret Memorandum of S. Witte on the Industrialization of Imperial Russia', *Journal of Modern History*, 26, (1954), p. 70.
102. Ellison (1965), pp. 537–8.
103. Cited by McKay (1970), pp. 25–8.
104. Cited by von Laue (1963), p. 287.
105. Sontag (1968), pp. 529–41.
106. McKay (1970), p. 29.
107. Barkai (1973), p. 360.
108. *Ibid.*, p. 362.
109. Gerschenkron (1968), p. 228.
110. *Ibid.*, pp. 237–9.

111. Miller (1926), pp. 48–9.
112. Von Laue (1963), p. 184.
113. Miller (1926), pp. 46, 55, 60.
114. Barkai (1973), p. 370.
115. A. S. Suvorin quoted by von Laue (1969), p. 261.
116. Rashin (1958), p. 582.
117. The opinion of a hostile ministerial colleague, Lobko, that Witte permitted 'the artificial and excessive growth of industry . . . out of proportion to the growth of the consumer market' suggests that even conservative thinking allowed some room for some of the necessary qualifications. Cited by von Laue (1963), p. 220.
118. Quoted by von Laue (1963), p. 193.
119. McKay (1970), p. 10 (my emphasis).
120. Miller (1926), p. 299.
121. *Ibid.*, p. 299.
122. Von Laue (1963), pp. 211–14.
123. Gerschenkron (1947), p. 152.
124. Quoted by Gerschenkron (1963), p. 154.
125. Gerschenkron (1962), p. 142.
126. Volin (1966), p. 123.
127. Gerschenkron (1968), p. 231.
128. Redemption payments were to be halved in 1906 and abolished altogether in January 1907.
129. Gerschenkron (1968), pp. 237–41.
130. Volin (1966), p. 124.
131. Gerschenkron (1968), p. 243.
132. Male (1971), pp. 18–19.
133. Miller (1926), p. 99.
134. Crisp (1967), pp. 206–8. Also Yaney (1971), pp. 6–7.
135. Gerschenkron (1968), p. 244.
136. Yaney (1971), p. 6.
137. Chayanov (1966).
138. Miller (1926), p. 63n. Note 1 pood = approximately 17.2 kilogram.
139. Calculated from main crop totals given in Mitchell (1975), p. 262, cols. 1–6.
140. Metzer (1974), pp. 544–9. However, Metzer is not sufficiently exact as to the period in which he considers this increased responsiveness to *originate*.
141. Miller (1926), p. 92.
142. Crisp (1967), pp. 208–9.
143. Miller (1926), p. 93.
144. Metzer (1974), pp. 544–5.
145. Portal (1974), p. 165.
146. This estimate is a Soviet one, by P. A. Khromov. But assessments pitched around one-third of total industrial output have widespread currency. See Crisp (1976), p. 48. Further, the recent reassessment of Russian national income in 1913 by M. E. Falkus implies an even larger share of net industrial output attributable to *kustar*, a figure of 37.9 per cent for the area that was to become USSR territory. See Falkus (1968), pp. 58, 71.
147. Lenin (1957).
148. Shanin (1972); also *idem* (1971), pp. 222–35.
149. Shanin (1971), p. 228.

150. *Ibid.*, pp. 223–4.
151. Volin (1966), p. 121.
152. Gregory (1972), pp. 426–7.
153. Roosa (1972), p. 395.
154. Miller (1926), pp. 223–30.
155. McKay (1970), pp. 184, 306.
156. *Ibid.*, pp. 117–18.
157. *Ibid.*, p. 143.
158. *Ibid.*, p. 116.
159. *Ibid.*, pp. 193–6.
160. *Ibid.*, p. 199.
161. The number of pupils in rural elementary schools increased from 1.75 m. in 1885 to over 7 m. in 1914 and the number of teachers from 24,389 in 1880 to 109,370 in 1911. Kahan (1971a), p. 302. Between 1860 and 1913 employed workers in industry, construction and railways multiplied by 4.3 times, but pupils in elementary and secondary schools increased by sixteen times. See Kahan (1971b), p. 372.
162. Cipolla (1969).
163. Rashin (1958), p. 582.
164. Bowman and Anderson (1963).
165. Vickers Archive: Letter Books, Nicolaiev Commission to London, 18 Nov. 1912.
166. McKay (1970), p. 186.
167. Portal (1974), p. 175.
168. US Department of Commerce (1905b), cf. p. 112, 'It is a common practice of Russians to attend German industrial schools of all the better grades . . . Everywhere the Russian has found his way into the halls of learning of the German Empire.'
169. Limitations persisted, however. Even in 1914 the vast bulk of the Empire's own educational provision remained at the elementary level. Out of the total student enrolments for 1914–15, 91.8 per cent were at the elementary level, only 6.9 per cent at secondary level, and a miniscule 1.3 per cent at higher education level. Kahan (1971b), p. 373.
170. McKay (1970), pp. 187–9.
171. Roosa (1972), pp. 397–417.
172. Lyashchenko (1970), pp. 669–70. By 1914, 40 per cent of Russian industrial labour worked in plants employing more than 1000 men; again this proportion was twice the American level (Rimlinger, 1961, p. 210).
173. Lyashchenko (1970), pp. 679–80.
174. McKay (1970), p. 137.
175. *Ibid.*, pp. 279–80.
176. Although a lesser form of integration was achieved in the engineering sector in 1912 and was extended during the First World War.
177. Garvy (1972), pp. 876–8.
178. Crisp (1967), pp. 201, 221.
179. *Ibid.*, pp. 196–9, 210–16; Miller (1926), pp. 81–7.
180. Crisp (1967), Tables VII.5–8, pp. 192–5.
181. Gindin (1927) cited by Crisp (1967), p. 230.
182. Cameron (ed.) (1967), pp. 301–5.
183. *Ibid.*, p. 298.

184. Gregory (1972), p. 432.
185. Yaney (1971), pp. 5–8.
186. Haimson (1964), pp. 633–7.
187. Volin (1966), p. 122.
188. *Ibid.*, pp. 121–3.
189. See for instance, Lyashchenko (1970), p. 634 *passim*.
190. Vickers Archive: Microfilm 214.
191. McKay (1970), p. 349.
192. Shimkin (1949), p. 30.
193. Crisp (1967), p. 226.
194. McKay (1970), pp. 235, 277.
195. Crisp (1967), pp. 230–1.
196. Garvy (1972), p. 884.
197. Cited by Miller (1926), pp. 84–8.
198. Cited by Garvy (1972), p. 881 (my emphasis).
199. McKay (1970), p. 237 gives some brief argument to the contrary, while Gindin (1927), and Bovykin (1959), pp. 109–20 are notably more committed.
200. Explanatory Note to Proposed Budget, 1913, cited by Miller (1926), p. 132.
201. Lyashchenko (1970), p. 534.
202. Bovykin (1959).
203. Shatsillo (1968), p. 209, provides a notably more modest estimate of 350 m. roubles actually expended 1907–12 upon *naval* construction only. Recent research suggests that the sums approved for actual expenditure on all armament heads *within* the period 1906–14 may have totalled 2050 m. roubles, or 11 per cent of the national income for 1913 (calculated from Gattrell, 1979, pp. 15–16). But the amount *spent* on all weaponry accounts may again have been less, perhaps 1100 m. roubles.
204. Falkus (1968), p. 57.
205. Lyashchenko (1970), pp. 555, 739, 769.
206. Trebilcock (1973), pp. 254–76.
207. Vickers Archive: Microfilm 215.
208. Rosenberg (1963), pp. 220–4.
209. As indeed some was from wartime Russian advances in shell and fuse manufacture. I am indebted to important work upon the tsarist war economy and the Vankov organization by P. W. Gattrell for this information. This is described in his thesis 'Russian Heavy Industry and State Defence, 1908–18; Pre-War Expansion and Wartime Mobilization' (unpublished Ph. D. thesis, Cambridge, 1979).
210. See Trebilcock (1969), p. 475.

CHAPTER FIVE

The Powers of Deprivation: Italy, Austria-Hungary, Spain

The ground for considering these three countries within a single comparative structure are considerable. All three were marginal international powers; Italy trembling upon the brink of great power status, her lavish naval programmes already imitating the expenditure patterns of the élite; the Habsburg Empire, territorially the second largest state in Europe but slowly crumbling towards disintegration; and Spain, divested of her overseas possessions in the Spanish-American War of 1898, her international role terminated in all but rhetoric by collision with the surfacing bulk of the transatlantic democracy. Economically, too, there were strong similiarities: all three were late and slow developers; all three retained massive estate agricultures and somehow missed the chance of land reform; all three experienced severe problems of regional under-development; all three attracted the attentions of 'penetrative' foreign capital; all three harboured military ambitions which outran their budgetary resources. Yet the similarities were not all oppressive ones; by 1914 each nation had constructed a modern sector – the steel, engineering, and automobiles of northern Italy; the heavy manufactures of metropolitan Austria and the arma-ment industries of Steyr and Skoda; the shipbuilding and metals of Bilbao and Viscaya – which clearly lifted it beyond the reach of chronic, and into the realm of moderate, backwardness. Starting around 1800 from a level of peasant primitivism not far removed from the Russian, each economy by 1914 had created notable successes in both manufacture and agriculture, and at least two of them – Italy and metropolitan Austria,[1] through probably not Spain – had outpaced Russia in the quest for 'modern economic growth'. The similar-ities are such that inter-country comparisons should yield significant results: recently Nadal has argued that 'discussion of the Italian example can help to enrich discussion of the Spanish problem',[2] and it is not unlikely that extra enrichment can be drawn from the plentiful eccentricities of the Habsburg Empire. As a group these countries should provide an additional testing ground for the major Gerschenkronian hypotheses. Theoretically, these are economies in which one would expect to find 'big spurts', development biased towards capital goods industries, active direction by the state, and, somewhat later, the rise of growth-promoting investment banks. It remains to be seen whether the unstable, dualistic, 'colonial' and belligerent realities of these states could stretch, or be stretched, to include these promising indications.

THE MODEST PROFILES OF GRADUAL GROWTH

Certainly, much recent analysis has considered at least some of these countries as suitable candidates for discontinuous or spurt-like patterns of development. Unusually but not unreasonably, however, Spain has largely escaped such attentions: there may be marginal disagreement about her exact level of archaism – Nadal considering her predicament as 'less that of a latecomer, than of an attempt, largely thwarted, to join the ranks of the firstcomers',[3] Carr judging the economy even of the 1960s as 'only a *candidate* for sustained growth'[4] – but there are few differences concerning either the pace or the chronology of the bid for modernization. Broadly, this fell into three phases: a period (1715 – 1830) of proto-industrialization of the characteristic type, although in this case, its bases of small-scale textile production and old-regime cameralism were much weaker than was common further north; a period (1830–90) of low-order technological development and primary exportation, mainly of minerals and wine, but displaying more sustained forms of factory production in light manufactures; a period (1890 onwards) of increasingly capital-intensive industrialization resting upon development in steel, engineering, and shipbuilding, as well as upon a scattering of higher technologies. At no point in this process did a fully fledged national take-off become established.

The early developments were unusually weak: in 1719 the Crown attempted a 'substitute' for large-scale enterprise by establishing the woollen manufactory at Guadalajara, but the bulk of industry remained small-scale, artisanal, and capital-starved. In Valladolid in 1781 there were 91 producers of woollens and serges with an average equipment per unit of only 2.6 looms.[5] Expanding agricultural output and improving productivity in Catalonia, 1715 – 35, followed by rising agricultural costs after 1750, provided in sequence both the means and the incentive for the pursuit of an industrial alternative to agricultural profit-taking.[6] Even so, the Catalan cotton industry – perhaps Spain's most convincing exponent of proto-industrialization – was slow to apply advanced English methods before the 1800s, and was badly damaged by the Napoleonic Wars while still at an impressionable stage. Convincing signs of incipient industrialism came only in the second phase, when, in the 1830s and 1840s, the economy executed if not a leap, at least a hop. Under the sting of high wage costs and the emollient of repatriated capital, returning from the colonies confiscated by the Vienna Settlement, the cotton textile industry was pushed forward virtually to full mechanization in the spinning, and to semi-mechanization in the weaving, branch by 1860. At this point, the Catalan mills were consuming raw cotton at ten times the rate of 1820 and had overtaken the total output of the Belgian and Italian cotton industries.[7] The half-century between 1830 and 1880, the heyday of the eastern textile industry,

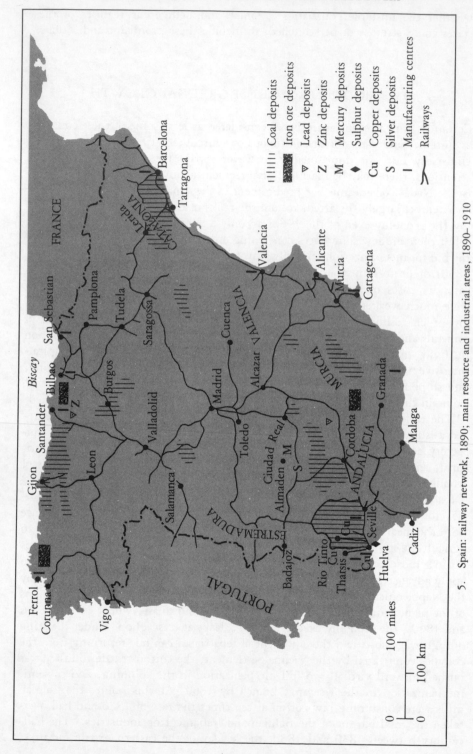

5. Spain: railway network, 1890; main resource and industrial areas, 1890–1910

witnessed the domination of Catalonia within the Spanish manufacturing economy. Yet, during the same years, the rapid adoption of the Bessemer process by the metal industries of the continent greatly expanded demand for the high-quality iron ore of the Spanish south-eastern region and the happy progress of *Phylloxera vastatrix* through the French vineyards equally encouraged European enthusiasm for the wines of Malaga, Gerona, and Tarragona. From mid-century the appetite of a bibulous continent gave wine the premier place among Spanish exports, carrying viticulture to a peak performance between 1882 and 1892. When these successes are augmented by the upswings in railway investment of 1878–80 and 1882–84, intimations of take-off perhaps begin to stir. Unfortunately, they are not true guides: in the Spanish case, the presence of lead sectors, expanding overseas trade, and technological adaptation merely denotes passing advantages and false starts. The Catalan mainstay continued to suffer from over-small production units, deficiencies in raw materials – especially iron and coal – and an excessive dependence upon the harvest. At its best the textile industry accumulated only half the average spindle-count of the other European producers and recorded an output per man less than half that of the USA.[8] From the 1880s the growth in cotton production began to slow, and, during the 1900s, as agricultural crisis strangled domestic demand and international crisis disposed of Catalonia's irreplaceable colonial markets, output turned balefully downward. Meanwhile, the 'best practice' of European metallurgy moved on, leaving Spanish ores to one side, and the worst habits of *Phylloxera* spread to Spain – initially by 1876, devastatingly by 1892 – killing the wine export in the bud. As a take-off, these attempts developed critical failures in propulsive power; as a leap they lacked grace or balance.

Higher standards were reached in the third phase, in new regions, and with different materials. The upsurge after 1885, based on the minerals of Viscaya and Santander and the modern heavy industries of Bilbao represented the Spanish economy's best efforts prior to 1914 (see Table 5.1). Nevertheless, the 'Basque industrial revolution' was embarrassingly situated: it lay to the west of the superannuated economic system of Catalonia, to the north of the de-industrialized zones around Malaga, and within an archaic national economy which still permitted agriculture to occupy 68 per cent of the workforce and

Table 5.1   Mining, processing, and export of Spanish iron ore (thousand tons)

	Total Spanish extraction	Mined in Vizcaya	% of total smelted in Spain	% of total ore exported
1861–70	2,579	47.1	–	–
1871–80	12,551	63.3	–	–
1881–90	49,425	72.0	7.7	92.3
1891–1900	66,349	74.5	8.2	91.8
1901–1910	87,246	53.5	8.8	91.2
1861–1913	245,919	61.7		

Source: Adapted from Nadal (1973), p. 582.

to generate 38.4 per cent of national income.[9] Not even the dockyards, steel-mills, and cement works of the northern 'renaissance' could carry a complete industrialization in such abrasive company. Across the three growth phases, Spanish economic performance displays no dramatic turnabouts; rather it is gradual, sometimes stumbling, forever replacing collapsed prospects with fresh hopes, both continuous and suppressed.

Curiously, the not dissimilar growth patterns of Austria-Hungary and Italy have generated much more dissension than the behaviour of the Iberian economy. Once more, a period of proto-industrialization is common ground, running in Italy from the mid-eighteenth century to the 1860s,[10] and in Austria over the approximate period 1720–1867. In each case, this prolonged preparation contained an acceleration in the 1830s, not unlike the increased Spanish tempo of that time, and, as so frequently throughout Europe, drew its momentum largely from the textile industries. Within the Habsburg Empire, Vienna and Voralberg offered a wide selection of cloths, with cotton gaining ground from the 1720s, while Bohemia-Moravia boasted cotton, linen, and woollen manufactures.[11] The organization of production combined domestic outputting, a majority of semi-rural workers, and urban facilities for skilled processess, but some operations were on the largest scale: the Linz manufactor-ies in Upper Austria drew upon nearly 12,000 domestic employees by 1773 and 16,000 by 1790 while major integrated mills were in existence at the Horni Litvinov and Nova Kdyne factories by 1775.[12] Generally, the most impressive manufacturing achievements were centred upon Bohemia: by 1798 the textile industries provided more than 80 per cent of Bohemia's non-agricultural jobs and occupied 17.5 per cent of the population, while the foremost cotton mills were leading Europe in the application of English-style mules. In turn, the needs of the large textile manufactories set up a demand for sophisticated machines which, as early as 1821, were being satisfied by workshops like that of Scholl and Luz of Brno, effectively laying the founda-tions for the engineering sector of the whole Empire. Industrial prospects in the Czech lands were sufficiently bright by the 1820s and 1830s to attract yet another seminal group of British technologists, machine-builders like Bail-don (at Brno), Edward Thomas (at Lieberec), Thomas Bracegirdle (at Jab-lonec), David Evans and Joseph Lee (both at Prague) or ironmasters like David Thomas and William Jones (both at Vítkovice). It is not surprising that by 1830 commentators were drawing the usual comparisons with Britain, one arguing that 'Bohemia can feel flattered that it can be for the Continent, a little England', while Klima himself observes that the Czech developments were 'quite similar' to the contemporary advances in industrialized Belgium.[13] To restore perspective within the Empire, however, it is worth recording that, even before 1750, the Alpine regions were converting their rich iron ores into such high-grade products as steel cutlery, scythes, and sickles.

In Italy the initial mix was very similar: by the 1780s the silkmasters around Turin and Como employed nearly 300 reels and 16,000 workers, while the cotton mills around Milan could enlist as many as 500 workers apiece. Again, higher grade processes such as glass-making, metal-working, and

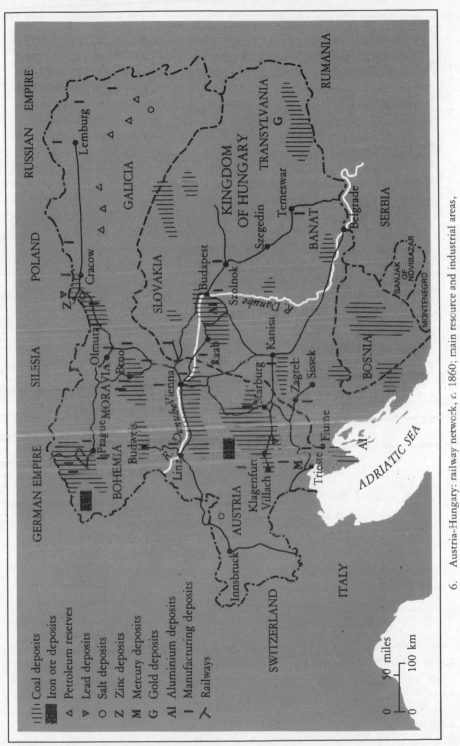

6. Austria-Hungary: railway network, c. 1860; main resource and industrial areas,
   1860–1910

7. Italy: railway network, *c.* 1870; main resource and industrial areas, 1870—1910

sugar-refining grew up in Brescia and Tuscany between 1750 and 1790, while paper-making expanded at Fabriano and Bologna. Moreover, in this respect unlike Spain, both Italian and Habsburg economies drew advantages from the Napoleonic Wars and the Continental System. The textile centres of Bohemia-Moravia and Lower Austria obtained their English-style machinery in good time and drew both rich profits and further mechanization from the markets left vacant by Napoleon's autarky. Conversely, Italy benefited from the internationalism *within* the system, acquiring her new technology from France after 1808, together with enterprising projectors from many corners of the conquered territories. French capitalists were attracted especially to Lombardy, while Alsatians, Swiss, and Germans brought large-scale ventures and advanced methods to Piedmont.[14] After a brief period of post-war readjustment, both the Italian states and the Empire, once more in step with Spain, profited from the worldwide expansion in the textile market which occurred between 1830 and 1860. By 1840 the cotton-spinning centres of Lower Austria, Voralberg and Lieberec, like the woollen spinning centres of Vienna and Brno, were almost entirely machine-powered, while modern large-scale organization had spread across the majority of the Empire's silk textile industry.[15] No less than 41 per cent of total industrial output was contributed by the textile sector by 1841 (with a good half of the total cotton-spinning yield accounted for by the single province of Bohemia), while the metal and metal-products sector achieved only a 13.4 per cent share. Similarly, the Italian states of Piedmont and Lombardy – the latter an Austrian satellite until 1859 – had absorbed much of their cotton-spinning capacity into large and advanced mills by 1848; together they could amass some sixty installations averaging 3,000–3,500 spindles. But, according to Cafagna, it was the silk industry which played leading sector to the pre-*risorgimento* economy, drawing land-owning and financial capital into its first non-agricultural investment, educating a factory workforce, and providing an export spearhead for the century after 1815. By 1850 the Piedmontese and Lombard centres contained 700–800 silk-throwing mills and a labour force of 150,000.[16] Yet it was a measure of the change in economic climate between 1830 and 1860 that textiles were no longer alone as large-scale contributors to industrialization. In Austria, the iron industry advanced to provide a twin leading sector, increasing its output between 1841 and 1847 by 98 per cent[17] and amassing some sixty-three modern puddling furnaces by 1846. Perhaps more surprisingly, the spindle count of the Austrian cotton industry exceeded that of the German Customs Union by 1840, and the production per head of the imperial iron industry also drew ahead of the German competitor for a period around 1850. In each case, these Austrian industries were joining the European leaders.[18] If not quite of this stature, the iron industries of Lombardy, Tuscany, Piedmont, and Calabria did profit over this period from the expanding military requirements of the individual Italian states. Similarities were probably more pronounced in railway development: Austria completed her first (horse-drawn) line from Linz to Budweis in 1832, while Italian construction was equally precocious, commencing the Naples–Portici connexion in 1830 and the Milan–Monza in 1832. By the late 1850s, the engineering industries of the Genoa–Turin–Milan triangle were responding to railway activity and the important enterprise of Ansaldo (Genoa) began assembling imported locomotives as early as 1855. When capital-intensive and technology-intensive metal industries and railway workshops began to join the textile mills, with their relatively modest capitals, easily recycled profits, and undemanding skills, the proto-industrial phase was clearly drawn to a close.

But for all three countries, the transition remained a partial one. If the spinning of yarn in each case was widely mechanized by 1850, weaving frequently remained a handicraft occupation beyond 1900. If iron production made progress, it also confronted massive internal constraints. In Italy scarcity of coal forced the retention of charcoal-smelting, restricted the application of new technology, and cramped the growth of firms, much as it had done in France. In Austria-Hungary, rare and poorly located coking coal, miniaturized Alpine furnaces, and the vested interests of timber-raising estates hampered advances in practice and organization. In both cases, the utilization of steam-power, and the engineering industries to provide it, were severely impeded by shortages of essential minerals; and these, in turn, ensured that traditional systems of water-power remained attractive. In Spain, iron manufacture was effectively confined to the Malaga region before 1850, while nearly three-quarters of the entire national output flowed from just two of this district's furnaces. Here the problem was less deficiency of raw materials than foreign occupation of the chief resource areas; the 'exploitation de type primitif' ascribed by Gille to foreign interests in Italy finds ready and powerful Spanish parallels.[19] Furthermore, the railway developments, which in all three countries formed an important market base for the heavy technologies, remained poorly developed in scale and profitability: in the mid-1850s Spain could boast only 500 kilometres of operational track, the Italian states 1,207 kilometres and the Empire 2,145 kilometres. Around mid-century, Gille considers Italy's industrial economy to have been 'sinon artisanale, du moins peu orientée vers les formes modernes du capitalisme';[20] and again very much the same might go for its Austrian and Spanish neighbours. Broadly speaking, then, there is substantial agreement that, down to 1850 or 1860, the three economies followed a more or less similar pattern: gradual advance based largely on textile spinning, insecure but accelerating after 1830; strong retained elements of domestic industry; lingering primitivism in non-textile industrial developments.

After 1850, however, agreement is a stranger to the economic history of Austria-Hungary and Italy, if not to that of Spain. In metropolitan Austria, the hunt has been for the take-off, something resembling which has been detected in every conceivable quarter: by Gross in the period 1851–73,[21] by Purs in the same period for the Czech provinces,[22] by Marz,[23] Herz,[24] and Rudolph[25] in the decade before 1914, not to speak of the renegrade spurt sighted by Blum in the 1840s.[26] In Italy, a similar pursuit roused twin hares: the period of 'primitive accumulation' placed by Romeo in the 1860s and 1870s, and trailing a notable upsurge in manufacturing at its heels,[27] an interpretation sustained to some extent by Eckhaus[28] and contested vigorously by Gerschenkron[29] and Luzzatto,[30] among others; and the period of the 'big spurt' proposed by Gerschenkron for the period 1896–1908[31] and distrusted by Eckaus,[32] Golzio,[33] and Cafagna,[34] among others.

Certainly, the claims for an early Austrian take-off are supported by impressive growth rates – 4.09 per cent 1865–85 (real industrial output) against 3.42 per cent for the competing period 1880–1911 – but the underpinnings elsewhere are not especially robust. Again, the regional differences within the Empire proved crucial. If coal consumption rose by an annual rate of 10.4 per cent for metropolitan Austria 1851–73, and at the even more impressive rate of 11.5 per cent for her Hungarian partner, only the Czech section of the Empire possessed sufficient coal actually to satisfy the area's industrial needs; the upswing merely took the other manufacturing centres to the verge of a resource constraint.[35] Similarly, if the entire Empire increased its consumption of raw iron by 7 per cent p.a. 1851–73, domestic output scarcely sufficed to meet this requirement. Indeed the imperial iron industry continued to take more than half its smelt from an archaic charcoal technology well into the 1880s (the world average was 10%). Even the major railway-building spurts of 1855–60 and 1867–73 – expanding operational track within the Empire from 1748 to 15,597 kilometres – while they created a new lead sector for the Habsburg economy, were accompanied by a major deceleration in the performance of the *previous* lead sector, the cotton textiles industry. The total count of cotton spindles within Austro-Hungarian territory, after rising from 1 m. to 1¼ m. over the eight years 1841–48 took another quarter-century to reach 1½ m. In agriculture, too, despite the serf emancipation measures of 1848, there remained sufficient mire to weigh down the economic machine: in 1869 67 per cent of the Empire's labour force remained in the primary sector (64% in 1900), a proportion larger than that borne by any country which *did* achieve take-off before 1914. Italy's comparable figure of 61 per cent in 1871 perhaps measures her rather higher chances of take-off, while Spain's rating of 70 per cent in 1877 measures her greater distance from it. The ingenuity of efforts designed to place Austria-Hungary within the upswing of the second Pan-European Kondratiev cycle may thus command applause but not trust. To be explicit, however, most of the 'optimistic' observers claim not a take-off but merely the most dramatic growth rates of the Empire's nineteenth-century experience; and usually they are careful to present these developments as 'a *continuation* of the impact of early industrializing changes in the second quarter of the century'.[36] This emphasis appears correct: the shortcomings within the Habsburg economic surge, especially those of endowment, are clearly related to the constraints upon earlier developments and would surely rule out any major discontinuities in performance.

Until recently, measurement of the mid-century acceleration would anyway have been considered secondary to proper appraisal of the Austrian Great Depression of the 1870s and 1880s, apparently a recrudescence of backwardness sufficiently savage to submerge any tentative approach to industrialization. But now even this negative discontinuity can be removed: the recession in metropolitan Austria, like many of this generation, has turned out a mythical beast; its growth rates in industrial production of 4.3 per cent p.a. 1880–96 (Rudolph) and in bank assets *per capita* of 4.43 per cent 1873–96 (Good) are, in fact, more impressive than those of the 'spurt' period of the 1900s (2.7% and 3.84% p.a. respectively).[37] There is no strong reason for distrusting the recent statistical evaluations; they may be viewed as an important revision, especially since Good's broadly based sample of financial assets would appear to deliver an effective answer to one of the most common, if not particularly substantial, 'pessimistic' claims – that the banking sector was particularly seriously afflicted during the 1870s and 1880s. Given the weakened stature of the intervening recession, the recent calculations are able to suggest a continuity between the strong growth of 1870–1900 and that of the period 1900–14, permitted to retain its reputation for industrial dynamism with new 'German' technologies such as electro-technicals and chemicals joining the more traditional lead sectors of textiles, metals, and sugar-refining. Moreover, the fact that the period 1865–85 (Gross) and the period 1873–96 (Good) may have moderately exceeded the pre-war years in industrial growth rates does not greatly assist the claims of the earlier eras to be considered as 'take-off' phases: the transition in growth rates between all major subperiods is noticeably gentle. Indeed Good is able to calculate the probability that Austria experienced take-off at any stage before 1914,[38] and finds it extremely low. As the very multiplicity of the alternative claims for industrial acceleration might imply, the most convincing interpretation of pre-war Habsburg economic achievement should probably emphasize the gradualness, constancy, and lack of discontinuity in economic performance. Like Spain – and less closely like France – Austria-Hungary demonstrated that the slow, halting but persistent approach to industrialization constituted as plausible a model for nineteenth-century developers as the dramatic convolutions of the more favoured or more regimented economies. By 1914 both these wasting empires had been industrializing over nearly two centuries but neither had taken off. Equally clearly, with growth rates never exceeding 4–5 per cent for any sustained period, the prospects of a 'great spurt' are scarcely convincing.

With Italy, the matter is more complex still. The merits of two major growth bursts, one in the decade or so after unification, the other at the turn of the century are disputed with more seriousness and detail than anything in the Austrian experience, yet they are separated by a 'Great Depression' in the 1880s much less prone to revision than the Austrian. The problem turns around the 1860s and 1870s: if these were years of healthy advance and orderly preparation, Italian industrial development could be seen as a smoothly continuous process of adaptation, interrupted only by the temporary 'transition' of the 1880s; if, however, these early years were ones of deprivation and economic failure, and were followed by further bouts of dislocation in the 1880s, then the subsequent development of the 1890s and 1900s might be construed as a 'leap' out of backwardness. The basis of modern gradualism is supplied by Romeo's proposition that the absence of deliberate economic reforms within the *risorgimento* process in no way compromised Italy's chances of substantial industrial growth; on the contrary, traditional estate agriculture could accumulate capital ready for industrial application and underdeveloped regions could be tapped for resources in the interest of the modern sector. Precisely the exploitative aspect of old-style agriculture would serve as a means of 'primitive capitalist accumulation'.

Undoubtedly, there is support for the idea that the unification of the Italian state and governmental structure was accompanied by a definite upsurge in manufacturing, however disunified its *economic* bases might remain. Textiles continued to build upon their early successes: the cotton mills, centred mainly on Piedmont, doubled their intake of raw materials, 1871–75, and almost doubled spindle capacity, 1871–76, while similar rates of output advance were recorded in silk between 1865 and 1871. Metals, too, did well: the production of lower quality iron semi-finished articles tripled, 1860–80, and the raising of ores increased spectacularly, by 500 per cent for iron, 1860–81, 250 per cent for lead and zinc. Within the transport sector, the characteristic European pressures of the 'railway Kondratiev' appeared to be present: track length increased by three and a half times, 1861–81 (from 2,773 to 9,506 kilometres). Even in an agriculture normally discounted for its poor cultivation, an average growth rate in value added of 1.96 per cent p.a. was achieved in 1861/65–1881; corn production doubled, rice more than doubled, and wine advanced by 50 per cent, 1855–75. Eckaus concludes that the mining sector grew in the decade or so after unification faster than, and the agricultural sector as fast as, at any time in the nineteenth century.[39]

But, even with these factual reinforcements, the Romeo structure does not function well. For all the agricultural upturn, Italy's performance remained comparatively very weak: the complete crop of the 1860s and 1870s did not exceed one-quarter of the French,[40] and, embarrassingly for Romeo, total output displayed an almost immediate reluctance to expand on its post unification successes, retaining a marked upward stickness throughout the period 1876/80–1896/1901.[41] Deficient markets and capital supplies held productivity at distinctly low levels, allowing Luzzatto to select 'a complete lack of progress' for his judgement upon performance in the important grain sector. Painted in these colours, Italian agriculture does not make a convincing engine of original accumulation. Nor, indeed, is there much evidence to suggest that capital accumulation or transfer in fact occurred. The spurt which should have succeeded the earlier foundation-building did not materialize at its appointed time in the 1880s and the behaviour of Italian savings is not such as to suggest the existence of a powerful underlying stream of agricultural replenishment. Savings rates were negligible after unification, rose to a modest 4 per cent in the 1870s, and reached their peak of 6 per cent around 1880, on the eve, not of an economic upswing, but of a deep recession. The rate of gross investment varied in the meagre range 7.9–9.8 per cent of GNP, 1860–80, and its embodiment in the preparatory apparatus for industrialization was the reverse of generous: for instance the share of public works in GNP *fell* throughout the period and did not regain the low level of 1860 until 1881–85.[42] The initial advances in railway construction were financed, virtually as an enclave operation, and, much as in Spain, by foreign, and pre-eminently French, capital, its primary purpose not the extension of the Italian economy but the exploitation of Italian raw materials. Even then, the resulting networks were, again comparatively, of limited scope – some 9,500 kilometres in 1881 against 24,249 kilometres for France and 34,381 kilometres for Germany – and many of them suffered declining revenues after 1861. If this style of accumulation was sufficiently modest, so too were its industrial consequences: the post-1860 economic upturn was rapidly qualified from the middle of the decade by severe deterioration both in the overseas trade balance and in public finances, now required to support the chauvinistic policies of an ambitious new nation. Ferrara concluded, 'there would be very little in the economic order to show the observer that a great nation has been formed . . . what little sporadic industrial activity there is, is nothing but the artificial and ephemeral activity of a government whose only industrial aim is to clothe soldiers and make guns'.[43] Certainly, with national income advancing at only 0.3 per cent p.a. 1861–70, and falling by 0.23 per cent p.a., 1871–80, there is little indication anywhere on the economic scene of the primitive savings spree required for an early Italian take-off.

As in Austria and Spain, the first attempts at adjusting a traditional to a modern fashion of industrial growth were largely ineffectual: in company with the Austrian spurt of 1851–73, or the Spanish upturn of the 1830s, the Italian development of the post-unification era emerges as a continuation of growth patterns drawn earlier in the century, rather than as any significant break in trend. Therefore, none of these countries can be comfortably fitted into the general mid-century upsurge which saw the industrialization of the 'second-generation' powers. Unlike Austria and Spain, however, Italy's fortunes in the succeeding years of the 1880s and early 1890s were sufficiently luckless for the *downward* discontinuity of a 'Great Depression' to achieve some relevance. Romeo is entirely isolated in ascribing 'discreetly rapid growth' to this period, and even this is a somewhat obviously determined attempt to derive the necessary consequences of his hypothesis from theoretical expectations rather than real conditions; most observers find the growth so discreet as to be entirely concealed. More accurately, perhaps, the period should be assessed as one of stagnation and Gerschenkron's estimate of 0.3 per cent p.a. advance in industrial output 1888–96 stands as representative of its least promising capabilities.[44] The chief disruptive influences at work during the 1880s and early 1890s were a gathering agricultural depression and a debilitating swing in investment away from industry towards housing, public works, and urban expansion, especially that of Rome. Where an urbanization boom had galvanized the more advanced economy of France after 1896, a parallel event drew a vast movement of capital out of the more directly productive investment in plant and equipment which Italy's more backward economy required, and prevented it from growing, as both the Spanish and Austrian economies had done, through the 'general' European depression. Additionally, the banking sector entrusted with the administration of this real-estate bonanza was damaged by the attendant speculative excesses to a point not far short of total destruction. Throughout the 1880s, fixed capital formation in housing and public works, quite remarkably, consumed as much investment as the entirety of industrial capital formation; not until after 1897 did the balance tip back, more conventionally, towards the manufacturing option.[45] Eckaus' proposition that these venturesome funding operations actually provided the social capital to underpin the accelerated growth after 1896 is probably over-generous. More likely, the Italian economy was subjected to one of the disadvantages of economic lateness: the diversion, due to demonstration effects from more advanced countries, of much-needed investment funds to areas of high prestige but marginal utility at a relatively much earlier stage of development than was usual with the industrial forerunners. At any event, while the Italians used French money to beautify their cities, the economy slowed to a tempo from which, according to Gerschenkron, only a 'great spurt' could rescue it.

Certainly, strongly revived expansion based on developments in banking, steel, engineering, and chemicals filled the period between 1896 and 1908. The more sanguine estimates put growth rates at 6.7 per cent p.a. average for industrial output 1896–1908 and 5.4 per cent p.a. for 1896–1914 (Gerschenkron), the more moderate at 4.3 per cent p.a. for 1896–1914 (Istat). By 1901–10 capital investment in plant and equipment was 114 per cent higher than during the period of urban expansion, 1881–90.[46] Some improvement in the economy's performance is undeniable, but the dimensions of the great spurt are by no means beyond question. Against the measure of other candidates for spurt-like development – Sweden with its 12 per cent p.a. average growth rate of industrial output 1888–96, Japan with its 8.5 per cent p.a. of 1907–13, Russia with its 8 per cent p.a. of 1891–1900 – even against the measure of the stronger established economies – Germany with its creditable 5.5 per cent p.a. average of the 1890s – Italy's achievement was at best moderate. Moreover, the sectors of the economy which were generating this momentum were arranged in a narrow band: not until 1901–05 did manufacturing account for more than 17 per cent gross private product, not until 1911–15 for more than 21 per cent;[47] not until 1906–10 did the new leading sectors of the mechanical technologies surpass the traditional cotton textile sectors as the major industrial contributors to national income.[48] These restrictions in turn were echoed by the much smaller proportion of the working population committed to occupations in mining–manufacture than was conventional for countries with large rural populations – 4.7 per cent for Italy in 1911 against 7.7 per cent even for France in 1900 or 10.1 per cent for Germany around 1907–10. Strictly considered, the Italian expansion of 1896–1908 contained insufficiently dramatic growth rates, insufficiently developed manufacturing sectors, and excessively durable traditional industries to be convincingly rated as a 'big spurt'. However, if the Italian economy passed up this special variety of violent acceleration, it is likely that by 1914 it had at least achieved take-off: the makeshift checkpoint at which gross savings and investment first exceed 10 per cent GNP was successfully negotiated between 1896 and 1900.

Modern research has tended, therefore, to reduce the drama of Italian development: *both* the spurts of 1861–75 and 1896–1914 have undergone cuts in power and speed, while only the intervening deceleration has been left untouched.

The result is a scenario of Italian growth which is extremely close to that for Spain or Austria: a series of jerks towards industrialization, each linked fairly closely to its predecessor, none of outstanding force, frequently interspersed with periods of hesitation. By 1914, clearly, Italy had travelled a greater distance in this gradualist style, becoming the first industrial power of the

Mediterranean area, but, essentially, she had merely pushed further within the same basic terrain. The Dual Monarchy lagged some way behind, and Spain further still. Neither can be dismissed, however. The Habsburg autocracy on the eve of the First World War was not, as Jaszi would have us believe, 'already a defeated empire from the economic point of view',[49] nor as Rostow pretends, merely in the 'early preconditions stage, a rural based traditional society breaking up'.[50] Probably by 1900 it was more developed than its tsarist rival, and certainly in some of the more advanced technologies such as motor cars, electro-technical equipment, and armament, it could compare favourably with Italy. Indeed, if metropolitan Austria alone were set against Italy, the backwardness rankings would probably reverse, promoting the western component of the Habsburg duarchy above its Mediterranean competitor.[51] Spain, quite certainly, offered no challenge to either of her two partners in this comparison, but, by 1914, had surpassed, in her turn, other contenders in the development race; she remained, 'backward in comparison with the other western nations . . . yet ahead of those other nations whose industrialization *began* only in the nineteenth century'.[52] Nevertheless, to all three of these economies, backward in different measures, the great spurt, supposedly a feature of backward economies, remains a stranger; like most other forms of growth, the escape from backwardness proceeds according not to one but to a considerable variety of possible patterns. The problem then is to examine why in these cases the patterns were very similar, why they were so modest in their similarity, and why in their modesty — among other ways — they digressed so markedly from some of the best current expectations concerning the behaviour of backward economies.

ENDOWMENTS: NATURAL SPOILS AND THE SPOLIATION OF NATURE

At first sight, the distribution of raw materials between these economies appears entirely perverse: the least well endowed, Italy, grows most strongly; the most richly endowed, Spain, grows most weakly; and the intermediate case, Austria-Hungary, displays an almost neutral relationship between physical resources and industrial achievement. Italy's deficiencies were at least obvious. She possessed generous and unique sulphur deposits in Sicily exploited first by the French, later by the native chemical industry; a little iron ore in the Val d'Aosta, at Terni in Umbria, around Como, and, in the highest quality, on the island of Elba; and the natural hydraulic installation of the Alps for which the appropriate technical release came only at the end of the century. These apart, the land was practically destitute: only half the surface area was cultivable and what it lacked in fertility, the subsoil lacked in energy resources. Coal reserves were so lean that in 1913 Italy could raise only one-four-hundredth of the British coal haul, and, since imported coke remained beyond her pocket, could afford to erect no modern furnace equipment before

1900. The only relief was in natural gas, undetected before the First World War, unexploited before the Second World War. And if the land was deprived, it was also contorted and inconveniently disposed: there were too few major rivers, too many mountain barriers – almost as troublesome to transportation as the transverse ranges which so afflicted Spain – and, for outlook, a whole ocean long since stagnant as a major trading area. The total constituted an extreme case of resource starvation; anything that the Italian economy achieved would be in the face of nature.

For Spain matters were quite other. Some of the topographical problems did indeed recur: the interior is as mountainous as Switzerland, with the Castilian sierras rising to 2,400 metres, while the capital is over 300 kilometres from the sea in any direction, and much of the land surface is, or was, effectively desert. The consequences in the nineteenth century were perpetual transportation crisis[53] – the economy literally walking with the staggering gait of the pack mule until the locomotive conquered the sierras – and almost perpetual agricultural crisis. But nature offered compensation in mineral form: there was iron ore in Murcia, Almeria, Santander, and Viscaya, much of it high quality; there was lead in the sierras of Gador, Almagrera, and Cartagena and in the central south; there were massive copper reserves in the famous lodes of Rio Tinto and Tharsis; and, most precious of all, there was the mercury of Almaden. In Asturias and Cordoba there was even fairly plentiful coal. Resources like these virtually guaranteed *some* degree of success in extraction: correspondingly, Spanish pig-lead production succeeded the British, and anticipated the American, in the domination of world markets over the period 1869–98; similarly, the area of Huelva in its peak year (1912) accounted for 66 per cent of world pyrites production, and its richest mine, Rio Tinto, for 44 per cent. The problem here was not the feebleness of nature but rather of Spanish administration, both entrepreneurial and bureaucratic. Under native management, even the mines of Rio Tinto contrived to make financial losses; under foreign management they averaged a 70 per cent return on capital, 1879–1908. Under the pressure of a needy Treasury, the government in 1868 devised a mining law which amounted simply to a speculators' charter: the authorities openly bartered mineral concessions for short-run pecuniary relief. The result was to transfer Spain's best resources, the best use of these resources, and the best profit from them to the account of foreign capitalists. By 1913 29 per cent of Spanish mining companies and about half of Spanish mining capital lay in overseas control. Between 1881 and 1913 over 90 per cent of the iron ore mined in Spain was exported (see Table 5.1). Between 1870 and 1900 the Rothschilds, by now world monopolists in mercury, snatched 54 per cent of the returns from the Almaden concession leaving the Spanish Treasury with the minor share.[54] Given the excision of untreated ores entirely from the Spanish economy, the coal industry, most unusually among its European counterparts, suffered from a critical lack of *demand* for smelting fuels. Well before the mismanagement stopped – and that was after 1914 – the final irony was rung: the much exploited riches of Spain turned out to be temporary riches. The iron ores were mainly non-phosphoric, less suitable for the advanced metallurgical methods of 1900 than for those of the 1850s, and the pyrites were largely superseded by the apparently limitless resources of North America. Spain and Italy thus lie at reciprocal points on the scale both of resource endowment and resource utilization: Italy is pitifully endowed but rises above foreign exploitation to make the best of what she has; Spain ranks high in nature's favour but lacks the entrepreneurial talent to capitalize upon her assets before they run to waste.

With the Habsburg Empire, *both* a measure of under-endowment and a measure of mismanagement are in evidence, and the diagnosis is correspondingly confused. Bóth Warriner[55] and Gross[56] emphasize under-supply in coal and iron with the implication that, when the economy was at full stretch, resources were probably insufficient to service current demand. On the other hand, Blum[57] and Rothschild[58] stress the Empire's natural benefits: iron ore disposed in all but three provinces and many regions equipped with reserves of timber, lignite, coal, or hydro-power. While lamenting the Empire's impeding mountains, ill-disciplined rivers, and horrendous transportation, European observers as early as the 1830s were impressed by the resources even of the eastern regions: Hungary was pictured as a reservoir from which the industrial concentrations of the German, Silesian, and Austrian states could draw at need, while one assessment of 1839 ranked Hungarian iron ore second in quality only to the Swedish.[59] Problems in coal supplies lay largely in uneven distribution: the Viennese, Alpine, and Magyar industrial regions did experience shortages of cokeable fuels while Moravia-Silesia and Bohemia enjoyed substantial and secure supplies. In 1873, however, the Empire as a whole cut more lignite than bituminous coal and the latter remained generally more expensive than peat, charcoal, or 'brown coal'. Consequently, charcoal forges and water-wheels held the coke-furnaces and steam-engines of modern practice at bay for some considerable time. Nevertheless, these fuel deficiencies do not seem to have formed genuinely binding constraints. In the iron industry much of the methodological conservatism could be attributed to the fragmented and miniaturized production structure rather than to limitations upon resources. Estate control over both ore deposits and timber stands could also frequently create a bias in favour of charcoal technology. Certainly, management standards among the Hungarian ore-mines left much to be desired: English observers applauded the quality of the metal but deplored the conduct of the extraction. Even Gross admits that the fuel curbs could have been much reduced by more energetic exploitation;[60] with stronger leadership in business and government and a more definite emphasis upon economic development as a desirable objective, the problems imposed by coal shortages could have been substantially qualified.

On balance, the Habsburg resource problem leans more closely towards the Spanish than towards the Italian comparison: both the eastern European and the western Mediterranean economies enjoyed natural endowments of considerable substance, and, in some items, of high quality, but in neither was the quality of the resources matched by the quality of resource utilization. In the Austrian case, however, mismanagement did not proceed so far as to surrender the mineral base to massive foreign control, and, to this extent, the Dual Monarchy conserved its natural gifts more carefully.

All three cases powerfully confirm the contention that resource endowment and economic growth are linked in no direct or automatic relationship. Indeed a further, and more powerful, proposition is suggested: that natural endowment combines with human (entrepreneurial) endowment to create a practically limitless selection of growth or stagnation effects. That the most resource-deprived of these economies should attain the best level of economic performance offers striking confirmation of the view that natural endowments define (superable) problems for solution rather than (insuperable) constraints for observance.

POPULATION: THE LEAKING SOCIETIES

In some respects, however, the quality of the human resource varied little between the three societies. Each was encumbered with a large peasant community poorly equipped for efficiency as a rural or industrial workforce: illiteracy rates around mid-century were chronically pronounced in both Spain (75%) and Italy (75–80%), although somewhat better in the Dual Monarchy (40–45%). All three experienced demographic expansion which was, by European standards, unusually slow: Spain's average performance of 0.63 per cent p.a. 1797–1860 and 0.49 per cent p.a. 1860–1910,[61] Austria's of 0.83 per cent p.a. 1857–1910[62] and Italy's, just before the First World War, of 0.67 per cent p.a.[63] were far inferior to the comparable German (1.09% p.a. 1857–1910) or British (1.18% p.a. 1861–1911) achievements. And all three experienced major 'leakages' of population prior to 1914, placing them among continental Europe's very largest exporters of population; between 1870 and 1912 Spain lost about one-third of her natural population increase to emigration, Austria-Hungary approximately one-sixth, and Italy over a half. Significantly, also, the massive Italian losses were unevenly distributed, with the southern provinces surrendering 62 per cent of the natural increase in 1901–11 and the northern provinces 32 per cent. The total number of individuals 'exported' between 1870 and 1910 represented 3.7 per cent of the Austro-Hungarian population in 1910, 12.3 per cent of the Spanish population in 1910, and 18.3 per cent of the Italian population in 1910 (see Table 5.2).

Once again, however, the economic consequences of demographic growth, deflated by lethargic natural increase and enthusiastic emigration, conform to no set pattern. Two of these countries exhibit signs of underpopulation relative to economic requirement, weakly in the case of Austria-Hungary, emphatically in the case of Spain; the third reveals heavy traces of overpopulation mitigated only by emigration. Despite the large absolute size of the Austro-Hungarian community (49.5 m. in 1910–11), the onset of demographic feebleness is sufficiently apparent: in Austria in 1866 deaths exceeded births, and in Hungary between 1871 and 1875 the population actually contracted in

Table 5.2   Emigration from continental Europe, 1861–1910: selected countries

Country of origin	1851–60	1861–70	1871–80
Austria-Hungary	31,000	40,000	46,000
France	27,000	36,000	66,000
Germany	671,000	779,000	626,000
Italy	5,000	27,000	168,000
Netherlands	16,000	20,000	17,000
Portugal	45,000	79,000	131,000
Russia	–	–	58,000
Spain	3,000	7,000	13,000
Sweden	17,000	122,000	103,000

Source: Abstracted, with adaptations, from Woodruff (1966), p. 106

size.[64] On top of this, emigration, given the higher literacy of the Empire's subjects, probably represented a substantial drain of talent and resources: the economy bore the dependency and educational burden of some 2 m. individuals from whom it derived little or no return. In Spain the problem was more acute: after the leachings of the *reconquista* and the New World adventures, Spain simply became destitute of Spaniards: by 1800 only 40 towns housed more than 10,000 individuals and only 2 of her 29 provinces accommodated more than 50 individuals to the square kilometre.[65] Between 1700 and 1860 the Spanish population was engaged largely upon recovering its earlier size, upon erasing a backlog while still embarrassed by highly traditional birth/death-rate patterns; at no point in this period did demographic capacities press against economic resources. Consequently, Spain joins that select group of countries – headed perhaps by France – where the stimulus accorded to economic change by population growth is noticeable by its absence. Yet, in the peninsula, the theoretical benefits of slow population growth – such as high savings rates – were also minimized due to the advanced poverty of the rural populace and the dramatic skewness of income distribution. Of all European countries Spain perhaps bears most clearly the traumata of population deprivation.

Italy, on the other hand, drew substantial benefits from her demographic peculiarities. Without her massive emigration, the rate of natural increase would have been uncomfortably high – about 2.08 per cent p.a. at the century's turn – and unemployment would have weighed more heavily even than it did. Here there was demographic oversupply rather than demographic frailty, and emigration acted to relieve pressure upon overstretched resources rather than to deny stimulation for their more effective utilization. Nor is there much possibility that population 'leakage' deprived the economy of valuable talents or labour inputs: in the south every job opportunity was oversubscribed several times and the maintenance of labour stocks in these circumstances would merely have issued in the institutionalization of immiserization. Moreover, illiteracy was so high – 84 per cent in the south in 1871 – and the state's investment in human capital so meagre, that few sacrifices in forgone

310

1881–90	1891–1900	1901–10	Total	Rank
248,000	440,000	1,111,000	1,916,000	4
119,000	51,000	53,000	352,000	8
1,342,000	527,000	274,000	4,219,000	2
992,000	1,580,000	3,615,000	6,387,000	1
52,000	24,000	28,000	157,000	9
185,000	266,000	324,000	1,030,000	6
288,000	481,000	911,000	1,738,000	5
572,000	791,000	1,091,000	2,477,000	3
327,000	205,000	224,000	998,000	7

returns attached to the labour outflows. Indeed, one highly specialized characteristic of Italian emigrants probably allowed them to contribute more to the economy by leaving it than by working within it. The transfer of Italians to higher-earning occupations overseas achieved this unusual effect by encouraging the repatriation of 'foreign' income to relatives still in the homeland.[66] Such was the scale of this thoughtful gesture that the dividend on Italy's export of human capital provided by 1901–13 about one-half of the country's net invisible earnings (roughly 6,000 m. lire) and allowed the correction of a large visible trade deficit. Earnings brought home by Italy's highly versatile seasonal migrants – typified by the *golondrina* (swallow) who might follow the autumn harvest to Argentina and the spring sowing back to Piedmont[67] – no doubt also contributed to this valuable subsidy. No evidence exists to suggest that feedbacks from emigration accrued on anything like this scale to either of the other two economies. Where Spain's demographic endowment operated as a strongly negative factor in development, and Austria-Hungary's probably as marginally negative, the population resources of Italy deployed themselves in an original and at least partly creative style. Yet if these resources supplied economic benefits, they also contained very severe imbalances. Emigration was a safety valve which released a fortuitously rich by-product, but, inside the containing vessel, critical pressures could persist. The container in question was the Italian south, the *mezzogiorno*, for the major shortcomings of Italian population was its failure to expand in a nationally uniform style. The safety valve was located in the maritime centres of the north, but it was the rate of population advance in the south – close to the world's highest, and exceeding northern rates, among the world's lowest, by a factor of three – which generated the pressure. The *mezzogiorno* experienced the classic trauma of demographic explosion in a backward economy: between 1861 and 1936 its inhabitants increased by 5.7 m., but its economically active workforce by only 200,000; the participation ratio fell from 76 to 50 per cent.[68] Unlike Spain or Austria-Hungary, the southern Italian section did experience population pressure upon economic resources – and of overbearing and stupefying rather than stimulative dimensions.

If, therefore, the population variable takes on different values across the three national cases, it also fluctuates in regional impact *inside* at least one of them. Demographic resources in Italy were distributed dualistically, heavily in one geographical sector, thinly in another. The result was overpopulation in the south which was relieved, but not extinguished, by migration northwards,[69] and thence overseas. This inter-regional disparity was to become a recurring pattern: in many areas alongside those of demographic endowment, the unevenness of resource distribution came to exert more influence upon economic development than the total size of the resource.

DUALISM: THE SPLIT ECONOMIES

The diffuse style in which nature distributed its bounty extended so far in these three cases as to create entirely separate economic systems within the political frontiers. In more advanced economies, like the French, a similar untidiness of distribution could create highly regionalized economies, but within the poorer countries the inherently more pronounced skewness of endowment gave rise to explicitly dualistic economic structures: modern sectors of some sophistication lay alongside sectors less traditional than overtly primitive. Respectively growth-generating and growth-resisting, these sectors shared, incongruously, similar cultures and the same government. Frequently, also, the economic divergence was reinforced by geographical features – alps sierras, and unfriendly hillsides – which impeded inter-regional trade, transportation, and communication. In Italy, notoriously, the consequential economic fragmentation, opposing the prosperous industrial north to the ravaged and barren *mezzogiorno*, yielded in no way to the acts of political unification during the 1860s. Less acknowledged, however, is the repetition of similar patterns in Austria-Hungary and Spain.

In the Habsburg lands, of course, economic advance was accompanied, unusually, by *increasing* politically disparateness. But while the writ of Vienna maintained its tenuous hold in the provinces, the unity of economic experience was subject to more advanced erosion. Broadly, the main divide fell between the manufacturing regions of the west, Bohemia-Moravia, metropolitan Austria, especially the Vienna basin, and their appendages in Styria and Carinthia, and, on the other hand, the fertile agriculture of Galicia and the great grain plains of the Magyar east. If the primary sectors of the imperial domain possessed more potential for development than the sterile *mezzogiorno*, the economic structure of quasi-feudal Hungarian estate agriculture nevertheless contrasted dramatically with that of Austrian heavy industry or Bohemian craft production. Thus the western provinces supplied 35–36 per cent of the Empire's iron smelt in the 1840s against Hungary's 17 per cent, 41 per cent in the 1860s against Hungary's 32 per cent: only after 1870 did Hungary approach parity in this manufacture, and it was one of the few in which it did. For most of the nineteenth century the Habsburg east, like the Italian south or the Spanish centre, displayed a genuine analogy with the underdeveloped economies of the present century. Yet the tensions between the mining/capital goods/forestry/livestock system of Austria, the coal/craft-manufacture/sugar-beet system of Bohemia, and the extensive cereal system of Hungary amounted to something more complicated even than dualism. Some imperial provinces were able to pull away from the Austro-Hungarian economic framework and establish more profitable international liaisons, much as the border areas of France and Germany had done: Bohemia pursued German markets and found outlets through the Elbe and Hamburg; isolated beyond the Alpine ring, Galicia, Bukovina, and Dalmatia naturally inclined away from the imperial heartland; the western textile centres found their natural partners amidst the Swiss-Suabian manufacturing complex around Lake Constance.

'International' economic conflicts within the Empire were paralleled by international affiliations outside it. As with Germany, the industrial potential of the Dual Monarchy tended to burst through its political boundaries, establishing once again the trans-national nature of the industrial revolution. But where the German economy resembled a very dense star, affecting 'extra-territorial' industry by its gravitational force, the Austrian economy favoured rather the dying nebula, diffuse, random, its core less integrated or defined. The Empire thus had to contend with the international implications of industrial development, while lacking a coherent or unified national economy. Even in 1914, the forces of economic centralization – the waterway system, the railroads, the financial and commercial services of Vienna – had made few inroads upon the regional enclaves. And when the economy was peopled by minorities of Czechs, Slovaks, Poles, Rumanians, Serbs, Croats, and Italians to the value of 30 m., ruled by an ascendancy of 12 m. Austrians and 10 m. Hungarians, this was as true of demographic resources as of any other. Where in Italy economic unification refused to accompany political unification, in Austria-Hungary political fragmentation reinforced economic fragmentation. The result, logically enough, was the unedifying combination of interior dualism with marginal raggedness.

In Spain, the economy was less intricately but no less damagingly split. From the seventeenth century, Spanish development had been constrained by the differential growth rates of the responsive periphery – Catalonia, Valencia, Vizcaya – and the stagnant central domain of old Castile. With the important manufacturing developments of the nineteenth century again disposed at the margins and agricultural advance restricted to the remarkable citrus groves of Valencia and the sugar-beet fields of the Ebro and Guadalquivir basins, the centre was left, as so often, with the residue: the primitive cereal monoculture of the *secano* lands, the desert cultivation of 'true Spain'. Even sheep-farming was cramped by land resources of this quality so that 40 per cent of the available pasture could support only two animals to the hectare.[70] Naturally enough, by 1860 entirely separate capitalistic and subsistence economies had emerged from these divergent endowments.[71]

And, down to 1914, even the capitalistic sector developed in a pronounced and unusual regional style: as one province created manufacturing capability,

313

so, too frequently, it seeped away from another. Thus Catalonia constructed the initial foundations for Spanish industrialization, but after 1880, as the impulsion of the textile industry declined, found that its deficiencies in coal and iron prevented diversification towards the heavier technologies. Catalan manufacturers were so infected by parochialism that they considered Asturian coal as a foreign commodity and demanded protection against the competing shipping trade growing out of Biscay. As they lost confidence and direction, Spain's industrial centre of gravity became unfixed, wobbling precariously between provinces, creating both regional activity and regional displacement. Iron output, for instance, centred first on Malaga and Seville but then drifted northwards towards the cheap fuel of Asturias: the southern furnaces controlled 55.1 per cent of total iron output in 1861 but only 4.7 per cent by 1868; they 'faded away owing to lack of coal'.[72] From the late 1870s, Asturias in turn yielded to Vizcaya, itself a backward iron-producing region at mid-century, but controlling 22.7 per cent of natural cast-iron output 1861–79, and 65–74 per cent 1880–1913. This halting reallocation brought severe distress to the early developers: the withering of Andalusian metallurgy, followed rapidly by a similar deceleration in textiles, imposed a fairly thorough *counter*-industrialization upon the Spanish south, very much as it was imposed upon the Italian south in the post-*risorgimento* decades. In such cases dualism not only set deserts and development areas in counterpart; it also created industrial development in some areas at the price of industrial suppression in others. From this contorted evolution no national industrial vertebrate emerged before 1914.

At the same point, Italian evolution had produced one modern industrialized 'country', much like the smaller manufacturing nations of Europe, and one chronically underdeveloped· 'country', as backward as anything to be found around the Mediterranean. The north held the ores of Como and Terni, the water-power of the Alps, the passably productive agriculture of the Po delta, and the main industrial concentrations of Liguria, Lombardy, Tuscany, and Umbria; the south possessed a small-scale squatter agriculture scarcely above subsistence and the few, insecurely based, manufactures of the Neopolitan region. By 1911 the three most advanced north-western provinces contained only 21.6 per cent of the nation's population but 58 per cent of its factory workforce (units of ten and above) and 49 per cent of its mechanical horse-power. The contrast here is exceptionally clear and vivid: Italy specialized not so much in the economic fragmentation as in the dramatic chasm between a few economic regions, the northern and southern halves in the conventional interpretation, the northern, central, and southern thirds according to Eckaus.[73]

But that is all which remains clear concerning Italian dualism; immense controversy surrounds the reasons for its existence. Variously, the 'southern problem' has been put to the account of rogue governments, ill-timed economic feebleness, or long-run under-endowment. Broadly, the conspiratorial case, as argued by Vochting,[74] or Nitti,[75] has proposed that the two regions possessed equal chances at unification and that southern opportunities were spoiled by the exploitation of an imperialist Piedmontese rival. There is little in this: the south was not mulcted of taxes; rather it paid less to the national treasury than to the provincial fiscal agencies, and received back, in proportion to its payments, a larger share of total government expenditure than its northern neighbour. Thus the southern allocation of railway facilities increased from 7.2 per cent of the total track in 1861 to 32 per cent in 1875.[76] Similarly, it is highly dubious that the replacement of regional protection by the light Piedmontese tariffs could further, or seriously, have harmed a southern agriculture which by nature and climate was already inherently fragile. Government action did not create the southern problem; it simply failed to relieve a disease that was inherited rather than acquired.

Yet it is clear that by the 1860s the south was producing 'a quite notable industrial advance'. Between 1825 and 1860, metallurgical, machine, textile, glass, and shipbuilding industries took root in the south and during the *risorgimento* period, activity in the production of castings, hulls, and steam-engines was substantial.[77] In 1867 the southern littoral accounted for 60 per cent of Italian ship construction by value (but only 18% by tonnage).[78] From such developments stem the propositions that Italy's economic regions were roughly equally balanced by the 1860s. However, any correct interpretation of the southern upsurge requires recognition of its transitory nature and its lack of underlying substance. Given the regional inheritance, it could scarcely be otherwise. From the first Roman occupation through Angevin and Spanish suzerainty to Napoleonic annexation, the area had been the object of determined imperialistic exploitation. Moreover, it lacked secure commercial foundations, having failed to claim its due share of Italy's trading successes in the medieval and early modern periods: the great marts and seaports of the past were, almost without exception, northern cities – Genoa, Florence, Milan, Venice. Even geography worked against southern aspirations: where the northern provinces looked across the Alps to Europe's industrial heartland, profiting readily from technological diffusion and demonstration effects, the south, in contrast, confronted only the somnolent waters of the Mediterranean economic system. Like Austria-Hungary – an area also circumvented by the major trade routes of the later medieval period and equally deprived of substantial commercial experience – southern Italy was damaged by the powerful force-field of the 'Atlantic trade magnet'. Add the impediments of convoluted topography and an agriculture blending the worst features of estate and peasant cultivation, and it becomes clear that the *mezzogiorno*'s brief industrial flowering under the last Bourbons occurred upon a frail and rootless plant.

More plausibly, Italian dualism should be attributed to an inter-regional disjunction which long anticipated political unification. Since, in the early 1860s, the northern and central provinces already contained 92.8 per cent of the nation's railways, 87.5 per cent of its roads, 78 per cent of its silk production, and 68 per cent of its agricultural output, it was virtually predetermined that the two halves of the economy should tear apart. Every trick of endowment suggested this outcome. The fertile delta of the Po was larger than any comparable southern resource. The iron ore of the north was most imperfectly matched by the southern sulphur, lead, and zinc, inadequate supports at that time for the development of heavy industry. No commercially exploitable river existed in the south to compete with the waterways of the Po or the water-power of the Alps. Long-run disparities of this kind were not susceptible to cure by a limited burst of activity in the manufacture of glassware and fishing boats. By 1876 when the southern areas had accumulated only 7 per cent of total Italian manufacturing capital, 9 per cent of housing capital, and 16 per cent of bank capital[79] this was already sufficiently established. Dualism, therefore, was the work of nature rather than of governments; and it could be corrected neither by the illusory 'dynamism' of the south, nor by acts of political unification.

This last was unfortunate; after all, the German states had included economic objectives in their strategy of unification and, in that case, political fusion had secured a substantial measure of economic integration. For Italy, it was an acute paradox that economic union should have been so imperfectly achieved when economic arguments had been so frequently invoked in the campaign for political integration. The most realistic Italian liberals, the Lombard journalists, understood the interrelation of economic and nationalist interest, idolized England as much for her industrialism as for her liberalism, and encouraged the spread of railways as much for political as for economic gain.[80] Similar preoccupations even achieved a position of strategic influence after 1861, for Cavour's interest in water-power and railroads was no less perceptive. Why then were there so few returns? After all, the *risorgimento* had been made in the shape of a good bourgeois revolution by lawyers (Crispi, Rattazi), doctors (Farini, Bertani), and ex-officers (Cavour), a movement of the middle and professional classes[81] as solid as that of the French revolutionary leaders. Why then were not the economic claims of the Italian bourgeoisie as firmly cemented into the settlement of Unification as those of the French into the revolutionary settlement? Was it because the Italian middle class was, in fact, more frail than its French counterpart,[82] unable to defeat particularism and vested interest in the campaign for a bourgeois state and a compact nation? Partially, this is true, but there are more important variables. Centrally important is the contrast between the political and the economic doctrine of the new regime: precisely the brand of liberal 'autonomist' nationalism needed to contrive political unification carried with it as inevitable accompaniment the style in *laissez-faire* economics least likely to rectify severe economic imbalance.[83] Cavour believed that there was a 'coiled spring of enterprise' awaiting release in the south; and he was prepared to liberate it only with a limited commitment to public expenditure. He was wrong: there was no 'coiled spring' and the region required a form of major surgery which a non-interventionist administration could not bring itself to perform. The *mezzo-giorno* needed more than governmental restraint from despoliation, more than well-mannered liberalism; it required a thorough-going rescue operation implemented with the full apparatus of the modern *dirigiste* state. Before 1914, of course, this was unavailable: desultory state schemes for reafforestation, extended public works, and fiscal concessions began in 1904 but came to little. Only since 1950 has the Casa por il Mezzogiorno confronted the problem with a scale of resources roughly – and then only roughly – appropriate to the task in hand. Germany, after all, contained no economic imbalance half so acute and was governed by no regime half so liberal.

Dualism in one sense exists, of course, in all economies; it is in the nature of the 'modern' industrial sector to open a growth gap between itself and the 'traditional' agricultural sector. This is the dualism of growth; and its destructive effects are relatively modest. There is also the dualism created by the imposition of a modern foreign 'enclave' upon a primitive 'colonial' economy. This is the dualism of imperialistic exploitation; and, if the two sectors are almost entirely isolated from one another, as they often are, the development of the modern sector may not extensively disrupt the *future* growth prospects of the host economy. The worst effects seem to be concentrated among the intermediate cases: the late developers attempting industrial growth but carrying the incubus of large, geographically defined, regions of immiserization. This is the dualism of backwardness. Historically, it has proved extremely damaging, and it is probable that its ill-effects may intensify rather than diminish as growth is achieved in the modern sector. This is particularly true of the 'backwash' effects: as the modern sector grows, so it sucks capital and labour away from the traditional sector, intensifying *both* its own development and the pauperization of the primitive region, stretching the gap from both sides. In Italy, the south could offer as an economic attribute only its cheap labour supply, but the quantity was excessive and the quality offered no guarantee even of low unit costs. Both labour and capital, in consequence, flowed towards more attractive prospects in the north. The chasm between wholly opposed socio-economic systems progressively widened until modern northern Italy was driven to reinvest part of the receipts, drawn from the widening process, in a programme to bring its underdeveloped partner into the twentieth century. In Austria-Hungary, the existence of widely diverging economic regions within a free-market system, and in the absence of any deliberate compensating policy, ensured the perpetuation and accentuation of painful disparities.[84] And in Spain, the *various* economies were subjected to fission rather than fusion by the process of industrialization; even manufacturing regions were wrenched apart as the industrial plasma swelled and then receded. Some of these economic regions, in fact, like some Habsburg regions, related more closely to industrial areas in other countries than to their Spanish counterparts: thus the rise of the Basque industries generated a mutual trade in coal and iron ore along the 'Cardiff–Bilbao axis',[85] *replacing* the earlier Bilbao–Gijon connexion which had tapped the coal of neighbouring Asturias. Here, economic advance paradoxically distributed both industrialization and counter-industrialization among the 'advanced' regions, greatly complicating the existing conflicts between the industrial and the agriculturally primitive sectors. Once established, therefore, dualism made increasing inroads upon the economic fortunes of all three economies down to 1914.

Perhaps the most considerable, among the many, costs of this economic fracture lay in the small size of the viable market which dualism imposed even upon nations of large territorial and demographic size. Primitive sectors could retaliate for their accelerating pauperization at the hands of the industrial regions by denying to the latter significant shares of the 'national' market. Thus, in the Italian case, *per capita* consumption remained largely constant 1871–95, but the leverage of the primitive areas ensured that the share going to basic needs (food, shelter, etc.) actually increased.[86] Even though the normal definition of a 'small' country might be one with less than 10 m. inhabitants, the pressure of dualism could create problems of smallness within economies of 40–50 m. inhabitants, and more. Italian experience was exactly of this type: metal industries found themselves so constrained by domestic demand that they were unable to mount effective export campaigns; shipbuilding, railway engineering, and electrical engineering industries frequently laboured under wide margins of excess capacity. In particular, steel production was bedevilled by high costs and uneconomically scaled plants, manifestations of shortage in outlets rather than in raw materials.[87] Precisely similar were the market deficiencies of the Spanish coal, iron, and steel industries: not before 1850 did demand advance sufficiently to awaken the languishing coal industry of Asturias, and, into the 1860s, orders for Spanish iron products were so undependable that importation was frequently preferred to domestic production. Under such market conditions, output, when it is forthcoming, is likely to arrange itself within an array of undersized and uncompetitive producers and to require extensive tariff protection. Certain unpleasant consequences are inevitable: technical progress will be retarded; external diseconomies of scale will arise; in some markets monopoly will represent the optimal scale of trade. Within a dualistic economic structure, therefore, the modern sector will pay for its progress in some very antiquated coin.

THE EXPORT MARKET: DUALISM ESCAPED OR DUALISM REFLECTED?

Opinions differ as to how far a small-market economy may compensate for its domestic tribulations by the cultivation of export opportunities. It is widely held that available economies of scale are controlled by the structure of *home* demand and that foreign trade can offer little effective substitution: in this view, an economy will only succeed – as Italy may have done – in exports for which there is also a strong domestic requirement.[88] On the other hand, it is contended that external markets, despite their lesser homogeneity and greater riskiness, may offer the single salvation for demand-starved economies, and, if approached with relevant strategies, may also offer success to manufacturers wholly dependent upon a foreign clientele. Since economies with small markets do not respond rapidly to changes in demand, the appropriate export strategies usually amount to a search for 'niches' in world trade which can be filled with products combining standardization with speciality appeal – for instance, Belgian sulphuric acid, Swiss luxury textiles and watches, Dutch butter, Danish furniture or Swedish motor ships.

For the three split economies, however, the recipe was not so easily found. Small in markets, they were physically sufficiently large, and also sufficiently primitive, for bottlenecks of transportation to interpose themselves between the exportable product and the export market. This remained a critical problem for Spanish exportation throughout the century, and, in the vast Hungarian *Alföld*, as late as 1869, a simple deficiency of roads – where they did exist, the only truly impassable areas of the grainlands – was said to be crippling its development as an exporting prairie economy.[89] For all three countries, long-term isolation from the main continental, and especially 'Atlantic', trade routes compounded these problems of communication. Further, where such forlorn and intractable developers were also rich in raw materials, the obvious homogeneity and rarity of these items, and thus their suitability for an export 'niche', could seduce the possessor into relinquishing for immediate trading gain the constituents of prospective manufacturing advance. Combined with transportational difficulties, this over-hastiness in the surrender of the natural inheritance frequently meant that the backward country could export only what the advanced nations required and only what they would come – with investment in railways and ports – to fetch. In Spain, the 'penetrative' character of British and French capital, in Italy, of French and German capital, in Austria-Hungary, largely of German capital, worked to bias overseas trade in this fashion. 'Imitating Esau', as Carr puts it, gave minerals pride of place among Spanish exports – with one-third of the total 1899–1911 – but left to the foreign concessionaire the commercial whiphand.[90] Being less well endowed, the other countries suffered less from the problems of Esau but these, nevertheless, registered their presence: Gille is entirely convinced that the advanced powers were seeking a comprehensively exploitative relationship with the Italian states in the early part of the century,[91] and Hungary, for its part, made noteworthy surrenders of its assets to outsiders. Dualism, therefore, did not only create a deficiency of home demand; by imposing under-utilization of valuable endowment, by constricting mobility of resources, by inclining advanced sectors towards relations with other advanced economies rather than with their own hinterlands, it stimulated a form of foreign trade which was asset-reducing rather than growth-inducing. 'Niches' of this kind were a poor bet, literally purchasing an export effort from the industrialized nations with a tribute of under-priced minerals, a profitless forfeit of the materials for growth forgone.

Furthermore, since dual economies will tend by definition to be retarded developers, late entrants to world trade, they will find many 'niches' already occupied and will lack the technical sophistication needed to capture many of the remainder. 'Genuinely' small economies of compact size, modest population, and developed skills may encounter fewer problems. But for the dual economy, the pressures making for an hurried or unwise choice of 'niche' are considerable. Significantly, for most of the century, all three of these countries relied upon primary products or luxury consumer articles for their export staples – Spanish ore, oranges, and wine; Hungarian grain; Italian silk, cheese,

(a) Table 5.3   Composition of Spanish exports by main categories, 1850–1913 (% of total exports)

1850			1883			1893		
Rank	Item	%	Rank	Item	%	Rank	Item	%
1	Wine, etc.	28.3	1	Wine, etc.	48.4	1	Minerals	28.3
2	Wool	9.3	2	Minerals	20.4	2	Wine, etc.	18.7
3	Pig lead	9.1	3	Fruit	8.4	3	Cotton goods	10.9
4	Wheat and flour	7.1	4	Olive oil	3.7	4	Fruit	9.7
5	Dried fruit	7.0	5	Animals	3.5	5	Olive oil	5.5
6	Cork stoppers	3.8	6	Cork stoppers	2.0	6	Footwear	5.2
7	Cochineal	3.2	7	Cotton goods	1.5	7	Cork stoppers	4.6
8	Silver and coin	3.1	8	Footwear	1.4	8	Animals	2.1
9	Olive oil	2.9	9	Wool	1.3	9	Wool	1.1

Sources: Calculated from Nadal (1973), p. 618 and Vicens Vives (1969), p. 700

(b) Composition of Italian exports by group, 1881–1915 (% of total exports)

Group	1881–85	1886–90	1891–95
Raw Materials	14.4	16.2	18.3
Foodstuffs	34.9	32.0	30.8
Semi-finished industrial products	34.8	38.9	36.1
Finished industrial products	15.9	12.9	14.8

Source: Abstracted from Clough (1964), pp. 112–13.

(c) Comparison of Spanish and Italian exports by group, 1881–1915 (% of total exports)

Group		1881–85	1886–90	1891–95
Raw Materials	Italy	14.4	16.2	18.3
	Spain	21.7[a]		29.4[b]
Foodstuffs	Italy	34.9	32.0	30.8
	Spain	64.0[a]		36.0[b]
Semi-finished Industrial Products	Italy	34.8	38.9	36.1
	Spain	–		–
Finished Industrial Products	Italy	15.9	12.9	14.8
	Spain	4.9[a]		20.7[b]

[a] 1883; [b] 1893; [c] 1903; [d] 1913

Source: Abstracted and calculated from foregoing tables

and fruit (cf. Table 5.3 for Italy and Spain) – hardly an indication that foreign demand succeeded in alleviating the market deficiencies experienced by domestic *manufacturing*. Thus, although Italy expanded the industrial sector of her export trade by an average of 7.2 per cent p.a. 1892–1910, finding new

1903			1913		
Rank	Item	%	Rank	Item	%
1	Minerals	35.9	1	Fruit	13.0
2	Fruit	13.2	2	Minerals	12.2
3	Wine, etc.	11.3	3	Wine, etc.	11.9
4	Olive oil	6.7	4	Metals	11.6
5	Cork stoppers	5.0	5	Preserved foods	4.4
6	Animals	3.2	6	Cotton goods	3.9
7	Cotton goods	4.4	7	Cork stoppers	3.7
8	Footwear	2.4	8	Vegetables	2.6
9	Wool	1.9	9	Olive oil	2.5

1896–1900	1901–05	1906–10	1911–15	Averages 1881/85–1911/15
17.2	15.8	14.0	13.4	15.6
28.0	25.5	27.0	28.9	29.6
33.7	35.4	33.4	24.3	33.8
21.1	23.3	25.6	33.4	21.0

1896–1900	1901–05	1906–10	1911–15	Averages 1881/85–1911/15
17.2	15.8	14.0	13.4	15.6
	37.8[c]		12.2[d]	25.3
28.0	25.5	27.0	28.9	29.6
	34.4[c]		34.4[d]	42.2
33.7	35.4	33.4	24.3	33.8
			11.6[d]	–
21.1	23.3	25.6	33.4	21.0
	11.8[c]		7.6[d]	11.3

markets in South-east Europe, the Near East, and Asia, she had to deal predominantly in textiles; her steel, machinery, and chemicals, some of them high in quality, could make little headway against those of the advanced powers. And in Spain the domination of external trade by the raw materials—

foodstuff group was maintained virtually entire down to 1914 (see Table 5.3). Only at the end of the period did characteristically specialist manufactures emerge from some of these economies into the market-places of the world, and, even then, none came from Spain. It was left to Italian motor cars, Hungarian electrical products, and Austrian small-arms to fulfil the terms of the model and occupy their slots in world trade.

And if dualistic backwardness narrowed the selection of exploitable 'niches', the complications of great power status were more than effective in narrowing the range of exploitable markets. Here Spain was the greatest sufferer: the Treaty of Utrecht of 1715 did for her what the Treaty of Vienna later did for France, extinguishing colonial markets, rocking the nexus between the New and the Old World, suppressing commerce as a potential leading sector. Since for Spain overseas trade *per capita* never surpassed one-quarter of the equivalent measure for France,[92] such abrogations were even more cruel than for her Gallic neighbour. The tariffs of 1882 and 1891 instructed the last remnants of empire to buy Spanish, but the loss of Cuba scarcely a decade later negated such efforts entirely: with unfriendly warships penning up 60 per cent of Spain's export market, the Spanish-American War completed with ironical symmetry the work begun at Utrecht. Austria-Hungary, in contrast, drew economic debits less from her problems as a crumbling empire than from her preferences as an isolationist autocracy. The unsuccessful diplomatic contest with the upstart politico-economic power of the *Zollverein* in the 1840s and 1850s encouraged the Habsburgs towards a policy of minimum commitment to foreign trade – and thence into the masochistic delights of self-inflicted technological constraint. Prior to 1848, even Hungarian exports to metropolitan Austrian were subject to penal duties. Where, in the case of Spain, the notions of other powers helped stifle the development of a commercial leading sector, in the case of Austria-Hungary, home-grown notions as to the Empire's proper place in Europe achieved similar results with only limited outside aid. For Italy, aspiring to the standing which Spain and Austria-Hungary were gradually surrendering, the problem was different: involvement in the power game implied the use of an economico-diplomatic vocabulary with which the established powers were incontestably more adroit. Thus Italy's resort to tariff policies from 1879 involved competitive frictions which developed into all-out tariff war against France during the 1880s. Moreover, it assumed a conventional protectionist shape which, some observers believe,[93] was damaging to the country's most promising industries. Here, economic nationalism borrowed a style from an increasingly strident chauvinism, almost certainly at the price of some commercial prosperity.

Whatever the proper export objectives for small-market economies, therefore, the problems of dualistic, weakly muscled, and over-sensitive great powers offer substantial obstacles to their fulfilment. Neither dualism nor political control could be escaped in the export market; peculiarities both of domestic economy and of national state operated powerfully to influence the content and direction of the export effort.

AGRICULTURE: MISSING REVOLUTIONS

Within the classically dualistic economy, the strongest and most important distinguishing feature will clearly be its agricultural endowment. In turn, this endowment will exhibit several obvious and unfortunate characteristics: it will be very large (see Table 5.4); it will produce little surplus; its productivity will be low; its agricultural practice will be conservative. Almost by definition, it will not have undergone the process of agricultural revolution. This last part is critical. Much work has gone into the assertion that these countries (and others like them) did not submit to the modernizing experience by which a (usually bourgeois) revolution or a (usually enlightened) bureaucracy successfully dismantles feudalism, and by shuffling the pieces, creates a sturdy independent proprietorship of small landholders equipped to carry the gospel of profit and market into the countryside. The most powerful statement was Gramsci's, denouncing the bourgeoisie of the *risorgimento* for sleeping on their historical mission and engineering only a 'rivolutione agricultura manquata',[94] while in Spain, J. Sole-Tura[95] produced a parallel indictment reproaching the Catalan bourgeoisie for their ineffectiveness as apostles of rural enlightenment. However, these apparently incontrovertible arguments have not been allowed to rest: it is suggested that there are more ways than one of skinning the farmyard cat and that the reformed rural bourgeoisies are not – in some cases definitely not – the indispensable architects of agricultural progress. *Unreformed* agricultures, in the hands of the revisionists, become positively virtuous since the great estates are held to be more efficient accumulators of capital than the 'revolutionized' peasant plots and more ready suppliers of the investment required to inaugurate modern industrial growth.[96] Hence both the 'missed' agricultural revolution and the agricultural revolution proper are installed as institutions of economic *development*, the one less active but not necessarily less useful than the other. The proposition brings variety to economic analysis, realistically permits the conjunction of divergent endowments with economic advance, but whether it captures the historical realities of dualistic economies is another matter. However, since all three of these economies had the opportunity of missing their agricultural revolution – Austria-

Table 5.4   Percentage share of agriculture/forestry/fisheries in economically active population (male and female)

	Austria	Hungary	Italy	Spain
1870	65.2[a]	69.8[a]	60.9[b]	66.3[f]
1880	55.6	58.7	51.4[c]	70.2[g]
1890	64.1	71.0	—	69.4[h]
1900	59.7	69.7·	58.7[d]	68.1
1910	56.9	64.0	55.4[e]	56.3

[a] 1869; [b] 1871; [c] 1881; [d] 1901; [e] 1911; [f] 1860; [g] 1877; [h] 1887.
Source: Calculated from Mitchell (1975), pp. 153–61.

Hungary in the emancipation provisions of 1848; Italy in the *risorgimento* settlement of the 1860s; Spain in the nationalization of mortmain lands finalized in 1855 — and each gratefully accepted the chance, the point is a relevant and material one.

Habsburg agriculture between 1750 and 1914 covered the range between peasant monopoly and estate monopoly, in a rather specialized sense, but almost always with unhappy consequences. Moreover, this spectrum of misfortune was located inside an industry of enormous macro-economic importance: not until 1934 did the contribution of manufacturing to the GDP of metropolitan Austria outweigh that of agriculture and forestry, while in Hungary in 1914 the primary sector supported over 60 per cent of the population and generated half the exports.

Stirrings of reform had begun in the imperial domains as early as the eighteenth century with the peasant protection policies of Maria Theresa and the emancipation proposals of Joseph II, but these tentative provisions, while creating a genuine measure of personal security for small cultivators[97] — Transylvania, immune from these changes, was agriculturally the worse for it — scarcely penetrated the crust of farming practice. Despite the liberating decrees bestowing personal freedom upon all Habsburg subjects, the peasantry were still bound by manorial officialdom and by unreformed systems of tenure and labour dues. If they were no longer legally tied to the land, as in Russia, they were still expected to generate produce rents and to support state and nobility with a work regime which many landlords made oppressive. Up to, and probably after these partial adjustments, the Austrian peasantry exhibited strong tendencies towards under-production, cultivating no more perhaps than one-quarter to one-third of estate acreage. Similarly, in Hungary, only one-third of cultivable land was under exploitation as late as 1839. Facing punitive taxation levels — which before the Josephine reforms snatched up to 60 per cent of peasant income — Austrian small producers developed an aversion for surplus and a positive liking for marginal farms.[98] In this state, and little occurred to amend it before 1848, peasant cultivation conformed to the revisionist model, offering few growth prospects, revolutionary or otherwise; instead it operated as a peasant monopoly pegging output at subsistence level.

Better chances to establish the agrarian revolution, or to miss it more consructively, came with the wide-ranging reform measures of mid-century. The Habsburgs made a fairer hand at peasant emancipation than their Romanov cousins, with measures both more accurate and more generous. Essentially, the peasantry was freed of all forms of lordly obligations and permitted to retain all pre-reform holdings, while the lords were awarded compensation only for loss of income and found even this calculated at equity or sub-market rates: thus *robot* (labour) dues were assessed at one-third of wage-labour cost, agricultural output at tax-assessment levels, and in Hungary, where acreage provided the basis of compensation, land at one-third of its market value. Compared with the swingeing extortion of tsarist emancipation, and the rigour of the Stein–Hardenberg reforms, the eastern autocracy handled the transfer of land to peasant ownership and the attendant redemption — in which both central and local government assisted – with exemplary even-handedness. In Hungary the peasantry were even discharged from involvement with redemption and the state itself assumed the obligation.[99] The overall result might appear perilously close to an agricultural revolution. In Austria, certainly, an upsurge of peasant proprietorship did follow upon emancipation, and, in Hungary, some half-million urbarial peasants began suspiciously to resemble a substantial farming middle class, especially in the south-east. But these were false indicators. When examined for growth-inducing capabilities, the emancipation settlement displays omissions more brightly than provisions. The rigid social hierarchy of the countryside was untouched; the enclosure or consolidation of holdings went unattempted; the distribution of agricultural income remained chronically skewed. These deficiencies were most overt in the Magyar lands. Here the problem of the landless peasantry was carefully skirted, and, in consequence, a rural proletariat of 4½ m., scarcely smaller than the Italian, shambled painfully into existence. The liberated small cultivators enjoyed an extremely limited heyday in the 1850s and 1860s before surrendering their undersized plots to the expansionist appetites of the great estates, now greedy for the custom of the railroads and hungry for extra grainland.[100] At the same time, the gentry – the losers in the humanitarian redemption process enjoined by the autocracy – gave up the unequal struggle to convert their niggardly compensation into effective cultivation and were also gobbled by the estates. As Eddie's calculations show, land passed rapidly from this middling agricultural group, not to create a sturdy peasantry, but to make great landlords greater still.[101] Divergent inheritance systems – equal division and morcellation among peasantry and lesser gentry, single-heir transference among the aristocracy – reinforced the increasing polarization of land-holding. Consequently, rural reform in the Empire's most important agricultural regions was succeeded not by the decline of the traditional quasi-feudal estates but by a rapid recrudescence of their strength: the *latifundia* more than doubled in scale 1885–1914, absorbing an extra 11 per cent of the land area, while, as early as 1895, this process had placed a mere fraction of landholders (0.15%) in possession of very nearly one-third (32.3%) of the total land area. Even in metropolitan Austria 0.1 per cent of landowners held 34.1 per cent of the available land by 1903 (against a share of 10.3 per cent in Germany by 1895).[102] Effectively then, not a rural bourgeoisie but a second sectional monopoly, and a lordly one at that, emerged from the Habsburgs' commendable attempts at agricultural adjustment.

Austria-Hungary, therefore, missed the authorized route towards a western-style agricultural revolution. But did she miss it in the approved manner, selecting the alternative vehicle of the 'agricultural revolution manqué'? The great estates played their allotted role, growing larger by the decade, increasingly tapping a world market, and, presumably, expanding their powers as capital accumulators. Perhaps the traditional agriculture of the Empire's Hungarian granary did promote growth in the manner suggested by Romeo for the traditional agriculture of the *mezzogiorno*: as a coarse sponge mopping up primitive accumulations of capital for the refreshment of a new manufac-

turing community. Certainly, there was potential: German observers in the
1830s viewed Hungary as a reservoir of raw materials for her fortunate neighbours, while her flocks and vineyards, and the remarkable fertility of the
Banat prairie, persuaded English contemporaries to rank Magyar agriculture
among the most promising in Europe.[103] Similarly, both the arrival of the
railroad, and the sharpness of Vienna's fiscal punishment for the attempted
Hungarian secession of 1848, elicited a swing away from pastoral farming
towards the massive scale economies of extended cereal production. Under-
utilized plainlands succumbed to a tide of wheat pushed along by transportational opportunity and financial necessity. Undoubtedly, also, these new developments exerted leverage upon urban processing industries: by the century's turn the Hungarian milling industry ranked with the world's best; in
1898 nearly half the country's industrial output derived from the processing of
foodstuffs. Agriculture here took upon itself some of the characteristics of a
leading sector, increasingly establishing linkages with new manufacturing
prospects. But if there was potential, the outcome remained problematical,
and most of the problems went by the name of the Magyar nobility. Even by
the standards of eastern European aristocracy, the Hungarian magnates were
extravagant, apathetic, lawless, and 'remarkable for a spirit of antique incur-
able Asiatic indolence', their convictions immortalized in Petofi's eponymous
satire of the Magyar nobleman, 'I am idle; therefore I am alive'.[104] Agriculturists of this calibre were content to take revenue from grain, but had scarcely
an inkling of competitive production or of technological improvement. When
mechanization did invade the Hungarian prairies, late in the day, in the 1890s
and 1900s, it was for good reactionary reasons: to resist the pressure of agrarian socialism and its expression in strikes and emigration. Similarly, as the
estates expanded and tariff protection became increasingly available, the flexibility of aristocratic cultivation very probably *declined*: these reticent landlords
refrained from full commercial production and instead set about exploiting
their monopolistic position within imperial markets.[105] Nor was this missed
revolution much better at securing productive use for the rewards of restrained
production than at producing genuine commercial innovation. Gross, and increasing, inequality of income can as readily make for conspicuous consumption – at which the Magyar élite were expert – as for capital accumulation and
investment. Certainly, the heavy incidence of German and Austrian capital
within the Hungarian processing industries, as well as the attested unwillingness of noble fortunes to enter manufacturing,[106] suggests that in practice the
Magyar surplus rarely progressed further than the dining table or the hunting
lodge. Warriner is of the opinion that expanded *peasant* cultivation and *smaller*
estates would have created a more productive agriculture; the actual, and precisely opposite, trend revealed by Eddie, conforms closely to the requirements of the
'missed revolution', yet culminates only in the commercial conservatism of a
producers' monopoly. Given chronic polarization of land-holding and immense
skewness of income distribution, there may well be not capital accumulation
but temptation to the self-indulgent. Some particularly talented agriculturists, it would seem, can miss even 'agricultural revolutions manqués'

In Spain, however, they had also to do without decent agricultural lands; no less than one-quarter of the cultivable area was suitable only for cereals, and much of that only barely. The primary sector may have been large – it provided 66 per cent of national income in 1913 – but it lacked anything resembling the potential of the Hungarian plains. The main crops of the *secano*, supporting some 2 m. cultivators, were wheat, wine and olives, and, in the last third of the century, these needed an immense 'orthopaedic' tariff to keep them going. Such poor resources maintained a production which barely matched the very modest population advance; without the tariff many of these fields would have reverted to scrub. Where the railroad had brought the world's custom to the threshold of the Magyar nobleman, it transported only cheaper and more competitive products to the market-place of the Spanish farmer. The combined impact of low-cost New World grain and cheap steam carriage proved disastrous for Spanish cereals: from about 1850 American wheat cost less in Spanish ports than the native crop, and sometimes less even in inland provincial capitals. Viticulture was no better defended: once the French wine industry had conquered the aphids, its Spanish colleague stood little chance in an opened market; between 1889 and 1907 it relinquished its prosperity and nearly one-fifth of its land area. Practically, the sole benefit derived by Spanish agriculture from the coming of the railways was that the merino flocks now rode rather than ate their seasonal way across Spain. Clearly, the 'alternative' form of agricultural development could be postponed too long: the transport revolution of the years after 1870 offered few prospects to the agricultural latecomer whose missed revolution included – as the majority did – inherently high costs.

For Spain the chance of reform presented itself during the second third of the nineteenth century. In an attempt to rectify plunging national finances, the regime moved to nationalize all clerical, municipal, and royal estates, and to auction them off to the highest bidder: Although its fiscal origins offered few guarantees of success, this transaction, extending through the 1840s and 1850s, did contain opportunities for major adjustments to land-holding practice. Virtually all were disappointed. Most of the property moved simply from large-scale institutional ownership into the hands of large-scale absentee landlords, much like those of the Italian south and in no way superior to the magnates of Hungary, who, whatever else, were agriculturists to the core. If the beneficiaries were in any sense bourgeois, they were not the stalwart medium cultivators of a new *bourgeoisie rurale* but the scanty representatives of an established, isolated, and parasitical urban bourgeoisie. Once again an agricultural settlement prolonged, rather than suppressed, reactionary forms of land-holding; and, as before, the economic gains were not immediately obvious. Some expansion and enclosure of estate lands did follow – for grains in the highlands, for vines in Catalonia and Andalusia – but a high proportion were ill-situated and ill-considered. Until the early 1880s these adjustments did support a fairly consistent export surplus in grain, but thereafter the high proportion of marginal land within the total exerted a strong downward pressure, pushing even the cereal sector into an adverse trading balance.[107] Given the poverty of Spanish endowment, reliance for increased agricultural output upon simple extensions in the cultivated acreage necessarily entailed diminishing returns. Precisely how estate systems of this complexion were to act as capital accumulators remains painfully opaque.

In fact, there is a strong correlation between the regions displaying the poorest agricultural performance – for instance, southern Andalusia and Estremadura – and those with both the largest class of estate and the highest measure of absentee landlordism. In this context, it was especially unfortunate that the great estates should have exerted a dominion over the land-holding structure of Spain fully comparable with that jealously maintained by the magnates of Austria-Hungary. Indeed the bias within Spanish land-holding was, in some respects, even worse than that of the Habsburg domain: the tyranny of the *latifundia* is no less marked, but the band of middling holdings is even weaker and the concentration of plots in the miniature category even more pronounced (see Table 5.5). In 1900 a negligible proportion of Spanish landholders (0.1%) controlled a swingeing proportion of total cultivated land (33.3%), while small and medium farms together made up 3.6 per cent of all

Table 5.5 Comparison of distribution of landed property: Austria, Hungary, Spain around 1900 (% of total holdings and land area)

Size of property (hectares)	Austria 1903		Hungary 1895		Spain 1900	
	Number (%)	Area (hectares) (%)	Number (%)	Area (hectares) (%)	Number (%)	Area (hectares) (%)
0–5	79.2	10.3	72.8	14.8	96.0	29.6
5–10					2.0	6.1
5–20	15.1	23.2	24.7	30.9		
10–100					1.6	20.6
20–50	4.7	18.8	1.5	6.5		
50–100	0.6	5.3	0.4	3.8		
100–250					0.1	10.4
100–500	0.3	8.3	0.4	11.6		
250+					0.1	33.3
500+	0.1	34.1	0.15	32.3		

Source: for Spain Vicens Vives (1969), p. 639; for Austria and Hungary, Eddie (1967), p. 302.

Table 5.6 Distribution of agricultural land according to holding size: Spain, 1900

	Number	Area (hectares)
Latifundia (250 hectares +)	12,488	7,468,629
Large estates (100–250 hectares)	16,305	2,339,957
Medium holdings (10–100 hectares)	169,472	24,611,789
Smallholdings (5–10 hectares)	205,784	1,379,416
Minifundia (up to 5 hectares)	9,810,331	6,635,299

Source: Vicens Vives (1969), p. 639

328

holdings but cultivated just over one-quarter (26.7%) of available land. The plight of the Spanish peasantry is fully evoked by their proportions of holdings and land; they farmed 96 per cent of all holdings but had to make do with less than one-third of all farming land (see Table 5.6). Their plots were too small, usually little more than one hectare, and their practice too poor for anything but a perilously maintained hold on subsistence. Yet, where Spanish agriculture did exhibit flexibility and rapid advance – and not all cultivation was as bereft of promise as the *secano* – was where *modest* investment yielded dividends: with vegetables and fruit, in the market gardens of Catalonia, the potato fields of the *Maresme* and the orange groves of Levante.[108] The Spanish citrus industry, lying fourth in the schedule of export contributors by 1914, and achieving at peak the astonishing output growth of 12.5 per cent p.a. must rank as one of the most considerable agricultural successes in single products to be recorded in nineteenth-century Europe. But it was not won on the great estates. In Spain, as in Austria-Hungary, agricultural reform did not conjure forth a Frenchified species of substantial peasant; nor in Spain did it even carry capitalism to the great estates, which, after a fashion it had managed in Habsburg territory. Capitalistic successes in fact came from enterprise of medium scale in favoured regions, and of these, despite the revisionist fanciers of broad acres, both countries had too few.

On the face of it, the plea for the utility of the missed reform and the durable estate looks more convincing in its Italian homeland. Here a large traditional sector – providing 57 per cent GNP 1861–81 and 44 per cent GNP 1911–15 – succeeded for most of the period in expanding output sufficiently to compensate for food imports, economize on foreign exchange, and maintain a favourable balance of payments. This it achieved without any damping of domestic consumption in the Russian style: in contrast, the domestic intake of all consumables rose at a healthy rate, two and a half to three times more rapidly than population.[109] In the half-century after 1861, gross agricultural output notched up advances of 228 per cent in the southern provinces, 262 per cent in the central regions and 295 per cent in the north, while in some major products such as corn, wine, and olive oil, the south may have enjoyed an initial pre-eminence.[110] Is this then evidence that the agricultural rearguard could indeed cajole surpluses out of old-fashioned cultivation into new-fangled industrialization?

Av. area per unit (hectares)	% of all holdings	% of total farm area (hectares)
598	0.1	33.3
143	0.1	10.4
27	1.6	20.6
6	2.0	6.1
0.6	96.0	29.6

In the Italian context, the answer to this question depends on the valuation given to southern agriculture: whether it is seen as temporarily effective (Eckaus), deliberately if creatively sacrificed (Romeo), or totally and painfully deprived (Luzzatto, Hildebrand *et al.*). The 'optimistic' assumption underlying the first two interpretations, and involving a post-*risorgimento* upsurge in estate cultivation enduring for some one and a half decades, rests on frail foundations. It is not only that the behaviour of Italian savings stubbornly refuses to correlate with the imputed activation of the estates supposedly engaged upon their production. There is also the problem of the divergent regional patterns in the *per capita* output of wheat, an obvious estate staple: from the 1870s to the 1890s the northern provinces were the only ones to sustain a rising trend in wheat output per head, yet their southern counterparts were increasing wheat *consumption* per head – necessarily implying, not an increase in capital accumulation, but an actual decrease in self-sufficiency within exactly the estate system featured by the Romeo hypothesis. Nor did the southern seigneuries profit measurably from the advent of railways, as some of their archaic colleagues in other countries managed to do. After an initial bout of prosperity among the wheat farmers, the more enduring (and swiftly delivered) outcome of transportation advance proved to be more Spanish than Hungarian in style: in Magyar territory the railroad had suppressed the small producers and bolstered the estates; in the *mezzogiorno* they encouraged the deforestation of the *latifundia* and thus the exhaustion of their already arid soils. As it did in Spain, the locomotive placed the Italian south in contact with a more prosperous and efficient world, and delivered to its threshold, not the world's custom, but incontrovertible proof of the region's economic inferiority. Within such limits, small evidence of a surplus might be expected and small evidence is forthcoming: the most modest indicator of an agricultural balance, the amount of investment in farm improvement or additional cultivation, reveals that between 1861 and 1915 southern estate owners 'reformed' only 2,362 hectares against 329,000 hectares treated by northern farmers. This strongly suggests that the 'surplus' of the *mezzogiorno* managed to find productive employment no more frequently than its Magyar equivalent. Nor, if ploughback on the estates was neglected, is it likely that the returns garnered by absentee landlords found their way into industrial capital formation. More likely claimants were the demands of an urban life style or the requirements of the money-lenders. The advantages of the unregenerate estate, as preached by Romeo, wear embarrassingly thin against such friction, and it is the bleak view of Luzzatto, picturing a cultivation devoid of progress, which proves more durable.

The explanation for this disappointing result lies, much as in Spain, within a land reform which fumbled the opportunities for a French-style agricultural revolution without grasping those of its opposite: reform was missed but in the wrong style and with property transferred to the wrong hands. The Italian land problem lay not in the absence of ownership changes but in too little change in some directions and too much change in unsuitable directions. The reformist auction of ecclesiastical and crown lands beginning in 1867 offered an occasion both for the exchequer to gather much-needed revenue and for a rationalization of cultivation stemming from the liberation of land supplies. In the event, receipts of 294 m. lire were obtained by the state in 1867–70, and cultivation changed scarcely at all. Two-thirds of the early sales took place in the south and the majority of all sales transferred land to middling landowners, apparently creating the archetype of a landed bourgeoisie, classical competitor for the old nobility.[111] But, as so often, this bourgeoisie refused to run true to the thrusting capitalistic type; rather it was an exhausted bourgeoisie. Its resources were entirely consumed in the acquisition of land; it disposed of no further surplus with which to finance improvement; it could survive only by exploitation of its rural inferiors. Eckaus' musings as to why the southern middle classes did not turn to industrial or commercial investment are answered in the peculiar emaciation of this agricultural bourgeoisie.[112] By the same token, Romeo's prognostications for an estate-based 'primitive accumulation' of capital evaporate when confronted with the precarious and weakened estate owners of the post-unification era.

Mack Smith judges rightly that, 'feudalism had not been abolished, but had just changed names and changed hands';[113] certainly, new hands directed a cultivation scarcely more productive than the feudal. And they held it fiercely: as late as 1896, 86 per cent of sales of foreclosed land still fell in the south and still involved transfers to *latifondisti*, *gabellotti*, or the exploitive *mercanti di campagna*, that is, to hands traditional, ineffectual, or grasping. But if feudalism had not been abolished, this less-than-fresh adaptation *did* involve some changes, and few for the better: part of the land transfers simply went to swell the great estates; another part, however, passed from autocratic, but sometimes resourceful, control into new but largely paralysed bourgeois supervision. This revolution failed to strengthen the magnate 'sufficiently' and failed also in reaching a particularly enfeebled kind of middle cultivator too well.

It is true that, once the Italian countryside had pulled through the difficult post-*risorgimento* years, and through the full recession of the 1880s, notable improvements in practice did occur in some northern regions, Piedmont, Lombardy, Venetia, and Emilia-Romagna. Between 1896 and 1914 cereal production rose by one and a half times, and there were similar improvements in wine, citrus, and fruit, as well as in dairy produce. These results were achieved not by increased land input (it was static) nor by increased labour input (it declined) but by much extended chemical fertilization (imports rose by fifteen times, domestic output by ten times, 1887–90) and machine utilization (imports rose by twenty times, 1880–1910).[114] Yet this northern achievement took place within a fragment of Italian land surface: the area of improved yields covered only a handful of provinces. The Po Valley alone, with 13 per cent of the nation's cultivable land, accounted for 30 per cent of its output. Probably by 1900 no more than one-fifth of Italy's entire land area was subject to capitalistic exploitation. Not surprisingly, with a base so narrow, the improved cultivation of 1880–1900 managed to lift total national agricultural output only by 10 per cent against an increase in manufacturing over the same term of 40 per cent. The innovations of fertilization and mechanization had also accelerated from very small beginnings. In 1900 the research manpower investigating chemical fertilization and other aspects of agricultural science amounted to a meagre seventy individuals, while, even in a reasonably proficient agricultural region like Reggio, chemical fertilizers did not replace animal wastes until well into the 1900s. Widespread mechanization came, similarly, only with the pervasive agricultural strikes of 1901–02, curbing the landowner's usual inclination to substitute his immense reserve army of labour for expensive accumulations of agriculture capital.

Even in the north, agricultural technique was adversely affected by capital weakness and entrepreneurial conservatism. Thus the relatively sturdy wine industry of Reggio was hampered by patriarchal management and a chaotic variety of vine species; here only dairy farming, and then only strongly in the 1900s, provided evidence of successful modern methods. Nor were the more productive territories without their absentee landlords and peasant problems. Reggio province was characterized by very small units, tended by micro-farmers and share-croppers (*mezzadro*) and interspersed with large estates.[115] Even among the capitalistic farms of Lombardy, labour was still drawn from quasi-feudal bonded *braccianti*. Primitive multiple taxation requirements absorbed 25 per cent of peasant crops, inviting indebtedness and proletarianization and their inevitable sequels: as late as 1884 the Mantuan peasantry rebelled against starvation wages, and in 1896 two-thirds of Reggio Emilia's population was drawing charity. At the century's turn, therefore, the abrasive juxtaposition of great estates and micro-plots, peasant impoverishment, and oldstyle cultivation did not constitute a southern monopoly; they could be duplicated even in the most promising sectors of northern agriculture.

The performance of the Italian primary sector and its ability to generate investment surpluses, 1861–1914, may be described in three separate phases: the agriculture of 1861–80, too fixed in structure and effete in management to produce a surplus; the recessional agriculture of 1880–96, too impoverished to produce a surplus; the improving agriculture of 1896–1914, its own capital requirements too pressing to liberate a surplus. Northern farmers in this last period of renaissance reinvested virtually the totality of their proceeds in land improvement and had often to approach the banks on their own account for additional development finance. And if the *latifondisti* managed during this period of prosperity to siphon profits out of agriculture,[116] the likelihood that they were directed towards industry improves not at all.

In general, the most appropriate verdict upon Italian agriculture is that it was misused. The southern regions, like the Spanish centre, were subjected to an over-emphasis on grain, over-use of marginal land, fractionlization of peasant holdings, and surrender of the estates to incapable hands. Unsurprisingly, the Italian tariff on wheat was among Europe's highest by the 1890s, as much a crutch to the cereal sector as its Spanish counterpart. In the north, miniaturization of holdings, excessive taxation, and poverty of technique, enduring into the 1900s, took their toll. Probably, government action is the important variable here. It was state need and state policy which prompted

unproductive transfers of land. And it was official protectionism which preserved the inefficient grain-raising economy of the south. No doubt, Gerschenkron's argument that such cosseting was unnecessary, given the 'flexibility' of Mediterranean agriculture, founders upon the rock of southern deprivation; the removal of the tariff could scarcely have elicited a flexible response
from the *mezzogiorno* in the absence of other very considerable public measures
for agricultural improvement. But it was exactly such schemes which were the
critical omissions from policy. Not only in Italy but also in Austria-Hungary
and Spain, the vital remedial measures – involving irrigation, reafforestation,
and innovational promotion by public authorities – were relegated to the margin of government interest. In all three cases state-sponsored schemes of rural
regeneration arrived only in the 1900s, too late for any worthwhile effect and
insufficiently generous to correct the central problems of agricultural productivity. In northern Italy, the Cavour Canal, linking the Po and the Ticino,
brought irrigation to 500,000 hectares of Piedmontese and Lombard countryside, while land reclamations on the Lower Po and the Venetian coast
yielded some useful results. However, most such schemes in pre-war Italy
attracted more electoral rhetoric than concrete achievement. Similarly, in
Spain the still more resistant regime of Don Antonio Maura repudiated the
irrigation and public works proposals of the Gasset Plan (1906) in favour of
the more pressing demands of naval reconstruction. Before this initiative
Spanish finance ministers 'had prevented the allocation of all but a pittance'[117]
to similar proposals for agricultural assistance. If these regimes did not act to
perpetrate or maintain dualism, they did fail to fully confront the agricultural
problems raised by it.

What then is the contribution of agriculture to the development of the split
economies? Obviously, the reality of the missed revolution – which is sustained in all three cases – rules out the orthodox transfers of the agricultural
'precondition'. But, on the other hand, the behaviour of these rural systems
does not closely resemble the specifications laid down by Gerschenkron for the
agriculture of the *backward* economy. These imply a passive role for the primary sector, neglected by official policy except in its capacity as a resource bank
for periodic spoliation. Yet none of these agricultures is uniformly passive: the
Hungarian estates were, for a while, grain exporters of world stature, while
sectors of the Spanish (citrus, wine) and Italian (fruit, oil, wine, cheese) systems enjoyed production records of a dynamism not given to the conventionally backward agriculture. Again, none was deliberately subjected to resource
raids of the archetypal Russian variety; in Italy, on the contrary, agriculture
managed after the 1880s to maintain both domestic consumption *and* foreign
trade. Neglect of the primary sector by the state is perhaps evident in two
cases to some degree, but, in the Habsburg example, agriculture, although
requiring less assistance, is in fact awarded an especially favoured place within
imperial policy. One superficial resolution of these discrepancies is provided
by Romeo's version of the missed revolution which cuts entirely across Gerschenkron's appraisal of the backward agriculture: where the latter discounts

unreformed cultivation as a frictional force which governments must combat in their industrial policies, the former converts it into an *advantage* of backwardness. However, the flaw in Gerschenkron's interpretation is not that the backward agriculture is really an engine of accumulation in disguise. Rather, the experience of these countries suggests that there are probably as many ways of missing the agricultural revolution damagingly as there are of perpetrating it successfully. In Hungary, land settlement initially favoured the smaller farms, but then unleashed massive transfers to genuinely traditionalist estates; yet these proved to be capitalistic accumulators only to a limited extent and reactionary monopolists to a very large degree. In Spain, reapportioned land passed directly to parasitic absentee landlords – but these were neither accumulators nor capitalists in any real sense. In Italy, the revolution was neither achieved to the benefit of a sturdy peasantry, nor unequivocally missed to the benefit of the great landlords; it was half-missed to the dubious advantage of a powerless bourgeoisie.

Clearly then, the missed agricultural revolution is a dependable institution neither of primitive accumulation nor of agricultural backwardness, no more reliable as a determinant of growth or non-growth than the agricultural 'preconditions' which slip their chronological anchors or the agricultural revolutions which slide all too often into evolutions. Probably, the most useful formulation is that backward agricultures within dualistic economies do offer massive impediments to growth in the absence of determined government counter-action. Further, even well-endowed agricultures within dualistic economies will provide no more than partial support for growth in the presence of indulgent and socially biased state policy. In either case, agricultural revolution may be missed in a wide variety of ways according to the composition of the government's scheme of land settlement and the fitness of the major beneficiaries. The outcome will not invariably be positive when the recipients are magnates, nor invariably positive when the recipients are peasants. Other things being equal, *either* a wide-ranging peasant proprietorship or a traditional estate structure could offer prospects of surplus. This approach moves the emphasis away from the rearrangement of land tenure, in which conventional analysis has perhaps become over-interested, towards the processes for *making* other things equal, that is, the entire complex of policy – fiscal, tariff, social, educational, and infrastructural – available to the state in its vital role of agrarian engineer. In nineteenth-century experience, these processes were probably displayed most fully by the highly successful cultivation systems of Japan and Denmark. Elsewhere, it may be that the composition of the state ministeriat and bureaucracy too frequently prejudiced government against the innovations needed by backward agricultures. But it is at least certain that the missed agricultural revolution, however piquant its central paradox, is *not* an infallible recipe for the accumulation of surplus; and equally certain that there are an infinite number of attitudes which governments may take in respect of backward agricultures more useful than the automatic discount which Gerschenkron feels to be likely.

THE INTERVENTIONIST STATE: ARTIFICER OR OBSTACLE

One of the prime requirements for the backward economy, in the conventional understanding, is that it should demonstrate a high degree of government participation in the management of growth. The rapid spurt which is supposed to issue from the growing tension between the rapidly increasing prospects for technological advance and the realities of economic deprivation, together with the concentrated burst of technological imitation and borrowing involved in the spurt, require co-ordinating, administrative, and fiscal capabilities which are a monopoly of the central executive. Agriculture alone is excluded from the bailiwick of the interventionist state in Gerschenkron's proposals, and, as we have already seen, it was probably excluded unwisely. Admittedly, the Russian experience did reveal the classic array of rapid spurt, dominant government, and captive agriculture, but this is less corroboration of a general rule than indication of a very *rare* juxtaposition. For the smaller dual economies, the record is from the outset less impressive: the spurts are suppressed, the agricultures by no means uniformly neglected, and nowhere subjugated to non-agricultural objectives. Further afield again, of course, other developing nations boasted positively creative agrarian policies. What then remains of the state's *dirigiste* role in the secondary sectors – and particularly in the heavy industrial components – of the dual economies?

Immediately in Austria-Hungary, the model finds some confirmation: state intervention of a growth-inducing kind commenced in metropolitan Austria in the eighteenth century and then diminished over time as backwardness was moderated. Reassuringly, this is a pattern much like the Prussian. By the mid-nineteenth century, Austria, like the German states, was moving from a state-supervised to a bank-directed mode of growth, while its less advanced Hungarian satellite, obedient to the imperatives of an earlier development phase, was still initiating its own *dirigiste* policies. The Magyar economy even substantiated its passing resemblance to the Russian by throwing up a reputable counterpart to Count Witte – Count Széchényi, magnate and credit reformer, land reclaimer, regulator of the Danubian waterways, and planner of railroads. Unfortunately, however, not all the details fit as well as the increasing abstentionism of Vienna and the increasing interference of Széchényi; much of the discussion of the Habsburg state's role in economic affairs centres not so much around its creative interventionism as around its restraining obscurantism.

Most commonly, in fact, the imperial state, like its Spanish and perhaps Italian colleagues, is roundly dismissed as an obstacle to growth. Initial testing of this hypothesis may be applied simultaneously to Austria-Hungary and Spain since the development of state activity in these countries moved with remarkable parallelism from the mid-eighteenth to the early twentieth century; the more complex Italian experience may be left for later incorporation.

At the outset, the territorial peculiarities of the Habsburg system lent its economic government some highly idiosyncratic aspects. In the second half of the eighteenth century the Empire was already disposed as a pugnaciously independent and interiorated 'continental system', employing inter-regional specialization and treating the eastern provinces as reserve stores·for bargain-price foodstuffs. Obviously, the Spanish imperial economy was less tightly integrated and less coherently organized. Nevertheless, both regimes employed the growth-controlling instruments of the *ancien régime* extensively and in strikingly similar style. Subsidies to key manufacturers, finance for promising innovations, tax exemptions, scrutiny and maintenance of industrial standards, composed a common cameralist vocabulary, understood as readily in Vienna as in Madrid and as readily in both as in Berlin. Indeed, the occasion of its strenuous enunciation within Habsburg territory was supplied by Berlin: as the Seven Years War (1757–63) provided Prussia with the economic plunder of Silesia, so the loss of these same assets forced the Austrian Empire into active policies of economic compensation. The shape taken by this activity included control-systems of virtually Colbertist dimensions, and extended, in some opinions, towards a primitive form of economic planning. Certainly, in the post-war turmoil of the 1760s, the existing regional boards of commerce were instructed to draw up *operationspläne* for remit to a central board and consolidation into a master national plan.[118] Rough as it was, this may well have been the pioneer inkling of all concepts of central planning. Yet, remarkably, it was not without a genuine, if lesser, Spanish counterpart. The Real y General Junta di Commercio established in 1679 by Charles II, but administered effectively only from 1730, was designed 'to make these kingdoms laborious and industrious', and to do so as a formidable institution of the central government in Madrid. After 1750 its network of control also became more sophisticated as local *juntas* were set up in Barcelona (1758), Valencia (1762), and Malaga (1785).[119] On the face of things, these old regime proto-plans square impressively with Gerschenkron's expectations for curative interventionism. But it was only on the face of things: inherent limitations upon state activity were always more powerful than the state's capability for effective action. As was common elsewhere, the market context for these experiments in induced growth was exceedingly small, limited to the court and the army. Furthermore, the intrinsic composition of the *ancien régime* state, though it by no means precluded economic modernization, set particular limits upon the *form* of change, among them the preferences of the aristocracy, the army, and the church, each vital to the security of this governmental mode. Administratively, the more that was attempted, the more likely were these constraints to tighten. In Austria-Hungary and Spain, they were especially binding. Economic engineering was, therefore, directed away from any upheaval to these established interests. If industry was promoted, it was on the lowest level, with enterprises of a scale unlikely to attract disapproval. And, once promoted, it was conserved without regard to its efficiency – since established 'lame ducks' involved less threat to stability (though more misallocation of resources) than new enterprises. Such small-scale manufactories, together with the restricted flow of subsidies they attracted, could make but little dent on the chronic capital deficiencies of these economies. Perhaps most corrosive, however, were the internal problems of the economic administrations; once again, not only the type of the state administration but the character of the bureaucracy limited the effectiveness of official action. Within a traditional civil service, the established norms of the planning bodies soon became restrictive practices while official overview of industrial development easily converted to over-bureaucratization. Even when competent, however, the economic officials possessed insufficient authority and insufficient resources to pursue their objectives inside a power constellation which they were not permitted to threaten. Their own necessarily undefined jurisdiction and the massive indifference of their administrative colleagues to all matters economic combined to impose the interdepartmental wrangle (frequently with the fiscal authorities) as the most severe obstacle to policy implementation.

Nevertheless, these late-eighteenth-century developments represented something of a high point for deliberate economic stimulation; from this point, the trend for both Austria-Hungary and Spain is mostly downwards. The increasing dilution of interventionism was less the product of receding backwardness than of the advanced gaucheness of reactionary governments which rarely could intervene, and, when they could, intervened counter-productively. In Austria-Hungary, after the interlude of Josephine reform, the baton of *dirigisme* passed to the Vormarz regime (1815–48) and especially to the Emperor Francis I, a ruler endowed with an implacable repugnance for all novelty. Although undeniably meddlesome, this government was as unsympathetic to industrial modernization, as closely wedded to the old forms of agricultural and guild organization, as any in Europe. Its preference for traditionally strict protectionist policies formed one among many obstacles to industrial progress at a particularly sensitive point in the Empire's economic development. Even after Francis' death in 1835, the arts of procrastination at last failing him, his epileptic and cretinous son, Ferdinand was suitably served by the Archduke Louis, Metternich, and Kolowrat, the so-called *Greisenregiment*, whose combined age was 200 and whose genius for inactivity made them the true heirs of Francis. To the industrial surge of the 1830s and 1840s this administration contributed almost nothing, a few highways merely, mainly military roads serving Vienna and Milan, about one-twentieth of private construction over the same period. Any improvement to Austrian capitalism was made *despite* these governments; only where a still enlightened economic bureaucracy managed to preserve a shred of independence — again evidence of the fragmented nature of 'state intervention' — did official action retain any virtue. Against opposition from above, these officials could achieve little, but in commercial policy at least the removal of tariff discrimination against Hungary (1852) and the trade agreement with Prussia (1853) stand to their credit.

If Spain was seized by nothing so forbidding as the *Greisenregiment*, its governments, nevertheless, developed considerable skills in economic restrictionism. These were fully and convincingly displayed in the important Commercial Code of 1829; under its provisions, the formation of all share-companies was made subject to the veto of the government's Commercial Tribunal while the creation of issuing banks required nothing less than the royal consent. Despite these remarkable controls, the advent of financial crisis in 1847–48 convinced the state that its defences against unscrupulous speculation were insufficient: new measures were invoked to place banking developments under the supervision of the Cortes and to *ban* entirely all other company formations, unless they could demonstrate public utility. It was an autonomous economic upswing in the 1850s, and no governmental conversion, which dismantled this trap for the enterprising, simply by outgrowing the existing credit facilities and forcing new ones into existence. Indeed, the major reaction of the state to Spain's expanding mid-century prosperity was simply to mortgage away as many of the country's assets as possible: the land nationalization of 1868, and the subsequent ceding of national property were designed to compensate for the regime's prevailing revenue deficiencies by converting latent territorial wealth into rapid cash returns. The result was to preclude successful native exploitation of both agricultural and mineral resources. As in Austria-Hungary, capitalist achievement could be secured only by evading the reach of such heavy-handed administration.

In the final pre-war half-century, the mood of official policy in both countries was quieter, if scarcely intentionally constructive. Austrian governments were pressured by nationalistic tensions into composing policies favourable to the stabilizing elements among the middle classes and white-collar workers,[120] and in this there were rewards for business. Factory insurance on German lines brought equilibrium to the workforce, while greater ministerial toleration for cartels permitted the coalescence of a business structure by 1900 probably more densely integrated even than the German (if smaller, and less weighty). In Spain, the tariff laws of 1882 and 1891 rallied colonial markets to the support of the mother economy, although in the longer run they helped provoke colonial resentment and the subsequent loss of these same customers. However, in both economies the dominant trend of the period was towards Gladstonian budgetary orthodoxy: in Austria during the 1890s, Finance Minister Dunajewski successfully balanced the national accounts while his Spanish counterpart Villaverde produced a spotless run of surpluses, 1901–08. From the manufacturing standpoint, this preoccupation with retrenchment economics was probably unfortunate. Barkai's suggestion that Russian austerity policies failed to provide a match between government promotion of supply and the necessary expansion of demand (see above, pp. 226–7) – a case of left and right hand pulling in opposite directions – might perhaps be applied more appropriately to other over-faithful follower economies. Acceptance of the ruling budgetary proprieties of the late nineteenth century may well have imposed artificial obstacles to demand upon a wide range of late developers. Of these three countries, ironically enough, only Italy escapes this snare, since, up to 1897, she was forced into an energetic expansion of the money supply by the very immensity of her debts. Not only powerful executives and competent bureaucracies but also appropriate theoretical assumptions – or enforced deviations from inappropriate assumptions – make up essential ingredients of effective *dirigiste* policy.

Between 1750 and 1914 Austria-Hungary and Spain passed through three matching phases in which their governments adopted distinctive attitudes *vis-á-vis* the economy: a proto-planning phase during the second third of the eighteenth century, a reactionary phase in the second third of the nineteenth century, and a Gladstonian phase from the last quarter of the nineteenth century. At no point did their provisions resemble the growth-aiding policies of the Gerschenkron model: in the first phase, they were inevitably deficient in economic technique: in the second, post-Napoleonic, phase, wary of all forms of change; in the third phase, excessively influenced by a *non*-interventionist economic philosophy. Almost certainly – and outside the special terrain of Széchényi's Hungary – these states did more to obstruct than to clear the path of the backward economy.

For Italy, there is less certainty. Here discussion centres on the post-unification period; before the 1860s there were too few competent agencies and too many competing overlords to support a plausible prehistory of *dirigisme*. However, this does not lessen the problems of interpretation. Rather paradoxically, but in no uncertain terms, Gerschenkron has always denied to the Italian government the qualities which he approves in the Russian: Mediterranean officialdom, it appears, was dilatory in its economic activities, less rather than more evident in the management of the 'big spurt', over-committed to the least deserving sectors of the economy, and unskilled at contriving appropriate 'substitutes'.[121] More charitably, but no more optimistically, Luzzatto argues that Italy, unlike France or Britain, retained antiquated social values and structures, and so narrowed the economic band in which the state could manoeuvre that it was '*forced* to be the greatest obstacle to a policy of rehabilitation'.[122] Others like Cafagna and Eckaus have produced more enthusiastic valuations. Most of the argument has centred around three areas of policy-making: tariffs, shipping subsidies, and metal industries, especially the first.

To Gerschenkron, the tariff policies with which Italy initiated her swing away from free trade in 1878 made uninformed and destructive choices: they favoured old, moderate-growth industries like cotton textiles or – in a country starved of coal and importing British coke at twice the Newcastle price – fuel-intensive technologies like iron and steel.[123] Moreover, these were choices which prejudiced the metal-*consuming* industries like engineering, potentially among the brightest of Italian growth prospects. For Luzzatto also, the tariffs of 1878 and 1887 were internally inconsistent, and, worse still, highly damaging to Italy's commercial relations throughout the century's last two decades, especially to the vital relations with France.[124] Protectionist competition between the two neighbours sufficed to close the French capital market to Italian issues, and, more unfortunately, to deny French custom to the especially vulnerable agricultural producers of the Italian south; since France provided the major share of Italy's foreign credit and consumed some 40 per cent of Italian exports, this was a high price to pay for commercial autonomy. Even if, in principle, Italy needed protection, Hildebrand concludes that the government's timing was ill-considered: the economy of the 1880s needed access to cheap foreign iron and steel, and tariffs could have waited until a later date.[125] There is something in this indictment of trade policy, particularly in the allegations concerning the detrimental effects of tariff war, but in general it is probably overdrawn. Agricultural protection was indispensable, and, given political dispositions – a solidarity block combining established manufacturers and price-sensitive landowners – some industrial equivalent was unavoidable. What was provided was almost certainly less damaging than Gerschenkron imagines. Despite their 'ill-judged' protection, the major industries were not precisely impeded: cotton textiles supported the very reputable growth rate of 5.82 per cent p.a. between 1881 and 1913, while the harshly criticized metal-making industries progressed at 9.3 per cent p.a. The first of these performances was appreciably in excess of the all-industry annual average of 3.8 per cent p.a., and the second dramatically so. Similarly, the 'neglected' industries, the partially defended engineering industry, which Gerschenkron considers the premier claimant for protection, and the entirely undefended chemical industry, achieved rates well above the average – 4.7 per cent p.a. for engineering (12.2% over the shorter period 1896–1908) and a phenomenal 11.3 per cent p.a. for chemicals. Intriguingly, the engineering sector performed least well (negative rate of 7.4% p.a.) in the period immediately *after* it received most tariff assistance (1888–96).[126]

It would appear clear from this that the retardative effect of tariffs upon the major protected industries must have been slight – cotton and metal-making industries are unlikely to have suffered much growth forgone when their actual growth rates were 5.82 and 9.3 per cent respectively – and that the disadvantage suffered by the least protected sectors was also slight. No doubt, adjustment of the protective weights between industries would have achieved marginally different results, but, with engineering advancing at 12.2 per cent p.a. during the 'spurt' period, 1896–1908, it is difficult to accept Gerschenkron's contention that, given more appropriate tariff assistance, its growth rate 'would have been a *multiple* of the one actually achieved'.[127] Any prejudice to engineering caused by tariff choices was probably counterbalanced by the state's activity in the promotion of shipbuilding and in the special direction of railway purchasing:[128] the Baccarini Law of 1882 provided privileged quota contracts for Italian machine and equipment producers. As Cafagna rightly emphasizes, the effective constraints upon engineering expansion lay in the small size of the domestic market (which the state did something to rectify) and the deficiencies of labour skills, rather than in misshapen tariffs. Crucially also, more substantial protection of engineering would have damaged the widely spread consumers of machinery more than it assisted the engineers.[129] Since Gerschenkron is solicitous of the metal-consuming interests, it is oddly inconsistent that he should discount the machine-using interests, surely a strategic area of decision-making in a developing economy. Given, then, that protection, like budget-balancing, fell within the conventional.international armoury of statist economics in the late nineteenth century, it was virtually certain that new industrial economies would employ the device. That allowed, it appears that Italy's selection of tariff structure was little worse than any other country's. It gave necessary aid to a precarious cereal culture, facilitated respectable growth performances from established industries, and did not preclude energetic expansion of new high-technology sectors. Certainly, there is little evidence that it impeded growth; much that it co-existed with substantial growth.

In respect to official patronage for key industries – mainly steel, iron, and shipbuilding – Gerschenkron does allow some credit to the Italian state, but finally categorizes its efforts as 'desultory' and 'one-sided'[130] (although how those interests are more 'one-sided' than Russian preoccupation with capital goods industries is left unclear). Here again there appears to be inconsistency. Within the steel industry the state played a major role in its take-over, jointly with the banks, of the large Cassian Bon works at Terni in 1884, and the provision there from 1886 of modern full-cycle mills: thanks to this assistance, the works grew to become one of Europe's biggest, providing three-quarters of Italian needs by 1890. Gerschenkron does concede that the Terni venture provided the outstanding example of government launching aid, but does not permit the state full credit for countering the limitations of the country's lean market in this strategic commodity. By supporting and expanding a large-scale producer in the key metallurgical sector from an early date, the state surely secured an input base of considerable value for the economy's future growth.

If he is severe upon steel policy, Gerschenkron is no more generous to the state's attempts to promote ship construction and ore extraction. It is true that Italian shipping subsidies did proceed by instalments – subsidies for home-built hulls in 1877, revised subsidies from the Depretis government in 1885, additional bounties for construction and subsidies for navigation in 1896 and that at least the first two instalments failed to revitalize the industry in the desired way. However, the provisions, as finally amended, did succeed in lifting construction from 7000 tons p.a. before 1896 to 63,294 tons p.a. by 1900, and the 667 m. lire of state aid which flowed towards shipping between 1861 and 1914 did achieve the dividend of doubling the steam fleet. The 'desultory' or apathetic nature of Italian *dirigisme* is, in fact, partly illusory; it arises largely because Italian intervention, as with the shipping subsidies, was less grandly drawn than cautiously and persistently probing. This pattern is repeated in the official handling of the important iron ore industry. The first efforts by the bureaucrats conferred upon the Elba ore-fields a series of generous subsidies, tariff protection to the value of 40 per cent and a sequence of carefully selected entrepreneurial concessionaires. Unfortunately, the sequence was necessary since many of the early managerial provisions – the recruitment of the Banca Commerciale to form the Ferriere Italiano in 1880, for instance, or the involvement of Belgian financiers – proved unworkable. But, just as in other sectors, the officials persisted, and eventually they did contrive a successful solution. In 1902 the Elba lode was placed under the effective supervision of one outstanding manager, Count Raggio, and, in 1905, it passed under the control of the equally impressive ILVA syndicate. This surely does not compose a tally that is 'woefully inadequate'. It is true that Italian interventionism was not as comprehensive as the Russian, nor as smoothly modulated as the German; it proceeded slowly, by expedient rather than masterplan, and it made mistakes. Perhaps, however, it did not need to mount the committed onslaught against underdevelopment to which both Witte and Széchényi were driven, and, free of this obligation (outside the south) it scored its successes in more modest style. Certainly, it does not depart so far from the requirements of the growth-inducing state as the designer of the backwardness model would have us believe.

Nor, unlike the Austro-Hungarian or Spanish regimes, does the Italian appear most often as an *obstacle* to growth. True, the post-unification governments faced the common destructive paradoxes of underdevelopment: a pronounced need for growth finance; an inability to attract foreign portfolio investment while hampered with a reputation for economic frailty; the consequential need to provide gold backing for the national currency as an earnest of international respectability; the requirement for export successes to meet the cost of the gold standard; and, finally, as the snake seizes its tail, the need for growth in order to procure successful exportation. Like many other administrations, including the Spanish and Russian, the Italian authorities resolved this vicious cycle only by massive borrowing overseas on government account, and, like Spain, with its interest rates up to 11½ per cent, Italy could only borrow expensively, averaging about 7–8 per cent. For a major part of the period after 1850, therefore, Italian state obligations imposed heavy burdens upon the economy, with the public debt soaring from 2.4 billion lire in 1861 to 12.1 billion in 1890.[131] But the Italian government offered more compensation even for these impositions than its Spanish or Austrian counterparts. Its financial necessities, for instance, provided it with some unexpected but useful powers for the manipulation of demand. Official emphasis upon debt funding entailed the side effect down to 1890 of rapid currency expansion with its implications for the widening of the market. But, on the other hand, the regime's fiscal preferences, featuring heavy indirect taxes and substantial levies on property, could be directed so as to redistribute income away from casual consumption towards increased purchasing of capital equipment and increased investment in capital assets.[132]

Moreover, the Italian state, unlike its colleagues, appears to have improved its interventionist record over time. To begin with, the intensely held liberal principles of the early Italian governments restrained all *dirigiste* commitments, despite wise contemporary recommendations for programmes of education, reafforestation, and transportation. Here political variables outweighed economic ones, defying the requirement that backwardness should of itself provoke determined remedies from government. The late political integration of the Peninsula, and the liberal-autonomist type of politics needed to achieve it, exerted more influence upon the content of state policies than did the measure of Italy's industrial underdevelopment. Subsequently, although Cavour's *laissez-faire* principles proved stubbornly durable, the regime's willingness to intervene did advance significantly, at least from the 1880s. Again, this had little to do with the measure of backwardness; that condition certainly did not intensify; indeed certainly it receded. More to the point was the fact that the *political* curbs on the economic activities of government also receded. This pattern fails even superficially to fulfil Gerschenkron's expectations – perhaps disposing him to distrust the *quality* of Italian statism. Viewed from another angle, however, that same pattern defines a form of cumulative and strengthening policy commitment perhaps more likely to assist long-run growth than the Austrian or Spanish equivalents.

There remain, however, two areas of state interest which are not fully controlled by these generalizations: defence policy and railway policy.

THE COSTS AND BENEFITS OF WAR AND DEFENCE

As with many states ambitious beyond their slowly growing strength, or empires self-important beyond their slackening muscles, these countries allocated large shares of their budgets and industrial capacity to warlike activities. Their occasional resort to outright hostilities, also conventionally, exercised entirely unpredictable economic effects. Such campaigns could secure territorial gains, cash indemnities, and industrial boom, or, quite as easily, financial embarrassment, trade disruption, and damaging inflation. These three powers experienced most of the possible combinations. Thus, Austro-Hungarian industry enjoyed increased demand as a result of the numerous wars and deficits of the Theresan–Josephine era, and, after the loss of Silesia, became the object of the state's attempts at planned development. Simple military necessity was the motivating force: with agriculture already taxed to the hilt, the wherewithal for future security could be drawn only from the revenue of industry. Generally, the outcome of these entanglements was economically positive. On the other hand, Austria's ineffectual mobilization during the Crimean War raised international suspicions, overturned state finances, and interrupted railway construction, while the two lost wars of 1859–66 against the secessionist Italian states cost the Empire the rich captive markets of Lombardy and Venetia. Throughout the entire period 1848–90 the costs of war and warlike attitudes prevented budgetary stability and institutionalized permanent and chronic shortfalls. Financially, this pattern was similar to the Russian experience with military over-spending, and, commercially, to Spain's experience with colonial forfeitures. But for Spain, in turn, the effects of war were not limited to the loss of overseas possessions. The civil wars of the Carlist era from the 1830s to the 1870s imposed problems of indebtedness close to the Austrian in scale, and the Spanish-American War of 1898–99 cost the exchequer £1.6 m. per month. Only the Italians seem to have enjoyed a credit balance in belligerence, no doubt initially because their fortunes were the reciprocal of Austrian fortunes, as, at a later date, the Japanese were of the Russian. The Wars of Liberation triggered currency devaluation and thus a well-timed stimulus to Italian exports, while in 1870, the quarrels of competitors, in the shape of the Franco-Prussian War, brought further expansion to trade. Even the Ethiopean fiasco of 1896, by discrediting the Crispi government, facilitated *rapprochement* with France and the resumption of credit arrangements. Clearly, however, these results are capricious: there is no way of systematizing the effects of war, nor of connecting certain types of economy with certain varieties of wartime gain.

This is not true of war *preparation*. These economies shared with Russia and a number of other developing countries (e.g. Japan, China, Turkey, Greece), the need to create modern defence industries amidst general economic backwardness. Since the technology could be imported, and since the states concerned had special reasons (generally they accorded high respect to arguments of security) for acquiring and sustaining this technology, the defence sector of such economies could provide means for the systematic incorporation of advanced capital goods industries and their attendant externalities. Nationalism as a galvanic force within late-developing economies, although conventionally underrated, can make considerable contributions to growth by this means. Indeed, Kahan has argued that it was the technological requirements of advancing military science, rather than a simple chauvinistic concern for national economic performance, which placed the emphasis upon state policy as a means of building the sophisticated economy and complex administration of the modern great power.[133] Certainly, the international diffusion of high-quality armament manufacture should be ranked in developmental effectiveness alongside the major technological transfers brought about by the railway and agricultural machinery workshops which sprang up across Europe in the half-century after 1850.[134]

The process of technological borrowing through the defence sector is visible in each of these economies and transcends the differences noted in other areas of state activity. German, and especially British, defence technology was absorbed into the developing economies through the arsenals and dockyards of Skoda and Fiume, Ferrol and Cartagena, Spezia, Pozzuoli, and Ansaldo. Once assimilated, it generated an important demand for high-quality inputs from indigenous supplying industries, threw off innovations relevant for civilian production, and defined 'best practice' levels of technique and management for other heavy industrial concerns. In some cases also, entirely homegrown armament concerns achieved their own standards of excellence and produced similar benefits for the civilian sector. For, even within the host economy, defence orders directed to native suppliers frequently involved items of advanced technology, rigorously standardized for interchangeability, and required in numbers sufficient to invite a mass production response. New products, processes, and tools issued from these pressures and found non-military applications faster than would otherwise have been the case.

In Spain and Italy, the pressures stemmed from maritime need and from the adoption of British defence technology, in Austria-Hungary from land service requirements and the application of indigenous or German technology. By the 1880s the Spanish shipbuilding industry was in the doldrums, the nation importing 97 per cent of its iron ships, and its own slipways 'utterly powerless in the face of the competition of the Scottish shipyards'.[135] By 1900 most of the antique Spanish navy, recently trapped by the Americans with boilers cold and guns shipped in the fiascos at Manila and Santiago – 'the most complete naval disasters of modern times', according to Carr[136] – lay rusting on the ocean bed. In this context, the Laws of the Construction of the Fleet of 1887 and 1908 had an entirely deliberate dual purpose: to create, and then to maintain, a modern naval force, and to regenerate, and then to expand, native shipbuilding and engineering capabilities. The generous financial provisions of the naval laws – 190 m. pesetas for construction in 1887, 200 m. in 1908, roughly equivalent to one-fifth of the Spanish annual budget or to approximately 2 per cent of national income by 1906 – acted as a 'substantial subvention to the infant capital goods industry'.[137] Much neglected, however, have been the intermediaries needed to deliver this 'subvention'; as in Russia, they were the major British armament concerns. In the large industrial project known as La Sociedad Española de la Construccion Naval, the Spanish government succeeded in recruiting the British armourers to refurbish the great dockyards at Ferrol and Cartagena, and later the state arsenal at La Carraca, and to produce with the renovated plant an entire new navy. In the process it bound them explicitly to 'encourage the national industries as far as possible',[138] and the trade interests themselves described the project as designed 'to bring together various important branches of the national industry such as naval, metallurgical, machine-building and banking societies'.[139]

The form taken by this encouragement and co-ordination was extensive: technical transfers were governed by contract as the British firms promised to make their shipbuilding expertise and all relevant patents available for use in Spain; financial participation to the extent of 60 per cent was reserved for Spanish interests, including the ample shareholding assumed by Altos Hornos, the largest native metallurgical concern; skilled British management and labour was supplied for instructional purposes; and, perhaps most important, contracts for such advanced items as special steels, condensers, machinery, and boilers were directed to the leading sectors of Spanish industry – the Bilbao steel mills; the foremost engineering works such as the Maquinista Terrestre y Maritima, builders of Spain's first locomotives, and the new high-technology producers such as the Industria Electrica.[140] These procedures proved so successful for the main participants that the armament interests widened their field of activity to include overtly commercial undertakings, notably the Matagorda shipyard, acquired in 1914, the Reinosa steelworks, and the Sestao shipyard on the Bilbao estuary, commenced in 1915. The technological contribution of 'spun-off best practice' at this point became accumulative, penetrating not one but several layers of the industrial structure. Within the dockyards themselves, Vickers noted contentedly that the work was 'brilliantly designed and executed', and, by 1916, considered Spanish construction sufficiently improved to justify the withdrawal of the British advisors.[141] Nor was this the only return to the domestic economy: La Naval, like many defence projects in the less developed economies, became the largest shipbuilding and engineering undertaking in Spain, paid fat dividends from 1908 until its decline in the 1930s, and involved a significant section of the economy's most important industrial installations in work of unusually high quality. Measured by the adjustments to domestic practice, the policy for the 'encouragement of the national industries' provided one of the happier interludes in the development of Spanish technology. By 1913 both the national shipbuilding and railway engineering industries had advanced considerably in sophistication.[142]

Many of these patterns were repeated in Italy. Here native defence technology was more advanced than the Spanish – though less advanced than the Austro-Hungarian – and produced its own 'spin-offs' from an early date. By 1862 Turin contained four arsenals equipped to the highest standards, drawing inputs such as machine-tools, pumps, and hydraulic machinery from civilian industry and providing supplies of skilled labour for the commercial engineering works.[143] By the early 1900s the Fiat concern could supply weaponry of the best quality, including an excellent submarine and the dependable Fiat-Revelli machine-gun. Such articles most particularly required advanced design methods (for pressure-resistant hulls) and production disciplines (for standardized production of automatic weapons) from which civilian manufacturers could learn much. Given this native competence in defence technology, foreign suppliers naturally emphasized the heavier and more intricate weaponry in their dealings with the Italian government. These, the great ships and guns of the pre-war armament contest, the ambitious new nation found irresistible: between 1901 and 1912 alone, the Italian authorities planned to disburse £50–60 m., equivalent to 3.3 per cent of the national income for 1901, on modern naval equipment.[144] Once again, and with similar methods, the British armourers proved the major beneficiaries. Duplicating the interest in very large concerns displayed in Spain, the Newcastle firm of Armstrong turned its skilled attention upon the engineering works of Pozzuoli near Naples as early as 1885, converting the undertaking into the chief supplier of war material to the Italian navy, the most important industrial establishment in the south, and the largest machine-shop in the world.[145] By 1914 Pozzuoli had become virtually an extension of the British armament complex and had been joined within the Armstrong empire (from 1904) by the huge Ansaldo engineering works, possibly Italy's most sophisticated industrial venture, and, according to Saul, 'one of the few significant machine-tool makers in Europe in the less advanced countries'.[146] By 1914, thanks to the participation of foreign armament expertise, the slipways of Ansaldo had released dreadnoughts of the largest international class, probably Italy's most impressive engineering constructions up to that time. But the sponsorship provided by Armstrong was at least matched by that of their Sheffield rivals, for, in the 1900s, Vickers broached the Italian market with highly characteristic tactics: they struck an alliance with the important Italian ship constructors Frattelli Orlando and N. Odero e Cie, extended a contractual promise to provide the Italians with their most modern designs and patents, assumed a shareholding (of 28%, leaving 53% to the shipbuilders and 19% to Italian steel interests[147]) in the new Vickers–Terni Società Italiana d'Artiglierra ed Armamenti, and accepted an undertaking to construct an entirely new arsenal at Spezia on the Gulf of Genoa between 1906 and 1910. The equipment installed by Vickers for this scheme, 'brought knowledge of altogether new types of machine-tool techniques to Italy',[148] and by 1911 the arsenal could tackle the problems of hydraulic engineering raised by the manufacture of battleship gun turrets, some of the most intricate of the era.

The increment to Italian technological growth from both indigenous and imported defence skills was again obviously substantial. The impact of new manufacturing procedures left clear marks, as, in an economy starved of scale, did the armourers' habitual preference for generosity of organizational size. The possibility even exists that the military–industrial complex provided the *main* stem of Italian industrialization, that the development of the capital goods sector relied almost entirely upon defence contracts.[149] Certainly, military demand provided the essential element of width in markets without which the expansion of the metal industries in Italy would have been scarcely worth while. The steel mills of Terni cut their teeth on armour-plate contracts and fed their reserves with easy credit from the Admiralty. The national shipping line, the Navigazione Generale, promoted for largely strategic and colonial reasons, formed a concentration of capital and demand without which 'the other elements of heavy industry might never have come into being at all'. The economy's best civilian producers, the railway and automobile workshops, found that military work was the most profitable work and subsidized their everyday business with lucrative armament contracts. For the heavy shipbuilding industry, soon to be a successful exporter of the largest vessels, naval orders constituted 'perhaps the only way such an organization could survive in Italy then'.[150] Here the fortunes of the capital goods industries – largely because of the few readily imaginable alternative sources of demand for their products – were tied to the military customer with a closeness which few other economies have displayed.[151]

Among these three cases only the Habsburg Empire records a rather modest value for the impact made upon the economy by the diffusion of international armament technology. But this was due only to the strength of the indigenous defence industries. Some connexion did exist between Krupp and the great private armoury of Skoda, and, from the 1860s, the English concern of Whitehead had maintained facilities at Fiume (Rijeka) on the Adriatic coast which by the 1900s could manufacture torpedoes and submarines to British and American designs. But the strength of the Empire's own armouries – again Skoda, and, most especially, Jacob Werndl's great rifle plant at Steyr – severely limited the penetration of foreign technology. Even Vickers' well-rehearsed attempt to provide 'the whole of their experience in the manufacture of war material' for an Hungarian arsenal scheme to rank alongside Tsaritsyn or Spezia failed in 1911, due to political complications and a certain lack of imperial urgency.[152] Instead, the native arsenals took the lead as instructors for the rest of industry. Remarkably, for a backward economy, Austria could boast in Skoda an enterprise of such force (not least due to the financial participation of the Rothschild's Kreditanstalt) that it became the only gunworks of genuinely international calibre outside the ownership or supervision of the great West

European defence industries. It was sufficiently formidable as a competitor for Vickers to aim their scheme of 1911 at an expropriation of its markets. Clearly, a heavy industrial concern, ranking even approximately with Vickers, Krupp, or Schneider-Creusot would be well placed to exert technological leverage within an economy poised to develop its capital goods sector. Probably, however, this was even more true of Steyr. Werndl's remarkable enterprise – replacing the traditional cottage gunmaking centre around Ferlach – became a repeat-production small-arms producer of the most advanced type, the biggest concern of its class anywhere by the 1890s, and by 1914 the home of Europe's most successful export-earning rifle, the Mannlicher. The Austrian small-arms industry – effectively Steyr – was among the first of all European industries to apply mechanized mass production. Moreover, it maintained its international competitiveness – sufficient to win orders from French and German governments between 1860 and 1900 – primarily by excellence in research and design. Detectable 'spin-offs' emanated from its work upon rapid-fire rifle mechanisms – notably in fine steels and strain-resistant spring systems – and the arsenal's classic requirements for high-grade materials created useful linkage effects with the Austrian steel industry, most especially with the Bohler Steel Co.[153] The military preoccupations, even of ailing empires, were therefore not entirely destructive; in the Habsburg case precisely these preoccupations carried specialized capital goods and machine-intensive industries to a place of eminence unusual in economies of comparable achievement.

As long as war could be avoided, therefore, the aggressive instincts of these powers placed an imperative behind technological development which was positively useful and which probably could not have been duplicated in equivalent strength from any other source. Naturally, considerations of opportunity cost – beneficial alternatives forgone as a result of defence expenditure – are relevant here; obviously, it would have been preferable if the large slices of national income devoted to warlike activity had been directed instead towards peaceful projects of superior economic or technological return. But it must be realized that not all defence expenditure is unproductive, even in terms of social gain: some proportion represents a genuine price of security, the cost of deterring aggression, and thus *sustaining*, rather than 'burdening', the existing economic order. Another proportion purchases facilities – roads, railway equipment, accommodation – which are similar, and convertible, to civilian facilities and which involve services or employment which might otherwise fall upon civilian budgets. And an important proportion finances technological transfers useful for commercial purposes and frequently deprived of alternative parentage by the lower priorities given to science-intensive manufacture outside the military sector. Furthermore, the transfer of state funds between heads of expenditure (and implicitly, *away* from military expenditure) requires highly sophisticated governmental processes: the perception by the executive of a schedule of alternatives for its outgoings; the existence of effective lobbies or pressure groups able to articulate demand for these alternatives; the willingness of the executive to recognize the pressure groups as proper claimants. In the absence of these conditions, the true alternative to substantial military expenditure may well be merely a smaller total for official expenditure. Before 1914 the actual historical conditions included: a marked international disequilibrium, pitching the genuine price of security at a high level; a failure among governments to recognize a range of claims upon the exchequer of anything like the present-day width; a selection of pressure groups arranged in a restricted 'élitist' rather than the modern 'pluralist' pattern.[154] In these circumstances, military investment might be taken as a given and any economic bonus welcomed as a free good. Further, 'among regimes ideologically resistant to *other* types of public expenditure' – and, on both reactionary and liberal grounds, few were more 'resistant' than Austria-Hungary, Spain, and Italy – military investment can play a useful role as technological sponsor and 'general stimulus to the economy'.[155]

RAILWAYS: THE MISSED KONDRATIEV

General stimulation is conventionally more readily ascribed to the mid-nineteenth-century outburst of railway construction than to the later outburst of armament construction. With these three countries, however, it might not be impermissible to reverse the weights. Having missed the benefits of agricultural revolution, it is not inconceivable that their chronology of growth was such as to ensure that they missed also the benefits of the railway revolution. If they did so, of course, a further demerit would have to be placed against the state's role in the supervision of growth, balancing the somewhat fortuitous credit secured by its military endeavours. In each country, the benefits of rail transportation fall under question in a number of areas: the strategic accuracy of the planners' railway design; the efficiency of bureaucratic surveillance over major public utilities; the measure of foreign capital participation; and, the most significant contrast with the defence sector, the viability of the railroad's linkages with the manufacturing economy.

None of these dual economies succeeded in creating transportation networks which met the indigenous requirements of their industries and markets: both Austria-Hungary and Spain constructed 'star' systems, centring inappropriately upon their capital cities, while Italy dealt in vertical 'spines' which ignored the country's regional fragmentation. Initially, Solomon Rothschild had attempted to provide the Habsburgs with a series of 'industrial' lines connecting Vienna with the coalfields of Moravia and Silesia and the salt deposits of Galicia, but his early proposals had been thwarted by the hostility of the Emperor and the conservatism of Austrian capital.[156] Similarly, the bankers' ambitious projects for an Austrian railway imperialism in northern Italy – an example of modernizing economic forces overspilling national frontiers, much as with Germany's railway conquests – were foiled by political complications.[157] Plans to push a major Munich–Vienna spur through Verona, and to achieve commercial expansion eastwards to the Orient through the railhead at Trieste and westwards into Europe through another at Livorno, crumbled against the force of the Italian independence movement. Actual performance was more humble: from 1841 the state sent military feeder lines to the Saxon and Bavarian frontiers and into the northern Italian provinces, while private construction extended the *Nordbahn* to meet the European track system and probed south to the Adriatic and east into Hungary. But even in the 1860s the imperial network was embarrassingly fixated upon the metropolis: mobilization of regional forces in the war of 1866 against the Prussians consequently proceeded with dangerous slowness, and, with only one Austrian line servicing Bohemia, victory went as much to the Prussian train-drivers as to the Prussian generals. If the Empire could not move military materials in bulk towards its major European frontiers, there was little hope that economic materials could escape the tether of an over-centralized transportation system.

In Spain, as French capital and engineers apparently strove to replicate the centripetal tendencies of the early French railways, identical problems of lateral communication arose. But here the domination of foreign interests created an over-emphasis not only upon the hub, but also upon the individual points of the spokes, upon ports and frontier posts. Where most imperial railroads ran *to* Vienna, most Spanish railroads ran *out* of Spain, their purpose not internal communication but foreign extraction. Consequently, the transport of Spanish commodities between Spanish centres remained prohibitively expensive while foreign goods could be deposited in Spanish ports at overwhelmingly competitive prices. Even the attempts of the early 1900s to construct genuine feeder lines proved misbegotten and never met the freight they were intended to convey.[158]

The basic characteristic of inept railway planning – the misalignment of construction with major traffic requirements – also featured strongly in Italy. D'Azeglio was confident that 'railways will serve to sew up the Italian boot', and, even before unification, Petitti's national plan, endorsed by Cavour, cast two long seams along the axes Milan–Bologna–Brindisi and Genoa–Rome–Naples.[159] The dispositions of 1859 certainly required energetic stitching: at this point the 'Italian network' consisted of four separate railway enclaves; Naples, Rome, and Florence each acted as terminus for its own provincial system, while another, larger, one embraced Turin, Venice, and Bologna, an arrangement which neatly isolated the Venetian from the central, and the Tuscan from the northern, lines. Unfortunately, when the connexions were made, many fell in the wrong place: between 1861 and 1911 railway construction was greatest in the southern provinces, although the expansion of traffic here was least, and the availability of freight, both actual and potential, most unpromising. The planners' mistaken assumption – companion of the 'coiled spring' hypothesis – was that railways would generate their own traffic, and, since they had supported this confident insight by guaranteeing the revenue of all participating contractors, the costs of misalignment were high: the receipts of the Southern Railway Company were, in the event, composed of one-third operating profits and two-thirds government compensation. Again, since Italian railways, no less than the Spanish, followed their foreign sponsors into 'penetrative' patterns, connecting ports to centres of consumption, and then, as a second step, moved into areas where 'self-generated' traffic failed to respond, average revenue per kilometre tended actually to fall after 1861.[160] In each of these cases, therefore, railroads failed to deliver the prime communications services and the uniform reductions in transportation costs which, in classical cases, formed their major contribution to the modernizing economy.

Given the average competence of state control over the development of these railway systems, the outcome is not greatly surprising. In each country it was hesitant, or fluctuating, or dominated by economic stringency, or irresponsible; and sometimes it was all of these. Although Austria had constructed one of the continent's first lines, the horse-drawn service from Linz on the Danube to Budweiss on the Moldau (1832) for the carriage of government monopoly salt, the Emperor Francis opposed further construction 'lest revolution might come into the country';[161] not until he was safely interred in imperial soil could the Rothschilds commence excavating it for large-scale railway works. Although private undertakings continued fitfully during the 1830s, the authorities took a full decade to discover the military possibilities of steam, then to lay down, a few of their own lines and reserve the right to plan, control, or acquire all others (1841). Neither in Austria-Hungary, nor in Italy were such powers well used. By 1848 half of the Empire's modest 1,070 kilometres of track was state-constructed, by 1854 half of all networks state-administered, but, nevertheless, the really large constructional peaks of the 1850s and 1867–73 were financed mainly from private resources with the state maintaining merely a supervisory role. Dereliction of control in this form followed in both Austria-Hungary and Italy from acute pressure on national finances: each government concluded, the Austrian in 1854, the Italian in 1865, that railway systems formed mobile assets which, in lean times, could be auctioned to private interests for cash return. The Habsburg state maintained a policy of selling state lines and offering ninety-year private concessions for almost three decades;[162] only from 1881 did it resume a policy of full nationalization, winning back some 80 per cent of Austria's 19,000 kilometres and a lower proportion of Hungary's 22,000 kilometres by 1913.[163] In Italy the state veered from a budgetary emphasis on railway construction (claiming 20% of official expenditure in the early years) to the complete abandonment of its one-sixth share in the networks. However, the violence of this manœuvre created such inefficiency and diseconomy among private operators that the authorities were forced to resume control from 1868, and, on an extensive scale from 1873, as economic recession ate into the independent companies. By 1884 the nationalized proportion of Italy's 9,867 kilometres had reached 60 per cent, but, in the very next year, the state resorted to another surrender, a scheme combining government ownership with private operation and equal division of the spoils. Only in 1905, too late to assist the spurt of 1896–1908, did the government assume unified control over all rail facilities.[164] Not even the large amounts spent by the state on construction – by 1913 some 12,600 m. lire, equivalent to the entire national income of 1900 – could compensate for the damage to efficiency caused by the tergiversations in management. The penalties attached to these policies ran in parallel for the Italian and Austro-Hungarian governments: uneconomical operation by inexperienced, undersized, and sometimes corrupt, private interests; a lack of continuity in planning; major disincentives to long-run investment by private projectors.

In Spain, the railway problem was less complex but no less destructive. At least there were no variations in control of the networks; they remained solidly in foreign hands, while an extraordinarily misconceived official policy provided lavish subsidies and concessions to make the process of foreign exploitation more efficient. The consequential boom in the funding of the railway enclave no doubt competed with, and compromised, the mobilization of capital for more utilitarian industrial purposes. By the mid-1860s, the investment capital amassed by the rail companies exceeded that available to manufacturing concerns by fourteen or fifteen *times*; as Tortella concludes, 'the Spanish railways were constructed *at the expense* of the manufacturing sector they were supposed to help'.[165]

In these instances, *dirigiste* measures aimed at resolving the rigidities of the backward economy in no way exhibited the productive characteristics expected of them. And since the area of social overhead capital is one in which the participation of government is conventionally assumed to be peculiarly necessary, the indictment is all the more damaging. It is significant also that in the railway sector at least, Italy is hardly less damaged than its colleagues in underdevelopment.

At least part of the weakness in the governmental direction of these railroad systems followed from the need to associate foreign capital in their creation. Probably, the Dual Monarchy suffered this dependence least; although some of its early services owed much to French capitalists, and, after the Franco-Habsburg estrangement, later developments drew substantially upon German support. But, in metropolitan Austria, the independent weight of the Viennese banks reduced the need for external credit, a fact which in no way prevented these same banks from driving a 'foreign' body of railway capital into Hungary and tapping the eastern grain-plains in fully colonial style. However, such sinister motifs were generally more familiar to the Mediterranean countries. Spanish railroad development, led by the Ferrocariles del Norte and the Ferrocaril de Madrid, was very rapid after 1860, but like these companies, financed respectively by Péreire and Rothschild, it was scarcely an indigenous affair. With 80 per cent of Spain's 4,828 kilometres of operational line owned by French interests in 1865 and 85 per cent of 11,378 kilometres controlled by foreign undertakings in 1914,[166] the railroad sector was effectively an alien implantation for which Spain provided merely the subsoil, both as track-bed and as cargo. Colonialist exploitation was here not a tone but a dominant theme. In Italy, also, it achieved some resonance, at least to begin with. Very probably, the Habsburg plan to unify the Italian railway network – to the imperial advantage and with the Rothschilds as executors – failed during the last decade of Austrian domination only by a slender margin,[167] while, in the 1860s, the railroad sector came to rival the public funds as the special preserve of foreign capital. Overseas contractors like Thomas and Brassey were prominent in rail construction and, by 1862, foreign capital controlled all lines in Lombardy, Venetia, and central Italy. During the 1860s only one large undertaking, the Società Italiana per le Strade Ferrate Meridionali sported Italian ownership, and even this was not beyond doubt.[168] The tightening grip of the state upon the railway industry in the last decade before the war represented not only a substitution of official for private ownership but also an overdue and costly replacement of external by domestic control. In contrast to the Spanish government, the Italian did succeed with its railway *reconquista*, but at the eleventh hour and only after a half-century of effective foreign suzerainty. With incursions upon economic sovereignty of these dimensions, it was little wonder that the railway policy of governments proved defective.

It remains to be seen whether this misdirected development of social overheads nevertheless evoked useful linkages with the manufacturing sectors of the host economies. Saul argues that, throughout the continent, the demand for railway goods and maintenance did call forth new technological capabilities. Even for Italy and Austria-Hungary he can cite instances: 'before unification in Italy . . . railway construction had brought with it those typical beginnings of a future industrial complex in the Genoa, Turin, Milan areas. Ansaldo of Genoa was just the most famous of the firms to be boosted along the path of becoming a major engineering complex through locomotive repair', and, within the Dual Monarchy by 1900, 'In Vienna the State Locomotive Works were turning out 140 locomotives a year and the Budapest Works half as many again.'[169] Alongside these precocious engineers might be placed the Maquinista Terrestre y Maritima, assembling locomotives in Spain from the 1850s. The detail is interesting and establishes that a measure of steam-driven 'spin-off' did link railway and manufacturing sectors, even within these backward economies. But the thrust of the argument requires substantial qualification for Italy, Spain, and Austria-Hungary. Italian governments may have intended that railways should form 'le moteur d'un essor économique générale du pays' (Gille), but the reality was a good deal humbler. In practice, foreign participation often included foreign equipment: contracts for capital goods were most usually directed by overseas managements to *overseas* suppliers of steel and engineering products. The Alta Italia company between 1861 and 1878 purchased 602 locomotives abroad, but only 39 in Italy, and the Romana company refused to give a single contract to Italian producers while it remained under French control. Ansaldo, and the large Milanese shops, in fact mostly made do with truck and coach manufacture.[170] Only after renationalization in 1905 did large-scale railway orders – between 1905 and 1909 some 1,000 locomotives and 25,000 trucks – form useful linkage effects between the Italian railroad sector and the Italian engineering sector.[171]

In Spain, the bias towards foreign suppliers was even more marked, despite the desperate need of the domestic capital goods industries for an expanded market. Under stricter controls, railway development could well have supplied the necessary custom, but, in the event, foreign operators and ineffectual governments converted infrastructural development into an occasion for massive importation. Between 1861 and 1865 overseas purchases of iron products exceeded the volume of domestic production by 100 per cent, while British and Belgian hardware, French and Belgian rolling-stock, dominated the railway market until 1914. In both of these economies, railway demand was sold abroad rather than concentrated upon the lead sectors of the home economy. In each case, also, it was poorly synchronized with the major swings of industrial activity. Italy's rate of advance 1896–1908 may well have been depressed by the fact that most of the railroad construction had been completed *before* industrial growth accelerated; during the great spurt of 1896–1908, an addition of barely 10 per cent was made to existing networks, against the contrasting figure of 70 per cent for the Russian spurt of 1886–1900.[172] In Spain also, railway growth anticipated the surge of manufacturing development by an embarrassingly wide margin. Linkages with the capital goods industries could not occur since they 'required levels of production which the country had not [yet] reached'.[173] As one contemporary expert perceived, railways might 'help to encourage the growth of industrial production; but where the latter does not exist, *they do not improvise it*'.[174] Although transportation formed a critical bottleneck in nineteenth-century Spain, the irony remained that industrial development was insufficiently advanced to permit traffic levels capable of covering the high costs of construction. The outcome of this was a *negative* linkage: the feedback of accumulating railway losses to bring financial disaster to the Spanish banking system during the 1860s. The peaks of track construction in 1856–66, 1878–80, 1882–84, and 1893–99 brought the Spanish network to completion too early. By 1914, before domestic industry had drawn from it any worthwhile transportational or technological benefits, yet not before Spanish finance had taken from it some near-lethal blows, the railroad system was already sinking into disrepair, requiring a second bout of capital formation to fit it for the industrial expansion yet to come.

Once again, Austria-Hungary provides a contrast, encountering fewer transportational impediments than its counterparts, perhaps experiencing some linkages as early as the 1840s. But even here well-used refrains are repeated: the major proportion of the imperial lines were laid out between 1850 and 1875, an era of 'relatively free trade so that important linkage effects were . . . diverted to foreign countries'.[175] Too often the railway workshops cited by Saul received less benefit from construction programmes than was their due and were left to play second fiddle to the great established factories of the capital-exporting nations. Too often, also, the native workshops were merely harbingers of technical advance, drawn into precarious activity by railway programmes which long preceded the advent of widespread manufacturing activity.

In several ways, therefore, government activity in the transport sector was *less* productive than its dealings in the defence sector. The upsurge of railway construction coincided much less precisely with the major acceleration of capital goods manufacture than did the great armament schemes of 1890–1914. The capitals of railway companies were much less protected from foreign monopoly – and thus from export of the financial linkage – than those of the arsenal and dockyard schemes, carefully preserved for compelling reasons of national interest. And, perhaps most importantly, during the railway era, governments were much less insistent that major investment programmes should be employed to 'develop the national industries' than they had become by the time of the pre-war defence projects. Here, Spain with its total neglect of railway linkages at the mid-nineteenth century yet its insistence upon securing the full benefits of the early-twentieth-century defence schemes provides the most striking example. However, the *uniformity* with which governments wasted the benefits of railway construction – with the Italian case on past record the most puzzling – remains a conundrum in need of resolution. One answer might be that the 'advantages of backwardness' simply reverse themselves in sectors both of great lumpiness and of great appeal for foreign capital. Chronic underdevelopment may place costly infrastructure projects beyond the reach even of the state authorities and attract the only alternative brand of assistance: over-lavish capital flows from the advanced nations, precocious in arrival and distorting in effect.

The beneficial tension observed by Gerschenkron between the growth opportunities inherent in the industrialized powers and the actual performance of the underdeveloped nations becomes subject to dangerous redirection: rather than useful international 'borrowing' the outcome may be the forceful *implantation* by external interests of advanced systems linked to the host economy in only the most tenuous manner and lying well beyond its current needs. Since this redirection may well bring about the completion of a 'precondition' decades before the manufacturing sector can employ it, the risks are that an *obstacle* to growth will be created – expensive scrap which will require renovation before genuine economic benefits can be reaped. Furthermore, the costliness of such steam-driven follies may exert additional leverage *against* industrial advance by diverting resources away from direct investment in production and by straining youthful financial intermediaries to the breaking point. If the need to create modern transport facilities under these conditions is ranked systematically as a 'disadvantage of backwardness', the similarities between the railway programmes of these countries is partially explained.

BACKWARDNESS: RECONFIRMED IMPEDIMENTS

Gerschenkron's attractive paradox that backwardness conferred advantages of imitation and rapid growth upon underdeveloped nations of the last century is cast generally into doubt by the experience of these economies. Not only do the characteristically brusque growth patterns fail to materialize in these instances; and nor is it only that the 'imitation' of the railway sectors proved of highly equivocal utility. More wide-ranging reservations also occur, suggesting that the 'covering laws' of backwardness in fact cover historical situations only up to a certain *measure* of underdevelopment. Beyond this point, effects occur which extinguish the potential 'advantages' of backwardness. In this dangerous area, underdevelopment is likely to include severe regional differences in the levels of pauperization, some of them attached to local economies so derelict that no activity within the modern sector can offer prospects of reconstruction. When the 'big push' is geographically so restricted, large proportions of the economy will not only stay disadvantaged but, as 'backwash' effects take place, will grow increasingly disadvantaged. And since the modern sector will need eventually to invest in rectifying the divergence, this 'advantage of backwardness' bears a high price for all parties. In place of Gerschenkron's rapid surge, this style of dualism might well permit only a gradual process of adaptation in the modern sector and an enduring, perhaps insoluble, absence of adaptation in the primitive sector. By the same token, such acute problems are less likely to invite the effective counter-action of determined governments than to outrun the capability of states to design remedies. Nor is there any historical law requiring the current state of the economic art to include the interventionist methodology needed by late developers. Consequently, imitation of the advanced nations provides no infallible remedies for the late starters: the orthodoxies suitable for established prosperity – especially the *laissez-faire* principles of the nineteenth century – bear little obvious relevance to the problems of the economically underprivileged. Probably, this also applies outside the realm of economic theory: the pressure for imitation falling upon the latecomer, by virtue of the tension between its performance and that of the early starters, may well lead to the selection of technologies ambitious beyond its endowments and capabilities.

The conjunction between the modernism of the advanced economies and the primitivism of the dual economies issued in other than merely beneficial tensions. And international diffusion could feature forces other than the growth–promoting. Among the worst were the strains developed in the area of labour relations. Owing to international demonstration effects, the late developers encountered labour problems of a modern kind at a relatively much earlier stage of their industrial careers than did the advanced economies. Where the more successful nations had experienced upward pressures upon living standards only after the initial growth phases had been safely negotiated, the follower countries found their early development complicated, and perhaps deflated, by such intrusions. In Italy, for instance, precocious union demands for higher wages may have exerted an important depressive leverage upon economic performance.[176] In the early 1900s, Giolitti was forced into a profession of state neutrality in wage bargaining, and Italian governments between 1890 and 1913 were menaced by a swelling tide of strikes, reaching flood between 1899 and 1908, and including a crest of spectacular rural violence in 1901–02. Probably this force was insufficient to drown the Italian industrial surge of 1896–1908 (real investment rose by 9.4% p.a. during the worst strike phase),[177] but, almost certainly, did choke off growth prospects *after* 1908. An uprush in unit labour costs, growing at 1.3 per cent p.a. and a decline in investment, followed in *immediate succession* to the most intense labour agitation and simultaneously with the scarcely lesser upheavals of 1908–13. Similar patterns were evident in the other deprived economies. Barcelona metal-workers mobilized in a general strike in 1902, and, in the following year, the Spanish economy lost 52 m. working days to strike action.

356

Even in Hungary, the great rural strikes of 1897 and 1905 could halve the grain harvest and force even Magyar landowners into an expensive substitution of capital for labour. For the workforce, the advantage of lateness lay in the exchange of traditionally deferential labour relations for the tactical devices of western Europe's more mature, and internationally inclined, union organizations, but the returns for industrial performance were in no way liberating. Employers encountering cost-push and work disruption of this kind would not have relished the twist of Gerschenkron's paradox.

The advantages of backwardness constitute no systematic promises for underdeveloped economies. Russia, it is true, secured some of the returns. But backwardness elsewhere, perhaps because of differing relative levels of dereliction, perhaps because of different starting points on the time schedule of development, perhaps because of different factor mixes, perhaps entirely *unsystematically*, engendered quite other prospects. In the Austro-Hungarian, Spanish, or Italian style, it was more likely to create permanently split economies and powerless governments than to evoke efficient *dirigisme* and dramatic spurts. Exchanges between countries, in this company, were less likely to feature galvanizing technologies than inappropriate theories and corrosive labour practices. The precise type of growth which may follow from international imitation, bureaucratic supervision, and a low rank upon the development ladder appears, once again, to be a highly variable experience. The Russian case carries towards Gerschenkron's prescription, but the more southerly laggards vary strongly in the opposite direction.

BACKWARDNESS AND PRODUCER GOODS: THE OMITTED EMPHASIS

Also variable is the technological mode selected by these economies. According to the requirements of backwardness, developing countries are supposed theoretically to favour the capital goods sector which can best sustain the onerous requirements of the big spurt. In practice, however, neither backwardness on the one hand, nor the tendency of advanced economies to supply inappropriate processes on the other, can fully explain the technological choices made by the lesser economies. Certainly, the bias towards the heavy producer industries is very far from uniform. Spain, in fact, found it difficult to create these classic constituents of the spurt,[178] and turned to lighter pursuits such as chemicals and the generation of electricity. In 1910 Madrid was supplied by the longest high-tension line in Europe, and, four years later, electric power proved instrumental in rescuing Catalan industry from a threatening fuel crisis. After the loss of the Cuban textile market, Catalan manufacturers had re-equipped themselves to provide, not heavy equipment, but automobiles, chemicals, beer, and electric power. The slant of these developments was as much towards consumer-orientated goods and services as towards inputs for other manufacturers.

This tendency was even more marked in Austria where the major consumer sectors (textiles, clothing, food, drink, and tobacco) accounted for as much as 64 per cent of industrial output in 1880 and 49 per cent even in 1911 (see Table 5.7). During the critical phase of industrial growth between 1841 and 1880, the metals and metal products share of total output actually contracted (from 14 % to 13 %) and did not achieve 20 per cent until 1911. Even at this point, it controlled a smaller proportion of the workforce than the equivalent sector of German industry, whereas, according to Gerschenkron, the weights should have been reversed in favour of the more backward economy. Similarly, in Hungary, more backward still, the highest ranking industries in the output tables by the 1890s were the food-processing facilities such as flour-milling and distilling, while the most powerful capital goods industry, machine-making, claimed only third place.[179] Even here, the machinery industry possessed special values which both warn against the conventional exaggeration of Habsburg backwardness and question the accuracy of the familiar correlation between backwardness and the expansion of the heavy industries. For these machine-building industries were not at all conventional. By 1900 Budapest's 400 factories certainly included powerful shipyards and locomotive works, but its most successful manufactures issued from the new high-technology, and by no means entirely 'heavy', industrial sector of electrical engineering: the city's machine-shops found custom as far afield as St Petersburg or Monaco, served clients as advanced as the Italian hydroelectric plant at Tivoli or the Piccadilly Line of the London Underground. Their product range stretched from the largest generating plant to a much less predictable specialism in light equipment such as milking machines. This excellence in high-quality manufacturing practice duplicated an emphasis upon new technological developments already evident in metropolitan Austria. Here, alongside the mass production and export mastery of Steyr's light armament industry, there was also the accumulating force of Ferdinand Porsche's work in automobile engineering: by 1914 Austria possessed an indigenous motor-car technology and a growing international reputation in this line.[180] Technological backwardness, and the escape from it through the producer goods sector, forms too simple a description for these complex blends of consumer goods, processing, and science-related industrial disciplines.

Perhaps this is best revealed in the case of Italy. Gerschenkron's estimate for heavy industrial expansion lives up to expectations to the extent that the capital goods share of industrial output advances from 28 per cent in 1881–96 to 42 per cent in 1908 and 47 per cent in 1913.[181] But other estimates are less obliging. The leading contributors to industrial value added in 1914, ferrous metals, machines, chemicals, and electrical power, make a somewhat heterogeneous selection, and had only just achieved their premier ranking (see Table 5.7), while the share of total industrial output attributable to this same group is assessed by Clough at only 12 per cent in 1901, against 26 per cent of German output falling to the equivalent industries.[182] More precisely, Hildebrand allocates only 20 per cent of industrial value added to the heavy manufactures and 45 per cent to small-scale industry, for the period 1901–

Table 5.7 Relative sector shares of output, Austria and Italy: contribution of individual industries to total industrial output or total industrial value added (%)

Austria	1841	1865	1880	1911		
Textiles and clothing	41	41	34	24		
Tobacco and foodstuffs	18	11	30	25		Total
Glass, clay, etc.	15	6	7	8	%	Industrial
Metals and products	14	16	13	20		Output
Chemicals, fuel, power	2	2	4	10		
Wood, leather, paper	10	24	10	14		

Italy	1861–65	1881–85	1891–95	1911–15		
Textiles and clothing	37	35	32	24		
Tobacco and foodstuffs	45	38	35	26		Total
Metals and products	12	17	18	30		Industrial
Other minerals	2	3	4	3	%	Value
Chemicals, fuel, power	4	6	8	13		Added
Rubber, paper	1	2	2	4		

Sources: for Austria, Gross (1973), p. 274; for Italy, calculated from Clough (1964), p. 83.

05; textiles alone are awarded a larger slice of total production than the combined share of all capital goods industries before 1906,[183] and probably retained a 20 per cent share in value added as late as 1913.[184] The performance of textile consumption goods was, in fact, highly impressive: the expansion of Italian cotton spinning was faster than any other nation's in the 1900s, while woven Italian silk expanded from 6 to 17 per cent of total exports between 1885 and 1913, outdistancing its French rival in many important markets. This expansion of the lighter industries was based, moreover, upon the development of a high-technology power sector: by 1911 electrical energy had replaced about 20 per cent of imported fuels and accounted for half of all industrial motive power. As Austria-Hungary ranked among the pioneers in electro-technical production, Italy led Europe in the *use* of electrical power: the continent's first electric lighting plant was erected at La Scala, Milan; Rome was the first major city to employ hydroelectric power on a large scale; the first Italian tramway was wired for electricity as early as 1890, the first textile mill from 1899, the first railway from 1901.

However, Italian performance was notable not only for its successes in textiles and power generation but also for the wide selection of consumer industries, light manufactures, and sophisticated processes employed by the economy. Cirio founded the celebrated jam and preserves industry in 1875; Pirelli began making bicycle tyres from 1890; the Olivetti works at Ivrea commenced production in 1911. But the most significant achievements were in cycle and automobile engineering, rated by Cafagna as 'probably one of the most brilliantly effective examples of Italian industry's participation in the *new international movement of these years*'.[185] Between 1899 and 1907 some forty automobile plants started up, among them the entrepreneurial leader, Fiat,

359

and by 1914, most of the great marques, Lancia at Turin, Romeo and Bugatti at Milan. If the typical scale of these firms was small, their combined weight reserved to them some five-sixths of the Italian market by 1914. Successful construction of this durable-consumer base in turn provided important derived demand effects for machine-tools, aluminium, steel, and other heavy industries. Here an important modern consumer industry supplied linkages to the more reticent capital goods manufacturers. Similarly, significant developments in areas much influenced by consumer demand occurred in the production of rayon, dyestuffs, and cement (the latter galvanized by the building upsurge of the 1880s), while the formidable chemical fertilizer industry, spearheaded by Montecatini, brought a high-technology capability to the problems of rural productivity. Although the great engineering works like Ansaldo or Breda, and the big steel-mills at Terni or Cornigliamo, were busily occupied during this period, the full Italian technology mix again escapes the narrow pronounced specialism in capital goods, both simple and sophisticated.

In these economies, the single-minded emphasis upon metal-making and fabricating, machine-building and railroad construction which formed the centrepiece of Witte's economic design finds no close parallel. The greater heterogeneity of industrial types found to the south is striking but not accidental; it may be explained in several ways. Firstly, the arrival of electric power, a heavily exploited device in all three economies in the pre-war quarter-century, provided a new lease of life for small-scale manufacture; it brought something like efficiency to the tiny workshops which littered these industrial sectors and reduced the advantages of large-scale production. Moreover, it could substitute for mineral fuel endowments where these were scarce, and, in the Italian case, could unlock and transport the massive, hitherto wasted, dynamo of the Alpine watercourses. Since it could convey this energy source economically to the humblest Milanese workbench or the greatest Umbrian furnace, it was effectively scale-neutral. And since many units of small scale were consumer goods producers, new possibilities for competitiveness were opened in this area.

Secondly, Gerschenkron's emphasis on capital goods does not allow for the fact that the latecomer may have to find for itself an export 'niche' in a world already well peopled with capital goods producers. Even where a backward country does lean towards the heavy manufactures – as Hungary partially did – this may be less for the purposes of rapid industrial growth than to fill a niche with an *exportable* product of highly specialized design. Capital goods created by small countries under these conditions are often tailor-made, advanced in technology, and weakly linked to domestic industrial requirements.

Thirdly, it is clear that many processes adopted by these latecomers were drawn from the fashionably *avant-garde* manufactures of the day – motor-cars, chemicals, electro-technicals. It may be that Gerschenkron has mistaken for a covering law of backwardness what is the product simply of a technological—chronological conjunction: those backward economies which commenced development in the second third of the nineteenth century, when capital goods were at the forefront of world best practice, naturally turned to these indus-

360

tries for their technological lead sectors. But, in contrast, the later developing economies, entering an impressionable stage just as world best practice moved on to incorporate lighter, consumer, and high-technology products, tended to select industries featuring these varied elements for their manufacturing vanguard. Within these terms, it is perhaps Russia which is an aberration, held to the selection of an earlier era by the state's monopolistic adherence to Listean doctrine. Under free-market conditions, it was less the inclination of technologies towards producer goods than their ranking in the current league of best practice which caught the interest of industrialists. Selection of fashionable technologies, according to this model, can, of course, involve either heavy *or* light manufactures. And, equally, it can involve choices which may be appropriate – but as easily may not be appropriate – to the economy's present endowment or future development needs.

If the backwardness of these economies is defined by their dualism and their unreformed agricultures; if it is largely uncorrected by government action or by transportational development; if it is partially qualified by high-technology borrowings in the defence sector and more extensively reduced by exploitation of 'civilian' high technologies, we require still to identify accurately both the forces which supported these mitigating developments and those preserving backwardness against mitigation.

ENTREPRENEURIAL UNDER-FULFILMENT

Within societies so enmired with ancient cultivations and besprinkled with feudal survivals, little aid to development could be expected from unsupported private enterprise. As in Russia, the bourgeoisie remained a withered arm of the body social down to the First World War; both its size and its strength posed grave problems for entrepreneurial recruitment. In Austria-Hungary, the Empire's most sophisticated bourgeois group, the German-speaking Austrians, were hamstrung as an effective economic force by their loyalty to a political anachronism. Convinced that the supra-national structure of the Habsburg ascendancy served its special interest, this bourgeoisie could not assume the lead in economic processes damaging to the Empire's fragile institutional framework. Believing, then, that political stability and protected markets were preferable to the risks of parliamentarianism and social flux, the Austrian bourgeoisie exploited the full range of tactics open to the species and settled for a highly un-revolutionary bargain: in exchange for a circumscribed prosperity, it accepted the quasi-feudal values of the traditional élites. The net which, in consequence, was cast across the entrepreneurial stream might fail to hold the occasional maverick like Werndl, or the tinsmith's son, Ferdinand Porsche, but generally its mesh was both fine and durable.

In Spain, the traps for the adventurous were still more formidable, and the adventurous correspondingly even less plentiful. Once again, a tiny bourgeoisie made accommodation with existing imperial values. The remnants of empire supplied a hide-bound exchequer with funds and a somnolent society with sustaining illusions. Even in the 1920s – when half the province of Cordoba was still owned by 5 per cent of its population – the middle class of an average small town consisted of a tiny handful of doctors, chemists, vets, shopkeepers, prostitutes, and policemen. This was scarcely an arena for industrial enterprise. And nor, it seems, were the major industrial regions much better endowed. The spoliation under Spanish management of the fabulous prospects at Rio Tinto might convince the cynical observer that, in Spain, no resource was too rich to be ruined by the human element. Certainly, the critical path for Spanish enterprise – combining to best advantage the exploitation of cheap ores and the husbanding of dear fuel in the manufacture of semi-finished products – was convincingly missed by all parties. The application of tariff protection to the profitless metal and engineering industries of Catalonia in 1891 formed simply a less demanding alternative to the detection and pursuit of the critical path. For precisely similar reasons, fiscal prophylaxis also appealed to the iron interests of Biscay and the grain interests of Castile. The alliance of these unenterprising groups composed perhaps the most enervated solidarity bloc in Europe, yet it gathered tariffs directly in proportion to its fragility: by 1906 Spanish manufacturers were currently the most heavily protected upon the continent.

Italian prospects were less bleak. The *risorgimento* had, after all, called out a classically reforming bourgeoisie unprepared to settle on the old terms. Admittedly, enterprise was hampered, much as in France, by the small scale of business characteristically employed by this group, especially in textiles, engineering, and chemicals. And the high representation of family firms, common in Latin countries, did nothing to counter this trend. But the restrictions upon business size in Italy probably derived less from restrictive social forces than from the limited size of the national market. This supposition gains weight from the forceful export performance of Italy's small-scale producers – especially in textiles – and the considerable technical prowess implied in their product range – notably with motor-cars, chemicals, and rayon. The alert watchdogs of Italy's most promising industrial ventures, the German directors of the Banca Commerciale, were impressed by the quality of Italian entrepreneurs and feared, not a deficiency, but rather an excess of zeal; when such verve was balanced by the clear-sighted caution of German assistants and accountants, they considered the resulting entrepreneurial blend to possess true quality.[186] The divergence between the managerial endowments of Italy and those of its dualistic partners is consistent with this economy's greater competence in the new technologies and its closer approach – even if still tentative – to a spurt-like pattern of growth after 1896. One of the identifying features – if by no means the entire physiognomy – of Italian industrial development is supplied by this measure of entrepreneurial sophistication.

FOREIGN PARTICIPATION: FROM ENERGIZER TO ENCLAVE

Where domestic managerial cadres proved deficient, it was a commonplace of nineteenth-century development that the forces of international capitalism stepped in with manpower and money-power. In this connexion, and in varying degree, all three economies were, like Russia, client states of the great lending powers, primarily of France, secondarily of Germany. The points at issue are: to what extent did foreign enterprise and capital substitute for, or usefully complement, indigenous resources; and, alternatively, to what extent did foreign collaborators aim at the creation of enclave systems complementary only to the interests of the creditor nations? Among these three countries, a full range of possibilities is covered with Spain at one extreme and Italy at the other.

While its Mediterranean neighbour inched slowly upwards along the slope of insolvency to reach a precarious financial independence, Spain tumbled down it and into the pocket of western capital. Her problem was revealed with brutal simplicity in the shrinkage of government revenue – a diminution of 25 per cent between 1800 and 1830 – and in the consequent heavy borrowing on official account. The state's rapidly gathering impecuniosity involved considerable damage to normal investment processes: potentially useful capital was drained away into highly profitable, if unproductive, accommodation with the Treasury and the formal money markets converted all too readily into dens of speculation. When the bills were presented for the First Carlist War of 1833 39, and for the revolution of 1868, large stakes of foreign capital were also placed in the game. With the French directing one-third of their foreign securities investment into Spanish public issues, 1816–51, and the British devoting nearly one-quarter of their European lending to Spain, 1869–73, the government in Madrid accumulated the continent's second largest official debt. However unlike its still more indigent Russian colleague, the Spanish regime was unable to prevent the growth of this irritation into the incubus of enclave development. The attempt to control the spiral of debt by employing Spain's natural resources to underwrite the nation's borrowing proved a cardinal and ineradicable error. Anxious to win credit in the hard eyes of western capitalists, the government merely opened the mineral vaults to their acquisitive hands. As the *conquistadores* had plundered the Inca cities for gold, the westerners plundered the Spanish interior for pyrites, lead and mercury. By 1913 foreign capital controlled one-half of the entire Spanish mining industry. And, since in Spain, railways merely formed the connexion between foreign-owned mines and foreign-owned ships, the enclave smoothly extended to incorporate the transport sector. At the zenith, the French alone had disposal over no less than 56 per cent of the entire railway capital of Spain. The final additions to the spreading complex of foreign control in the years before 1914 were, logically enough, the public utilities serving the main commercial centres. Even if Spain lacked the entrepreneurs and risk capital for native exploitation of endowment, the role played by foreign capital was scarcely an effective substitute. Rather, foreign leverage worked to tip the economy into the lop-sided development most commonly produced in the colonial world by the ministrations of economic imperialism. Of all the European economies, Spain's was the most nearly colonialized.

At mid-century, the prospects facing Italy were ominously similar. The unification of the debt, and its great expansion in the 1860s, surrendered huge liabilities to the Parisian market. By 1869 the French had achieved their characteristic predominance in the control of the Italian public funds. Furthermore, the infrastructural needs of the newly integrated nation necessarily involved appeals to external capital. Here, too, French financiers displayed their usual appetite for other peoples' railway systems, while the Austrians retained important shares even after 1861. The implied threat, however, never materialized. Beyond railways and government loans, foreign capital in Italy comported itself with some timidity: external investment in Italian manufacturing was probably less significant between 1850 and 1880 than at the start of the century and its commitment to the extractive industries was always limited. The prime foreign interests lay rather in utilities and urban expansion which in the 1880s attracted huge sums, storing up a destabilizing, but by no means ruinous, foreign contribution to the financial crises of the 1890s. Yet the share of overseas funds in the mobilization of Italian manufacturing after 1885 remained modest; the acceleration was made possible 'only to the extent that Italian investment was attracted to it'.[187] By 1896 the external interests, far from occupying the strategic enclaves in the Spanish style, were concentrated in the more humdrum categories of tramways, gas, and water; these sectors contained more alien funds than mining, railway, or navigational facilities.[188]

Partly, this moderate foreign participation is explained by the volatility of Italy's financial relationship with France. After the débâcle at Sedan, the Parisian market necessarily ranked Italian issues well below the more pressing requirements of French war indemnities, and, when diplomatic relations between Rome and Paris themselves became strained during the 1880s and 1890s, the French maintained the lower profile out of choice. In consequence, very large withdrawals of capital from the Lombard and Roman railways took place in this period.[189] No doubt, the retreat of the French opened opportunities for the Germans, but the newcomers were selective investors, aware that they were amassing their portfolios at a time of expanding indigenous capabilities. Indeed, within a few years of the rupture with France, in one of its major economic achievements of the pre-war period, the Italian government was able to repatriate over one-half of its enormous foreign-held debt (see Table 5.8). Nationalization of foreign-dominated assets was also carried fur-

Table 5.8 Italian government bonds held abroad (m. lire)

	1889–90	1890–91	1894–96
London	171	147	152
Paris	2111	1818	730
Berlin	571	1424	736
Total	2853	3389	1645

Source: Gille (1968), pp. 351, 358.

ther during the 1900s with the state's resumption of control over the railroad network.

On balance, foreign capital contributed usefully to Italian infrastructure growth and operated as a genuine subsidy to economic modernization. Penetrative and exploitative features did exist but never reached the proportions of enclave development; in the end, any threatening characteristics were suppressed by state counter-action. Foreign capital itself rarely strayed outside the utilities or the public funds, whereas in Russia it strayed creatively into the heavy industries and in Spain damagingly into the extractive industries. If external funding was occasionally attracted to projects of low utility – lavish disbursements on urban expansion providing the best case in point – it mostly concerned itself, and was only permitted to concern itself, with projects where the prospects of economic subversion were slight. This result was due not least to the accomplishments of native enterprise and to the efforts of a state bureaucracy which proved that it could design viable economic solutions, even if it took decades to do so. Again, the formulae usually applied to non-European capital importers may capture a part of the Italian experience: where (as in Spain but not in Italy) entrepreneurial resources were insufficient to benefit from incoming capital flows, enclave or 'imperialist' exploitation was common; where (as in Italy but not in Spain) native enterprise could creatively employ the available credit, some accommodation of interest was usual from which both creditor and debtor might draw benefit.

Between these two cases lies Austria-Hungary. From the start of its industrial career, the Habsburg monarchy had drawn upon the international pool of talent and capital to supplement its own resources. Thus the important development of Danubian navigation was undertaken by the Englishmen, Andrews and Pritchard, and their considerable fleet – over forty vessels by 1847 – proved instrumental in expanding Austro-Hungarian commerce. English capital was also involved in Viennese utilities from the 1840s, and English technologists provided irreplacable contributions to the early development of the crucial machine industries. But it was the insatiable French appetite for supplying Europe's weaker treasuries (and her need to seek allies in low places) which first carried large-scale foreign involvement into the imperial economy. Two of the most important early railroads, the Southern Railroad and the State Railroad were funded from Paris, while, until their collapse in the 1880s, the Banque de Lyons et Loire and the Union Générale gave extensive support to the public funds, the banks, and the ports, as well as to the railways.[190] The French taste for government issues, a marked feature of both Italian and Spanish financial relationships, reappeared with respect to both partners in the Dual Monarchy: until 1890 the Parisian market was a heavy customer for Austrian bonds and the largest single customer for Hungary's official loans. A wide range of connexions was completed by French institutional involvement with the Länderbank and the Austrian and Hungarian mortgage banks. Yet the loyalty of Paris was a weathercock held steady only by the most balmy of diplomatic breezes; as the wind from the east increasingly carried rumours of disreputable Habsburg affiliations, the indicator veered abruptly around, pointing rigidly away from Vienna during the 1890s, and from Budapest after 1908–09. Like Italy, the Empire found that failure to meet the Quai d' Orsay's high standards for faithfulness among its pensioners received short shrift and a ruptured credit line. For Austria-Hungary, this was sufficiently painful to cause upheavals among the public issues of the 1900s, some of these even foraging as far afield as the costly American market in search of placement.

The Empire's declining place in French affections is revealed by the apportionment of Parisian long-term overseas lending: in 1900 Austria-Hungary received nearly 13 per cent of the French capital committed to Europe and ranked third in preference; by 1914 the country held 8 per cent of French capital deployed in Europe and ranked fifth.[191] Like Italy, however, the Dual Monarchy found new friends willing and partially able to replace the minatory French: by 1914 the Empire provided accommodation for nearly three-quarters (8 billion marks) of Germany's capital commitment to European debtors. The Darmstädter Bank, working in alliance with Rothschild, led German finance into Austria-Hungary and assisted it to establish 'intimate connections in all fields of banking and industry'.[192] As it did so, a familiar sequel occurred: German entrepreneurs in the high technologies set out upon their own conquest of the new territories, erecting satellite plants, notably of AEG and Siemens-Schuckert, upon imperial soil (as they had also done in Italy and Spain).

Clearly, the Empire drew important infrastructural assistance, production facilities, and credit on government account from its succession of foreign backers. Yet there was never serious question either of a subordination of imperial economic interests to those of exploitative creditors, nor of a determined effort to replace foreign holdings with domestic capital. The international standing of the Dual Monarchy would anyway have been sufficient to rule out the first; probably the strength of the country's own financial institutions excluded the need for the second. Initially, of course, the Rothschilds had pulled off a considerable coup against the Péreires by establishing the Kreditanstalt as an Austrian institution deserving of international respect and capable of leading other Viennese banks into fresh fields of endeavour. It is significant that the Darmstädter chose to pursue its eastern projects in alliance with the Rothschilds, a mark of respect to a sitting tenant which no agency in Italy or Spain could have commanded. Similarly, thanks to this indigenous financial sophistication, Vienna could participate in the international exchange of capital from the creditor's side as well as from the debtor's; thus Austrian funds went into Bosnian iron-mines and Hungarian and Lombard railways, sometimes even creating its own enclaves. Neither Spain nor Italy possessed the financial equipment to execute operations of this scale. Austria is a hybrid: a client state, but never one subordinated in the Spanish style, yet neither one to re-establish its independence in the Italian style, a client state throughout, but also a creditor nation in the thinly populated second league of international lenders.

In none of these countries did foreign enterprise and capital effectively or extensively 'substitute' for missing native capabilities. For Spain, the external influences merely aggravated existing problems and distorted prevailing economic structures. For Italy, foreign funds brought some benefits, if also some dislocations, to infrastructure development, but became dispersed in areas of low return; they did not penetrate either directly or in quantity to the strategic manufacturing sectors. For Austria-Hungary, foreign capital was more widely spread across infrastructural, governmental, and manufacturing uses, but it was provided by enterprises not distinctly superior to the advanced financial intermediaries already funtioning in Vienna. Despite these generally negative results, some clue to the relative development of the three economies is provided by their respective dealings with foreign capital. All three experienced a phase of close involvement with foreign finance between 1850 and 1890, and some lessening of this connexion in the period before 1914. Not unnaturally, the corrective movement was weakest in the economy most enthralled by exploitative capital and strongest in the economy which built most energetically upon it. The two more advanced nations, and more considerable powers, each advertised their greater stature – and in Italy's case it was a definite pronouncement of growing stature – by their ability to outface their creditors. Thus, each experienced a 'French', and then after mounting disagreement, a 'German' period of borrowing. Finally, Austria-Hungary, though by no means more financially skilled than Italy by 1914, once more provides evidence of a characteristically patchy economic sophistication: she possesses a small number of institutions on a footing with those of the creditor nations and employs them for very similar purposes.

GREAT BANKS ABROAD

Where dualism sunders economies, where agricultures miss revolutions and railways miss Kondratiev cycles; where entrepreneurs omit to mass and foreigners prove unhelpful; where, above all, bureaucracies fail in percipience and authority; there, if anywhere, managerial substitutes are most keenly required. According to Gerschenkron, they were most satisfactorily supplied, wherever entrepreneurial gaps opened up among Europe's less privileged economies, by the industrial investment bank. In this familiar view, the financial agency is not passive, nor even neutral, but energetically promotional: the bank becomes a maid of all work, a nursemaid tending the manufacturing enterprise from infancy to senility. As a 'substitute' for 'missing prerequisites', the specialized bank can elicit growth where otherwise there would have been only frustrated potential. But the potential must not be too frustrated; the investment bank is essentially a creature of *moderate* backwardness, a preference of habitat perhaps borne out by its appearance in Austria in the 1850s, but not in Hungary before 1900, by its successful adaptation to the Italian economy of the 1890s, but not of the 1880s. However, 'the degree of backwardness' is a singularly elusive unit of measurement and scarcely a dependable operational concept. Certainly, its influence appears most opaque when the first establishment of the investment bank in Austria, Spain, and Italy may be traced in *each* case to the 1840s or 1850s: surely the 'degree of backwardness' was not exactly 'moderate' for all three of these economies at this same juncture? Moreover, we have already noted, from comparisons between the French and German data, that the promotional value of the investment bank did not remain constant between cases. Rather, this financial device operated like any other innovation, no doubt a high-quality innovation, ranking perhaps with the steam-engine or the machine-tool, but equally dependent for its economic worth upon the skill with which it was exploited, that is, upon the entrepreneurial verve with which it was wielded. Interestingly, the most recent comparative study of continental banking – Cameron's second anthology of cases[193] – improves upon its immediate predecessor – the first anthology appeared to accept the *autonomous* macro-economic leverage of innovations in banking[194] – and argues that the investment banks should be seen as functions of their economic context, most particularly of government policy and of market demand for financial services. An entrepreneurial 'substitute', itself reliant upon the quality of entrepreneurial inputs, or upon the quality of business demand for its products, raises some interesting problems of circularity.

Although the Austrian case is often taken as an example of the transference of German-style *bankinitiative* to a developing country, closer study throws doubts upon its relevance to the concepts either of entrepreneurial substitution or of bank-induced growth. Prior to the formation of the Austrian great banks, the financial arena was ruled by a highly restrictive central bank (founded in 1816) and by a set of apathetic private houses well satisfied with their aristocractic clientele. Yet industrial growth was nevertheless evoked, at a gradual tempo, by an army of small entrepreneurs employing mercantile funds, family savings, or dowries to meet their limited capital needs. Precisely the style of growth most readily associated with moderate backwardness proceeded, therefore, on the basis not of bank-finance but of self-finance; similarly it generated its own supply of entrepreneurship and required no 'substitution'. When the large investment banks did arrive – the Niederösterreichische Escompte Gesellschaft in 1853, the Banca Commerciale Triestina in 1854, and the huge Kreditanstalt für Handel und Gewerbe in 1855 – it was because the demands of railway funding required them; yet, paradoxically, they approached this prime line of business with the utmost caution. Reserve rather than risk-orientation was to become the hallmark of the Austrian great banks. Even the Rothschilds were insistent upon official guarantees before they would take on ventures in transportation and navigation, a demonstration of entrepreneurial timidity which reveals new facets of their involvement with the early Austrian railroads.[195] If the Péreires were beaten to the draw for the *mobilier* trade by the local branch of the great banking family, this does not necessarily represent the clear triumph for German-style *bankinitiative* which some observers have claimed.[196] Similarly, if the Austrian great banks were participants in the industrial surges of 1867–73 and 1896–1908, the style of their involvement is instructive: they suspected industrial investment, and where they did entertain it, selected established ventures, mergers between established businesses, or successful undertakings with their major risks already exist-inguished – the 'plump juicy firms with favourable prospects'[197] – for their attention.

Moreover, between the two instalments of industrial expansion, the banks were so alarmed by the Bourse crash of 1873, and so afflicted by the decline in the industrial demand for credit following the regime's introduction of swinge-ing taxation upon incorporated companies, that they *reverted* to conventional current account business. Between 1873 and 1888, the retreatist financiers concerned themselves scarcely at all with promotion and restricted their in-dustrial dealings to connexions formed before the crash or to clients of unim-peachable, and preferably aristocratic, pedigree. Once more, this directs a rather special light upon Good's calculation that the growth in assets of Aus-trian financial intermediaries proceeded at the 'good average' rates of 5.1–5.5 per cent per annum, 1881–1913;[198] even if it did so, the con-straints upon the effective *use* of the accumulated resources were obviously severe. Even after 1890, when demand revived, and the banks relinquished some of their hesitation, both adjustments proceeded slowly. In 1907 the number of Austrian incorporated concerns remained at a level one-eighth of the German and one-third of the Russian, while industrial and railway secur-ities accounted for only 2.3 per cent of all issues in Austria, against 29 per cent in Germany, 20 per cent in Italy, and 16 per cent in France. Perhaps this level of demand was insufficient to elicit *bankinitiative*. Bankers certainly seem to have acted upon this assumption; their resumed *mobilier* activity after 1890 religiously followed rather than enterprisingly led the economy's upswings – to the displeasure of Finance Minister Steinbach who drew pointed compari-sons with Germany – and their interest continued to revolve around the eco-nomy's soundest firms. Consequently, much of the growth in heavy industry was financed by very varied means, including large measures of reinvested profits, while the expansion of the electro-technical industry again attracted bankers only in the support of enterprises already provenly successful. Down to 1914, it appears that the Austrian great banks were growth-accommodating rather than growth-inducing, their industrial participation less a substitute for missing entrepreneurship than a reward for already pro-ficient entrepreneurship.

Revisionism, however, is indigestible if taken to excess; it is most palatable in moderate portions. The concession must be allowed that financial caution did not prevent the investment banks from acting as a curb upon the 'penetra-tion' of foreign capital; for they were most active precisely where foreign capi-tal was most in evidence – within the railway sector. Since the Empire was alone among underdeveloped countries in possessing entirely indigenous banks of advanced design, their 'protective' value should be given due weight. Within the context of industrial finance, however, the banking contribution suggests once more that the innovational potential of the investment agencies was only as good as their managerial controllers. Where the entrepreneurial class was poorly developed, it is not surprising that there should have been shortages *both* of risk-taking bankers and of credit-hungry industrialists. Yet it is not helpful to exaggerate the dependence of the bankers upon the manufacturers' appetite for credit, since this may in itself frequently depend less upon entrepreneurial inclinations than upon government policies. In Austria the fiscal impositions and other impediments upon incorporation (lifted only in 1899) worked to deter potential *customers* for industrial investment, while, in the wider capital market, an overweighty bureaucracy again gobbled funds and captured creditors with the lure of extravagant interest rates. Without these officially induced distortions, the market for industrial credit would probably have been sufficiently active to justify more consistently energetic bank policies, and possibly sufficiently active to encourage the transition to a fully 'German' *bankinitiative*. Caution may well have been an appropriate response to a market which contained the Habsburg autocracy, reappearing in its familiar role of economic 'obstacle', and perhaps the prime limitation upon the Empire's absorption of fully fledged investment banking. Certainly, it represented a constraint which no amount of entrepreneurial *élan* could circumvent.

Many of these trends were duplicated in Spain: an avidly competitive official appetite for funds, government restrictions upon incorporation, inadequate levels of demand for industrial credit. But Spain, as in other sectors, possessed no curbs upon foreign participation. Consequently, a common European affliction was here expanded to enormous proportions: where other nations underwent railway mania, Spain, thanks largely to external financial pressures, contracted railway neurosis, a disorder which proved lethal for industrial and commercial banking.

Early developments in the capital market had been dominated by the Central Bank: founded in 1829, it quickly developed into the government's chosen instrument for reordering its extremely messy budgetary problems; throughout its career to 1873, it transacted four times as much business with the public as with the private sector. Although it became more involved in growth promotion in the 1890s and 1900s, it allowed crucial opportunities for stimulating and regulating the capital market to slip away in the 1850s and 1860s.[199] The country's second largest issuing bank, the Bank of Barcelona, similarly, loaned six times as much to the state as to private industry between 1858 and 1866, despite its situation within Spain's most industrialized city.[200]

Much of the initial capital formation had therefore to depend upon the repatriated fortunes of Spain's own colonial 'nabobs', driven home from the now inhospitable territories of Latin America. These savings were converted into small-scale manufacturing, developed as in Austria, not from entrepreneurial substitution by bankers, but *despite* the apathy of existing financial intermediaries. Even the half-dozen or so joint-stock banks created during the 1840s (including the Bank of Barcelona of 1844) defaulted upon their promise of greater financial aid for industry, and, by suffering or sinking during the crisis of 1848, provided both confirmation for the bureaucracy's suspicion of corporations and grounds for penal restraints upon further corporate formations.[201] These controls endured for some two decades and were as pernicious in the breach – during the 1850s they were set aside in favour of railway and banking, but not of manufacturing companies – as in the observance. By 1858 there were four times as many joint-stock banks as there had been a decade previously. Yet the partial waiver of corporate restrictions merely opened the way for the foreign banker and his main preoccupation: railway finance. The new banking ventures were dominated by schemes hatched in the boardrooms of Paris, by two very ambitious *mobiliers* from Péreire (Credito Mobiliario) and Prost-Gilhou (General Credit) and by a relatively modest Rothschild commitment (Sociedad Mercantil y Industrial).

Capital support for the mid-century bank flotations was overwhelmingly foreign: Rothschild's attempts to tap native savings failed miserably, while the Credito Mobiliario, with 85–95 per cent of its equity controlled by external interests, summarized more accurately the going conventions. Domestic attempts at financial emulation like the Credito Mobiliario Barcelones or the Credito Castellana proved ineffectual counters to the foreign invaders; here there was no Kreditanstalt or its colleagues to safeguard investment autonomy. Not until the second third of the present century did the Spanish, and especially Biscayan, banks recover control of the nation's industrial and commercial finance. Effectively also, the banking innovations of the mid-nineteenth century were monopoloid in interest as well as in ownership: credit supplies were restricted not only to foreign control but also to railway employment. In the years immediately following their creation, the leading trio of 'Spanish' *mobiliers* locked up between three-fifths and three-quarters of their total investment in railway ventures and ranked even their secondary preferences – public funds, public works, real estate, or mining – well above manufacturing.

The railway obsession was general: native ventures like the Sociedad Catalana General de Credito (1856) might be promoted as industrial banks yet nevertheless ended up fully entangled in railroads. In total, the railway sector probably consumed something around 70 per cent of the assets of the largest non-issuing banks.[202] Consequently, when railway fortunes failed, revealing the full unwisdom of the initial investments, the banking sector was torn asunder: chronically over-concentrated interests destroyed nearly 60 per cent of its membership in the recession of 1865–74. Reconstruction of the financial mechanisms in the period down to 1914 necessarily proceeded cautiously amidst the debris from this collapse: the successor-banks were conservative in the extreme, only the Bank of Bilbao (1857) involving itself usefully in industrial affairs. In Catalonia, especially, the banking reflexes became sclerotically rigidified as extensive capitals were immobilized within the region's run-down textile mills and deteriorating railroads. As in Austria, financial crisis extinguished promotional activity among investment banks whose dynamism was anyway under question. But in Spain, the crisis issued from the inherent design of the banking facilities themselves, was triggered by a system of auto-destruction, and produced more enduring repercussions.

Tortella is of the opinion that the Spanish investment banks, far from providing entrepreneurial substitutes, turned out to be 'docile instruments of a

371

misguided policy', both protagonists and victims of a 'nation-wide economic miscalculation'.[203] Here again, government is cast in the role of villain, greedily consuming bank services, restricting the market for industrial investment, and then, far more culpably than its Austrian colleague, creating in the railroad sector a single financial focus where overcapitalization, foreign penetration, and perilous maldistribution of risk could accumulate unchecked. Once more, the *employment* of the investment-banking instruments is critically suboptimal. No doubt a more comprehensive explanation of this misuse would feature, not only the state's impact upon the financial mechanism, but also the low level of entrepreneurial development and the naturally modest level of financial demand. But probably a more important refinement is possible. It is significant that some banks working within the Spanish market, and presumably aware of its formal limitations, nevertheless *planned* ambitious industrial undertakings – the Péreires intended to attach a manufacturing empire to their transport interests, as did the Catalan General Credit Co. – yet were *unable* to progress beyond the stage of railway finance. Given the prevailing standard of industrial enterprise, the implication is that the alternative to railway-based bank growth may have been simply a virtual absence of investment-bank development. And, since railway-based growth proved extremely damaging, this in turn suggests that Spanish investment banking may constitute a further example of an advanced technology pressed into service by foreign intermediaries before the host economy could efficiently absorb it. It is the timing and concentration of the foreign presence which explains a level of destruction far higher than that perpetrated by the similarly extensive implantations within the Russian or Italian banking systems.

According to Gerschenkron, however, Italy's adaptation to financial change was far happier than that of her underdeveloped counterparts, and featured indeed a classic demonstration of the institutional remedies for moderate backwardness, 'the deliberate application of the techniques of investment banking evolved in Germany . . . the importation of the great economic innovation of German banking in its most developed and mature form'.[204] These agencies provided the 'discipline of production' for the accelerated Italian growth of the 1890s and 1900s. Here the demand for capital was high. With its lean markets and indifferent raw materials, Italy could not attract large subventions from foreign creditors and such supplies as were available anyway risked political interruption throughout the growth period. For its part, agriculture remained too preoccupied with its own self-improvement to render up a surplus. Yet the growth rate of incorporated concerns was far faster than in Spain or Austria-Hungary, and could not be readily financed by reinvested profits.[205] Industrialization for Italy, therefore, was particularly 'lumpy' in its financial requirements and most authorities are agreed that the essential responses to this problem were provided only by the banking innovations of the 1890s.[206]

However, this fortunate conjunction of demand and supply did not always appear likely in the period following unification. By the 1860s the Houses of Rothschild and Hambro had established a mastery in the financing of the Italian public debt and were moving towards the familiar infiltration of the railway sector. As in Spain, the indigenous competition was not impressive; it experienced severe difficulties prior to unification and proved unable either to mobilize local capital or to attract sufficient external support. Moreover, the models for banking reform employed in the mid-century period were French and the results were not encouraging. Even the bank promotions of the 1870s (the Banks of Venice and Turin and the Banca Generale in 1871; the Bank of Piedmont in 1873; the Bank of Milan in 1874) retained the French style, and, ominously in view of Spanish experience, were both necessary for, and deeply involved in, the construction of the Italian railroads. Worse still was the gravitation of the larger finance houses towards the other Gallic preoccupation – urban construction and public utilities, a connexion which, in the 1880s, 'prevented a generous and far-sighted *industrial* policy on the part of the old banks'.[207]

Once again, as in Spain from 1866 and Austria from 1873, it was financial crisis which initiated an unfortunate adjustment in financial development: the Italian *Gründerkrise* of the early 1870s brought an immense casualty rate (20 per cent to incorporated companies) and thus narrowed the risk margins between industrial ventures and speculative real-estate transactions. Though the largest of the 'old, French' banks, the Banca Generale and the Credito Mobiliare had built up considerable commitments in the manufacturing sector, their major interests now rapidly settled upon the property market: over half the Credito's losses after 1887 were caused by failures in this sector.[208] With large-scale French participation, the conventional 'railway bias', and a single area of pronounced overcapitalization, the Italian banking sector of the 1880s appeared set to repeat the disasters of its Mediterranean colleague to the west.

Two peculiar features prevented this outcome. One was that financial penetration progressed neither so far nor so persistently as in Spain. French efforts to sequester the Italian banking structure in fact fell off distinctly in the 1880s,[209] and, after the diplomatic breach between the two countries, the flow of credit towards Italy diminished further. The other was that the inevitable speculative crash emanated from the property sector at a time when Italian business resources (unlike the Spanish of the 1860s or Austrian of the 1870s) had strengthened sufficiently to maintain their own demand for credit. Consequently, the financial breakdown of the early 1890s could both kill off French-style banks, along with their characteristic investment preferences, *and* provide a beneficial shock to the credit structure. For the Italian financial system proved sufficiently robust to respond to crisis by swiftly replacing the defunct French-style *mobiliers* by a fresh set of German-style investment banks, most notably the Banca Commerciale (1894) and the Credito Italiano (1895). Foreign capital was, of course, still heavily involved: the Commerciale was controlled by German, Austrian, and Swiss interests, the Credito by German and Swiss, the Elecktrobank to the extent of 76 per cent of equity by German. Similarly, all but one of the German Great Banks participated in the large Italian government loan of 40 m. lire in 1893.[210] However, a second bout of penetration was largely averted by the Germans' need to allay Italian suspicions concerning the new banks: within the investment houses deliberate policies of 'Italianization' were pursued and their German directors were careful to deploy their resources in furtherance of Italian economic interests, and in no imperialistic style.[211] Very largely also, these banks acted as mobilizers of Italian rather than of foreign funds. This positive policy was reinforced by new developments in the behaviour of external capital supplies: firstly, their total volume contracted, and, secondly, direct investment fell off, as in Russia after 1900, in favour of investment *through* the newly responsible bank system. The volatile nature of foreign investment was thus matched in Italy after 1890 by improving methods of control. Moreover, any bias towards a Teutonic monopoly of the financial system – and the Bank of Italy, despite Gerschenkron, did sometimes fear, '1' influence lourde et envahissante de l'Allemagne dans le système bancaire Italien'[212] – was counterbalanced by the revival of a much-chastened French capital interest from 1899.

Once established in this judicious style, the Italian Great Banks did much to substantiate Gerschenkron's hypothesis that they provided the major institutional 'substitutes' within Italy's developmental processes. Their two largest representatives controlled 60 per cent of the nation's bank assets and operated as 'discriminating monopolists'[213] distributing credit rations to industrial clients selected for profitability and market power. Naturally, there were flaws within their lending schedules – their customers from the metallurgical sector remained high-cost producers, while the Banca Commerciale failed to detect the value of the new motor-car industry – but, generally, the record displays promotional verve in consistent measure. The new banks operated almost exclusively with high-technology – that is, the most risky – industries, and, for their special protégés, like those within the electro-technical sector, they provided a level of sponsorship which would not have disgraced their colleagues in Berlin. With the private and incorporated banks devoting 40 per cent of their assests to industrial and commercial investment by 1900, it was clear that the main external source of manufacturing credit now lay with the professional financiers. The high degree of bank integration and the widespread use of interlocking directorships further operated in the classic style to convert the creditor relationship into an entrepreneurial relationship. With the rapid acceleration in the size and muscularity of the financial sector after 1890 (see Table 5.9), this entrepreneurial capability broadened to match the gathering pace of industrial advance.

Table 5.9   Asset and sector shares of financial institutions

	Ratio of total financial assets to all primary securities	Ratio of debt held by financial system to national income
1880–84	0.38	15.7
1890–94	0.56	25.0
1900–04	0.62	31.9
1910–14	0.88	44.2

Source: Cohen (1972), pp. 74–5

Perhaps the more advanced state of Italy's managerial and social development might explain why investment banking should succeed there, while failing in Spain and remaining stylistically cramped in Austria. But, this would in turn imply that, even in Italy, the concept of an entrepreneurial 'substitute' is not entirely a happy one: far from replacing autonomous business talents, the investment banking process appears to require at least their partial development as a precondition for its own effectiveness. Yet if the necessary custom for credit was consequently forthcoming, it was not the only variable within the Italian financial context which turned out positively. Cohen believes that, in the 1890s, some adjustment to the risk-factor of banking innovation was essential if the depressive tendencies of the 1880s were to be eradicated, and proposes that the necessary rectification of the financial balance was provided by the Italian government, and through the agency of the Bank of Italy (1892). There is virtue in this analysis and injustice in Cameron's opposing (and characteristic) view that government policy – primarily in the expansion of the public debt and the discrimination against foreign capital – acted as an obstacle to financial progress in Italy as well as in Spain and Austria.[214] The intelligent and restrained deployment of the new Italian Central Bank[215] throughout the 1890s and 1900s resembled the discrete style of the Russian State Bank much more than the ill-judged policies of its Spanish or Austrian counterparts, and surely gives the lie to Cameron's doctrinaire contention. The bank provided an institutional antidote to the financial panics which had recurrently afflicted the pre-1890 economy; it substituted the confidence-inspiring gambit of a national currency for the previously endemic monetary chaos; and, most usefully, it curtailed the risks for the new banking innovations by acting as a reliable lender of last resort. Its attempt in 1911 to rationalize the Italian metallurgical sector so as to protect the bankers from the consequences of industrial instability strongly resembled the Russian rescue operations of 1900 and 1912. Clearly, government action is an important variable in the financial development of these three countries, weighted positively in one case, negatively in the other two. Again, this conclusion sits well with the generally greater (if still modest) proficiency of the Italian state in its attempts at directed growth.

At a higher level of abstraction, two further points of importance arise from this comparative exercise: one concerns the immensely flexible value of the investment banking innovation; the other relates to a dangerous indistinctness in the concept of degrees of backwardness. Comparative testing reveals that the investment bank is not only an entrepreneurial substitute: under widely differing conditions, it proved able to *stifle* industrial entrepreneurship in Spain, *reward* already successful entrepreneurship in Austria, or *supplement* existing entrepreneurship in Italy. This variability in performance confirms the view that the investment bank is, in reality, a piece of technology as open to creative or destructive employment by suppliers (bankers), customers (industrialists), or supervisors (governments) as any item of industrial hardware. Its status within the Gerschenkron scheme as autonomous force, a stripe-suited fairy godmother appointed to transform the withered pumpkin of under-

375

development into the steel chariot of industrial advance, should be revised accordingly.

Secondly, the comparative treatment displays in two cases, Spain and Austria, an awkward collision between two of Gerschenkron's entrepreneurial substitutes, the investment bank (for economies of medium backwardness) and the *dirigiste* state (for economies of pronounced backwardness). In *these* two instances of medium backwardness (defined, presumably, by the presence of investment banks), the state declined to make way for the financial substitute and adopted policies positively damaging to it. This strengthens the proposition that substitutes (and stages of backwardness) may in fact intermingle, and indeed entangle, as the exact degree of backwardness (and its appropriate institutional equipment) remains a highly unrevealed truth. There is no controlling requirement that the 'telescoping' or interpenetration of growth stages, a process frequently encountered among imitative latecomer economies, should in fact turn out positively, as it largely did in Russia and Italy. On the contrary, in severely backward economies, the state's general inability to design remedies could well embrace definite but misconceived polices *vis-à-vis* the bank sector. Additionally, it seems likely that Gerschenkron's state of 'moderate backwardness' occupies a painfully slender band of industrial achievement, far narrower than most observers have assumed. For the investment bank to operate in accordance with Gerschenkron's specifications, it appears necessary that the economy should be poised at a very particular point upon the development curve: the financial and managerial capabilities for large-scale industrial activity must be underdeveloped (allowing *some* room for substitution); yet, on the other hand, an incipient and expansible demand for financial services must exist (implying *some* measure of entrepreneurial activity). The balance is so delicate that it is surprising, not that some countries have failed to produce growth-inducing banking systems, but that a few others, among them Germany, Russia, and Italy have succeeded in doing so. However, this surprise is slightly mitigated by an important secondary characteristic of successful investment banking: its highly cosmopolitan nature. It was this which permitted the practised and timely erection of German-designed, and frequently German-managed, institutions within non-German economies. Here the *imported* expertise could easily outpace domestic capabilities, yet might also possess sufficient discrimination, both diagnostic and financial, to strike an effective partnership with the best of the home-grown talent.

CONCLUSIONS

Lessons of development are particularly difficult to extract from the experience of these three powers. Austria-Hungary, an international system as variegated in economic endowment as in race, did not provide in its industrial performance to 1914 any simple analogue for its accelerating political disintegration. With its high technologies like motor cars and small-arms, its celebrated universities and technical schools, its indigenous banking facilities, and the rich, if reactionary, agriculture of its eastern provinces, its level of economic attainment was probably superior to that of tsarist Russia in 1914 (if not perhaps in 1916).[216] Political and governmental decrepitude and social stagnation set genuine limits upon this attainment, but are often incorrectly interpreted as indications of its entire absence. Suitably, the pace of development, as in Italy, and even moreso in Spain, was gradual down to the First World War. At that point, however, Austria-Hungary experienced perhaps the most traumatic check to continuing economic development to befall any of the continental powers, not excluding even Russia. For exactly those forces which had restrained growth to 1914 now involved the Empire in the tumultuously inept conduct of a disastrous war and the shattering consequences of an abject peace. For the shrunken Austria which emerged from the armistice settlement, stripped of its imperial titles and territories, the edicts of Versailles represented a more total deprivation than that meted out to the French or Russian empires at Vienna or Brest-Litovsk. Chronic 'size-pessimism', the conviction that the miniaturized nation was inviable both politically and economically, served to imprison Austria's growth potential throughout the inter-war period.[217] Nor, unlike her Soviet partner in adversity, could the new Austria devise any governmental therapy against her post-war shock. The economic promise exhibited by a shaky empire on the eve of the First World War was not made good by its successor state until the morrow of the Second World War. This dualistic great power provides, therefore, an instance of frustrated or interrupted development, through which runs a strong political and cultural drag.

For Italy, most of the backward nation's checkpoints of development are passed but only barely passed: spurts are suppressed, governments cautious in their intervention, investment banks dependent upon benign foreign participation. And, in a sense, they are passed at the second attempt. Cameron argues that, in the 1860s, Italy possessed the experience of a decade of past growth, a newly unified market, a vigorous spate of railroad construction, 'with both direct and indirect benefits', and a lively inflow of foreign entrepreneurship – and consequently that an industrial spurt might have been expected at this time.[218] No explanation is offered as to why this surge did not materialize, but, in fact, the reasons are fairly straightforward: the past growth was insecurely, and, in the south, freakishly, based; the newly unified market was meagre in volume; the railway system exported most of its linkages; the foreign capital did not flow to the sectors of maximum utility. For its second chance Italy rectified these mistakes: after 1861 more securely based capitalistic experience was accumulated in the north; the market was enlarged, to an extent, by government action and military demand; the railroad system was domesticated; foreign capital was tamed and set to work through the agency of the investment bank. The Italian economy sailed close to the wind, but eventually found a course which took it out of backwardness in a style not excessively unconventional.

With Spain, however, the interruptions are more intense and the second chances longer deferred: Tortella identifies not merely stagnation but a definite cataclysm, the collapse of an attempted industrialization in the second third of the nineteenth century.[219] The example is a rare one: an economy reaching precariously for modern economic growth, but slipping, and toppling backwards into long-lived underdevelopment. Possibly, it is also an instructive example: a nineteenth-century LDC (less developed country) anticipates the ambitions of twentieth-century LDCs from a similar background of deprivation and colonialization – and reveals at least one style in which such ambitions are better not pursued. Railways, foreign capitalists, and investment banks did not suffice to bring modern growth to Spain; this was achieved after extended delay by the motor lorry, the construction industry, the tourist resort, and the more dispassionate foreign assistance of the International Monetary Fund.

Components of these failures and frustrations may grow into useful generalizations. Despite the desperate sea-change meted out to convert the 'agricultural transformation' into the 'missed agricultural revolution', the relationship between rural and industrial progress within developing economies remains highly variable. In Britain and Germany 'agricultural revolution' coincided with manufacturing advance, in France with economic quiescence; in Spain the 'missed agricultural revolution' was accompanied by industrial stagnation, in Italy by some waxing of industrial talents. Clearly, the operational concepts need to be more closely specified: the degree of agricultural transformation (the German greater than the French) or failure (the Italian less than the Spanish), the composition of change or stagnation (tenure or technique), and the regionalization or uniformity of innovation must all exert heavy leverage upon the value of revolutions both accomplished and abandoned. All that appears permissible as a statement is that the most complete rural transformations do ease the industrial pathway of smoothly developing economies, while partially missed revolutions do not prevent hesitant and spasmodic versions of capitalism from arising in agriculture or industry. Similar variety attaches, in practice, to the operation of both financial prerequisites *and* financial substitutes. As the Spanish case suggests, badly designed financial systems may, in extreme cases, act merely as prerequisites for economic disaster. And, as both the Austrian and Spanish cases suggest, the entrepreneurial substitute may prove powerless at very low levels of managerial development; in reality, there is no substitute for a certain measure of entrepreneurial evolution. The utility range of the investment bank, as measured from the Spanish to the German extremes, argues that it has no given or predictable capacity to engineer growth.

Much the same might be said of social overhead capital: in these three countries, it resolutely declined to serve as Rostow's 'precondition', Schumpeter's 'carrier' or Gerschenkron's preserve of the contriving state. Indeed this set of national growth patterns suggests that preconditions may be supplied to an untimely tempo, quite out of step with the requirements of general industrialization, that 'carriers' may go without cargoes and states succumb to destructive over-contrivance. Certainly, the attempts to generate manufacturing development via excess capacity in social overheads (building railways ahead of demand) proved deeply damaging to the economies of Spain and southern Italy. Development by shortage, following upon more lavish investment in manufacturing (railways built to answer demand), would have been virtually assured of superior results.[220] Once more the point is made that state action, the most powerful entrepreneurial substitute, is as likely in historical as in contemporary terms to involve inappropriate policy, reversed priorities, or bad theory. Not only does the state sometimes prove a dubious engine of growth, it, too, is a sufficiently variable term in the economic formulae to act occasionally as an undoubted engine of obstruction. Spanish disentailment, Austrian, Spanish, and Italian railroad policy, Austrian tariff policy provide examples of 'substitution' which the host economies could well have done without. In nineteenth-century continental experience, there are few such powerful correctives to expectations of creative *dirigisme* as those provided by the Spanish government, an economic obstacle of heroic proportions. However, if the worth of state intervention varies sharply between countries, it is perhaps significant that, in these three cases, economic success or failure seems to be geared unusually closely to the overall quality of government policy. And this seems less to do with the ability of Italian regimes to promote than with the inability of Spanish or Austrian regimes to do any other than impede. It is within the interrelationship between the entrepreneurial and the bureaucratic communities, within the development or underdevelopment of the former and the matching class monopolies of the latter, that perhaps the most potent forces affecting the growth prospects of these nations was generated.

NOTES AND REFERENCES

Full publication details are given in the bibliography.
1. In this chapter 'Austria-Hungary' is used as a synonym for the entire Habsburg Empire. 'Austria' or 'metropolitan Austria' is used to describe the western 'half' of the dual system into which the monarchy was divided by the settlement of 1867. Taken literally, the western section was composed of the lands under the jurisdiction of the Reichsrat, but it is conventional historical usage to name these lands, Austria.
2. Nadal (1973), p. 565. A rather fuller statement of Nadal's argument is available in *idem* (1975), an enlarged and separately published version of the original essay.
3. Nadal (1973), p. 617.
4. Carr (1966), p. 428 (my emphasis).
5. Callahan (1968), pp. 522, 525n.
6. Vilar (1962).
7. Nadal (1973), p. 606.
8. Carr (1966), p. 392.
9. The matching proportions for industry-mining around 1900 were 17 per cent and 25.9 per cent.
10. 'Italy' is here taken to mean the various pre-*risorgimento* states, including those

which were, until the successful wars of independence, ending in 1866, Austrian provinces.

11. Gross (1973), pp. 245–6, see also *idem* (1968), pp. 88–101.
12. Klima (1974), pp. 54–5.
13. Klima (1975), pp. 49–77.
14. Gille (1968), pp. 69–70.
15. Blum (1943), p. 34.
16. Cafagna (1973), pp. 280–1.
17. Blum (1943), p. 36.
18. Klima (1975), p. 74; Gross (1973), p. 266.
19. Gille (1968), p. 73.
20. *Ibid.*, p. 265.
21. Gross (1973), p. 269.
22. Purs (1960), pp. 183–272.
23. Marz (1965).
24. Herz (1947), pp. 45–51.
25. Rudolph (1972), pp. 29ff.
26. Blum (1943), pp. 32–8.
27. Romeo (1959).
28. Eckaus (1961), pp. 308–13.
29. Gerschenkron (1962b), pp. 90–118 and *idem* (1968), pp. 98–127.
30. Luzzatto (1969), pp. 203–25.
31. Gerschenkron (1962a), pp. 72–89.
32. Eckaus (1961), pp. 308, 310ff.
33. Golzio (1952).
34. Cafagna (1973), pp. 297–300.
35. Gross (1971), pp. 902–7.
36. Gross (1973), p. 269 (my emphasis).
37. Good (1974), pp. 74, 79.
38. *Ibid.*, pp. 82–3.
39. Eckaus (1961), p. 307.
40. Luzzatto (1969), p. 218.
41. Istituto Centrali de Statistica (1958).
42. Gerschenkron (1962b), pp. 110–11; see also Table 7.7.
43. Cited by Luzzatto (1969), p. 203.
44. Gerschenkron (1962a), pp. 76, 409.
45. Cafagna (1973), p. 300.
46. *Ibid.*, p. 298.
47. Hildebrand (1965), pp. 317–18.
48. Clough (1964), p. 66.
49. Jaszi (1961), p. 210.
50. Rostow (1960), p. 118.
51. Many of the tests carried out in Chapter 7 produce precisely this result.
52. Nadal (1973), p. 617 (my italics).
53. Ringrose (1968), pp. 51–79.
54. See the excellent summary in Nadal (1973), pp. 567–94; also, Vicens Vives (1969), pp. 657–64.
55. Warriner (ed.) (1965), p. 7.
56. Gross (1973), p. 249.

57. Blum (1943), p. 35.
58. Rothschild (1963), p. 168.
59. Cited Warriner (ed.) (1965), pp. 66–7.
60. Gross (1973), pp. 249–50.
61. Livi Bacci (1968), p. 84; also Nadal (1971).
62. Gross (1973), p. 275.
63. Hildebrand (1965), p. 109.
64. Gross (1973), p. 275.
65. Ringrose (1968), pp. 55–6.
66. Kindleberger (1965), pp. 237–9.
67. Thistlethwaite (1964), p. 77.
68. Hildebrand (1965), pp. 288–9.
69. Lutz (1961), pp. 389–94; compare Ackley and Spaventa (1962).
70. Carr (1966), p. 426.
71. Sanchez Albornoz (1968). See also *idem* (1975), pp. 725–45 for data on price divisions between major agricultural regions.
72. Nadal (1973), p. 602.
73. Eckaus (1961), pp. 286–7.
74. Vochting (1952), p. 67.
75. Nitti (1900).
76. Clough and Livi (1963), p. 366.
77. Hildebrand (1965), p. 278.
78. Eckaus (1961), p. 297.
79. Clough and Livi (1963), Table 3, p. 363.
80. Greenfield (1965), pp. 157, 205.
81. Mack Smith (1954), pp. 15–30.
82. Gramsci (1949).
83. Cf. Mori (1975), pp. 79–94 for the argument that *risorgimento* politicians 're-jected any form of protectionist programme designed to protect either possible nascent industries or even those weak concerns which already existed' (p. 85).
84. Gross (1973), p. 241.
85. Nadal (1973), p. 604.
86. Cohen (1972), pp. 67–8.
87. Marsan (1963), pp. 155–6.
88. See *ibid.*, p. 153.
89. Patterson cited by Warriner (ed.) (1965), p. 87.
90. Carr (1966), p. 391.
91. Gille (1968), p. 73.
92. Carr (1966), p. 400.
93. Cf. Gerschenkron (1962a), pp. 80–3.
94. Gramsci (1949), esp. pp. 65–70.
95. Sole-Tura (1967).
96. Romeo (1959).
97. Warriner (ed.) (1965), provides useful coverage of the more constructive aspects of the eighteenth-century reforms, esp. pp. 39–45.
98. Soltys (1978), pp. 200–26.
99. Eddie (1967), p. 295.
100. Cushing in Warriner (ed.) (1965), p. 33.
101. Eddie (1967), pp. 293–309.

102. *Ibid.*, pp. 297–302. In Spain, the proportions were very similar: in 1900, 0.1 per cent of landholders controlled 33.3 per cent of total cultivated land. See pp. 328–9

103. Warriner (ed.) (1965), cf. pp. 36, 87–8, 90–1.

104. *Ibid.*, p. 59.

105. Cf. Eddie (1971), p. 585.

106. Anton Gavafda, *Die Entwicklung der ungarischen Industrie* cited by Eddie (1967), p. 293n.

107. Nadal (1973), pp. 557–8; Vicens Vives (1969), pp. 647–9.

108. Carr (1966), pp. 400–1.

109. Cafagna (1973), p. 301.

110. Eckaus (1961), pp. 308–9.

111. Luzzatto (1969), pp. 219–21.

112. Eckaus (1961), p. 317.

113. Mack Smith (1954), p. 29.

114. Cohen (1972), pp. 88–9.

115. The references concerning Reggio are drawn from the thesis recently completed by Moses K. Anafu, *The Co-operative Movement in Reggio Emilia, 1889–1914* (Cambridge, 1980), and I am most grateful to him for allowing me to use them.

116. Cohen (1972), pp. 88–9.

117. Harrison (1974), p. 623.

118. Freudenberger (1967), pp. 506–7.

119. Callahan (1968), pp. 519, 524.

120. Gross (1973), p. 258.

121. Gerschenkron (1962a), pp. 79–86.

122. Luzzatto (1969), p. 205 (my italics).

123. Gerschenkron (1962a), pp. 80–3.

124. Luzzatto (1963), pp. 224–7.

125. Hildebrand (1965), p. 307.

126. Growth rates from Gerschenkron (1962a), p. 76; Eckaus (1961), p. 314 (for cotton growth rate).

127. Gerschenkron (1962a), p. 83n.

128. Saul (1972), pp. 48–55; also Webster (1975), pp. 106–112.

129. Cafagna (1973), pp. 318–19.

130. Gerschenkron (1962a), p. 80.

131. Cohen (1972), p. 87.

132. *Ibid.*, p. 69.

133. Kahan (1968), p. 19.

134. Trebilcock (1973/1974); Saul (1972), pp. 48–55.

135. Nadal (1973), p. 598.

136. Carr (1966), p. 387.

137. Nadal (1973), p. 605.

138. Vickers Archive: *La Naval* File.

139. Vickers Archive: Report of Advisory Committee of La Naval, 9 June 1910.

140. Trebilcock (1973), p. 261.

141. Vickers Archive, *La Naval* File.

142. Nadal (1973), p. 605.

143. Saul (1972), p. 53.

144. Naval programme costs from *Brassey's Naval Annual*; shares of national income

calculated from Kuznets (1955–57), pp. 53–94.

145. Newbold (1916), pp. 6–9.
146. Saul (1972), p. 53.
147. Vickers Archive: Document 22 of Material prepared for *Royal Commission on Private Manufacture and Trade in Arms*, 1935–36, Cmd. 5292.
148. Saul (1972), p. 54; cf. my argument for Russia in Trebilcock (1973) pp. 265–6.
149. Webster (1975), pp. 106–116.
150. *Ibid.*, pp. 77, 96–7, 116.
151. Japan is perhaps the most readily comparable case, over a rather similar period, 1870–1914.
152. Vickers Archive: Letter Books, *Draft Agreement for Hungarian Gunworks*, 19 June 1911.
153. I am grateful to Andrew Wheatcroft for allowing me to see his unpublished manuscript, 'The Divided Army', which has useful material on Steyr.
154. Lieberson (1971).
155. Benoit and Lubell (1967), p. 59 (my italics).
156. Blum (1943), p. 31.
157. Gille (1968), pp. 148–98.
158. Carr (1966), pp. 409–11.
159. Clough (1964), pp. 26–7.
160. Luzzatto (1969), pp. 213–14.
161. Cited by Blum (1943), p. 26.
162. During the depression of the 1870s financially embarrassed lines were, however, purchased by the state.
163. Gross (1973), p. 261.
164. Gerschenkron (1962a), p. 84.
165. Tortella (1972), pp. 98, 118.
166. Nadal (1973), p. 596; Cameron (1961), p. 275
167. Gille (1968), p. 148.
168. Luzzatto (1969), p. 211.
169. Saul (1972), pp. 48–9.
170. Luzzatto (1969), p. 214.
171. Cohen (1972), p. 71.
172. Gerschenkron (1962a), p. 84.
173. Nadal (1973), p. 551.
174. Martinez Alcibar cited by Nadal (1973), p. 552 (my italics).
175. Gross (1973), p. 272.
176. Lutz (1958), pp. 322–3.
177. Hildebrand (1965), pp. 345–8.
178. Carr (1966), pp. 405, 408–9.
179. Cf. Warriner (ed.) (1965), pp. 34, 100–2.
180. Hopfinger (1962), pp. 15–30.
181. Gerschenkron (1962a), pp. 77–8.
182. Clough (1964), p. 82.
183. Hildebrand (1965), pp. 324–5.
184. Cafagna (1973), p. 305.
185. *Ibid.*, p. 315 (my italics).
186. Gerschenkron (1968), pp. 106–7.
187. Gille (1968), p. 319.

188. *Ibid.*, p. 364.
189. *Ibid.*, p. 318.
190. Feis (1961), p. 201.
191. *Ibid.*, p. 51.
192. *Ibid.*, p. 74.
193. Cameron (1972).
194. Cameron (1967), cf. p. 320, 'it should be evident from the historical record that the banking system is a strategic location with a large leverage for economic development'.
195. Cf. Blum (1943), p. 31.
196. Gerschenkron (1962), p. 20.
197. Rudolph (1972), p. 43.
198. Good (1974), p. 83; Goldsmith (1969), p. 188, App. I and II.
199. Tortella (1972), p. 100. See also *idem* (1970).
200. Nadal (1973), p. 541.
201. Tortella (1972), pp. 102–3.
202. *Ibid.*, pp. 109–15.
203. *Ibid.*, pp. 120–1.
204. Gerschenkron (1962a), pp. 88–9.
205. Cohen (1972), p. 64.
206. Gerschenkron (1962a), pp. 87–9; Cohen's chapter in Cameron (ed.) (1972) strikes a similar note, as does his article, *idem* (1967), pp. 363–82.
207. Gerschenkron (1968), p. 106 (my italics).
208. Cohen (1972), p. 82.
209. Gille (1968), p. 323.
210. *Ibid.*, pp. 354–7.
211. Gerschenkron (1968), p. 388.
212. Gille (1968), p. 375. It appears that the fears were largely groundless. Recent research by Webster confirms that the German controllers of the great Banca Commerciale consistently furthered Italian interests against those of their 'first fatherland' and demonstrated 'how financial institutions of clearly "cosmopolitan" origin soon acclimatized themselves to the nation state' (Webster, 1975, p. 162).
213. Cohen (1967), pp. 386–9.
214. Cameron (1972), p. 19.
215. The Bank of Italy was developed from the Bank of Sardinia in 1892 after the collapse of the important regional bank, the Banco Romana and the absorption of its equally embarrassed Tuscan equivalent.
216. Stone (1975), Ch. 9.
217. Rothschild (1963), pp. 168–72.
218. Cameron (1972), p. 18.
219. Tortella (1972), p. 91; although Nadal (1973) employs a similar general concept, he is nowhere quite so precisely damning.
220. Hirschman (1966), p. 93.

CHAPTER SIX

Anti-models

A convenient method of conclusion – though scarcely of rendering final judgement – is to review the more important assumptions and models which have been employed in the analysis to this point. The object is to discover whether, after experiencing the stress of conflicting individual and comparative cases, these assumptions and models still point in the original, or indeed any definite, direction. As Youngson has remarked, 'When thinking about economic progress, the most important thing to decide is what not to think about.' With this reflection in mind, it is probably true that the inescapable commitments of this study are owed to the models which describe the relationship between industrialization and developments in: agriculture, overseas trade, resource utilization, population growth, investment banking, state administration, entrepreneurship, and, more generally, economic backwardness.

AGRICULTURAL MODELS: CONTENTION IN THE FARMYARD – CHICKENS, EGGS, AND RATIONAL PEASANTS

Here the models have been left in some disarray, with neither the 'agricultural prerequisite' nor its hostile relation, the 'missed revolution', providing a convincing performance. Both depend for their thrust towards development upon the generation of surpluses: the properly executed agricultural revolution, by improving productivity, generates transfers of 'excess' labour, capital, and output for the modern sector; its opposite, the failed agricultural revolution, by increasing accumulation through the exploitative and near-feudal policies of the surviving great estates theoretically raises the economy's level of savings and thus its capacity to invest in modernization. Yet, historically, the problem is that the 'positive' prerequisite rarely occurs at the appropriate point in development (France, Italy, Russia) and that the 'negative' revolution rarely proves an efficient accumulator (Italy, Spain, Hungary).

Probably, the concept of the 'missed agricultural revolution' contains a single lonely virtue: its realization that there is no good logical reason why an upsurge of agricultural dynamism *should* have preceded or evoked industrialization, or, as Bairoch believes, 'first aroused and then fostered the Industrial Revolution'.[1]

In this at least the protagonists of the 'negative' revolution score over the peddlars of prerequisites, for, in reality, agricultural and industrial developments relate in far more various ways than are implied by the optimistic strategists of the stage theories, laying out their 'agricultural transformations' neatly in advance of their 'industrial revolutions'. In fact, both the operational connexions and the sequence of events may be very much more complicated than this, running in many possible directions. For instance, agricultures capable of improved output may well be held back by a failure in productive response on the other side of the hedge, among their prospective customers in the urban – industrial sectors: potential agricultural surpluses may not emerge if the town economy cannot offer desirable commodities for exchange or terms of trade attractive to farmers. Alternatively, the obstacle between the stimulus from agriculture and the response from manufacture may be provided by the state: the sophisticated cultivations of antiquity (China, Rome) tended less to encourage the emergence of modern sectors than to provoke the fiscal appetite of bureaucratic revenue states pledged to defence or conquest; their surpluses were taxed into military campaigns.[2] Or, once more, an equally effective impediment could be constructed by population growth: many evolving agricultures have witnessed their potential to inspire economic expansion fall victim to powerful demographic surges and the attendant downward pressures on productivity and income growth; their surpluses were absorbed by additional mouths. Yet again, when agriculture is isolated, most frequently by political decision, within an 'enclave' or a deliberately restricted cash-cropping system, resembling that of colonial economies, the fertile connexions between domestic agriculture and domestic industry have no chance to gain a footing (perhaps Russia before 1905). It is not even obvious that a particular *type* of agriculture can be readily connected with the successful process of 'arousing and fostering' economic modernization: share-cropping systems proved a dead-end in the Mediterranean (Italy) but not in Asia (Japan); peasant-owners blocked change in one corner of nineteenth-century Europe (France) only to encourage it in another (North-west Germany); the great estate proved a capitalistic success in some quarters (East Elbia) only to fail elsewhere (Spain, Italy, and, arguably, Russia). Not even the peasant type of agriculture can guarantee a specific economic outcome: conventionally, it has been seen as a constraint upon output growth, but, with the spreading discoveries of 'rational' peasant cultivators not only in their customary habitats (Japan, Denmark) but also in some very untraditional ones (Germany;[3] Russia after 1905[4]), even this now lies in question. Probably, as Rostow observes, 'the efficiency of the large unit in agriculture has been over-estimated and that of the peasant under-estimated'[5], but the product of this realization is a discomforting instability: peasant agriculture, like most other types, can support a wide *range* of relationships with economic progress. The ways in which the agricultural stimulus is generated, therefore, cover an embarrassing proliferation of possibilities, but this variety becomes even more intense if the accent within the growth relationship is shifted towards the industrial sector, conventionally seen simply as the recipient of the stimulus.

For it is entirely possible that 'aroused' agricultures may need to be supplied with preconditions of their own from *outside* the rural framework. Given that the 'industrial revolution' requires prerequisites, why not the 'agricultural revolution'? And where are they to come from? If it is difficult to conceive of any source, other than the agricultural, for the surpluses required for early industrialization, it is equally difficult to conceive of farmers increasing output in the absence of rising demand, and difficult to contemplate the existence of sufficiently widespread demand without reference to a *pre-existing* development of the urban market. Kindleberger has explicitly conceded that, 'after a time' – although the duration and location of that time is open to debate – 'there is just as much reason for industry to furnish demand and savings to agriculture as vice versa'.[6] Certainly, at a rather early time, the vitally important market-based farming economy of late-medieval Flanders, a region destined to become an agricultural diffusion centre of enormous power, could not have developed without the expanding demand of the nearby and prosperous textile towns; and they made up in their day the 'largest concentration of manufacturing in northern Europe'.[7] And at a much later point, Dovring contends, the modernizing agricultures of some nineteenth-century economies were still advancing under the sting of demand from industrializing societies.[8] In place of the agriculturally galvanized economy or perhaps alongside it – one might readily imagine the industrially galvanized primary sector. Not only might urban–industrial, or, at worst, urban–commercial, sectors provide the essential demand needed to draw out agricultural production, they might also supply, in the shape of consumption goods, the necessary incentives for farmers to market their produce, so that, 'in a free economy the agricultural precondition has its *own* pre-condition –a bigger supply of manufactured goods'.[9] Equally, industrial advance, by sucking manpower off the land, could force upon agriculturalists the use of labour-economizing implements or equipment, themselves supplied by industry – hence the rapid mechanization of German and Hungarian prairie cultivation in the nineteenth century's final third amidst general lamentations concerning the accelerated seepage of rural manpower.

Still earlier in its modern career, and for reasons more generally concerned with the maintenance of productivity growth, a transforming agriculture might require such factory-produced inputs as improved hand-tools, iron ploughs, or drainage ceramics; somewhat later, simple hand- or horse-powered machinery and artificial fertilizers; later still, fully mechanized draft and process power. Even within the western European cultivations of the period 1780–1815, harvesting efficiency, as Collins has clearly demonstrated, depended upon the availability of factory-produced steel scythes.[10] The *absence* of sufficient factory-power to generate such inputs could act as a definite constraint upon agricultural progress. Probably, the inadequate application of the iron plough in France followed from the slow modernization of the country's metallurgical industries, and the more widespread adoption of the scythe was made possible only by those improvements in metal production which *were* secured between 1800 and 1850. Indeed, as early as the 1790s, the French government had responded to the prospects for agricultural advance with a programme to sponsor an efficient scythe-making industry, a clearly perceived *manufacturing prerequisite* for rural improvement.[11] But over the nineteenth century, as a whole, the most valuable 'spin-off' from factory to field almost certainly came in the shape of artificial fertilizers, implanted in agricultural 'best practice' by the parallel discoveries of Boussingault, von Liebig, and Lawes in the 1840s. Mid-century gas-works yielded up ammonia-sulphate for the sugar-beet fields; Gilchrist—Thomas furnaces from the mid-1880s surrendered their unlikely tribute to farmers in the shape of basic slag; while, most spectacularly, the Haber—Bosch process, pioneered by the German chemical industry in the early 1900s, contrived to snatch from the air itself the nitrates required for the grain plains.

It was no accident that the continent's most industrialized nation was also the power to make the most extensive use of artificial fertilizers and to achieve with them some of the world's most impressive yields: against the minimum effective target application of 60 kilograms of fertilizer per hectare of land, Germany by 1900 scored 50 kilograms, while the other powers, in declining order, matched their fertilizer use against their degree of manufacturing development, France achieving 40 per cent of the German performance, Italy 28 per cent, and Spain 8 per cent. To this extent, the efficiency of the various European primary sectors was controlled by the level of sophistication of their respective manufacturing counterparts. Rather similarly, at a later stage of development, the world's most scale-intensive cultivations appear to have required the development of comprehensive agricultural mechanization before their full productive capability could be released.[12] Thus the tractor and the combine, as Lenin loudly proclaimed, represented true industrial prerequisites for the exploitation of the Soviet countryside. Whatever else fails to emerge from such propositions, one point is secure: the wholly independent or self-generated form of agricultural change, frequently assumed though it may be, is in practice rarely distinguishable amidst the highly interconnected ligatures of nineteenth century development.

Measured against this intricate weave of intersectoral relationships, the customary 'model' which traces force lines directly from agricultural prerequisite to industrial response appears dangerously frail. It is therefore surprising to find it still current and even restated with increased strength. Recently, Paul Bairoch has roundly contended that, 'in general, the speeding up of agricultural development preceded that of industry by 30—50 years',[13] and has set his 'agricultural revolution' firmly in the Britain of 1700, the France of 1750—60, and the Germany of 1800. While admitting that an economy could, in theory, develop industrially without an agricultural precondition — by exchanging surplus industrial production for essential agricultural supplies via the foreign trade mechanism — he argued that this would require significant productivity differences between primary and industrial sectors. These would be necessary in order to provide industry with an income advantage sufficient to finance the considerable transport costs involved in a major expansion of trade. However, an outcome of this kind is deemed unlikely, since it would require ' a fairly advanced degree of *previous* economic development'.[14] Finally, and most daringly, it is suggested that the vital initial demand impulses for one component of the early industrial structure, the iron-processing industry, issued not, as is often assumed, from the railway sector, but from the much earlier expansion of agriculture, with its requirement for iron ploughs – the elimination of the fallow by the new crop rotations may have raised the ploughing commitment by 45 per cent – and for iron horseshoes. The English case, with perhaps 30–50 per cent of the demand for iron accounted for by the farm sector, is taken as prototype. Since this is an influential revival of a highly durable model, it is worthy of careful rebuttal; with the hope that a superior solution may emerge in the process.

In the first place, and with the exception of the German case, Bairoch's 'agricultural revolutions' are very dubiously dated. The claims for England 1700 for the 'agricultural revolution'; 1760 for the 'industrial revolution' – entirely fail to conform with the sophisticated gradualistic interpretation which has become the new orthodoxy in domestic economic history.[15] For France the choice of 1750–60 for the agrarian watershed manifestly compels the selection of the singularly unconvincing date of 1815 for its industrial equivalent; clearly, to have employed the more conventional take off date of 1850 70 would have raised even more uncomfortable problems of continuity. In *either* case, however, the lack of fit remains sufficient to leave an embarrassing time lapse – into which Crouzet mischievously inserted the economic 'catastrophe' of the revolutionary period – between rural stimulus and industrial response. Moreover, the discontinuous interpretation of agrarian change chimes discordantly with the more precise, and pessimistic, long-run estimates of French agricultural performance suggested by Morineau. In fact, the 'agrarian revolution' in France was largely a matter of crop changes, while advances in consolidation of holdings, technical practice, and yields proceeded at a very *gradual* pace.[16]

In the more general vein, it is probable that Bairoch misidentifies the problems of the economy which approaches industrialization without first having secured its agricultural prerequisite, both exaggerating the magnitude of the trade-transport problem and underplaying the width of the productivity gap between the rural and manufacturing sectors. When he does encounter economies which managed the transition to industrial or commercial prosperity without significant agricultural assistance (the Italian marts of the fifteenth, the Dutch of the seventeenth, centuries), he explains these aberrations by their 'special advantages', traditional maritime capabilities or favoured geopolitical situations. Yet it is exactly such favourable endowments – perhaps maritime resources and skills acting to mitigate the burden of transportation costs – which underpin such processes as commercial and industrial revolutions. 'Special advantages' do not excuse deviation from one model; they suggest alternative models. If one set of special factors could allow the Dutch and

Italian trading centres to break out of the agricultural stranglehold, further special factor mixes might allow other countries to perpetrate the 'gradual breakout' of industrialization without benefit of agricultural precondition.

Even the statistical evidence suggests that the prospects for this type of advance were brighter than Bairoch allows: the gap in productivity between the primary and secondary sectors in fact diminishes as measurement moves from poorer to richer countries,[17] implying that it *could* be very considerable in the early stages of development, and thus *well placed* to finance expensive transportation requirements. Finally, there is the problem of the iron industry: in eighteenth-century England, indeed, the demand for 'agricultural' ironware must have been colossal (although not all horseshoes did rural work), but what might be true of the capitalistic English countryside can in no way be assumed amidst the traditional teneurial system of France or the estate systems of central and eastern Europe. There, neither demand nor supply could be guaranteed. And where in France there *was* demand for iron ploughshares, the charcoal forges of an essentially rural iron industry failed for many years effectively to meet it.

Concealed behind these evidential conflicts lies an alternative pattern of agricultural growth, less a pattern of revolution – missed or otherwise – than of evolution. It implies a process of change that is, on the one hand, gradual and, on the other, contemporaneous with manufacturing change, itself therefore reckoned to be long drawn out. Support for parts of this contention has come recently from Collins who has recognized the striking simultaneity of industrial and agricultural change in the European theatre[18] and from Boserup who has emphasized the relationship between successful industrialization and a 'preceding *or concurrent* expansion of agricultural output'.[19] The alternative surrendered here is a most valuable one, for the concept of simultaneous change greatly alleviates the problem of the 'two-way' prerequisite – agricultural surpluses for industry, industrial demand and industrial artefacts for agriculture. The problem, of course, is the means by which this mutually balancing system is to be *initiated*. Here, the concept of gradualism is of most use. It is, in fact, clear that for some considerable time – much more than thirty years – before the industrial surge of the nineteenth century, the relationship between the primary and secondary sectors of the European economies was being adjusted from *both* sides, even within regions of high backwardness. The extent to which the pre-industrial European economies were *entirely* agricultural systems is commonly overplayed; in the decades preceding the acceleration of manufacturing activity most countries had no more than 80 per cent of their population on the land with the rest already resident in urban–commercial–manufacturing sectors, arguably supplying something like Bairoch's 'fairly advanced degree of previous economic development'. This, in turn, possessed two further implications. For the more prosperous regions, it suggested that an enlarging home market for rural products may have been forming in the urban–manufacturing sector well in advance of the main expansion of cultivation. For the less prosperous, it suggests that the productivity differential between rural and urban sectors may have developed by accretion over the long run and may, on the eve of industrialization, have reached substantial proportions, sufficient certainly to finance the transportation effort required for the provision of new commodity outlets overseas. In this connexion, it is important that Jones and Woolf place the advent of the exchange goods essential for the mobilization of an industrial surplus, that is food imports, far earlier than does Bairoch, arguing that, well before the end of the eighteenth century, north-western, central, and southern Europe could draw grain supplies at need from East Elbia.[20] It would seem, therefore, that *either* the 'two-way' prerequisite or the 'trade alternative' was available to many nineteenth-century economies, the choice depending upon level of backwardness, but, in each instance, stemming from a long-run process of adjustment between sectors. However, for the very late developers of the century's last decades this situation was complicated by the arrival of some ambivalent novelties: the enormously expanded world trade in primaries, the ready availability of high-productivity industrial processes *and* the ready availability of high-productivity agricultural processes.

From the 1870s, the possibilities for importing cheap foodstuffs, and, hypothetically, for specializing upon industrial production were better than ever before, while the productivity gap between the two sectors become a matter of more governable choice. On the other hand, the world market was already overflowing with industrial exporters and the new methods, both in industry and in agriculture, were expensive. In practice, however, the dilemma was resolved by the poor response to the prospects of innovation among Europe's more conservative agriculturalists – the standard bearers of the 'missed revolution' – which worked effectively to preserve the productivity advantage of the industrial sector. In these cases, and perhaps in these alone, the returns were meagre: lacking a convincing history of agricultural adaptation *and* robbed of the opportunity successfully to export manufacturers by the achievements of their industrial predecessors, this group exhibited strong tendencies towards the cash-cropping 'solution'. Here the problem was less the lack of an agricultural revolution – in some cases practice did notably improve – but precisely the lack of an extended period of adjustment between the two sectors.

But for many countries outside this group, the assimilation of the revised 'British' model – featuring lengthy, parallel, and mutually reinforcing processes of change in both sectors – offers the best prospects of a convincing chronology, and the most inclusive summary of the very varied relationships between agriculture and manufacture. This is unlikely to represent the only occasion when gradualism acts as an enemy to received models.

TRADE MODELS: THE EXPORT PROPELLER

For many analysts the contrast between the closed economy and the open economy is a contrast between stagnation and growth. And the difference is represented by international trade. Here the model connects together commercial and industrial expansion and trade is made to break the ground for manufacturing. Primarily, the export sector is seen as a source of initial demand for industrial products within economies where agriculture cannot provide this service. Undoubtedly, the activation of the export sector can procure major benefits for an industrializing economy, perhaps the most obvious being: the economies of scale derived from the large external market; the concentration upon goods in which the economy has a comparative advantage, a choice encouraged by the wide product selection inherent in international trade; or the increased efficiency stemming from international specialization of labour. Powerful linkage effects may also connect the export trades to other sectors: foreign trade will require the development of specialized credit services, shipping services, and maritime construction industries; by accumulating merchant fortunes, it will create a capital surplus for investment in manufacturing; by absorbing larger proportions of the workforce in high-productivity, scale-intensive industries, it will create additional income and expand the domestic market. The problems lie in the security of these gains and in the precise sequence of manœuvres for 'opening' the economy.

In fact, the export sector can influence total economic performance in a style scarcely less various than that exhibited by its agricultural counterpart. Even the scale effects of the export market have a double edge: in some instances, involving industrial systems prone to overproduction, export demand may act partly to alleviate, but also partly to sustain and even inflate, already excessive reserves of capacity (late-nineteenth-century Germany). Similarly, comparative advantages may *retard* industrialization if the economy's advantage lies in primary production. Here, the export sector may help to purchase foreign capital goods, but otherwise its impact upon the economy will be slight. Owing to the heavy inertial pressures exerted by the existing patterns of world trade, the requirements of the advanced economies for raw materials and their stranglehold upon the trade in manufactures, the export system dealing in primary products will face grave obstacles in any attempt to alter its internal composition and progress beyond its enclave status; instead, it may endure extended periods as a quasi-colonial producer (Russia, Spain). Nor, even if the export sector lies outside agriculture, is there any guarantee that it will be a best-practice sector: comparative advantage can as readily fall upon sectors of peasant or artisanal manufacture, or upon sectors of primitive mineral extraction, as upon high-productivity factory industries (Japanese handicrafts, Spanish mining). If it *is* a best-practice sector, its linkage effects may still lack in security; the prospects for strong technological connexions are best in the context supplied by a well-developed economy and perhaps least strong in the early growth stages when the export sector may be an *isolated* best-practice sector, separated by an uncomfortably wide 'technology gap' from its less advanced industrial colleagues. Similarly, for follower economies, best-practice export sectors may be available only within rigidly specified areas: such economies commonly encounter problems in finding an export 'niche'

within an already crowded world market and may settle upon highly specialized products, efficient in commercial terms, but offering restricted opportunities for linkage to the remainder of domestic industry. The apparently
straightforward proposition that the export sector may act as a particularly
powerful lead sector in the early stages of industrialization is thus hedged with
many necessary qualifications.

Moreover, the process by which the export sector moves into the lead is
greatly neglected in most interpretations. Once more, the autonomy of the
'opening' process is taken for granted and inquiry is insufficiently concentrated
upon the *mechanisms* for acquiring export propulsion. In particular, it is difficult to identify precisely how some of the conventional suggestions for the
major trade stimuli such as 'a favourable change in demand abroad' or 'an
innovation reducing costs at home'[21] – *could* lead independently to the emergence of an export lead sector. 'Unilateral' changes in foreign demand for an
economy's products are exceedingly unlikely to encourage enthusiastic responses from the export sector: it is scarcely likely, for instance, that Britain's
overseas customers in the late eighteenth century judiciously elected to cease
consuming luxury re-exports and take cottons instead. Rather, producers will
examine the *domestic* market closely for shifts in demand, will respond to these
more readily perceived adjustments, and may, at a later stage, apply solutions
devised for the home market to suitable foreign trades. Flows of information
will be more dependable, risks more readily assessable within the home market, and the preparation of new products and production strategies will naturally commence there. By the same token 'cost-reducing innovations at home'
are unlikely to emerge as purpose-built initiators of export-led growth; these
too will be developed for 'domestic' trades and later transferred to the export
industries. Here the line of causation runs from the economy to the export sector not vice versa; and, once more, the foreign trade activity expands
in parallel with industrial production (France 1856–65 and 1896–1913 provides good examples).[22] This form of export expansion does not readily explain
the 'opening' of the economy since, at this level, it appears simply as an
extension of developing internal capabilities, and by no means as an antidote
to internal 'stagnation'. An abrupt form of 'opening' can be achieved, of
course, by a political decision to reverse isolationist policies (Russia after
1857; Japan after 1868). More usually, however, the pressures towards an
outward swing of the economy are provided by characteristics intrinsic to the
prosperity and endowment of the domestic economy. Fairly obviously, the
nature of the national market may heavily condition the need to export: low
domestic income levels (Japan 1868–1914) or insufficient consumers (Germany 1890–1914) may drive an economy into exportation.

In rare cases (the pre-1914 *Kaiserreich*) the market imbalance may follow
pre-eminently from elephantiasis of *production*, rather than from any real failure
on the part of domestic demand, and, in such instances, the plunge into the
export pool depends in a special sense upon an independent push from the
supply side. Alternatively, rich domestic markets with high income levels

may generate a demand for luxury imports which can be paid for only by increased exports (Britain 1750–1800). In either case, exports are propelled by the economy rather than the reverse. Very similar propositions can be constructed from considerations of factor endowment. Deficiencies in natural resources will require compensating imports of raw materials and these in turn will constitute an import 'trigger', firing off export commodities as repayment for overseas purchases (Japan, Germany). Similarly, inferior endowment in human capital will encourage an appetite for imported technology and expertise, and these again will be financed by a (probably agricultural) export effort (Russia, Italy). Pressure upon the import trigger perhaps represents the most common, and also most underrated, reason for the development of export lead sectors. Hirschman's powerfully refined assessment of the role of *imports* in industrialization – presenting them as development catalysts revealed by the economy's commercial arm – is not far removed from this valuation. According to Hirschman, imports 'fulfill the very important function of demand formation and demand reconnaissance for the country's entrepreneurs . . . they reconnoiter and map out the country's demand'.[23] Here imports not only press the trigger for the export explosion, they also help construct and aim the weapon. They achieve this by signalling to entrepreneurs exactly which goods industry should be producing, replacing those that the economy is currently buying in. Imports, therefore, help both to determine the economy's overall range of products and to condition its technological level, as well as requiring it to balance the books through its export earnings. It remains to emphasize, however, that imports are not *imposed* upon healthy, developing economies by the independent pressures of the world market; rather, they are selected by most (non-colonial) economies in compensation for commodities which they do not possess or cannot yet manufacture competitively. Once more, the acquisition of benefits by trade depends upon the current possessions and performance of the host economy.

From this it is clear that trade models, like farmyard models, do not make convincing prime movers. Export development depends on the prevailing level of economic achievement as defined by the exploitation of the domestic market and the importation of overseas commodities. It advances as total industrial output advances. Indeed it may even lag slightly, since not all domestic production will activate an import 'trigger' for inputs, and, perhaps more importantly, industrial producers will prefer to construct a secure domestic base wherever possible, before adventuring into foreign fields. At a later stage, selection of the foreign market may prove important as a means of adding scale to an *existing* production base. In these terms, the export sector is much more likely to sustain an existing growth trajectory than to initiate one. Shaped by the foregoing development of the domestic market, viewed as a response to import needs defined by foregoing development, the export lead sector ceases to be an instrument of discontinuous growth and becomes, like its rural cousin, an agency of gradually unfolding development.

MODELS OF RESOURCE: THE CONTEST OF ENDOWMENT AND INNOVATION

Until 1914, and possibly later, models featuring natural endowment or physical resources were taken to be the most powerful explanatory systems for historical economic growth. In this stern gospel, rich resources were believed to facilitate industrialization, and, more pertinently, poor resources to impede or even prohibit it. According to Jevons, for instance, coal was *the* indispensable prerequisite for a modern industrial civilization, fulfilling the 'same role of ultimate constraint . . .as land supply does in the Ricardian model'.[24] However, where confrontation with a largely illusory apocalyse moved Victorian economists to pessimism, and J. S. Mill to address the Commons on the imminent exhaustion of Britain's fuel reserves, confrontation with the apparently looming twentieth-century apocalypse has, paradoxically, encouraged some modern economists to lighter spirits. The basic philosophy is encapsulated in Hirschman's contention that so-called physical 'obstacles' to continued growth are less real constraints upon development than symptoms of inadequate economic organization (i.e. inferior deployment of entrepreneurial or institutional capabilities in problem-solving).[25] Thus, efficient development does not depend upon a particularly 'fortunate' inheritance of resources; rather, efficient development will marshal skills to bring about a superior use of whatever resources there are. Encouraged no doubt by the obvious relevance of current shortages in vital materials, more recent analysts have added several important insights to this central perception. On the more optimistic reading, an immense creative force is allocated to technology itself, assuming that it will 'continue to be ingenious in finding substitute materials for those that become scarce',[26] while the pessimists are soundly drubbed for neglecting 'the impressive array of adaptive mechanisms through which a market economy responds to shifting patterns of resource scarcity'.[27] Economic history is specifically invoked to suggest 'the reasonableness of a number of alternative scenarios to the essentially Malthusian one'.[28] In particular, Rosenberg has most perceptively suggested that even the British industrial revolution stemmed less from the richness of the nation's endowment than from the development of techniques for circumventing a contemporary resource constraint of great strength, the British economy's acute deficiency in a conventionally 'vital' fuel – timber.

In this interpretation, the wheel has turned another segment: technological change is not limited by factor shortages, rather technological change becomes a synonym for factor substitution. By making it possible to exploit resources which previously could not be worked, the technological dynamic (Gilchrist–Thomas, Haber–Bosch) is effectively supplying a continuous stream of *additions* to the stock of endowments. Similar adjustments in the use of resources can operate to economize upon, or substitute for, endowments in short supply – that is, high-quality endowment – by the more extensive exploitation of endowment in plentiful supply – that is, low-grade endowment. In fact, no economy has ever faced *absolute* resource constraints; typically, nature distributes small quantities of premium resource unevenly, and much larger quantities of inferior resource much more generally. The utilization of the latter is a matter of process and cost, not of supply. Classically, technological *coups* such as those which permit the extraction of nitrogen from air or magnesium from sea-water have both added to the resource base and substituted abundant, low-quality resources for scarce and valuable ones. At this point the wheel comes full circle: technology growth is not limited by resource shortage; rather, technology growth creates its own resources.

Just as modern industrial growth cannot be traced to prior development of the rural or commercial sectors, but rather by its own expansion rolls these sectors with it through the processes of accumulative development, so a similar formula covers the relationship between the resource base and the manufacturing top-hamper. For, in fact, it appears that the infrastructure and the superstructure can exchange places: when the 'conventional' resource foundations are slender, the high-technology layer may itself act as a base for the acquisition of new resources and the intensive exploitation of familiar ones. Again, the resource model frequently seen as providing 'prerequisites', 'constraints', or controls upon industrialization must abandon these claims and accept absorption within a system of technologically flexible industrial change, one capability of which is to transform the relevance and even the composition of the resource base. Assuming, that is, that the niceties of economic organization are scrupulously observed.

POPULATION MODELS: PEOPLE AS GROWTH-OBSTACLES AND GROWTH-INDUCERS

'There can be no general rule as to whether population produced industrialization or industrialization called forth extra population. Neither process can stand by itself. To say that it is a continuous process of interaction is merely to hedge.'[29] So writes Professor Eversley and leaves, it might well be thought, very little for the rest of us. Kindleberger, too, is non-committal: 'For our period (1850–1950) there is no short-run link between economic growth and population change, nor any clear-cut model of the secular connexions running between bigger population and greater prosperity.'[30] Clearly, demographers are natural pessimists and demographic problems sufficient to reduce even the strongest economic minds to bafflement. Moreover, the native intractability of the subject-matter has tended to divert the burden of demographic inquiry away from the influence of population growth on industrial progress and towards a preoccupation with the causation of population growth itself. According to the somewhat sketchy models which do exist, the increase in numbers will register its impact upon economic change, primarily by its effect on three variables: labour supply, market demand, and investment capacity. All these raise very hard questions. And, in much of the literature, they are not addressed but delicately skirted.

Unfortunately, direct confrontation with these issues is little better at producing conclusions. Observe, in the first instance, the connexion between population, labour supplies, and industrialization. If it is true that too few workers may impose the burden of high wages upon infant industries, it is equally true that too many may impose the special limitation of cheap labour, the disincentive for managers to employ best-practice machinery which is often both expensive and labour-*saving*. In this context the industrialist may see little point in replacing plentiful and economical labour with costly but more efficient machines. For any but the pioneer industrial economy, necessarily limited to a relatively simple labour-intensive technology, the fruits of labour plenty may be as bitter as those of labour scarcity. Similarly, for any given economy, the precisely beneficial number of consumers is a highly elusive quantity. Too few consumers will narrow the market and create major deterrents for enterprise. Too many will expand demand to the point where customers compete for commodities, pushing prices upwards along the inflationary spiral and living standards downwards along the subsistence spiral. In general, demand will advance satisfactorily only if the increase in consumers is accompanied by a similar increase in income. If, on the contrary, the growth in average remuneration is less than the growth in population, the effect on demand may not be beneficial for industrialization: total purchases may expand in volume but they will concentrate at a lower point within the demand structure or 'schedule', preferring agricultural necessities to manufactured 'decencies'. If the increase in income and the increase in population are roughly matched, demand will expand in volume, while retaining its earlier structure. And if average remuneration expands faster than population, demand should both enlarge in volume and move up the schedule towards 'decencies' and even luxuries. On another front, if the increase in incomes is less than the increase in consumable commodities, the threat of over-production will materialize once more. If it is significantly higher, the result will again be price-inflation, and this will leave the industrial market in a state of over-dependence upon the high-income groups with their relatively few consumers. In these circumstances identification of a line running discriminatingly between 'excessive' and 'sufficient' supplies of workers and consumers constitutes a frontier which the research has scarcely inspected, let alone explored. What is clear is that the European experience of the past two centuries must have included an equilibrium between demographic and economic expansion which – measured against either the traditional supply of crises or the modern incidence of 'Third World' crises – was both highly unusual[31] and, of necessity, since the point of balance is so elusive, perilously achieved. And even then, some members of the European community demonstrated the low tolerances within the system: while most risked, and mostly avoided, the various economic 'drains' of over-large societies, nearby France laboured under *scarcities* both of workers and of demand.

With regard to the effect of population growth on investment, the models are scarcely more decisive. Broadly speaking, most recent analysis has taken a pessimistic or 'neo-Malthusian' direction in which higher rates of population growth are held to depress incomes and savings, and, by extension, investment, while slower rates are believed to assist in the increase of *per capita* income and savings. The more optimistic, or Keynesian, employment models, in which population growth, by guaranteeing labour supplies and good expectations of rising demand, *encourages* investment, have not fared well against the historical record. The most common working assumption is that population growth creates an *obstacle* to income growth and thus to economic advance. This assumption is grounded upon a significant long-term observation. It appears that, prior to 1914, population growth in the pre-industrial parts of Europe proceeded, generally, at modest rates but was accompanied by very little in the way of economic change. On the other hand, where and when industrialization took hold, it was frequently accompanied by a much more rapid form of population growth. The suggestion follows that this accelerated type of demographic expansion was 'induced' by industrial change. Yet, once released, this expansion of the community itself operated to rein back the further progress of industrial change.

Behind the paradoxes, the explanatory mechanism for these relationships is reasonably straightforward. First, industrialization, by expanding output, raises national income and personal income. Next, rising income itself calls forth more persons, since advancing prosperity helps finance earlier marriages and healthier environments for new infants. But then the resulting upsurge in live births will expand the proportion of non-workers within the community. This will raise the total cost of dependence to the economy. Furthermore, the expansion of the non-working population will cause difficulties in sustaining the expansion of output per head. As the circle is completed, these pressures will act once more to bear down upon *per capita* income. As the induced population spurt changes the balance in the community between producers and dependent consumers, the rise in income per head will be constrained and perhaps reversed.

In the early stages of industrialization, rising incomes generate rising fertility. In the later stages, however, families confronted by slipping income and threatened living standards will commence to prefer lower birth rates. Some time will probably be required for this perception to crystallize and to become the basis of action. In the meantime, the community's ability to save and invest will shadow the path taken by personal income, rising as it rises, falling back as it dips downwards. Since income per head is merely the product obtained by dividing national income by total population, it is self-evident that the outcome is controlled by the relationship between economic growth and population growth. The central assumption is that income per head determines the nation's capacity to invest. And the central proposition is that industrialization works to increase *both* national income and total population. In effect, it unleashes a race between population growth and income growth. But, unfortunately, at least in the short term, the destination of the race appears to be a 'trap' for income and investment.[32]

However, it does seem that the term of the entrapment is short. Few economies before 1900 recorded patterns of *sustained* income depression. The economies which experienced induced upsurges in population, and then pressure upon income levels, also experienced a sequel: a delayed but substantial downward adjustment of birth-rate which finally sprang the 'trap'. In most early developers the interval between the initial upswing and the eventual 'correction' of the population balance consumed some seven or eight decades; in later developers it has diminished to as little as three. The content of this 'correction' – or 'demographic transition' – is the decision to restrain birth rates and thus population growth; it is the culmination of the drift towards smaller families. Its relevance in the race for investment growth is clear: national income can at last pull away from its demographic rival, personal income resumes an upward path, and the community becomes heir to a substantial increment in investable funds, an increment which may be as much as 40 per cent of current savings. In this interpretation, often christened the 'income trap hypothesis', population does act as an obstacle to industrialization but not – as long as the demographic transition is successfully negotiated – as an enduring or insurmountable obstacle.

Much recent demographic investigation has produced results consistent with this reading. Empirical evidence certainly suggests a low rate of pre-industrial population advance before 1780, at about 0.3 per cent p.a. average over most of the European continent; further proposes a marked acceleration 'almost everywhere' by 1820 (commencement of 'induced' expansion); and draws the pattern to a close in a general deceleration ('transition') in the century's final third, 'the age of emigration and birth control'.[33] Perhaps more significantly, the discovery, in the regions west of the St Petersburg–Trieste 'demographic axis', of a distinctively 'European' pattern of marriage featuring high age at marriage for women and low fertility rates, and quite unlike patterns elsewhere, has given a convincing personality to the pre-industrial form of population movement.[34] This arrangement would have left sufficient demographic slack to be taken up later by the 'induced' upsurge accompanying industrialization and would conform with the generally modest estimates of pre-industrial population growth. An additional suggestion is added, however, that this specialized marriage pattern made a significant preparatory contribution to European economic growth. According to Spengler, the low rate of population advance which it entailed, permitted a 'slow and intermittent accumulation' of savings for investment, and protected European resources, particularly agricultural land, from the despoiling effects of excess numbers. The age structure of societies would have tilted towards the more productive working age groups in the range fifteen to forty, probably by a proportion close to 5 per cent, while the improvement in savings rates would most likely have been somewhat better than 5 per cent.[35] The 'European marriage pattern' then not only guaranteed an appropriate level of pre-industrial population growth but helped prepare the materials for an industrialization which would release its 'induced' counterpart.

At the other end of the population 'race' important clarifications have been achieved concerning the working of the demographic transition. Professor Eversley, in his statement that, 'the history of the last 150 years has shown us that a country may first experience a rapid rise in fertility as prosperity increases; [but] in the next stage, the standard of living may reduce fertility to danger point',[36] both assumes phases in which population growth is induced and incomes are reduced and then suggests a simple mechanism for the transfer to a third, more prosperous, era. Here it is precisely the pressure upon living standards which triggers an evasive manœuvre towards lower fertility rates and the revived incomes which these permit. Plausible suggestions for this trigger mechanism have also been built around a selection of socio-economic effects: a decline in infant mortality which removes the need for large families; the spread of education which both takes the child out of employment and diffuses knowledge of fertility limitation; the relative rise in the cost of living space brought about by urbanization and the consequent inconvenience of families which consume large spaces; and increases in welfare legislation which both restrict the employment of children and reduce the need to invest in large families as an insurance against old age.[37] Leibenstein has employed the somewhat looser formulation that the 'fluidity' of the social structure created by industrialism placed a premium upon mobility in occupation, location, and social status, and that, consequently, the response to these new requirements was expressed in lower birth-rates and smaller families. Whichever version is preferred, the more precise operational descriptions of recent research have effectively established the fertility transition as an institution of growth patterns which are first population-obstructed and then population-released.

Generally, then, the demographic pessimists have conquered most of the field; and they have succeeded in establishing a powerful descriptive vocabulary in which voracious populations 'swallow' economic growth or the 'downstream elevator' carries economic man, struggling purposefully but fruitlessly in attempted ascent, always lower towards a tumultuous oblivion of fertility. Moreover, the addition by the 'partial' Malthusians of an eventually relenting fertility goddess prepared to release industrial growth from the income trap by means of the demographic transition, has greatly improved the descriptive range of this approach. Such is the 'openness' of the demographic issue, however, that even these powerful phrases and concepts may be overturned with a simple twist of assumptions. Hirschman's determination to cast population growth as a positive force for economic change is a particularly effective example of this. Taking as his controlling assumption the observation that societies *resist* erosion of their living standards, he contends that the downward pressure exerted upon income growth by rising numbers will elicit *counter-pressures* as the community seeks to defend its current standards from 'dilution'. Even more to the point, the economy's growth prospects, thanks to this experience, may actually be *improved*, since, in the contest, society will undergo a learning process, equipping it more readily 'to control its environment and organize itself for development'.[38] Empirical evidence certainly suggests that institutions faced with the educational, residential, transportational, and welfare demands of expanding populations do respond with innovating systems of management and expenditure.[39] And Hirschman argues that these

responses will be strongest when population increases are sudden and dramatic, inviting society to rally against a clearly perceived attack on living standards; or when population increase is combined with urbanization, thus presenting a vivid need for improvements to social capital; or, most easily, when
population growth occurs in a context where there are slack resources available
for embodiment in the counter-attack. This last point is important since, at
the outset of development, economies *will* possess some slackness in resource
utilization, whereas all Malthusian interpretations assume that resources are
fully employed. To this extent, the developing economy is better qualified to
mount campaigns of 'resistance' than the Malthusian models allow.

Ingenious as this is, it remains a very long way from conclusive. Even
Hirschman admits that population growth provides only a *weak* inducement
for further industrial growth, since it functions by eliciting a response to a
diminution of income, and does so by processes and stages which cannot be
operationally specified. Obviously enough, 'the resisting society' is a creature
of assumption rather than of proven existence and its reflexes cannot be
guaranteed. In fact, actual societies are more likely to provide only a *part* of
their response to a demographic overload in a constructive manner – by expanding *essential* social overheads and support systems, and probably only
these – while supplying the remainder in a gesture less of resistance than of
avoidance: the deliberate downward adjustment of fertility growth rates. Some
learning processes may be achieved within such communities, but their successful economic development will still depend upon the ease with which they
negotiate this demographic turn-round.

All in the end remains uncertain. Connexions between demographic and
economic development have attracted as many models – income-reducing, em-
ployment-creating, dilution-resisting – as there are demographic theorists and
as much contention as there are economic historians. The problem, as Rostow
succinctly identified it, is 'a question of the balance between the need for a
supply of workers . . . and enough consumers' demand to stimulate activity
without diverting resources from investment',[40] but exactly how these three
terms may be juggled into equilibrium remains a puzzle. Take, for instance,
the notion of connecting demographic and industrial expansion by casting the
former as prerequisite for the latter. This possibility is immediately complicated by the fact that, in western European experience, pre-industrial or
'autonomous' population growth was notably gentle and that the main population upsurge occurred *simultaneously* with early industrialization, and may even
have been induced by it. Scarcely more specifically geared to the course of
events is the Spengler–Jones–Woolf suggestion that a demographic *lull* may
have provided the essential preparation for economic change. The problem
here is that the emergence of the 'European marriage pattern' was not a closely
pre-industrial phenomenon but a matter of gradual crystallization, of 'diffusion rather than innovation',[41] over a period beginning in the late sixteenth
century. In this respect, the demographic precondition becomes subject to the
chronological stretching process which recent research has shown to have
afflicted most, if not all, of Rostow's prerequisites; its early incidence, in fact,

interestingly parallels the precocious accumulation, during the continent's pro-to-industrial phase, of the sources of agricultural demand. Yet here again there are further problems, for, where some analysts cast demographic acceleration in the role of prerequisite, an increasing number are coming to extol the economic virtues of an early demographic *deceleration*. Where Leibenstein stress-es the galvanizing effects of population upsurge, requiring an industrial effort fit to leap the demographic hurdle, Spengler points to the gradually accruing advantages of more decorous population patterns. And if it is true that the main additions to the community are not only contemporaneous with, but also dependent upon, the forward push of industrialization, where lies the de-mographic precondition, whether accelerating or decelerating? Can it be that the prerequisite for the first industrial stirring is a low rate of population advance, for the industrial quickening a rapid rate, and for sustained indus-trial advance a repetition of low rates? If so, the complexity of the demographic prerequisite, given the present state of knowledge, can only be admired from afar. Faced with it, Kindleberger could only report that he had experienced a hunch that 'we are in the presence of collinearity, that population changes in response to other influences which also affect economic growth in the long run, with differential effects in the short'.[42] Since this was written, the state of knowledge has advanced only a little. But it has advanced. Perhaps the most useful product of recent inquiry, and one of the few useful products in this difficult area, is the demonstration that the unique European population patterns, like so many of the interwoven strands of continental modernization, were spun with much gradualness, over the very long run. The 'autonomous' population pattern is no longer economically sterile and the hurdle-avoiding leap is – conveniently in view of the moderate pace of much recorded indus-trial advance – no longer the only economically viable response to the problem of demographic pressure. But beyond this the visible connexions remain slender, the substantial connexions undiscovered.

A CHANGE OF MODELS

Alongside the models which describe the ponderable forms of economic wealth – fertile cultivations, rich mineral stocks, favourable maritime and mercantile capacities, well-peopled communities – historians have sensibly arranged a number which deal with the less tangible benefits supplied by human enter-prise, whether individual or institutional. These systems attempt to connect certain forms of financial, bureaucratic, or entrepreneurial activity with the inculcation of modern economic growth. Frequently, they also imply that the relationship between the physical endowment and the man-made contrivance contains certain self-balancing elements. Certainly, meagre endowments may provoke only meagre responses (Spain, southern Italy), but there are powerful expectations amidst the literature (and growing more powerful in an era of resource stringency) that the community's scientific, technological, or organizational ingenuity will frequently make up for the oversight and inegalitarianism of Nature. As Gerschenkron taught, the managerial input, whether of banker, functionary, or independent manufacturer may 'substitute' for deficiencies in the objective endowment. Indeed, within the backwardness model, the self-compensating nature of the relationship between the resource and the resourceful innovator, between 'objective' and 'subjective' elements emerges especially powerfully, since it is precisely the *lack* of orthodox economic benefits which conditions the supply and design of the institutional or entrepreneurial response. If conclusive analytical results are not to be found among agricultural revolutions, resource crises, trade miracles, and demographic surges, they must clearly be pursued amidst the talents for substitution displayed by bankers, civil servants, and industrialists, and even amidst the curious dietaries of backwardness itself, which, for all their measures of gristle and bone, apparently possessed the ability to nourish talent. From the outset, however, it is wise to reserve a suspicion: that too frequently the independent leverage of administrative 'substitutes' is exaggerated, that in reality their successful operation depends upon the strength of feedback from other sectors, the current level of demand from industry for their services, the existing development of the classes from which the bureaucracy is recruited, etc. Too often this *deus ex machina* is only a ghost *within* the machine, and quite dependent upon the quality of his acolytes.

BANK MODELS: GAMES OF RISK – OR OF RISK AVOIDANCE?

In the early development of Britain's pioneering industrial economy, with its relatively simple technologies and its well-distributed reserves of wealth, the financing of capital formation raised few problems; for the most part, the costs of industrial expansion could be met out of reinvested profits, while informal markets in credit would take care of the needs for working capital. With the follower economies, facing more expensive initial requirements in industrial equipment and leaner supplies of investable capital, the position was quite other; in these cases later entry to the industrial process both raised the cost of obtaining a progressively advancing technology and ensured a relative poverty in the resources for funding it. Here, specialized institutions were needed to deal with the capital gap. Indeed, it has become rather an axiom of continental economic history that, 'under conditions of moderate backwardness . . . an *aggressive* banking system provided a more *centralized* response to capital and entrepreneurial deficiencies'.[43] The underlying logic is clear, since, in a context of *moderate* backwardness, in which a small entrepreneurial vanguard would already be active, the demand for bank services would not be so suppressed as to deprive financiers of custom, nor the supply of capital so lavish as to leave manufacturers contentedly supported by local or informal credit sources. Moreover, where managerial capabilities remained at least partially underdeveloped, the banker's influence as creditor might expand naturally into that of participant or entrepreneur – a suggestion accepted by authorities as diverse as Gerschenkron, Cameron, Good, or Gille. And from this suggestion, the model of *bank-directed* development in a context of medium backwardness follows naturally.

Even recent quantitative evaluation has seemed to confirm several important expectations attached to this model. Measurement of the annual growth in the ratio of bank assets to GNP has revealed much faster bank expansion in 'middle industrializers' like Germany (with the highly significant exception of France) than in 'early starters' like England or 'late developers' like Russia (see Tables 6.1 and 6.2). Alone among the industrial generations, the moderately backward economies embarked upon modern economic growth with bank sectors of small size and then experienced sudden and rapid financial expansion. Allowing for the considerable managerial potential attached to bank growth of this type, Good believes that the high growth rates in the bank asset/GNP ratio may be 'rough proxies' for the entrepreneurial influence exerted upon the moderately backward economy by its financial sector.[44]

Table 6.1   Ratios of Bank assets to GNP: selected countries

	1783	1803	1829	1849	1870	1884	1896	1904	1913
England	0.18	0.30							0.46
France			0.06	0.09					0.56
Germany				0.05	0.16				0.42
Russia						0.18		0.23	0.52
Italy							0.22		0.32

Source: Good (1971), Table 1; fn., p. 850

Table 6.2   Rate of growth in ratios of bank assets to GNP over take-off period, (%av. p.a.)

England	1783–1803	2.4
France	1829–1849	2.0
Germany	1850–1870	6.3
Russia	1884–1904	1.3
Italy	1896–1916	2.5

Source: Good (1971), Table 1

Much of this is consistent with the general strategy of the foregoing analysis. True, the *sudden* emergence of dynamic bank sectors among the middle industrializers would seem to breach the gathering preference for gradualistic growth patterns. But this is not altogether so. Rapid bank expansion is *confined* to the small group of middle industrializers; both the early and the late developers initiated industrialization with relatively large and well-prepared bank structures which had been gradually accumulated and which continued to grow gradually. Important implications regarding the growth patterns of extremely backward economies follow from this: even these countries, by selective and sustained financial borrowing from more advanced neighbours, may help to 'telescope' the growth stages, and by long-run compilation of growth materials, *reduce* the discontinuity of their development process. Quickfire application of the financial 'substitute' among middle industrializers may indicate only that a gradually gathered macro-economic potential has achieved a sufficiently critical pressure and a sufficiently critical focus to bring rapid development in a single strategic sector: while industrial forces accumulate in the long term, a vocabulary for their convincing expression may be found in the short. And in this connexion, it is significant that the sudden bank advances, where they did occur, did not come about in an immediately preindustrial era, nor in the livery of financial prerequisites; rather the high bank asset/GNP growth rates coincided in time with the acceleration in manufacturing performance and – suitably enough for entrepreneurial 'proxies' – formed one manifestation of that acceleration.

In other ways, the bank model does not satisfy so readily. In much of the literature which has described it, the industrial bank, investment bank, *mobilier*, or *banque d'affaires* has been treated as a device interchangeable between countries and, by implication, growth-inducing in effect wherever it is set down. Like the railway, it has been cast as a virtually autonomous carrier of change: and indeed its effectiveness as an entrepreneurial 'substitute' depends largely upon the assumption of its autonomy. However, that this is the best means of evaluating the investment bank must be open to severe doubt. As Gille has recently pointed out,[45] the great omissions in the studies of European bank development concern matters as vital as the degree of esteem accorded by industrialists to the financial fraternity – and thus, critically, the demand for bank services – and the attitudes maintained by bankers towards involvement in industry – and thus, critically, the measure of entrepreneurial substitution they were prepared to provide. In all probability, it is ignorance upon these points which has led directly to the current overestimates of the forceful autonomy of 'bank-directed growth'. Nor are these points the only ones we need to resolve before we can be clear about the part played by banking in continental development: the demand for bank services is controlled by many forces over and above the affections of industrialists for bankers; and the extent of entrepreneurial verve generated by bankers is controlled by forces larger than their suspicions of industrialists. At present the models dealing with bank development are biased towards a preoccupation with the supply side and towards the technicalities of financial procedure. At the very least, we need to know more about the market-place for bank 'commodities', including the economic attitudes of bank customers and much more about the reserves of entrepreneurial talent actually present within the financial community (clearly greater in Germany than in France), including the means by which banker-entrepreneurs were selected and recruited. For the time being, and in the absence of this information, it is safer to deny the investment bank the role of autonomous growth-inducer and to consider it instead as a piece of financial technology in itself economically neutral and dependent for its effective operation upon the nature both of financial 'producers' and financial 'consumers'. Like any piece of technology, it may be transported at will, but will vary in local performance according to factor availability and market conditions.

The most recent investigations have given force to these reservations. Many of the early *mobiliers*, it turns out, despite their proclaimed ambitions in general company promotion, were so constrained by market conditions that they proved unable to break out of their initial attachment to railway funding. Nor was this true only of a backward market like the Spanish, for it appears that many French institutions, including the Crédit Mobilier, laboured under similar restrictions.[46] Consequently, in many parts of Europe (Austria, Spain, Italy, France) market characteristics ensured that a real distinction was established between the activities of the 'railway *mobiliers*' and those of the genuine industrial investment agencies. In France, indeed, no institution comprehensively specialized in *industrial* credit grew up before 1872 (the Banque de Paris et des Pays Bas) and it found no successor before 1904 (the Banque de l'Union Parisienne); and even then both institutions followed the customary French bias towards foreign business. Inadequate demand for bank services – whether due to industrial underdevelopment or to industrialists' suspicions of bankers – has featured increasingly in recent interpretations of financial development in both Austria[47] and France[48]. Moreover, throughout Europe, the distrust and dislike of bankers expressed by industrialists – even those as successful as Cavallier, Citroën ('banking is the death of spirit'), Rathenau, or Skoda – supplies evidence of a much-neglected failure in *rapport* between financial and manufacturing businessmen. It is even possible that these relationships deteriorated further as the rise of the large-scale *mobilier*, with its far-reaching (for businessmen, 'dangerous') plans for industrial reform, replaced the small-scale, familiar, and provincial (that is, 'safe') banking house. And, in the more backward parts of the continent, of course, bank credit was regarded as scarcely more appetizing than outright debt, while debt itself remained anathema. Such vitally important reactions to bank finance are, as yet, only scantily documented and substantial comment is restricted almost exclusively to the French case. There, it is clear, industrialists actively resented financial schemes for industrial rationalization and found retaliation in an organized invasion of the directing boards of the joint-stock banks, thus securing a financial voice which they promptly employed to *restrict* the flow of bank finance towards industry.[49] In Germany, however, instances of friction between bankers and industrialists seem to be confined to powerfully individual manufacturers such as Rathenau or Thyssen and their general relevance is unclear. Certainly, Gille's claim that German bank boards were 'colonized' by industrialists[50] appears badly overplayed and entirely neglects the immensely powerful migration running in the opposite direction: here, it seems that bank and industrial interests remain combined in a more creative and less distrustful relationship, with the financiers maintaining a guiding voice for the majority of the period, losing perhaps a little influence to the very greatest industrial concerns in the final decade (from which almost all of Gille's examples are drawn). Yet even here we still know a quite inadequate amount concerning the attitudes involved in the bank–industry connexions.

On the supply side, it is certainly true that the response of bankers to the prospects of industrial promotion was by no means invariably that of growth-inducing enterprise assumed by Gerschenkron, at least implicitly, as a constant. The involvement of many *mobiliers* in railroad work seems to have been less a promotional than a banker's ploy, and a fairly conservative one at that: with many states prepared to guarantee the yield on railway shares, these could be regarded by bankers as gold-encased securities rather than as risky equities, and enjoyed for the least enterprising of reasons. As readily as they could be attracted by the high profitability of industrial involvement proper, the financiers might, equally, be deterred from such involvement by the fear that bank aid to industry would start up an insatiable credit commitment which, at some future and painful time, they might have to terminate. Very various methods were employed to cover this possibility: French bankers simply fled from industrial entanglements, Austrian bankers sought to cushion their risks among well-heeled clients of impeccable repute, while the more adventurous Germans were sometimes forced into desperate expedients in order to satisfy their manufacturing customers. Of these, only the last was a genuinely enterprising response, but the others may not have been less *reasonable* readings of the problem. What is critical here is the quality of the evaluation available to the contemporary financiers concerning the profitability of industrial investment It is a matter of information. For instance, it is perfectly possible that the advice supplied to the financial staff of the German banks by their industrial departments was more expertly prepared than that provided by the engineers who counselled the French bankers. But if it is possible, it remains to be proved.

While important questions concerning the relationship between the investment bank and continental industrialization have still to be asked, it is at least now certain that the 'financial substitute' did not operate in a uniform or predictable manner as it travelled the width of the continent. While it could be found from Rome to St Petersburg and from Paris to Vienna, its developmental value varied enormously with location. While in Germany (and, after 1890 in Italy) the investment bank actually did play the classic entrepreneurial role of the financial 'maid-of-all work', in Russia it acted frequently as a precondition only for the foreign control of industrial finance, in Spain (and before 1890, in Italy) too frequently as a precondition for financial collapse, and in Austria consistently as a precondition for timid risk-*avoidance*. Whatever the intrinsic value of the equipment, it could obviously be used and abused in many different ways. However, a few of the controlling factors are becoming more evident. In countries with ample capital supplies and traditions of industrial reinvestment, that is, with fixed and sturdy patterns of demand for credit, bank 'substitution' was not necessary and did not readily emerge. The conditions in which it thrived occurred in countries with moderately acute capital shortage – pressing upon financial innovation – but with moderately developed reserves of enterprise, both in industry – creating demand for capital – and in banking – creating credit supply. This balance was delicate and few countries may have struck it. Germany's pre-eminence in the banking field rested upon a conjunction of the necessary conditions which was unusually favourable: good entrepreneurial reserves from which to recruit talented bankers, solid credit demand from a rapidly concentrating business structure, and, not least, a classically quick and well-timed expansion of financial institutions (1850–70). The prospects for bank-led growth in Germany, therefore, remain fairly bright, but this implies neither that bank development could proceed without its *own* preconditions (supplied, once more, by an existing measure of industrial development), nor that this mixture could be readily imitated elsewhere. In fact, distortions in the volume and type of the *demand* for credit created over-specialized and unstable banking systems in many countries (Spain, Italy). And, in some others, distortions in the *supply* of enterprise among both industrialists and bankers produced very erratic results when banks attempted to guide economic development (France, Austria). Deficiencies in *both* the demand for, and the supply of, French industrial credit would be enough to explain why, alone among the group of middle industrializers, France displayed a slow rate of growth in bank assets/GNP.

Among the late industrializers, of course, more pronounced levels of backwardness would act upon both demand and supply in the credit market, depressing both. Such conditions offered few attractions for home-grown investment banks, but sometimes encouraged other institutions, usually foreign banks or native governments, in efforts to fill the gaps, the western financiers attempting to lead demand, the home bureaucracy more concerned with the supervision of supply. At this level, the utility of the investment bank to the home economy could be compromised by its management in the alien interest (possibly Russia, certainly Spain) or entirely negated by obstructive or inept official policy, (Austria, Spain). On the other hand, however, as extremely backward countries gradually built up their financial equipment and the more competent among their governments consciously borrowed financial methods from the international stock of development aids, it could no longer be true that the investment bank remained simply an institution of *medium* backwardness.

Bank models depend on too many feedbacks in enterprise and demand to offer either a dependable supply of financial preconditions or a convincing measure of entrepreneurial substitution. They are too delicately tuned to be universally applicable, and may have operated well in rather few cases. Yet they are spread too widely by the process of international imitation and diffusion to attach only to one category of developing countries or to one type of backwardness. They are too readily captured by governments and too reliant upon capitalistic verve to be entirely separated either from the role of the state in development or from the role of the entrepreneur in development. In the end, they appear to describe *dependent* variables of a high order of technical sophistication, rather than independent inducements to economic modernization.

STATE MODELS: INTERVENTION, INTEREST GROUPS, AND INFORMATION

Where the models of bank-led growth have been subjected to at least some critical interpretation, those describing state-directed development have been employed in a remarkably stereotyped fashion. Economic historians, in both distaste and enthusiasm, have applied the concept of 'state intervention' to all manner of nineteenth-century economies, as if it were some standard black box guaranteed to provoke growth, whatever the climate or context. Initial attempts to create a framework for comparative judgements have drained away into the sands of specific national instances and unsatisfactory summary.[51] And even Gerschenkron teaches only that the strength of state intervention – still mysterious in design – will intensify as the level of backwardness rises. More especially, in economies of chronic backwardness, where enterprise, capital, and demand are all deficient, the state will form the only agency of sufficient power and range to supply substitutes and to 'induce' development. But the compulsions for it to do so are still very imperfectly understood, as indeed are the means. Perhaps in reaction to this lack of headway, a significant proportion of the recent literature has occupied itself with industrialization as an *international* experience, thereby necessarily imputing a low or constant economic leverage to the various national state administrations.[52] One distinguished economic historian of the twentieth century was even moved to write of the nineteenth, though admittedly in somewhat casual company: 'If such things [as the 'role of the state'] played any role in German economic development, it was perfectly comparable with the role they played elsewhere in Europe in similar circumstances at the same time.'[53] Presumably, that is to assume that the German civil service, communications, and costs of information were as one with their counterparts all over Europe; yet, presumably, to assume this is also absurd. At least in part, the drift towards international explanations – though these make a genuinely useful contribution of their own – seems to follow from our ignorance of the workings of the nineteenth-century nation-state. A similar point was recently touched upon by J. B. Cohen in the important observation that, 'the government's decisions are influenced by its objectives and these depend on the political power of groups within the system and on their goals. . . . Political scientists seem much more aware of these relationships than economists.'[54]

Some attempt to defend the profession's good name, and an almost unique attempt, has been made by Professor Supple. Commencing from the assumption that, 'frontiers are more than lines on a map; they frequently define quite distinctive systems of thought and action', he argues powerfully that, 'the state must be seen as part of society, reflecting particular social forces and representing (however confusedly or narrowly) specific group or class interest. . . . The state, like the entrepreneur or the labour movement is a *social phenomenon*', and necessarily concludes that there is not a single 'role of the state' but rather 'a variety of roles', stretching 'from a permissive shaping of prerequisites to a positive and autocratic mobilization of capital'.[55] These are brave and perceptive statements and they constitute an excellent basic framework upon which to effect a more extensive interweaving of concepts from political science and economic history. However, the analysis may be improved. For one thing, it perhaps does not fully describe the controlling factors which apportion the variety of state roles *between* individual countries or fully identify the 'particular social forces' to be found in individual states. The proposition, for instance, that state policy will be controlled by a variety of interest groups within society is used by Supple simply to question the famous categorization by Hoselitz which divides economic growth into an 'autonomous' form generated by free-enterprise capitalism and an 'induced' form directed by the state apparatus.[56] Yet this, in itself imaginative, insight does not capture a further important reality: that the particular social groups responsible for 'autonomous' growth, on the one hand, and for 'induced' growth, on the other , are highly unlikely to be similar or even compatible. While bourgeois industrialists, with their taste for non-interventionist government policies, still loom large in the explanation of Britain's autonomous development and tsarist functionaries, with their commitment to *dirigiste* policies, in the explanation of Russia's induced growth, virtue may still adhere to Hoselitz's formulation. For another thing, Supple's analysis, as it stands, provides little measure of the *effectiveness* of nineteenth-century government policy, whatever its variety. A more comprehensive appraisal of the factors influencing both the style and the utility of state intervention might perhaps be obtained by consideration of: the constitutional structure of the state and its constituent interest groups; the level of sophistication of the national economy; the social composition of the bureaucracy; the scale and information costs of the national government; the quality of the available economic theory.

To begin with, it is clear that all nineteenth-century states, whatever their constitutional complexion, accepted *some* measure of economic interventionism, that is, the preparation of the framework for economic enterprise (involving currency reform, design of company legislation, extension of patent law, etc.) which Supple terms 'negative interventionism'. Neglect of this minimum assistance for free-enterprise development would have indicated not anti-*dirigiste* preferences but merely inept administration. More at issue are the large-scale operations, undertaken on grounds of social benefit, to inaugurate or protect economic ventures which would not have been commenced or maintained under the aegis of private profit alone. Here the form of government is critical. Autocratic systems possess advantages over other types in their ability freely to dispose of resources and to execute economic programmes rapidly and without compromise (although this, of course, includes the freedom to make large mistakes rapidly and without compromise). Perhaps most importantly, authoritarian political systems possess the coercive power to mobilize major investment programmes upon the basis of forced savings extracted from the community. To this extent, and leaving aside the high social cost, there may well be an affinity between autocracy and high industrial growth rates (Russia, Japan).

410

On the other hand, the autocratic system requires at least some political approval from the body politic and often turns to specialist minorities for this support. Under nineteenth-century conditions, such needs encouraged autocratic governments to protect the interests of reactionary agrarian aristocracies, virtual monopolists in the supply of approval for authoritarian rule. Rather similarly, the political imperative requiring autocratic systems thoroughly to subjugate entire national communities often cuts across the social fluidity which normally accompanies and assists the formation of the new industrial order. For both these reasons, autocracies may pursue rapid industrialization within a framework of rigid social control which will eventually set limits to economic change (Russia). Within democratic structures, in contrast, political approval must be sought across a wider social band and power is not centralized but traded, 'exchanged for desired policies in a political transaction between party and electorate'.[57] Outside a context of national emergency, neither forced-draft policies nor the uncompromising thrusts of induced development will find a place within this consensus structure. Further, the need to reflect a variety of interests within economic policy may jeopardize its internal coherence, and when the interest groups are 'delinquent' (France), this will certainly be so. Broadly speaking, since the interest groups most frequently reflected by advanced democratic systems in the nineteenth century were bourgeois ones, that is, those most interested in unrestricted profit, the increasing sensitivity of political representation worked to turn state policy in non-interventionist directions (Britain). While autocratic systems are more liable to procure rapid, if potentially socially disruptive, industrialization by direct and massive intervention, democratic systems are more likely to reflect a carefully balanced array of economic interest groups in a context of moderate growth and non-interventionist policy. If, before 1914, autocratic systems are counted as backward political systems, it follows that the level of state interventionism in the economy may be conditioned less by economic than by political backwardness.[58]

Modern political science offers useful refinement of these hypotheses. Under present-day conditions, analysts employing an 'élitist' frame of measurement have argued that national policy-making is frequently controlled by a narrow range of interests, while their 'pluralist' adversaries see policy rather as the product of an extensive array of contending interest groups. Most significantly, the 'élitists' have proposed that the dominant interest group, exhibiting unique scope and co-ordination in action, has frequently proved to be the military lobby. Moreover, it may have exerted a particular influence upon policy-making in the area embracing both military and industrial affairs.[59] No historical dimension has been given to these propositions, but it is a simple matter to construct one: namely, that backward political systems are broadly 'élitist' in behaviour and that they become increasingly 'pluralistic' as modernization takes hold. Or, as Kahan has argued, 'nationalistic economic policies historically developed from policies furthering particular or group interests [here a military élite] to policies epitomising an over-all view of the national interest'.[60] This interpretation conforms closely to recorded events:

411

military expenditures were at their maximum relative to state budgets in the *early* modern period when many states still employed authoritarian methods. In 1752, for instance, Prussia committed 90 per cent and in 1784 France committed 70 per cent of state revenue to defence activities, clearly underlining the 'élitist' expenditure patterns of backward autocracies. But this approach also offers a convincing *motive* for the connexion between authoritarian rule and economic interventionism. For autocracies usually win support as political systems by the military proficiency of their ruling cliques. Industrial structures created by more advanced rival states will disturb the security of autocratic governments by opposing powerful modern weaponry to their traditional military skills. Yet, when copied by backward states, these same structures offer means for repairing dented prestige and tarnished reputations. International industrialization thus forces the challenged military – autocratic élite into the specialized development patterns of 'reactive nationalism'. Among many possible examples, this pattern is most beautifully displayed by Russia: each military disaster, from the Crimean surrender of 1857, through the Berlin Congress of 1878, (nullifying tsarist gains in the Turkish War) to the Tsushima débâcle of 1905, set the autocracy scrabbling for countermeasures. Each military fiasco could consequently be reinterpreted as the starting point for a new phase of economic modernization. Something of this is grasped in Kahan's statement that 'it was chiefly the development of a new military technology requiring an elaborate and modern industrial base that demanded a forced pace of industrialization and *thus elevated economic growth to prominence among the objectives of nationalism in nineteenth century Europe*'.[61] More usefully, however, Gerschenkron recently recognized that there is an operational linkage not only between backwardness and state intervention but between backwardness and a policy preference for military development[62] – and *thus* with programmes of economic modernization. The élitist structure of autocratic states can be presented, therefore, as the engine of a very particular form of industrialization, an industrialization in the strategic interest. Moreover, the strong resistance of this kind of structure to *alternative* forms of creative investment reduces the historical opportunity costs and the 'unproductiveness' which is usually alleged against most kinds of large-scale expenditure on the military.[63] Finally, as economic modernization takes place, itself creating powerful new interest groups, the increasing complexity of society will widen the range of factions which attempt to influence policy, and, in due time, *alter* the composition and style of state intervention.

One major flaw remains within this analysis. If backward states are now almost conventionally said to require extensive state intervention, whether for economic or military reasons, there is a perfectly respectable body of opinion which holds that the degree of governmental activity rises with the level of *maturity* of the advanced economy. On this reading, it is swelling national wealth, and not the outmoded military, which requires the protection of lavish defence services and armament industries; it is urban expansion, not agricultural stagnation, which requires increased expenditure upon social control; and it is the poverty of the industrial towns, not the poverty of the benighted countryside, which requires the tourniquet of modern welfare services. Within a pluralist political system, the pressures upon government to provide the necessary services of protection, control, and rescue need not be imagined; they are everyday facts. Either backwardness or forwardness, élitism or pluralism, it therefore seems, means the death of *laissez-faire*. Nevertheless, one or two important distinctions can be made. The interventionist exercises of élitist systems are normally aimed at the *initiation* of growth; they are themselves induced only by a lack of previous growth and are intended to be correctives to backwardness. Mature economies (and states), however, deal in intervention for the relief of pressures *caused* by forgoing growth; this form of *dirigisme* is induced by growth rather than growth-inducing. And, as Hirschman contends, state activity of this type is likely to retain a passive mood within free-enterprise systems. For, inside a pluralistic structure, the only kind of intervention likely to please a wide selection of interests will need to serve social purposes, avert crises, avoid risk or clear unprofitability, and yet to incur a minimum of planning, effort, or expense. Consequently, 'it takes an unusually enterprising and risk-accepting government to engage in novel manufacturing methods instead of going on with its port and highway projects'.[64] If both backward and advanced states intervene in economic affairs, therefore, they do so for different strategic reasons, usually in different sectors (broadly defence versus welfare, though there will be some overlap), and always under the pressure of different groupings of vested interests.

So much, however, concerns only the state's *will* to meddle with economic affairs; other forces control its ability to meddle effectively. Thus, where the nature of the constitutional balance might inculcate a desire for state-led growth, the strength of the government's administrative arm might still limit the success of its endeavours. Broadly speaking, the administrative systems, the bureaucracies, or at least their senior elements, are recruited from the prevailing social ascendancies of their respective states and possess effective connexions with their cousins in the legislature, in the armed services, or at court. They constitute a force not lightly to be dismissed. Where, normally within a pluralistic structure, the bureaucracy reflects a wide range of social interests, its professional capacity to administer intricate change is probably highest, although, ironically, the demand for such change is probably low under these conditions. Within a backward, early developing, or élitist system, however, the bureaucracy will be drawn mainly, and possibly solely, (Prussia) from the traditional landed classes. Whatever the developmental ambitions generated within the ruling circles, this group may still find its own interests threatened by development and may react strongly against it. Acting as a sensitively placed proxy for conservative interests, the bureaucracy may ensure the surrender of concessions which cut across growth objectives. Thus, European tariffs (especially in Germany and Italy) were commonly slanted towards the preservation of established, rather than the protection of new, economic interests; and where gentry-administrators retained influence, policies of agrarian control were preferred to those of agrarian reform (Russia, Hungary). Progressive administration under these conditions became either the monopoly of an embattled bureaucratic minority (Russia) or a bargaining counter to be surrendered only upon proper recognition of archaic vested interests which in turn constrained progressive administration (Germany). In this sense the Junker-bureaucrats of Prussia were very far from being at one with the French functionaries from the *grandes écoles*. On a rather similar tack, political scientists have recently argued that bureaucracies may only be introduced or improved where there are 'free-floating' resources of manpower, funds, and cultural values not tied to ascriptive or particularist groups.[65] Precisely the reverse situation, of course, obtains within traditional agrarian societies on the eve of industrial modernization. Nor are such societies likely to possess many of the 'resource-freeing' mechanisms, such as urban growth, expanding literacy, or political adjustments displacing the established interests. The bureaucratic thrust, therefore, will not feature as a constant between nations. Across frontiers the variations in the affections and education of state servants, in the finance and quality of administrative equipment, may well prove considerable. Paradoxically, the bureaucratic capability for effective intervention was probably least in the backward states most urgently requiring it and most developed within the advanced states requiring it least (to 1914). Nor, frequently, could much utility be extracted from the latter situation, since the more efficient administrative systems, often remained oversupplied with personnel but undersupplied with tasks.

As bureaucratic resources – the supply feature – varied between countries, so too did the scale problems of government – the demand features. In order to formulate policy, governments need information; in order to administer, they must deliver information to the relevant points within the body politic or economic. Under modern conditions, the costs of these information flows are roughly constant between continental nations. Under nineteenth-century conditions, these costs varied enormously, mainly in relation to the quality of the railway network and the other communications services of the various powers. On these criteria, a large power like Germany was intrinsically more 'governable' than a large power like France and a small country like Britain infinitely more governable than a vast empire like Russia. To some extent at least, 'state intervention' must depend for its efficiency upon the state's ability to identify problems or prospects within the economic structure and to manifest its will at the correct points and times. If the costs of information are too high, either development programmes will be seriously impaired, or major infrastructural and bureaucratic reforms will be required to bring costs down.

Finally, there is the small matter of theory. In the present day, almost any act of government intervention may be made the subject of intricate technical debate – yet the most common valuation of economic science is to bemoan its powerlessness in face of the sequence of traumas thoughtlessly supplied by providence. How much then is to be expected of governments confronting their own economic traumas decades before the advent of the Keynesian revolution and the planning revelation? To what extent in these circumstances is the concept of 'state intervention' a theoretical anachronism, to be entirely distinguished from the fumbling acts committed by governments under the pressure of their controlling interest groups? Here it is a major irony of history that, for the nineteenth-century states most bent upon economic development and committed to interventionist policies, the longest-lived, most internationally influential, and most rigorously articulated economic principles of the era were strongly *opposed* to the expansion of government's role within the economy. Admittedly, Gerschenkron is correct in his recent argument that it was simple *ideology* – the sum of borrowings from, and corruptions of, theory, and in itself simply the product of the crude socio-political pragmatism of the day – and not theory proper, which controlled the formulation of nineteenth-century economic policy.[66] The improved German investment banks were 'altogether unsupported either by past or by contemporaneous economic theories'; German tariffs were affected by theory not 'by one jot',[67] and remained 'an instinctive rather than reasoned conviction';[68] connexions between Marxism and Russian industrialization stayed 'wholly on the surface'.[69] Effective transfer between theory and practice appears, therefore, to have eluded all schools, not excluding that of the great *laissez-faire* thinkers. But for the *dirigiste* bureaucrats, even the stock of appropriate theories available for corruption was painfully small. Most of the half-way relevant hypotheses had been put forward by Mordvinov, List, or the Saint-Simonians before the turn of the half-century, were descriptive rather than operational, and failed to reach an acceptable logical standard: Schumpeter, for instance, contended that Saint-Simon's contribution to economic analysis was nil. Even if Count Witte is made out to be the century's most successful disciple of List, the crucial point is that, in the end, Listean theory disappointed the Finance Minister: the heavy industrial core of the national economy proved insufficient support in itself, agriculture collapsed under the strain, and no adequate principles were available for the management of the demand side of the economy. The sober truth of the matter is that nineteenth-century states were forced to rely upon an interventionist equipment not of glistening theoretical devices but of rudely cobbled expedients, often obvious, sometimes archaic: traditional remedies like subsidies, fiscal concessions, and state monopolies, dating back to the *ancien régime*; fashionable social overheads like railroads, clearly too costly for private budgets and decorated with military enticements; protective tariffs loudly advertised by persistent and influential sectional interests.

Almost invariably, within democratic systems, state intervention came about as a simple reflex reaction to particularist lobbying, within authoritarian systems as a simple coercive response – since coercive power was more readily understood by nineteenth-century regimes bent upon large tasks than was creative power – to élitist ambitions and preoccupations. Gerschenkron's conclusion, the correct one, sounds the death-knell for nineteenth-century economics as a discipline for the practical interventionist: 'Had the theories been more operational', he writes, 'had there been, that is, a sufficiently large stock of empirical knowledge to support them, their impact upon events would have been much greater.'[70] But as it was, they were not operational, and one of the most important guidelines for the twentieth-century *dirigiste* state was denied its earlier counterpart.

415

'State intervention' then does not survive as the magic black box. It is not an international constant. It relates all too closely to the power dispositions of the individual political structures which deploy it, faithfully mirroring the weaknesses both of pluralist and élitist systems, the competition between groups and the delinquent communities of the first, the over-centralization and social rigidities of the second. It occurs in both backward and mature economies, but for different reasons, and may be either growth-inducing or growth-induced. It varies between countries according to political structures, bureaucratic dynamism, and even distance. It may fail for almost as many reasons as it may be inaugurated: owing to excessive delinquency among controlling groups (the Third Republic), or to friction from powerful bureaucratic traditions (Germany, Russia), or to inadequate support from contemporary theory (Russia, South Italy). Once even some of the controlling variables are revealed, it seems scarcely likely that the nineteenth-century state made a more convincing guarantor of economic progress than its luckless present-day descendants. Scarcely likely either, given these governmentally induced peculiarities, is the proposition that industrialization was a process generally careless of frontiers. Though it no doubt possessed internationalist implications, it was clearly unable to escape the clutch, however unsure, of these highly individual state administrations.

ENTREPRENEURIAL MODELS: ON THE TRAIL OF THE 'CREATIVE DESTROYER'

With the entrepreneur the analytical buck comes clumsily to rest. Efficiency in agrarian change, trade expansion, resource utilization, or population mobility all require, in one form or another, appropriate entrepreneurial decision-making. The bankers who 'lead' growth are merely financial entrepreneurs recruited from the general constituency of business talent; the development-inducing state is simultaneously a segment of, and a reflector of, society, and will either react to entrepreneurial pressures or attempt to emulate entrepreneurial behaviour in corporate form (although its objective then will be less the capitalistic maximization of profit than the autocratic maximization of periods of existence[71]). But if the entrepreneur claims pride of place as 'the central figure in modern economic history',[72] penetration of the logistic maze which surrounds him reveals not even Minotaur but rather Enigma. Despite the massed biographies, business histories, industrial studies, and quasi-philosophical essays, a comprehensive operational description of the interrelationships between entrepreneurial development and economic change is still lacking. Even the notable output from the Harvard Research Centre in Entrepreneurial History raised more hopes than it provided answers and subsided over-frequently into a curiously sterile discussion of entrepreneurial *functions*, avoiding the more fundamental requirement of explaining *why* entrepreneurship occurs, and why it differs in strength between individual economies. The upshot is that the models regarded by some as the most crucial of all are agreed by almost everyone to be among the least articulated of all. This fact may possibly explain why recent advances in the methodology of economic history – particularly in econometric analysis – have tended to shy away from entrepreneurial explanations. The trend may be regretted (although some reversal is fortunately in sight): at present entrepreneurial models require not rejection but refinement. Certainly, if entrepreneurship is understood, in the conventional rubric, as 'the utilization by one productive factor of the other productive factors for the creation of economic goods',[73] an approach which emphasizes all productive factors *except* entrepreneurship appears positively unwise.

Again, despite prevailing uncertainties, certain margins of doubt or malpractice may be usefully narrowed. Basically, only two approaches to the problem of entrepreneurship are possible: one describes the general *economic* function performed irrespective of social context; the other relates entrepreneurial activities to a constellation of economic, political, and social conditioning factors. Most analysts would also append to this a scale of entrepreneurial dynamism in which routinized entrepreneurship (sometimes, and perhaps better, described simply as management) and innovative entrepreneurship occupy the polar extremes. Within this scale, the necessary distinction between the select ranks of the pathbreaking entrepreneurs and the more populous ranks of the imitative entrepreneurs – the distinction between the leadership and the followership groups – is fairly readily accomodated. But the central problem, and the source of much malpractice, is that the investigation of the general entrepreneurial function draws upon a neo-classical theory of the firm which is unable effectively to represent the *innovative* responsibility of the entrepreneur. According to available theory, the only motivation attributable to the businessman is that of profit maximization, a preoccupation so outrageously monolithic that it has moved entrepreneurial historians to point out unkindly that 'automaton maximizers'[74] or 'rational automatons maximising profits'[75] do not, to put it at its lowest, constitute the majority of actual businessmen and that for any individual capitalist, 'the assumption of crass money-making'[76] will not represent his single objective in business. Moreover, the means of maximizing profit, by 'improving efficiency within the limits of the *known* technology', by functioning as 'a *passive calculator* that reacts mechanically to changes imposed upon it by fortuitous external developments'[77] make of the theoretical archetype a very poor kind of entrepreneur, indeed no entrepreneur at all but rather an unembroidered manager. The true entrepreneur acts as an innovating leader, identifying and applying new processes, concerned not with mechanical reactions but with organizing the major *deviations* in economic processes. For enterprise at this level, according to Leibenstein, 'not all of the markets exist or operate perfectly and the entrepreneur, if he is to be successful, must *fill in for market deficiencies*.'[78]

Clearly, the adventurous 'gap-filling' and 'input-completing' roles, the leadership functions, compose crucial omissions from current economics. Yet, equally clearly, the economic historian needs concepts to fit these important activities, and, to a certain extent, though he has no embracing theory of entrepreneurial behaviour, he has attempted to build these concepts. More

417

building is required, but poor practice does not issue from the bids at construction. It comes rather from the application of theory describing managerial behaviour to the measurement of entrepreneurial performance. At present the economist, for lack of better instruments, must persevere with established practice until something better comes along. But the cliometricians – who have not been friendly to entrepreneurial explanations – have, in effect, *chosen* to apply an inferior measure of business behaviour for its methodological convenience: the concept of the rational manager, the careful housekeeper, who dependably optimizes use of measurable resources and can only react to measurable inputs, has obvious procedural attractions in historical analysis. But the outcome is that the 'automaton maximizer' has conquered new fields and that the econometric analysis of historical problems contains an intrinsic discount on entrepreneurial behaviour. For the rationality of the businessman in the new economic history is the rationality of the manager, not of Schumpeter's 'creative destroyer'. The irony is that, in their debates about entrepreneurship, the 'old' and the 'new' economic historians have been discussing *different* economic figures and functions. Moreover, the espousal by the cliometricians of theoretical positions which many economists are increasingly prepared to question does not necessarily appear as the more scientific of the two approaches.

However, in the most recent, and, as it happens most perceptive, econometric studies, a more generous understanding of the developmental role of the human factor has made a reassuring appearance. Abramovitz and David have suggested that the conventional econometric measurement of the residual (the element 'left over' when quantifiable elements are accounted for, and taken to represent changes in the quality of labour, capital, etc.) has entirely failed to capture significant interrelationships between human capital (i.e. labour and entrepreneurs, and particularly the skills embodied in each) and ponderable capital (i.e. plant, and particularly its technological level). On the one hand, they acknowledge that it is mistaken 'to simply dismiss the significant historical part played by human capital in promoting the exploitation of technological innovations'; on the other hand, they contest the usual, and unsupported, cliometric assumption that 'technological change has been "neutral" in its potential impact upon factor supply',[79] arguing instead that it is the nature of technological change to pose an ongoing demand for *improvements* in the factor of human capital which are achieved by adjustments to educational practice. More advanced technology requires more sophisticated entrepreneurs and these, once produced, will help generate more advances in technology. It may be deduced that if society does not respond with additional educational efforts, it is perfectly possible for a mismatch to occur between a lagging supply of high-quality human capital and the potential supply of best-practice technology (Britain, 1870–1914); once this is admitted, the 'automation maximizer' is banished the scene and the possibilities for both 'entrepreneurial failure' and 'heroic entrepreneurship' re-enter the lists. Further, it becomes possible for a society to place particular emphasis upon 'uncoventional capital deepening' through education and to reap high technological returns from this form of investment (Germany). The relevance of this for the conventional residual is clear: the various factors within it are not independent – the quality of technology can amend the quality of human capital and will, in turn, be amended by it. The responsibility allotted to human capital is not predictable because it is both experiencing feedback pressures from the capital embodied in new plant and creating its own pressures upon technical change. Abramovitz and David rightly conclude, with rare econometric modesty, that 'until we are able to articulate the reciprocal interactions between technical and social innovations and alterations in the available factors of production, the "residual" as we have known it must remain at best a lower-bound measure of our ignorance of the process of economic growth'.[80]

Although Abramovitz and David are dealing with the whole range of human capital, their arguments have important implications for entrepreneurial studies in particular. The segment of human capital which 'promotes innovation' is, of course, entrepreneurial, as is part of that which experiences the educational demands of new technology. The implications are that econometric studies have not succeeded in disposing of entrepreneurial explanations and that more sensitive handling of cliometric techniques might once more bring the methodologies together. But here both the econometrician and the economist perhaps need to come some way towards the economic historian.

What remains then for the economic historian himself to contribute to the entrepreneurial model? As Easterbrook emphasizes, the main analytical failure up to now has lain less in poor description of the entrepreneurial function than in the inability to associate it 'with any specific set of conditions, institutional and ideological'.[81] Although many sources talk enthusiastically of the entrepreneur as if he were a universal type dispensing rugged individualism even-handedly throughout history, the contexts which have supported the 'creative destroyers' have in fact been few and select. Results might therefore be expected from a more rigorous application of the assumption that entrepreneurship is culturally determined – a view which would unite a large group of analysts including Cochran, Cole, Jenks, and Landes – to comparative testing of these contexts. Criticism of the culture-determined view of entrepreneurship has most frequently come from economists for whom the constant reiteration by entrepreneurial analysts of the 'cultural obstacles to growth' easily becomes an implicit denial of the economic discipline itself; in reaction, much economic writing has overplayed the power of economic growth to amend cultural patterns so that growth will be progressive. The truth of the matter is that some cultures are more resistant to economic change than others, and that the economic historian urgently requires an accurate identification of at least some of the types. To date, an 'adjusted' social-value explanation has probably offered the best prospects. If society is acknowledged to contain a mass of contending value systems with negative, positive, and neutral attitudes to capitalistic growth, it remains possible for the whole structure of forces so to resolve itself as to tilt in a particular direction, either favouring or obstructing the wide spread of economic innovation. Since the balance between groups may change over time, and since a sufficient rise in

419

economic prospects may overcome a previously obstructive but relatively mild adverse 'tilt', the model has dynamic capabilities. Certainly, it offers useful descriptions of cases as diverse as the French (predominance of anti-capitalistic values giving a moderate adverse tilt), the German (extensive spread of authoritarian, state-service, and state-building values giving a strong positive tilt) or the Russian (chronic adverse tilt permitting enterprise only from markedly isolated 'deviant' groups) – and does so within a comparative structure of wide application. True, it can sometimes appear obscure as to whether social values control economic performance or whether the reverse is true. It has been argued, for instance, that values and attitudes rooted in a historical context where economic growth has been slow may prove a grave obstacle to *future* rapid advance.[82] But a route around even this obstacle may be found in the useful hypothesis that the traditional culture represents a *resource* and requires only the application of appropriate techniques to release its growth potential.[83]

However, even the adjusted value system model requires much further improvement, and, as yet, only pointers towards possible refinement are available. Easterbrook's system of 'securities' required for satisfactory entrepreneurship – the security for risk-taking, security from want, ethical security (virtually, 'social approval'), and political security[84] – offers another, wider, and almost wholly neglected instrument for comparative testing. Similarly, Leibenstein has suggested some interesting controls upon the supply of 'gap-fillers'.[85] Essentially, their presence in sufficient numbers will depend upon opportunity costs. In other words, individuals who occupy 'outsider' or 'deviant' positions within society, remaining barred from other careers by its structure of sanctions, will have lower opportunity costs as entrepreneurs, that is, they will sacrifice less in terms of alternative careers forgone, than social conformists. Therefore, they will be attracted in disproportionate strength to the business occupations. Once there, their efficiency in gap-filling will depend heavily on the supply of assets available to them through family, kin group or clique connexions. And outsider or deviant groups, by virtue of their status as tightly integrated minority communities, will possess special advantages in the mobilization of assets for use by their members. But if the 'gap-fillers' will often be social deviants, they must not deviate too far – which means that 'social-value' or 'security' systems must contain enough support for rank-and-file entrepreneurship – otherwise, 'the leaders will have no followers'.[86] Alternatively, Baumol recommends that attention should be concentrated upon those elements in the socio-economic context which most bear upon risk-taking and innovation, and emphasizes particularly those forces which reduce the marginal cost of entrepreneurial risk-taking and those which make it economically easier to pursue the research and development necessary for innovation. This approach provides a bridge between those hypotheses, like Easterbrook's, which dwell upon the optimal conditions for an enterprising response to risk, and those like Abramovitz and David's which emphasize the need to raise the quality of the entrepreneurial factor itself. The connexion holds because improvements in human capital will smooth the path for more and better research, and this, in turn, will lower the risk barriers surrounding innovation. Operationally, also, Baumol's methodology produces results: in Russia, for instance, not only deficiencies in social approval but, more particularly, shortcomings in business organization, in educational provision, in transportation and in the supporting talents in auxiliary sectors *increased* the marginal costs of entrepreneurial risk-bearing; in Germany, however, an intricately interleaved business structure, the servicing of the great banks, and high-quality scientific support worked to reduce these costs.

Until these possibilities are more fully explored, preferably in detailed comparative exercises run over rather small sets of matched countries, there will be no entirely convincing model of entrepreneurial behaviour. In a sense, we know too much about ideal-type entrepreneurs and too little about the socio-economic landscapes they inhabited. We may suspect that 'the central figure in economic history' does lurk somewhere in these environs, but, as yet, we have studied only his footprints, and in no thorough way the terrain which nourishes and supports him. As direction-indicators, footprints are better than nothing, and not to be thoughtlessly discarded, but they are not as good as maps.

MODELS OF BACKWARDNESS: THE PRIZES AND PENALTIES OF UNDERDEVELOPMENT

In many ways, the device which traces an anatomy of growth, not from the operation of single factors or institutions but from the galvanizing tensions of an entire economic condition, has a superior ring to it. Moreover, where the foregoing models turn out to possess rather low measures of independence – banking developments are controlled by entrepreneurial resources, state administrations by constitutional and social structures, entrepreneurs by social values – the concept of 'growth-inducing backwardness' offers forces sufficiently strong to play a directing role, *controlling* the behaviour patterns of banks, governments, and entrepreneurs. Yet even this interpretation cannot be left unadjusted.

Quantitative testing, comparing the level of backwardness (defined mainly by levels of *per capita* income and labour shares in agriculture) with the date and speed of the industrial acceleration has broadly confirmed Gerschenkron's expectation that the speed of industrial development rises in step with the level of deprivation from which industry is escaping. For at least four of the continental powers, over a sample composed of France, Germany, Italy, and Russia, the higher measures of backwardness correlated strongly with both the lateness and the rapidity of the manufacturing surge.[87] However, the limitations of this group are obvious: the inclusion of Italy as a country experiencing a 'great spurt' may be questioned and the exclusion of powers such as Austria-Hungary and Spain for which the 'great spurt' was a great deal more than questionable merely demonstrates the extremely narrow range of countries upon which the backwardness model can be deployed. Even amidst the somewhat wider sample of the continental great powers the examples of Austria-Hungary and Spain suggest that certain types of backwardness may contain more growth-frustrating than growth-inducing forces, and that the resulting pattern of advance may offer a hesitant and spasmodic alternative to the powerful, though equally unbalanced, onrush of the 'spurting' economy. As so often, the experience of backwardness appears more various than the neatly designed model can readily accommodate.

There are also more uniform effects with which it has little affinity. The most important result to emerge from Barsby's statistical evaluation of the Gerschenkron hypothesis concerns its emphasis upon the connexion between the escape from backwardness and the selection of capital goods industries as the vehicles of escape. Although the sample countries display the anticipated correlation between backwardness and the *size* of the producer goods sector, they signally fail to display a match between measures of backwardness and *speed of expansion* in the producer goods sector (see Table 6.3). It seems that an early developer like Germany can generate very high growth rates in capital goods output while late developers like Russia or Italy may experience rather modest progress in this area. All that may be allowed to the backwardness model is the generalization that, the later an economy's start on industrialization, the larger will be the capital goods share *with which it will start*. But this possesses critically important implications. Firstly, it establishes that the backward country is capable of sustaining a *gradual* assimilation of the heavy technologies in the phase *before* take-off, and, that, in consequence its subsequent industrialization may come about as 'a continuation of a trend of absorption . . . established in the past'.[88] This argument clearly works to mix an element of gradualistic growth into the backwardness model and to reduce its heavy emphasis upon discontinuity in economic performance. National examples like the Austro-Hungarian and Spanish, as well as the Russian and Italian, might benefit from this amendment in interpretation. Secondly, Barsby's results are consistent with the hypothesis that the association between the backward economy and producer goods industries may be fixed less by any universal logistic of growth than by simple chronology. Economies industrializing in a period when world technology was biased towards capital goods processes will – like Germany in the second third of the last century – reflect this bias in their own technological 'mix'; during the industrial surge this 'mix' is therefore unlikely to be diluted by rapid advance in the lighter technologies. But, for still later developers, this will not hold true: in subsequent time periods, the blend of world technological best practice will incorporate new elements and become more variegated, and although prior absorption of technology by backward economies may have led to the gradual accumulation of large producer industry shares, new possibilities in other sectors will deflate the rate of growth in the capital goods sector during the phase of industrial acceleration; in the absence of strict planning controls, some dilution of the heavy technology 'mix' is probably unavoidable. Beyond a certain point, therefore, backwardness need not correlate with any particular style or content of industrial advance.

Table 6.3   Share of producer goods industries in total industrial output (%)

	I		II		III		Rate of change pa. (II/III)	Attributed Backwardness rank
	Share	Date	Share	Date	Share	Date		
France	11.0	1829	10.8	1839	10.7	1849	−0.1	1
Germany	7.0	1850	11.0	1860	17.0	1870	+4.5	2
Russia	28.0	1884	32.1	1894	36.9	1904	+1.4	3
Italy	35.0	1896	40.3	1906	47.0	1916	+1.5	4

Notes: All dates in col. I are estimated
Source: Barsby (1969), Table 2, p. 455; Table 5, p. 457; Table 9, p. 460

Perhaps the major shortcoming of the backwardness model is its failure accurately to describe the extreme sensitivity to time and circumstance displayed by the concepts of medium backwardness and pronounced backwardness. The flaws which permit gradual growth and technological 'dilution' to escape the model follow from its lack of any adequate time dimension. In fact, however, its specification of the characteristics of medium backwardness and pronounced backwardness are likely to hold true only at very particular points in world economic development. This criticism is capable of wide application. The efficient operation of the growth-leading investment bank, supposedly the classic institution of medium backwardness, in reality depends upon a very delicate balance of entrepreneurial development and credit shortage which cannot frequently occur. Similarly, the growth 'advantages' of pronounced backwardness will retain force only when the latecomer's pursuit of industrialization can be executed *prior* to the operation of modern growth impediments such as refractory labour unions or obsolescence in social overheads. A good instance of the last point is provided by the railway networks of nineteenth-century underdeveloped economies; often laid down decades before industrialization began, they were in no fit state to support it when, eventually, it did arrive. If development materializes still later than this – in an early-twentieth-century context, for example – not only will these same frictional forces come into play, but they will be qualified in their turn by technological characteristics which will cause further deviations from the model: the availability of electric power to the countries industrializing at the very end of this period, for instance, considerably modified the latecomer's dependence on large-scale plant and gave the small workshop a renewed role to play in development. It may well be true that Gerschenkron's 'advantages of backwardness' apply only to industrial activity within a highly select time span and are subject to diminishing returns outside that span. This is particularly true of the contribution made to development by the state. Here Supple has advanced the interesting proposition that, during Europe's mercantilist phase, the prevailing level of backwardness worked to stifle, rather than to activate, effective state management of economic affairs: 'the "direct action" policies of the eighteenth century', he writes, 'were *premature* until a more appropriate environment for directly productive activity had evolved'.[89] Yet at the opposite end of the time scale for European industrialization, the late developers encountered an 'appropriate environment' of very limited duration, bounded on one side by backwardness itself, and, on the other, by diminishing returns to the 'advantages of backwardness'. This favourable environment, then, is less a historical constant, available to backward economies at any time, than a special historical moment to be exploited only by those few economies equipped to derive benefit from it. It is an easy matter to set a time boundary at its far extent, perhaps around 1900. By this time the average context for economic underdevelopment would be likely to contain many of the modern growth obstacles, together with a dualistic schism of accumulating seriousness, and, for good measure, perhaps a colonial inheritance of confused values and overheated national ambitions. In this landscape, the already limited economic armoury of the state – and even its extended armoury after 1920 – would make of the battle for growth less an elegant *coup de main* than a long and arduous infiltration.

Once a certain point in world industrialization, and in the backwardness of the tardiest latecomers, is passed, it is probable that the 'disadvantages of backwardness' increase in step with the level of deprivation more powerfully than do the matching 'advantages'. Occasionally, Gerschenkron displayed an awareness of this possibility, recognizing the growth obstacles formed by 'sinister' social tensions or medically induced population growth where industrialization has been long postponed[90] and imagining the logistic problems, 'should it become clear that *diminished advantages* of backwardness are coupled with *increased disadvantages* of delayed economic development'.[91] However, it is likely that the degree to which the developers of the pre-1914 world were afflicted by these difficulties has been underrated; and at no point has any scheme of backwardness disadvantages been presented as a pair for the more celebrated apparatus of backwardness advantages.

Nevertheless, it is possible to delineate the rudiments of an alternative model of pronounced backwardness, emphasizing not the developmental but the restraining characteristics of that economic state, and meant not to substitute for, but to supplement and partly to modify, Gerschenkron's formulation:

(a) The greater the backwardness, the more likely is the spurt to be retarded by the developer's absorption, alongside its advanced technology, of the constraints embodied in advanced industrial systems (high wage expectations, labour unrest, inherited obsolescence, even, in some circumstances, low death rates). Clearly, it is a mistake to hold that only the positive elements in economic growth are subject to the diffusion process.

(b) The greater the backwardness, the more likely is the developing economy to incorporate portions of the currently fashionable technology which may have very little to do with capital goods, and thus less to do with rapid spurts of growth.

(c) The greater the backwardness, the greater the likelihood of geographically unbalanced or sectoral growth, leaving important regions untouched by modernization. Dualism will result and will intensify. Gerschenkron's belief that agriculture will play little part in the growth process of backward economies may be converted into this more pessimistic valuation as huge primary sectors remain resistant both to autonomous development and to official rescue programmes.

(d) The greater the backwardness, the more likely is the state to encounter problems which it lacks the equipment or the expertise to solve.

Although some advantages of backwardness will survive, this model will apply with progressive force once the highly specialized stage of medium backwardness is passed and remaining latecomers move forward into a new generation of obstacles. Even models of backwardness, perhaps the most comprehensive we have encountered, can thus be made to cut in more than one direction.

CONCLUSION

The models and assumptions employed in the study of European economic history emerge at the end as rough instruments; they are signposts rather than micrometers, giving the approximate directions rather than the exact calibrations of growth potential and performance. Even though the indications that they provide may lead us to suspect that the most basic reasons for the industrial divergences between nations are entrepreneurial ones, there is, as yet, no satisfactory means of verifying this suspicion. The lack of finish in the design of these models is unsurprising given the methods most often employed in their formulation: in many cases explanatory systems purporting to describe the general economic experience of nations are in fact deduced from the characteristics of very few, and sometimes single, cases – as the backwardness model was generalized largely from Russian materials, the resource model initially from British, the banking model from German, and the 'social-value' model (in historical practice) mainly from French. Of course, this need not necessarily constitute any vital deficiency. Gerschenkron long emphasized that the proper investigative procedure with regard to any explanatory model consists of an attempt to 'discover the limits of its applicability and . . . to discard it when those limits have been ascertained';[92] thus the excessively constricted model would simply succumb to testing, and those with narrow origins but wider relevance would gain in persuasive power under testing. In reality, however, it may well be that many of the modelled systems we are offered are so derived that, from the start, they diverge from more instances than they resemble; it is merely that the process of ascertaining this fact, based as it is upon the painstaking accumulation of detail and insight, is intrinsically more time-consuming than the work of model-designing. Even the most frail of constructs, therefore, may endure for some time before sufficient data are amassed to delimit its proper sphere of influence. Moreover, the process of discarding used models is described more readily than it is enacted: for some unclear reason, the spectacle of eminent scholars delivering their ingenious,

425

provocative, but in the end unsatisfactory, creations to the scrapyard is so uncommon as to invite disbelief. The more usual reaction to any sustained bout of critical testing is a doughty defence conducted upon the letter of the original.

An alternative procedure is required which will combine specificity with range, avoiding both the excessive inflation of microscopic characteristics and the individualized anatomization of unique instances. One answer might lie in comparative international analysis conducted under rather rigorous controls, that is across quite small 'sets' of matched and similar national cases – small 'sets' in order to retain validity within the generalizations, similar cases in order to preserve administrative coherence. The aim would be to distinguish significant convergences and divergences within the sets and to establish covering rules specific to each set. Comparison of the rule systems between sets would follow as a second stage. The virtue lies in the accumulative construction of broader claims from matched, detailed, and catalogued cases, rather than from the more or less random application of a model of unspecified pedigree to each and any national instance, which passes for the common form. Careful comparison of bureaucratic types, such as the models of state intervention badly need, trans-national description of the socio-economic conditions favourable to capitalistic growth, such as the entrepreneurial models still lack, would fit readily into this framework. And since economic historians already employ a kind of informal hierarchy of national groups – Britain and America; Britain and Germany; Germany and France; Russia and Japan; Austro-Hungary, Italy, and Spain – there should be little trouble in composing suitable sets; indeed merely to give systematic operational description to those international comparisons which are casual commonplaces of the vocabulary of European economic history, employed usually at chance or to illuminate a particular point, would advance inquiry further than any single model has yet been able to do. We require not further floods of detail but the application of analytical tools to manageable samples and the improvement of the analytical tools by controlled grinding on the comparative wheel.

NOTES AND REFERENCES

Full publication details are provided in the bibliography.
1. Bairoch (1973) p. 454.
2. Jones and Woolf (eds) (1969), pp. 1–4.
3. Hunt (1974), pp. 311–31.
4. Metzer (1974), p. 549.
5. Rostow (ed.) (1963), p. 434.
6. Kindleberger (1964), p. 210.
7. Jones and Woolf (eds) (1969), p. 6.
8. Dovring (1966), pp. 608–17.
9. Singer in Rostow (ed.) (1963), p. 427 (my italics).
10. Collins in Jones and Woolf (eds) (1969), pp. 60–94.

11. Collins, *op. cit.*, p. 87.
12. Cf. Dovring (1966), p. 671. 'Those who foretold rapid industrialization of agriculture in the late nineteenth century had miscalculated the magnitude of the *industrial* tasks involved' (my emphasis).
13. Bairoch (1973), pp. 460, 470–1.
14. *Ibid.*, p. 475 (my italics).
15. See, for instance, Chambers and Mingay (1966) or Jones (1964).
16. Morineau puts the important adjustments in yields in the *second* half of the nineteenth century; Dovring places the effective consolidation of French peasant holdings in the twentieth century. Morineau (1968); Dovring (1966), pp. 629–30.
17. Singer in Rostow (ed.) (1963), p. 427.
18. Collins (1969), p. 70.
19. Boserup (1963), pp. 202–3.
20. Jones and Woolf (eds) (1969), p. 8.
21. Kindleberger (1964), p. 265.
22. *Ibid.*, pp. 267–8.
23. Hirschman (1966), pp. 121–3.
24. Gordon (1973), p. 108.
25. Hirschman (1966), p. 25.
26. Fisher and Ridker (1973), p. 82.
27. Rosenberg (1973), p. 111.
28. *Ibid.*, p. 111.
29. Eversley in Glass and Eversley (eds) (1965), p. 66.
30. Kindleberger (1964), p. 86.
31. Eversley (1965), pp. 63–5.
32. Leibenstein (1963), pp. 174–81; see also *idem* (1957), Ch. 10.
33. Eversley (1965), p. 58.
34. Hanjal (1965), pp. 101–40.
35. Spengler (1972), pp. 96–8.
36. Eversley (1965), p. 66.
37. Heer in Glass and Revelle (eds) (1972), pp. 103–10.
38. Hirschman (1966), p. 177.
39. Peacock and Wiseman (1967); Andic and Veverka (1964).
40. Rostow (ed.) (1963), p. 409.
41. Glass in Glass and Eversley (1972), p. 2; cf. Carlsson (1966), pp. 149–74.
42. Kindleberger (1964), p. 87.
43. Good (1971), p. 846 (my emphasis).
44. *Ibid.*, pp. 849–50.
45. Gille (1973), p. 256.
46. Tortella (1972), pp. 95–8; Gille (1973), p. 294.
47. Rudolph (1972), p. 28.
48. Gille (1973), pp. 278–84.
49. *Ibid.*, pp. 283–4.
50. *Ibid.*, pp. 285–7.
51. See, for example, Aitken (ed.) (1959).
52. See, for example, Pollard (1973).
53. Milward reviewing Henderson (1975) in *The Times Higher Education Supplement*, 2.1.1976.
54. Cohen in Cameron (ed.) (1972), p. 64 and fn.

55. Supple (1973), pp. 301, 306–7, 351 (my italics).
56. Here the terms 'autonomous' and 'induced' are used to describe the degree of state direction of the economy; in population studies the same terms are used to describe the degree to which demographic expansion is controlled by industrial expansion. For the Hozelitz hypothesis, see his contribution to Aitken (ed.) (1959), pp. 325–49.
57. Downs (1957), pp. 135–50.
58. There will obviously be operational connexions between economic and political backwardness. Just what they are is the reverse of obvious.
59. Lieberson (1971).
60. Kahan (1968), p. 23.
61. Ibid., p. 19 (my italics).
62. Gerschenkron (1969), pp. 3–4.
63. Trebilcock (1971), pp. 446–8.
64. Hirschman (1966), p. 166.
65. Eisenstadt (1972); see also idem (1963), Ch. 10, esp. pp. 291–2.
66. Gerschenkron (1969), p. 8.
67. Ibid., pp. 13–16.
68. Schmoller (1902); II, p. 353.
69. Gerschenkron (1969), p. 15.
70. Ibid., pp. 16–17.
71. Easterbrook (1965), p. 70.
72. Cole (1965), p. 37.
73. Ibid., p. 33.
74. Baumol (1968), pp. 67–8.
75. Jenks (1965), p. 80.
76. Cole (1965), p. 87.
77. Baumol (1968), pp. 65, 67 (my emphasis).
78. Leibenstein (1968), p. 73 (my emphasis).
79. Abramovitz and David (1973), pp. 432, 433.
80. Ibid., p. 438.
81. Easterbrook (1965), p. 69.
82. Aitken (1965), p. 117.
83. Ibid., p. 118.
84. Easterbrook (1965), pp. 71–5.
85. Leibenstein (1968), p. 81.
86. Aitken (1965), p. 117.
87. Barsby (1969), pp. 455–6. Here backwardness was defined by date of industrialization and labour share in agriculture. Per capita income measures of backwardness yielded no significant results.
88. Ibid., p. 461.
89. Supple (1973), p. 316 (my italics).
90. Gerschenkron (1962), pp. 27–8.
91. Ibid., p. 187.
92. Gerschenkron (1968), p. 46.

CHAPTER SEVEN

Statistics and Structures

Table 7.1 Coefficients and ranks of backwardness (measured by *per capita* income, share of labour in agriculture and the date of the industrial spurt)

Country	Income coefficient	Rank	Agricultural labour coefficient	Rank	Date of spurt	Rank
	I		*II*		*III*	
England	100	1	100	1	1780	1
France	229	4	244	2	1829	2
Germany	182	3	266	3	1850	3
Austria	311[a]	5	447	4	1880	4
Russia	338	6	739	8	1884	5
Italy	427	7	500	5	1896	6
Hungary	617[b]	8	731	7	as at 1910	7 =
Spain	127[c]	2	659	6	as at 1910	7 =

[a] Territory of contemporary Austria for 1911–13. But note that the coefficient for Austria-Hungary in 1874 was 345. Data of a more exact comparability is wanting.
[b] Territory of contemporary Hungary, 1911–13.
[c] 1911–13.

Sources: Abstracted and amended from Barsby (1969), Table 2, p. 455. Estimates for Austria, Hungary, and Spain were added to Barsby's own sample and were calculated, following his methodology (p. 454) viz.:

$$\frac{\text{British per capita income at date } x}{\text{Backward economy per capita income at date } x} \times 100$$

for income coefficient and

$$\frac{\text{Backward economy agricultural labour share at date } x}{\text{British agricultural labour share at date } x} \times 100$$

for the agricultural labour coefficient. Data for income coefficients for Austria, Hungary, and Spain calculated from Clark (1957), pp. 99, 138–9, 151, 180. Data for agricultural labour coefficients from Mitchell (1975), pp. 153–63.

Observations: The degree of relative backwardness is obtained by taking the ratios of *per capita* income and agricultural labour share between the selected follower economy and the pioneer economy of England on the eve of the industrial acceleration of the former. The coefficients rise in value with the degree of backwardness.

Note that Barsby selects a mediumly early date for the commencement of the French spurt.

With the exception of the aberrational income coefficient for Spain, the resulting rankings are broadly consistent with the structure employed in the foregoing chapters

Note particularly the creditable performance of Austria and the enormous dead-weight exerted by Russian agriculture.

Table 7.2   Indices of manufacturing output for dates ten and twenty years after the commencement of the spurt.

Country	Date	10-year index	Rank	20-year index	Rank
Britain	1780	145	4	195	4
France	1829	141	2	180	1
Germany	1850	143	3	189	2
Austria	1880	134	1	190	3
Russia	1884	172	5	297	6
Italy	1896	185	6	256	5

Sources: For all countries except Britain and Austria the figures are from Barsby (1969), Table 3, p. 456. Data added for Austria calculated from Mitchell (1973), p. 768–9. Data for Britain derived from Hoffmann (1955), Table 54, p. 331.

Observations: Barsby uses data of this type to test the proposition that the greater the relative backwardness of a country, the more sudden and rapid was the growth of industrial output. The procedure is to correlate relative backwardness as measured by the three methods displayed in Table 7.1 against industrial growth performance as measured in Table 7.2. Barsby found that the proposition was broadly correct, but the strength of the correlation depended upon the manner in which backwardness was defined. In Barsby's sample there turned out to be no significant relationship between relative backwardness, as measured by the level of *per capita* income, and the rate of manufacturing growth over the spurt period. In the sample shown above that relationship (evaluated by the Spearman *r* coefficient) is even weaker. But if the shares of agriculture or the lateness of the spurt are used as indicators of backwardness, the correlation becomes more definite, both for the Barsby sample and for this sample. Here, however, the correlation is still far from emphatic. Low rankings, of course, indicate relatively gradual growth over the spurt period and, therefore, *should* attach to the less backward economies.

The features which disturb the correlation – and which make generally important points about the growth patterns of the economies involved – are primarily: (a) the unseasonably rapid thrust of the early starter, Britain, over the spurt period; (b) the suppressed performance of late starter, Austria, over the first ten years of its industrial acceleration. Neither of these economies are included in the Barsby sample.

However, two points emerge: (1) the proposition that lateness of development is associated with rapidity of development holds, up to a point. But the doubts about the vitality of some late developers, discussed in the text, here find some statistical corroboration; (2) lateness of spurt or agricultural labour coefficients are the most efficient indicators of backwardness and will consequently be employed in later tables where a guide to the 'anticipated level of backwardness' is required.

In relation to the measure of the *anticipated* level of backwardness, however, three problems arise. Firstly, Barsby's most contentious choice of date for the spurt period concerns France, and thus the most crucial issue of the ranking as between France and Germany. Secondly, it will often prove necessary to gauge the relative backwardness of economies not at the commencement of the spurts but at the end of the period, in the vicinity of 1914. Thirdly, it is possible that the backwardness rankings within this sample of economies may vary over time due to unusually energetic or unusually lethargic performance by individual members. As it happens, the only pronounced instance of this kind within this set of countries again concerns the important matter of the relative placings allocated to France and Germany.

On two grounds an adjustment to the rankings given in Table 7.1 is required:
(a) Many observers prefer to place the commencement of the French acceleration not around 1830 but around 1850, that is, contemporaneously with the German acceleration.
(b) If the agricultural labour ratios are recalculated for a date as near as possible to 1914, the rankings given in Table 7.2a are achieved.

Table 7.2a   Revised rankings for 'anticipated levels of backwardness'

Country	Date of spurt	Rank	Agricultural labour coefficient c. 1914	Rank	Overall rank
England/UK	1780	1	100	1	1
France	1850	2=	468	3	2=
Germany	1850	2=	421	2	2=
Austria	1880	4	650	5	4
Russia	1884	5	680	7	6
Italy	1896	6	633	4	5
Hungary	as at 1910	7=	731	8	8
Spain	as at 1910	7=	659	6	7

Table 7.3   Indices of industrial output by value, 1855–1913

	UK	France	Germany	Austria	Russia	Italy
1855–64	100	100	100	–	100	100
1865–74	134	116	161	–	139	124
1875–84	166	138	220	100	236	145
1885–94	193	160	302	134	399	158
1895–1904	233	194	459	190	749	187
1905–13	273	235	666	256	1030	289
Rank in 1905–13	2	1	4	n.a.[b]	5	3
Anticipated rank[a]	1	2=	2=	4	6	5

[a] Derived from Tables 7.2a.
[b] Not applicable due to different date of base.

Source: Calculated from Mitchell (1973), pp. 768–9.

Observations: Note that the ranks for 1905–13 are listed from the lowest to the highest index figures. Early starting economies, having begun well before 1855–64 could be expected to produce the lowest index figures for 1905–13 (assuming an index base of 1855–64). Follower economies starting from low absolute bases of production around or near the period 1855–64 could be expected to have high index figures by 1905–13. In fact, however, France produces a lower value than Britain, testifying to the sluggish French performance of the nineteenth century. Italy, too, displays a surprisingly low figure for a late-starting economy suggesting again that the 'spurt' of 1896–1908 was relatively suppressed. Austria does rather better than Italy, allowing for its later base year, and neither Italy nor Austria fare as well as Germany or Russia, both of which show the high terminal values expected from late developers. In fact, of course, Germany was not a late-developing economy, and therefore displays an extraordinarily high index value, and testifies to a remarkably *sustained* pattern of high growth rates, for a country which commenced its industrialization among the 'second generation' follower economies of the mid-nineteenth century.

For the sake of completeness, annual average growth rates of industrial output are also provided in Table 7.3a. These data again reveal the rather modest performance of Italy (1880–1900 only) and Austria, although, on these figures, Italy does better than Austria over the (approximately) twenty-year periods. Germany again displays notably high growth rates.

431

Table 7.3a Annual rates of growth in industrial output

	UK	France	Germany	Austria	Russia	Italy	World
1860–80	2.4	2.4	2.7	–	–	–	3.2
1880–1900	1.7	2.4	5.3	4.3[a]	6.4	4.5	4.0
1900–13	2.2	3.7	4.4	2.7[b]	4.8	5.6	4.2
Rank in							
1880–1900	1	2	5	3	6	4	
Rank in							
1900–13	1	3	4	2	5	6	
Anticipated							
rank	1	2=	2=	4	6	5	

[a] 1880–96; [b] 1896–1913.

Sources: All except Austria from Patel (1963), p. 72.
Austrian data from Good (1974), p. 74.
Anticipated (backwardness) rank from Table 7.2a.

Table 7.4 Proportion of national product by sector of origin

Country	Date	Agriculture	Industry	Construction	Transport	Commerce
UK	1788	40	21	–		12
	1821	26	32	–		16
	1850	21	35	–		19
	1861	18	38	–		20
	1871	15	40	–		23
	1881	11	40	–		24
	1891	9	41	–		24
	1901	7	43	–		25
	1907	6	34	4	10	19

Anticipated backwardness rank: 1
Ranking by size of agricultural sector c. 1910: 1

France	1815	51	22	–	–	7
	1847	45	29	–	–	7
	1859	45	30	–	–	7
	1872	43	30	–	–	7
	1882	41	30	–	–	7
	1892	37	32	–	–	7
	1909	35	36	–	–	7

Anticipated backwardness rank: 2=
Ranking by size of agricultural sector c. 1910: 3

Table 7.4   (Cont.)

Country	Date	Agriculture	Industry	Construction	Transport	Commerce
Germany	1850	47	21	–	1	7
	1860	45	23	–	1	8
	1870	40	28	–	5	8
	1880	36	32	–	3	8
	1890	33	37	–	4	8
	1900	30	40	–	5	9
	1910	25	43	–	6	9

Anticipated backwardness rank   2=
Ranking by size of agricultural sector c. 1910:   2

Russia	1880	66–71	14–15		14–20	
	1900	60–63	24–26		11–16	
	1913	58–60	28–30		10–14	

Anticipated backwardness rank: 5+
Ranking by size of agricultural sector c. 1910:   7

Italy	1861	57	19	3	2	15
	1870	57	18	2	2	15
	1880	57	15	2	3	16
	1890	51	17	3	4	17
	1900	51	17	2	4	16
	1910	42	22	3	6	17

Anticipated backwardness rank: 4+
Ranking by size of agricultural sector c. 1910:   5

| Hungary | 1899–1901 | 43 | 20 | – | 8 | 6 |
| | 1911–13 | 44 | 24 | – | 8 | 6 |

Anticipated backwardness rank: 7+
Ranking by size of agricultural sector c. 1910:   6

| Spain | 1914 | 38 | 26 | – | – | – |

Anticipated backwardness rank: 6+
Ranking by size of agricultural sector c. 1910:   4

Note: Anticipated backwardness rankings from Table 7.2a. Since Austria was included in the original sample, but, for data reasons cannot be included here, an intentional margin of variation is given to the backwardness rankings greater than 4.

Sources: For all countries except Russia and Spain, Mitchell (1975), pp. 799–804. For Russia, Goldsmith (1961). For Spain, Nadal (1973), p. 616.

Observations: Modern economic growth characteristically includes rapid shifts in the sector shares of agriculture, industry, and services. Classically, the agricultural share shrinks from a pre-modern level of 50–65 per cent to a minimum of 10–20 per cent of total product, while the industrial share expands classically from a pre-modern level of 20–30 per cent to a maximum of 40–50 per cent. All the sample economies display starting levels close to these prototypes. But in the subsequent redistribution of sector shares, there is wide variety. Britain and Germany execute patterns which are near to the characteristic profile. In Germany, however, although the industrial share develops strongly, the rural proportion, in conformity with the socio-economic complexion of the *Kaiserreich*, remains somewhat high and there is little of the movement from the manufacturing towards the service sector which is a character-mark of the mature economy – and which, by 1907, is appearing in the UK. In France, again, the pace is dragging: the decline in the agricultural, and advance in the industrial, share are notably slow for a fairly early developer. In Italy and Russia, both late developers, the redistribution is again notably incomplete by 1913. Russia is unique in the enormous preponderance of agriculture, massive even by the standards of the superficially comparable estate–peasant system of its cereal-farming East European colleague, Hungary.

Table 7.5 Index of level of agricultural development by productivity (100 = net annual production of 10 m. vegetable-based calories per male worker in agriculture)

	1810	1840	1860	1880	1900	Rank in 1900	Anticipated rank
UK	140	175	200	235	225	1	1
France	70	115	145	140	155	3	2=
Germany	–	75	105	145	220	2	2=
Austria	–	75	85	100	110	4	4
Russia	–	70	75	70	90	5	6
Italy	–	40	50	60	60	7	5
Spain	–	–	110	70	75	6	7

Source: Bairoch (1973), p. 472. Anticipated backwardness rankings from Table 7.2a.

Table 7.5a Percentage increase in agricultural productivity (final product per male agricultural worker)

		% change
UK	1841–1901	+ 45
France	1859–1909	+ 21
Germany	1840–1900	+ 190
Austria	1840–1900	+ 45
Russia	1840–1900	+ 30
Italy	1840–1900	+ 50

Sources: Bairoch (1973), p. 484 for all except UK and France. Estimates for UK and France calculated from Mitchell (1975), pp. 155, 163, 782–804.

Table 7.5b   Agricultural workforce as percentage of total active population

			Rank around 1900	Anticipated rank
UK	1841 : 22	1901 : 9[a]	1	1
France	1866 : 52	1901 : 43	3	2=
Germany	1871 : 45	1895 : 36	2	2=
Austria	1869 : 65[a]	1900 : 60[a]	5	4
Russia	1890 : 87	1910 : 86	8	6
Italy	1850 : 70	1901 : 59	4	5
Spain	1860 : 66[a]	1900 : 68[a]	7	7
Hungary	1869 : 70[a]	1910 : 64[a]	6	8
(Silesia-Bohemia	1890 : 50	1900 : 38)		

Sources: All except those marked [a] from Dovring (1969), pp. 604–9ff. [a] Calculated from Mitchell (1975), pp. 153–63. Anticipated backwardness rank from Table 7.2a.

Table 7.5c   Application of chemical fertilizer: 1910–13 (kg per hectare) of Arable Land

UK	28	Italy	14	Denmark	?5
France	?0	Spain	4	Netherlands	164
Germany	50	Belgium	69		

Source: Dovring, (1969), p. 656.

Observations: As one might expect from a comparison of Tables 7.2a and 7 5b, the backwardness rankings derived from the shares of agricultural population in the total active community accord fairly closely with the 'anticipated' backwardness rankings. There is one notable exception: the huge numerical predominance of the Russian peasant horde manages to reverse the expected ranking even against the rival prairie system of the Magyar plains. This makes it somewhat surprising that the Russian productivity performance (Tables 7.5 and 7.5a) was as healthy even as it was – though this surprise must be partly tempered by recognition of the low level of the starting point in 1840. Tempering, however, will not eliminate the *relative* strength of Russian productivity in 1840 – at least in terms of Bairoch's vegetable-based calories and at least in comparison with the French results for 1810 or the pathetically modest Italian ones for 1840. This, of course, reflects more upon the feebleness of the French record – note, particularly, the poor productivity increment of 1859–1909 – and upon the special nature of the Italian sickness, largely expressed here by the relentless *accadie* of the southern sector, rather than upon any native vigour in the Russian countryside. Austria again produces a surprisingly 'mature' profile with a starting point in productivity equal to the German and a creditable finishing point. But the outstanding success story once more is Germany, building upon that merely average starting point to produce, between 1860 and 1900, the most remarkable agricultural dash to be found among the nineteenth-century continental powers – remarkable, that is, as long as efficiency of output alone is considered and commercial content is not. Table 7.5c gives a good part of the explanation: Germany applied science not only to industry but also to agriculture, achieving fertilizer inputs which were exceeded by no other large country. Only a few small nations, suffering physical shortages of cultivable land, had a better record.

Generally, the more dismissive valuations of the 'agricultural prerequisite' are well sustained. There is a little upward flexibility in these figures for French productivity 1810–40 and for Austrian 1840–80, but almost none for Russia 1840–80, while for Spain there is an actual decline after 1860. The best performance is produced by a country strongly launched upon industrialization (after 1850), and, in no small part, because of that industrialization. The importance of the 'industrial prerequisite' for the 'agricultural revolution' is provocatively displayed.

THE INDUSTRIALIZATION OF THE CONTINENTAL POWERS

Table 7.6 Capital formation as a proportion of National Product: Gross National and Net National Capital Formation (CF) as % GNP and NNP

UK

	GNCF/GNP	NNCF/NNP
1801/11–1821/31	–	7.5
1860–69	11.6	10.0
1870–79	13.4	11.8
1880–89	12.4	10.9
1890–99	11.7	10.1
1900–09	13.3	11.7
1909–14	14.4	13.0

France

	GNCF/GDP[a]	NNCF/NDP[a]
1788–1839	–	3.0
1835–44	17.7	–
1839–52	20.5	8.0
1855–64	–	–
1852–80	19.2	12.1
1865–74	19.8	–
1875–84	–	–
1880–92	–	12.9
1885–94	19.3	–
1892–1902	21.3	12.4
1895–1904	–	–
1902–12	–	12.2
1905–14	21.0	–

Germany

	GNCF/GNP	NNCF/NNP
1851–60	–	8.6
1851–70	14.4	–
1861–70	–	9.7
1871–80	–	13.5
1871–90	21.0	–
1881–90	–	14.0
1891–1900	–	15.4
1891–1913	24.1	–
1901–1913	–	16.5

Italy

	GNCF/GNP	NNCF/NNP
1861–70	7.5	2.4
1871–80	9.6	4.1
1881–90	10.6	5.0
1891–1900	10.9	5.0
1901–10	17.4	11.1
1906–15	15.2	–

Norway

	GNCF/GNP	NNCF/NNP
1880–89	11.1	6.4
1890–99	8.6	3.0
1900–09	8.0	2.2
1905–14	12.2	6.8

USA

	GNCF/GNP	NNCF/NNP
1869–78	20.3	13.4
1879–88	20.6	13.0
1889–98	23.1	13.9
1899–1908	22.8	13.8
1904–13	21.8	12.6

a National product aggregates for France are Gross Domestic and Net Domestic Product.

Sources: GNCF: For UK, Italy, Norway, USA – Kuznets (1961) pp. 58, 69, 80, 92. For Germany, Kuznets (1966). pp. 236–9. For France, calculated from Marcovitch (1966).

NNCF: For UK, Germany, Italy, Norway, USA – Kuznets (1961), pp. 58, 54, 69, 80, 92. For France, Marczewski (1963). p. 121.

Observations: Norway and USA, for which data are available permitting a broad comparability, are included in order to extend the otherwise limited selection of countries for which comparisons are possible.

According to Rostow, the onset of modern economic growth requires an expansion in the share of *net* national product 'productively invested' from below 5 per cent to above 10 per cent. In fact, in the experience of most developing economies before 1914, capital formation did fall within the range of 5–15 per cent NNP. But it is widely accepted that the progression from below 5 per cent to above 10 per cent was very rarely achieved within the short span of twenty to thirty years required for Rostow's 'take-off'. In several important cases (Britain, France, Germany, Norway, USA) the net capital formation proportion had already reached, and, in some cases surpassed, 5 per cent *before* the industrial acceleration occurred; and, often, it then required a fairly extended period from *this* point before the 10 per cent barrier was breached. If the 5/10 per cent 'rule' is taken, as it often is, to imply a need to *double* the capital formation proportion with which take-off is commenced, then it is even more clear from the NNCF/NNP columns that this manoeuvre could not be executed in short order. Within these data, the only case which clearly demonstrates a 'Rostowian' pattern is Italy; and it is quite exceptional both within this sample of countries and within the larger sample investigated by Kuznets.

It also appears that *many* different levels of capital formation were associated with successful industrial development. Within this sample there is a tendency by 1914 for the NNCF/NNP proportions of the more advanced economies to cluster in the range 12–16 per cent. But if the GNCF/GNP proportions are taken, even for this group, the scatter widens to 14–24 per cent. And if a larger selection of six economies with flourishing industrial systems is taken for the two decades before 1914, the range of GNCF/GNP proportions expands further to 9–24 per cent (the six were USA, UK, Japan, Germany, France and Sweden). Given this fact, and also the absence of data for the more backward economies, it is pointless to rank the sample economies in respect of the capital formation proportions. Nevertheless, a number of significant features do emerge:

(a) The relatively economical nature of the investment effort (in relation to national product) required of early industrializing economies like the UK.

(b) The rising 'threshold' price of industrialization for follower economies as time elapses and technology becomes more complex and expensive. This effect is suppressed in the case of Italy (net ratios), again suggesting a relative weakness in the *content* of the industrial surge in this economy. Nor is it yet pronounced in the case of Norway, where the major adjustments to the capital formation proportions lie in the future.

(c) The enormous investment effort of Germany by 1914, producing the highest capital formation proportions of the era, and surpassing even the USA by the end of the period. This investment was heavily concentrated in industrial and infrastructural fixed capital (non-residential construction + canals, roads, railways + equipment accounted for 53 per cent NDCF in 1851–60, 62 per cent NDCF in 1901–13); and it does appear to correlate with the high level of industrial efficiency of this economy. No doubt its size and composition owed something to the strategy of the *Kreditbanken*.

(d) The surprisingly sturdy performance of French gross capital formation, although the figures are only broadly comparable since the aggregates are GCF/GDP. Nevertheless, they are notably high, and are probably influenced by the French leaning towards hefty foreign investment. Even the net proportions (NNCF/NDP) are highly respectable.

Table 7.7 Central government expenditure as proportion of National Product

	UK	France	Germany	Italy	Russia	Hungary	Spain
1845–54	–	9.2	–	–	–	–	–
1850	10.3	–	–	–	–	–	–
1855–64	–	9.4	–	–	–	–	–
1860	10.4	–	–	10.4[b]	–	–	–
1865–74	–	9.4	–	–	–	–	–
1870	7.1	–	8.6[a]	11.9	–	–	–
1875–84	–	12.3	–	–	–	–	–
1880	5.8	–	2.9	10.0	–	–	–
1885–94	–	12.2	–	–	–	–	–
1890	6.0	–	4.5	12.8	–	–	–
1895–1904	–	12.4	–	–	–	–	–
1900	9.4	–	4.5	11.1	28.6	58.7[c]	–
1905–13	–	11.2	–	–	–	–	10.5[c]
1910	7.0	–	5.6	11.3	–	–	11.4
1913	7.1	–	6.2	12.2	28.6	61.1[d]	14.5

[a] 1872; [b] 1862; [c] 1899–1901; [d] 1911–13; [e] 1906.

Sources: All values, with the exception of those for Germany, calculated from Mitchell, (1975), pp. 697–702; 781–90. German values from Andic and Veverka (1964), Table A-7, p. 244. National product aggregates are GNP for all cases except France (GDP) and Hungary (NNP). All underlying data are in current prices.

Table 7.7a Ratios of central government shares in National Product.

	1870	Rank	1913	Rank	Anticipated rank[a]
UK	100	1	100	2	1
France	143	2	165	3	2=
Germany	165	3	87	1	2=
Italy	168	4	172	4	4+
Russia	–	–	403	6	5+
Hungary	–	–	861	7	7+
Spain	–	–	204	5	6+

[a] Derived from Tables 7.2a. The absence of Austria again requires a margin of variation in rankings greater than 4.

Sources: Calculated from Table 7.7, employing Barsby's methodology, as in Table 7.1, for measurement of the performance of backward economies relative to that of the British industrial prototype: viz.

$$\frac{\text{Backward economy government share in GNP at date } x}{\text{British economy government share in GNP at date } x} \times 100$$

Table 7.7b Total government expenditure (central + local) share in National Product

	UK	Germany
1870	9.4	–
1880	10.2	–
1881	–	10.0
1890	8.9	–
1891	–	13.2
1900	14.4	–
1901	–	14.9
1907	–	16.5
1910	12.7	–
1913	–	14.8

Sources: For Britain, Peacock and Wiseman (1967), pp. 37, 42: for Germany, Andic and Veverka, (1964). Table A-5, p. 243. All underlying data in current prices.

Observations: The primary sources of interest are Table 7.7 and Table 7.7a. The main controlling forces upon the share of national product committed to central government expenditure appear to be military precociousness and economic backwardness. The high values for Britain 1850/60 and 1900 and for France and Germany around 1870 owe a good deal to the pressures of war expenditure. But the level of economic sophistication of the subject economy appears to be a more persuasive long-run influence on the state share in GNP. This proportion is notably lower in the countries which commenced industrialization before or around 1850 (UK, France, Germany) than in the countries which commenced industrialization around or after 1880 (Italy, Russia, Hungary, Spain). Gerschenkron's proposition that the degree of state participation in the economy increases with the level of backwardness is roughly substantiated by this result. This is particularly clearly displayed in the ratios for 1913 given in Table 7.7a. The leverage exerted by programmes of state promotion shows up especially vividly in the cases of Russia and Hungary. But central government expenditure is not, of course, the whole story. Germany and the UK, particularly, witnessed considerable public spending *outside* the central government, through provincial state and local government agencies. Even allowing for those disbursements, however (Table 7.7b), the *total* government shares of these two major industrial economies around 1910 remained definitely modest, especially given that the shares of other state administrations would also have expanded if non-central government spending were included, though to a lesser degree. On any reading, the government shares of industrial economies, advanced by the standards of 1913, are dwarfed by the massive public commitments of backward economies such as Russia or Hungary. Noteworthy once more is the modest government share of Germany in 1913, again emphasising the basically free-market complexion of the *Kaiserreich* economy. In this connexion it is worth recording that the rather surprising relationship between Britain and Germany in 1913 (ratios of 100 and 87 for central government alone) is reversed if *total* government expenditure is measured in place of central government spending (giving equivalent ratios of 100 and 117). In either case, however, the relationship is strikingly close.

By contrast, the French government share is high for a 'second-generation' follower economy and begs a comparison rather with the more restrained members of the 'third generation' such as Italy, or, perhaps, Spain. This is consistent with the many contemporary criticisms of 'big government' under the Second Empire and the Third Republic.

Table 7.7c The military share in government spending: total defence as % total government expenditure.

UK		Germany		France		Italy		Russia	
1890	26.7	1881	24.4	1855/64	33.1	1862–66	39.5	1894	29.0
1895	27.5	1891	23.6	1865/74	25.2	1867–71	18.5	1903	24.8
1900	48.0	1901	20.8	1875/84	28.0	1872–76	19.0	1911/13	22.9
1905	26.1	1907	19.2	1885/94	27.2	1877–81	19.7	1913	26.6
1910	27.3	1913	19.7	1895/1904	26.1	1906/07	16.5	1914	35.0
1913	29.9			1905/13	31.6	1909/10	19.5		
						1913/14	30.0		

| Rank at end period | 2 | 1 | 4 | 3 | 5 |
| Anticipated backwardness rank[a] | 1 | 2= | 2= | 4+ | 5+ |

[a] As in previous tables, again allowing for the absence of Austria.

Sources: For UK – calculated from Peacock and Wiseman (1967), Table 3, p. 55 and Table A-15, p. 186.

For France – calculated from Crouzet (1974), pp. 292–3, 305 and Mitchell (1975), pp. 698–700.

For Germany – calculated from Andic and Veverka (1964), Table A-5, p. 243 and A-22, p. 262.

For Italy – Webster (1975), p. 45; Romeo (1959), p. 141.

For Russia – various estimates as in text, Table 4.3, with the addition of an estimate for 1911/13 calculated from Shatsillo (1974), pp. 37–9, 86.

Observations: Clearly the military share in government expenditure is inflated by active engagement in hostilities – the figures for Britain in 1900 (Boer War) and Italy 1862/66 (Wars of Unification) or 1913/14 (Libyan War) fully display this pressure. Preparation for hostilities also acts to swell the military share in some cases (France, 1909–13; Russia 1914) but, in others, the arms race was financed fairly cheaply in terms of the strain on public resources (Germany).

The sample is too small for any strong correlations to emerge, but there is *some* indication that the military share rises with the level of backwardness. For a good part of the period, the proportion is low in the case of advanced Germany and high in the cases of backward Russia and Italy. But imperial commitments also ensure that it is on the high side in the case of advanced Britain. And the consistently lavish French disbursements on the military certainly act to disturb the pattern further, although, once more, these extravagant appetites conform with the view that the government bulked uncomfortably large within the French economy. By 1913 there is really very little in the differences between the French, British, and Italian military shares, despite the very different economic standing of these countries. There is some irony in the modest military commitment of 'belligerent' Germany when set against the more determined programmes of the Entente powers.

The outcome is some rather qualified support for the view that economically backward states tend also to be politically backward, and thus to exhibit a leaning towards authoritarian structures with pronounced military castes. Equally, however, advanced economic (and political) systems may generate such commercial ramifications that they take aboard pronounced colonial obligations – and then, necessarily, the expensive defence apparatus that these entail.

THE INDUSTRIALIZATION OF THE CONTINENTAL POWERS

Table 7.8 Central government revenue as proportion of National Product.

	UK	France	Germany	Italy	Russia	Hungary	Spain
1845–54	–	7.6	–	–	–	–	–
1850	10.6	–	–	–	–	–	–
1855–64	–	7.7	–	–	–	–	–
1860	10.0	–	–	5.3[b]	–	–	–
1865–74	–	7.9	–	–	–	–	–
1870	7.1	–	1.1[a]	8.6	–	–	–
1875–84	–	10.7	–	–	–	–	–
1880	5.9	–	1.6	9.7	–	–	–
1885–94	–	11.7	–	–	–	–	–
1890	6.3	–	2.9	11.9	–	–	–
1895–1904	–	12.4	–	–	–	–	–
1900	6.8	–	2.7	11.2	25.9	56.4[c]	–
1905–13	–	11.3	–	–	–	–	11.4[e]
1910	8.5	–	3.1	10.4	–	–	10.7
1913	7.3	–	3.3	9.9	28.9	53.5[d]	12.1
Rank in 1913	2	4	1	3	6	7	5
Anticipated backwardness Rank[f]	1	2 =	2 =	4 +	5 +	7 +	6 +

[a] 1872; [b] 1862; [c] 1899–1901; [d] 1911–13; [e] 1906;
[f] as in previous tables, again allowing for the absence of Austria.

Sources: All values with the exception of those for Germany, calculated from Mitchell (1975), pp. 706–26, 781–90. German GNP values from Andic and Veverka (1964), Table A-5, p. 241. National product aggregates are GNP for all cases except France (GDP) and Hungary (NNP). All underlying data are in current prices.

Observations: Proportions again run roughly with the current of backwardness, rising as the level of economic development falls. This effect is no doubt conditioned by the need to finance the larger government expenditure shares of the more backward economies. The basic profiles are very similar to those shown in Table 7.7 for public spending. Note the rather high proportion of national product claimed by the revenue in France, another indication of the large size and high cost of the French administrative machine.

442

Table 7.9 Railway construction 1890–1913, (kilometres).

Country	Open track 1890	Open track 1913	Rank	Increase	Rank
Russia (incl. Finland)	31,000	62,200	2	31,200	1
Germany	42,900	63,700	1	20,800	2
Austria-Hungary	27,100	46,200	4	19,100	3
France	36,900	51,200	3	14,300	4
Spain	9,900	15,400	7	5,500	5
UK	32,300	37,700	5	5,400	6
Italy	12,900	17,600	6	4,700	7

Source: Miller (1926), p. 214.

Table 7.9a Comparative densities of railway networks, 1913. Length of open track (kilometres) per each 100 square kilometres of territory.

Country	Track Km. per 100 sq. km.	Rank	Area of country (square kilometres)	Rank
Belgium	30	1	188,464	8
UK	12	2=	241,169	7
Germany	12	2=	573,272	3
France	10	4	531,044	4
Austria-Hungary	7	5	674,046	2
Italy	6	6	294,873	6
Spain	3	7	498,900	5
Russia (imperial territory)	1	8	21,226,058	1

Source: Miller (1926), p. 215.

Table 7.9b Comparative densities of European railway networks, 1850–1913 (ratios of railway track in kilometres per square kilometre of territory)

	UK	Germany	France	Italy	Austria-Hungary	Spain	Russia
1850	0.041	–	–	–	0.002	–	–
1860	0.061	–	–	–	0.004	0.003	–
1870	0.089	0.033	0.029	0.022	0.009	0.011	0.001
1880	0.104	0.059	0.043	0.032	0.017	0.015	0.001
1890	0.115	0.075	0.063	0.046	0.023	0.020	0.001
1900	0.125	0.090	0.072	0.056	0.029	0.026	0.003
1910	0.133	0.107	0.076	0.061	0.034	0.029	0.003
1913	0.135	0.111	0.077	0.064	0.034	0.030	0.003
Rank in 1870	1	2	3	4	6	5	7
Rank in 1913	1	2	3	4	5	6	7

Sources: Calculated from Mitchell (1975), pp. 581–4 and Miller (1926), pp. 30–1; 214–5.

Observations: By 1913 the largest countries, Russia, Austria-Hungary, and Germany have the largest railway systems and have made the largest additions over the period 1890–1913 (Table 7.9). However, a more exact measure of the efficiency of the transport service is provided by estimation of railway density in relation to total national area. Here, the economic penalties of the size of nations strongly assert themselves and both Russia and Austria-Hungary score poorly on the scale of railway densities. Russia's disability in this respect, with a land area more than thirty times that of the rival empire of the Habsburgs, is particularly striking. Among the group of very large countries, only Germany is able to combine a big scale of transport industry with a high density; again, the investment effort required to effect this is enormous (Table 7.6). Small countries, like Italy, can produce rather modest construction programmes but achieve creditable densities. It is notable, however, that for late developers like Spain or Italy, the small additions to the transport networks in the period 1890–1913 deny these economies stimulation from the multiplier effects of powerful railway lead sectors at particularly sensitive stages in their careers. Austria-Hungary, in contrast, perhaps because of its military–imperial commitments, as well as its territorial scale, does rather better on this count.
The modest differences between density figures given here and some cited in the text reflect different sources and bases of calculation. They do not affect the issue.

Table 7.10 Ratios of bank density to national population

	England and Wales	France	Prussia	Russia
1750	0.06	–	–	–
1785	0.21	–	–	–
1800	0.48	0.03	–	–
1820	–	–	0.3	–
1840	0.77	0.10	–	–
1850	–	–	0.27	–
1860	–	–	0.34	–
1870	–	0.12	–	–
1914	–	–	–	0.17

Source: Cameron (ed.) (1967), pp. 296–9

Observations: The spread of data from this source is not especially helpful. French bank density is surprisingly low even in 1870, Russian surprisingly high in 1914. As might be expected, the Prussian results are creditable throughout the period 1820–60, but the absence of data for imperial Germany reduces the force of the comparison. Table 6.1 gives a wider spread of perhaps more reliable indicators of bank power (bank assets/GNP ratios); see p. 404.

Table 7.10a Deposits in commercial banks as proportion of GNP

	UK	France	Germany	Russia	Italy
1870	–	–	1.4	–	–
1880	35.7	–	3.0	–	–
1890	42.9	–	6.5	–	–
1900	41.1	–	10.6	8.2	–
1905–13	–	23.4	–	–	–
1910	39.8	–	20.9	–	–
1913	39.6	–	19.4	21.5	6.7
Backwardness ratios 1913[a]	100	169	204	184	595
Rank	1	2	4	3	5

[a] Calculated by Barsby's methodology adapted for bank proportions, i.e.

$$\frac{\text{Bank asset proportion of UK at date } x}{\text{Bank asset proportion of follower economy at date } x} \times 100$$

445

Sources: Calculated from Mitchell (1975), pp. 681–3, 781–9. German GNP from Andic and Veverka (1964), Table A-5, p. 241. Aggregates for France are GDP as before.

Observations: By 1913 France, Russia, and Germany fall in very much the same band, though the comparison must be made with caution due to the GDP aggregate employed for France. With these margins of difference between cases, however, it is unlikely that the difference in aggregate would affect the outcome in rankings. The strong position of Russia by 1913 testifies to the very rapid diffusion of investment banking to the tsarist empire after 1900. And the French position in respect to *deposits* is stronger than one might expect from the data on bank density. It is likely, however, that the deposit proportion bears witness more directly to the *savings* patterns of communities rather than to the investing propensities of bankers. Certainly, the large size of the British deposit proportion belies the aloof policies of British bankers and the rather modest German proportion gives no guide to the enthusiastic industrial involvements of the *Kreditbanken*.

Table 7.11 Literacy: proportion of bridegrooms or military recruits able to write(%)

	England and Wales[a]	France[b]	Prussia[a]	Italy[a]	Russia[b]
1835	–	50	–	–	–
1848	–	60	–	–	–
1850	–	–	–	–	–
1853–55	70	–	90	–	–
1863	–	70	–	–	–
1868–70	80	–	–	–	–
1873	–	80	–	–	–
1878	–	–	–	–	–
1886	90	–	–	50	–
1888	–	–	–	–	–
1890	–	90	–	–	30
1892	–	–	–	–	–
1896	–	–	–	60	–
1901	–	–	–	–	40
1905	–	–	–	–	50
1907	–	–	–	70	60
1919	–	–	–	80	–

[a] Bridegrooms; [b] military recruits.

Source: Adapted from the display of Cipolla's data given in Mitchell (1973), p. 802.

Observations: Again, England, France, and Prussia group together with relatively early achievement, in the period approximately 1850–75, of the 'second threshold' of 80 per cent male literacy, the level required for the high-technology phase of development. The paucity of data for post-unification Germany is especially inconvenient in this field. All countries in this sample, with the exception of Russia, would have passed the 'first threshold' of 40 per cent literacy, the level required for initial industrialization, by 1850–60 – by some margin in the case of England, France, and Prussia, only barely in the case of Italy. Russia's arrival at this point is predictably belated. The actual assessment of literacy achieved by these measures is, of course, tendentious; ability to sign one's name is a highly problematic indicator of ability to do anything else. However, in the absence of anything better, this procedure is something of a convention.

446

Table 7.11a   Proportion of population in primary schools, secondary schools, and universities (%)

Primary schools	UK	France	Germany	Austria	Hungary	Italy	Spain	Russia
1850/51	1.9	9.3	–	8.3	–	–	–	0.7[b]
1860/61	4.1	–	–	–	6.5[c]	4.0	8.0	–
1870/71	5.9	11.7[a]	–	8.4[b]	7.5[d]	6.4	–	2.0[i]
1880/81	11.6	14.3	–	11.0	10.3	6.9	10.6[e]	–
1890/91	13.4	14.6	–	13.3	12.0	–	10.5[f]	–
1900/01	15.0	14.4	15.9	14.2	12.0	8.4	–	–
1910/11	14.9	14.5	15.9	15.9	11.8	9.7	7.7[g]	5.19[j]
Rank c. 1910	3	4	1=	1=	5	6	7	8
Anticipated backwardness rank	1	2=	2=	4	8	5	7	6

Secondary schools:	UK	France	Germany	Austria	Hungary	Italy	Spain	Russia
1850/51	–	0.13	–	0.13	–	–	–	–
1860/61	–	0.15	–	–	0.19[c]	0.06	0.14	0.2
1870/71	–	0.19	–	0.21[e]	0.21[d]	0.13	–	–
1880/81	–	0.23	–	0.30	0.25	0.12	–	–
1890/91	–	0.24	–	0.30	0.24	–	–	–
1900/01	0.05	0.27	–	0.39	0.33	0.28	–	–
1910/11	0.46	0.33	1.56	0.55	0.37	0.47	0.24[i]	0.39[i]
Rank c. 1910	4	7	1	2	6	3	8	5
Anticipated backwardness rank	1	2=	2=	4	8	5	7	6

Universities:							
1850/51	—	—	—	—	0.07	—	—
1860/61	—	0.06	0.03	0.01[c]	—	—	—
1870/71	—	—	0.05	0.02[d]	0.06[b]	—	—
1880/81	—	—	0.04	0.03	0.06	—	—
1890/91	—	0.09[f]	—	0.03	0.07	0.06	—
1900/01	—	—	0.08	0.05	0.09	0.09	—
1910/11	0.07[j]	0.10[i]	0.08	0.07	0.14	0.11	0.07
Rank c. 1910	6=	4	5	6=	1	2=	6=
Anticipated backwardness rank	6	7	5	8	4	2=	1

[a] 1866; [b] 1869; [c] 1857; [d] 1869; [e] 1877; [f] 1887; [g] 1908; [b] 1856; [i] 1885; [j] 1914.

Anticipated backwardness ranks from Table 7.2a.

Sources: Calculated from Mitchell (1975), pp. 19–24, 750–9, with the following exceptions. Data for Russia from Kahan (1971), pp. 366, 369, 372–3. Data for UK from Sanderson (ed.) (1975), p. 242.

Observations: As might be expected, Germany scores heavily in all three sectors. Austria, however, does remarkably well for a third-generation follower economy and even leads the pack in higher education. France and Britain, true to their reputation, score very moderately in primary and secondary education, given their economic status. France, matches Germany closely in the higher education sector, however, and this is consistent with some of the foregoing analysis (see p. 195). Elsewhere, Hungary in primary and secondary education, Italy in secondary, and Spain in university education perform more creditably than their economic rank would suggest. The Russian performance, though predictably weak in primary education, reflects the regime's increasing emphasis on secondary school training towards the end of the period. The British performance in university provision, ranking with the Hungarian and the Russian, is, of course, a saga in its own right.

448

Table 7.11b Proportion of children in age group 5–14 attending primary and secondary schools (%)

	UK	France	Germany	Austria	Hungary	Italy	Spain
1850/51	–	52.3	–	–	–	–	–
1860/61	–	68.8[b]	–	–	–	22.8	–
1870/71	–	74.0[c]	–	42.4	34.3	31.2	–
1880/81	–	83.0	–	54.3	44.7	35.2	–
1890/91	–	84.5	–	63.5	54.7	–	–
1900/01	77.7[a]	87.5	80.4	67.9	55.6	40.6	–
1910/11	76.7	87.7	79.1	73.5	54.3	47.5	43.1[d]
Rank at 1910/11	3	1	2	4	5	6	7
Anticipated backwardness rank[e]	1	2=	2=	4	7+	5	6+

[a] 1904; [b] 1865; [c] 1876; [d] 1914; [e] Derived as before from Table 7.2a with allowance made for the absence of Russia.

Source: Calculated from Mitchell (1975), pp. 29–54, 750–9.

Observations: There are two distinct bands. Advanced economies group in the range 77–88 per cent by 1914. Backward economies group in the range 43–54 per cent by this date. The Austrian performance is again sound. Note the very low starting point of Italy in relation to those of Austria and Hungary. But most striking is the improvement in the French position, when this measure is employed, as against the result obtained by comparing the school population with *total* population (Table 7.11a). In itself this is testimony to the 'top-heavy' nature of the French age structure, with an unusually high proportion of the community *above* school age.

449

THE INDUSTRIALIZATION OF THE CONTINENTAL POWERS

Table 7.12 Population size of major nations (m.)

	Austria	Hungary	France	Germany	Italy	Russia	Spain	UK
1850/51	17.5	13.2	35.8	34.0	24.4ᵈ	68.5	15.3ᵉ	20.8
1860/61	18.2ᵃ	14.3ᵃ	37.4	36.2	25.0	74.1	15.7	23.1
1870/71	20.4ᵇ	15.4ᵇ	36.1ᶜ	40.8	26.8	84.5	16.2	26.1
1880/81	22.1	15.7	37.7	45.2	28.5	97.7	16.6ᶠ	29.7
1890/91	24.0	17.5	38.3	49.4	30.3	117.8	17.6ᵍ	33.1
1900/01	26.2	19.3	39.0	56.4	32.5	132.9	18.6	37.0
1910/11	28.6	20.9	39.6	64.9	34.7	160.7	20.0	40.8

ᵃ 1857; ᵇ 1869; ᶜ 1872; ᵈ 1852; ᵉ interpolated estimate; ᶠ 1877; ᵍ 1887.

Table 7.12a Indices of population growth of major nations (1850/51 = 100)

	Austria	Hungary	France	Germany	Italy	Russia	Spain	UK
1850/51	100	100	100	100	100ᵈ	100	100ᵉ	100
1860/61	104ᵃ	108ᵃ	104	106	102	108	103	111
1870/71	117ᵇ	117ᵇ	101ᶜ	120	110	123	106	125
1880/81	126	119	105	133	117	143	108ᶠ	143
1890/91	137	133	107	145	124	172	115ᵍ	159
1900/01	150	146	109	166	133	194	122	178
1910/11	163	158	111	191	142	235	131	196
Rank in 1910/11	5	4	1	6	3	8	2	7
Anticipated backwardness rankʰ	4	8	2 =	2 =	5	6	7	1

ᵃ⁻ᵍ As Table 7.12, ᵇ from Table 7.2a.

450

Sources: Table 7.12 taken from Mitchell (1973), p. 747. Table 7.12a calculated from the same source.

Observations: The most significant features of Table 7.12 are the enormous predominance of Russia throughout the period and the marked reversal in the relative positions of France and Germany.

Table 7.12a is perhaps the more revealing, however. The countries are ranked for population growth achieved over the period 1850/51–1910/11 from the lowest increment upwards. The underlying assumption is that the most developed nations may display the lowest rates of population advance. This assumption is not borne out. Indeed *no* significant correlation between rate of population growth and economic status emerges from these data. The countries with the highest rates of population expansion compose the discordant trio, Germany, UK, and Russia, while those with the lowest rates, France, Italy, and Spain are equally mismatched in level of economic achievement. The high level of ambiguity in the relationship between population and industrial growth, already revealed in the foregoing analysis, is here much in evidence. Even the political partners, Austria and Hungary, so divergent in manufacturing prowess, display only marginally discrepant population patterns. Perhaps the most outstanding features are:

(a) the marked weakness of long-run demographic forces in France even given the notable effect produced by territorial losses in 1871;
(b) the rather similar demographic feebleness of Spain;
(c) the concealment of the high regional growth rates of the Southern Italian population within a moderate national performance;
(d) the remarkably high growth rates of the Russian national community, even given its remarkable size at the outset.

Table 7.12b Birth rates per 1000 of population

	Austria	Hungary	France	Germany	Italy	Russia	Spain	England and Wales
1840	38.6	–	27.9	36.4	–	–	–	32.0
1850	39.6	–	26.8	37.2	–	–	–	–
1860	38.2	39.7[a]	26.2	36.4	38.0[b]	49.7[a]	36.7	35.6
1870	39.8	42.1	25.9	38.5	36.8	49.2	36.6	34.6
1880	37.5	42.8	24.6	37.6	33.9	49.7	35.5	33.6
1890	36.2	40.7	21.8	35.7	35.8	50.3	34.4	30.4
1900	35.0	39.4	21.3	35.6	33.0	49.3	33.9	28.7
1910	32.5	35.4	19.6	29.8	33.3	45.1	32.7	25.1
1914	29.7[c]	34.5	13.1	26.8	31.0	43.1	29.9	23.8 Mean 1914 = 29.61
Rank in 1914	4	7	1	3	5	8	5	2
Backwardness rank[d]	4	8	2=	2	5	5	7	1

451

[a] 1861; [b] 1862; [c] 1913; [d] as in previous tables.

Source: Abstracted from Mitchell, (1975), pp. 105–20.

Observations: Most cases group quite closely with a span of 35.6–39.7 per 1000 covering all but two countries in 1860, and one of 26.8–29.9 per 1000 covering all but three countries in 1914. The two major exceptions – France and Russia at each date – are enormous exceptions. Much of the ominous weakness of French demographic performance and much of the ominous strength of Russian demographic performance must be traced to these extraordinary birth-rate patterns. The tendency towards a general decline in fertility, affecting all cases by 1880/90, is striking. As might be expected, the birth-rate rankings rise fairly closely in step with the level of backwardness. Significantly, in view of the foregoing analysis, the Russian birth-rate ranking is considerably higher than its backwardness ranking and the Spanish birth-rate ranking considerably lower. Elsewhere the agreement is quite good.

Table 7.12c Death rates per 1000 of population

	Austria	Hungary	France	Germany	Italy	Russia	Spain	England and Wales
1840	30.4	–	23.7	26.5	–	–	–	22.9
1850	32.9	–	21.4	25.6	–	–	–	20.8
1860	26.8	32.2[a]	21.4	23.2	30.9[b]	35.4[a]	27.4	21.2
1870	29.4	33.5	28.4	27.4	29.9	35.0	31.6	22.9
1880	29.7	37.8	22.9	26.0	30.8	36.1	30.1	20.5
1890	29.1	32.5	22.8	24.4	26.3	36.7	32.1	19.5
1900	25.2	27.0	21.9	22.1	23.8	31.1	29.0	18.2
1910	21.2	23.4	17.8	16.2	19.9	31.5	23.1	13.5
1914	20.3[c]	23.4	18.5	19.0	17.9	27.4	22.2	14.0 Mean 1914 = 20.34
Ranking in 1914	5	7	3	4	2	8	6	1
Anticipated backwardness rank[a]	4	8	2=	2=	5	6	7	1

[a]–[d] As in Table 7.12b.

Source: As in Table 7.12b.

452

Observations: There is less convergence in the death-rate pattern for 1860 than in the birth-rate pattern, but, by 1914, leaving aside the extreme cases of England and Wales, and Russia, a fairly narrow band of 17.3–23.4 per 1000 covers the remaining cases. Again, it is broadly time that the death-rate ranking rises with the level of backwardness, but the spectacular exception perpetrated by Italy demands special note. Even more striking is the fact that the 'special cases' of European population performance – Russia and France – are much less special in death-rate behaviour than in birth-rate behaviour and deviate much less from the 1914 mean for mortality than for natality. Again there is a universal tendency for death rates to decline from c. 1880.

Table 7.12d Marriage rates per 1000 of population

	Austria	Hungary	France	Germany	Italy	Russia	Spain	England and Wales
1840	15.9	–	16.5	16.2	–	–	–	15.6
1850	19.3	–	16.7	17.0	–	–	–	17.2
1860	16.9	18.8ᵃ	15.9ᵇ	16.1	16.4ᵇ	23.2ᵃ	16.2	17.1
1870	19.6	19.8	12.2	15.4	14.6	20.8	12.8	16.1
1880	15.2	18.3	14.9	15.0	14.0	19.2	12.4	14.9
1890	15.0	16.4	14.0	16.1	14.6	16.8	15.8	15.5
1900	16.4	17.8	15.5	17.0	14.4	17.8	17.7	16.0
1910	15.1	17.4	15.6	15.4	15.6	16.8	14.1	15.0 Mean 1910 = 15.63
1913	13.5	18.4	15.0	15.3	15.0	–	13.6	15.7 Mean 1913 = 15.21
Rank in 1913	1	8 ?	3=	5	3=	7 ?	2	6
Anticipated backwardness rankᶜ	4	8	2=	2=	5	6	7	1

ᵃ 1861; ᵇ 1862; ᶜ as in previous tables; 1914 was an aberrational year for marriages; hence the use of 1913 as terminal date

Source: As in Table 7.12b.

Observations: There are few deductions that can be drawn about the relationship between marriage rate and level of economic backwardness and certainly there are none provoked by these rankings. Once more, it is interesting that the French and Russian patterns – with the exception of the Russian starting point – are not powerfully divergent from the pattern of the sample as a whole. Perhaps the major implication of Tables 7.12b–7.12d is that the peculiarities of the very weak French and the strong Russian population development owe more to fertility factors than to any others. This would be consistent with the hypothesis that the institutions of equal inheritance and communal tenure exerted decisive influence upon family size.

Bibliography

CHAPTER ONE: HISTORICAL MODELS OF GROWTH

H. G. J. Aitken (ed.) (1965) *Explorations in Enterprise.* (Cambridge, Mass.).

R. Aron (1967) *Eighteen Lectures on Industrial Society* (London).

W. Ashworth (1977) 'Typologies and evidence: Has nineteenth century Europe a guide to economic growth?', *Economic History Review*, 30.

A. K. Cairncross (1963) 'Capital Formation in the Take-off' in W. W. Rostow (ed.), *The Economics of Take-off into Sustained Growth* (London).

R. E. Cameron (1961) *France and the Economic Development of Europe 1800–1914* (Princeton).

D. C. Coleman (1972) *What Has Happened to Economic History?* (Cambridge).

A. Gerschenkron (1962) *Economic Backwardness in Historical Perspective* (Cambridge, Mass.).

A. Gerschenkron (1968) *Continuity in History* (Cambridge, Mass.).

H. J. Habakkuk (1963) 'The historical experience on the basic conditions of economic progress' in B. E. Supple (ed.) *The Experience of Economic Growth* (New York).

H. Hauser (1917) *Germany's Commercial Grip on the World* (London).

A. O. Hirschman (1966) *The Strategy of Economic Development* (New Haven).

A. C. Kelly, J. G. Williamson and R. J. Cheetham (1972) *Dualistic Economic Development: Theory and History* (Chicago).

S. Kuznets (1966) *Modern Economic Growth* (New Haven).

D. N. McCloskey (1971) 'International differences in productivity? Coal and steel in America and Britain before World War I'. in D. N. McCloskey (ed.) *Essays on a Mature Economy: Britain after 1840* (London).

B. R. Mitchell (1975) *European Historical Statistics, 1750–1970* (London).

T. Parsons and E. Shils (eds) (1951) *Towards a General Theory of Action* (Cambridge, Mass.).

S. Pollard (1973) 'Industrialization and the European economy', *Economic History Review*, 26.

H. Rosovsky (1961) *Capital Formation in Japan* (New York).

W. W. Rostow (1960) *The Stages of Economic Growth* (Cambridge).

W. W. Rostow (ed.) (1963) *The Economics of Take-off into Sustained Growth* (London).

J. **Schumpeter** (1942) *Capitalism, Socialism and Democracy* (New York).

J. **Schumpeter** (1969) *Business Cycles* (New York).

B. E. **Supple** (ed.) (1963) *The Experience of Economic Growth* (New York).

C. **Trebilcock** (1973) 'British armaments and European industrialization, 1890–1914', *Economic History Review*, 26.

CHAPTER TWO: GERMANY

D. H. **Aldcroft** (1964) 'The entrepreneur in the British economy, 1870–1914', *Economic History Review*, 17.

S. **Andic and J. Veverka** (1964) 'The growth of government expenditure in Germany since the unification', *Finanzarchiv*, 23.

K. D. **Barkin** (1970) *The Controversy over German Industrialization, 1890–1902* (Chicago).

A. **Bergengrün** (1908) *Staatsminister August Freiherr von der Heyt* (Leipzig).

V. R. **Berghahn** (1970) 'Zu den Zielen des deutschen Flottenbaus unter Wilhelm II', *Historische Zeitschrift*, 210.

V. R. **Berghahn** (1971) *Der Tirpitzplan* (Düsseldorf).

V. R. **Berghahn** (1973) *Rustung und Machtpolitik* (Düsseldorf).

H. **Böhme** (1966) *Deutschlands Weg zur Grossmacht. Studien zum Verhältnis von Wirtshaft und Staat Während der Reichsgrundungszeit* (Frankfurt-Main).

H. **Böhme** (1979) *Introduction to the Social and Economic History of Germany* (Oxford).

K. **Borchardt** (1973) 'Germany 1700–1914' in C. M. Cipolla (ed.) *The Fontana Economic History of Europe: 4 The Emergence of Industrial Societies*, Vol. I, (London).

R. **Bowen** (1950) 'The roles of government and private enterprise in Germany 1870–1914', *Journal of Economic History*, Supp. 10.

R. A. **Brady** (1943) 'The economic impact of imperial Germany', *Journal of Economic History*, Supp. 3.

W. F. **Bruck** (1962) *The Social and Economic History of Germany, 1888–1939* (New York).

H. **Calwer** (1900) *Handel und Wandel* (Berlin).

R.E. **Cameron** (1956) 'Founding the Bank of Darmstädt', *Explorations in Entrepreneurial History*, 9.

R. E. **Cameron** (1967) *Banking in Early Stages of Industrialization* (New York).

W. **Conze** (1969) 'The effects of nineteenth-century liberal agrarian reforms on social structure in Central Europe' in F. Crouzet, W. H. Chaloner and W. M. Stern (eds) *Essays in European Economic History* (London).

F. **Crouzet** (1958) *L'Economie brittanique et le Blocus continental, 1806–13*, 2 vols (Paris).

F. **Crouzet** (1964) 'Wars, blockade and economic change in Europe 1792–1815', *Journal of Economic History*, 24.

F. **Crouzet** (1974) 'Récherches sur la production d'armaments en France,

1815–1913 Conjunctures économiques, structures sociales; hommage à Ernest Labrousse (Civilizations et Sociétés, 47; Paris; The Hague).

S. M. Eddie (1967) 'The changing pattern of landownership in Hungary, 1867–1913', *Economic History Review*, 20.

F. Eicholtz (1962) *Junker und Bourgeoisie in der Preussischen Eisenbahn geschichte* (East Berlin).

E. Eistert (1970) *Die Beeinflussung des Wirtschaftswachstums in Deutschland von 1883 bis 1913 durch das Bankensystem* (Berlin).

G. Eley (1974) 'Sammlungspolitik, social imperialism and the navy law of 1898', *Militargeschichteliche Mitteilungen*, 1.

H. Feis (1961) *Europe, the World's Banker* (New York).

F. Fischer (1975) *War of Illusions, German Policies from 1911 to 1914* (London).

W. Fischer (1960) 'The German Zollverein, a case study in customs union', *Kyklos*, 13.

W. Fischer (1963) 'Government activity and industrialization in Germany, 1815–70' in W. W. Rostow (ed.) *The Economics of Take-off into Sustained Growth* (London).

R. W. Fogel (1964) *Railroads and American Economic Growth* (Baltimore).

R. Fremdling (1975) *Eisenbahnen und deutsches Wirtschaftswachstum, 1840–1879: Ein Betrag zur Entwicklungstheorie und zur Theorie der Infrastrucktur* (Dortmund).

R. Fremdling (1977) 'Railroads and German economic growth: a leading sector analysis with a comparison to the United States and Great Britain', *Journal of Economic History*, 37.

R. Fremdling and R. Tilly (1976) 'German Banks, German Growth and Econometric History', *Journal of Economic History*, 36.

A. Gerschenkron (1943) *Bread and Democracy in Germany* (Berkeley).

A. Gerschenkron (1963) *Continuity in History* (Cambridge, Mass.)

B. Gille (1973) 'Banking and industrialization in Europe, 1730–1914' in C.M. Cipolla (ed.) *The Fontana Economic History of Europe: 3, The Industrial Revolution* (London).

T. S. Hamerow (1958) *Restoration, Revolution, Reaction: Economics and Politics in Germany, 1815–71* (Princeton).

H. Hauser (1917a) *Germany's Commercial Grip on the World* (London).

H. Hauser (1917b) *Les méthodes allemandes d'expansion économique* (7th edn, Paris).

W. O. Henderson (1955–56) 'Peter Beuth and the rise of Prussian industry, 1810–45', *Economic History Review*, 8.

W. O. Henderson (1958) *The State and the Industrial Revolution in Prussia, 1740–1870* (Liverpool).

W. O. Henderson (1960) *The Zollverein* (London).

W. O. Henderson (1960–2) 'The rise of the metal and armament industries in Berlin and Brandenburg', *Business History*, 3–4.

A. O. Hirschman (1966) *The Strategy of Economic Development* (New Haven).

W. Hoffmann (1963) 'The take-off in Germany' in W. W. Rostow (ed.) *The*

Economics of Take-off into Sustained Growth (London).

E. D. Howard (1907) *The Cause and Extent of the Recent Industrial Progress of Germany* (London).

J. C. Hunt (1974) 'Peasants, grain tariffs and meat quotas; imperial German protectionism re-examined', *Central European History*, 7.

J. C. Hunt (1975) 'The egalitarianism of the Right; the Agrarian League in south-west Germany', *Journal of Contemporary History*, 10.

T. Kemp (1969) *Industrialization in Nineteenth Century Europe* (London)

C. P. Kindleberger (1964) *Economic Growth in France and Britain, 1850– 1950* (Cambridge, Mass.).

H. Kisch (1962) 'The impact of the French Revolution upon the Lower Rhine textile districts', *Economic History Review*, 15.

M. Kitchen (1978) *The Political Economy of Germany, 1815–1914* (London)

E. von Knorring (1970) *Die Berechnung makroökonomischer Konsumfunktionen fur Deutschland, 1851–1913* (Tubingen).

W. Köllman (1964) 'The population of Germany in the age of industrialism' in H. Moller (ed.) *Population Movements in Modern European History* (New York).

A. Kraus (1965) *Die Unterschechten Hamburgs in der ersten Hälfte des 19 Jahrhunderts* (Stuttgart).

S. Kuznets (1961) 'Long-term trends in capital formation proportions', *Economic Development and Cultural Change*, 9.

S. Kuznets (1966) *Modern Economic Growth* (Yale).

D. S. Landes (1965) 'Japan and Europe; contrasts in industrialization' in W. W. Lockwood (ed.) *The State and Economic Enterprise in Japan* (Princeton).

D. S. Landes (1969) *The Unbound Prometheus* (Cambridge).

H. Lebovics (1967) 'Agrarians versus industrializers; social conservative resistance to industrialism and capitalism in late-nineteenth-century Germany', *International Review of Social History*, 12.

R. Liefman (1932) *Cartels, Concerns and Trusts* (London).

A. Marshall (1920) *Industry and Trade* (London).

E. Maschke (1969) 'An outline of the history of German cartels from 1873 to 1914' in F. Crouzet *et al.* (eds) *Essays in European Economic History* (London).

A. Milward and S. B. Saul (1973) *The Economic Development of Continental Europe, 1780–1870* (London).

B. R. Mitchell (1975) *European Historical Statistics, 1750–1970* (London).

W. J. Mömmsen (1973) 'Domestic factors in German foreign policy before 1914', *Central European History*, 6.

H. Neuburger and H. Stokes (1974) 'German banks and German growth, 1883–1913; an empirical view', *Journal of Economic History*, 34 (1974); see also the critique by R. Fremdling and R. Tilly (1976).

R. R. Palmer (1964) *The Age of the Democratic Revolution*, Vol. II (Princeton).

W. N. Parker (1954) 'Entrepreneurial opportunities and response in the German economy', *Explorations in Entrepreneurial History*, 7.

W. N. Parker (1959) 'National states and national development: French and German ore mining in the late nineteenth century' in H. G. J. Aitken (ed.) *The State and Economic Growth* (New York).

A. Peacock and T. Wiseman (1967) *The Growth of Public Expenditure in the UK* (London).

S. Pollard (1973) 'Industrialization and the European economy', *Economic History Review*, 26.

N. G. Pounds (1959) 'Economic growth in Germany' in H. G. J. Aitken (ed.), *The State and Economic Growth* (New York).

H-J. Pühle (1966) *Agrarische Interessenpolitik und preussischer Konservatismus in Wilhelminischen Reich* (Hanover).

W. J. Reader (1970) *A History of I.C.I.:* Vol. 1. *The Forerunners* (London).

J. Riesser (1911) *The German Great Banks and their·Concentration in Connection with the Economic Development of Germany* (Washington).

H. Rosenberg (1967) *Grosse Depression und Bismarckzeit* (Berlin).

W. W. Rostow (ed.) (1963) *The Economics of Take-off into Sustained Growth* (London).

G. Schmoller (1894) *Zur Geschichte der Kleingewerbe im 19 Jahrhundert* (Halle).

J. Schumaker (1912) *Address to Conference of the British Royal Economic Society.*

J. Schumpeter (1939) *Business Cycles*, Vol. I (New York).

Sir Swire Smith (1916) *The Real German Rivalry* (London).

D. Stegmann (1970) *Die Erben Bismarcks, Parteien und Verbände in der Spätphase der Wilhelminischen Deutschlands Sammlungspolitik, 1897–1918* (Cologne).

J. Steinberg (1964) 'The Kaiser's navy and German society's *Past and Present*, 28

J. Steinberg (1965) *Yesterdays Deterrent: Tirpitz and the Birth of the German Battlefleet* (London).

A. H. Stockder (1932) *Regulating an Industry: The Rhenish-Westphalian Coal Syndicate, 1893–1929* (New York).

R. Tilly (1967) 'Germany 1815–70' in R. E. Cameron (ed.) *Banking in the Early Stages of Industrialization* (Oxford).

F. B. Tipton (1974a) 'National consensus in German economic history', *Central European History*, 7.

F. B. Tipton (1974b) 'Farm labour and power politics in Germany, 1850–1914', *Journal of Economic History*, 34.

F. B. Tipton (1976) *Regional Variations in the Economic Development of Germany during the Nineteenth Century* (Middleton, Conn.).

S. R. Tirrell (1951) *German Agrarian Politics after Bismarck's Fall* (New York).

C. Trebilcock (1966) 'A "special relationship" government, rearmament and the cordite firms', *Economic History Review*, 19.

C. Trebilcock (1969) '"Spin-off" in British economic history: armaments and industry, 1760–1914', *Economic History Review*, 22.

W. Treue (1962) 'Wirtschafts-und Socialgeschichte Deutschlands in 19 Jahrhundert' in B. Gebhardt (ed.) *Handbuch der deutschen Geschichte* (8th edn, Stuttgart), III.

US Department of Commerce (1905) *Industrial Education and Industrial Conditions in Germany*, Special Consular Reports, Vol. 33, (Washington).

T. Veblen (1939) *Imperial Germany and the Industrial Revolution* (London).

H. Wagenblass (1973) *Der Eisenbahnbau und das Wachstum der deutschen Eisen- und Maschinenbauindustrie, 1835—60* (Stuttgart).

F. Walker (1906) 'The German steel syndicate', *Quarterly Journal of Economics*, 20.

P. Barrett Whale (1930) *Joint Stock Banking in Germany* (London).

E. E. Williams (1896) *Made in Germany* (London).

CHAPTER THREE: FRANCE

D. H. Aldcroft (1964) 'The entrepreneur in the British economy, 1870—1914', *Economic History Review*, 17.

R. Aron (1967) *Eighteen Lectures on Industrial Society* (London).

C. B. Behrens (1962—63) 'Nobles, privileges and taxes in France at the end of the ancien régime', *Economic History Review*, 15.

M. Blanchard (1969) 'The railway policy of the Second Empire' in F. Crouzet *et al.* (eds) *Essays in European Economic History* (London).

M. Bloch (1960) *Les Charactères Originaux de l'Histoire rurale française* (Paris).

J. Bourgeois-Pichat (1951) 'The general development of the population of France since the eighteenth century', *Population*, 6.

J. Bouvier (1961) *Le Crédit Lyonnais de 1863 à 1882* (Paris).

J. Bouvier (1970) 'The banking mechanism in France in the late nineteenth century' in R. E. Cameron (ed.) *Essays in French Economic History* (Homewood, Ill.)

M. J. Bowman and C. A. Anderson (1963) 'Concerning the role of education in development', in C. Geertz (ed.) *Old Societies and New States* (Glencoe, Ill.).

R. E. Cameron (1961) *France and the Economic Development of Europe, 1800—1914* (Princeton).

R. E. Cameron (1963) 'Economic growth and stagnation in France' in B. E. Supple (ed.) *The Experience of Economic Growth* (New York).

R. E. Cameron (ed.) (1967) *Banking in the Early Stages of Industrialization* (Oxford).

R. E. Cameron (ed.) (1970) *Essays in French Economic History* (Homewood, Ill.).

F. Caron (1970) 'French railway investment, 1850—1914' in R. E. Cameron (ed.) *Essays in French Economic History* (Homewood, Ill.).

J. C. Christopher (1951) 'The desiccation of the bourgeois spirit' in E. M. Earle (ed.) *Modern France* (Princeton).

J. Clapham (1936) *The Economic Development of France and Germany, 1815—1914* (Cambridge).

S. B. Clough (1939) *France: A History of National Economics, 1789–1939* (New York).

S. B. Clough (1946) 'Retardative factors in French economic development', *Journal of Economic History*, Supp. 6.

D. N. Collins (1973) 'The Franco-Russian alliance and the Russian railways', *Historical Journal*, 16.

F. Crouzet (1958) *L'Economie britannique et le Blocus continental, 1806–13*, 2 vols (Paris).

F. Crouzet (1964) 'Wars, blockade and economic change in Europe, 1792–1815', *Journal of Economic History*, 24.

F. Crouzet (1967) 'England and France in the eighteenth century: a comparative analysis of two economic growths' in R. M. Hartwell (ed.) *The Causes of the Industrial Revolution in England* (London).

F. Crouzet, W. H. Chaloner and W. Stern (eds) (1969) *Essays in European Economic History* (London).

F. Crouzet (1970) 'An annual index of French industrial production in the nineteenth century' in R. E. Cameron (ed.) *Essays in French Economic History* (Homewood, Ill.).

F. Crouzet (1972) 'Western Europe and Great Britain; "catching up" in the first half of the nineteenth century' in A. J. Youngson (ed.) *Economic Development in the Long Run* (London).

F. Crouzet (1974) 'Récherches sur la production d'armaments en France, 1815–1913' in *Conjoncture économique, structures sociales; hommage à Ernest Labrousse* (Paris; The Hague).

L. Dansette (1954) *Quelques familles du patronat textile* (Paris).

C. Dupin (1827) *Forces productives et commerciales de la France*, 2 vols (Paris).

H. Feis (1961) *Europe, The World's Banker* (New York).

C. Fohlen (1956) *L'Industrie textile au Temps de Second Empire* (Paris).

C. Fohlen (1970) 'The industrial revolution in France' in R. E. Cameron (ed.) *Essays in French Economic History* (Homewood, Ill.).

C. Fohlen (1973) 'France, 1700–1914' in C. M. Cipolla (ed.) *Fontana Economic history of Europe*: 4, *The Emergence of Industrial Societies*, vol. I (London).

A. Gerschenkron (1953) 'Social attitudes, entrepreneurship and economic development', *Explorations in Entrepreneurial History*, 6; and see the replies by D. S. Landes (1954) and J. Sawyer (1954) in *Explorations*, 6.

A. Gerschenkron (1962) *Economic Backwardness in Historical Perspective* (Cambridge, Mass.).

A. Gerschenkron (1968) *Continuity in History* (Cambridge, Mass.).

C. J. Gignoux (1952) *L'Industrie française* (Paris).

B. Gille (1968) *Les Investissements français en Italie, 1815–1914* (Turin).

B. Gille (1973) 'Banking and economic development' in C. M. Cipolla (ed.) *Fontana Economic History of Europe*: 3, *The Industrial Revolution* (London).

M. Gillet (1969) 'The coal age and the rise of the coalfields in the north and the Pas de Calais' in F. Crouzet et al. (eds) *Essays in European Economic History* (London).

R. Girault (1973) *Emprunts russes et investissements français en Russie, 1887–1914* (Paris).

E. O. Golob (1944) *The Méline Tariff: French agriculture and nationalist economic policy* (New York).

W. O. Henderson (1961) *The Industrial Revolution on the Continent* (London).

L. Henry (1965) 'The population of France in the eighteenth century' in D. V. Glass and D. E. C. Eversley (eds) *Population in History* (London).

S. Hoffman et al. (eds) (1963) *France, Change and Tradition* (London).

P. Hohenberg (1972) 'Change in rural France in the period of industrialization, 1830–1914' *Journal of Economic History*, 32.

C. Kent (1972) 'Camille Cavallier and Pont à Mousson: An Industrialist of the Third Republic' (unpub. Ph.D. thesis, Oxford).

J. M. Keynes (1924) 'Foreign investment and national advantage', *The Nation*, 9.8.1924.

C. P. Kindleberger (1964) *Economic Growth in France and Britain, 1850–1950* (Oxford).

D. Kirk (1951) 'Population and population trends' in E. M. Earle (ed.) *Modern France* (Princeton).

C. E. Labrousse (1933) *Esquisse du mouvement des prix et des revenus en France au dix-huitième siècle*, 2 vols (Paris).

C. E. Labrousse (1944) *La Crise de l'économie française à la fin de l'Ancien Régime* (Paris).

G. Lamèyne (1958) *Haussmann* (Paris).

D. S. Landes (1949) 'French entrepreneurship and industrial growth', *Journal of Economic History*, 9.

D. S. Landes (1951) 'French business and the businessman, a social and cultural analysis' in E.M. Earle (ed.) *Modern France* (Princeton).

D. S. Landes (1954) 'Social attitudes, entrepreneurship and economic development: a comment', *Explorations in Entrepreneurial History*, 6.

D. S. Landes (1969a) 'The old bank and the new: The financial revolution of the nineteenth century' in F. Crouzet et al (eds) Essays in European Economic History (London).

D. S. Landes (1969b) *The Unbound Prometheus* (Cambridge).

G. Lefebvre (1924) *Les Paysans du Nord* (Lille).

G. Lefebvre (1929) 'La place de la révolution dans l'histoire agraire de la France', *Annales d'histoire économique et sociale*, 4.

P. Léon (1960) 'L'industrialization en France en tant que facteur de croissance économique du dix-huitième siècle à nos jours' in *Première conférence internationale d'histoire économique, Stockholm, 1960* (Paris).

M. Lévy-Leboyer (1968) 'La croissance économique en France au dixtionale dans la Première Moitié du Dix-neuvième Siècle* (Paris).

M. Lévy-Leboyer (1968) 'La croissance économique en France au dix-neuvième siècle', *Annales; Economies, Sociétés, Civilizations*, 23.

T. J. Marcovitch (1966) 'L'industrie française de 1789 à 1964; Conclusion Générale', *Cahiers de l'ISEA*, 7.

D. McCloskey and L. Sandberg (1971) 'From damnation to redemption; judgements on the late Victorian entrepreneur', *Explorations in Economic History*, 9.

J. Marczewski (1961) 'Some aspects of the economic growth of France, 1660–1958', *Economic Development and Cultural Change*, 9.

J. Marczewski (1963) 'The take-off hypothesis and French experience' in W. W. Rostow (ed.) *The Economics of Take-off into Sustained Growth* (London).

J. Marczewski (1965) 'Le produit physique de l'économie française de 1789 à 1913', *Histoire quantitative de l'économie française*, vol. 4 (Paris).

A. Marshall (1920) *Industry and Trade* (London).

P. Mathias and P. K. O'Brien (1976) 'Taxation in Britain and France, 1715–1800: A comparison of the social and economic incidence of taxes collected for the central governments', *Journal of European Economic History*, 5.

A. Milward and S. B. Saul (1973) *The Economic Development of Continental Europe, 1780–1870* (London).

B. R. Mitchell (1975) *European Historical Statistics, 1750–1970* (London).

C. Morazé (1952) *La France bourgeoise* (Paris).

M. Morineau (1968) 'Y-at-il une révolution agricole en France au dix-huitième siècle?', *Revue historique*, 239.

M. Morineau (1972) 'Budgets populaires en France au dix-huitième siècle', *Revue d'histoire économique et sociale*, 50.

C. Mourre (1900) *D'où vient là décadence économique de la France?* (Paris).

G. Palmade (1972) *French Capitalism in the Nineteenth Century* (Newton Abbot).

R. R. Palmer (1959) 'Lefebvre, the peasants and the French Revolution', *Journal of Modern History*, 31.

R. R. Palmer (1964) *The Age of the Democratic Revolution*, 2 vols (Princeton).

W. N. Parker (1959) 'French and German ore-mining in the late nineteenth century' in H. G. J. Aitken (ed.) *The State and Economic Growth* (New York).

S. Patel (1965) 'Rates of industrial growth in the last century, 1860–1958' in B. E. Supple (ed.) (1965) *The Experience of Economic Growth* (New York).

J. R. Pitts (1963) 'Continuity and change in bourgeois France' in S. Hoffman et al. (eds.) *France, Change and Tradition* (London).

R. Poidevin (1969) *Les Relations économiques et financières entre la France et l'Allemagne de 1898 à 1914* (Paris).

R. Price, (1975) *The Economic Modernization of France* (London).

W. J. Reader (1970) *A History of ICI: Vol. 1 The Forerunners* (London).

R. B. Rose (1959) 'Eighteenth century price riots: the French Revolution and the Jacobin maximum', *International Review of Social History*, 3.

W. W. Rostow (ed.) (1963) *The Economics of Take-off into Sustained Growth* (London).

G. Rudé (1954) 'Prices, wages and popular movements in Paris during the French Revolution', *Economic History Review*, 3.

G. **Rudé** (1964) *The Crowd in History* (New York).

J. **Sawyer** (1954) 'In defence of an approach; a comment on Professor Gerschenkron's social attitudes', *Explorations of Entrepreneurial History*, 6.

A. **Siegfried** (1951) 'Approaches to an understanding of modern France' in E. M. Earle (ed.) *Modern France* (Princeton).

J. **Spengler** (1951) 'France's response to her declining demographic growth', *Journal of Economic History*, 11.

C. **Trebilcock** (1969) '"Spin-off" in British economic history: armament and industry, 1760–1914', *Economic History Review*, 22.

J. **Vial** (1967) *L'Industrialization de la Sidérurgie Francaise;* '1814–64 (Paris; The Hague).

R. K. **Webb** (1963) 'The Victorian reading public', in *From Dickens to Hardy* (London).

H. D. **White** (1933) *French International Accounts, 1880–1913* (Cambridge, Mass.).

J. B. **Wolf** (1951) 'The élan vital of France: a problem in historical perspective' in E. M. Earle (ed.) *Modern France* (Princeton).

E. A. **Wrigley** (1969) *Population and History* (London).

CHAPTER 4: RUSSIA

H. **Barkai** (1973) 'The macro-economics of tsarist Russia in the industrialization era: monetary development, the balance of payments and the gold standard', *Journal of Economic History*, 33.

A. **Baykov** (1954) 'The economic development of Russia', *Economic History Review*, 7.

V. T. **Bill** (1959) *The Forgotten Class, The Russian Bourgeoisie to 1900* (New York).

C. E. **Black** (ed.) (1960) *The Transformation of Russian Society* (Cambridge, Mass.).

W. L. **Blackwell** (1965) 'The old believers and the rise of private industrial enterprise in early nineteenth-century Russia', *Slavic Review*, 24.

W. L. **Blackwell** (ed.) (1974) *Russian Economic Development from Peter the Great to Stalin* (New York).

J. **Blum** (1961) *Lord and Peasant in Russia from the Ninth to the Nineteenth Centuries* (Princeton).

V. I. **Bovykin** (1959) 'Banki i voennaya promyshlennost' Rossii nakanune pervoi mirovoi voiny', *Istoricheskie zapiski*, 64.

M. J. **Bowman** and C. A. **Anderson** (1963) 'Concerning the role of education in development', in C. Geertz (ed.) *Old Societies and New States* (Glencoe, Ill.).

M. J. **Bowman** and C. A. **Anderson** (eds.) (1971) *Education and Economic Development* (London).

R. E. **Cameron** (ed.) (1967) *Banking in the Early Stages of Industrialization* (New York).

A. Chayanov (1966) *On the Theory of Peasant Economy* (eds D. Thorner, B. Kerblay and R. E. F. Smith) (Homewood, Ill.).

C. M. Cipolla (1969) *Literacy and Development in the West* (Harmondsworth).

D. N. Collins (1973) 'The Franco-Russian alliance and the Russian railways', *Historical Journal*, 16.

O. Crisp (1967) 'Russia, 1860–1914' in R. E. Cameron (ed.) *Banking in the Early Stages of Industrialization* (New York).

O. Crisp (1976) *Studies in the Russian Economy before 1914* (London).

I. M. Drummond (1976) 'The Russian gold standard, 1897–1914', *Journal of Economic History*, 36.

H. J. Ellison (1965) 'The economic modernization of imperial Russia', *Journal of Economic History*, 25.

T. Emmons (1968) *The Russian Landed Gentry and the Peasant Emancipation of 1861* (Cambridge).

M. E. Falkus (1968) 'Russia's national income, 1913: a revaluation', *Economica*, 35.

D. Field (1976) *The End of Serfdom: Nobility and Bureaucracy in Russia, 1855–61* (Cambridge, Mass.).

M. T. Florinsky (1953) *Russia: A History and an Interpretation*, 2 vols (New York).

G. Garvy (1972) 'Banking under tsars and soviets', *Journal of Economic History*, 32.

P. W. Gattrell (1979) 'Russian Heavy Industry and State Defence, 1908–18; Pre-War Expansion and Wartime Mobilization' (unpub. Ph.D. thesis, Cambridge).

A. Gerschenkron (1947) 'The rate of industrial growth in Russia since 1885', *Journal of Economic History*, Supp. 7.

A. Gerschenkron (1962) *Economic Backwardness in Historical Perspective* (Cambridge, Mass.).

A. Gerschenkron (1963) 'The early phases of industrialization in Russia' in W. W. Rostow (ed.) (1963).

A. Gerschenkron (1968) 'Russia: agrarian policies and industrialization, 1861–1917' in *Continuity in History* (Cambridge, Mass.), reprinted from *Cambridge Economic History of Europe*, Vol. 6, ed. M. M. Postan and H. J. Habbakuk (Cambridge, 1965).

A. Gerschenkron (1970) *Europe in the Russian Mirror* (Cambridge).

I. Gindin (1927) *Bankii i promyshlennost' v. Rossii* (Moscow).

R. W. Goldsmith (1961) 'The economic development of tsarist Russia, 1860–1914', *Economic Development and Cultural Change*, 9.

P. Gregory (1972) 'Economic growth and structural change in tsarist Russia: a case of modern economic growth?', *Soviet Studies*, 23.

P. Gregory and J. Sailors (1976) 'Russian monetary policy and industrialization, 1861–1913', *Journal of Economic History*, 36.

L. Haimson (1964) 'The problem of social stability in urban Russia, 1905–17', *Slavic Review*, 23.

A. Kahan (1965) 'Continuity and economic activity: policy in post Petrine

Russia', *Journal of Economic History*, 25.

A. **Kahan** (1967) 'Government policies and the industrialization of Russia', *Journal of Economic History*, 27.

A. **Kahan** (1971a) 'Determinants of the incidence of literacy in rural nineteenth-century Russia' in M. J. Bowman and C. A. Anderson (eds.) (1971).

A. **Kahan** (1971b) 'The development of education and the economy in tsarist Russia' in M. J. Bowman and C. A. Anderson (eds) (1971).

H. P. **Kennard** (1911) *The Russian Year Book for 1911* (London).

J. W. **Kipp** (1972) 'The consequences of defeat: modernising the Russian navy, 1856–63', *Jahrbücher fur Geschichte Osteuropas*, 20.

J. W. **Kipp** (1975) 'M. Kh. Reutern on the Russian state and economy', *Journal of Modern History*, 47.

V. I. **Lenin** (1957) *The Development of Capitalism in Russia* (Moscow).

P. I. **Lyashchenko** (1970) *The History of the National Economy of Russia to 1917* (New York).

D. J. **Male** (1971) *Russian Peasant Organisation before Collectivization* (Cambridge).

J. P. **Mckay** (1970) *Pioneers for Profit: Foreign Entrepreneurship and Russian Industrialization* (Chicago).

J. **Metzer** (1974) 'Railway development and market integration; the case of tsarist Russia', *Journal of Economic History*, 34.

D. A. **Miliutin** (1959) 'Ob opastnosti prodolzheniia v 1856g.. voennykh deistvii', in I. V. Bestuzhev (ed.) *Istoricheskii archiv* (Moscow).

M. S. **Miller** (1926) *The Economic Development of Russia, 1905–14* (London).

W. E. **Mosse** (1958) *Alexander II and the Modernization of Russia* (London).

B. R. **Mitchell** (1975) *European Historical Statistics, 1750–1970* (London).

A. A. **Nesterenko** (1954) *Ocherki istorii promyshlennosti i polozhenia proletariata Ukrainy v kontse XIX i nachale XX reka* (Moscow).

A. **Nove** (1972) 'Russia as an emergent country' in A. J. Youngson (ed.) *Economic Development in the Long Run* (London).

G. W. **Nutter** (1962) *The Growth of Production in the USSR* (Princeton).

G. **Pavlovsky** (1930) *Agricultural Russia on the Eve of Revolution* (New York).

P. N. **Pershin** (1922) *Uchastkovoe zemplepol'zovanie v Rossii i Khutora i otruby i ikh vastprostranenie za desyatiletie, 1907–16* (Moscow).

P. N. **Pershin** (1925) in *Krestyanskaya sel'skokhozyaistvennaya entsiklopediya*, III, (Moscow).

R. **Portal** (1965) 'The Industrialization of Russia' in the *Cambridge Economic History of Europe*, Vol. 6, ed. M. M. Postan and H. J. Habakkuk (Cambridge).

R. **Portal** (1974) 'Muscovite industrialists: the cotton sector' in W. L. Blackwell (ed.) *Russian Economic Development from Peter the Great to Stalin* (New York).

A. G. **Rashin** (1958) *Formirovanie rabochego Klassa Rossii* (Moscow).

G. V. **Rimlinger** (1960) 'Autocracy and the factory order in early Russian industrialization', *Journal of Economic History*, 20.

G. V. **Rimlinger** (1961) 'The expansion of the labour market in capitalist Russia, 1861–1917', *Journal of Economic History*, **21**.

G. T. **Robinson** (1932) *Rural Russia under the Old Regime* (New York).

R. A. **Roosa** (1972) 'Russian industrialists and state socialism, 1906–17', *Soviet Studies*, **23**.

N. **Rosenberg** (1963) 'Capital goods, technology and economic growth', *Oxford Economic Papers*, **15**.

H. **Rosovsky** (1954) 'The serf-entrepreneur in Russia', *Explorations in Entrepreneurial History*, **4**.

W. W. **Rostow** (ed.) (1963) *The Economics of Take-off Into Sustained Growth* (London).

W. W. **Rostow** (1971) *The Politics of the Stages of Growth* (Cambridge).

T. **Shanin** (1971) 'Socio-economic mobility and the rural history of Russia, 1905–30', *Soviet Studies*, **23**.

T. **Shanin** (1972) *The Awkward Class* (Oxford).

T. **Shanin** (ed.) (1971) *Peasants and Peasant Societies* (Harmondsworth).

K. F. **Shatsillo** (1968) *Ruskii imperializm i razvitie flota nakune pervoi mirovoi voiny* (Moscow).

D. B. **Shimkin** (1949) 'The entrepreneur in tsarist and Soviet Russia', *Explorations in Entrepreneurial History*, **2**.

A. **Skerpan** (1964) 'The national economy and emancipation' in A. D. Ferguson and A. Levin (eds), *Essays in Russian History* (Hampden, Conn.).

J. P. **Sontag** (1968) 'Tsarist debts and tsarist foreign policy', *Slavic Review*, **27**.

S. G. **Strumilin** (1969) 'Industrial crises in Russia, 1847–67' in F. Crouzet et al. (eds.) *Essays in European Economic history* (London).

P. **Struve** (1913) *Krepostnoye Khozyaystvo* (Moscow).

C. **Trebilcock** (1969) "Spin-off" in British economic history', *Economic History Review*, **22**.

C. **Trebilcock** (1973) 'British armaments and European industrialization, 1890–1914', *Economic History Review*, **26**.

US Department of Commerce and Labor (1905a) *Commercial Russia in 1904* (Washington).

US Department of Commerce and Labor (1905b) *Industrial Educations and Industrial Conditions in Germany* (Washington).

L. **Volin** (1966) 'Land tenure and land reform in modern Russia' in C. K. Warner (ed.) *Agrarian Conditions in Modern European History* (New York).

L. **Volin** (1970) *A Century of Russian Agriculture* (Cambridge, Mass.).

T. H. **von Laue** (1960) 'The state and the economy' in C. E. Black (ed.) *The Transformation of Russian Society* (Cambridge, Mass.).

T. H. **von Laue** (1961) 'Russian Peasants in the Factory, 1892–1904', *Journal of Economic History*, **21**.

T. H. **von Laue** (1962) 'Tsarist Labour Policy, 1895–1903', *Journal of Modern History*, **34**.

T. H. **von Laue** (1963) *Sergei Witte and the Industrialization of Russia* (New York).

T. H. von Laue (1964) *Why Lenin, Why Stalin?* (New York).

T. H. von Laue (1969) 'Problems of industrialization' in T. Stavrou (ed.) *Russia under the Last Tsar* (Minneapolis).

W. S. Vucinich (ed.) (1968) *The Peasant in Nineteenth Century Russia* (Stanford).

J. N. Westwood (1965) 'John James Hughes and Russian metallurgy', *Economic History Review*, 17.

J. N. Westwood (1973) *Endurance and Endeavour: Russian History, 1812–1971* (Oxford).

G. L. Yaney (1964) 'The concept of the Stolypin land reform', *Slavic Review*, 23.

G. L. Yaney (1971) 'Agricultural administration in Russia from the Stolypin land reform to the forced collectivization' in J. R. Millar (ed.) *The Soviet Rural Community*, (Urbana, Ill.).

CHAPTER 5: THE POWERS OF DEPRIVATION: ITALY, AUSTRIA-HUNGARY, SPAIN

F. Ackley and L. Spaventa (1962) 'Emigration and industrialization in southern Italy; a comment', *Banca Nazionale del Lavoro Review*, 15.

M. K. Anafu (1980) 'The Cooperative Movement in Reggio-Emilia, 1889–1914' (unpub. PhD. thesis, Cambridge).

E. Benoit and H. Lubell (1967) in E. Benoit (ed.) *Disarmament and World Economic Interdependence* (London).

J. Blum (1943) 'Transportation and Industry in Austria, 1815–48', *Journal of Modern History*, 15.

L. Cafagna (1973) 'The industrial revolution in Italy, 1830–1914' in C. M. Cipolla (ed.) *The Fontana Economic History of Europe: 4, The Emergence of Industrial Societies*, vol. I, (London).

W. J. Callahan (1968) 'A note on the Real y General Junta de Comercio, 1679–1814', *Economic History Review*, 21.

R. E. Cameron (1961) *France and the Economic Development of Europe 1800–1914 (Princeton)*.

R. E. Cameron (1967) *Banking in the Early Stages of Industrialization* (Oxford).

R. E. Cameron (ed.) (1972) *Banking and Economic Development* (New York).

R. Carr (1966) *Spain, 1808–1939* (Oxford).

S. B. Clough (1964) *The Economic History of Modern Italy* (New York).

S. B. Clough and C. Livi (1963) 'Economic growth in Italy: an analysis of the uneven development of North and South' in B. E. Supple (ed.) *The Experience of Economic Growth* (New York).

J. B. Cohen (1967) 'Financing industrialization in Italy, 1894–1914: the partial transformation of a latecomer', *Journal of Economic History*, 27.

J. B. Cohen (1972) 'Italy' in R. E. Cameron (ed.) (1972).

R. Eckaus (1961) 'The North–South differential in Italian economic development', *Journal of Economic History*, 21.

S. M. Eddie (1967) 'The changing pattern of landownership in Hungary, 1867–1914', *Economic History Review*, 20.

S. M. Eddie (1971) 'Farmers' response to price in large estate agriculture', *Economic History Review*, 24.

H. Feis (1961) *Europe, The World's Banker* (New York).

J. Freudenberger (1967) 'State intervention as an obstacle to economic growth in the Hapsburg monarchy', *Journal of Economic History*, 27.

A. Gerschenkron (1962a) 'Notes on the industrial growth rate of Italy, 1881–1913' in *Economic Backwardness in Historical Perspective* (Cambridge, Mass.).

A. Gerschenkron (1962b) 'Rosario Romeo and the original accumulation of capital' in *Economic Backwardness in Historical Perspective* (Cambridge, Mass.).

A. Gerschenkron (1968) 'The industrial development of Italy; a debate with Rosario Romeo' in *Continuity in History* (Cambridge, Mass.).

B. Gille (1968) *Les investissements français en Italie* (Turin).

R. Goldsmith (1969) *Financial Structure and Development* (New Haven).

S. Golzio (1952) *Sulla misura della variazione del reddito nazionale Italiano* (Turin).

D. Good (1974) 'Stagnation and take-off in Austria, 1873–1913', *Economic History Review*, 27.

A. Gramsci (1949) *Il Risorgimento* (Turin).

K. R. Greenfield (1965) *Economics and Liberalism in the Risorgimento* (Baltimore).

N. T. Gross (1968) 'An estimate of industrial production in Austria in 1841', *Journal of Economic History*, 28.

N. T. Gross (1971) 'Economic growth and the consumption of coal in Austria and Hungary, 1831–1913', *Journal of Economic History*, 31.

N. T. Gross (1973) 'The industrial revolution in the Hapsburg monarchy, 1750–1914' in C. M. Cipolla (ed.) *The Fontana Economic History of Europe: 4, The Emergence of Industrial Societies*, Vol I, (London).

R. J. Harrison (1974) 'British armaments and European industrialization: the Spanish case re-examined', *Economic History Review*, 27.

R. J. Harrison (1978) *An Economic History of Modern Spain* (Manchester).

F. Herz (1947) *The Economic Problem of the Danubian States* (London).

G. Hildebrand (1965) *Growth and Structure in the Economy of Modern Italy* (Cambridge, Mass.).

A. O. Hirschman (1966) *The Strategy of Economic Growth* (New Haven).

K. B. Hopfinger (1962) *Beyond Expectation; The Volkswagen Story* (London).

Istituto Centrali di Statistica (Istat) (1958) *Sommario di statistiche storiche Italiane, 1861–1955* (Rome).

O. Jaszi (1961) *The Dissolution of the Habsburg Monarchy* (Chicago).

A. Kahan (1968) 'Nineteenth-century European experience with policies of economic nationalism' in H. G. Johnson (ed.) *Economic Nationalism in Old and New States* (London).

C. P. Kindleberger (1965) 'Emigration and economic growth', *Banca*

Nazionale del Lavoro Review, 18.

A. **Klima** (1974) 'The role of domestic industry in Bohemia', *Economic History Review*, 27.

A. **Klima** (1975) 'The beginning of the machine-building industry in the Czech lands in the first half of the nineteenth century', *Journal of European Economic History*, 4.

S. **Kuznets** (1955–57) 'Quantitative aspects of the growth of nations, I,' *Economic Development and Cultural Change*, 5.

S. **Lieberson** (1971) 'An empirical study of military–industrial linkages', *American Journal of Sociology*, 76.

M. **Livi Bacci** (1968) 'Fertility and nuptiality changes in Spain from the late eighteenth century to the early twentieth century', *Population Studies*, 22.

V. **Lutz** (1958) 'The growth process in a dual economic system', *Banca Nazionale del Lavoro, Review*, 11.

V. **Lutz** (1961) 'Some structural aspects of the southern problem; the complementarity of emigration and industrialization', *Banca Nazionale del Lavoro Review*, 14.

G. **Luzzatto** (1963) *L'economia italiana dal 1861 al 1914: I, 1861–1894* (Milan).

G. **Luzzatto** (1969) 'The Italian economy in the first decade after unification' in F. Crouzet et al (eds.) *Essays in European Economic History* (London).

D. **Mack Smith** (1954) 'Italian peasants and the risorgimento' in Istituto Italiano di Cultura di Londra, *Italia e Inghilterra nel Risorgimento* (London).

V. A. **Marsan** (1963) 'The experience of Italy', in A. E. G. Robinson (ed.) *The Economic Consequences of the Size of Nations* (London).

E. **Marz** (1965) 'Zur Genesis der Schumpeterschen Theorie der Wirtschaftsruchen Entwicklung' in *On Political Economy and Econometrics* (Warsaw).

B. R. **Mitchell** (1975) *European Historical Statistics, 1750–1970* (London).

G. **Mori** (1975) 'The genesis of Italian industrialization', *Journal of European Economic History*, 4.

J. **Nadal** (1971) *Le Poblacion espanola, Siglos XVI a XX* (Barcelona).

J. **Nadal** (1973) 'The failure of the industrial revolution in Spain' in C. M. Cipolla (ed.) *The Fontana Economic History of Europe: 4, The Emergence of Industrial Societies*, vol. 2, (London).

J. **Nadal** (1975) *El fracaso de la Revolucion industrial en España, 1814–1913* (Barcelona).

J. W. T. **Newbold** (1916) *The War Trust Exposed* (London).

F. S. **Nitti** (1900) *Nord e Sud* (Turin).

J. **Purs** (1960) 'The industrial revolution in the Czech lands', *Historica*, 2, (Prague).

G. **Ranki** and I. T. **Berend** (1974) *Hungary: A Century of Economic Development* (Newton Abbot).

D. R. **Ringrose** (1968) 'Transportation and economic stagnation in eighteenth century Castile', *Journal of Economic History*, 28.

R. **Romeo** (1959) *Risorgimento e capitalismo* (Bari).

W. W. **Rostow** (1960) *The Stages of Economic Growth* (Cambridge).

K. W. Rothschild (1963) 'Size and viability; the lesson of Austria' in A. E. G. Robinson (ed.) *The Economic Consequences of the Size of Nations* (London).

R. Rudolph (1972) 'Austria, 1800–1914' in R. E. Cameron (ed.) (1972).

R. Rudolph (1976) *Finance and Industrialization in Austria-Hungary* (Cambridge).

N. Sanchez Albornoz (1968) *España hace un siglo: una economia dual* (Barcelona).

N. Sanchez Albornoz (1975) 'Congruence among Spanish economic regions in the nineteenth century', *Journal of European Economic History*, 4.

S. B. Saul (1972) 'The nature and diffusion of technology' in A. J. Youngson (ed.) *Economic Development in the Long Run* (London).

J. Sole-Tura (1967) *Catalanisme i revolucio burgesa* (Barcelona).

M. J. F.X . Soltys (1978) 'Austrian Agriculture; Lower Austrian Estates and the Peasantry, 1751–87' (unpub. M. Litt. thesis, Cambridge).

N. Stone (1975) *The Eastern Front* (London).

F. Thistlethwaite (1964) 'Migration from Europe overseas in the nineteenth and twentieth centuries' in H. Moller (ed.) *Population Movements in Modern European History* (New York).

C. Trebilcock (1973/1974) 'British armaments and European industrialization, 1890–1914', *Economic History Review*, 26, 27.

G. Tortella (1970) 'El banca de Espana entre 1829 y 1929' in *El Banca de Espana: Una historia economia* (Madrid).

G. Tortella (1972) 'Spain, 1829–74' in R. E. Cameron (ed.) (1972).

J. Vicens Vives (1969) *An Economic History of Spain* (Princeton).

P. Vilar (1962) *La Catalogne dans l'Espagne Moderne* (Paris).

F. Vochting (1952) 'The industrialization or pre-industrialization of Southern Italy', *Banca Nazionale del Lavoro Review*, 21.

D. Warriner (ed.) (1965) *Contrasts in Emerging Societies* (London).

R. A. Webster (1975) *Industrial Imperialism in Italy, 1906–14* (Berkeley).

W. Woodruff (1966) *The Impact of Western Man* (London).

CHAPTER SIX: ANTI-MODELS

M. Abramovitz and P. David (1973) 'Reinterpreting economic growth: parables and realities', *American Economic Review*, 63.

S. Andic and J. Veverka (1964) 'The growth of government expenditure in Germany since the unification', *Finanzarchiv*, 23.

H. G. J. Aitken (ed.) (1959) *The State and Economic Growth* (New York).

H. G. J. Aitken (ed.) (1965) *Explorations in Enterprise* (Cambridge, Mass.).

P. Bairoch (1973) 'Agriculture and the industrial revolution' in C. M. Cipolla (ed.) (1973).

S. Barsby (1969) 'Economic backwardness and the characteristics of development', *Journal of Economic History*, 29.

W. J. Baumol (1968) 'Entrepreneurship and economic theory', *American Economic Review, Papers and Proceedings*, **58.**

M. Boserup (1963) 'Agrarian structure and take-off', in Rostow (ed.) (1963).

R. E. Cameron (ed.) (1972) *Banking and Development* (New York).

G. Carlsson (1966) 'The decline of fertility; innovation or adjustment process?', *Population Studies*, **19.**

J. D. Chambers and G. E. Mingay (1966) *The Agricultural Revolution* (London).

C. M. Cipolla (ed.) (1973) *The Fontana Economic History of Europe: 3, The Industrial Revolution* (London).

C. Clarke (1957) *The Conditions of Economic Progress* (London).

A. H. Cole (1965) 'An approach to the study of entrepreneurship' in Aitken (ed.) (1965).

E. J. T. Collins (1969) 'Labour supply and demand in European agriculture 1800–80' in Jones and Woolf (eds) (1969).

A. Downs (1957) 'An economic theory of political action in a democracy', *Journal of Political Economy*, **66.**

F. Dovring (1966) 'The transformation of European agriculture' in M. Postan and H. J. Habakkuk (eds) *The Cambridge Economic History of Europe*, Vol. 6 (Cambridge).

W. T. Easterbrook (1965) 'The climate of enterprise' in Aitken (ed.) (1965)

S. N. Eisenstadt (1963) *The Political System of Empires* (New York).

S. N. Eisenstadt (1972) *Bureaucracy and Bureaucratization* (New York).

J. L. Fisher and R. G. Ridker (1973) 'Population growth, resource availability and environmental quality', *American Economic Review*, **63.**

A. Gerschenkron (1962) *Economic Backwardness in Historical Perspective* (Cambridge, Mass.).

A. Gerschenkron (1968) *Continuity in History* (Cambridge, Mass.)

A. Gerschenkron (1969) 'The history of economic doctrines and economic history', *American Economic Review*, **59.**

B. Gille (1973) 'Banking and industrialization in Europe, 1730–1914' in C. M. Cipolla (ed.) (1973).

D. V. Glass and D. E. C. Eversley (eds) (1965) *Population in History* (London).

D. V. Glass and R. Revelle (eds) (1972) *Population and Social Change* (London).

D. Good (1971) 'Backwardness and the role of banking in nineteenth-century European industrialization', *Journal of Economic History*, **31.**

S. Gordon (1973) 'Natural resources as constraints in economic growth: today's apocalypse and yesterday's', *American Economic Review*, **63.**

J. Hanjal (1965) 'European marriage patterns in perspective' in Glass and Eversley (eds) (1965).

D. M. Heer 'Economic development and the fertility transition' in Glass and Revelle (eds) (1972).

W. O. Henderson (1975) *The Rise of German Industrial Power, 1834–1914* (London).

471

A. O. Hirschman (1966) *The Strategy of Economic Development* (New Haven).

J. C. Hunt (1974) 'Peasants, grain tariffs and meat quotas', *Central European History*, 7.

L. H. Jenks (1965) 'Approaches to entrepreneurial personality' in Aitken (ed.) (1965).

E. L. Jones (1964) *Agriculture and the Industrial Revolution (Oxford)*.

E. L. Jones and S. J. Woolf (eds) (1969) *Agrarian Change and Economic Development* (London).

A. Kahan (1968) 'Nineteenth-century experience with policies of economic nationalism' in H. G. Johnson (ed.) *Economic Nationalism in Old and New States* (London).

C. P. Kindleberger (1964) *Economic Growth in France and Britain, 1850– 1950* (Oxford).

H. Leibenstein (1957) *Economic Backwardness and Economic Growth* (New York).

H. Leibenstein (1963) 'Population growth and the take-off hypothesis' in Rostow (ed.) (1963).

H. Leibenstein (1968) 'Entrepreneurship and development', *American Economic Review, Papers and Proceedings*, 58.

S. Lieberson (1971) 'An empirical study of military–industrial linkages', *American Journal of Sociology*, 76.

H. Metzer (1974) 'Railway development, and market integration; the case of tsarist Russia', *Journal of Economic History*, 34.

B. R. Mitchell (1975) *European Historical Statistics, 1750–1970* (London).

M. Morineau (1968) 'Y a-t-il une révolution agricole', *Revue Historique*, 239.

A. Peacock and T. Wiseman (1967) *The Growth of Public Expenditure in the U.K.* (London).

S. Pollard (1973) 'Industrialization and the European economy', *Economic History Review*, 26.

N. Rosenberg (1973) 'Innovative responses to materials shortages', *American Economic Review*, 63.

W. W. Rostow (ed.) (1963) *The Economics of Take-off Into Sustained Growth* (London).

R. Rudolph (1972) 'Austrian banking 1800–1914', in R. E. Cameron (ed.) (1972).

G. Schmoller (1902) *Jarbüch fur Gesetzgebung* (Leipzig).

J. Spengler (1972) 'Demographic factors in early modern economic development' in Glass and Revelle (eds) (1972).

B. E. Supple (1973) 'The State and the Industrial Revolution' in Cipolla (ed.) (1973).

G. Tortella (1972) 'Spain, 1829–74' in R. E. Cameron (ed.) (1972).

C. Trebilcock (1971) '"Spin-off": a reply', *Economic History Review*, 24.

CHAPTER SEVEN: STATISTICS AND STRUCTURES

S. **Andic and J. Veverka** (1964) 'The growth of government expenditure in Germany since the unification', *Finanzarchiv*, 23.

P. **Bairoch** (1973) 'Agriculture and the industrial revolution' in Cipolla (ed.) (1973b).

S. **Barsby** (1969) 'Economic backwardness and the characteristics of development', *Journal of Economic History*, 29.

R. E. **Cameron** (ed.) (1967) *Banking in the Early Stages of Industrialization* (Oxford).

C. M. **Cipolla** (ed.) (1973a) *The Fontana Economic History of Europe: 4, The Emergence of Industrial Societies*, Vol 2 (London).

C. M. **Cipolla** (ed.) (1973b) *The Fontana Economic History of Europe: 3, The Industrial Revolution* (London).

C. **Clark** (1957) *The Conditions of Economic Progress* (London).

F. **Crouzet** (1974) 'Récherches sur la production d'armements en France, 1815–1913' in *Hommage a Ernest Labrousse* (Paris; The Hague).

F. **Dovring** (1969) 'The transformation of European agriculture' in Postan and Habbakuk (eds) (1969).

R. W. **Goldsmith** (1961) 'The economic growth of tsarist Russia, 1860–1913', *Economic Development and Cultural Change*, 9.

D. **Good** (1974) 'Stagnation and take-off in Austria, 1873–1913', *Economic History Review*, 27.

W. G. **Hoffmann** (1955) *British Industry, 1700–1950* (Oxford).

A. **Kahan** (1971) 'The development of education and the economy in tsarist Russia' in M. J. Bowman and C. A. Anderson (eds) *Education and Economic Development* (London).

S. **Kuznets** (1961) 'Long-term trends in capital formation proportions,' *Economic Development and Cultural Change*, 9.

S. **Kuznets** (1966) *Modern Economic Growth* (New Haven).

T. J. **Marcovitch** (1966) 'L'industrie française de 1789 à 1914', *Cahiers de l'I.S.E.A.*, 7.

J. **Marczewski** (1963) 'The take-off hypothesis and French experience' in W. W. Rostow (ed.) *The Economics of Take-off into Sustained Growth* (London).

M. S. **Miller** (1926) *The Economic Development of Russia, 1905–14* (London).

B. R. **Mitchell** (1973) 'Statistical appendix' in Cipolla (ed.) (1973a).

B. R. **Mitchell** (1975) *European Historical Statistics, 1750–1970* (London).

J. **Nadal** (1973) 'The failure of the industrial revolution in Spain' in Cipolla (ed.) (1973a).

S. **Patel** (1963) 'Rates of industrial growth in the last century, 1860–1958' in B. E. Supple (ed.) *The Experience of Economic Growth* (New York).

A. **Peacock and T. Wiseman** (1967) *The Growth of Public Expenditure in the U.K.* (London).

M. M. **Postan and H. J. Habbakuk** (eds) (1969) *The Cambridge Economic History of Europe*, Vol. 6 (Cambridge).

R. **Romeo** (1959) *Risorgimento e Capitalismo* (Bari).

M. **Sanderson** (ed.) (1975) *The British Universities in the Nineteenth Century* (London).

K. F. **Shatsillo** (1974) *Rossiya pered pervoi mirovoi voiny* (Moscow).

R. **Webster** (1975) *Industrial Imperialism in Italy* (Berkeley).

Index

Aachen, 30−2

Abramovitz, M., 419

Adams, H., 255

Addington, 118

AEG, 48, 70, 98: in Austria-Hungary, 366; in Italy, 190

agrarian reform: Austro-Hungarian, 301, 323−6; French, 121−2, 133−5; German, 33−7, 106−7nn; Italian, 329−33; Russian, 207−10, 239, 257−65; Spanish, 327−9, 338

agrarian revolt, 121−2, 254, 257

Agrarstaat, 101

agricultural depression: French, 156−7, 162; German, 83−6; Russian, 254; Spanish, 295

agricultural revolution 5, 378, 385−91: Austro-Hungarian, 324−6, 333−4; French, deficiencies of, 133−5, 149, 151, 190−1, 201n; German, 34−7, 45; Italian, 303, 323, 329−33; Russian, after 1900, 258−65, failure of, 213−19, 228−9, mechanization, etc., 260−1, Witte and neglect of, 247−51; Spanish, 323, 327−9; and agricultural evolution, 390−1; and agricultural preconditions, 385−91, 427, 434−5; 'missed' agricultural revolution, 323−34, 378, 385−91

Alexander II, 207−8, 212, 226

Alexandrovskii Steel Co., 266

Allarde, decree of, 126

Almaden, 307

Almagrera, 307

Almeria, 307

Alsace-Lorraine, 52, 55, 59, 90, 131, 140−1, 145, 155−6, 164, 167−72, 194, 195, 197

Altos Hornos, 345

ancien régime: Austro-Hungarian, 336−7; French, 114−25, and agrarian problem, 121−2, and bourgeois reaction, 123−4, and fiscal inflexibility, 118−20, and price crisis, 122−3, undervaluation of economic potential of, 128; German, and industrial promotion, 22−9; Spanish, 336−7

Andalusia, 314, 327 8

Anderson, C.A., 194, 267

Andrézieux, 144

Anglo-French Commercial Treaty (1860), 153, 162, 186

Aniline Dyes Manufacturing Co., 70

Ansaldo Engineering Works, 299, 344, 346, 353, 360

Antonovich, A.I., 272

Anzin Mining Co., 140, 171

armament industry: Austro-Hungarian, 344, 347−8, 358; French, 132, 187; German, and *ancien régime*, 26−9, and excess capacity, 111n, and 'spin-off', 110n; Italian, and engineering industry, 346−7; and linkages compared to railways, 354, and markets for capital goods, 347, and metal industries, 304, 344; Russian, 224, and economic development, 282−4, expenditure on, 281−2, internationalism of, 278; Spanish, 344−6

ArmstrongWhitworth, Sir W.G. and Co. Ltd, 278, 282, 346

475

concentration, financial: see investment banks

consumer goods industries: Austrian, 358–9; French, 141; Italian, 358–60; Russian, 237–8, 255, 262–3

Continental System, 30–1, 129–32: and Austria-Hungary, 298; and Italy, 298–9

copper industry: Russian, 270; Spanish, 307

Cordoba, 307, 362

Corps des Mines, 170–2, 184–5

Cortes, 338

Côte de Dijon, 156

Côte d'Or, 64, 156

cotton industry: Austro-Hungarian, 296–8, as lead sector, 301; French, and Continental system, 129–31, coal costs, 167, comparisons with G.B., 112, 162, decline as lead sector, 151, high growth rates, 145, mechanization, 128, 140, merchant entrepreneurs, 142, slow growth, 146, 200–1n, take-off, 140, 143, technological lags, 132, 145; German, 27, 45, 46; Italian, 296, 298, 359; Russian acceleration of, 211, and depression of, 255, low levels of mechanization, 207, neglect of, 237–8, serf entrepreneurs in, 210–11; Spanish, late mechanization of, 293–4, international comparisons, 293–4

Council of State, (French): and agricultural interest, 197, and Restoration conservatism, 147, 150; and Second Empire, 152

Crédit Agricole, 152, 177

Crédit Foncier, 152

Crédit Industriel et Commercial, 153

Crédit Lyonnais, 153, 177, 183: in Russia, 279

Crédit Mobilier, 43, 107n, 152–3, 174, 186, 406

Credito Castellana, 371

Credito Italiano, 373

Credito Mobiliare, 373

Credito Mobiliario, 371

Credito Mobiliario Barcelones, 371

Crespel, 142

Crimean War, 205, 208, 220, 225, 343, 412

Crisp, O., 210–12: on peasant cyclical mobility, 264

Crouzet, F.: on *belle époque*, 158; on 'catas-trophe' of French Revolution, 117, 132, 389; on comparisons of France and G.B., 112, 114; on Continental System 132; on disaster of Sedan, 156; on entrepreneurship, 198; on French take-off, 142, 146, 150, 153–4; on growth rates, 158; on *industries de pointe*, 145; on late recovery, 158; on 'slavish imitation' in technology, 141

Cuba, 322, 357

Daimler, G., 77

Darmstädter Bank, 43, 95, 97, 107n, 366

David, P., 418–19

Décazeville, 1

Decembrists, 214

Decretot, 140

de Cyon, 280

defence expenditure: Austro-Hungarian, 343–9; French, 184, 187; German, 24–9, 81–3; Italian, 343–9; Russian, 226, 242–3, 281–2, 291n; Spanish, 343–9; and opportunity cost, 348–9

de-industrialization: French, 130–1,; German, 49–50; Spanish, 295

Delbruck, 81

'democratic revolution', 34

'demographic transition', 399–401

'demographic axis', 399

Depretis, A., 341

de Tocqueville, 138

Deutsche Asiatische Bank, 81

Deutsche Bank, 44, 95, 97–9

'developmental serfdom', 219, 229, 251, 281

de Wendel, 96, 142, 170, 189, 195

diffusion, technological, 18, 27–8, 64, 116, 129, 132–3, 141, 223–4, 266–7, 282–4, 285, 296, 315, 343–9

Dingley tariff, 83

Direktionprinzip, 27

Diskonto-Gesellschaft, 43, 78, 92, 97–9

Dneiper, 266

Don, 248, 254

Donets, 205, 234, 254

Donets Steel Co., 266

Donetsk, 224

Dortmunder Union, 70, 96

Dovring, F., 387

Dresdner Bank, 44, 78, 95, 97

Ponts et Chaussées, 166
population: Austrian, 309–11; French, 163–
7, 199n, 397, and savings levels, 165;
German, 53–4, 76n; Hungarian, and
emigration, 309–11; Italian, and
emigration, 309–12; Spanish, underpopulation, 309–11; and agricultural
surplus, 386; and 'demographic axis',
399; and 'demographic transition', 399–
400; and 'demographic trap', 399; and
growth models, 396–402; and Malthusian models, 397–8, 400–1; as prerequisite, 41–2; growth, birth, death,
marriage rates, 451–4
population mobility, 53–4, 165, 309–12
Porsche, F., 358, 361
Portal, R.: on Russian emancipation, 212;
on Russian entrepreneurs, 218; on Russian textiles, 237
potassium, 48, 52
Potsdam, 26
Pounds, N., 170
Pozzuoli Works, 344, 346
Prague, 296
preconditions, 4–8, 378–9, 385ff: French,
135, 154–5, 197; German, 44–5, 105;
Russian, 256–7, 277, 280, 284; and
dualistic economies, 333–4, and population, 401–2; financial precondition,
404–5; precocious preconditions as
obstacles to growth, 353–4, 423–4
'primitive capitalistic accumulation', 300,
302–4
private banks: Austrian, 368; French, 148;
German, 26, 92–3
Prodameta, 270
Prodarud, 270
Prodvagon, 270, 278
Prokhorov, 268
Prost-Gilhou, 371
proto-industrial developmental: Austro-
Hungarian, 296; French, 116–17, 132,
142, and technological lags, 145; German, 26–7, 38; Italian, 296–9; Russian, and automonous stream of enterprise, 210–11; Spanish, weakness of,
293–5
Prussia: and ancien régime, 22–9, 75–6,
133; and bank restrictions, 92–3; and
Napoleonic Wars, 32–4; and railways,

56; nature of state intervention, 75; rural
nature of, 41
Pugachev rebellion, 208, 214
Purs, J., 300
Putilov Works, 282
pyrites, 52, 307, 363

Quai d'Orsay: and foreign investment, 178–
9, 365–6

Raggio, 341
Raiffeissen credit cooperatives, 101, 103
railway imperialism: Austrian, 349–50;
German, 89–91
railways: Austro-Hungarian, and agricultural expansion, 326, and engineering industry, 353, and government, 351–2,
383n, and investment banks, 368–9,
and negative linkages, 354–5, as lead
sector, 299–300, inefficiencies of, 349–
50, strategy of, 349–50; French, and
government, 166, 169, 185–6, and investment banks, 152–3, and market integration, 151–2, 153, and railway 'multiplier', 144, as lead sector, 144–5, 151–
2, 155, 185–6, capital burden of, 152,
inadequacy of, 147, 166, 169, total construction and investment, 144, 151–2;
German, and industrial location, 59, and
'railway Kondratiev', 46, 49, and take-
off, 37–8, 40, as lead sector, 43, 59–
60, dispensability of, 59–61, 108n,
efficiency of, 55–7; Italian, 299–300,
303, and agricultural weakness, 330, and
dualism, 315, and engineering industry,
353–4, and foreign capital, 303, 352–
3, 364, and government, 351–2, and
negative linkages, 354–5, and withdrawals of French capital, 364–5, inefficiency of, 350–1, strategy of, 350–
1; Russian, and early Finance Ministers,
223, and engineering industry, 270–1,
and imperial railway ukaz, 220, and
nationalisation, 226, and state guarantees, 223, and Witte System, 233–6,
first lines, 205–6, inadequate provision,
234–5, military purpose of, 235; Spanish, 300, 307, and agricultural decline,
327, and banking system, 354, and
'crowding out' of national investment,

INDEX

Tulle, 132
Turgot, A.R.J., 116, 125
Turin, 296, 299, 346, 353, 360
Tuscany, 298, 299, 314

Ukraine: and dualism, 145; and high technologies, 237, 255; and railways, 234
Umbria, 306, 314, 360
Unckell, A., 67
underpopulation: French, 163–7; Spanish, 310
Union Générale, 365
Urals: and bank-induced development, 274; and emancipation, 218; iron industry, 205, 207; mining, 237, 255
urbanization: French, 151–2, and market integration, 151–2, 157, comparisons with Germany and UK, 165–6, slowness of, 191; German, 54; Italian, 304–5; Russian, 248, 262–3
U.S. Steel, 69
Utrecht (Treaty), 322

Vainshtein, 245
Val d'Aosta, 306
Valencia, 313, 336
Veblen, T.: on German railways, 56; on German raw materials, 51; on German state intervention, 74
Venetia, 331, 353
Versailles, (Treaty), 377
Vial, J.: on bank-industry relations in France, 177; on industrial training in France, 194; on rural iron industry in France, 142, 188–9
Vickers, Ltd., 278, 282–3, 346–7
Vienna, 1, 296, 299, 312–13, 336, 349, 353, 366
Vienna (Treaty), 131, 293, 377
Villaverde, 338
Viscaya, 295, 307, 313–14
Vitkovice, 296
Vladimir, 266
Vochting, F., 314
von Berlepsch, 81
von Heinitz, 27–8, 77
von Humboldt, 34
von Laue, T.H.; on Russian government expenditure, 242, 253; on Witte and Nicholas II, 231, 253
von Moltke, 88, 156
von Liebeg, 388
von Reden, 27–8, 77
Vormarz regime, 337
Vyshnegradskii, I.A., 227–8, 248–9, 251

war, and industrial development: 24–36, 46, 49, 105, 129–33, 155, 205, 208, 220; and currency, 227; and foreign debt, 225; and internal reforms, 412; and markets, 322, 343–9; and railway, 350–1
Wars of Liberation, (Italian), 343
Warriner, D., 308, 326
water power, 142, 145; see also hydroelectric power
Werndl, J., 347–8, 361
Westende mine, 96
Westphalia, 29, 32, 50, 56
Westphalian Coal Syndicate, 69
White, H.D., 182
Wilhelm II, 88, 105
Wilkinson, J., 28, 31
wine Industry: French, and *phylloxera*, 156–7; Italian, inefficiency, 332; Spanish, and competition, 327, and *phylloxera*, 295
Witte, S.I., 16, 29, 212, 223, 231–54, 280–1, 342: estimate of foreign capital in Russia, 245
Witte System, 231–54: and agricultural stagnation, 247–51; and budgetary policy, 238–44; and deficiencies in economic science, 253, 415; and economic performance, 233; and education, 252; and gold standard policy, 239–42; and neglect of Urals industrial region, 237, 274; and overcommitment to capital goods industries, 236–8, 283–4, 289, 341, 360; and railways, 233–6; and state capitalism, 232; and taxation, 238–9; as public relations campaign, 253–4; collapse of, 251; derivativeness of, 251; encroachment on other policy areas, 252; 'gamble' of, 238; incorrect assumptions of, 252–3
Wolf, J.B., 137
Woolf, S.J., 391, 401

494